STUDIES IN LEGAL HISTORY

Published in association
with the American Society
for Legal History

EXECUTIVE PRIVILEGE: A CONSTITUTIONAL MYTH

RAOUL BERGER

Harvard University Press Cambridge, Massachusetts 1974

Third printing, 1974
Library of Congress Catalog Card Number 73–93837
ISBN 0–674–27425–3
Printed in the United States of America

To Carly, Andy, and Patty

PREFACE

WHEN "executive privilege" dawned on the national consciousness in 1954, in the midst of the McCarthy-Army Hearings, it seemed like an overdue presidential riposte to congressional excesses, to the bullying, abusive tactics of Senator Joseph McCarthy, which had become the object of widespread aversion. To many it merely represented a jurisdictional squabble between the legislative and executive branches, best worked out in a spirit of accommodation. Few discerned that the Eisenhower administration's claim of "uncontrolled discretion" to withhold information from Congress might become a shield for executive unaccountability and thus a matter of critical concern to the nation. That first emerged for me in 1963, in the quiet of a university chamber, when I began a study that was published in 1965.[1] At the time the issue was quiescent because President Kennedy had drastically curtailed executive invocation of the privilege. The genie, in the words of Congressman John E. Moss, had been bottled, although he prophetically foresaw that it would again emerge.

Emerge it did; and when I began a restudy of the problem in 1971 a very marked change had taken place. Information was being withheld in areas of vital public interest; for example, Secretary of Defense Melvin Laird had advised the Senate Foreign Relations Committee that disclosure to it of the Pentagon Papers—an inside study critical of the Vietnam War escalation—was against the "national interest," notwithstanding that Congress is the senior partner in warmaking. Executive privilege had become an iron curtain which shut off crucial information from Congress and the people.

Now I experienced at first hand the difficulties met by a scholar who would dispassionately survey the conflicts that agitate his fellows. With them he is swept on by the current of his times. Here my experience as a lawyer came to my aid. Every lawyer learns the cost of distorting, or ignoring, adverse facts. Adversaries who well know how to exploit such blunders will blow his case out

1. Raoul Berger, "Executive Privilege v. Congressional Inquiry," 12 UCLA L. Rev. 1043, 1287 (1965).

of the water. Caution, let alone the duty of a scholar who dedicates himself to the pursuit of "truth," dictates that one face up squarely to everything that militates against his views. The test of a scholar is not that he has no thesis, or if he has one, that he presents it in colorless ("neutral") fashion, but rather that it is documented and takes account of everything that may vitiate his analysis. It has been my constant effort to unearth and be faithful to the facts; to the best of my knowledge I have left no argument in favor of executive privilege unexamined. Indeed, what seem to me the most telling historical data in favor of executive privilege —Madison's statement in the Jay Treaty debate and Jefferson's reliance on remarks during the Robert Walpole proceedings in 1741–1742—were first uncovered by me.

If my strictures against the modern foundation stone of executive privilege, the 1958 memorandum of Deputy Attorney General William P. Rogers, seem oversevere, I may say with Gibbon, that "I have tediously acquired, by a painful perusal, the right of pronouncing this unfavorable sentence."[2] Let the reader judge whether I have made out my case. In his brilliant "The Limitations of Science," J. W. N. Sullivan stated, "The vigorous criticism, the complete lack of indulgence, that is shown by the scientific world, is one of its most agreeable characteristics. Its one simple but devastating criterion, 'Is it true?' is perhaps the chief characteristic that makes it seem such an oasis for the spirit in the modern world."[3] That criterion should commend itself to the law.

In the eight years that have elapsed since publication of my 1965 articles, no advocate of executive privilege has come to grips with my critique. Perhaps this book will arouse the sleeping dogs, and I may learn from my critics.

It is a pleasure to acknowledge the helpful criticism of my editor and friend, Professor Stanley N. Katz. My thanks are also due to the following editors for permission to use the respective materials: UCLA Law Review, "Executive Privilege v. Congressional Inquiry" (1965); Michigan Law Review, "The Presidential Monopoly of Foreign Relations" (1972); and University of Pennsylvania Law Review, "War-Making by the President" (1972).

R. B.

Concord, Massachusetts
January 1974

2. 4 Edward Gibbon, *The History of the Decline and Fall of the Roman Empire* 60 n. 111 (New York, Nottingham Press, n.d.).
3. Pp. 173–174 (New York, 1952).

CONTENTS

CONTENTS

ABBREVIATIONS

1 Annals of Cong.	*Annals of Congress*, vol. 1, 1789, 2d ed. (Washington, Gales & Seaton, 1834; print bearing running head "History of Congress")
Berger, *Congress v. Court*	Berger, Raoul, *Congress v. the Supreme Court* (Cambridge, Mass., 1969)
Berger, Executive Privilege	Berger, Raoul, "Executive Privilege v. Congressional Inquiry," 12 UCLA L. Rev. 1044, 1288 (1965)
Berger, *Impeachment*	Berger, Raoul, *Impeachment: The Constitutional Problems* (Cambridge, Mass., 1973)
Bishop	Bishop, Joseph, "The Executive's Right of Privacy: An Unresolved Constitutional Question," 66 Yale L.J. 477 (1957)
Chandler	Chandler, Richard, *History and Proceedings of Parliament from 1621 to the Present*, vol. 13 (London, 1743)
Commager	Commager, Henry Steele, *Documents of American History*, 7th ed. (New York, 1963)
Corwin, *Control*	Corwin, Edward S., *The President's Control of Foreign Relations* (Princeton, 1917)
Corwin, *President*	Corwin, Edward S., *The President: Office and Powers*, 3d ed. (New York, 1948)
Corwin, *Total War*	Corwin, Edward S., *Total War and the Constitution* (New York, 1947)
Elliot	Elliot, Jonathan, *Debates in the Several State Conventions on the Adoption of the Federal Constitution*, 2d ed. (Washington, 1836)
E.R.	English Reports
Ervin Hearings	Hearings on Executive Privilege: The Witholding of Information by the Executive Before the Senate Subcommittee on Separation of Powers (92d Cong., 1st Sess., 1971)
Executive Agreements Hearings	Hearings on Transmittal of Executive Agreements to Congress Before the Senate Foreign Relations Committee (92d Cong., 1st Sess., 1971)
Farrand	Farrand, Max, *The Records of the Federal Convention of 1787* (New Haven, 1911)
Federalist	*The Federalist* (New York, 1937)
Fulbright Hearings	Hearings on War Powers Legislation Before the Senate Committee on Foreign Relations (92d Cong., 1st Sess., 1971)
Halberstam	Halberstam, David, *The Best and the Brightest* (New York, 1972)

Hamilton, *Works*	Hamilton, Alexander, *Works,* ed. H. C. Lodge (New York, 1904)
Henkin	Henkin, Louis, *Foreign Affairs and the Constitution* (Mineola, N.Y., 1972)
Jefferson, *Writings*	Jefferson, Thomas, *Writings,* ed. P. L. Ford (New York, 1892–1899)
Kramer & Marcuse	Kramer, Robert, and Herman Marcuse, "Executive Privilege: A Study of the Period 1953–1960," 29 Geo. Wash. L. Rev. 623, 827 (1961)
McDougal & Lans	McDougal, Myres, and Asher Lans, "Treaties and Congressional-Executive or Presidential Agreements: Interchangeable Instruments of National Policy," 54 Yale L.J. 181, 585 (1945)
Madison, *Writings*	Madison, James, *Writings,* ed. G. Hunt (New York, 1900–1910)
Mollenhoff	Mollenhoff, Clark, *Washington Cover-Up* (Garden City, N.Y., 1962)
Moorhead Hearings	Hearings on U.S. Government Information Policies and Practices before a Subcommittee of the House Committee on Government Operations (92d Cong., 1st Sess., 1971–1972)
Morison	Morison, Samuel Eliot, *Oxford History of the American People* (New York, 1965)
Moss Hearings	Hearings on Availability of Information from Federal Departments and Agencies before a Subcommittee of the House Committee on Government Operations, part 16 (85th Cong., 2d Sess., 1958)
Pent. Pap.	Sheehan, Neil, et al., *The Pentagon Papers* (New York, 1971)
Poore	Poore, Ben P., *Federal and State Constitutions, Colonial Charters* (Washington, 1877)
Richardson	Richardson, James D., *Compilation of the Messages and Papers of the Presidents, 1789–1897* (Washington, 1897)
Rogers memo	Memorandums of the Attorney General, "The Power of the President to Withhold Information from Congress," Senate Subcommittee on Constitutional Rights (85th Cong., 2d Sess., 1958)
Trevelyan	Trevelyan, Sir G. M., *Illustrated History of England* (London, 1956)
Wilson, *Works*	Wilson, James, *Works,* ed. R. G. McCloskey, 2 vols. (Cambridge, Mass., 1967)
Wormuth, Vietnam War	Worthmuth, Francis, "The Vietnam War: The President versus the Constitution," in R. Falk, ed. 2 *The Vietnam War and International Law* (Princeton, 1969)
Youngstown Case	Youngstown Sheet & Tube Co. v. Sawyer, 343 U.S. 579 (1972)

EXECUTIVE PRIVILEGE: A CONSTITUTIONAL MYTH

The right of freely examining public characters and measures, and of free communication thereon, is the only effective guardian of every other right. —James Madison

A popular Government, without popular information, or the means of acquiring it, is but a Prologue to a Farce or a Tragedy; or perhaps both. Knowledge will forever govern ignorance: And a people who mean to be their own Governors, must arm themselves with the power which knowledge gives.—James Madison

No nation has ever found any inconvenience from too close an inspection into the conduct of its officers, but many have been brought to ruin, and reduced to slavery, by suffering gradual impositions and abuses, which are imperceptible, only because the means of publicity had not been secured. —Edward Livingston

A frequent recurrence to the fundamental principles of the constitution . . . [is] absolutely necessary to preserve the advantages of liberty and to maintain a free government.—Massachusetts Constitution of 1780, drafted by John Adams

6 Madison, *Writings* 398; 9 Madison, *Writings* 103; Livingston quoted in *Reynolds v. United States,* 192 F. 2d 987, 995 (3d Cir. 1951); Massachusetts Constitution of 1780, drafted by John Adams.

1

INTRODUCTION

"EXECUTIVE privilege"—the President's claim of constitutional authority to withhold information from Congress[1]—is a myth.[2] Unlike most myths, the origins of which are lost in the mists of antiquity, "executive privilege" is a product of the nineteenth century, fashioned by a succession of presidents who created "precedents" to suit the occasion. The very words "executive privilege" were conjoined only yesterday, in 1958.[3] Of late years

1. It also embraces withholding from the "judicial branch." Assistant Attorney General William H. Rehnquist, Hearings on Executive Privilege before Senate Subcommittee on Separation of Powers, July–August 1971, p. 421 (hereafter cited as Ervin Hearings). But discussion will chiefly be addressed to withholding from Congress.

2. A seasoned administrator, George Ball, former Under Secretary of State, said that "the myth of Executive privilege, and it is indeed a myth, for I find no constitutional basis for it, has tended to be greatly exaggerated." Hearings on War Powers Legislation before Senate Committee on Foreign Relations, March–October 1971, p. 626 (hereafter cited as Fulbright Hearings). See statement by Congressman Richard M. Nixon in 1948, quoted in Ch. 8, text accompanying n. 108.

3. Deputy Assistant Attorney General Mary C. Lawton testified that "the term is of recent origin." Hearings on Availability of Information to Congress before a Subcommittee of the Committee on Government Operations of the House of Representatives, p. 116 (April 1973). So far as I could find, the words "executive privilege" were first combined in a private litigation by Assistant Attorney General Doub, in Kaiser Aluminum & Chem. Co. v. United States, 157 F. Supp. 939, 943 (Ct. Cl. 1958), and were picked up by Justice Stanley Reed, sitting by designation. A series of articles, Herman Wolkinson, "Demands of Congressional Committees for Executive Papers," 10 Fed. B.J. 103, 223, 319 (1949), which are an apologia for presidential discretion to withhold information from Congress, make no mention of "executive privilege." When Deputy Attorney General William P. Rogers adopted these articles *in haec verba*, without attribution, in the memorandum he submitted to the Senate in 1958, he likewise left "executive privilege" unmentioned, and entitled his memorandum, "The Power of the President to Withhold Information from the Congress," Memorandum of the Attorney General, Senate Subcommittee on Constitutional Rights (85th Cong., 2d Sess.) (hereinafter cited as Rogers memo).

Without pretending to an exhaustive search, I found no reference to "executive privilege" in the detailed reasoning of President Tyler in 1843, infra, Ch. 6, text accompanying nn. 118–120; nor in Attorney General Robert H. Jackson's 1941 opinion, 40 Ops. Atty. Gen. 45. Both referred to presidential discretion to withhold. So too, in a private litigation, United States v. Reynolds, 345 U.S. 1 (1953), the government claimed an "executive power to suppress documents," and the Court referred to the "privilege against revealing military secrets, a privilege which is well established in the law of evidence"; ibid. 6–7.

assertions of "executive privilege" have assumed swollen proportions,[4] realizing the extreme claim of Deputy Attorney General William P. Rogers that the President has "uncontrolled discretion" to withhold information from Congress.[5]

Rogers owned that "We live in a democracy in which an informed public opinion is absolutely essential to the survival of our nation and form of government. It is likewise true that Congress must be well informed if it is to do its legislative job realistically and effectively."[6] An "uncontrolled discretion" to refuse information to Congress, however, leaves Congress, and therefore public opinion, at the mercy of the President; they learn only what he considers they should know, with the consequence that Congress is disabled from functioning "as a truly coequal branch of government."[7] "The country," said Woodrow Wilson, "must be helpless to learn how it is being served" unless Congress have and

---

Professor Arthur Schlesinger, Jr., also concluded that the term " 'executive privilege' seems to be of very recent American usage . . . I cannot find that any President or Attorney General used it before the Eisenhower administration. You will look in vain for it as an entry in such standard reference works as the Smith-Zurcher 'Dictionary of American Politics,' or 'The Oxford Companion to American History,' or Scribner's 'Concise Dictionary of American History.' " It is not even to be found, I was dismayed to discover, in 'The New Language of Politics,' compiled by William Safire of Mr. Nixon's very own White House staff"; Wall Street Journal, Mar. 30, 1973, p. 8.

4. See infra, Ch. 8. Former Chief Justice Earl Warren stated that "over the last two decades, deep and disturbing changes have been occurring in the relationship of the executive and legislative branches. Now, even secretaries of state can decline to discuss major policy decisions with appropriate Senate Committees. In doing so, they join a growing line of officials who apparently can escape from reporting to the elected representatives of the people"; N.Y. Times, Feb. 12, 1973, p. 27.

5. Rogers memo 1. So too, former Assistant Secretary of State William P. Bundy testified in 1971 that "if I read the law correctly, the executive privilege could be invoked on anything"; Ervin Hearings 323.

6. W. P. Rogers, "Constitutional Law: The Papers of the Executive Branch," 44 A.B.A.J. 941 (1958). Under Secretary of State William B. Macomber testified in 1971 that "the zealous protection of the people's right to know is of absolutely critical importance to all Americans . . . critical to the survival of free government." Hearings on U.S. Government Information Policies and Practices, before a Subcommittee of the Committee on Government Operations, House of Representatives, part III, p. 899 (June 1971–June 1972) (hereafter cited as Moorhead Hearings). See infra, Ch. 2, n. 169.

7. Senator Charles McC. Mathias, Jr., Ervin Hearings 15. Senator Mathias justly insisted that "to carry out its constitutional responsibilities in foreign affairs, [Congress] must have access to the same information the President has—access to the documents, the recommendations, the advisers"; ibid. 17. Senator J. W. Fulbright also stated that Congress lacked "the information it required in order to discharge its constitutional responsibilities"; ibid. 23. Arthur J. Goldberg, former Secretary of Labor, Justice of the Supreme Court, and Ambassador to the United Nations, stated: "I cannot conceive that Congress can carry out its duties unless it is adequately informed; "1 Moorhead Hearings 25.

"use every means of acquainting itself with the acts and disposition of the administrative agents of the government."[8]

Our democratic system is bottomed on the legislative process; a "government of laws" premises first and foremost a lawmaking body, the legislature. "With all its defects, delays and inconveniences," said Justice Jackson in rejecting a presidential power-grab, "men have discovered no techniques for long preserving free government except that the Executive be under the law and that the law be made by parliamentary deliberation."[9] Since lawmaking confessedly needs to be based on an informed judgment, this requires the widest access to information.[10] With the help of Congress, the Executive has developed the greatest information-gathering apparatus extant; it is a national asset, not an exclusive executive preserve. To duplicate these worldwide facilities in order that Congress may obtain the information it considers essential for performance of its duties would be an intolerably costly folly.[11] Rather, as Roger Sherman, who had been a Framer, said in the First Congress, "as we want information to act upon, we must procure it where it is to be had. Consequently we must get it out of this officer," the then Secretary of the Treasury, Alexander Hamilton.[12]

Then too, the Constitution contemplates executive accountability to Congress, as the Article II, §3 provision that the President "shall take care that the laws be faithfully executed" alone should show. Who has a more legitimate interest in inquiring whether a law has been faithfully executed than the lawmaker? So thought Montesquieu, the high priest of the separation of powers—the doctrine which is again and again invoked by the

8. Woodrow Wilson, *Congressional Government* 297, 303 (Boston, 1913).

9. Youngstown Sheet & Tube Co. v. Sawyer, 343 U.S. 579, 655 (1952) (concurring).

10. Infra, Ch. 8, text accompanying nn. 80–83.

11. For example, Senator Fulbright testified, "We have had to hire staff and send our own staff to Southeast Asia, including Laos, to get the information we need directly. This is very unwieldy; it is not practical to do this all over the world . . . We have done that in desperation because of the realization that we are not being told the truth about the operations in Laos"; Ervin Hearings 206. For what that concealed "truth" was, see infra, n. 35, and Ch. 4, n. 2.

When the General Accounting Office went to the Philippines, Thailand, and Korea at the behest of the Senate Foreign Relations Committee, it met with departmental obstruction that has to be read in detail to be appreciated; Ervin Hearings 306–307, 311, 312, 315. See Justice Story, infra, Ch. 2, text accompanying n. 139; Ch. 5, n. 123.

12. I Annals of Cong. 607 (1789).

Executive branch in defense of executive privilege.[13] The legislature, said he, "has a right, and ought to have the means, of examining in what manner its laws have been executed," in which the English enjoy an advantage over some governments where public officers "gave no account of their administration."[14] The accountability of the executive branch to Congress is underlined by the Article II, §4 provision for impeachment of the President and "all civil officers." Impeachment lies for corruption, bribery, and other high misdemeanors, and, as Blackstone stated, for action contrary to law,[15] as well as for subversion of the Constitution, that is, usurpation of power.[16] From early times it was preceded by parliamentary investigation.[17] Such considerations were summarized by Woodrow Wilson:

> Quite as important as legislation is vigilant oversight of administration; and even more important than legislation is the instruction and guidance in political affairs which the people might receive from a body which kept all national concerns suffused in a broad daylight of discussion . . . The informing function of Congress should be preferred even to its legislative function.[18]

13. President Richard Nixon, Ervin Hearings 46; Attorney General W. P. Rogers, supra, n. 6 at 1010–1011, repeated by him as Secretary of State, Ervin Hearings 473; Assistant Attorney General W. H. Rehnquist, ibid. 430; W. P. Bundy, former Assistant Secretary of State, ibid. 319; former Secretary of State Dean Rusk, ibid. 350.

14. 1 C. de S. Montesquieu, *The Spirit of the Laws* 187 (Philadelphia, 1802). Justice Holmes "saw it as a basic value in the separation of powers that ultimate surveillance should rest in the legislature." J. W. Hurst, *Justice Holmes on Legal History* 99 (New York, 1964). A severe critic of investigatory abuses stated, "the law-making prerogative would be a nearly empty one if it did not also imply a right to call the Executive to account for the administration of the laws. Inseparable from the power to legislate is the power to inquire into the efficacy of legislation and the efficiency with which it has been carried into effect"; Alan Barth, *Government by Investigation* 15–16 (New York, 1955). This, as will appear, was the long-time practice of Parliament.

15. 1 Sir William Blackstone, *Commentaries on the Law of England* 244 (Oxford, 1765–1769).

16. Raoul Berger, *Impeachment: The Constitutional Problems* 33, 86 (Cambridge, Mass., 1973).

17. Infra, Ch. 2.

18. W. Wilson, supra, n. 8 at 297, 303. In this Wilson merely echoed J. S. Mill, *Essay on Representative Government*, quoted H. V. Wiseman, *Parliament and the Executive* 122 (London, 1966): "the proper office of a representative assembly is to watch and control the Government; to throw the light of publicity on its acts; to compel a full exposition and justification of all of them which any one considers questionable; to censure them if found condemnable."

Bagehot held similar views; he regarded the "informing function" as "the second function of Parliament in point of importance . . . it makes us hear what otherwise we should not," and need to know; Walter Bagehot, *The English Constitution* 153 (London, 1964).

Performance of these functions has increasingly been made to run an executive gauntlet, and this on the basis of made-to-order "precedents" of very recent vintage.

One who would espouse the claim of Congress to be fully informed must face up to the fact that the rampant excesses of the McCarthy Senate investigations left the investigatory process in ill repute.[19] In 1971, Dean Acheson paraded the ghost of Senator McCarthy, when he opposed an innocuous proposal that no executive official should plead executive privilege without presenting an express presidential authorization.[20] It is true, as Senator J. W. Fulbright acknowledged, that the excessive-information-withholding "evil" was born of "the desire of the Eisenhower administration to protect its officials from the attacks of the late Senator McCarthy."[21] McCarthysm was but the full-blown exemplar of the earlier post–World War II Committee practices,[22] which the Supreme Court said represented "a new kind of Congressional inquiry unknown in prior periods of American history."[23] Many, Senator Fulbright stated in 1971, "were revolted by some of the actions in Congress," and there grew up "a feeling that the Congress was not worthy of trust."[24] The McCarthy witch-hunts left the more enduring impress because the Senate never saw fit to curb nor censure him for his perversion of the investigatory function.[25]

But, as a critic of the McCarthy era pointed out, "if Congressional use of power to investigate produced occasional excesses, it also produced tremendous boons."[26] We need only recall the

19. For details see Barth 24–26, 40–65, 83, 154–155; Telford Taylor, *Grand Inquest* 112–135, 266–269, 184–185 (New York, 1955).

20. Ervin Hearings 260.

21. Ibid. 24.

22. See Walter Goodman, *The Committee* (New York, 1968).

23. Watkins v. United States, 354 U.S. 178, 195 (1957).

24. Ervin Hearings 208. Even Justice Frankfurter, the once perfervid admirer of the investigatory function—"The power of investigation should be left untrammeled [re Teapot Dome]"; Felix Frankfurter, "Hands off the Investigations," 38 New Republic 329, 331 (1924)—was impelled to recognize "wide concern . . . over some aspects of the exercise of the Congressional power of investigation"; United States v. Rumely, 345 U.S. 41, 44 (1953).

25. "It is especially noteworthy, as Senator Monroney pointed out on the closing day of debate, that Senator McCarthy was not censured for his misuse of the Senate's investigatorial prerogatives, for his attack on the executive branch, or for his treatment of any one other than his fellow-senators. He was censured only for his sulphurous reaction to the Senate's undertaking to investigate and judge him—i.e. for *obstructing* rather than for *abusing* the Senate's power"; Taylor 134.

26. Barth 14. Taylor, 83, wisely cautions that "we must not allow general conclusions about congressional investigations to be determined by our own personal

benefits which flowed from the Senate investigation of the Teapot Dome scandal. Corruption and mismanagement repeatedly have been exposed over strenuous executive opposition only because of congressional investigation.[27] The starting point, therefore, must be a congressional function which again and again has proved its value over the years.[28] Growing resort by the Executive branch to "uncontrolled discretion" to withhold information robs the country of the benefits which flow from legislative inquiry into executive conduct.[29] That information is more frequently fur-

---

approval or disapproval of individual investigators, be they Senator McCarthys or Ferdinand Pecoras."

27. Writing in 1924 of the Teapot Dome investigation, Professor Felix Frankfurter stated that "the bills filed by the government against the Sinclair and Doheny leases are based upon the findings of the Walsh committee, namely, corruption and conspiracy rendered possible through Secretary Fall's corruption and Secretary Denby's guileless incompetence; the disgrace of, and pending grand jury inquiry into a recent member of the Cabinet—Fall; the resignation of another member through incompetence—Danby; the dismissal of a third member—the Attorney General [Harry Daugherty] because of an enveloping, malodorous atmosphere"; Frankfurter, supra, n. 24 at 329–330. "For nearly two years," he stated, "the efforts to uncover wrong-doing in the disposal of our public domain were hampered by every conceivable obstruction on the part of those in office"; ibid. 329.

28. A few earlier examples were inquiries into defalcations in the New York Customs Service, attributed to ineffectual supervision by the Secretary of the Treasury, Marshall Dimock, *Congressional Investigating Committees* 93 (Baltimore, 1929); into successive frauds in the Bureau of Indian Affairs, ibid. 94; into charges of fraud against President Buchanan which contributed to the election of Lincoln, ibid. 109–111; into the conduct of the Civil War—battles, surrenders, war contracts, ibid. 111–112; fraudulent mail contracts, ibid. 112.

From 1789 to 1925 there have been "about 285 investigations by the select and standing committees of the House and Senate . . . the houses of Congress have employed the inquisitorial function over a wide range of governmental activity . . . Congressional Committees have scrutinized the conduct of all the wars in which the United States has engaged except the Spanish-American war, when President McKinley forestalled legislative inquiry by appointing the Dodge Committee"; George Galloway, "The Investigative Function of Congress," 21 Am. Pol. Sci. Rev. 47, 48 (1927). See also infra, Ch. 2, text accompanying nn. 164–171. The list can be expanded by examples drawn from our own times; see infra, Ch. 8, text accompanying nn. 21–31, 32–37, 136–137.

29. Senator George Norris, who shed luster on the Senate, stated: "Whenever you take away from the legislative body . . . the power to look into the executive department . . . you have taken a full step that will eventually . . . destroy any government such as ours"; quoted at Ervin Hearings 31. See also supra, n. 4; and infra, Conclusion, text accompanying n. 20.

Former Assistant Attorney General Robert Kramer, an ardent proponent of executive privilege, stated that "undue secrecy may seriously cripple the legislature and promote official arrogance and inefficiency as well as fiscal laxity . . . government without investigation might easily turn out to be democratic government no longer"; Robert Kramer and Herman Marcuse, "Executive Privilege—A Study of the Period 1953–1960," 29 Geo. Wash. L. Rev. 623, 827, 915–916 (1961). The Supreme Court also has adverted to the "danger to effective and honest conduct of the Government if the legislature's power to probe corruption in the executive branch were unduly hampered"; Watkins v. United States, 354 U.S. 178, 194–195 (1957).

nished than withheld is beside the point: investigation is hobbled at the outset if the Executive branch may determine what Congress shall see and hear. How can that determination safely be left to the object of investigation? That it cannot was pointed out by William Pitt in 1741: "this enquiry, Sir, will produce no great information if those whose conduct is examined, are allowed to select the evidence."[30] Since 1954 it has become executive practice to refuse on the flimsiest grounds information which should underlie the appropriations of billions of dollars or the passage of vital legislation. Recoil from the McCarthean excesses has engendered a cure that is worse than the disease.

Only the tip of the iceberg is represented by the formal claim of executive privilege. Bureaucrats engage in interminable stalling when asked for information. The Secretary, and his underlings, of a Department which owes its very creation and continued existence to Congress, advise the senior partner in government, for so Congress was regarded by the Founders,[31] that is is "contrary to the national interest" or "inappropriate" for it to see the requested information![32] Such refusals are merely part of a wider pattern of concealment: "executive agreements" which are suspected of making large-scale military and financial commitments are not disclosed to Congress or the people.[33] They learn of the costly invasion of Cambodia, the mining of Haiphong Harbor after

30. 11 Parl. Hist. Eng. 1009 (1741).

31. See Madison, infra, Ch. 3, text accompanying n. 9. The "chief executive departments are all the work of the first and succeeding Congresses. No constitutional duty demanded their institution; no constitutional duty demands their continuance. Congress may abolish them at its pleasure, redistribute them, consolidate or divide them"; James M. Landis, "Constitutional Limitations on the Congressional Power of Investigation," 40 Harv. L. Rev. 153, 196 (1926).

32. Ervin Hearings 5–6, 38. An example is afforded by the efforts of the General Accounting Office on behalf of the Senate Foreign Relations Committee, then by the Committee itself, to obtain a five-year plan prepared within the Department of Defense for military assistance to foreign nations for purposes of a foreign aid authorization bill, running from May 21, 1969, to Aug. 30, 1971, when a threatened cutoff of funds produced a plea by President Nixon of executive privilege; ibid. 27, 40–46.

A memorandum to the Departments from President Nixon, Mar. 24, 1969, stated that "Executive Privilege will not be used without Presidential approval"; ibid. 36–37. Nevertheless, without citing such authorization, the Department refused to turn over the information for upward of two years. William B. Macomber, Deputy Under Secretary of State, testified: "I know there is no authority to deny a document or information to the Congress unless . . . the President invokes executive privilege. No subordinate in the executive branch, no matter how high his rank, has a right to refuse a document or information to Congress that is being formally requested and published without the authorization of the President"; 3 Moorhead Hearings 918.

33. Infra, Ch. 5, text accompanying nn. 123–126.

the fact, notwithstanding that the predominant role in warmaking was confided to Congress.[34] The costs of such undercover presidential policy were evidenced by a massive revulsion against the Vietnam War. Whether President Lyndon Johnson candidly communicated his plans for escalation of American involvement in Vietnam, whether he advised Congress of all the relevant facts before requesting the Gulf of Tonkin Resolution—widely debated issues—is not nearly so important as the existence of a large body of opinion that he practiced concealment.[35]

A zealous apologist for the Johnson war policy and the alleged power of the President, single-handed, to commit the nation to war, recognized that "The tension between public opinion and the behavior of the government [read President] is much too great for safety. That tension has already destroyed the careers of . . . Johnson; divided the nation."[36]

Even the spokesman for the conservatives on military matters, Senator John Stennis, Chairman of the Senate Armed Services Committee, who long held up the arms of the President, stated in 1971, "Vietnam has shown us that by trying to fight a war without the clear-cut support of the American people, we . . . strain the very structure of the republic."[37] Vietnam teaches, to borrow the words of the Chairman of the Foreign Relations Committee, Senator Fulbright, that "secrecy and subterfuge are themselves more dangerous to democracy than the practices they conceal."[38]

As if to temper Rogers' "uncontrolled discretion" claim, Assistant Attorney General (now Justice) William H. Rehnquist, stated that the "President's authority to withhold information is *not an unbridled one.*" But he immediately washed out this concession by asserting that "it necessarily requires the exercise of *his* judgment" whether disclosure "would be harmful to the national

34. Infra, Ch. 4.

35. E.g., William E. Colby, Deputy Director for Operations of CIA, testified that "the congressional intent embodied in the 1947 law creating the agency had probably been violated when the agency was directed in 1964 to support a secret war in Laos"; N.Y. Times, July 3, 1973, p. 1. See also infra, text accompanying n. 68; Ch. 9, n. 2; cf Ch. 9, text accompanying nn. 101–108. David Halberstam, *The Best and the Brightest* 144 (1972).

36. Eugene V. Rostow, "Great Cases Make Bad Law: The War Powers Act," 50 Texas L. Rev. 833, 899 (1972).

37. N.Y. Times, Oct. 7, 1971, p. 3. Former Justice Goldberg stated respecting the escalation of the Vietnam War: "it was never thrashed out and adequately debated under our system, and it should have been"; 1 Moorhead Hearings 27.

38. Ervin Hearings 20.

interest."[39] Thus the President is "bridled," but it is a bridle that only he himself can check! Since Congress admittedly must "obtain information in order to aid it in the process of legislating," a conflict is presented with the President's claim of power to "withhold documents or information in his possession."[40] On this boundary dispute, Attorney General Rogers unabashedly asserted, "the President and heads of departments must and do have the last word";[41] a view reiterated by Assistant Attorney General Rehnquist in blander terms: the issue "necessarily requires the exercise of his [President's] judgment." Although Mr. Rehnquist quoted Madison's statement in Federalist No. 49 that "neither the executive nor the legislative can pretend to an exclusive or superior right of settling the boundaries between their respective powers,"[42] he did not draw the inescapable conclusion that some other tribunal than one of the boundary disputants must therefore determine the issue.[43] For Madison merely followed the centuries-old common law rule that no man may be judge in his own cause, not even the King,[44] a rule that has the greater urgency when the executive judgment would render Congress subordinate and dependent.[45]

39. Ibid. 422; emphasis added. Rogers' claim to "uncontrolled discretion" to withhold information has been rejected by Professors Joseph Bishop, "The Executive's Right of Privacy: An Unresolved Constitutional Question," 66 Yale L.J. 477, 478 n. 5 (1957); Norman Dorsen, Ervin Hearings 367; Bernard Schwartz, "Executive Privilege and Congressional Investigatory Power," 47 Calif. L. Rev. 3, 13 (1959); Ralph Winter, Ervin Hearings 256, 301. The General Counsel of the Defense Department, J. F. Buzhardt, considered that executive privilege is "not entirely absolute"; Ervin Hearings 447. The Rogers memo is dissected, infra, Ch. 6.

Nevertheless, Secretary of State W. P. Rogers continued to rely on Attorney General Rogers' memo, Ervin Hearings 472; and former Assistant Secretary of State William P. Bundy, in reliance on that memorandum, testified that "the executive privilege could be invoked on anything"; ibid. 323. But Assistant Attorney General Rehnquist stated that the power is "not absolute in the sense that the President could willy-nilly withhold any number of things requested by Congress just because he did not feel like giving them"; 2 Moorhead Hearings 370. No wielder of power may safely be left to judge finally the limits of his own power. Infra, Ch. 11, n. 127 and accompanying text.

Not the least remarkable aspect of Rogers' continued reliance on his earlier memo is the fact that he completely ignores the harsh strictures against his views.

40. Ervin Hearings 421.

41. Rogers Memo 46.

42. Ervin Hearings 420.

43. Infra, Ch. 11, text accompanying nn. 126–135.

44. In 1621 Coke stated in the Commons, "the king cannot be judge of his own cause, therefore the case must be judged by the Lords"; 2 W. Notestein, F. H. Relf and H. Simpson, *Commons Debates: 1621*, p. 195 (New Haven, 1935). Earlier he had stated the rule in Dr. Bonham's Case, 8 Co. Rep. 113b, 77 E.R. 646 (1610).

45. "What," asked Judge Learned Hand, "could be better evidence of complete dependence than to subject the validity of the decision of one 'Department' as to its

In seeking to ascertain the boundaries between the conflicting claims of Congress and the President, questions of practical convenience need to be separated from the issue of constitutional power. For the source of the powers we must look to the Constitution and its history. If the scope of the congressional power be ascertainable, it cannot be diminished by presidential fiat, notwithstanding the President believes revision is required by the "national interest." The fact that Congress may exercise a power unwisely, even abuse it, is not the test of its existence,[46] still less a justification for its curtailment by the President. In the words of John Marshall, "The peculiar circumstances of the moment may render a measure more or less wise, but cannot render it more or less constitutional."[47]

Consequently, my analysis will focus first on the constitutional issue and then proceed to evaluate the practical arguments for and against executive privilege, which should sway judgment only if the constitutional sources are equivocal. A few further preliminary remarks may serve as a road map to the subsequent discussion and anticipate questions that may arise in the mind of the reader. Neither the congressional power of inquiry nor executive privilege are expressly mentioned in the Constitution. Since the Congress was patently modeled on the two Houses of Parliament,[48] since the colonial assemblies long asserted for themselves the various powers and privileges of Parliament,[49] and since Jefferson, when formulating the rules of the Senate, went back to parliamentary practice for his prototype[50]—indeed, earlier searched out English precedents on the very issue of congressional inquiry and executive disclosure—[50a] we are justified in turning to parliamentary history for the existence and scope of legislative

authority on a given occasion to review and reversal by another whose own action was conditioned upon the answer to the same issue? Such a doctrine makes supreme the 'Department' that has the last word"; Learned Hand, *The Bill of Rights* 4 (Cambridge, Mass., 1958). See infra, Ch. 11, text accompanying n. 148.

46. The Founders were well aware that the powers which they delegated might be subject to abuse. Berger, *Impeachment* 191–192. "The contention is earnestly made . . . that this power of inquiry . . . may be abusively and oppressively exerted. If this be so, it affords no ground for denying the power"; McGrain v. Daugherty, 273 U.S. 135, 175 (1927).

47. Gerald Gunther, *John Marshall's Defense of McCulloch v. Maryland* 190–191 (Stanford, 1969).

48. Hamilton, *The Federalist*, No. 65 at 425 (New York, 1937).

49. Infra, Ch. 2, text accompanying nn. 105–107.

50. 3 Dumas Malone, *Jefferson and His Times* 454 (1962).

50a. See infra, Ch. 6, text accompanying n. 37.

inquiry and executive withholding.[51] The Supreme Court turned to that history when it held in *McGrain v. Daugherty* that

power to secure needed information [by investigatory means] has long been treated as an *attribute* of the power to legislate. It was so regarded in the British Parliament and in the Colonial legislatures before the American Revolution.[52]

Inasmuch as the congressional power of inquiry is thus based on parliamentary practice, that practice should likewise serve as the index of the *scope* of the power. With but one exception that scarcely ruffled the historical stream, I found no objection by the Crown or any Minister to what was virtually untrammeled parliamentary power of inquiry into executive conduct.[53]

Adherents of "executive privilege" rely heavily on the "separation of powers,"[54] apparently viewing the doctrine as a self-evident foundation for executive immunity from inquiry. Such reliance overlooks Montesquieu's unqualified statement that the legislature has the *right* to examine how "its laws have been executed";[55] and it puts the cart before the horse. To rely on the separation of powers is to assume the answer, to postulate that there is a pre-existing exemption which invokes the protection of the separation of powers. Before we conclude that an executive "power" to withhold information from Congress is protected by the separation of powers, it needs to be *established* that such a power existed at the adoption of the Constitution. The first step is to establish that information-withholding was a recognized *attribute* of the executive power in 1787. For the separation of powers, as the 1780

51. "The language of the Constitution cannot be interpreted safely except by reference to the common law and to British institutions as they were when the instrument was framed and adopted." The Framers "expressed them[selves]in terms of the common law, confident that they could be shortly and easily understood"; Ex parte Grossman, 267 U.S. 87, 108–109 (1925). See also Berger, *Impeachment* 87 n. 160.

52. 273 U.S. 135, 161 (1927); emphasis added.

53. Infra, Ch. 2.

54. Supra, n. 13. Assistant Attorney General Rehnquist stated that the doctrine of executive privilege "is implicit in the separation of powers"; 2 Moorhead Hearings 359. To the same effect, Secretary of State W. P. Rogers, Ervin Hearings 473; former Assistant Secretary of State W. P. Bundy, ibid. 319.

President Nixon invoked the "precedents on separation of powers established by my predecessors," ibid. 46, "precedents" that, as will appear, are utterly without precedential value.

55. Supra, n. 14. In the 1792 debate on a proposed examination into the conduct of the Secretary of the Treasury, Alexander Hamilton, Madison stated that it was the Secretary's duty "to inform the House how the law had been executed"; 3 Annals of Cong. 934.

Massachusetts Constitution—the handiwork of John Adams[56]—spells out, was designed to prevent one department from exercising the powers of another.[57] Only if there is encroachment by the legislature on a pre-1787 attribute of the executive power, or if that attribute can be traced to a constitutional grant, does the separation of powers become relevant.

It was because the "power of inquiry [prior to 1787] . . . was regarded and employed as a necessary and appropriate attribute of the power to legislate—indeed, was treated as inhering in it," that the Supreme Court concluded that "the constitutional provisions which commit the legislative functions to the two houses are intended to include this attribute."[58] But because the power of inquiry is an historical attribute of, and therefore "implicit" in, the legislative power, it does not follow, as Assistant Attorney General Rehnquist mistakenly assumed, that the executive withholding power is equally "implicit."[59] *No pre-Convention history* was cited by Messrs. Rogers and Rehnquist to prove that the right of the executive to refuse information to Congress for the protection of the "national interest" was "firmly rooted in history and precedent."[60] Instead they relied on alleged "precedents" thereafter drawn out of thin air by a number of presidents, which will not bear the construction placed on them. Assume that those "precedents" are susceptible of the claimed construction, it was yet not open to the President to remodel the "Executive power" by exercising an authority theretofore unknown to the law,[61] particularly with the design of cutting down an established legislative power of inquiry. *This* in truth is such an encroachment on the powers of another department as violates the separation of powers.

Nor does the presidential claim of power to withhold gain much comfort from the records of the several Conventions. Repeatedly the Founders, by their references to the role of the House as "Grand Inquest of the Nation," assumed that the investigatory function, which was an attribute of the Grand Inquest, resided in

56. 1 Page Smith, *John Adams* 440 (Garden City, N.Y., 1962).

57. Article XXX of Part the First recites: "the legislative department shall never exercise the executive and judicial powers," etc. 1 B. P. Poore, *Federal and State Constitutions, Colonial Charters* 960 (Washington, 1877).

58. McGrain v. Daugherty, 273 U.S. 135, 175 (1927).

59. Ervin Hearings 429.

60. Ibid. 421.

61. "An agent cannot new model his own commission," said Hamilton; *Letters of Camillus*, 6 *Works* of Alexander Hamilton 166 H. C. Lodge ed. (New York, 1904).

the House.[62] On the other hand, there is not a single utterance in the Conventions nor in *The Federalist* which remotely suggests that the executive was or should be empowered to withhold information from the Grand Inquest. Given the established parliamentary practice of all but unlimited inquiry into the executive, some solid evidence is required to demonstrate that the Founders' references to the Grand Inquest postulated a more limited function than that enjoyed by Parliament, or to point to an intention to curtail the familiar legislative power by establishing an innovative executive power to withhold information from the legislature. That burden is not met by newly minted, self-serving "precedents" that are a post-Convention product, nor by crystal-gazing into the "executive," "commander-in-chief," or "foreign relations" roles of the President, which from time to time are alleged to afford a cloak for secrecy. These, history will show, were severely limited roles, designedly subordinate to Congress, or, as in the case of the "treaty-power," at most concurrent with the Senate, and in which the Senate was fully to participate. Of an intention to confer by these roles a power of executive secrecy, there is not of course the slightest intimation.

It needs also to be borne in mind that the claim of executive privilege—the right to determine what Congress shall see—asserts a paramountcy over the legislature that the Crown itself could no longer maintain. When the obstinate George III exhibited unwillingness in 1782 to submit to the verdict of the House of Commons, his Prime Minister, Lord North, reminded him that he could not "oppose the deliberate resolution of the House."[63] The Framers did not endow the President with more power than the King had, but with less; they removed notable powers formerly exercised under the Crown prerogative and lodged them in Congress, not the President. All this was subsumed by Madison when he wrote in Federalist No. 51 that "in a republican form of government, the legislature necessarily predominates."[64] Congress, it cannot be unduly emphasized, was to be the senior partner, from whom, it follows, no junior could conceal the state of the Union.

Americans have a historical aversion to secrecy. There is a

62. Infra, Ch. 2, text accompanying nn. 91, 127–130.

63. Sir Herbert Butterfield, *George III and the Historians* 281 (London, 1969).

64. *Federalist* at 338. Justice Brandeis referred to the deep-seated conviction of the English and American people that they "must look to representative assemblies for the protection of their liberties"; Myers v. United States, 272 U.S. 52, 294–295 (1926) (dissenting; Holmes, J., concurring).

"strong 'public feeling against secrecy of any kind in the administration of the Government,' " stated President Polk;[65] and that the feeling has endured is recognized in Assistant Attorney General Rehnquist's statement that "the claim of executive privilege is an unpopular one."[66] The price of secrecy, as one who was within the inner circle of the Lyndon Johnson administration stated, is "an actual loss in public confidence in the Government itself,"[67] what has come to be known as the "credibility gap."[68] At bottom, the issue concerns the right of Congress and the people to participate in making the fateful decisions that affect the fortunes of the nation. Claims of presidential power to bar such participation or to withhold on one ground or another the information that is indispensable for intelligent participation undermine this right and sap the very foundations of democratic government. More than extravagant legend is required to sustain such claims, nothing less than demonstrable constitutional sanction, and, even then, proof that a presidential iron curtain is demanded by the highest wisdom.

65. Charles Warren, "Presidential Declarations of Independence," 10 Bost. U. L. Rev. 1, 16 (1930); see also infra, Ch. 6, text accompanying nn. 186–204.

66. Ervin Hearings 428.

67. George Reedy, ibid. 455. As Senator J. W. Fulbright said, "When a government refuses to put its trust in the people, the people in turn will withdraw their trust from that government"; ibid. 19. We need look no further than President Lyndon Johnson's decision not to run for re-election. For a good discussion of the pros and cons of secrecy by W. B. Pearce, see ibid. 590–594.

68. See Bruce Ladd, *Crises in Credibility* (New York, 1968); W. McGaffin and E. Knoll, *Anything But the Truth: The Credibility Gap* (New York, 1968).

2

HISTORY OF LEGISLATIVE INQUIRIES INTO EXECUTIVE CONDUCT

A. *Parliamentary Inquiries*

Parliamentary inquiry into executive conduct is met at least as early as 1621, in connection with a number of ensuing impeachments.[1] That inquiry should precede accusation is simple common sense: "Would not a Physician be a Madman," said a member of the House of Commons in 1742 (when it was considering an inquiry into the regime of the fallen Robert Walpole), "to prescribe to a Patient, without first examining into the State of his Distemper, the Causes from which it arose."[2] Coke acknowledged that the House of Commons "have no power to judge," but said "we may examine."[3]

The power of inquiry as a prelude to impeachment, all but unnoticed in our time,[4] goes far to establish the parliamentary

1. Parliamentary inquiries were initiated in 1571 with respect to election disputes for seats in Parliament. Marshall Dimock, *Congressional Investigating Committees* 48 (Baltimore, 1929); James M. Landis, "Constitutional Limitations on the Congressional Power of Investigation," 40 Harv. L. Rev. 153, 160 (1926).

2. 13 Richard Chandler, *History and Proceedings of Parliament from 1621 to the Present* 85 (London 1743). The King had asked for the "Counsel and Assistance" of the Commons, and A. H. Campbell said that knowledge of the facts was a prerequisite. Sir W. W. Wynne asked, "could the Parliament, previous to any Inquiry, ever have such proofs against a Minister?"; ibid. 93. As Wynne's statement indicates, a determination to impeach need not precede an inquiry. William Pitt explained the "Difference between a Motion for Impeachment, and a Motion for an Inquiry. If any Member were to . . . move for impeaching a Minister, he would be obliged to charge him with some particular Crimes or Misdemeanors, and to produce some Proof, or to declare that he was ready to prove the facts. But any gentleman may move for an Inquiry, without any particular Allegations, and without offering any Proof . . . because the very Design of an Inquiry is to find out the particular facts and particular Proofs . . . This, Sir, has always been the practice"; ibid. 170.

3. 3 W. Notestein, F. H. Relf, and H. Simpson, *Commons Debates: 1621*, p. 24 (New Haven, 1935). Sergeant Ashby stated: "We have power to examine"; ibid.

4. Barenblatt v. United States, 360 U.S. 109, 111–112 (1959): "Since Congress may only investigate into those areas in which it may potentially legislate or appropriate it cannot inquire into matters which are within the exclusive province of one of the other branches of the Government." McGrain v. Daugherty, 273 U.S. 135, 175 (1927): the "power of inquiry . . . was regarded . . . as a necessary and

oversight of executive functions, to which Montesquieu much later adverted. C. D. Bowen remarks upon

Parliament's extraordinary zeal in searching out corruption of government and trade [in 1621] . . . President Judge Bennet of the High Commission was found guilty, Attorney General Yelverton . . . "I am ashamed," James told Parliament, "and it makes my hair stand upright."[5]

When corruption was laid at the door of Lord Chancellor Francis Bacon, the King, perhaps to dilute the forces of the Commons, offered to "give both the houses his commission to examine what should be alledged in this matter," and "proposed a commission, 6 of the Higher House and 12 of the Lower House" to examine into it upon oath.[6] But the House of Commons already had appointed a Committee for Grievances with "Power to send for what or whom they thought fit to be questioned";[7] and Coke cautioned, "we should take heed the Commission did not hinder the manner of our parliamentary proceedings."[8] Ever jealous of its privileges, Parliament preferred to travel under its own steam: "the commission was liked by neither of the houses as being prejudicial to Parliamentary liberty."[9] In Notestein's masterly compilation of diaries of various members of the 1621 Parliament, no hint of an objection by the Crown to this independent procedure appears; nor is there any record of any challenge made on behalf of the Lord Chancellor, or Attorney General Yelverton, et al. to the right of Parliament to inquire or to the scope of inquiry into executive conduct. Rather, one diarist recorded, "Note that Blun-

appropriate attribute of the power to legislate"; see also ibid. 161; and Quinn v. United States, 349 U.S. 155, 160–161 (1955); Louis Henkin, *Foreign Affairs and the Constitution* 87 (Mineola, N.Y., 1972). For early American perception of the correlation between impeachment and inquiry, see infra, text accompanying nn. 133–155.

In fact, as Lord Chief Justice Denman pointed out, "The Commons . . . are not invested with more of power and dignity by their legislative character than by that which they bear as the grand inquest of the nation"; Stockdale v. Hansard, 112 Eng. Rep. 1112, 1156 (Q.B. 1839).

5. Catherine D. Bowen, *The Lion and the Throne* 435 (Boston, 1957). Sir John Bennett was Judge of the Prerogative Court and "Master of the Chauncery"; 3 Notestein, supra, n. 3 at 24. For the inquiry, see 2 ibid. 291, 298; 3 ibid. 3, 151, 310; 4 ibid. 248. For the inquiry into Sir Henry Yelverton, Attorney General, see 2 ibid. 159, 188; 6 ibid. 48, 394.

6. 6 ibid. 385; 2 ibid. 244–245.

7. 5 ibid. 475. There was likewise a Committee for Grievances in 1628, with "Power to send for Records, and Witnesses"; 1 H.C. Jour. 873.

8. 2 Notestein, supra, n. 3 at 245.

9. 6 ibid. 385.

dell and Mompesson are called in person to answere, though they were the King'es servaunts."[10] It is reasonable to infer that Parliament exercised an unqualified right to examine the "King'es servaunts," in which the Crown and its highest ministers acquiesced. In 1624, Bacon, who had been impeached and removed from office in 1621, pungently summarized the parliamentary practice. Congratulating the Treasurer on his advancement, Bacon declared that "he had one rule for all great officers of the Crown: 'Remember, a Parliament will come.' "[11] Bacon's "rule" received striking confirmation in 1715, when a Committee of Secrecy under the leadership of Robert Walpole examined into the conduct of the "Last Ministry," and charged it with "treasonable negotiations for the peace of Utrecht," whereupon the Commons impeached Bolingbroke, Ormond, Oxford, and Strafford. Once again parliamentary inquiry into executive conduct served as a prelude to impeachment.[12]

It is not my purpose to attempt a compendious history of parliamentary inquiries into executive conduct but to brush in some evidence for what, before the end of the eighteenth century, was to harden into established practice. Let us pass therefore to the Restoration period and view the scene through the eyes of the noted diarist, Samuel Pepys, who then served as Surveyor General of Victualing and was to become Secretary to the Admiralty. On June 29, 1666, he recorded, "I do think that . . . the Parliament's taking the whole management of things into their hands, and severe inquisitions into our miscarriages will help us."[13] On July 25 he wrote, Parliament "will fall foul upon the faults of the Government; and I pray God they may be permitted to do it [i.e., without prorogation by the King], as nothing else, I fear, will save the King and kingdom than the doing it betimes."[14] Pepys moved in the highest executive circles, and his remarks express recognition of the power to which Bacon forty-five years earlier had bowed. Upon this scene burst first the investigations, then the impeachments of Peter Pett, Commissioner of the Navy, and of his fellow Commissioner, Sir William Penn, the Vice Admiral of England, as a result of an inquiry into "mis-

10. 5 ibid. 35.
11. Bowen, supra, n. 5 at 462.
12. 59 *Dictionary National Biography* 184 (London, 1899); infra, text accompanying nn. 46–51.
13. 7 *Diary of Samuel Pepys* 216 (New York, 1904).
14. Ibid. 260.

carriages" in the war against the Dutch.[15] The right to call executive officers had been spelled out in 1664: in the course of preparing a bill to prevent the embezzlement of "Stores of Powder and Ammunition," a Committee was empowered to "send for Persons, Papers and Records; and receive Information from the Officers of the Navy, or any persons whom they shall think necessary."[16]

Inquiries into the conduct of a war became commonplace. In 1668, Sir John Harman was examined for not pursuing the Dutch fleet.[17] In 1689, "the burghers of Londonderry endured the famous siege, facing starvation . . . These men held England's bridgehead in North Ireland till reinforcements could be shipped over."[18] Dissatisfaction with the conduct of the war led to an inquiry into "the Occasion of the Delays in sending Relief over into Ireland."[19] Another Committee was appointed in the same year to inquire "into the Miscarriages in the Victualing of the Navy; and the Transportation of the Army; and all other Things relating to the War, both by Sea and Land."[20] Hallam said of these committees, "No courtier has ever since ventured to deny this general right of inquiry."[21] An inquiry into the Miscarriages of the Fleet in 1691 called for the Admiralty papers, which two of the Commissioners, Admiral Russel and Lord Falkland, laid before the Commons; subsequently, Russel and Sir John Ashby, commander of the Fleet, testified.[22] A similar inquiry was made in 1693; Sir Christopher Musgrave asked, "Shall it ever be said to the disgrace of the house of commons that we do not examine Miscarriages?"[23]

15. Pett had been charged by the Duke of Albemarle, joint commander of the Fleet, who appeared before the Committee appointed to inquire, with neglect of orders "to remove the Royal Charles above the Dock" in the Thames, in consequence of which the ship was burned by the Dutch; 9 H.C. Jour. 4, 11, 13, 42, 43. The Committee of Accounts furnished evidence that Penn had embezzled Prize Goods; ibid. 81, 82; see also 4 Parl. Hist. Eng. 409–410 (1667).

16. 8 H.C. Jour. 630.

17. 9 ibid. 82. A Committee was appointed in 1667 "to inquire into the Miscarriage of Affairs in the late war"; 9 ibid. 4, 49, 53, 55.

18. Sir G. M. Trevelyan, *Illustrated History of England* 483 (London, 1956).

19. 10 H.C. Jour. 162 (1689).

20. 10 H.C. Jour. 278. The Comptroller of the Navy and the Victualler were summoned; 5 Parl. Hist. Eng. 405, 448, 451 (1701).

21. 3 Henry Hallam, *Constitutional History of England* 143 (London, 1884). If it was questioned earlier, I found no record of it.

22. 5 Parl. Hist. Eng. 657, 658, 710, 712, 714. In 1742 a Committee report recalled to the House of Commons a prior inquiry into the "Conduct of the Lord Commissioners of our Admiralty," who were censured and then deprived of the "Direction of that Branch of the publick Business"; 13 Chandler 208.

23. 5 Parl. Hist. Eng. 778. In the course of the 1742 debate on a motion to inquire into the Walpole administration, Mr. Phillips asked, "Shall there be the least sus-

Investigation into executive conduct of a war was therefore a recognized prerogative of Parliament.

Accountings for expenditures of public moneys were also called for. A number of instances are to be found in 1664. A Committee was appointed "to examine and state the Accompts touching the Monies payable to the indigent loyal officers . . . and to send for Persons, Papers and Records."[24] Another was appointed "to inspect the Rolls and returns in the Exchequer of Chimney-Money, and the Farmers and Farmers Books,"[25] meaning those to whom the collection of certain revenues had been "farmed" out. Reference is made in the 1666 Journal of the Commons to "taking an Accompt of the Publick Monies, upon Oath" and to provide a "just Account of how the said Moneys have been disbursed."[26] In 1668, Sir George Carteret, Treasurer of the Navy, was found guilty of a misdemeanor by the Commons on the basis of evidence furnished by the Committee of Accompts.[27] Inquiry penetrated into Crown circles. The Lords, in 1691, ordered the Commissioners of Accounts (the prototype of our own General Accounting Office) to furnish their accounts; they reported that "When we called for the accounts of the King's Household, we found some accounts had not been made up in ten years."[28] In 1695 the Commons ordered the Lord Commissioners of the Treasury "to lay before this House, a State of the Revenue with the Loans, Debts and Charges," and the Commissioners complied, even submitting a report of payments under "Secret Services."[29] Inquiry into the receipt and disbursement of public funds may therefore be regarded as an established branch of parliamentary inquiry.

Another head of investigation was inquiries designed to furnish

---

picion of Mismanagement and a *British* House of Commons not inquire into it?"; 13 Chandler 149.

24. 8 H.C. Jour. 630.

25. Ibid. 637.

26. Ibid. 660. Trevelyan 453 notes that in 1666, "the Commons insisted on searching the royal account books to trace the actual use made of money voted for the maritime war with Holland."

27. 9 H.C. Jour. 112.

28. 5 Parl. Hist. Eng. 666, 669.

29. Ibid. 865–866, 878. In 1691, a Treasury officer testified with respect to money for secret services that "it was for a service of such nature" as ought to "remain confidential," but if the Commons "insisted upon it, they should have it." Ibid. 670. In 1703 the Commissioners of Public Accounts reported an examination of the Earl of Ranelagh, Paymaster General of the Army; he was expelled from the House for misapplication of several sums of the public moneys, a "high misdemeanor"; 6 Parl. Hist. Eng. 97, 127.

a basis for legislation. In 1664 a Committee was "appointed to inspect the Act concerning Customs; and to hear such complaints as shall be offered to them . . . and to consider expedients for settling the Table of Fees between Customer [customs officer] and Merchant."[30] Another Committee was "appointed to look into the former Laws against Atheism, Profaneness" and to inquire "whether there be any Neglect in putting the Laws in Execution."[31] In 1667 a Committee was "appointed to peruse the Act against importing *Irish* cattle" and to inquire what "Frauds and Abuses there are in the Execution of that Law; and how the same may be remedied."[32] Here we have exemplification of Montesquieu's statement that the lawmaker has a right to examine "how its laws have been executed."[33] Legislative inquiry as a basis for legislation is perhaps most clearly spelled out in an order of the Commons in 1729:

That the Committee, appointed to inspect what Laws are expired, or near expiring, and to report their Opinion to the House, which of them are fit to be revived, or continued, and who are instructed to inspect the Laws relating to Bankrupts, and consider what Alterations are proper to be made therein, have Power to send for Persons, Papers, and Records, with respect to that Instruction.[34]

Before existing laws were to be altered, repealed, or left standing, Parliament desired information as to how they had functioned and had been administered.

In sum, legislative supervision of administration in plentitude, exemplified by inquiries into executive conduct, including the conduct of war, the execution of the laws, the expenditure of appropriations, and to lay a foundation for legislation, had be-

30. 8 H.C. Jour. 550. Reference to a "Committee appointed to peruse the old Laws, and also the Acts lately made concerning the Highways; and to see wherein they are defective"; ibid. 583 (1664).

31. Ibid. 630.

32. 9 H.C. Jour. 27. How such policing functioned may be gathered from a 1668 order to Sir Peter Pindar, Collector of the Customs in Chester, to appear before the Committee on Grievances and give an account of exacting duties contrary to law; ibid. 70, 95.

33. Supra, Ch. 1, n. 14.

34. 21 H.C. Jour. 223 (1728). Landis, supra, n. 1 at 161 cites an earlier instance, a 1628 report from the Committee for the Examination of the Merchants Business, in reliance on W. Petyt, *Miscellania Parliamentaria* 108 (London, 1681). Petyt records that the Committee found Acton, Sheriff of London, "in prevarications and contradictions," and the House, because he was "so great an officer of so great a city," sentenced him to the Tower; ibid. 109. Nothing in the Petyt account suggests that the purpose of the Committee was to lay a predicate for legislation, and the Journals of the Commons for 1628, so far as I could discover, make no mention of this incident.

come a familiar parliamentary function. The highest officers of the land responded to such inquiries. Judges too were questioned by the Commons, which went so far in 1689 as to interrogate Chief Justice Francis Pemberton and Justice Thomas Jones as to the basis of their decision in a certain case.[35] Hallam, after adverting to the investigations of 1691 and 1694 into the Admiralty and sundry admirals, concluded, "it is hardly worth while to enumerate later instances of exercising a right which had become indisputable, and, even before it rested on the basis of precedent, could not reasonably be denied to those who might advise, remonstrate and impeach."[36]

Was any exception made for foreign affairs, about which American presidents have drawn a curtain of secrecy, not to be drawn aside even by the Senate?[37] No such exception crossed my ken; indeed there is evidence which rebuts its existence. Perhaps the most extensive claim to participation in foreign affairs was made by the House of Commons in a petition of December 9, 1621, which stated with respect to matters of peace and war, "we cannot conceive that . . . the state of your kingdom, are matters at any time unfit for our deepest consideration in time of Parliament."[38] The constitutional changes in the conduct of foreign affairs during the revolutionary seventeenth century—by which the Founders were more influenced than by eighteenth-century developments—[39] have been admirably described by E. B. Turner, and

35. S. A. Ferrall, *The Law of Parliament* 316–329 (London, 1837). They were then ordered into the custody of the sergeant-at-arms; ibid. 329. For a similar proceeding in the House of Lords (1697) against Chief Justice Holt and Justice Eyres, ibid. 332–343. In 1667 the Commons examined into abuses charged against Chief Justice Keeling (Kelynge?) and he humbled himself before the House. 9 H.C. Jour. 35; 2 Lord John Campbell, *Lives of the Chief Justices of England* 170 (New York, 1874). A Committee was appointed in 1680 "to examine the proceedings of the Judges in Westminster Hall"; 4 Parl. Hist. Eng. 1228.

36. 3 Hallam, supra, n. 21 at 144.

37. Infra, Ch. 5, nn. 11, 12, 113.

38. Joseph R. Tanner, *Constitutional Documents of the Reign of James I, 1603–1625*, 281 (Cambridge, 1960).

39. Bernard Bailyn, *The Ideological Origins of the American Revolution* viii, xi, 34–35, 53 (Cambridge, Mass., 1967). Compare colonial reliance on Coke for judicial review, notwithstanding Blackstone had plumped for "parliamentary supremacy"; Berger, *Congress v. Court* 23–30; and the colonists' frequent references to Stuart absolutism; Berger, *Impeachment* 5, 99. "The founding fathers owed their mental sustenance much more to seventeenth century England than to the England with which they were contemporary." Edward Corwin, *Twilight of the Supreme Court: A History of Our Constitutional Theory* 102 (New Haven, 1934); see also Julius Goebel, "Constitutional History and Constitutional Law," 38 Colum. L. Rev. 555, 563 (1938).

In particular, it was the revolutionary Parliament of the seventeenth century upon which the colonists fixed their gaze. It needs to be borne in mind that "The privileges

for present purposes a few examples drawn from Turner may suffice. By virtue of its powers over supplies, Parliament constrained the headstrong James I to promise "to make no treaty without first acquainting parliament and requesting its advice."[40] When "the long parliament was sitting the king informed the members of the alliance which he was about to make with the Dutch, and asked for advice."[41] After the Restoration, "the commons aimed at nothing less than direction and control . . . More and more information was called for, and the commons insisted on a share in foreign policy if they were to supply the means of carrying it out."[42] In 1673, "the lord chancellor declared . . . that 'the King . . . hath made your counsels the Foundations of all His Proceedings [abroad].' "[43] To keep Parliament in the dark was to risk harsh retaliation, as when Parliament objected that negotiations respecting the second partition treaty (1700) "had been carried through without the advice of parliament," and "then proceeded to impeach those who had assisted William in making it."[44] In the Hanoverian period the "participation of

---

of the House of Commons, for which the people had fought in the seventeenth century, which they had then held to be synonymous with their liberty had by now (the nineteenth century) become nearly as odious as the rigours of martial law. Why? Because the seventeenth century conflict took place between the Crown and Parliament. But from the middle of the eighteenth century onwards a realignment in this conflict had occurred, leaving the people on one side, and Crown and Parliament combined on the other." Parliament "had now drawn unto itself all of the vices and all of the unpopularity of executive government." John Clive, *Macaulay* 124, 125 (New York, 1973). The American Constitution, stated J. H. Plumb, "was designed to avoid the seeming corruption of the British Constitution in the 18th century, in which the executive—headed by the king—appeared to dominate the legislature to its own corrupt advantage"; Plumb, "Notes from London," N.Y. Times, June 6, 1973, sec. 6, pp. 20, 24.

40. E. B. Turner, "Parliament and Foreign Affairs, 1603–1760," 38 Eng. Hist. Rev. 172, 174 (1919).

41. Ibid. 175.

42. Ibid. 176. Trevelyan 453 states of this period "Till Parliament could control policy and expenditure, it would not consent to open wide the public purse."

43. Turner, supra, n. 40 at 177. In 1701 the Commons advised the King to act in concert with the States General in treaty negotiations with France "to conduce to their security"; the King responded that he had done so; 5 Parl. Hist. Eng. 1243 (1701). The King communicated the posture of negotiations and in closing said, the "safety of England . . . does very much depend upon your Resolution in this matter"; ibid. 1250. In 1709 both Houses advised Queen Anne as to measures for a secure peace. 6 Parl. Hist. Eng. 788.

44. Turner, supra, n. 40 at 183. In 1715, the Commons "impeached Oxford [of high treason] because . . . he had misrepresented negotiations to the queen and hence to parliament, and so 'prevented the just Advice of the Parliament to her Majesty' "; ibid. 188. Was it sheer coincidence that James Iredell told the North Carolina Ratification Convention that if the President "has concealed important intelligence" from the Senate and so induced them to consent to a treaty, he could be

parliament in foreign affairs and even its supervision of them was . . . fully recognized, but not its power to direct them."[45] By 1714, "Parliament had established a degree of control over the executive and over all its actions—including foreign policy."[46] In the words of Trevelyan, Parliament had emerged "as the leading partner."[47]

The cost of concealment from the "leading partner" was again illustrated in 1715 by the inquiry into the Treaty of Utrecht carried through under the aegis of Robert Walpole, who was himself to become the subject of inquiry in 1742. The Committee of Secrecy had before it books and papers relating to a number of negotiations, among them "the extraordinary *Measures* pursued to form the Congress at *Utrecht*," the "*Clandestine Negotiations*" with the French agent Mesnager, "*Bolingbroke's* journey to *France* to negotiate a *Separate Peace*."[48] Two of the intermediaries, Matthew Prior and Thomas Harley (brother of the Earl of Oxford who, with Bolingbroke led the Ministry), had been authorized as agents of the Ministry to communicate with France.[49] Prior and Harley were taken into custody, examined, and Harley was committed for prevarication.[50] The papers of the Earl of Strafford, member of the Privy Council, Ambassador Extraordinary to Holland, were seized.[51] This inquiry was of very broad scope; it entered into examination of the negotiating envoys and documents, in relation to foreign affairs of utmost confidentiality.[52] In the upshot, Bolingbroke, Ormond, Oxford, and Strafford were impeached of high treason for making a dishonorable peace.[53]

---

impeached?" 4 Jonathan Elliot, *Debates in the Several Conventions on the Adoption of the Federal Constitution* 127 (2d ed. Washington, 1836).

45. Turner, supra, n. 40 at 188.

46. Christopher Hill, *The Century of Revolution* 2 (New York, 1961).

47. Trevelyan 472.

48. A. Boyer, *History of the Impeachment of the Last Ministry* 3 (London, 1716).

49. Ibid. 6–7, 27–28, 79, 94, 244–245.

50. Ibid. 2, 124–125, 245–247.

51. Ibid. 262–263.

52. Henry Fox explained in 1742 that "they could not make their Inquiry compleat without having all such Papers" of State; 13 Chandler 153.

53. Oxford, Boyer, supra, n. 48 at 127; Bolingbroke, ibid. 223; Ormond, ibid. 234; Strafford, ibid. 248. For example, Bolingbroke promised the Dutch, an ally in the war against France, that he would "make no step towards a peace but in concert with them," and negotiated with France behind the back of the Dutch; ibid. 4–5. Walpole, who himself prepared the 1715 Report, charged "the late ministry with treasonable misconduct in the negotiations for the Peace of Utrecht." 59 DNB 184. Both Bolingbroke and Ormond fled; Boyer, ibid. 240–241; 59 DNB 184. In opposing an inquiry into the Walpole administration in 1742, Henry Fox commented on the actors of 1715, "a most glorious War had been put an end to by most infamous peace; our allies had been deserted, if not betrayed"; 13 Chandler 153.

Just as there exists no executive limit on the parliamentary power to impeach, so there can be no executive limit on the power of Parliament to *inquire* whether executive conduct amounts to impeachable misconduct. No executive officer can bar the portals to impeachment or to preliminary inquiry, be the field domestic or foreign affairs.[54] But I would not suggest that the parliamentary power to inquire into executive conduct derives from the impeachment power alone; it rests upon the fullest legislative supervision of administration, exhibited by inquiries into executive miscarriages, expenditures of public moneys, and execution of the laws, as a basis for legislation and the like.

For Americans special interest attaches to a number of incidents in the last days of the Walpole regime, because Thomas Jefferson, in an unofficial note, cited them for his view that the executive ought to refuse papers to the Congress, "the disclosure of which would injure the public."[55] Since the Jefferson dictum has become a central pillar for presidential claims of executive privilege it behooves us to look closely at what these Walpole incidents actually involved. By 1742 Sir Robert Walpole had exercised control over the administration for twenty-one years and his government was tottering. Certain papers of State had been presented to the Commons in January 1742, presumably in response to its request, and were ordered "to lie upon the Table for the Perusal of the Members." William Pulteney moved that the papers be referred to a Select Committee for examination and report.[56] Such an inquiry might extend beyond the papers and open up matters that the administration might prefer to keep in the dark. Speaking in opposition, Henry Pelham conceded that he had been "zealous" for such an inquiry in 1715, but maintained that the timing was inopportune because the nation was now "involved in a dangerous foreign War."[57] The times were indeed stormy: England was at war with Spain; the opposition rattled the bones of disrupted alliances; they raised the dread specter of civil war; they played a tattoo on the multitudinous dangers that would flow from a parliamentary inquiry.[58] "If anything has been done amiss," Pelham stated, "we may soon find a proper Time for

54. Supra, n. 2; cf. infra, text accompanying n. 102.
55. 1 Thomas Jefferson, *Writings*, P. L. Ford, ed. 189–190 (New York, 1892). For full discussion of this note, see infra, Ch. 6, text accompanying nn. 32–52.
56. 13 Chandler 70.
57. Ibid. 77, 100.
58. Ibid. 82, 86, 89, 99, 154, 195.

inquiring into it, but the present is far from being so."[59] The *power* to inquire, it needs to be stressed, was never questioned; it was the inconvenient timing that the opposition pressed.

In passing Pelham remarked that when the curiosity of the members "prompts them to desire a sight of any Papers of State, they move for having them laid before the House, and their Motion is always complied with, when consistent with the publick safety"[60]—a truly novel claim of a right to withhold information from the Commons.[61] Even so, it was sharply limited by Sir William Yonge, also speaking for the opposition to Pulteney's motion, who picked up Pelham's suggestion but stated that, "with regard to *domestick* Affairs, we have a much greater Latitude, because we may more freely call for *all* Papers relating to any such Affairs."[62] Pulteney's motion was defeated by a narrow margin, 253 to 250.[63] So far as this incident has *any* precedential value it *excludes* a claim of executive privilege for information pertaining to *domestic* affairs. In fact, however, it is altogether without precedential value, for reasons now to be stated.

Immediately following this vote, the Commons resolved to ask for copies of correspondence with the King of Prussia, "relating to the State of War in the Empire."[64] On behalf of "His Majesty," it was replied that the request would be "carefully examined, in order to see how far the same may be complied with without prejudice to the Publick, and consistently with the confidence reposed in him by other Princes."[65] The historian J. B. Owen states that Walpole "pointed out that there was a negotiation pending with the King of Prussia which might well be unfavorably affected if the details were made public at this juncture. Consequently it was suggested [on December 18] that those particular papers should be withheld until the end of January."[66] This was not a claim of an absolute right to withhold,[67] but a temporizing

59. Ibid. 81.

60. Ibid. 82.

61. "On numerous occasions" in the Hanoverian period "treaties or papers . . . were asked for, and invariably transmitted thereupon"; Turner, supra, n. 40 at 188.

62. 13 Chandler 98–99; emphasis added.

63. Ibid. 104.

64. Ibid. In "December 1740 Frederick of Prussia, by invading Silesia, was instrumental in entangling England in a continental conflict in support of the Queen of Hungary"; J. B. Owen, *The Rise of the Pelhams* 2 (London, 1957).

65. 13 Chandler 106–107.

66. Owen, supra, n. 64 at 25.

67. Ibid. But Pelham "tactlessly asserted that it might not be in the national interest to reveal all the papers relevant to the existing transaction, even after its conclusion";

answer which made it premature to bring the issue to a vote. Then too, this was no contest between King and Parliament, for by Walpole's time "parliament had become absolute. He maintained this supremacy."[68] "His Majesty's" reply therefore represented the voice of the Prime Minister rather than that of the King.[69] So long as Parliament was dominated by his adherents—as for years had been the case—the Prime Minister could withhold information from the Commons whose servant he was supposed to be. But the Commons could at any time terminate his power; indeed Walpole resigned in February 1742, when he saw that he had lost the confidence of the Commons.[70] Hence this incident does not represent an assertion by the Crown of a constitutional right to withhold information from Parliament, to which its right was established, but at best the exercise of transient political control of an acquiescent Parliament by its own servant, and in a situation that did not really call for immediate rejection by Parliament.

Confirmation for this analysis is supplied by the fact that after control of Parliament had passed from Walpole, the Commons, on May 20, 1742, by a vote of 202 to 182, resolved upon an Address requesting all papers "relating to the Convention between Great Britain and Spain" of 1739, a sore subject.[71] On June 4, Sir Conyers Darcy told the Commons that "he had received his Majesty's command to lay before them . . . copies of all papers" requested by the Address of May 20, "as there had been Time to prepare . . . Copies of the remaining Papers are preparing with the utmost diligence to be laid before the House,"[72] an acknowledgment of Parliament's right to the information it requested.

Shortly after Walpole left the scene, on March 8, 1742, Lord Limerick moved for an inquiry "into the conduct of our affairs at home and abroad, during the last twenty years."[73] The motion was defeated by a vote of 244 to 242, in no small part because of

ibid. If there was an established right to withhold such information from Parliament, a reference to it could hardly be "tactless."

68. 59 DNG 203. Trevelyan 475 states that "from 1689 onwards no King . . . ever attempted to govern . . . contrary to the votes of the House of Commons."

69. Replying to the statement that facts stated in the King's Speech from the Throne could not be controverted, Pitt said, "Everyone knows that in Parliament, the King's Speech is always considered as the Speech of the Minister"; 13 Chandler 178.

70. 12 Parl. Hist. Eng. 455.

71. 13 Chandler 246.

72. Ibid. 268.

73. Ibid. 139.

the neglect of a number of anti-Walpolians to attend.[74] A subsequent motion to inquire into Walpole's conduct during the last "Ten Years of his being First Commissioner of the Treasury, and Chancellor and Under-Treasurer" of the Exchequer was adopted 252 to 245.[75] There was oft-voice suspicion that the Ministry had employed public moneys "for gaining a corrupt Influence, both at Elections and in Parliament."[76] For the opposition Henry Fox blandly agreed that "to apply the publick Money towards corrupting the Members of this House, or the Voters at any Election, must by all Men be allowed to be a Crime," which, Walpole's son, Horatio, stated, "ought to be punished."[77] "That we have a Right to inquire into the Conduct of our own publick Affairs," said Pelham, "no Gentleman will deny." But he called for "well-grounded Suspicion of Misconduct."[78] Where is your "proof?" asked Fox in effect, knowing well that the administration sat on the "proofs." It was "impossible," said Horatio Walpole, that such criminal practices could "be done in a hidden manner."[79] In the event it proved not at all "impossible"; the Commons' Committee of Secrecy documented the charge that Walpole had caused his subordinates to employ the "Secret Services" and other public moneys to corrupt elections and Members of Parliament.[80] Trevel-

74. 12 Parl. Hist. Eng. 448, 530–531. Hampered by a number of absences, the proponents faced "a firmly united Old Corps which, with one exception, stood by its former leader"; Owen, supra, n. 64 at 101.

75. 13 Chandler 190, 245.

76. Ibid. 140, 202, 212–213, 215. There were also suspicions that preferment went to those who voted with Walpole; ibid. 144. Pitt charged that Walpole made it "his constant Rule never to give a Post, Pension or Preferment, but to those who vote for his Measures . . . Has he not declared in the Face of this House, that he will continue to make this his Practice?"; ibid. 213. J. B. Owen, who stresses the absence of parties at this time, the shifting allegiances of various groups, and the swing role of the independent country gentlemen, notes that in a House composed of about 550 members, 124 of Walpole's supporters "actually held places of profit under the Crown"; another 28 "either sat for Government boroughs or owed their seats to patrons who were themselves friends of the Administration"; Owen, supra, n. 64 at 45. "Of the 44 army officers in the House in 1742, only two had consistently voted with the Opposition," their promotion was facilitated by "ministerial patronage"; ibid. 58.

It is not my purpose to assay how large a role corruption and placemen played in the twenty-one-year reign of Walpole, but rather to indicate that the proposed inquiry was not unfounded.

77. 13 Chandler 151, 192.

78. Ibid. 161. Pelham was the brother of "the arch-corruptionist Newcastle"; Trevelyan 534. He himself served in the lucrative post of Paymaster General of the Armed Forces. 24 H.C. Jour. 311 (1741).

79. 13 Chandler 151, 194.

80. The Report is printed as an appendix to 13 Chandler, and at 12 Parl. Hist. Eng. 627, 11 ibid. 1066. Owen states that the Commons elected a "composite Committee"; the Walpolians "managed to insinuate five of their number into the very body

yan states that Walpole allowed his "power to rest on the obvious and traditional basis of Parliamentary corruption."[81] The existence of corruption may be palliated[82] but hardly denied. This episode, parenthetically, illustrates the executive effrontery—from time to time since duplicated in the United States—with which the Executive has sought to screen its corruption. Let it be admitted that such inquiries are politically motivated;[83] nevertheless, they serve to cleanse the Augean stables, as our own Teapot Dome inquiry testifies. Note too that Nicholas Paxton, Solicitor of the Treasury, refused to testify on the ground that he should not be compelled to "accuse" himself and was thereupon clapped in jail.[84]

Jefferson did not cite the Paxton episode but the page of the Committee report[85] that recounts the refusal of John Scrope (Secretary of the Treasury and a Walpole instrument)[86] to testify about the Secret Service money on the ground that the disposal of the money "requires the utmost Secrecy" and that His Majesty could not "permit him to disclose any Thing on that subject."[87] Horatio Walpole recorded Scrope's answer "that he was fourscore years old, and did not care if he spent the few months he has to live in the Tower or not; that the last thing he would do should be to betray the King, and next to him the Earl of Orford [Walpole]." The Committee "was outraged," states J. B. Owen, "but the new Treasury could not afford to dispense with Scrope's intimate knowledge of financial administration."[88] His "intimate knowledge" of the Treasury Board forced even Pulteney to admit he was irreplaceable."[89] No immunity from disclosure to Parlia-

established to enquire into the conduct of their former leader [and six other members who were the choice of both sides], and had succeeded in rejecting from the Committee such virulent antagonists of Walpole as Wynne, Cotton, Philips and Dodington"; Owen, supra, n. 64 at 107–108. No dissent to the Report was filed.

81. Trevelyan 534. "There cannot be much question that votes had from time to time been secured by direct payments." 59 DNB 201.

82. Trevelyan 460 states that Danby (1674–1678) "secured his majority in the House by systematizing the bribery of individual Members which began at the Restoration and continued in the era of Walpole and George III"; and that "when the elder Pitt . . . tried to rule solely on the strength of [an appeal to national pride and conscience] he fell at once"; ibid. 534.

83. Compare the political motivation that has colored both English and American impeachments. Berger, *Impeachment* 94–97.

84. 13 Chandler 224–225; ibid. apps. 2–3.

85. 1 Jefferson 190.

86. 13 Chandler apps. 36–39.

87. Ibid. 44–45.

88. Owen, supra, n. 64 at 46.

89. Ibid. 108.

ment can be wrested from its forbearance to jail the aged and indispensable Scrope.[90]

A word about the place of "secrecy." William Pitt, destined to become a great Prime Minister, said:

> We are called the Grand Inquest of the Nation, and as such it is our Duty to inquire into every Step of publick Management, either Abroad or at Home, in order to see that nothing has been done amiss . . .[91] It is said, by some Gentlemen, that by this Inquiry we shall be in Danger of discovering the Secrets of our Government to our enemies . . . We have had many Parliamentary Inquiries into the Conduct of Ministers of State, and yet I defy any one to shew, that any State affair was thereby discovered which ought to have been concealed, or that our own publick affairs, either Abroad or at Home, ever suffered by such Discovery.[92]

To Thomas Winnington's question "Whether we can find Twenty-one Persons [the Committee membership], in this House, fit to be intrusted with all the Secrets of our Government,"[93] Lord Percival replied, "and yet, it seems, that one Man may be found proper to be intrusted, for twenty Years together, with the whole Revenues, . . . the sole power of this Government without Controul."[94] If, Percival emphasized, secrecy is to veil ministerial acts from examination, Ministers are "left to act in what Manner they think fit," without fear of "being called to Account."[95] The arguments for secrecy can scarcely weigh in the scales of a democratic society against the perils of such unaccountability.

"This very session has afforded us convincing Proof," Pitt stated, "how little Foundation there is for saying, that a Parliamentary Inquiry must necessarily discover the Secrets of our Government. Surely, in a War with *Spain*, which must be carried on chiefly by Sea, if our Government have any Secrets, the Lords of the Admiralty must be intrusted with the most important of

90. Ibid.

91. Member after member spoke for the right and the duty to inquire into the conduct of the administration and its ministers, "from the lowest to the highest"; 13 Chandler 157, 93, 94, 96, 101, 139–140, 149, 150, 158, 161, 210. Opposition to the inquiry was not based on a denial of the power but on injudicious timing, ibid. 148, 169, 192, 195; and an opposition spokesman confirmed that no man would deny that "we have a Right to inquire into the Conduct of our publick affairs"; ibid. 161. For a similar concession by Horatio Walpole, see ibid. 195.

92. Ibid. 172–173.

93. Ibid. 88.

94. Ibid. 102.

95. Ibid. 102–103.

them; yet we have in this very Session, and without any Secret Committee too, made an Inquiry into the Conduct of the Lords Commissioners of our Admirality," with the consequence that those Commissioners were no "longer intrusted with the Direction of that Branch of the publick Business."[96] Pitt referred to an inquiry into the instructions given by the Admiralty to Rear Admiral Haddock, who had charge of naval operations against Spain.[97] A batch of instructions from the Commissioners were delivered to the Commons in response to its request,[98] and this with respect to an *ongoing war*. Pitt remarked,

> our time cannot be more usefully employed during a war, than examining how it has been conducted, and settling the degree of confidence that may be reposed in those to whose care are entrusted our reputations, our fortunes, and our lives.[99]

Pitt's summation of the established right of Parliament to have such information as it requests, be the subject domestic or foreign affairs, is amply confirmed by history. And the Walpole incidents do not represent a curtailment of that right or a restoration of Crown prerogative but rather the Prime Minister's domination of a subservient majority in the Commons. The achievement of parliamentary supremacy meant ministerial responsibility to Parliament rather than the King, and management of foreign affairs by ministers who, under orthodox theory, were under the control of Parliament. What such control could mean is illustrated by a resolution passed by the House of Commons in 1782 condemning the "farther prosecution" of the war with the American colonies on the ground it was the means of "weakening the efforts of this country against her European enemies" and increasing the "mutual enmity, so fatal to the interests both of Great Britain and America." When the Ministry disregarded this resolution, a second resolution declared that "this House will consider as enemies" those who advise the "farther prosecution" of the war "for the purpose of reducing the revolted Colonies to obedience by force." Now Lord North buckled and bowed to the opinion of the Commons.[100] Indeed, when the willful George III showed

96. Ibid. 208.
97. 11 Parl. Hist. Eng. 1002–1010 (1741). In the summer of 1740, "Haddock and Norris had failed to prevent French and Spanish fleets from combining and sailing to the West Indies"; Owen, supra, n. 64 at 2.
98. 24 H.C. Jour. 148, 172–174 (1741).
99. 11 Parl. Hist. Eng. 1009.
100. 22 Parl. Hist. Eng. 1071, 1085, 1089, 1090, 1107 (1781–1782).

unwillingness to yield to the verdict of the Commons, Lord North reminded him that "the Prince on the Throne, cannot, with prudence, oppose the deliberate resolution of the House of Commons."[101]

The inferences here drawn as to the parliamentary power and scope of inquiry are confirmed by the words of Justice Coleridge in 1845:

That the Commons are, in the words of Lord Coke, the general inquisitors of the realm, I fully admit . . . it would be difficult to define *any limits* by which the subject matter of their inquiry can be bounded . . . they may inquire into every thing which it concerns the public weal for them to know; and *they themselves*, I think, are entrusted with the determination of what falls within that category.[102]

My earlier references to a "virtually" untrammeled power of inquiry do not reflect the discovery of any executive limits on that power in English history, but rather deference to the fact that our generation is inhospitable to absolutes, and that the Supreme Court from time to time has tempered seemingly absolute guarantees. But such tempering, particularly when curtailment of established legislative rights is involved, is a judicial, not a presidential, function.

B. *Colonial and Early State Materials*

In surveying the colonial scene, it needs to be borne in mind that, while the assemblies were elected by the colonists themselves, the colonial governors and judges were appointed by the Crown. Impeachment of Crown appointees was not in the scheme of things, as some of the colonial assemblies appreciated.[103] But

101. Sir Herbert Butterfield, *George III and the Historians* 281 (London, 1969). See also supra, n. 68.

The rejection of parliamentary precedent as "judicial" in Kilbourn v. Thompson, 103 U.S. 168 (1881), has been shown to be unhistorical. Landis, supra, n. 1 at 159–160; C. S. Potts, "Power of Legislative Bodies to Punish for Contempt," 74 U. Pa. L. Rev. 691, 692–696 (1926). See also Berger, *Impeachment* 18–20. Coke disclaimed a judicial function in the Commons; 3 Notestein, supra n. 3 at 54. United States v. Rumeley, 345 U.S. 41, 46 (1953), noted the Potts-Landis criticism and remarked upon the "inroads" made by McGrain v. Dougherty, 273 U.S. 135 (1927) upon Kilbourn v. Thompson.

102. Howard v. Gossett, 10 Q.B. 359, 379–380, 116 E.R. 139, 147 (1845); emphasis added. This was in essence repeated on appeal in Gossett v. Howard, 10 Q.B. 411, 451, 116 E.R. 158, 172 (1845).

103. "The judiciary," and by the same token the executive, was "put beyond the assembly's reach, for the power to erect and constitute courts was vested in the governor and council, creatures of the King." 1 Julius Goebel, *History of the*

though the Crown denied to the assemblies some privileges enjoyed by Parliament,[104] the assemblies themselves staked out the broadest claims,[105] among them a power of inquiry into the conduct of executive officers. The right to be represented in an assembly by their own elected officials, New York maintained from 1683 on, did not flow from the Crown but was "part of the inheritance of Englishmen." The assemblies claimed in matters of legislation powers "coequal in most particulars" with those of Parliament, accompanied by concomitant authority to effectuate them.[106] "In a pioneer study, C. S. Potts concluded that The Colonial assemblies, like the House of Commons, very early assumed, usually without question, the right to investigate the conduct of other departments of the government.[107] He instanced the 1722 inquiry by the Massachusetts House into the conduct of Colonel Walton and Major Moody in the field, maintaining a privilege "to demand of an Officer . . . an account of his Management while in the Public Imploy."[108] Like the House of Commons, the Pennsylvania Assembly had a standing committee to audit and settle the accounts of treasury officials, a practice, Potts states,

---

Supreme Court of the United States 12 (New York, 1971). The South Carolina House rejected a suggestion by the Council to impeach Chief Justice Nicholas Trott, saying that the "governor and council . . . were not a House of Lords nor a proper jurisdiction before whom any impeachment will lie." Quoted in M. P. Clarke, *Parliamentary Privilege in the American Colonies* 42 (New Haven, 1943). In Pennsylvania the Governor refused to try impeachment charges against an agent of the Proprietor, distinguishing the "transcendent power" of Parliament from the assembly which "had no power except as it was specifically granted in the Charter"; ibid. 40–41. Cf. Potts supra, n. 101 at 710.

104. When the Pennsylvania Assembly sought to punish one Moore for an indignity to a prior assembly, a matter of its own privilege, they were advised in 1759 that the English Attorney General Pratt and Solicitor General Yorke considered that "this unusual power could not be tolerated in the inferior Assemblies in the Colonies"; Clarke, supra, n. 103 at 220 n. 34.

105. Potts, supra, n. 101 at 700–712, cites examples wherein the colonial assemblies laid claim to the privileges of Parliament.

106. E. J. Eberling, *Congressional Investigations* 23–24 (New York, 1928). The "miniature parliament" of Virginia "was ludicrously yet reverently imitative of the mother assembly that sat beneath London spires." L. G. McConachie, *Congressional Committees* 10 (New York, 1898). The extent to which the assemblies modeled themselves on Parliament is illustrated by the Pennsylvania "Votes of the Assembly," Jan. 12, 1683: "The Speaker reads to the House the orderly Method of Parliaments, and the Demeanour of the Members thereof observed in England, which he recommended to them, as civil and good: as also the Method observed by the English in Committees"; ibid. 2. In "later colonial times legislators read and common-placed the books of the ancient parliamentarians"; ibid. 11. Virginia followed parliamentary use of Select Committees; several had "taken the names of the old-time English grand committees"; ibid. 19.

107. Potts, supra, n. 101 at 708.

108. Ibid.

that "was true of most of the colonies."[109] In 1758 the Pennsylvania Assembly conducted an investigation of Judge William Moore, who was charged with "corrupt" practices, though it was apparently conceded that removal was in the sole power of the Governor.[110] Admittedly the records are sparse, and it remains to carry further the study initiated by Potts, but enough emerges to demonstrate colonial awareness that the inquisitorial power exercised by the Commons was an attribute of a legislative assembly. That awareness shines forth in James Wilson's 1774 essay "On the Legislative Authority of the British Parliament," wherein he stated that the House of Commons

> have checked the progress of arbitrary power, and have supported, with honor to themselves, and with advantage to the nation, the character of grand inquisitors of the realm. The proudest ministers of the proudest monarchs have trembled at their censures; and have appeared at the bar of the house, to give an account of their conduct, and ask pardon for their faults.[111]

Destined to be one of the leading architects of the Constitution, Wilson was hardly one to let this prized legislative attribute go by default.[112]

Not surprisingly, virtually every early state constitution, following the English model, lodged the power of impeachment of all officers in the lower house;[113] and with impeachment, as we have seen, went the power of preliminary inquiry. The Massachusetts and New Hampshire constitutions expressly styled the house of representatives as the "grand inquest."[114] Georgia spelled out that "every officer of the State shall be liable to be called to account by the house of assembly";[115] and Maryland even more explicitly provided that the House "may call for all public or official papers

109. Ibid. 709. In 1770 the house "ordered the assessors and collectors of Lancaster County to appear before the audit committee and to bring with them their books and records for the preceding ten years"; ibid.

110. Ibid. 710.

111. 2 James Wilson, *The Works of James Wilson* 731 (Cambridge, Mass., 1967); see Keeling, C.J., supra, n. 35. For a later expression by Wilson, see infra, text accompanying n. 129.

112. Cf. infra, text accompanying n. 129.

113. Delaware, 1 Poore 277; Georgia, ibid. 383; Massachusetts, ibid. 964; New Hampshire, 2 Poore 1287; New Jersey, ibid. 1312; New York, ibid. 1337; North Carolina, ibid. 1413; Pennsylvania, ibid. 1545; South Carolina, ibid. 1624; Vermont, ibid. 1863; Virginia, ibid. 1912.

114. Massachusetts, 1 Poore 964; New Hampshire, 2 Poore 1287.

115. 1 Poore 383.

and records, and send for persons, whom they may judge necessary in the course of their inquiries."[116] What was thus spelled out was implicit in the several state constitutions.[117] In no constitution was there an intimation that the inquiry could be limited in any way by the executive branch. But I would not pin my conclusions on the colonial and early state practices, for the gaze of the Founders went beyond these to the English prototype.[118] Finally, the Continental Congress, in creating a Department of Foreign Affairs presided over by a Secretary, provided that "any Member of Congress shall have access [to '*all* . . . papers of his office']: provided that no copy shall be taken of matters of a secret nature without the special leave of Congress."[119] Here we have a clear reflection of British tradition, demonstrating that not even "secret" matters pertaining to foreign affairs could be withheld from the legislature.[120] Looking back at the colonial and early state practices, the Supreme Court stated that at the adoption of the Constitution

> the power of inquiry—with enforcing process—was regarded and employed as a necessary and appropriate attribute of the power to legislate —indeed, was treated as inhering in it . . . [T]he constitutional provisions which commit the legislative function to the two houses are intended to include this attribute.[121]

116. Ibid. 822.

117. "Similar powers," states Taylor 12, "were exercised quite as freely, and without objection, in the states with constitutions which were silent on the subject." Cf. Potts, n. 101 at 713–714.

118. So far as the Convention Records reveal, early American experience ultimately did not exercise as much influence as the English practice. For example, when removal by Address was proposed, references were made, not to the four state constitutions which provided for such removal (Maryland, 1 Poore 873; Massachusetts, ibid. 968; New Hampshire, 2 Poore 1290; South Carolina, ibid. 1625), but to the English Act of Settlement. 2 Max Farrand, *The Records of the Federal Convention of 1787* 428–429 (New Haven, 1911). John Dickinson said in the Federal Convention respecting the English practice of originating money bills in the Commons: "Shall we oppose to this long experience, the short experience of 11 years which we had ourselves"; 2 Farrand 278. Hamilton stated that the impeachment process was modeled on that of England. *Federalist* No. 65 at 425. When Vice-President Jefferson was preparing his Manual of Parliamentary Practice for the Senate some ten years later, "he went back to the [English] prototype, not contenting himself with such modifications of the historic practices as had been made in particular American legislatures." 3 Dumas Malone, *Jefferson and His Time* 454 (Boston, 1962). Jefferson's Manual is studded with citations to parliamentary records.

119. 22 Jour. Contl. Cong. 88 (1782).

120. The argument that this sheds no light on the later tripartite government is discussed infra, text accompanying n. 151.

121. McGrain v. Daugherty, 273 U.S. 135, 175 (1926). This had been emphasized at ibid. 174. Rogers attempt to restrict the force of McGrain is discussed in Appendix B.

C. *The Founders*

The Framers, after the English model,[122] provided for impeachment by the House and trial by the Senate. Since the power of impeachment historically was accompanied by a power of inquiry into the conduct of public officers, it should require some evidence that the Framers intended to withhold any part of this power from Congress. Of such evidence there is not a trace; and without it we cannot conclude that the inquisitorial power, asserted by colonial assemblies, expressly picked up in several state constitutions, was inexplicably curtailed by the Framers.[123] Such a conclusion must also account for the fact that the Framers vested many prerogatives of the Crown in Congress and denied them to the President.[124] On what ground, then, can it be concluded that American officers now enjoy an immunity to which no member of the English ministries laid claim? Again and again the Framers evidenced their intention to make the "ministers" of the President, that is, the Department heads,[125] indeed the President himself,[126] impeachable, and thus accountable to Congress.

In the Convention, the Committee of Detail referred to the House as the "grand inquest of the Nation,"[127] as did Fisher Ames in the Massachusetts Ratification Convention and Archibald Maclaine in that of North Carolina.[128] Justice James Wilson, who had extolled the inquisitorial function of the Commons in 1774, stated in his 1791 Lectures that "The house of representatives . . . form the grand inquest of the state. They will diligently inquire into grievances."[129] When the Washington administration was confronted with a congressional investigation into the disastrous St. Clair campaign, Jefferson searched the English precedents and

122. Constitution, Article I, §2(5), §3(6); *Federalist* No. 65 at 425 (Hamilton).

123. See infra, Ch. 3, text accompanying n. 12; and see infra, Ch. 5, n. 205.

124. Compare Hamilton's assurance that the Commander-in-Chief function of the President would be "much inferior" to that of the British King, the bulk of whose powers "would appertain to the legislature." Federalist No. 69 at 448.

125. In the Federal Convention, Gouverneur Morris stated that "certain great officers of State, as minister of finance, of war, of foreign affairs, etc. will be amenable by impeachment to the public justice"; 2 Farrand 53–54. See also George Nicholas, 3 Elliot 17; Patrick Henry, ibid. 512; Francis Corbin, ibid. 516; Henry Pendleton, 4 Elliot 263.

126. James Iredell adverted to the maxim that the King can do no wrong and exulted in the "happier" American provision which made the President himself triable; ibid. 109.

127. 2 Farrand 154.

128. 2 Elliot 11; 4 Elliot 44.

129. 1 Wilson, *Works* 415.

concluded that "the House was an inquest, therefore might institute inquiries into executive conduct."[130]

It bears repetition that while inquiry began as a prelude to impeachment, it broadened to cover the whole spectrum of government, as William Pitt observed in 1742 and Justice Coleridge confirmed in 1845.[131] Striking echoes of such views dot our early history. In 1796 Congressman Lyman affirmed that the "power of impeachment . . . certainly implied the right to inspect every paper and transaction in any department, otherwise the power of impeachment could never be exercised with any effect."[132] Washington recognized this right in rejecting the claim of the House to the Jay Treaty documents, on the ground that it was not empowered to participate in treatymaking, declaring that "the inspection of the papers" was not "relative to any purpose of the House except that of impeachment which the resolution has not expressed."[133] Thus, he plainly confirmed that inquiry is an auxiliary of impeachment; although he was mistaken in calling on the House for a prejudgment that it "purposes" to impeach before it can investigate. Moreover, as grantee of the "sole power" to impeach, it is for the House to determine how to go about it. A House committee summarized the matter cogently in 1843:

> The right of the House to information in possession of the Executive, if it exists at all, is an original right, and not acquired by asserting

130. 1 Jefferson 189–190. True, he concluded in mistaken reliance on the 1742 Walpole debate that there might be cases in which information might be withheld, but, as we have seen, no claim of Crown "privilege" can be drawn from those materials, and such an inference would run counter to the long parliamentary practice. For further examination of the Jefferson memorandum, see infra, Ch. 6, text accompanying nn. 32–52.

Professor Bernard Schwartz concluded that "American courts have rejected the notion that legislators are 'the general inquisitors of the realm,'" relying upon Kilbourn v. Thompson, 103 U.S. 168 (1880) for the proposition that the "investigatory authority could properly be employed only 'in aid of the legislative function.'" 1 B. Schwartz, *A Commentary on the Constitution of the United States* 126 (New York, 1963). Apart from the fact that the authority of Kilbourn has been undermined, Raoul Berger, Executive Privilege v. Congressional Inquiry, 12 UCLA L. Rev. 1044, 1054 n. 46 (1965), he himself notices that "The concept of the Congress as a 'grand inquest' is peculiarly appropriate to investigations by either House into the workings of the executive branch. In such inquiries, the legislative authority is at its maximum, for the Congress is patently acting in pursuance of a legitimate legislative function—i.e. that of supervision of administration"; ibid. 128. That is not only "appropriate" but was contemplated by the Founders, particularly as a preliminary to impeachment.

131. Supra, text accompanying nn. 92, 102.

132. 5 Annals of Cong. 601 (1796).

133. Ibid. 710–712. For more detailed discussion, see infra, Ch. 6, text accompanying nn. 53–97.

> that it is about to resolve itself into a court of impeachment . . . the right of the House to demand information from the Executive is possessed by it in its character of grand inquest of the nation . . . it is in this character it acts, whether engaged in the investigation of a petty fraud committed by some inferior officer of the Government, or in the impeachment of the President for the crime of high treason. It does not acquire the power necessary to pursue investigations by the act of proceeding to investigate . . . The right to demand and compel information is not merely an accidental right, but an original one, inherent in it, and not an incident of some particular duty.[134]

Those views had been anticipated by Congressman Nicholas in 1796: as the "grand inquest of the nation," the House had a right to "superintendence over the officers of government" which gave it a right to demand a sight of those papers, that should throw light upon their conduct," a view shared by a great majority of the House, among them the respected Edward Livingston.[135]

Then there is a constitutional provision, too little noticed, which by imposing a duty to supply information recognized the reciprocal legislative right to require it from the Executive. Originally the Framers made it "his duty to inform the Legislature of the Condition of the U.S. so far as may respect his Department."[136] Thereby he was placed under an unqualified duty to inform Congress as to matters within the Executive department. The final version in Article II, §3 represents a broadened and stylistically improved articulation of that duty: the President "shall from time to time give to the Legislature information of the State of the Union." One to whom a duty runs, said Chief Justice Marshall, has a correlative right to require performance of the duty;[137] what the President is under a duty to furnish to Congress "from time to time" could be *requested* at its convenience. That the President was given no discretion as to what to furnish or refuse emerges from the next following clause of Article II, §3: "and recommend to their consideration such measure as he shall judge necessary and expedient." No such discretion limits his duty to supply information and it is reasonable to conclude that none was conferred.[138]

134. H. Rept. No. 271, 27th Cong., 3d Sess. 13 (1843). For powerful confirmation see President Polk's statement, infra, Ch. 8, text accompanying n. 145.

135. 5 Annals of Cong. 444, 629 (1796); for additional citations see Berger, Executive Privilege 1089–1092.

136. 2 Farrand 158.

137. Marbury v. Madison, 5 U.S. (1 Cranch) 137, 162–166 (1803).

138. Compare T.I.M.E. v. United States, 359 U.S. 464, 471 (1959): "We find

The "State of the Union" clause has too mechanically been associated with annual presidential messages, but Justice Story properly read it more broadly. The President, he stated,

> must possess more extensive sources of information, as well in regard to domestic as foreign affairs, than can belong to Congress. The true working of the laws . . . are more readily seen, and more constantly under the view of the executive . . . There is great wisdom, therefore . . . in requiring the President to lay before Congress all facts and information which may assist their deliberations.[139]

An annual message does not exhaust the duty to furnish information "from time to time"; the duty to furnish such information is the reciprocal of the familiar legislative power to inquire.

Were confirmation of a plenary power of investigation needed, we have a practical construction of the legislative power by the First Congress, unmistakably expressed in the Act of September 2, 1789.[140] The First Congress, in which sat a goodly number of Framers, was, in the words of Charles Warren, "almost an adjourned session" of the Federal Convention;[141] and it followed the furrow plowed by the original version of the "State of the Union" clause, making it

> the duty of the Secretary of the Treasury . . . to make report, and give information to either branch of the legislature in person or in writing (as he may be required), respecting *all matters* referred to him by the House of Representatives, or *which shall appertain to his office.*[141a]

---

it impossible to impute to Congress an intention to give such a right to shippers under the Motor Carrier Act when the very sections which established that right in Part I [for railroads] were wholly omitted in the Motor Carrier Act." In Article II, §3, the two differing provisions are cheek by jowl, drawn by most fastidious draftsmen, reinforcing the conclusion that the omission of discretion in the "state of the Union" clause was deliberate.

139. 2 Joseph Story, *Commentaries on the Constitution of the United States* §1561 (Boston, 1905). Senator Edmunds said in 1886 that "The 'state of the union' is made up of every drop in the bucket of the execution of every law and the performance of the duties of every office under the law"; 17 Cong. Rec. 2215.

140. 1 Stat. 65, 66, now 5 U.S.C. §242 (Supp. V 1959–1963); emphasis added.

141. Charles Warren, *Congress, the Constitution and the Supreme Court* 99 (Boston, 1925).

141a. Act of July 31, 1789, 1 Stat. 65–66, cited supra, n. 140; emphasis added.

Later, when the House was debating a number of Resolutions charging Alexander Hamilton, Secretary of the Treasury, with grave derelictions, among them, with violation of the terms of an appropriation law, Madison, an advocate of the Resolutions, said that "it was the duty of the Secretary, in complying with the orders of the House, to inform the House how the law had been executed . . . to explain his own conduct"; 3 Annals of Cong. 905, 907, 934 (1792).

No provision for executive discretion to withhold information appears in the text of the statute, and there is no intimation in the legislative history of an intention to give the President discretion to withhold information. This provision was drafted by Alexander Hamilton,[142] who, as a member of the Convention and coauthor of *The Federalist*, knew full well whether a duty to give information to Congress could constitutionally be imposed.

As originally proposed, the bill made it the duty of the Secretary to "digest and *report plans* for the improvement and management of the revenue, and support of the public credit."[143] Opponents of the proposed duty to "report plans" strongly objected that it would give rise to executive invasion of the House's exclusive prerogative to originate revenue measures,[144] "an interference of the Executive with the Legislative powers."[145] Objection was made to the creation of "a legal right in an officer to *obtrude* his sentiments perpetually on this body."[146] But there was no dispute about the power to *call* for information; indeed there was recognition that, in the words of Elias Boudinot, "this power is essentially necessary to the Government . . . it is absolutely so."[147] Roger Sherman said, "as we need information to act upon, we must procure it where it is to be had, consequently we must get it out of this officer, and the best way of doing so, must be by making it his duty to bring it forward."[148] Noting that "no gentleman . . . had objected to his [the Secretary] preparing a plan, and giving it *when it was called for*," Thomas Fitsimons suggested that "harmony might be restored . . . by changing the word report into prepare," and he so moved.[149] The motion was "carried

142. Louis Koenig, *The Invisible Presidency* 58 (New York, 1960).

143. I Annals of Cong. 592; emphasis added.

144. Elbridge Gerry, ibid. 601, 604; Thomas Tucker, ibid. 593.

145. Tucker, ibid. 593; John Page, ibid. 594.

146. Thomas Hartley, ibid. 600; emphasis added. Tucker said "However useful it may be to obtain information from this officer, I am by no means for making it a matter of right in him to intrude his advice"; ibid. 606. See also Page, ibid. 595.

147. 1 Annals of Cong. 599. For the other side, Hartley said: "it is necessary and useful to take measures for obtaining other information than what members can acquire in their characters as citizens; therefore I am in favor of the present bill . . . modified so as to oblige him to have his plans ready for this House when they are asked for"; ibid. 600. So too, Page said: "I have no objection to our calling upon this or any other officer for information; but it is certainly improper to have him authorized by law to intrude upon us"; ibid. 594–595.

148. 1 Annals of Cong. 607. This view had been expressed by Fisher Ames: "if this House is to act on the best knowledge of circumstances, it seems to follow logically, that the House must obtain evidence from that officer; the best way of doing it will be . . . by making it his duty to furnish us with it"; ibid. 595.

149. Ibid. 604; emphasis added.

by a great majority";[150] no dissent was registered from the proposition that information might be required of the Secretary.

Not only was this a constitutional interpretation by the First Congress, of which Chief Justice Taft said that its "constitutional decisions have always been regarded, as they should be regarded, as of the greatest weight in the interpretation of that fundamental instrument,"[151] but it secured the approval of President Washington, who had served as presiding officer of the Convention. This authoritative construction is the first illustration of the fact that both Houses, as the Supreme Court remarked, "early in their history" "asserted and exerted" the power to inquire into the executive branch.[152] In declaring the right of Congress, in unqualified terms, to require information of the Executive branch, the Act of 1789 faithfully reflected parliamentary history and the Founders' understanding of that history. The fact that Hamilton drafted and Washington endorsed the Act constitutes unmistakable executive acknowledgment that such unqualified inquiry was not considered to invade executive prerogatives.

The foregoing history abundantly confirms the Supreme Court's conclusion that at the adoption of the Constitution the power of inquiry was regarded as an *attribute* of the "legislative power,"[153] and that the House, according to the understanding of the Founders, would possess the familiar powers of the Grand Inquest. There is no complementary history to show that it was an "attribute" of the "executive power" either to determine how far such an inquiry should go or how much information could safely be furnished to the legislature. One vainly searches for an inkling that an executive officer, Lord Chancellor Bacon, for instance, could determine how far an inquiry preliminary to impeachment could go. On the contrary, when Nicholas Paxton sought to withhold information as to the disbursement of "secret service" moneys, the Commons clapped him in jail.

Those who argue that "the same logic which holds that Congress has the power to investigate so that it may effectively exercise its legislative functions supports the proposition that the President has the power to withhold information when the use of the power is necessary to exercise his Executive functions

150. Ibid. 607.

151. Myers v. United States, 272 U.S. 52, 174–175 (1926).

152. McGrain v. Daugherty, 273 U.S. 135, 174, 161 (1927); see supra, text accompanying n. 119.

153. Ibid. 175 "power to legislate."

effectively"[154] can derive comfort from an ill-considered 1879 Report of the House Judiciary Committee, quoted by Attorney General William P. Rogers:

The Executive is as independent of either House of Congress as either House of Congress is independent of him, and they cannot call for records of his action or the action against his consent, any more than he can call for any of the journals and records of the House or Senate.[155]

That Report overlooked a House Report of 1843, which, accurately reflecting parliamentary practice, stated:

The House has the sole right of impeachment . . . a power which implies the right of inquiry on the part of the House to the fullest and most unlimited extent."[156]

It overlooked the House Report of 1860, wherein the Covode Committee, cognizant of the long legislative "oversight" tradition, said that "The conduct of the President is always subject to the constitutional supervision and judgment of Congress; while he, on the contrary, has no such power over either branch of that body."[157]

The appeal to logical symmetry was long since rejected by the Supreme Court in *Anderson v. Dunn*, when it was urged that the argument for an implied legislative contempt power would equally sustain "a superstructure of implied powers in the executive." The Court replied that "neither analogy nor precedent would support the assertion of such powers in any other than a legislative or judicial body."[158] Not logic but history is the test of executive power to withhold information, and history speaks plainly against it. It can no longer be doubted that Congress is empowered to investigate the conduct of the Executive departments. Congress, said the Supreme Court in *McGrain v. Daugherty*, may investigate "the administration of the Department of Justice, whether its functions were being properly discharged or were being neglected or misdirected, and particularly whether the Attorney General and his assistants were performing

154. Kramer & Marcuse 899. For similar expressions by Dean Acheson, Ralph Winter, William P. Bundy, and Dean Rusk see Ervin Hearings 265, 301, 319, 339.

155. Ervin Hearings 563.

156. 3 Hinds Precedents 183. This was richly confirmed by President Polk in 1846, quoted infra, Ch. 8, text accompanying n. 145.

157. 2 Hinds Precedents 1044. For more detailed discussion of "oversight" see Berger, Executive Privilege 1098–1099.

158. 19 U.S. (6 Wheat.) 204, 233–234 (1821).

or neglecting their duties in respect of the institution and prosecution of proceedings to punish crimes and enforce appropriate remedies against the wrongdoers."[159] It would be a self-defeating construction that would simultaneously endow the executive with "uncontrolled discretion" to withhold information needed for that purpose. Rather, we should say with Chief Justice Marshall,

> The power being given, it is the interest of the nation to facilitate its execution. It can never be their interest, and cannot be presumed to have been their intention, to clog and embarrass its execution, by withholding the most appropriate means.[160]

Then too, the accountability of the President is spelled out in the impeachment provisions with their corollary of preliminary inquiry. Where is the corresponding presidential power to examine into the Congress? Where is the executive analogue of the Article I, §6(1) provision that "for any speech or debate in either House [members] shall not be questioned in any other place"? Only Congress, by Article I, §5(3) was given discretion to keep its Journals secret; the omission to give the President similar authority indicates an intention to withhold it.[161] It cannot be maintained that because Congress is not accountable to the President, the President is not accountable to Congress.

History must be our guide as to the scope of both the "legislative" and "executive" powers, not merely because the Supreme Court turned to parliamentary history in *McGrain v. Daugherty* for existence of the investigatory attribute of the "legislative power," but because here as elsewhere the Framers thought in terms of English institutions and employed common law terms.[162]

159. 273 U.S. 135, 177 (1927). The Court went on to say, "This becomes manifest when it is reflected that the functions of the Department of Justice, the powers and duties of the Attorney General and the duties of his assistants, are all subject to regulation by congressional legislation, and that department is maintained and its activities are carried on under such appropriations as in the judgment of Congress are needed from year to year"; ibid. 178.

"The power of the Congress to conduct investigations . . . comprehends probes into departments of the Federal Government to expose corruption, inefficiency or waste"; Watkins v. United States, 354 U.S. 178, 187 (1957). In Sinclair v. United States, 279 U.S. 263, 294 (1929), the Court stated with respect to leases of naval oil reserves that Sinclair had made with Secretary of the Navy Denby and Secretary of the Interior Fall, that the Senate had power to investigate what "was being done by executive departments under the Leasing Act."

160. McCulloch v. Maryland, 17 U.S. (4 Wheat.) 316, 408 (1819).

161. See supra, n. 138.

162. Ex Parte Grossman, 267 U.S. 87, 108–109 (1925): "The language of the Constitution cannot be interpreted safely except by reference to the common law and to British institutions as they were when the instrument was framed and adopted. The

When those terms went beyond their needs, they deliberately cut them down, as when they tightly redefined treason.[163]

From the outset, members of the House, for example, insisted that "an inquiry into the expenditure of all public money was the indispensable duty of this House."[164] Mr. Randolph, in proposing the investigation of the War Department in 1809, put the matter sharply: "Among the duties—and among the rights, too—of this House, there is perhaps none so important as the control which it constitutionally possesses over the public purse. To what purpose is that control? The mere form of appropriating public money, unless this House rigorously examine into the application of the money thus appropriated; unless the House examine . . . if it be misapplied, that is, if money appropriated for one object be expended for another; unless we do this, sir, our control over the public purse is a mere name—an empty shadow."[165] So too, Congressman Macon said in 1810 that "the right to inquire into the state of the whole Army unquestionably gave the right to inquire into the conduct of the individuals composing it."[166] In this Congress claimed no more than was the established practice of Parliament.[167] Apparently unaware of the above history, Judge Learned Hand argued the power on grounds of practicality:

> Congress, especially now that appropriations for the armed forces are the largest items in the budget, should be allowed to inquire in as much detail as it wishes, not only how past appropriations have in fact been spent, but in general about the conduct of the national defense.[168]

Since then the Supreme Court has held that "the power of inquiry has been employed by Congress throughout our history . . . in determining what to appropriate . . . or whether to appropriate. The scope of the power of inquiry, in short, is as penetrating and far-reaching as the potential power to enact and appropriate under

---

statesmen and lawyers of the Convention who submitted it to the ratification of the Conventions of the thirteen States, were born and brought up in the atmosphere of the common law and thought and spoke in its vocabulary . . . When they came to put their conclusions into the form of fundamental law in a compact draft, they expressed them in terms of the common law, confident that they would be shortly and easily understood." See James Bayard's great statement in 1797; Berger, *Impeachment* 55 n. 9; and see ibid. 87, 131n., 203–204.

163. Constitution, Art. III §3; Berger, *Impeachment*, 54–55.
164. 3 Annals of Cong. 491 (1792).
165. 19 Annals of Cong. 1330–1331 (1809).
166. 21 Annals of Cong. 1748 (1810).
167. Supra, text accompanying nn. 17–29.
168. Learned Hand, *The Bill of Rights* 17–18 (Cambridge, Mass., 1958).

the Constitution."[169] To which may be added inquiry as a prelude to impeachment plus the across-the-board scope of investigation that had become a staple of parliamentary practice long before the adoption of the Constitution, the history of which was not before the Court.[170]

Throughout the first hundred years of our history there was a constant stream of investigations of the civil and military operations of the executive branch. The instances are too numerous to chronicle here, and such investigations have continued uninterruptedly down to the present day.[171] The Attorney General himself noted that the executive branch has failed to comply with Congressional demands for information in "relatively few instances."[172] Because Congress did not clap such recusants in the Capitol guardroom or run to the courts, Attorney General Rogers has spelled out more than "150 years of legislative acquiescence"

169. Barenblatt v. United States, 360 U.S. 109, 111 (1959). The Rogers memo acknowledges that "Intelligent legislation and the duty of the House and Senate to appropriate money for governmental expenditures, *require access* to information." But, it goes on to say, "However, we must not confuse *comity* and reasonableness . . . with the sometimes asserted right of the Houses of Congress to all information and papers in the executive branch"; Rogers memo 70, emphasis added. Congress is "justly entitled" to so much of the information which is "required" for legislation and appropriation as the executive by "comity" sees fit to disclose!

170. Note the Court's statement that Congress has jurisdiction to inquire into "the administration of the Department of Justice, whether its functions were being properly discharged or were being neglected or misdirected, and particularly whether the Attorney General and his assistants were performing or neglecting their duties"; McGrain v. Daugherty, 273 U.S. 135, 177 (1927). See Watkins v. United States, supra, n. 159.

171. To cite only a few early examples, the House "scrutinized the Treasury Department (1800 and 1824), the territorial government of Mississippi (1800), the War Department (1809 and 1832), the conduct of General James Wilkinson (1810), government 'clerks' generally (1818), the Post Office (1820 and 1822), the Bank of the United States (1832 and 1834), the New York Customs House (1839), the conduct of Captain J. D. Elliot commanding a naval squadron in the Mediterranean (1839), the Commissioner of Indian Affairs (1849), the Secretary of the Interior (1850), the Smithsonian Institution (1855). In the meantime the Senate had looked into General Andrew Jackson's conduct of the Seminole Wars in Florida (1818), the Internal Revenue Bureau (1828), the Post Office (1830), and John Brown's Raid at Harper's Ferry (1859). Soon after the outbreak of the Civil War, the Union disasters at Bull Run and Ball's Bluff led the House and Senate to establish a joint committee (the first such) 'to inquire into the conduct of the present war' "; Telford Taylor, *Grand Inquest* 33–34 (New York, 1955).

See also the "Covode Inquisition," an inquiry into President Buchanan's administration as to corrupt practices of spoils officials, and particularly into his attitude toward the Lecompton Constitution of Kansas. For a summary of its disclosures see 5 James Shouler, *History of the United States* 450–452 (New York, 1891). And see a list compiled by Senator Edmunds in 1886, 17 Cong. Rec. 2216 ff. (1886). See also supra, Ch. 1, n. 28. For more recent investigations see Clark Mollenhoff, *Washington Cover-Up* (New York, 1962), and Clark Mollenhoff, *The Pentagon* (New York, 1972).

172. Rogers memo 2.

in the assertion of executive power to withhold information from Congress.[173] It is a strange logic that would deduce from 175 years of persistent congressional demands for information and almost unfailing excoriation of executive refusals to furnish it,[174] an "acquiescence" in the withholding. Moreover, if the legislative power conferred by the Constitution indeed reflected parliamentary usage, as the Act of 1789 immediately demonstrated afresh, then subsequent "acquiescence" in resistance to its exercise is of no moment,[175] for a constitutional power no more can be abandoned by disuse[176] than it can be abdicated.[177] Lacking historical evidence that an executive *right to withhold* information from the legislature was an *attribute* of executive power at the adoption of the Constitution, we must search elsewhere for the basis of that right.

Without noticing the foregoing history, the Executive branch builds its case on the separation of powers.[178] But resort to the separation of powers assumes the answer; it postulates that the executive was given a withholding power upon which legislative inquiry encroaches.[179] But the separation of powers does not create or grant power; it only protects powers *conferred* by the Constitution. John Adams spelled out in the 1780 Massachusetts Constitution that the separation of powers was designed to prevent one department from exercising the powers of another.[180]

173. Ibid. 71.

174. See, e.g., Senator Edmunds' (chairman of the Senate Judiciary Committee) reply to President Cleveland in 1886. Philip Collins, "The Power of Congressional Committees of Investigation to Obtain Information from the Executive Branch: The Argument for the Legislative Branch," 39 Geo. L.J. 563, 569–573 (1951). Cf. the House Report filed in 1843. 3 Hinds Precedents 181–186.

175. In a pioneer critique of the extravagant claims made in the Rogers memorandum, Congressman George Meader stated: "Forbearance does not make law. The fact that Congress, in instances where the President has refused to comply with a congressional request for information, took no action does not prove there was any executive privilege. It proves nothing at all except that Congress chose not to assert its authority or test its powers"; 104 Cong. Rec. 3849 (Mar. 10, 1958).

176. United States v. Morton Salt Co., 338 U.S. 632, 647 (1950). In the Jay Treaty debate (1796) Mr. Havens "laid it down as an incontrovertible maxim that neither of the branches of the Government could, rightfully or constitutionally, divest itself of any powers . . . by a neglect to exercise those powers that were granted to it by the Constitution"; 5 Annals of Cong. 486. To the same effect, see the statement by Mr. Nicholas, ibid. 447.

177. Panama Refining Co. v. Ryan, 293 U.S. 388, 421 (1935).

178. For reliance on the separation of powers see supra, Ch. 1, n. 54.

179. Congressman Meader perceived in 1958 that "The doctrine of separation of powers can have no relationship to the problem at hand unless it is assumed that the power of Congress to obtain information is an invasion of the powers and prerogatives of the executive branch"; 104 Cong. Rec. 3283.

180. Art. XXX, 1 Poore 960.

Only after it is established, therefore, that a right to withhold information from the legislature was an attribute of the executive power at the adoption of the Constitution can it be maintained that that attribute is invaded by congressional inquiry. Since it was *not* an attribute of executive power to refuse information to the legislature at the adoption of the Constitution, since no such grant was made in the Constitution, a congressional requirement of information from the Executive branch does not violate the separation of powers. This is confirmed by Montesquieu, who was repeatedly cited by the Founders as the oracle of the separation of powers. The legislature, he said,—exhibiting his familiarity with English practice—should "have the means of examining in what manner its laws have been executed by the public officials."[181] Given repeated recognition of the Grand Inquest function of the House, something more than appeals to an abstract separation of powers is required to curtail the function. Unless evidence is inherently incredible, the courts have held, it is not to be defeated by speculation based on no evidence.[182] Then too, "the genius and spirit of our institutions are hostile to the exercise of implied powers,"[183] all the more when the effect of the power sought to be implied is to curtail an acknowledged, existing legislative power.

The fact that the separation of powers was not designed to reduce the Grand Inquest function may further be gathered from the Act of 1789, which made it "the duty of the Secretary of the Treasury" to furnish information to Congress "respecting *all* matters . . . which shall appertain to his office." Drafted by Alexander Hamilton, adopted by the First Congress in which sat some twenty Framers and Ratifiers of the Constitution, and signed by the presiding officer of the Constitution, President Washington—without expressing *any* claim to executive immunity—this Act must be deemed an authoritative construction that the separation of powers has no application to congressional inquiry. That is confirmed by the statement of Madison, the great architect of the Constitution, with respect to a 1793 inquiry into charges

181. Supra, Ch. 1, n. 10. Professor Alpheus T. Mason said: "Under the separation of powers principle, the Congress has a right to know"; Fulbright Hearings 318.

182. Phillips v. Gookin, 231 Mass. 250, 251, 120 N.E. 691 (1918) ("mere disbelief of testimony is not the equivalent of evidence to the contrary"); Mosson v. Liberty Fast Freight Co., 124 F. 2d 448, 450 (2d Cir. 1942); Eckenrode v. Pennsylvania R. Co., 164 F. 2d 996, 999 n. 8 (3d Cir. 1947). Cf. Miller v. Herzfeld, 4 F. 2d 355, 356 (3d Cir. 1925); Magg v. Miller, 296 Fed. 973, 979 (D.C. Cir. 1924).

183. Anderson v. Dunn, 19 U.S. (6 Wheat.) 204, 225 (1821).

against Secretary of the Treasury Hamilton that "it was the duty of the Secretary, in complying with orders of the House to inform the House how the law had been executed,[184] as, indeed, the Act of 1789 provided. Many years were to pass before a president bethought himself that the "separation of powers" might serve to shelter refusals to furnish information to Congress.

It remains to notice a glaring misapplication of the separation of powers—Attorney General Rogers' extension of executive privilege to the *independent agencies* on the "principle of the separation of powers," in reliance on the fact that Congress has subjected some agencies to "executive control," for example, that it has given the President power to remove agency members for neglect of duty and the like.[185] This limited executive control was *given* by Congress, and it affords slight basis for barring congressional inquiry. More important, Mr. Rogers' analysis runs head on into *Humphrey's Executor v. United States:*

> The Federal Trade Commission is an administrative body created by Congress to carry into effect legislative policies embodied in the statute in accordance with the legislative standard therein prescribed, and to perform other specified duties as a legislative or as a judicial aid. Such a body cannot in any proper sense be characterized as an arm or an eye of the executive. Its duties are performed without executive leave and, in the contemplation of the statute, must be free from executive control . . . To the extent that it exercises any executive function—as distinguished from executive power in the constitutional sense—it does so . . . as an agency of the legislative or judicial department of the government.[186]

Patently it is ludicrous to invoke the separation of powers in justification for withholding of information from Congress by such agencies; and as will appear, the executive "precedents" stand no better.

Finally, to argue from the bare fact of a tripartite system of government, without preliminary inquiry into the scope of each of the three powers, is like invoking the magic of numerology. And so I propose to inquire what did the Founders intend when they made the several grants of power to the President—the "executive power," the "war" power, the "foreign relations" power. Did they designedly lodge in the interstices of those powers

184. 3 Annals of Cong. 934 (1793).
185. Ervin Hearings 564.
186. 295 U.S. 602, 628 (1935).

a right to withhold information from the legislature theretofore not enjoyed by the "proudest" minister? Whence did Attorney General Rogers draw his bold assertion that "the President and heads of departments must and do have the last word?"[187]

187. Rogers memo 46.

3

PRESIDENTIAL POWERS: THE "EXECUTIVE POWER"

> The executive power is better to be trusted when it has no screen . . . [the President cannot] hide either his negligence or inattention . . . not a *single privilege* is annexed to his character — James Wilson*

AMONG the colonists, said Corwin, the prevalent belief was "that 'the executive magistracy' was the natural enemy, the legislative assembly the natural friend of liberty."[1] In considerable part this derived from the fact that colonial assemblies were elected by the colonists themselves, whereas governors and judges were placed over them by the Crown.[2] Then too, the House of Commons had been the cradle of liberty in the seventeenth-century struggle against Stuart absolutism,[3] a period that greatly influenced colonial thinking.[4] Little wonder that in most early state constitutions the Governor's office was "reduced almost to the dimensions of a symbol"; all roots in the royal prerogative were cut.[5] When the colonists assembled in the Continental Con-

* 2 Elliot 480.

1. Edward Corwin, *The President: Office and Powers* 4 (3d ed., New York, 1948). For survival of the colonial belief, see Justice Brandeis, supra, Ch. 1, n. 64; Justice Jackson, ibid. text accompanying n. 9.

2. James Wilson explained in 1791 that before the Revolution the executive powers were not derived from the people, but from a "foreign source" and "were directed to foreign purposes"; hence they were "objects of aversion and distrust." But "our assemblies we have chosen by ourselves . . . Every power which could be placed in them, was thought to be safely placed." At the Revolution "the same predilection, and the same jealous dislike, existed and prevailed"; 1 Wilson, *Works* 292–293. The persistence of this feeling may be gathered from his admonition in 1791 that it was "high time" to regard executive and judges equally with the legislature as the representatives of the people; ibid. 293. Then too, in the colonies, said Trevelyan, 550, the empire "was represented by Governors, Colonels and Captains [and judges] of the upper classes, often as little suited to mix with a democratic society as oil with vinegar."

3. Trevelyan 401.

4. Supra, Ch. 2, n. 39.

5. Corwin, *President* 4–5. For example, the Virginia Constitution of 1776 provided

gress and drafted the Articles of Confederation, they dispensed with an Executive altogether.

Before long the excesses of the state legislatures led to disenchantment,[6] expressed by Madison's well-known remark that the founders of the states "seem never for a moment to have turned their eyes from the danger to liberty" from a King to recollect "the danger from legislative usurpations, which, by assembling all power in the same hands, must lead to the same tyranny as is threatened by executive usurpations."[7] This was a plea for a strengthened executive to balance an overpowerful legislature; but it was addressed to a lively fear of executive tyranny, which persisted throughout the several conventions.[8] Nevertheless, Madison recognized in a subsequent issue of *The Federalist* that "In a republican government, the legislative authority necessarily predominates,"[9] both an explanation and justification of the disproportionate distribution made by the Constitution between the legislative and executive branches. One cannot improve on Professor Louis Henkin's summation:

> unhappy memories of royal prerogative, fear of tyranny, and distrust of any one man, kept the Framers from giving the President too much head. . . . In the end and over-all, Congress clearly came first, in the longest article, expressly conferring many, important powers; the Executive came second, principally as executive-agent of Congressional policy. Every grant to the President, including those relating to foreign affairs, was in effect a derogation from Congressional power, eked out slowly, reluctantly, and not without limitations and safeguards.[10]

---

that the Governor shall "exercise the executive powers of government, according to the laws of this Commonwealth; and shall not, under any pretense, exercise any power or prerogative, by virtue of any law, statute, or custom of England"; 2 Poore 1910–1911. Section 33 of the Maryland Constitution of 1776 made similar provision; 1 Poore 825. See also infra, text accompanying nn. 15, 40–44. Corwin justifiably concluded that, under the pre-1787 state Constitutions, "'Executive power' . . . was cut off entirely from the resources of common law and of English constitutional usage"; Corwin, *President* 5.

6. Berger, *Congress v. Court* 8–12.

7. Federalist No. 48 at 322.

8. In Federalist No. 67 at 436, Hamilton sought to overcome a carry-over to the President of "the aversion of the people to monarchy." Dread of monarchy surfaced again and again in the several Conventions; 1 Farrand 66, 83, 90, 101, 113, 119, 152, 425; 2 Farrand 35–36, 101, 278, 513, 632, 640; 3 Elliot 58, 60; 4 Elliot 311. Bagehot stated that the Constitution-makers feared that sovereign power "would generate tyranny; George III had been a tyrant to them, and come what might, they would not make a George III." Walter Bagehot, *The English Constitution* 218 (London, 1964).

9. Federalist No. 51 at 338.

10. Henkin 33. The "powers explicitly vested in [the President] are few and

To peer into the words "executive power" of Article II for light as to the scope of the power is to engage in crystal gazing. When former Justice Arthur J. Goldberg stated that "it is true that Article 2, vesting the Executive power of the United States in the President, necessarily implies that certain activities he conducts, either directly or through his staff and the Executive Departments are privileged,"[11] he assumed the answer. The fact that for 150 years English practice recognized no such "necessary implication" goes far to undercut its "necessity." And we should be slow to import into the words "executive power" an implication which curtails an established legislative power. For, as Chief Justice Marshall stated, it would

> be expected that an opinion which is to overrule all former precedents, and to establish a principle never before recognized, should be expressed in plain and explicit terms. A mere implication ought not to prostrate a principle which seems to have been so well established.[12]

The very word "executive" was a postrevolutionary creation. Professor Julius Goebel tells us that executive "as a noun, was not then a word of art in English law—above all it was not so in reference to the crown. It had become a word of art in American law through its employment in various state constitutions adopted from 1776 onward . . . It reflected . . . the revolutionary response to the situation precipitated by the repudiation of the royal prerogative."[13] For the scope of the "executive power," therefore, we must first look to the provisions of the several state constitutions. How slender were the powers there conferred may be judged from Madison's statement that state executives "are in general little more than Cyphers."[14] Even when the shortcomings of an omnipotent legislature under the Virginia Constitution of 1776 became apparent, Jefferson explained in his "Draft of a Fundamental Constitution for Virginia" in 1783 that "By Executive powers, we mean no reference to those powers exercised under our

---

seem modest, far fewer and more modest than those bestowed upon Congress"; ibid. 37.

11. 118 Cong. Rec. E 2996 (daily ed. Mar. 24, 1972).

12. United States v. Burr, 25 Fed. Cas. 55, 165 (No. 14693) (Cir. Ct. Va. 1807). Yet former Secretary of State Dean Acheson could state in 1971: "The privilege exists in him [the President] by reason of the delicate nature of his responsibilities and position. He is not accountable to the Congress"; Ervin Hearings 260. Such ipse dixits betray a sad unfamiliarity with the history of executive accountability.

13. Julius Goebel, Jr., "Ex Parte Clio," 54 Colum. L. Rev. 450, 474 (1954).

14. 2 Farrand 35; see supra, n. 5.

former government by the Crown as of its prerogative . . . We give to them these powers only, which are necessary to execute the laws (and administer the government)."[15]

This was the springboard for the Virginia Plan, submitted to the Convention by Governor Edmund Randolph; it dropped all reference to "administer the government" and proposed a "national executive . . . with power to carry into execution the national laws . . . to appoint to offices in cases not otherwise provided for."[16] That "executive power" was not conceived as a bottomless well into which the President could dip without limit was made clear by Madison's emphasis that preliminarily it was essential "*to fix the extent* of the Executive authority . . . as certain powers were in their nature Executive; and *must be given* to that departmt.," adding that the Executive power "shd. be confined and defined,"[17] as it was in the subsequent sparse enumeration of executive powers. Cut off from the royal prerogative, "confined and defined," the "Executive power" was hardly a cornucopia from which could pour undreamed of powers.

A close look at the Founders' conception of the executive power will disclose its meager scope. Roger Sherman "considered the Executive magistracy as nothing more than an institution for carrying the will of the Legislature into effect."[18] Although James Wilson was the "leader of the 'strong executive' " party,[19] the "only powers he conceived strictly Executive were those of executing the laws and appointing officers."[20] The explanation of executive power to the Ratifying Conventions reaffirmed these views. The President's powers were "precisely those of the governors," said James Bowdoin in Massachusetts, as did James Iredell

15. Quoted Charles Warren, *The Making of the Constitution* 177 (Boston, 1947). Compare with the Virginia Constitution, supra, n. 5.

16. 1 Farrand 62–63; for approval by the Convention on July 17, see 2 Farrand 32–33.

17. 1 Farrand 66–67, 70. Charles Pinckney stated to South Carolina, "we have defined his powers, and bound them to such limits, as will effectually prevent his usurping authority"; 4 Elliot 329. In the Pennsylvania Convention, Chief Justice McKean stated that executive officers "have no manner of authority, any of them, beyond what is by positive grant . . . delegated to them"; 2 Elliot 540. Such statements are at war with claims of presidential "inherent" power.

18. 1 Farrand 65.

19. Corwin, *President* 11. What a "strong executive" meant may be gathered from Charles Pinckney's remark in the South Carolina Convention: "we have . . . endeavoured to infuse into this department that degree of vigor which will enable the President to execute the laws with energy and dispatch"; 4 Elliot 329.

20. 1 Farrand 66.

in North Carolina.[21] "What are his powers?" asked Governor Randolph in Virginia: "To see the laws executed. Every executive in America has that power."[22] In Pennsylvania, James Wilson, in order to defend the President against the charge that he "will be the *tool* of the Senate," pointed first to the fact that he was to be commander-in-chief, and then added, "There is another power of no small magnitude intrusted to this officer. 'He shall take care that the laws be faithfully executed.'"[23] Charles Pinckney, a Framer, said in South Carolina that "His duties will be to attend to the execution of the acts of Congress"; and to ward off fears of "the danger of the executive," Pinckney stressed that the President cannot "take a single step in his government, without [Senate] advice."[24] Another Framer, William Davie, told the North Carolina Convention that "that jealousy of executive power which has shown itself so strongly in all the American governments, would not admit" of lodging the treaty powers in the President alone.[25] Here we have the heart of the matter, more forcibly expressed by Hamilton in *The Federalist*. "Calculating upon the aversion of the people to monarchy," he wrote, opponents of the Constitution "have endeavored to enlist their jealousies and apprehensions in opposition to the intended President . . . as the full-grown progeny of that detested parent."[26] To counter such fears he launched upon a minute analysis of each of the enumerated powers, downgrading them in the process, for example, the Commander-in-Chief was merely to be the "first General." Nothing, he continued, was "to be feared" from an Executive "with the confined authorities of a President."[27]

Further to dissipate any lingering talismanic aura that may surround the words "executive power," let us trace how these terms

21. 2 Elliot 128; 4 Elliot 107.

22. 3 Elliot 201. The Framers "relied almost exclusively upon what they themselves had seen or done . . . under the state constitutions and articles of confederation"; Max Farrand, *The Framing of the Constitution of the United States* 204, 128 (New Haven, 1913).

23. 2 Elliot 512–513.

24. 3 Farrand 111; 4 Elliot 258.

25. 4 Elliot 120. "Fear of a return of Executive authority like that exercised by the Royal Governors or by the King had been ever present in the States from the beginning of the Revolution"; Warren, supra, n. 15 at 173. See supra, n. 8.

26. Federalist No. 67 at 436.

27. Federalist No. 69 at 448; No. 71 at 468. Note his statement that the President's authority to receive ambassadors "is more a matter of dignity than of authority . . . without consequence"; ibid. at 451. Thomas Hartley stated that the President's "powers, taken together, are not very numerous." 1 Annals of Cong. 482.

came to be employed. Madison, it will be recalled, did not consider that the mere creation of an Executive gave rise to inherent powers, but rather that they "must be given" to the Executive, that it was necessary "to fix the extent of the Executive authority." Accordingly he moved, being seconded by Wilson, the insertion after the words "that a national Executive ought to be instituted" of the phrase "*with power* to carry into effect the national laws, to appoint to offices . . . and to execute such other powers as may from time to time be delegated by the national Legislature."[28] Upon Pinckney's motion, this was amended by striking the words "to execute such other powers as may . . . be delegated" on the ground that "they were unnecessary, the object of them being included in the 'power to carry into effect the national laws.' " Pinckney's motion was adopted,[29] and a power of appointment was added.[30] So it remained, with the addition of a veto power,[31] and so it appeared in an enumeration by the Committee on Detail of "his powers" which then included command of the land and naval forces.[32]

The phrase "the Executive Power of the United States shall be vested in a single person," the President, first appears in a James Wilson draft, accompanied by an enumeration of powers to grant reprieves and pardons, to serve as Commander-in-Chief, and with a Rutledge addition that "it shall be his duty to provide for the due and faithful execution of the Laws."[33] No explanation of the change from "power to carry into effect the national laws" to "Executive Power," appears; and it can hardly be assumed that James Wilson, who was chairman of the Committee of Detail,[34] and to whom the only conceivable executive powers were those of appointment and of "executing the laws," should have intended by the change in terminology to make a radical shift to unlimited executive powers. So to read "executive power" is to render meaningless the prior step-by-step addition of carefully enumerated

28. 1 Farrand 67; emphasis added.
29. Ibid.
30. 2 Farrand 121.
31. Ibid. 132, 146.
32. Ibid. 145–146.
33. Ibid. 163, 171. The report of the Committee on Detail changed the "faithful execution" phrase to "he shall take care that the laws of the United States be duly and faithfully executed"; ibid. 185. It was referred in this form to the Committee on Style, ibid. 572, 574; and that Committee shifted to, "The executive power shall be vested in a president of the United States of America . . . he shall take care that the laws be faithfully executed"; ibid. 597, 600.
34. Corwin, *President* 11.

powers which was carried over into the final draft, and to overlook the prevalent fear of executive usurpation.[35] Some explanation for such a reading is in order. It is not furnished by the fact that the Convention finally made the executive independent by substituting election by electors for appointment by the legislature.[36] Just as Madison separated the extent of the executive powers from the question whether the executive should be single or plural, so did Wilson impliedly separate the extent of the executive's powers from his right to exercise those powers independently. A "strong executive" Wilson could accept, but with powers limited to the execution of the laws. From the outset the executive powers were painstakingly enumerated and cautiously expanded; and the final phrase was merely the formula for settlement of the controversy whether the executive power should be lodged in more than one person, first expressed in the phrase "the Executive Power . . . shall be vested in a single person," and then in "the Executive Power shall be vested in a President."[37] The words "executive power" were thus no more than a label designed to differentiate presidential from legislative functions, and to describe the powers thereafter conferred and enumerated. To derive additional authority from this descriptive label is to pervert the design of the Framers and defeat their intention strictly to "define and confine" executive powers.

Chief Justice Taft stated in *Myers v. United States* that "the vesting of the executive power in the President was essentially a grant of the power to execute the laws";[38] but he then went on to suggest a broader interpretation on several grounds, first reaching for analogy to powers of the Crown. Faced with the fact that "at the time of the Constitutional Convention power to make appointments and removals had sometimes been lodged in the legislature or in the courts," he said that "such a disposition of it was really vesting part of the executive power in another branch of the Government," reasoning that

> in the British system, the Crown, which was the executive, had the power of appointment and removal of executive officers, and it was

35. See supra, text accompanying notes 1, 7–8, and note 8.
36. 2 Farrand 525.
37. "The records of the Constitutional Convention make it clear that the purposes of this clause were simply to settle the question whether the executive branch should be plural or single and to give the executive a title." Corwin, "The Steel Seizure Case: A Judicial Brick Without Straw," 53 Colum. L. Rev. 53 (1953).
38. 272 U.S. 52, 117 (1926).

natural, therefore, for those who framed our Constitution to regard the words "executive power" as including both.[39]

Nothing better illustrates the danger of attributing to our forebears views which may seem "natural" enough to us but which history shows were in fact alien to them. In the 1776–1787 constitutions of the various states, " 'Executive power' . . . was left to legislative definition and was cut off entirely from the resources of the common law and of English constitutional usage."[40] Jefferson explicitly divorced the "executive power" of the Virginia governors from the Crown prerogative, following the pattern of the 1776 Virginia Constitution.[41] James Wilson, leader of the "strong executive" contingent in the Convention, affirmed that "he did not consider the Prerogatives of the British Monarch as a proper guide in defining the Executive powers."[42] No voice was raised in opposition. Hamilton emphasized that the President's powers as Commander-in-Chief and his treaty powers were "much inferior" to those of the British King.[43] Madison and Wilson stated that the rights of "war and peace," enjoyed by the King, were not included in the "executive powers."[44] Patently the Framers were determined to cut all roots of the executive power in the royal prerogative.

Second, Chief Justice Taft, following the view expressed by Hamilton in 1793 in his "Pacificus" papers,[45] stressed the significant difference between the grant of the legislative power in Article I, which is limited to powers therein enumerated, and the more general grant of the executive power to the President in Article II.[46] Viewed alone, this "difference" might suggest an

39. Ibid. 118.
40. Corwin, *President* 5; see supra, n. 5.
41. Supra, text accompanying n. 15; and n. 5.
42. 1 Farrand 65. Referring to the maxim "the King can do no wrong," Iredell told the North Carolina Convention that a departure from the royal prerogative was made because "we have experienced that he can do wrong"; 4 Elliot 109. Later, Chief Justice Taney, remarking on the "wide difference" between the presidential and Crown powers, declared that "it would be altogether unsafe to reason from any supposed resemblance between them . . . where the rights and powers of the executive . . . are brought into question"; Fleming v. Page, 50 U.S. (9 How.) 603, 618 (1850). See infra, Ch. 4, text accompanying n. 18.
43. Federalist No. 69 at 448, 451.
44. 1 Farrand 65–66, 70.
45. Infra, Ch. 5, text accompanying nn. 96–97.
46. Myers v. United States, 272 U.S. 52, 128 (1926). A much narrower view had been taken by Mr. Taft in 1916: "There is no undefined residuum of power which [the President] can exercise because it seems to him to be in the public interest." This "undefined residuum . . . is an unsafe doctrine"; the Executive power "is

intention to create an unlimited executive, in contrast to a limited legislative power. But this does violence to the plainly expressed preference for a legislature that would be "predominant" over the executive; it overlooks the clear intention to create an Executive of rigorously limited powers, and the history of the words "Executive power." Of course the Convention moved to a "strong executive," but to one of *enumerated* functions, and one further limited by the legislature in important particulars. Treaties and certain appointments required Senate consent, and Congress was empowered to override the President's veto, thus being made the final arbiter of what laws are necessary, and a fortiori must be "executed" by the President. The "difference" in terminology between the grants of the legislative and executive powers cannot overcome the plain intention of the Founders to create a quite limited executive power.

Finally, Chief Justice Taft dismissed the specific enumeration of powers in Article II, saying that "the executive power was given in general terms, strengthened by specific terms where emphasis was regarded as appropriate."[47] Again, Taft totally misconceived what "enumeration" meant to those who adopted the Constitution. In the Virginia Ratification Convention, Governor Randolph, defending the Constitution, said that the powers of government "are enumerated. Is it not, then, fairly deducible, that it has no power but what is expressly given it?—for if its powers were to be general, an enumeration would be needless."[48] What Lee said in the Virginia Convention about Congress had no less application to the President: "When a question arises with respect to the legality of any power" the question will be *"Is it enumerated in the Constitution?* . . . It is otherwise arbitrary and unconstitutional."[49] James Iredell told the North Carolina Con-

limited"; William H. Taft, *The Chief Magistrate: His Powers*, 140, 144, 156 (New York, 1916).

47. Myers v. United States, 272 U.S. 118 (1926).

48. 3 Elliot 464.

49. Ibid. 186. In the Pennsylvania Convention, James Wilson referred to a "government consisting of enumerated powers"; 2 Elliot 436. Chief Justice McKean stated in that Convention that the powers of Congress being "therein enumerated and *positively* granted, can be no other than what this positive grant conveys"; ibid. 540. In South Carolina, General C. C. Pinckney said that "by delegating express powers, we certainly reserve to ourselves every right not mentioned in the Constitution," 4 Elliot 316, a statement soon to be nailed down in the 10th Amendment. See also Governor Samuel Johnston in the North Carolina Convention 4 Elliot 142. In the First Congress Richard B. Lee reminded the House that "this Government is invested with powers for enumerated purposes only, and cannot exercise any others whatever"; 1 Annals of Cong. 524.

vention, "It is necessary to particularize the powers intended to be given . . . but, after *having enumerated what we give up*, it follows . . . that whatever is done, by virtue of that authority is legal."[50] Conversely, lacking an "enumerated" power, action is illegal. All this merely reflects what Madison said at the outset: it was essential "to fix the extent of the Executive authority"; "certain powers . . . must be given"; the Executive power "shd. be confined and defined."[51] He later stated in Federalist No. 14 that the jurisdiction of the federal government "is limited to certain enumerated objects";[52] and repeated in Federalist No. 45 that the "powers delegated . . . to the federal government are few and defined."[53] Hamilton, after a minute analysis of several of the enumerated executive powers—downgrading them in order to counter "the aversion of the people to monarchy," stated that nothing was "to be feared" from an Executive "with the confined authorities of the President."[54] Without such assurances adoption would have foundered. Alexander White, who participated in the stormy and protracted Virginia Convention, said shortly thereafter in the First Congress, insisting that the federal government must adhere to the limits described in the Constitution:

> This was the ground on which the friends of the Government supported the Constitution . . . it could not have been supported on any other. If this principle had not been successfully maintained by its advocates in the convention of the State from which I came, the Constitution could never have been ratified.[55]

In is incongruous to attribute to a generation so in dread of executive tyranny an intention to give a newly created executive a blank check, and this at the very moment when it was cautiously

50. 4 Elliot 179; emphasis added.
51. 1 Farrand 66–67, 70.
52. *Federalist* at 82.
53. Ibid. 303.
54. Federalist No. 67 at 436; Federalist No. 71 at 468. And he concluded that

> The *only remaining powers* of the Executive are comprehended in giving information to Congress of the state of the Union; in recommending to their consideration such measures as he shall deem expedient; in convening them, or either branch, upon extraordinary occasions; in adjourning them when they cannot themselves agree upon the time of adjournment; in receiving ambassadors and other public ministers; in faithfully executing the laws; and in commissioning all the officers of the United States.

Federalist No. 77 at 501; emphasis added.

55. 1 Annals of Cong. 515; Berger, *Congress v. Court* 8–14. In the First Congress, also, Madison "acknowledged that the powers of the Government must remain as apportioned by the Constitution"; 1 Annals of Cong. 462.

enumerating the powers that were being granted, down to the veriest trifle—the express authorization to "require the Opinion in writing" of each department head which, as Justice Jackson stated, "would seem to be inherent in the Executive if anything is."[56] Justly did Jackson reject "the view that this [executive power] clause is a grant in bulk of all conceivable power but regard it as an allocation to the presidential office of the generic powers thereafter stated."[57] Not Taft's views but those of Justices Holmes and Brandeis have carried the day: "The duty of the President to see that the laws be executed is a duty that does not go beyond the laws."[58] This view was adopted by Justices Black, Douglas, Frankfurter, and Jackson,[59] and it is solidly anchored in history.

For the Founders the executive power extended little beyond the execution of the laws, and that little was "confined and defined." In this view executive assertion of a right to conceal from the lawmaker how the laws are being executed is a contradiction of parliamentary history and the understanding of Montesquieu, the oracle of the Founders. So far, then, as the "executive power" goes, there is not a scintilla of evidence in the constitutional records of a design to curtail the historical scope of legislative inquiry or to authorize executive withholding of *any* information from Congress.

56. Youngstown Case, 343 U.S. at 640–641, concurring. So thought Hamilton; Federalist No. 74 at 482. Nevertheless, the requirement of opinions received serious consideration, as may be gathered from Iredell's elaborate explanation to the North Carolina Convention of why the power was granted; 4 Elliot 108–110. His explanation of the pardoning power was even more extensive; ibid. 110–114. Time and again during the various Convention debates the smoldering distrust of centralized power flared up.

57. Youngstown Case, 343 U.S. at 641. See also infra, Ch. 4, n. 185.

58. Myers v. United States, 272 U.S. 52, 177 (1926), Holmes, J., dissenting. Justice Brandeis stated: "The President performs his full constitutional duty, if, with the means and instruments provided by Congress and within the limitations prescribed by it, he uses his best endeavors to secure faithful execution of the laws enacted"; ibid. 292, dissenting.

59. Black, J., Youngstown Case, 343 U.S. at 587; Frankfurter J., ibid. 610, concurring. Justice Douglas stated that "the power to execute the laws starts and ends with the law Congress has enacted," ibid. 633; and "Article II which vests the 'executive power' in the President defines that power with particularity"; ibid. 632, concurring.

4

PRESIDENTIAL POWERS: THE COMMANDER-IN-CHIEF

LATTERLY some of the most important executive refusals of information to Congress are clustered about the President's war powers, for example, the withholding of the "Pentagon Papers"—the inside story of the escalation of the Vietnam conflict—and other aspects of that war.[1] Expansion of the Vietnam War by the invasion of Cambodia without prior consultation with Congress[2] illustrates another facet of the problem. Such "war powers" as the President may lay claim to by constitutional grant rest almost entirely on the clause in Article II, §2(1), which constitutes him "Commander-in-Chief of the Army and Navy." Since the overtowering balance of the war powers is expressly conferred on Congress, it is necessary to consider those powers in juxtaposition. What is the "pattern" that Professor Eugene Rostow describes as "shared constitutional authority in this vital area"?[3] On what can the refusal of war information to Congress be rested?

A. *The Intention of the Founders*

1. *The Commander-in-Chief Clause*

The "Commander-in-Chief," as conceived by the Framers, bears slight resemblance to the role played by the President today, when, in the words of Justice Jackson, the clause is invoked for the "power to do anything, anywhere, that can be done with an

1. Senator J. W. Fulbright testified that the "Pentagon Papers"—the "history of the U.S. decision-making process on Vietnam policy"—were repeatedly denied to the Foreign Relations Committee on the ground that "it would be clearly contrary to the national interest" to furnish them; Ervin Hearings 30, 37–39.

2. American military forces were committed "to Cambodia in 1970, and to Laos in 1971, without the consent, or even the knowledge, of Congress"; S. Rep. No. 606 p. 8 (92d Cong., 2d Sess., 1972).

3. Eugene V. Rostow, "Great Cases Make Bad Law: The War Powers Act," 50 Texas L. Rev. 833, 847 (1972).

army or navy."[4] From history the Framers had learned of the dangers of entrusting control of the military establishment to a single man who could commit the nation to war.[5] Let a single quotation suffice. James Wilson, the "most learned and profound legal scholar of his generation," second only to Madison as an architect of the Constitution,[6] and who almost single-handedly carried the Constitution through to adoption by the Pennsylvania Convention, told that Convention that the power to "declare" war was lodged in Congress as a guard against being "hurried" into war, so that no "single man [can] . . . involve us in such distress."[7] For this reason it was that the vast bulk of the war powers was conferred on Congress, leaving to the President a very meager role. Wilson's summary of the constitutional provisions graphically illustrates the glaring disproportion between the allocations to Congress and President:

> The power of declaring war, *and the other powers naturally connected with it,* are vested in congress. To provide and maintain a navy—to make rules for its government—to grant letters of marque and reprisal —to make rules concerning captures—to raise and support armies— to establish rules for their regulation—to provide for organizing . . . the militia and for calling them forth in the service of the Union—all these are powers naturally connected with the power of declaring war. All these powers, therefore, are vested in Congress.[8]

To this may be added that Congress was also empowered to "provide for the common defense" and to make appropriations for the foregoing purposes. Since all the powers "naturally connected" with that of declaring war are vested in Congress, it follows, so far as warmaking goes, that they are not to be exercised by the President.[9] The President, said Wilson, "is to take care that the laws be faithfully executed; he is commander in chief of the army and navy"; like the Saxon "first executive magistrate" he has "authority to lead the army."[10] How narrowly the function

4. Youngstown Case, 343 U.S. at 642, concurring opinion.
5. Infra, text accompanying nn. 21–22.
6. R. G. McCloskey, Introduction, 1. Wilson, *Works* 2.
7. 2 Elliot 528.
8. 1 Wilson, *Works* 433; emphasis added. The several powers are set forth in the U.S. Constitution, Art. I, §8.
9. See infra, n. 40.
10. 1 Wilson, *Works* 440. In the Virginia Ratification Convention, George Mason "admitted to the propriety of his [the President's] being commander-in-chief, so far as to give orders and have a general superintendency; but he thought it would be dangerous to let him command in person"; 3 Elliot 496. Compare the New Jersey Plan, infra, text accompanying n. 15.

was conceived may be gathered from the fact that in appointing George Washington Commander-in-Chief, the Continental Congress made sure, as Professor Rostow remarked, that he was to be "its creature . . . in every respect";[11] in the words of the instruction drafted by John Adams, R. H. Lee, and Edward Rutledge,[12] "punctually to observe and follow such orders and directions . . . as you shall receive from this or a future Congress."[13]

Virtually every early state constitution made the Governor "captain-general and commander in chief," to act under the laws of the state, which is to say, subject to governance by the legislature.[14] In the Convention, the New Jersey Plan proposed by William Paterson provided that the Executive was "to direct all military operations" but not "on any occasion [to] take command of the troops, so as personally to conduct any enterprise as General."[15] In the plan Hamilton submitted to the Convention, he proposed that the Executive should "have the direction of war when authorized or begun," implying that it was not for him to "begin" a war.[16] The words "Commander-in-Chief" were adopted without explanation; but it is a fair deduction that Hamilton's explanation in *The Federalist* expressed the general intention.[17]

11. Rostow, supra, n. 3 at 840.

12. Fulbright Hearings 134.

13. Ibid. The instructions are also printed in ibid. 29. Distrust of executive power (supra, Ch. 3, text accompanying nn. 1–5, 7–10, 25–27), and of executive war-making propensities (supra, text accompanying n. 7, and infra, text accompanying n. 21) makes it altogether unlikely that the Framers meant to enlarge those powers beyond conduct of operations once war was commenced by Congress or by enemy invasion, as Hamilton confirms; infra, text accompanying nn. 16, 18, 47; and nn. 39, 92.

14. Article VII of the Massachusetts Constitution of 1780 provides that the Governor shall be "commander-in-chief of the army and navy" with power to "repel, resist, expel" those who attempt the invasion of the Commonwealth, and entrusts him "with all these and other powers incident to the offices of captain-general . . . to be exercised agreeably to the rules and regulations of the constitution and the laws of the land, and not otherwise." 1 Poore 965–966. For Delaware, Art. 9, ibid. 275; for New Hampshire (identical with Massachusetts), 2 Poore 1288.

Hamilton stated in Federalist No. 69 at 449: "the constitutions of several of the States expressly declare their governors to be commanders-in-chief . . . and it may well be a question, whether those of New Hampshire and Massachusetts, in particular, do not, in this instance, confer larger powers upon their respective governors, than could be claimed by a President of the United States."

15. 1 Farrand 244. The Virginia Plan contained no express provision on the subject, incorporating "the Legislative Rights vested in Congress by the Confederation"; ibid. 21. In North Carolina, Robert Miller demanded that "Congress ought to have power to direct the motions of the army"; 4 Elliot 114.

16. 1 Farrand 292. Similarly, the New Jersey Plan proposed that the President "shall have the direction of war when commenced"; 3 Farrand 624.

17. Corwin said of Federalist No. 78: "It cannot be reasonably doubted that

As Commander-in-Chief, said Hamilton, the President's authority would be "much inferior" to that of the British King; "it would amount to nothing more than the supreme command and direction of the military and naval forces, as first General and admiral . . . while that of the British King extends to the *declaring of war* and to the *raising* and *regulating* of fleets and armies—all which, by the Constitution . . . would appertain to the legislature."[18] Hamilton thus deflated this and other executive functions in order to defend against attacks by those who, "calculating upon the aversion of the people to monarchy," portrayed the President "as the full-grown progeny of that detested parent."[19] "[G]enerals and admirals," Professor Henkin reminds us, "even when they are 'first,' do not determine the political purposes for which troops are to be used; they command them in the execution of policy made by others"[20]—as was manifestly the intention of the Founders.

The severely limited role of the President was a studied response to what Madison called an axiom, an "axiom that the executive is

Hamilton was here, as at other points, endeavoring to reproduce the matured conclusions of the Convention itself"; Edward S. Corwin, *The Doctrine of Judicial Review* 44 (Princeton, 1914). In the North Carolina Convention there was apparently objection even to making the President Commander-in-Chief, and Richard Spaight, a delegate to the Federal Convention, said that he "was surprised that any objection should be made to giving the command of the army to one man; that it was well known that the direction of an army could not be properly exercised by a numerous body of men." 4 Elliot 114–115. Lofgren concluded that "the evidence indicates" that the Hamiltonian view with respect to " 'the President's authority as commander-in-chief' . . . accorded well with that of his contemporaries in the state debates." Charles Lofgren, "War-Making Under the Constitution: The Original Understanding," 81 Yale L.J. 672, 687 (1972).

18. Federalist No. 69 at 448.

19. Federalist No. 67 at 436. Referring to the proposal to vest appointive power in the President, John Rutledge said in the Federal Convention: "The people will think we are leaning too much towards Monarchy"; 1 Farrand 119.

Corwin commented on Hamilton's explanation of the commander role: "this appears to mean that in any war . . . the President will be top general and top admiral of the forces provided by Congress, so that no one can be put over him or be authorized to give him orders in the direction of the said forces. But otherwise he will have no powers that any high military or naval commander who was not also president might not have"; Corwin, *President* 276. Thus it appeared to Chief Justice Taney in 1850. Fleming v. Page, 50 U.S. (9 How.) 603, 615 (1850).

20. Henkin, 50–51. Until 1850, said Corwin, the Commander-in-Chief clause "was still . . . the forgotten clause of the Constitution." Edward S. Corwin, *Total War and the Constitution* 15 (New York, 1947). Mark President Buchanan's message of December 1859: "after Congress shall have declared war and provided the force necessary to carry it on the President, as Commander in Chief . . . can alone employ this force in making war against the enemy"; James D. Richardson, *Compilation of the Messages and Papers of the Presidents, 1789–1897*, at 569 (Washington, 1907). "Without the authority of Congress," Buchanan continued, "the President can not fire a hostile gun in any case except to repel the attacks of an enemy"; ibid. 570.

the department of power most distinguished by its propensity to war: hence it is the practice of all states, in proportion as they are free, to disarm this propensity of its influence.[21] The object, in Wilson's homelier phrase, was to prevent a "single man" from "hurrying" us into war. "Those who are to *conduct a war*," said Madison, "cannot in the nature of things, be proper or safe judges, *whether a war ought* to be *commenced, continued* or *concluded*. They are barred from the latter functions by a great principle in free government, analogous to that which separates the sword from the purse, or the power of executing from the power of enacting laws."[22] All appeals to the power of the President as Commander-in-Chief must therefore proceed from the incontrovertible fact that the Framers designed the role merely for command of the army as "first General." That a "first General" may not withhold from the legislature information about the conduct of a war is illustrated by parliamentary history;[23] the very notion offends against the democratic abomination of government by a "man on horseback."

2. *"Congress shall have power . . . to declare war"*

Under the Articles of Confederation the Continental Congress had the "sole and exclusive right and power of determining on peace and war."[24] That practice influenced the Framers; of the fifty-five Framers, thirty-five had been members of the Continental Congress. No reference was made to the warmaking power in either the Virginia or New Jersey plans; the former endowed Congress with the "Legislative Rights" of, the latter with all powers vested in, the Continental Congress.[25] Early in the Convention, Madison agreed with Wilson that "executive powers

21. *Letters of Helvidius*, 6 Madison, *Writings* 138, 174. In 1798 Madison wrote to Jefferson: "The constitution supposes, what the History of all Govts. demonstrates, that the Ex. is the branch of power most interested in war, & most prone to it. It has accordingly with studied care vested the question of war in the Legisl."; ibid. 312. Consequently, he rejected doctrines which "will deposit the peace of the Country in that Department which the Constitution distrusts as most ready without cause to renounce it"; ibid.

22. Ibid. 148. This is the logic of Jefferson's statement that "We have already given in example one effectual check to the Dog of war by transferring the power of letting him loose from the Executive to the Legislative body, from those who are to spend to those who are to pay"; 15 *The Papers of Thomas Jefferson* 397 (J. Boyd, ed., 1955), quoted in S. Rep. No. 797, 90th Cong., 1st Sess. 9 (1967).

23. Supra, Ch. 2, text accompanying nn. 15–23.

24. H. S. Commager, *Documents of American History* 113 (New York, 1963).

25. 1 Farrand 21, 243.

. . . do not include the Rights of war and peace."[26] The draft submitted by the Committee on Detail provided that the legislature should "make war,"[27] lifting this as well as other powers specifically granted to Congress "bodily from the old Articles of Confederation."[28] It was this provision that became the subject of debate.

Charles Pinckney opposed "vesting this power in the Legislature. Its proceedings were too slow";[29] he preferred the Senate, as Hamilton had proposed in his own Plan.[30] Pierce Butler, on the other hand, "was for vesting the power in the President"; but Roger Sherman considered that the Committee's provision "stood very well. The Executive shd. be able to repel and not to commence war."[31] Elbridge Gerry was astonished to hear "a motion to empower the Executive alone to declare war." George Mason also "was agst. giving the power of war to the Executive, because not safely to be trusted with it . . . He was for clogging rather than facilitating war."[32] The fact that no motion was made to substitute the President for Congress, and that the power was left in Congress, justifies the conclusion that presidential "commencement" of a war or his power "alone to declare a war" found no favor.

Any power to which the President may lay claim, apart from that of "first General," derives from a joint motion by Madison and Gerry to substitute "declare" for " 'make' war . . . leaving

26. Ibid. 65–66, 70. In *Letters of Helvidius*, Madison wrote in 1793, "In no part of the constitution is more wisdom to be found, than in the clause which confides the question of war or peace to the legislature, and not to the executive department"; 6 Madison, *Writings* 174. Earlier, when "John Adams argued that the issue of war should be one of those areas 'sacredly confined' to Congress, his views were adopted both in law and in practice"; Richard B. Morris, Fulbright Hearings 78.

Article 26 of the South Carolina Constitution of 1776 carefully spelled out that the governor "and commander-in-chief shall have no power to make war or peace, or enter into any final treaty, without the consent of the general assembly"; 2 Poore 1619. James Wilson stated that the war power is "legislative"; 1 Farrand 65–66.

27. 2 Farrand 182.

28. Charles Warren, *The Making of the Constitution* 389 (Cambridge, Mass., 1947). The "Framers of the Constitution were concerned . . . that the war powers would remain lodged in the legislative branch of the Government, wherein they had previously been vested"; R. B. Morris, Fulbright Hearings 79.

29. 2 Farrand 318.

30. 1 Farrand 292.

31. 2 Farrand 318. Pierce Butler later explained to the South Carolina legislature that the grant of power to "make war" to the President "was objected to, as throwing into his hands the influence of a monarch, having an opportunity of involving his country in a war"; 4 Elliot 263.

32. 2 Farrand 318–319.

to the Executive the power to repel sudden attacks."[33] The textual change from "make" to "declare" was approved; explanation of the change was furnished by Rufus King: " 'make' war might be understood to 'conduct' it which was an executive function,"[34] a function reserved to the Commander-in-Chief. But in that role the President was merely to act as "first General" of the army.[35]

The shift from "make" to "declare" has elicited varied explanations;[36] for example, Professor Ratner states that the "declare" clause recognized "the warmaking authority of the President, implied by his role as executive and commander-in-chief and by congressional power to declare, but not make, war."[37] No warmaking power, however, was conferred by the Commander-in-Chief clause; Madison and Wilson agreed that "executive powers . . . do not include the rights of war & peace."[38] So too,

33. Ibid. 318. The State Department distorted this interchange: "it was suggested that the Senate might be a better repository. Madison and Gerry then moved to substitute 'to declare war' for 'to make war,' 'leaving to the Executive the power to repel sudden attacks.' It was objected that this might make it too easy for the Executive to involve the nation in war, but the motion carried with but one dissenting vote"; Office of the Legal Adviser, U. S. Department of State, "The Legality of the United States Participation in the Defense of Vietnam," reprinted in 75 Yale L.J. 1085, 1101 (1966). From this one might infer that the Convention intended to "make it too easy for the Executive to involve the nation in war"; but in fact *no* objection was made to the Madison-Gerry motion, which merely gave effect to the Sherman-Madison-Gerry objections to the grant of warmaking power to the President, except to "repel sudden attacks." See Francis Wormuth, "The Vietnam War: The President versus the Constitution," in 2 R. Falk, ed., *The Vietnam War and International Law* 711, 714 (Princeton, 1969).

34. 2 Farrand 319. Story explains that the role of Commander-in-Chief gives the President "command . . . of the public force . . . to resist foreign invasion . . . and the direction of war." 2 Joseph Story, *Commentaries on the Constitution of the United States* §1491 (Boston, 1905).

Secretary of State William P. Rogers confirmed that the "change in wording" from "make" to "declare" was "not intended to detract from Congress' role in decisions to engage the country in war. Rather it was a recognition of the need to preserve in the President an emergency power—as Madison explained it—'to repel sudden attacks' and also to avoid the confusion of 'making' with 'conducting' war, which is the prerogative of the President"; Fulbright Hearings 488.

35. Leonard Ratner, "The Co-ordinated Warmaking Power—Legislative, Executive and Judicial Roles," 44 S. Cal. L. Rev. 461, 467 n. 29 (1971). Clinton Rossiter concluded that "the Court has refused to speak about the powers of the President as Commander in Chief in any but the most guarded terms . . . The breath-taking estimates of their war powers announced and acted upon by Lincoln and Roosevelt have earned no blessing under the hands of the judiciary"; Rossiter, *The Supreme Court and the Commander in Chief* 4–5 (Ithaca, 1951). Since he wrote, the Court gave such claims a decided setback in Youngstown Sheet & Tube Co. v. Sawyer, 343 U.S. 579 (1952).

36. E.g., Note, "Congress, the President, and the Power to Commit Forces to Combat," 81 Harv. L. Rev. 1771, 1773–1774 (1968) (hereafter cited as Harvard Note); S. Rep. No. 797, 90th Cong., 1st Sess. 8 (1967).

37. Ratner, supra, n. 35 at 467.

38. 1 Farrand 70.

the grant to Congress of *all* the powers "naturally connected" with the "declare" power (except the command function) excludes any warmaking power from the President's "role as executive." Only in a very limited sense—command of the armed forces plus authority to repel sudden attacks—can one accurately refer to a presidential warmaking power.[39] When Madison and Gerry proposed to leave to the President power "to repel sudden attacks" they plainly reflected Sherman's view that the "Executive should be able to repel and not to commence war." This is the true measure of the presidential power. Certainly Gerry did not mean to repudiate his rejection of the proposition that the Executive could "alone declare war," still less propel the nation into undeclared war.[40] It is we who have replaced their blunt realism with semantic speculation.

Viewed against repudiation of the royal prerogative, no more can be distilled from the Madison-Gerry remark than a limited *grant* to the President of power to repel attack when, as the very words "sudden attack" imply, there could be no time to consult with Congress. Despite the fact, therefore, that the replaced "make" is a verbal component of warmaking, the shift to "declare" did not deprive Congress of the war powers expressly enumerated and "naturally connected" with the power to "declare war." Instead, the change merely removed the power to *conduct* a war once declared, as Rufus King explained.[41] If the warmaking power did not remain in Congress, the exception for presidential power "to repel sudden attacks" was superfluous.[42]

39. In the Convention, Hamilton stated that the "Executive ought to have but little power." He proposed that the Senate should "have the sole power of declaring war" and that the Executive should "have the direction of war when authorized or begun"; 1 Farrand 290, 292. Compare supra, n. 14.

40. In the North Carolina Convention, James Iredell stated: "The President has not the power of declaring war by his own authority . . . Those powers are vested in other hands. The power of declaring war is expressly given to Congress"; 4 Elliot 107–108. Charles Pinckney said in South Carolina that "the President's powers did not permit him to declare war"; ibid. 287. These men did not contemplate that he could independently *make* war, leaving to Congress the empty formality of then "declaring" war. See Baldwin, infra, n. 45.

41. Supra, text accompanying n. 34. After the adoption of the Madison-Gerry motion, Butler "moved to give the Legislature power of peace, as they were to have of war"; 2 Farrand 319. His motion was adopted without objection, suggesting an understanding that the power of making war, except for "conduct" of the war, remained in Congress. See also Henkin 333, n. 60.

42. Speaking of the need to "provide for the common defense," vested in Congress by Art. I, §8(1), Wilson said: "Defence presupposes an attack . . . We all know . . . the instruments necessary for defence when such an attack is made," and then went on to list the powers conferred upon Congress; 1 Wilson, *Works* 433. This precludes an inference that the power to "repel sudden attack" was vested in the

And even the latter power was to some extent left subject to Congressional control for, at a time when standing armies were much feared, Article I, §8(15) left it to Congress "To provide for calling forth the militia . . . to repel invasions."[43] The exceedingly narrow scope of presidential war power may be gathered from Sherman's remark that the Executive should not be able to "commence war," Mason's statement that the Executive was "not safely to be trusted" with the war power, and Wilson's explanation that the power to "declare" war was lodged in Congress to prevent a "single man" from "hurrying" us into war—a "propensity" underscored by Madison.[44]

A powerful summation of the Framers' intention was made by Madison in 1793:

Every just view that can be taken of this subject, admonishes the public of the necessity of a rigid adherence to the simple, the received, and the fundamental doctrine of the constitution, that the power to declare war, including *the power of judging the causes of war, is fully and exclusively vested* in the legislature; that the executive has no right, *in any case,* to decide the question, whether there is or is not cause for declaring war; that the right of convening and informing congress,

President ab initio, but rather as a result of the adoption of the Madison-Gerry motion. So too, Chancellor R. R. Livingston, in the New York Ratification Convention, met objections that the Continental Congress did not have "the same powers" as the proposed Congress with the reply, "They have the very same . . . [including] the [exclusive] power of making war"; 2 Elliot 278. Compare Hamilton's statement that it is Congress "which is to declare or make war"; infra, n. 92.

43. Statement of Justice Jackson in Youngstown Case 644, concurring. Governor Randolph, a Framer, told the Virginia Ratification Convention that "With respect to a standing army, I believe there was not a member in the federal convention who did not feel indignation at such an institution . . . In order to . . . exclude the dangers of a standing army, the general defense . . . is left to the militia"; 3 Farrand 319. Cf. 2 Farrand 330 for statements by Luther Martin and Elbridge Gerry, and ibid. 326 for that of George Mason.

44. Professor Ruhl J. Bartlett therefore correctly stated that "the authority to initiate war was not divided between the Executive and the Congress; it was vested in the Congress and the Congress alone"; Hearings on United States Commitments to Foreign Powers before the Senate Committee on Foreign Relations 9–10 (1967).

"Now the original assumption of our Constitution framers, that the President could not engage in war on his own, was greatly strengthened by the elementary fact that he could not if he wanted to because there were no armies or navies with which to war. At the time of the ratification of the U.S. Constitution, the U.S. Army consisted of 719 officers and men, not a formidable force for military adventures"; H. S. Commager, Fulbright Hearings 10.

Professor John Norton Moore considers that it was left "uncertain which branch would have the authority to commit the nation to force short of war," as distinguished from "declared war"; ibid. 462. Such uncertainty, if any, was removed by the Supreme Court in Bas v. Tingy, 4 U.S. (4 Dall.) 37 (1800) which held that the power of Congress comprises the power to "declare a general war" and also to "wage a limited war." Cf. Talbot v. Seeman, quoted infra, text accompanying n. 103.

whenever such a question seems to call for a decision, *is all the right* which the constitution has deemed requisite or proper.[45]

On this score there was little difference between Hamilton and Madison; even after Hamilton had moved from a narrow[46] to a broader view of executive power, he still declared that it is the

> exclusive province of Congress, *when the nation is at peace*, to change that state into a state of war . . . *it belongs to Congress only, to go to war*. But when a foreign nation declares or . . . makes war upon the United States . . . any declaration on the part of Congress . . . is at least unnecessary.[47]

Hamilton was here criticizing Jefferson's request for congressional authorization to go beyond defense of American shipping against attacks by Tripolitan pirates;[48] but he was still confining himself to *reaction* against an attack upon American shipping, not arguing for presidential power to "commence" war.

Professor Alexander Bickel suggests that the " 'sudden attack' concept of the framers . . . denotes a power to act in emergencies in order to guard against the threat of attack, as well as against the attack itself, when the threat arises, for example, in such

45. *Letters of Helvidius,* 6 Madison, *Writings* 174; emphasis partially added. Surveying the labors of the Framers some forty years later, Story, §1171, said:

> The power of declaring war is . . . so critical and calamitous, that it requires the utmost deliberation, and the successive review of all the councils of the nation . . . The representatives of the people are to lay taxes to support a war [and to draft men for combat], and therefore have a right to be consulted as to its propriety and necessity.

In 1798 Abraham Baldwin, who had been a Framer, stated in the House that "He did not believe it was intended that this House should merely be the instrument to give the sound of war; the subject seemed to be placed wholly in the hands of the legislature. This was the understanding of the country when there was no Government in existence, and he believed this was the meaning of the Constitution"; 8 Annals of Cong. 1321 (1798).

46. Supra, n. 39.

47. *Letters of Lucius Crassus,* 8 Hamilton, *Works,* 249–250; emphasis partially added.

> The Founders considered the power to declare war too important to entrust to the President alone, or even to him and the Senate, and gave it to Congress (or left it there, as under the Articles of Confederation). There have been suggestions that the power of Congress was intended to be only a formal power to declare formal wars, and that wars can be fought by the President on his own authority if they are not "declared." That view is without foundation: the Constitution gave Congress the power to decide the ultimate question, whether the nation shall or shall not go to war.

Henkin 80.

48. This was a change of position on the part of Hamilton, infra, n. 92.

circumstances as those of the Cuban missile crisis of 1962."[49] Gerry and Madison, however, spoke of a "power to repel sudden attack," which connotes actual, not threatened, attack; and there is reason to believe that a restricted connotation should be given to their remark. Imminent danger of attack had been expressly provided for in the antecedent Articles of Confederation. In conferring the exclusive war power upon the Continental Congress, Article IX made an exception for Article VI, which provided, "No state shall engage in any war without the consent of the united states in congress assembled, unless such state be actually invaded by enemies, or shall have received certain advice of a resolution being formed by some nation of Indians to invade such state, and the danger is so imminent as not to admit of a delay, till the united states in congress assembled can be consulted."[50] Thus, resistance to invasion was limited to invasion of "such state"; it did not extend even to invasion of a contiguous state in the "league of friendship." Georgia was not authorized to resist the invasion of New York, let alone Canada. And danger of imminent attack permitted reaction only if there was no time for consultation with Congress. We are apt to think that devastating surprise is peculiar to our times, forgetting that the Founders had lived through sudden massacres in frontier settlements and well knew such havoc. It was that experience which led them to leave imminent danger of Indian attacks to the individual threatened state.

A provision similar to the Articles of Confederation exception for state resistance was recommended to the Convention by the Committee of Detail,[51] and was embodied in Article I, §10(3). The Framers well understood the distinction between actual invasion and imminent threat of invasion, and they expressly empowered a state to meet both. No mention whatever was made, however, in any of the Conventions of a *presidential* power to react to such imminent danger.[52] The omission is the more sig-

49. S. Rep. No. 606, 92d Cong., 2d Sess. 4 (1972). Professor Richard B. Morris also stated that "the war-making power of the President was little more than the power to defend against imminent invasion when Congress was not in session"; ibid. 15.

50. Commager 112.

51. The Committee of Detail recommended that no state should, without consent of Congress, "engage in any War, unless it shall be actually invaded by Enemies, or the Danger of Invasion be so imminent, as not to admit of a Delay, until the Legislature of the United States can be consulted"; 2 Farrand 169.

52. The explanation in part may be historical reluctance to permit executive deployment of troops outside the country. In 1701 an act provided that "Englishmen

nificant against the background of strictly enumerated presidential powers and pervasive jealousy of executive power.[53]

Expansion of the "sudden attack" remark in the Convention to include "imminent threat of invasion" requires great caution because it opens the door to a whole row of still other expansive readings of presidential power.[54] To be sure, there must be a means of meeting a Cuban missile crisis, but the path lies by congressional authorization, such as the Act of 1839 exemplifies and the Javits War Powers Bill of 1972 proposed.[55] For it is Con-

---

were not to be involved by a foreign king in war for the defence of territory not belonging to the English crown. Henceforth William was scrupulously careful to consult Parliament at every point"; Christopher Hill, *The Century of Revolution, 1603–1714*, p. 278 (New York, 1961). The Massachusetts Constitution of 1780, Art. VII, provided that the governor should not march inhabitants "out of the limits" of the Commonwealth without their consent or "the consent of the general court [legislature]"; 1 Poore 966. Lofgren, supra, n. 17 at 683, states that the presence of the state invasion provision "in the Constitution at least further suggests that Americans of that day need not have envisaged that the President as Commander in Chief would have an especially broad role in repelling sudden attacks." And Professor Henkin, 83, points out the significance of the fact that "the power to consent to wars or compacts by the States with foreign governments was given to Congress, not the President."

53. Supra, Ch. 3, text accompanying nn. 10, 25–27, 48–55.

Asserting "it can scarcely be doubted that the President possesses the authority to take whatever action is necessary to protect the interest of the United States in a threatened emergency," McDougal & Lans cite *Martin v. Mott*, 25 U.S. (12 Wheat.) 19 (1827), for the proposition that "the Supreme Court in dealing with the powers of the President to call out the militia and employ the armed forces of the United States, concluded that he was empowered to act not only in cases of actual invasion, but also when there was 'imminent danger of invasion.' This latter contingency was held to be a question of fact to be determined by the President"; Myres McDougal and Asher Lans, "Treaties and Congressional-Executive or Presidential Agreements: Interchangeable Instruments of National Policy," 54 Yale L.J. 181, 585, 612–613. *Mott* presented a challenge by one called into the militia under the Act of 1795, which authorized the President to call out the militia, "whenever the United States shall be invaded, or be in imminent danger of invasion." Of course it could not be left to a soldier to determine whether the emergency existed; the Court held that decision "whether the exigency has arisen belongs exclusively to the President"; 25 U.S. at 30. This express *statutory authorization* constitutes a delegation by Congress; it furnishes no foundation for a presidential claim of unlimited *constitutional* power to forestall "imminent danger of invasion."

Nevertheless, Secretary of State Rogers, testifying in 1971, also invoked *Martin v. Mott* for the proposition that "the President's power to repel sudden attacks undoubtedly includes the power to provide against the imminent threat of attack"; Fulbright Hearings 488 n. 13. The more dubious the power, the more "undoubted" the terms in which it is claimed.

54. My analysis leads me to dissent from the statement in the War Powers Report, S. Rep. No. 606, 92d Cong., 2d Sess., p. 4 (1972), that the authorization contained in §3 of the War Powers Bill to repel attacks on the United States and to forestall imminent danger of such attack "are recognized to be authority which the President enjoys in his independent Constitutional office as President/Commander-in-Chief." Historically his authority was limited to repel attacks on the United States.

55. For the Act of 1839, see text accompanying n. 67, infra. The Javits War Powers Bill, S. 2956, 92d Cong., 2d Sess. (1972) (reintroduced in 1973 as S. 440, 93d

gress, not the President, that was given virtually plenary power to deal with all facets of warmaking.

This brings us to the question whether a congressional authorization to the President to use the armed forces to forestall an imminent threat of attack on the United States, for example, Khrushchev's installation of missile sites in Cuba, would be an impermissible delegation. Professor Rostow defends prior delegations chiefly on the basis of *Zemel v. Rusk*,[56] where the Court, citing *United States v. Curtiss-Wright Export Corp.*,[57] stated that "Congress—in giving the Executive authority over matters of foreign affairs—must of necessity paint with a brush broader than that it customarily wields in domestic areas."[58] In opposition, Professor Francis Wormuth makes an extended analysis of the delegation cases and the history of prior attempts to delegate war powers,[59] and emerges with the principle that Congress may determine the general policy to be pursued and then "authorize the President to determine the facts which call the Congressional policy into play."[60] Although he cites the *Zemel v. Rusk* remark that Congress can not "grant the Executive totally unrestricted freedom of choice,"[61] he recognizes that war can not be made "perfectly automatic upon the occurrence of a future event,"[62] that is, given a "direct and imminent threat" of attack, the President cannot be left with no choice but to wage war. But he draws the teeth

Cong., 1st Sess.), roughly speaking, would authorize the President in the absence of a declaration of war by Congress only "to repel an armed attack upon the United States" or upon its armed forces "located outside the United States," and to forestall the "direct and imminent threat of such an attack," such use of the armed forces not to extend beyond thirty days without congressional authorization; ibid. §§3, 5. For a discussion of the constitutionality of the Javits Bill, see Raoul Berger, "War-Making by the President," 121 U. Pa. L. Rev. 29 (1972). The Bill was deemed constitutional by Professors Alexander Bickel, Henry S. Commager, Alfred H. Kelly, Alpheus T. Mason, and former Justice Arthur J. Goldberg; Fulbright Hearings 588, 31, 91, 98, 321, 774, 779.

56. 381 U.S. 1 (1965).

57. 290 U.S. 304, 324 (1936).

58. 381 U.S. 1, 17 (1965). Rostow, supra, n. 3 at 888–889. The analogical leap from the innocuous delegation of authority to embargo arms to the belligerents in the Gran Chaco war—the issue in Curtiss-Wright—to the delegation of authority to propel the nation into full-scale warfare cannot lightly be made.

59. Wormuth, Vietnam War 780–799; Wormuth, "The Nixon Theory of the War Power: A Critique," 60 Calif. L. Rev. 623, 692–697 (1972).

60. Wormuth, Vietnam War 792. For a more detailed treatment of the several underlying concepts, see Walter Gellhorn and Clark Byse, *Administrative Law: Cases and Comments* 85–102 (Brooklyn, 1960).

61. Wormuth, "The Nixon Theory of the War Power: A Critique," 60 Calif. L. Rev. 623, 695 (1972).

62. Wormuth, Vietnam War 796.

of this concession by concluding that the decision for war must be taken by Congress contemporaneously with the declaration of war,[63] which amounts to a total ban on delegation in the premises. Generally persuaded by Professor Wormuth's analysis, I find his approach too restrictive here. And because like him, I distrust any doctrine that builds on Justice Sutherland's vulnerable *Curtiss-Wright* opinion,[64] I shall outline at least two considerations which suggest a more flexible approach.

First, having concluded that the plenary warmaking power was vested in Congress, rather than the President, I would be guided by Marshall's statement in *McCulloch v. Maryland:*

> It must have been the intention of those who gave the powers, to insure . . . their beneficial execution. This could not be done, by confiding the choice of means to such narrow limits as not to leave it in the power of congress to adopt any which might be appropriate, and which were conducive to the end.[65]

McCulloch to be sure did not involve a delegation problem, but the principle has wide scope.

Second, the historical course of Congress, charted in part by Professor Wormuth, is not all one-way. It will be recalled that Article I, §8(15) empowered Congress "To provide for calling forth the militia . . . to repel invasion." Instead of providing a detailed expression of policy, Congress was content by the Act of 1795 to authorize the President to call forth the militia, "whenever the United States shall be invaded, or be in imminent danger of invasion,"[66] a policy no more detailed than the Javits' "direct and imminent threat of attack" formula. A similar course was pursued in the Act of March 3, 1839, which empowered the President to resist any "attempt" by Great Britain "to enforce, by arms, her claim to exclusive jurisdiction over" a disputed portion of Maine.[67]

Like Professor Wormuth, I little relish congressional issuance of a blank check to determine policy;[68] and I am aware that on

63. Ibid.

64. Wormuth, supra, n. 61 at 694–695. For a discussion of Curtiss-Wright, see text accompanying nn. 191–236 infra.

65. 17 U.S. (4 Wheat.) 316, 415 (1819).

66. Act of Feb. 28, 1795, Ch. 36, §1, 1 Stat. 424. Quoted in Martin v. Mott, supra, n. 53 at 30. It is not a little remarkable that the delegation point was not so much as mentioned in Mott.

67. Act of March 3, 1839, Ch. 89, §1, 5 Stat. 55.

68. Wormuth, Vietnam War 781; cf. ibid. 789.

the domestic front it was said in *Panama Refining Co. v. Ryan* that Congress must establish "a criterion to govern the President's course."[69] A criterion, however, can only be made as explicit as the particular circumstances admit; and the fact that the Framers themselves employed a formula hardly more specific—the Article I, §10(3) authorization to a state to engage in war if "in such imminent danger as will not admit of delay"—persuades that statutory criteria framed in similar terms are not unduly broad. In fine, the limits on delegation, which some consider a moribund doctrine,[70] must not be so rigorously applied as to deprive *both* Congress and the President of power to cope with the fearful exigencies of our contemporary world.[71] It need hardly be added that where powers are delegated by Congress to the President, there is not the shadow of an excuse for concealment from the principal of how the agency is being executed.

In summary, the transformation of the Madison-Gerry "repel sudden attack" exception into an alleged presidential power, without congressional authorization, to commit the armed forces to repel invasion of Korea or Vietnam can find no warrant either in the constitutional text or in the understanding of the Founders. About this there is virtually no dispute: the Legal Adviser of the State Department stated, "In 1787 the world was a far larger place, and the framers probably had in mind attacks upon the United States."[72] Instead, the executive branch relies on an extra-constitutional source, bootstrap "precedents" created by a succession of presidents in the nineteenth century, and rationalized by

69. 293 U.S. 388, 415 (1935). Zemel v. Rusk also stated that it was not true that "simply because a statute deals with foreign relations, it can grant the Executive totally unrestricted freedom of choice"; 381 U.S. at 17.

70. E.g., K. C. Davis, *Administrative Law Text* 32 (St. Paul, 1972).

71. When it concerns the powers of the *nation* as distinguished from those of the *President* we need to recall Hamilton's words respecting the "authorities essential to the common defense": "These powers ought to exist without limitation, *because it is impossible to foresee or define the extent and variety of means which may be necessary to satisfy them*"; Federalist No. 23 at 142. Any application of the delegation doctrine that would shackle the *nation* must yield to this necessity. "No government," said Chief Justice Marshall, "ought to be so defective in its organization as not to contain within itself the means of securing the execution of its own laws against other dangers than those which occur every day." Cohens v. Virginia, 19 U.S. (6 Wheat.) 264, 387 (1821). And Justice Holmes stated: "it is not lightly to be assumed that, in matters requiring national action, 'a power which must belong to and somewhere reside in every civilized government' is not to be found"; Missouri v. Holland, 252 U.S. 416, 433 (1920).

72. Legal Adviser's memo, supra, n. 33 at 1101. Professor Ratner, who takes a broad view of presidential warmaking, states that "in 1787, 'repel sudden attack' probably meant 'resist invasion' "; supra, n. 35 at 467.

academic apologists for presidential reallocation to himself of powers confided to Congress under the theory of "adaptation by usage." Let us begin with the "precedents."

B. *Presidential Usage: The "125 Incidents"*

The perspective in which presidential "usage" is to be viewed was happily expressed by Lord Chief Justice Denman: "The practice of a ruling power in the state is but a feeble proof of its legality."[73] "Since the Constitution was adopted," said the State Department, "there have been at least 125 instances in which the President has ordered the armed forces to take action or maintain positions abroad without obtaining prior Congressional authorization, starting with the 'undeclared' war with France (1799–1800)."[74] Professor Wormuth has located "the first serious discussion of the problem" in 1912, in a monograph by J. Reuben Clark, the Solicitor of the State Department, *The Right to Protect Citizens in Foreign Countries by Landing Forces*. There Clark "opined that, with the exception of our political interventions in Cuba and Samoa, all the earlier cases could be regarded as non-political interposition for the protection of citizens.[75] He suggested that they might fall within the President's constitutional power, but this opinion was 'with no thought or pretense of more than a cursory examination. It is entirely possible that a more detailed and careful study would lead to other or modified conclusions.' His tentative argument turned on the fact that the President possessed executive power . . . Clark made no reference whatever to the commander-in-chief clause."[76] As late as 1912, therefore, the legal theoretician of the State Department sought refuge in

73. Stockdale v. Hansard, 112 E.R. 1112, 1171 (Q.B. 1839).

74. Legal Adviser's memo, supra, n. 33 at 1101. Wormuth, Vietnam War 718, justly states of the "undeclared war" with France, "This is altogether false. The fact is that President Adams took absolutely no independent action. Congress passed a series of acts which amounted, so the Supreme Court said, to a declaration of imperfect war; and Adams complied with these statutes"; Bas v. Tingy, 4 U.S. (4 Dall.) 36 (1800) amply confirms that Adams acted under congressional authorization.

75. Secretary of State Rogers acknowledged that "The origin of the notion . . . that citizens have a right to protection abroad is unclear"; Fulbright Hearings 488 n. 13. Whatever the origin of the citizen's right, President Buchanan clearly recognized that the *power* resided in Congress: "I deem it my duty once more earnestly to recommend to Congress the passage of a law authorizing the President to employ the naval force . . . for the purpose of protecting the lives and property of American citizens passing in transit across the Panama . . . routes"; 5 Richardson 569 (Dec. 19, 1859).

"Protection" has wisely been confined to Americans in weak, undeveloped countries.

76. Wormuth, supra, n. 61 at 663.

the Constitution rather than appeal to the President's own practices for legitimation of prior presidential nonpolitical interpositions for protection of citizens.

From this frail seedling, in the short space of thirty-eight years, grew the present overweening executive claims. In 1950 President Truman committed troops to repel the sudden invasion of South Korea. Dean Acheson, then Secretary of State, recommended to Truman that he "should not ask for a resolution of approval, but rest on his constitutional authority as Commander in Chief." Later he wrote, "There has never . . . been any serious doubt . . . of the President's constitutional authority to do what he did. The basis for this conclusion in legal theory and historical precedent," he said, was a State Department memorandum of 1950 which "listed eighty-seven instances in the past century in which [Truman's] predecessors [had exercised "presidential power to send our forces into battle"]. And thus yet another decision was made."[77] Decisions can be made by executive fiat; but fiat cannot supply constitutional sanction.

The painstaking analysis of the "125 incidents" by Professor Wormuth cuts the ground from under the claims of Acheson and his followers.[78] Under Secretary of State Nicholas Katzenbach later stated that "most of these [incidents] were relatively minor uses of force."[79] The "vast majority" of such cases, said Edward Corwin, "involved fights with pirates, landings of small naval contingents on barbarous or semi-barbarous coasts [to protect American citizens], the dispatch of small bodies of troops to chase bandits or cattle rustlers across the Mexican border."[80] And

77. Dean Acheson, *Present at the Creation* 414–415 (New York, 1969). The argument had been anticipated by McDougal & Lans 612: "Now that the technology of war has made it imperative in the interests of national safety that aggressors be met with the threat of overwhelming force before they can commence their own military operations, it can scarcely be doubted that the President possesses the authority to take whatever action is necessary to protect the interests of the United States in a threatened emergency." Justices Douglas and Jackson held to the contrary, infra, n. 185.

78. See Wormuth, Vietnam War; see also Wormuth, supra, n. 61 at 652–664. Reveley states: "As precedent for Vietnam . . . the majority of the nineteenth century uses of force do not survive close scrutiny"; W. T. Reveley, "Presidential War-Making: Constitutional Prerogative or Usurpation?" 55 Va. L. Rev. 1243, 1258 (1969).

79. Cited Mora v. McNamara, 389 U.S. 934, 936 (1967) Douglas, J. dissenting. These were "mostly trivial episodes." Arthur Schlesinger, Jr., "Congress and the Making of American Foreign Policy," 51 Foreign Affairs 78, 87 (1972). See also J. N. Moore, Fulbright Hearings 463 ("relatively minor").

80. Edward Corwin, "The President's Power" in D. Haight and L. Johnston, eds., *The President's Role and Powers* 361 (Chicago, 1965). Elsewhere Corwin wrote,

almost all of these instances, adds Henry Steele Commager, represent the "use of presidential force . . . against small, backward and distraught peoples";[81] and they presented next to no possibility of armed conflict.[82] Hence there was no occasion to approach Congress for authorization to make war;[83] although even in these circumstances some Presidents sought authorization.[84] These incidents are far from "precedents" for sending our troops "into battle."[85]

Were they to be regarded as equivalent to Executive waging of war, the last precedent would stand no better than the first; illegality, the Supreme Court said, is not legitimated by repetition.[86] It is one of the ironies of history that such "precedents" should be invoked for vastly greater incursions[87] at a time when "gunboat diplomacy" has been discredited and abandoned.[88] To extrapolate from these "mostly trivial episodes"[89] to a right to commit the nation to a Vietnam War, which has cost 30 billion dollars a year, engaged upward of 500,000 men, and resulted in some 200,000 maimed and wounded and 45,000 dead, is to take a breathtaking analogical leap across a chasm of nonequivalence.[90]

"The vast proportion of the incidents . . . comprised . . . *efforts to protect definite rights of persons and property against impending violence*, and were defended on that ground as *not amounting to acts of war*"; Corwin, *Total War* 146. See also ibid. 147–148; Wormuth, Vietnam War 742–743, 746–748.

81. Fulbright Hearings 15.

82. Secretary of State Rogers stated that these incidents presented "no risk of major war," hence "there was no violation of Congress' power to declare war"; Fulbright Hearings 490.

83. Reveley, supra, n. 78 at 1258; Wormuth, Vietnam War 742–748.

84. Infra, text accompanying nn. 91–96, 113.

85. Perhaps President Polk's dispatch of troops into Mexico in 1846 may be deemed an exception, although when hostilities broke out he immediately asked Congress for approval. After bitter debate over his assertion that his actions were "defensive," Congress "authorized further hostilities"; Harvard Note, supra, n. 36 at 1780. In 1848, the House by a resolution in which Lincoln joined, condemned Polk's action. Wormuth, Vietnam War 726–727. See infra, text accompanying n. 112.

86. Powell v. McCormack, 395 U.S. 486, 546–547 (1969), reminded us "That an unconstitutional action has been taken before surely does not render that same action any less unconstitutional at a later date." In the Youngstown Case 588 the Court stated: "It is said that other Presidents without congressional authority have taken possession of private business enterprises in order to settle labor disputes. But even if this be true, Congress has not thereby lost its exclusive authority . . ."

87. Corwin, *President* 241, perhaps the most influential twentieth-century apologist for enlarged presidential powers, states that the President has gathered "to himself powers with respect to warmaking which ill accord with the specific delegation in the Constitution of the war-declaring power to Congress." Cf. n. 40 supra.

88. Reveley, supra, n. 78 at 1289.

89. Cf. Wormuth, Vietnam War 762.

90. Professor Bickel stated: "there comes a point when a difference of degree achieves the magnitude of a difference in kind"; S. Rep. No. 606, 92d Cong., 2d

Against such dubious "precedents" there is the testimony of great contemporaries of the Constitution.[91] In 1801 President Jefferson was confronted by Tripoli's declaration of war; when an American naval vessel was attacked, it disarmed but released the attacker. Jefferson explained to Congress, "Unauthorized by the Constitution, without the sanction of Congress, to go beyond the line of defense, the vessel, being disabled from committing further hostilities, was liberated with its crew. The Legislature will doubtless consider whether, by authorizing measures of offense also, they will place our forces on an equal footing with that of its adversaries."[92] In 1805 Spain disputed the boundaries of Louisiana; President Jefferson advised Congress that Spain evidenced an "intention to advance on our possessions . . . Considering that Congress alone is constitutionally invested with the power of changing our condition from peace to war, I have thought it my duty to await their authority for using force."[93]

Sess., p. 16 (1972). An exponent of a broad view of presidential powers, Professor Moore, states: "In view of the decision of the Constitutional Convention to lodge with Congress the power to commit the nation to major hostilities abroad, the expanded presidential role may have gone too far"; Fulbright Hearings 464.

91. These and other presidential utterances were collected by Albert Putney, "Executive Assumptions of the War-Making Power," 7 National U. L. Rev. No. 2, p. 1 (May 1927).

92. 1 Richardson 327. In December 1790, Secretary of State Jefferson submitted a report to Congress respecting American seamen captured at Algiers, stating, "it rests with Congress to decide between war, tribute, and ransom, as the means of re-establishing our Mediterranean commerce"; 1 American State Papers, Foreign Relations (1789–1815) 105 (Washington, 1832). As Secretary of State Jefferson said in 1793 of reprisal, "if the case were important and ripe for that step, Congress must be called upon to take it; the right of reprisal being expressly lodged with them by the Constitution, and not with the executive"; Wormuth, Vietnam War 758.

Hamilton, then in private life, attacked Jefferson's Tripoli position on the ground that a declaration of war by a foreign nation unleashes the President's defensive powers so that no congressional declaration of war was required for retention of the Tripolitan ship and crew; *Letters of Lucius Crassus,* 8 Hamilton, *Works* 246–252. This was a change of position, apparently in response to political considerations, if we may credit the explanation by his sympathetic editor, Henry Cabot Lodge, that the letter "really constitutes a defence of the Federalist party and an elaborate and bitter criticism of their opponents"; ibid. 246 n. 1. For, when in 1798 the French greatly endangered American shipping, Hamilton wrote Secretary of War James McHenry, "I am not ready to say that he [the President] has any other power than merely to employ ships or convoys, with authority to *repel* force by *force* (but not to capture), and to repress hostilities within our waters . . . Anything beyond this must fall under the idea of *reprisals,* and requires the sanction of that department which is to declare *or make war.* In so delicate a case, in one which involves so important a consequence as that of war, my opinion is that no doubtful authority ought to be exercised by the President"; 10 ibid. 281–282. In 1798 Hamilton was therefore in accord with Jefferson's view, reflecting his own earlier narrow view of presidential war powers. See text accompanying nn. 16, 18, 47, supra.

93. 1 Richardson 389.

The threat of invasion did not deter Jefferson from consultation with Congress.

James Madison, the leading architect of the Constitution, had taken a very narrow view of the presidential war power;[94] and after becoming President he adhered to that view. In his message of June 1, 1812, he called attention to English outrages on American commerce, to the failure of "our remonstrances," and referred the question whether we should oppose "force to force in defense of [our] national rights" to Congress as a "solemn question which the Constitution wisely confides to the legislative department of the Government."[95]

After adoption of the Monroe Doctrine, Colombia asked for protection against France in 1824. President James Monroe, a participant in the Virginia Ratification Convention, stated in a letter to Madison that "The Executive has no right to compromit the nation in any question of war"; and his Secretary of State, John Quincy Adams, replied to Colombia that "by the Constitution . . . the ultimate decision of this question belongs to the Legislative Department."[96]

Few presidents had a more jealous regard for presidential prerogatives than Andrew Jackson; yet when faced with recognition of Texas he referred the question to Congress, stating, "It will always be consistent with the spirit of the Constitution, and most safe, that it should be exercised, when probably leading to war, with a previous understanding with that body by whom war alone can be declared, and by whom all the provisions for sustaining its perils must be furnished."[97] Though he had chased Indian raiders back into Spanish Florida during the Monroe administration, "on the question of the war-making power he followed not his own example of 1817 but Jefferson's of 1801."[98] His view was later reiterated by Secretary of State Daniel Webster (1851),

94. Supra, text accompanying nn. 21, 45.

95. 2 Richardson 484–485, 489.

96. See Wormuth, Vietnam War 738. Professor Rostow expatiates on Monroe's instructions to General Andrew Jackson "to proceed into Spanish Florida to put down the Seminoles who were raiding settlements in Georgia from bases in Spanish Florida," on the ground of "Spain's inability to exercise effective control over her territory"; Rostow, supra n. 3 at 860. But Monroe well understood the distinction between such policing and committing "the nation in any question of war."

97. 3 Richardson 267. Earlier, Madison, Irving Brant points out, denied "the constitutional right of the President to take actions . . . that tend to deprive the Congress of a free choice between declaring war and not doing so"; Fulbright Hearings 147. For Madison letter, ibid. 154–156.

98. See Schlesinger, supra, n. 79 at 85.

when the issue was a possible attack by France on Hawaii: "the war making power . . . rests entirely with Congress . . . no power is given to the Executive to oppose an attack by one independent nation on the possessions of another."[99]

In brief, Jefferson and Madison did not regard attacks on American shipping on the high seas as dispensing with the constitutional requirement for consultation with Congress. And Monroe, Jackson, J. Q. Adams, and Webster did not view attacks on foreign nations, even though within the American sphere of influence, as a warrant to commit the armed forces without Congressional authorization. Misguided as is the construction put by the State Department on the actions of Madison, Adams, and Jefferson,[100] it yet concurs that "their views and actions constitute highly persuasive evidence as to the meaning and effect of the Constitution."[101] Their actions were faithful to the intentions of the Founders; and were that intention in doubt, they would fortify it by a contemporaneous construction which carries very great weight in the interpretation of the Constitution.[102]

To the contemporaneous construction by the great statesmen who participated in the formation and adoption of the Constitution, we may add the voice of Chief Justice Marshall, himself a vigorous participant in the Virginia Ratification Convention, who stated in *Talbot v. Seeman:* "The *whole power of war* being, by the constitution . . . vested in congress, the acts of that body can alone be resorted to as our guides in this inquiry."[103] Not even the crisis of the Civil War led the Court to depart in the *Prize Cases* from the earlier view: "By the constitution, congress alone has the power to declare a national or foreign war." The President "has *no power to initiate* or declare a war either against a foreign nation or a domestic State . . . If a *war* be made *by invasion* of a foreign nation, the President is . . . bound to *resist force* by force.

99. See Wormuth, Vietnam War 738–739. For other statements to the same effect by Presidents Buchanan, Benjamin Harrison, Cleveland, and Taft, see Putney, supra, n. 91 at 15–16, 24–29, 36–37.

100. Legal Adviser's memo, supra, n. 33 at 1106. It is a mark of the Legal Adviser's careless advocacy that he could argue against this background that "James Madison . . . and Presidents John Adams and Jefferson all construed the Constitution, in their official actions during the early days of the Republic, as authorizing the United States to employ its armed forces abroad in hostilities in the absence of any Congressional declaration of war"; ibid. 1106.

101. Ibid.

102. See infra, Ch. 6, n. 13.

103. 5 U.S. (1 Cranch) 1, 28 (1801); emphasis added.

He does not initiate the war, but is bound to accept the challenge."[104]

And so we come to Lincoln's "complete transformation in the President's role as Commander-in-Chief," by wedding it, says Corwin, to his duty to execute the laws to derive the "war power."[105] So far as the "original intention" is concerned, neither power taken alone conferred a "war-making power," and when nothing is added to nothing the sum remains nothing. In considering Lincoln's acts it must be remembered that they were triggered by a "sudden attack" on *American soil*, the firing upon Fort Sumter, and this when Congress was not in session,[106] exactly the situation envisioned by the Framers as the sole exception to the exclusive congressional war powers.[107] Congress was convened by Lincoln and met in about ten weeks;[108] in the words of Corwin, it accepted "willy-nilly"[109] when it did not expressly ratify the results of Lincoln's actions. It would be pointless to enter upon an examination of Lincoln's acts on the domestic scene, for they do not serve as a "precedent" for presidential resistance to a "sudden attack" on a *foreign* country.[110]

Such conduct had in fact been earlier condemned by Lincoln. When President Polk sent an army into territory disputed with Mexico, which engaged in battle (1846), Congress declared war

104. 67 U.S. (2 Black) 635, 668 (1862); emphasis added.

105. Corwin, *President* 275, 277.

106. Ibid. 277.

107. The dissenting Justices in the *Prize Cases* admitted that the war had been initiated by the South in a "material sense," but maintained that it did not exist in a "legal sense" as "within the meaning of the law of nations" in the absence of a declaration of war by Congress; 67 U.S. at 690. But the early statutes, which authorized the President to use the military and naval forces to suppress insurrection, would include a blockade as a measure of suppression; Act of Feb. 28, 1795, Ch. 78, 1 Stat. 424; Act of Mar. 3, 1807, Ch. 39, 2 Stat. 443. Whatever the merit the dissenting argument may have is dissipated by the fact that the Convention rejected the application of the law of nations to rebellion; 3 Farrand 158.

Against this background, McDougal & Lans are mistaken in stating that "the logic of the Civil War *Prize Cases* leads ineluctably to the conclusion that the President may recognize the existence or imminence of a war, which thereatens American interests, before there is an actual invasion of our territory"; McDougal & Lans 613. Lincoln held to the tenet that the Union is indissoluble, that no state can secede. The firing upon Fort Sumter therefore represented an "actual invasion of our territory"; and Lincoln was empowered by statute to suppress insurrection.

108. 6 Richardson 13; Corwin, *President* 277.

109. Corwin, *President* 282.

110. Cf. ibid. 279–280. "There is no suggestion," states Schlesinger, "that Lincoln supposed he could use this [war] power in foreign wars without congressional consent"; Schlesinger, supra, n. 79 at 89.

on Mexico.[111] But in 1848 the House adopted a resolution that the war had been "unconstitutionally begun by the President," and Lincoln, who voted for the Resolution along with J. Q. Adams, explained to Herndon:

Allow the President to invade a neighboring nation whenever he shall deem it necessary to repel an invasion, and you . . . allow him to make war at his pleasure . . . The provision of the Constitution giving the war-making power to Congress was dictated by the [fact that] . . . Kings had always been involving and impoverishing their people in wars . . . and they resolved to so frame the Constitution that no one man should hold the power of bringing oppression upon us.[112]

This was virtually a paraphrase of the Madison-Wilson remarks earlier quoted. That his conduct on the domestic front during the Civil War did not spell repudiation of his 1848 view may be gathered from the fact that his First Annual Message (December 3, 1861) referred to a prior authorization by Congress to American vessels to "defend themselves against and to capture pirates," and recommended an additional authorization "to recapture any prizes which pirates may make of United States vessels and their cargoes [in the Eastern seas specially]."[113] Clearly this constitutes a disclaimer of power to employ force abroad without the consent of Congress.

It was Congress rather than the reluctant President McKinley which clamored for the Spanish-American War and issued a declaration of war.[114] The nineteenth century, in sum, offers no example of a President who plunged the nation into war in order to repel an attack on some foreign nation.[115] That remained for the twentieth century.

It has been said that McKinley's dispatch of five thousand troops to China in 1900 to help "put down the Boxer Rebellion . . . marked the start of a crucial shift" from "police actions against private groups" to use of the armed forces "against sovereign states."[116] That is far from clear. The Boxers, set on expelling "foreign devils," besieged the legations in Peking; China, then too weak to suppress piracy and banditry,[117] was ill-prepared to

111. Wormuth, Vietnam War 726.
112. Ibid. 727.
113. 6 Richardson 47.
114. S. E. Morison, *The Oxford History of the American People* 801 (New York, 1965).
115. Putney, supra, n. 91 at 1–2; Harvard Note, supra, n. 36 at 1790.
116. Schlesinger, supra, n. 79 at 91.
117. Morison, supra, n. 114 at 807.

protect American citizens against the Boxers. The United States took part in a joint expeditionary force, not only to relieve the legations but to forfend the possibility that China "would be sliced up by the European powers"[118] acting in concert with Japan. In 1901, Corwin states, the Chinese government "formally conceded that President McKinley's action in joining the powers in defense of the Legations in Peking against the Boxers had not constituted an act of war."[119] If McKinley's response to the Boxer Rebellion was on a larger scale than earlier police actions, it was yet removed from commitment of troops to war with China.

Although World War I proved the truth of Madison's apothegm that "war is . . . the true nurse of executive aggrandizement,"[120] this was again largely on the domestic front, a development traced by Corwin.[121] Re-elected in 1916 on the slogan "He kept us out of war" Wilson asked Congress in February 1917 for authority to arm American merchant ships for their defense. The measure passed the House but was stalled in the Senate by a filibuster led by Senators Robert LaFollette and George Norris. Wilson then ordered the arming on his own,[122] and later acknowledged that the action was "practically certain" to draw us into war.[123] He summoned Congress to a special session on April 2; German submarines sank American shipping without warning; this, plus disclosure of the "Zimmerman note,"[124] fueled the rising war fever. Upon Wilson's request that Congress declare "the recent course of the German government to be, in fact, nothing less than war," it declared war.[125] Thus, he withstood the temptation "to resist force with force," single-handed to commit the nation to war. Much as Wilson expanded the war power for domestic purposes, his conduct gives scant comfort to the thesis that invasion of a foreign land affords an excuse for presidential warmaking.

Franklin Roosevelt also took measures which might have involved us in World War II; he exchanged fifty destroyers for

118. Ibid.

119. Corwin, *President* 241.

120. 6 Madison, *Writings* 174. "Taken by and large, the history of the presidency has been a history of aggrandizement"; Corwin, *President* 366.

121. Corwin, *President* 284–287.

122. Morison, supra, n. 114 at 859.

123. 55 Cong. Rec. 103 (1917).

124. The "Note" sent by the German Foreign Affairs minister proposed a German-Mexican alliance, Mexico to get New Mexico, Arizona, and Texas; Morison, supra, n. 114 at 858.

125. Ibid. 859–860; Edward Corwin, *The President's Control of Foreign Relations* 141 (Princeton, 1917).

British bases in the Western Atlantic and occupied Greenland and Iceland to insure the defense of America.[126] Doubts have been expressed as to the legality of the destroyer deal;[127] but it was soon ratified by Congress. While these measures might have involved the nation in war, they did not commit our troops to battle on foreign soil. In truth, the country, moving slowly from post–World War I isolationism, was sorely divided, and but for the Japanese attack on Pearl Harbor, which united the nation, Roosevelt might have had to remain content with measures "short of war."[128] Though torn by the German 1940 breakthrough into France, Roosevelt wrote Premier Reynaud that he could make no "military commitments. Only Congress can make such commitments."[129]

The historical record therefore confirms the statement by the Senate Foreign Relations Committee that "only since 1950 have Presidents regarded themselves as having authority to commit the armed forces to fullscale and sustained warfare."[130] In that

126. Corwin, *President* 288–289; Harvard Note, supra, n. 36 at 1786.

127. Corwin, *President* 289; Philip Kurland, "The Impotence of Reticence," 1968 Duke L.J. 619, 623. But see Justice Jackson, concurring in Youngstown Case, 343 U.S. 645 n. 14.

128. Morison, supra, n. 114 at 991, 995, 997, 1002.

Schlesinger states that "the poignant character of Roosevelt's dilemma was made clear when in August 1941 the House of Representatives renewed the Selective Service Act by a single vote. If Congress came that close to disbanding the army at home, how could Roosevelt have reasonably expected congressional support for his forward policy in the North Atlantic? His choice was to go to Congress and risk the fall of Britain to Hitler or to proceed on his own"; Schlesinger, supra, n. 79 at 93. T. A. Bailey, *The Man in the Street* 13 (New York, 1948) defends Roosevelt on the ground that since "the masses are notoriously shortsighted, and generally cannot see danger until it is at their throats, our statesmen are forced to deceive them into an awareness of their own long-run interests." See Alfred H. Kelly, Fulbright Hearings 89.

Against this view of a "great statesman who saved a nation in spite of itself," there is a school which considers that Roosevelt acted in disregard of a "national legislature and an electorate committed to staying out of war." Whichever view is espoused, comments Robert Dahl, "the conclusion is bound to be an unhappy one for a democratic society. According to one view, the Presidency is an institution of dangerously unlimited power to commit the nation without its consent. According to the other, the electorate is too incompetent to be granted choice over its own destiny"; R. A. Dahl, *Congress and Foreign Policy* 239 (New York, 1950).

A nation whose salvation must depend on the determination of a single man—today FDR, tomorrow a counterpart of Hitler—is in a parlous state; it is no longer a democracy. Professor Bickel reminds us that in one of his opinions Justice Holmes said that "ultimately the meaning of the Constitution is if the people . . . decide to go to hell in a basket it is his job to let them do so"; Fulbright Hearings 581.

129. Fulbright Hearings 266.

130. S. Rep. No. 797, 90th Cong., 1st Sess., p. 24 (1967). See H. S. Commager, Fulbright Hearings 8–9. Writing in 1951, Clinton Rossiter said, it is a "canon of our constitutional system that the nation cannot be finally and constitutionally committed to a state of war without the positive approval of both houses of Congress." Rossiter, supra, n. 35 at 66.

year President Truman ordered our troops to repel the sudden invasion of South Korea.[131] Acheson's conversion of "trivial episodes" into "historical precedents" for commitment to full-scale warfare[132] exhibits a high order of fantasy, but to elevate it to constitutional doctrine is something else again.

Whether or not the Tonkin Gulf Resolution (1964)[133] authorized President Johnson to commit the armed forces to war in Vietnam—a hotly debated issue—need not detain us because, like Acheson, Johnson claimed plenary power. "We did not think the resolution was necessary to do what we did and what we are doing."[134] Under Secretary of State Nicholas Katzenbach testified in August 1967 that President Johnson had "the constitutional authority" without the Tonkin Resolution, that repeal of that Resolution would not prevent him from continuing to exercise that authority.[135] When he was no longer burdened with the cares of office, however, Katzenbach testified on July 28, 1970, that "the constitutional authority to use our Armed Forces in Vietnam rests squarely on Tonkin and cannot otherwise be constitutionally justified."[136] The Resolution was repealed;[137] the war went on and was indeed extended by President Nixon to Cambodia and Laos.[138]

In summary, the nineteenth-century "incidents" mustered by the State Department for a presidential warmaking power are

131. The Senate Foreign Relations Committee observed that "President Truman committed American Armed Forces to Korea in 1950 without Congressional authorization. Congressional leaders and the press were simultaneously informed of the decision but the decision had already been made"; S. Rep. No. 797, 90th Cong., 1st Sess., p. 16 (1967). But Dean Acheson stated that Truman consulted with congressional leaders, and that at a second meeting several days later there was a "general chorus of approval"; Acheson, supra, n. 77 at 408–409, 413. See also Reveley, supra, n. 78 at 1263 n. 57. J. A. Robinson, *Congress and Foreign Policy Making* 48 (Homewood, Ill., 1962).

132. See supra, text accompanying n. 77. J. N. Moore comments, "the waging of a sustained major war in the Korean conflict without explicit congressional authorization, a war in which the United States sustained more than 140,000 casualties, seems a poor precedent"; Fulbright Hearings 464. Here the President "went too far"; ibid. 478.

133. H.R. J. Res. 1145, 88th Cong., 2d Sess., 78 Stat. 384 (1964).

134. Quoted in S. Rep. No. 797, 90th Cong., 1st Sess. 22 (1967).

135. Wormuth, Vietnam War 711 n. 1; Hearings on Commitments to Foreign Powers before Senate Committee on Foreign Relations 145, 147, 130, 141, 169 (Aug. 1971).

136. Quoted by Senator John Stennis, Fulbright Hearings 707.

137. But the repeal did not "direct the termination of Indo China hostilities, disapprove continuing combat, or correct the President's prior interpretation"; Ratner, supra, n. 35 at 474.

138. Supra, n. 2.

wide of the mark;[139] the acts of Wilson and Roosevelt in the twentieth century were provocative and might have drawn the nation into war, but they were still "short of war"; neither Wilson nor Roosevelt sent combat troops to engage in actual hostilities on foreign soil until Congress declared war. So far as the Korean war is viewed against the inflated claims of Acheson, it is a "precedent" created by the President only yesterday,[140] and thus far from "embedded" in the Constitution.[141] Justice Jackson gave such "precedents" short shrift in the *Youngstown* case, where he dismissed the Solicitor General's "seizure upon nebulous inherent [war] powers never expressly granted but said to have accrued to the office from the customs and claims of preceding administrations."[142] Abandoning Acheson's farfetched claims, Secretary of State Rogers testified that the "historical precedents" are not "dispositive of the constitutional issues," and "disavowed them as a precedent."[143]

It remains to notice the view that "the military machine has become simply an instrument for the achievement of foreign policy goals, which, in turn, have become a central responsibility of the presidency."[144] This is a choice example of the tail wagging the dog. "For the Framers," Professor Henkin justly states, "surely, war or peace was the paramount decision in foreign policy."[145] By endowing the President with authority to receive ambassadors and, with Senate consent, to appoint ambassadors and make treaties—such are the slight sources of his claim to be the sole organ for foreign relations[146]—the Framers hardly intended to undo all their labors, to confer upon him a power unmistakably withheld when the war powers were under consideration, the power single-handedly to "commence" a war.

The Senate Foreign Relations Committee handsomely acknowledged that "Congress . . . bears a heavy responsibility for its passive acquiescence in the unwarranted expansion of Presidential

139. Recognizing that such statements are mere advocacy, Justice Jackson dismissed as "self-serving" earlier statements he had made as Attorney General; Youngstown Case 647, concurring. See infra, Ch. 6, n. 6.
140. See Moore, supra, n. 132.
141. See Henry Monaghan, "Presidential War-Making," 50 Bost. U. L. Rev. 19, 31 (1970).
142. Youngstown Case 646–650, concurring.
143. Fulbright Hearings 490, 529.
144. Monaghan, supra, n. 141 at 27, 31.
145. Henkin 80.
146. Infra, Ch. 5, text accompanying nn. 17–18.

power,"[147] that "Congress has acquiesced in, or at the very least has failed to challenge, the transfer of war power from itself to the executive."[148] Various explanations have been proffered for this inertia,[149] the sufficiency of which need not here come in question. Coke long since said that no "Act of Parliament by non-user can be antiquated or lose [its] force."[150] Even less can Congress, by passivity or otherwise, divest itself of powers conferred upon it by the Constitution and accomplish the transfer of those powers to the President. It is a necessary consequence of the separation of powers that "none of the departments may abdicate its powers to either of the others."[151] Nor can any department, as John Adams was at pains to spell out in the Massachusetts Constitution of 1780, exercise the powers of another.[152] If powers, said the Supreme Court are "granted, they are not lost by being allowed to lie dormant, any more than non-existent powers can be prescripted by an unchallenged exercise."[153] The right of Con-

147. S. Rep. No. 606, 92d Cong., 2d Sess., p. 18 (1972). Referring to the Middle East debate in 1957, the 1967 Senate Report on National Commitments, S. Rep. No. 797, 90th Cong., 1st Sess., p. 18, stated: "Senator Fulbright, whose view has changed with time and experience, thought at the time that the President had power as Commander in Chief to use the armed forces to defend the 'vital interests' of the country." The report concludes, "The Gulf of Tonkin resolution represents the extreme point in the process of constitutional erosion"; ibid. 20.

148. S. Rep. No. 797, 90th Cong., 1st Sess., p. 14 (1967).

149. Ibid. 14, 20–21; S. Rep. No. 606, 92d Cong., 2d Sess., pp. 10–11 (1972); Reveley, supra, n. 78 at 1263, 1265–1271; Wormuth, Vietnam War 806.

150. 1 Sir Edward Coke, *Commentaries on Littleton* §81b (London, 1628).

151. Corwin, *President* 9; Panama Refining Co. v. Ryan, 293 U.S. 388, 421 (1935).

152. The Massachusetts Constitution of 1780 provides: "In the government of this commonwealth, the legislative department shall never exercise the executive and judicial powers . . . the executive shall never exercise the legislative and judicial powers . . . to the end it may be a government of laws, and not of men"; 1 Poore 960. The New Hampshire Constitution of 1784 is similar; 2 Poore 1283.

Charles Pinckney submitted to the Convention that the President "cannot be cloathed with those executive authorities, the Chief Magistrate of a Government often possesses; because they are vested in the Legislature and cannot be used or delegated by them in any, but the specified mode." 3 Farrand 111. In the Jay Treaty debate, Jonathan Havens "laid it down as an incontrovertible maxim, that neither of the branches of the Government could, rightly or constitutionally, divest itself of any powers . . . by a neglect to exercise those powers that were granted to it by the Constitution"; 5 Annals of Cong. 486 (1796). See also remarks of John Nicholas, ibid. 447.

Madison regarded the separation of powers as "a fundamental principle of free government"; 2 Farrand 56. In 1796 President Washington, speaking to the demand of the House for information about the Jay Treaty, said, "it is essential to the due administration of the government, that the boundaries fixed by the Constitution between the different departments should be preserved." 5 Annals of Cong. 761–762. No incident is more frequently cited for the separation of powers by the executive branch when the issue is the presidential claim of executive privilege. See supra, Ch. 1, n. 54.

153. United States v. Morton Salt Co., 338 U.S. 632, 647 (1950). See supra, n.

gress, therefore, to reclaim from the President powers vested in it by the Constitution seems to me clear.

At best, the "125 incidents" constitute bootstrap precedents which add up to a claim that the President may alter the constitutional distribution of powers by his own practices and reallocate to himself powers exclusively confided to Congress.[154] Few would maintain that he can revise the Constitution by proclamation. Why should his "practices" rise higher? To escape from the bonds of the Constitution, apologists for presidential expansionism have fashioned "adaptation by usage."

C. *"Adaptation by Usage"*

Not surprisingly, those who sit in the seats of power believe that they possess superior qualifications for the exercise of ever more power.[155] The greedy expansiveness of power was known to and feared by the Founders;[156] and to that fear, in large part, we owe the structure of our government.[157] What is remarkable is that scholars who have no stake in the exercise of power should, under the spell of this or that set of circumstances, set out to rationalize power grabs. A beautiful illustration of such result-oriented jurisprudence[158] was furnished in 1945 by Professor

86. Long before, Chief Justice Marshall stated, "It is not to be denied, that a bold and daring usurpation might be resisted, after an acquiescence still longer and more complete than this"; McCulloch v. Maryland, 17 U.S. (4 Wheat.) 316, 401 (1819).

154. "Past practices," said former Justice Goldberg, "cannot change" the Constitution; Fulbright Hearings 769. In the war powers area, he said, the President ought to share the responsibility "with Congress as the Constitution mandates"; ibid. 778.

155. At the time of the invasion of South Korea, Secretary of State Acheson remarked that "the argument as to who has the power to do this, that, or the other thing, is not exactly what is called for from America at this very critical hour"; quoted Schlesinger, supra, n. 79 at 95–96.

156. The colonists were unceasingly concerned with the aggressiveness of power, "its endlessly propulsive tendency to expand itself beyond legitimate boundaries." Bernard Bailyn, *The Ideological Origins of the American Revolution* 56–57 (Cambridge, Mass., 1967).

157. Explaining the separation of powers, Madison said that since "power is of an encroaching nature . . . it ought to be effectively restrained from passing the limits assigned to it"; Federalist No. 48 at 321. Such fears persisted. In the Virginia Ratification Convention, George Mason stated, "considering the natural lust of power so inherent in man, I fear the thirst of power will prevail to oppress the people"; 3 Elliot 32. Patrick Henry said, "your President may easily become a King"; ibid. 58; see also ibid. 60. In his Farewell Address, Washington adverted to the "love of power and proneness to abuse it"; 1 Richardson 219. See infra, text accompanying n. 204; Justice Frankfurter in Youngstown Case 593, concurring.

158. Result-oriented constitutional construction held no charms for me even when the "re-constructed" Court read into the Constitution predilections which I shared;

Myres McDougal and Mr. Asher Lans. Fired by zeal in the midst of World War II to prevent another holocaust by the building of a world union, and to forestall obstruction to such union by a "willful," "undemocratic" Senate minority—such as, under the leadership of Henry Cabot Lodge, blocked our adherence to the League of Nations—they went all out to lay a constitutional basis for "executive agreements" which circumvent Senate participation altogether, and in the event have proven more mischievous than McDougal and Lans probably anticipated.[159]

Since their view encountered formidable, if not insurmountable, difficulties in the text of the Constitution and the meaning attached by the Founders to the constitutional provisions, they resorted to "adaptation by usage,"[160] a label designed to render palatable successive usurpations whereby the President has taken over treaty functions confided to Senate and President jointly, and war functions exclusively granted to Congress and withheld from him, and thus disrupted the constitutional distribution of powers considered inviolable under the separation of powers.[161] For McDougal and Lans, one who opposes this claim is enslaved by "the words of the Constitution as timeless absolutes," a prey "to the mechanical, filiopietistic theory":[162] "Whether these powers are based on an *interpretation* of the language of the Constitution or on *usage* is strictly a matter of concern only for rhetoricians."[163] Impatiently brushing aside the "absolute artifacts of verbal archeology," "the idiosyncratic purposes of the Framers," they maintain that "continuance of [a] practice by successive administrations throughout our history makes its contemporary constitutionality unquestionable."[164] One hundred years earlier, it will

---

Raoul Berger, "Constructive Contempt: A Post-Mortem," 9 U. Chi. L. Rev. 602 (1942).

159. McDougal & Lans 187, 535, 536, 565, 567, 569, 575, 602. They hopefully anticipated that the President would consult Congress; infra, Ch. 5, n. 127.

160. Corwin had referred to the theory of "adaptive interpretation"; Edward Corwin, "Judicial Review in Action," 74 U. Pa. L. Rev. 639, 658–659 (1926), citing Marshall's dictum in McCulloch v. Maryland, discussed infra, text accompanying nn. 172–179.

161. See supra, n. 157. The Executive branch clings to the separation of powers when it claims a right to withhold information from Congress under the doctrine of "executive privilege." See supra, Ch. 1, n. 54a. Compare Justice Douglas in the Youngstown Case 632: "If we sanctioned the present exercise of power by the President, we would be expanding Article II of the Constitution and rewriting it to suit the political conveniences of the present emergency" (concurring opinion).

162. McDougal & Lans 212.

163. Ibid. 239, n. 104.

164. Ibid. 291, 444. Compare their comment, "The phrase 'treaty of peace,' when

be recalled, Lord Chief Justice Denman declared that "The practice of a ruling power in the State is but a feeble proof of its legality."[165] To give it conclusive weight is to hold that usurpation of power, if repeated often enough, accomplishes an amendment of the Constitution and a transfer of power. Although that view has commended itself to academicians,[166] it has not won the assent of the Supreme Court. In *Powell v. McCormack* the House of Representatives argued that the exclusion of Adam Clayton Powell on grounds not enumerated in the Constitution was supported by earlier, similar House exclusions; but the Court declared: "That an unconstitutional action has been taken before surely does not render that same action any less unconstitutional at a later date."[167] From George Washington on,[168] "usurpation" of power has not been a mere pejorative expletive but rather an expression of an abiding fear fed by the deepest wells of our constitutional history.[169]

bereft of the reification which makes it some mysterious, special kind of an agreement," excluded from the scope of presidential executive agreements (ibid. 286), with events in the Convention. Madison moved to "except treaties of peace" from presidential concurrence. Gerry objected that treaties of peace were of especial importance; and Hugh Williamson stated, "Treaties of peace should be guarded at least by requiring the same concurrence as in other Treaties"; 2 Farrand 540–541. The exception was rejected. For the Framers a treaty of peace was unmistakably a "special kind of agreement," for reasons which are not at all "mysterious."

165. Supra, n. 73.

166. A "practice so deeply embedded in our governmental structures should be treated as decisive of the constitutional issue"; Monaghan, supra, n. 141 at 31. "[H]istory has legitimated the practice of presidential war-making"; ibid. 29. For similar views see Ratner, supra, n. 35 at 467; cf. Reveley, supra, n. 78 at 1250–1257.

"If acts forbidden by a reasonable reading of the rules continue to be performed, it is highly unrealistic to regard the rules as complete statements of the law. To constitute 'the law' the course of conduct dictated by the rules must be the one followed in actual practice"; Reveley, ibid. 1253, citing M. McDougal, "Jurisprudence for a Free Society," 1 Ga. L. Rev. 1, 4 (1966). We cannot march "in the lockstep of the Framers' intent . . . upon occasion even the clear intent of the Drafters must be abandoned without the process of formal amendment, if the Constitution is to minister successfully to needs created by changing times"; Reveley, supra, n. 78 at 1253.

In justice to Reveley, he also condemns the automatic assumption that practice makes constitutional, and proffers a compromise, which all too shortly put is: "in determining the meaning of any constitutional provision, the ultimate criterion must be the long-term best interests of the country"; ibid. 1251, 1253–1256. Who is to determine that issue? If that decision is for the President, analysis is little advanced. The Constitution reserves that decision for the people by means of an Amendment.

John Quincy Adams arraigned President Tyler in 1842 for "gross abuse of constitutional power, and bold assumption of power never vested in him by law"; quoted in Charles Warren, "Presidential Declarations of Independence," 10 Bost. U. L. Rev. 1, 13 (1930).

167. 395 U.S. 486, 546–547 (1969). Cf. supra, n. 86 and text accompanying n. 142.

168. See text accompanying n. 204 infra.

169. Madison condemned "a usurpation by the Ex. of a legislative power"; 6

It is, therefore, McDougal and Lans, I suggest, who were word-intoxicated. For the issue is not one of words but of *power*. Whence does the President derive authority to transfer to himself exclusively the treaty power conferred by the Constitution on President and Senate jointly, or in the case of the war powers, almost entirely on Congress alone? To this McDougal and Lans would reply:

it is utterly fantastic to suppose that a document framed 150 years ago "to start a governmental experiment for an agricultural, sectional, seaboard folk of some three millions" could be interpreted today . . . in terms of the "true meaning" of its original Framers for the purpose of controlling the "government of a nation, a hundred and thirty millions strong, whose population and advanced industrial civilization have spread across a continent. Each generation of citizens must in a very real sense interpret the words of the Framers to create its own constitution."[170]

It is not enough to conclude that no generation can be fettered by the past; the question remains: from which "generation of citizens" did the President obtain a mandate to revise the Constitution under the guise of "interpretation"?

It is not as if the Framers did not foresee that the fledgling, seacoast nation would cover the continent and from time to time need to change the Constitution. For in Article V they provided a process of amendment, not, to be sure, made too easy;[171] but this was for protection of minorities against roughshod majorities. Because, in the words of McDougal and Lans, "the process of amendment is politically difficult, other modes of change have emerged."[172] Truly a marvelous non sequitur: because the amend-

---

Madison, *Writings* 313; see also Iredell, infra, n. 199; J. Q. Adams, supra, n. 166. For additional citations, see Berger, *Congress v. Court* 12–14, 24, 126, 127, 131, 132, 133, 136–140.

170. McDougal & Lans 214–215, quoting from Karl Llewellyn, "The Constitution as an Institution," 34 Colum. L. Rev. 1, 3 (1934). Ratner, supra, n. 35 at 467, tells us that "constitutional policy for ensuing epochs is not congealed in the mold of 1787 referants."

171. The Founders fully understood the difficulties of amendment. Thus, Patrick Henry argued in the Virginia Convention, "four of the smallest states, that do not collectively contain one tenth part of the population . . . may obstruct the most salutary . . . amendments"; 3 Elliot 49. But the prevailing view was expressed in the North Carolina Convention by James Iredell: the Constitution "can be altered with as much regularity, and as little confusion, as any Act of Assembly; not, indeed, quite so easily, which would be extremely impolitic . . . so that alterations can without difficulty be made, agreeable to the general sense of the people"; 4 Elliot 177. In Massachusetts, Charles Jarvis said, "we shall have in this article an adequate provision for all the purposes of political reformation"; 2 Elliot 116.

172. McDougal & Lans 293. Woodrow Wilson, in *Congressional Government* 242

ing process is cumbersome—and designedly so—the servants of the people may informally amend the Constitution without consulting them.[173] By a supreme irony of history, the President, who was excluded from the amendment process altogether—Article V confides it to Congress and the state legislators alone—would undertake "informally" to amend the Constitution. In a recent attack on the constitutionality of the Javits War Powers Bill, which merely seeks to restore the original distribution of powers, Professor Rostow upbraids the Senate for attempting by that Bill "to amend the Constitution without consulting the people."[174] Insistence that congressional restoration of the original constitutional allocation of war powers must proceed by amendment is incompatible with the view that the President is free unilaterally to alter the Constitution because, as his school maintains, amendment is difficult.

(Boston, 1913), likewise stated that "The legal processes of constitutional change are so slow and cumbersome that we have been constrained to adopt a serviceable framework of fictions which enables us easily to preserve the forms without laboriously obeying the spirit of the Constitution."! Because of the "difficulty of its formal amendment process, alteration by usage has proved to be the principal means of modifying our fundamental law"; Reveley, supra, n. 78 at 1252. Amendment is difficult: ergo, the President writes himself a blank check to act outside constitutional bounds.

173. In the First Congress, Elbridge Gerry, one of the Framers, stated: "If it is an omitted case, an attempt in the Legislature to supply the defect, will be in fact an attempt to amend the Constitution. But this can only be done in the way pointed out by the fifth article of that instrument, and an attempt to amend it any other way may be a high crime or misdemeanor." The people, he added, have "directed a particular mode of making amendments, which we are not at liberty to depart from . . . Such a power would render the most important clause in the Constitution nugatory"; 1 Annals of Cong. 503 (1789). The doyen of American legal historians, Willard Hurst, remarked in our own time that the informal amendment approach "is a way of practically reading Article V out of the Federal Constitution . . . [The Framers] provided a defined, regular procedure for changing or adapting it"; discussion in E. Cahn, ed., *Supreme Court and Supreme Law* 71, 74 (Bloomington, Ind., 1954).

The Supreme Court said of the amendment process "the framers of the Constitution might have adopted a different method . . . It is not the function of courts or legislative bodies, national or state, to alter the method which the Constitution has fixed"; Hawke v. Smith, 253 U.S. 221, 227 (1920). "Nothing can destroy a government more quickly than its failure to observe its own laws, or worse, its disregard of the charter of its own existence"; Mapp v. Ohio, 367 U.S. 643, 659 (1961).

174. Rostow, supra, n. 3 at 835. It is a mark of analytical confusion that at the very time that Secretary of State Rogers was saying of the Javits War Powers Bill, supra, n. 55, which seeks to restore congressional participation in decisions for hostilities, "I don't think you can change the Constitution, amend the Constitution, by legislation," he could also state, "the framers intended that decisions regarding the institution of hostilities be made not by the President alone . . . but by the entire Congress and the President together"; Fulbright Hearings 525, 488. He agreed that "the Constitution mandates a role for Congress in the making of decisions to use force"; ibid. 528; see also ibid. 500. In short, the President can change the Constitution by his practices, but Congress must restore the original by amendment!

"The people," said James Iredell, "have chosen to be governed under such and such principles. They have not chosen to be governed or promised to submit upon any other."[175] Conscious that a mandate for change must proceed from the people, McDougal and Lans argue that

> the crucial constitutional fact is that *the people* (Presidents, Supreme Court Justices, Senators, Congressmen *and electorate*) who have lived under the document for 150 years have interpreted it . . . [to] authorize the making of international agreements other than treaties on most of the important problems of peace or war.[176]

Now the inescapable fact is that such issues have never really been explained to the people;[177] much less has the judgment of the electorate ever been solicited. Would "the people," for example, have approved the Supreme Court's freshly minted "interpretation" of "due process" in the 1880's—whereby it repeatedly overturned ameliatory socioeconomic legislation—had they been told that up to that time "due process" connoted "procedural" due process only, which did not vitiate such legislation, and that the shift to a "substantive" content was a purely judicial construct without foundation in constitutional history?[178] Would "the

175. 2 G. J. McRee, *Life and Correspondence of James Iredell* 146 (1857); see also Berger, *Congress v. Court* 13–14.

176. McDougal & Lans 216; emphasis added. They also state that "In preferring to alter the Constitution by informal adaptation, the American people have also been motivated by a wise realization of the inevitable transiency of political arrangements"; ibid. 294.

177. Compare Professor Felix Frankfurter's advice to President Franklin D. Roosevelt in 1937: "the Supreme Court for about a quarter of a century has distorted the power of judicial review into a revision of legislative policy, thereby usurping powers belonging to the Congress." And "People have been taught to believe that when the Supreme Court speaks it is not they who speak but the Constitution, whereas, of course, in so many vital cases, it is *they* who speak and *not* the Constitution. And I verily believe that that is what the country needs most to understand." *Roosevelt and Frankfurter: Their Correspondence, 1928–1945*, Max Freedman, ed., at 384, 383 (Boston, 1967).

178. Charles P. Curtis, an ardent advocate of "adaptation" of the Constitution, states that when the Framers put "due process of law . . . into the Fifth Amendment, its meaning was as fixed and definite as the common law could make a phrase. It had been chiseled into the law so incisively that any lawyer and a few others, could read it and understand it. It meant a procedural process, which could be easily ascertained from almost any law book. We turned the legal phrase into common speech and raised its meaning into the similitude of justice itself"; Charles Curtis, "Review and Majority Rule," in E. Cahn, ed., *Supreme Court and Supreme Law*, supra, n. 173 at 170, 177. Robert G. McCloskey refers to "the years after 1877 when the slow accumulation of precedent was transmuting the due process clause and the commerce clause into the legal embodiment of a laissez-faire philosophy"; McCloskey, *The Modern Supreme Court* 206 (Cambridge, Mass., 1972). See also Walton Hamilton, "The Path of Due Process of Law," in C. Read, ed., *The Constitution Reconsidered* 167 (New York, 1938).

people" approve the presidential revision whereunder the President claims power, acting alone, to commit the nation to a Vietnam War, if they were told that the bloodletting is justified, not by constitutional text nor by the intention of the Framers (which runs clearly to the contrary), but by a bootstrap theory of power built upon successive usurpations?[179] Reveley, who is sympathetic to amendment by "usage," observes that the "general public takes a relatively blackletter view of the Constitution," and that the "subtleties" of amendment "by usage . . . would probably be lost on the general public."[180] It is therefore idle to impute informal ratification of the presidential power takeover to "the people." "The people" have been told that the President has exercised power conferred upon him by the Constitution, by which, in their benighted way, they understand textual warrant, not a long-continued progressive violation of the Constitution. Senator Barry Goldwater, a leading opponent of congressional attempts to curb presidential warmaking, agreed that "the American people believe that under the Constitution, Congress is supposed to participate in the initiation of hostilities abroad,"[181] a belief amply supported by historical fact.

Alexander Hamilton, the daring pioneer advocate of expanded presidential powers, stated with respect to the *express* presidential treaty powers (as distinguished from a power merely rested on "usage") that

> a delegated authority [for example, the President] cannot alter the constituting act, unless so expressly authorized by the constituting power. *An agent cannot new model his own commission.* A treaty *cannot transfer* the legislative power to the executive department.[182]

Now Hamilton's followers would claim that the President *can* by virtue of his own "usage" "new model his own commission" and "transfer the legislative power to the executive."

Adherents of "adaptation by usage" cite statements by Chief

179. Seeking to strike a compromise between "strict construction" and free "adaptation," Reveley, supra, n. 78 at 1293, states that "unless there is pressing need for its amendment, popular understanding of the rule of law dictates adherence to provisions whose language and initial intent seems clear. The power vested in Congress to declare war is a primal instance of such a provision."

180. Ibid. 1293, 1255 n. 31.

181. Fulbright Hearings 380. This was likewise the view of President Lyndon Johnson's Press Secretary George Reedy; ibid. 451.

182. *Letters of Camillus,* 6 Hamilton, *Works* 166; emphasis added. Madison stated in the Convention that "it would be a novel & dangerous doctrine that a Legislature could change the constitution under which it held its existence"; 2 Farrand 92.

Justice Marshall and Justice Frankfurter which have not received the close analysis they require. Thus, Professor Rostow paraphrases Marshall: "we should never forget it is a *constitution* we are expounding—a constitution intended to endure for ages to come, and capable of adaptation to the various crises of human affairs."[183] What such "adaptation" has come to mean may be illustrated by the words of the State Department: "in the 20th century the world has grown much smaller. An attack on a country far from our shores can impinge directly on the nation's security . . . The Constitution leaves to the President the judgment to determine whether the circumstances of a particular armed attack are so urgent and the potential consequence so threatening to the security of the United States that he should act without formally consulting the Congress."[184] Certainly that was not the view of the Framers, of Madison or Hamilton. What portion of the Constitution confers this astonishing power? Because the world is contracting it does not follow that the President's constitutional powers are constantly expanding at the cost of Congress.[185]

Marshall would have been the last to distill such a proposition

183. Rostow, supra, n. 3 at 844. McDougal & Lans, 213, rely on the Marshall statement for an "adaptive or instrumental" theory, which "treats the Constitution as 'an instrument of government' rather than as a 'mere text for interpretation.' This theory received its classic statement in Chief Justice Marshall's reminder in *McCulloch*." See also Corwin's earlier statement, supra, n. 160. But compare Marshall's statement in McCulloch, supra, n. 153.

184. Legal Adviser's memo, supra, n. 33 at 1101.

185. Justice Jackson said in the Youngstown Case 649–650: "The appeal . . . that we declare the existence of inherent powers *ex necessitate* to meet an emergency asks us to do what many think would be wise, although it is something the forefathers omitted. They knew what emergencies were, knew the pressures they engender for authoritative action, knew, too, how they afford a ready pretext for usurpation . . . Aside from suspension of the privilege of the writ of habeas corpus in time of rebellion or invasion . . . they made no provision for exercise of extraordinary authority because of a crisis. I do not think we rightfully may so amend their work." Emergency powers, Jackson continued, "are consistent with free government only when their control is lodged elsewhere than in the Executive who exercises them. That is the safeguard that would be nullified by our adoption of the 'inherent powers' formula"; ibid. 652. See also Professor Alexander Bickel, Fulbright Hearings 554.

The "emergency power" had been strongly urged by Justice Clark, 343 U.S. 660–662; but Justice Douglas also rejected it, saying the fact that speed was essential "does not mean that the President rather than the Congress has the constitutional authority to act"; ibid. at 629. Justice Frankfurter summed up the matter: "A scheme of government like ours no doubt at times feels the lack of power to act with complete, all-embracing, swiftly moving authority. No doubt a government with distributed authority, subject to be challenged in the courts of law . . . labors under restrictions from which other governments are free. It has not been our tradition to envy such governments. In any event our government was designed to have such restrictions"; ibid. 613.

from his dictum in *McCulloch v. Maryland*. *McCulloch* presented the question whether Congress had constitutional power to establish the Bank of the United States; the issue turned on whether a bank was a proper *means* for execution of expressly granted federal powers. In granting the powers, said Marshall, the Framers intended to

> insure . . . their beneficial execution. This could not be done, by confiding the *choice of means* to such narrow limits as not to leave it in the power of congress to adopt any which might be appropriate, and which were conducive to the end. This provision is made in a constitution, intended to endure for ages to come, and, consequently, to be adapted to the various *crises* of human affairs. To have prescribed the *means* by which government should, in all future time execute its powers would have been . . . [to give the Constitution] the properties of a legal code.[186]

Manifestly this is merely a plea for some freedom in the "choice of means," not for license to create a fresh power at each new crisis. For this we need not rely on inference, because Marshall himself made this plain in a debate with Judge Spencer Roane, the discovery of which we owe to the happy enterprise of Professor Gerald Gunther.[187]

McCulloch immediately had come under attack[187a] and Marshall leapt to its defense. Speaking directly to the abovequoted passage, he stated:

> it does not contain the most distant allusion to *any extension by construction of the powers* of congress. Its sole object is to remind us that a constitution cannot possibly enumerate the means by which the powers of government are to be carried into execution.[188]

Again and again he repudiated any intention to lay the predicate for such "extension by construction." There is "not a syllable

186. 17 U.S. (4 Wheat.) 316, 415 (1819); emphasis added; quoted by Rostow, supra, n. 3 at 891.

187. Gerald Gunther, *John Marshall's Defense of McCulloch v. Maryland* (Stanford, 1969).

187a. To Madison the Court's ruling seemed "to break down the landmarks intended by a specification of the powers of Congress, and to substitute, for a definite connection between means and ends, a legislative discretion as to the former, to which no practical limits can be assigned . . . [A] regular mode of making proper alteration has been providently inserted in the Constitution itself. It is anxiously to be wished . . . that no innovation may take place in other modes, one of which would be a constructive assumption of powers never meant to be granted"; H. C. Hockett, *The Constitutional History of the United States* 4 (New York, 1939).

188. Gunther, supra, n. 187; emphasis added.

uttered by the court," he said, that "applies to an enlargement of the powers of congress." He rejected any imputation that "those powers ought to be enlarged by construction or otherwise."[189] The Court, he stated, never intimated that construction could extend "the grant beyond the fair and usual import of the words."[190] Even the means were not to be "strained to comprehend things remote, unlikely or unusual."[191] Translated into terms of the present issue, a grant of power to "repel sudden attacks" on the United States is not to be construed as a presidential power to repel an attack by a foreign nation on Korea.[192]

Overmodestly appraising the impact of his discovery, Professor Gunther states:

> Clearly these essays give cause to be more guarded in invoking *McCulloch* to support the views of congressional power now thought necessary. If virtually unlimited discretion is required to meet twentieth century needs, candid argument to that effect, rather than ritual invoking of Marshall's authority, would seem to me more clearly in accord with the Chief Justice's stance.[193]

Enough of such incantations!

Against such misinterpretations of Marshall, there is the pledge of Jefferson, after his election to the presidency, to administer the Constitution, "according to the safe and honest meaning contemplated by the plain understanding of the people at the time of its adoption—a meaning to be found in the explanations of those who advocated . . . it."[194] Madison also clung "to the sense in which the Constitution was accepted and ratified by the Nation," adding, "if that be not the guide in expounding it, there can be no security for a consistent and stable government, more than for a faithful exercise of its powers."[195]

189. Ibid. 182, 184.

190. Ibid. 92; see ibid. 185.

191. Ibid. 168. "In no single instance does the court admit the unlimited power of congress to adopt any means whatever." Ibid. 186. Marshall emphasized that "in all the reasoning on the word 'necessary,' the court does not, in a single instance, claim the aid of a 'latitudinous' or 'liberal' construction"; ibid. 92.

192. "It is not pretended," said Marshall, "that this right of selection may be fraudulently used to the destruction of the fair landmarks of the constitution"; ibid. 173.

193. Ibid. 20–21.

194. 4 Elliot 446. On another occasion Jefferson stated, "Our peculiar security is in the possession of a written constitution. Let us not make it a blank paper by construction." Caleb P. Paterson, *Constitutional Principles of Thomas Jefferson* 70 (Austin, 1953).

195. 9 Madison, *Writings* 191, 372.

Justice Frankfurter stated in the *Youngstown* case:

It is an inadmissibly narrow conception of American constitutional law to confine it to the words of the Constitution and to disregard the gloss which life has written upon them. In short, a systematic, unbroken, executive practice, long pursued to the knowledge of Congress and never before questioned . . . may be treated as a gloss on the Executive Power vested in the President by §1 of Art. II.[196]

Those who rely on this "gloss of life" statement overlook that in the immediately preceding sentence Frankfurter said, "Deeply imbedded traditional ways of conducting government cannot supplant the Constitution or legislation, but they give meaning to the words of a text or supply them." What he meant is clarified by his concurring opinion in *United States v. Lovett*, where he distinguished such terms as "due process," the "broad standards" of which "allow a relatively wide play for individual legal judgment" from "very specific provisions" such as the prohibition of "bills of attainder," which must be read as "defined by history."[197] He was prepared to look to practice for the content of amorphous terms, but not to supplant or alter "very specific provisions." The Frankfurter who concluded in *Youngstown*, notwithstanding presidential "precedents," that presidential action had been *implicitly* barred by Congress, would hardly deny to Congress power *expressly* conferred by the Constitution because the President by a "gloss of life" had reallocated the power to himself. So too, the Marshall who declared in the Roane debate that the Court's exercise of the power of judicial review vested in it by the Constitution "cannot be the assertion of a right *to change that instrument*,"[198] would scarcely have agreed that the President's repeated exercise of power withheld from him and conferred upon Congress constituted a "gloss of life" which converted the usurpation into constitutional dogma.[199] Quite the contrary, as his own words demonstrate:

196. Youngstown Case, 343 U.S. 610–611, concurring; quoted by Rostow, supra, n. 3 at 843, and by J. N. Moore, "The National Executive and the Use of the Armed Forces Abroad," printed in R. Falk, ed., 2 *The Vietnam War and International Law* 808, 809 (Princeton, 1969).

197. 328 U.S. 303, 321 (1946).

198. Gunther, supra, n. 187 at 209; emphasis added.

199. To still fears of usurpation, James Iredell, leader in the fight for ratification in North Carolina, and later a Justice of the Supreme Court, said, "if Congress, under pretence of executing one power, should, in fact, usurp another, they will violate the Constitution"; 4 Elliot 179.

The people made the constitution, and the people can unmake it. It is the creature of their will, and lives only by their will. But this supreme and irresistible power to make or unmake, resides only in the whole body of the people; not in any subdivision of them. The attempt of any of the parts to exercise it, is usurpation, and ought to be repelled by those to whom the people have delegated their power of repelling it.[200]

The underlying reality, it may be countered, is that Marshall's acts were at war with his words, that he did in fact change the Constitution. This is to condone a divorce between words and deeds, to take a cynical view of adjudication, reminiscent of the lip-service paid by Renaissance Princes to Holy Church because religion made the masses more docile. "Realism" to be sure calls on us to look behind what courts say to what they do; but then ordinary honesty requires that the American people be told in plain words, which the man in the street can grasp, that the Court has assumed the function of amending the Constitution. Truth is the foundation of morality.

At bottom, the President lays claim to a power, as Corwin stated, "to set aside, not a particular clause of the Constitution, but its most fundamental characteristic, its division of powers between Congress and the President, and thereby gather into his own hands the combined power of both."[201] To a believer in constitutional government, in the separation of powers as a safeguard against oppression, even tyranny, there is no room for a takeover by the President of powers that were denied to him, and as our times demonstrate, denied with good reason. "Ours is a government of divided authority," declared Justice Black in 1957, "on the assumption that in division there is not only strength but freedom from tyranny."[202] If present exigencies demand a redistribution of power vested in Congress—a presidential power to propel the nation into war without consulting Congress—that decision ought

200. Cohens v. Virginia, 19 U.S. (6 Wheat.) 264, 389 (1821).
201. Corwin, *Total War* 65.
202. Reid v. Covert, 354 U.S. 1, 40 (1957). Justice Brandeis stated that the separation of powers was designed "to preclude the exercise of arbitrary power . . . to save the people from autocracy"; Myers v. United States, 272 U.S. 52, 293 (1926), dissenting. "The Founding Fathers were concerned with principles whose validity transcends the passage of time, principles as valid today as they were in the Eighteenth Century. These principles concern the danger of giving unchecked power to any branch of government, to any men or group of men"; Merrill Jensen, Fulbright Hearings 150.

candidly to be submitted to the people in the form of a proposed amendment,[203] not masked by euphemisms. The polestar should remain the advice given to the nation by Washington:

> The necessity of reciprocal checks in the exercise of political power; by dividing and distributing it into different depositories, and constituting each the Guardian of the Public Weal against invasions by the others has been evinced . . . To preserve them must be as necessary as to institute them. If in the opinion of the People, the distribution or modification of the Constitutional powers be in any particular wrong, let it be corrected by an amendment in the way which the Constitution designates. But let there be no change by usurpation; for though this, in one instance, may be the instrument of good, it is the customary weapon by which free governments are destroyed. The precedent must always greatly overbalance in permanent evil any partial or transient benefit which the use can at any time yield.[204]

D. *Inherent Presidential Power:* United States v. Curtiss-Wright Export Corporation

It remained for our time to furnish a powerful impetus to presidential expansionism in the shape of some ill-considered dicta in *United States v. Curtiss-Wright Export Corp.*, per Justice Sutherland,[205] to which the Court lent credit in *United States v. Pink.*[206] Despite searching criticism,[207] *Curtiss-Wright* has become the foundation of subsequent decisions and has all too frequently been cited for an omnipresent presidential power over foreign

203. In 1971, former Justice Arthur J. Goldberg, stated: "If our Constitution does not adequately permit what has to be done in a modern age to protect our security, our Constitution ought to be amended to permit it"; ibid. 772.

204. 35 *The Writings of George Washington*, J. Fitzpatrick, ed., 228–229 (Washington, 1940). The Massachusetts Constitution of 1780, Art. XVIII, states that the people "have a right to require of their lawgivers and magistrates an exact and constant observance" of the "fundamental principles of the constitution" which are "absolutely necessary to preserve the advantages of liberty and to maintain a free government."

How does Washington's advice square with the McDougal & Lans, 294, statement that the Constitution is "being ceaselessly adapted, *as its Framers intended*, to the problems of 'ages to come' "? Emphasis added. Marshall expressly disclaimed that his "ages to come" was meant to condone any enlargement of powers by construction. Supra, text accompanying notes 186–193. See Mapp v. Ohio, quoted supra, n. 173.

205. 299 U.S. 304 (1936). The Curtiss dicta were dismissed by Justice Jackson, who pointed out that Curtiss "involved, not the question of the President's power to act without congressional authority, but the question of his right to act under and in accord with an act of Congress"; Youngstown case, 343 U.S. at 635–636 n. 2.

206. 315 U.S. 203, 229 (1942).

207. E.g., David Levitan, "The Foreign Relations Power: An Analysis of Mr. Justice Sutherland's Theory," 55 Yale L.J. 467 (1946); Kurland, supra, n. 127 at 622–623.

relations. The case proceeded from a Joint Resolution which *authorized* the President, upon making certain findings and engaging in consultation with other American Republics, to declare unlawful the sale of munitions to countries then engaged in armed conflict in the Chaco, namely Bolivia and Paraguay, if it "may contribute to the re-establishment of peace between those countries."[208] The sole issue was whether this was an improper delegation,[209] a question that might adequately have been answered under the *Field v. Clark* line of cases.[210]

But the aims of Justice Sutherland soared beyond this modest goal; he would launch a theory of inherent presidential power over foreign relations.[211] To this end he confined the enumeration-of-powers doctrine to "domestic or internal affairs";[212] in foreign affairs, he explained, in terms recalling the descent of the Holy Ghost, "the external sovereignty of Great Britain . . . immediately passed to the Union."[213] In this he was deceived. It hardly needs more than Madison's statement in *The Federalist* that "[t]he powers delegated by the proposed Constitution are *few and defined* . . . [they] will be exercised principally on *external* objects, as war, peace, negotiation, and foreign commerce,"[214] to prove that powers over *foreign relations* were enumerated and "defined."

208. 299 U.S. at 312.

209. Ibid. at 315.

210. 143 U.S. 649 (1892). See also J. W. Hampton, Jr. & Co. v. United States, 276 U.S. 394 (1928). The cases are analyzed in Gellhorn and Byse, *Administrative Law*, supra, n. 60. Roughly, Congress may determine the general policy and leave to the Executive application of the policy to the facts. Alexander Bickel also questions Sutherland's view of the delegation issue; Fulbright Hearings 554–555. See also R. J. Bartlett, Executive Agreements Hearings 16.

211. As late as 1929, Willoughby wrote, "There can be no question as to the unconstitutional unsoundness, as well as the revolutionary theory" of inherent powers; 1 W. W. Willoughby, *The Constitutional Law of the United States* 92 (New York, 1929). For rejection of that theory by Justices Douglas, Frankfurter, and Jackson, see supra, n. 185. In 1971, former Justice Goldberg testified that he "reject[s] this concept of inherent power," and that the cases uttering broad language "about inherent powers . . . have not stood the test of time"; Fulbright Hearings 770, 777.

212. 299 U.S. 315–316.

213. Ibid. 317.

214. Federalist No. 45 at 303; emphasis added. Madison's statement undercuts Professor Henkin's attempt to bolster Sutherland's argument by the suggestion that "the Framers intended to deal in full only with the governance of domestic affairs where the distribution between nation and States was new and critical . . . but, with a few explicable exceptions, they did not deal with, enumerate, allocate powers in foreign affairs where the federal government was to have all"; Henkin 24. Henkin confirms, however, that the "Sutherland theory . . . carves a broad exception in the historic conception, often reiterated, never questioned and explicitly reaffirmed in the Tenth Amendment, that the federal government is one of enumerated powers only"; ibid. 24–25.

Deferring for the moment further comment on Sutherland's aberrant theory, let it be assumed that somehow the *nation* or Union obtained inherent powers over foreign relations, and it still needs to be shown how the power came to be vested *in the President*. For, as Justice Frankfurter pointed out, "the fact that power exists in the Government does not vest it in the President."[215] The "inherent power" theory, moreover, would circumvent the manifest intention of the Framers to create a federal government of limited and enumerated powers and defeat their purpose to condition presidential action in the field of foreign relations on congressional participation.

McDougal and Lans, who relied heavily on these dicta,[216] acknowledged that Sutherland's analysis "unquestionably involves certain metaphorical elements and considerable differences of opinion about historical facts," but concluded that he "may have been expressing a thought more profound than any involved in quarrels about the naming of powers."[217] This is to conclude that Sutherland was right for the wrong reasons. Apparently the "profound" thought was the "important fact . . . that the imperatives of survival have required the Federal Government to exercise certain powers."[218] No "imperatives of survival" were at stake either in *Curtiss* or in *Pink;* nor has there been any demonstration that the powers of the federal government were and are inadequate, still less how supraconstitutional powers came to rest in the President. The issue, which must be kept steadily in view, is whether the President may act without the participation of the Senate in the exercise of powers conferred on President and Senate *jointly*. The "quarrel," therefore, is not about the mere "naming of powers," but about presidential claims to exclusive power notwithstanding that the Constitution and Founders unmistakably meant the treaty power to be exercised jointly with the Senate.

The mischievous and demonstrably wrong dicta of Justice Sutherland deserve no further credence.[219] His view that the President

215. Youngstown Case, 343 U.S. at 604, concurring. Hamilton reiterated that the powers of the President with respect both to the war and treaty powers were less than those of the King; Federalist No. 69 at 448, 451.

216. McDougal & Lans 255–258. Dean Acheson, former Secretary of State, cited Curtiss to the Senate in July 1971; Ervin Hearings 260, 264.

217. McDougal & Lans 257–258. The Framers, we shall see, indulged in no such metaphors.

218. Ibid. This reasoning is followed by Craig Matthews, "The Constitutional Power of the President to Conclude International Agreements," 64 Yale L.J. 345, 348–350 (1955).

219. Professor R. J. Bartlett considers that the doctrine of Curtiss-Wright should

enjoys extraconstitutional powers outside the sphere of enumerated powers was based on the theory that

> since the states severally never possessed international powers, such powers could not have been carved from the mass of state powers but obviously were transmitted to the United States from some other source . . . [T]he powers of external sovereignty passed from the Crown not to the colonies severally, but to the colonies in their collective and corporate capacity as the United States . . . Sovereignty is never held in suspense. When, therefore, the external sovereignty of Great Britain in respect of the colonies ceased, it immediately passed to the Union. See *Penhallow* v. *Doane,* 3 Dall. 54, 80–81.[220]

Seldom have dicta more "obviously" been removed from the historical facts.

To the minds of the colonists, "thirteen sovereignties," as Chief Justice Jay said in 1793, "were considered as emerged from the principles of the revolution."[221] For this we need go no further than the Articles of Confederation, agreed to by the Continental Congress on November 5, 1777, signed by all the states save Maryland in 1778 and 1779, and ratified March 1, 1781.[222] Article II recited, "Each State retains its sovereignty, freedom and independence, and every Power . . . which is not . . . expressly delegated to the United States in Congress assembled." Article III provided, "The said states hereby severally enter into a firm league of friendship with each other, for their common defence." Mark that they entered into a "league"; they did not purport to create a "corporate" or "sovereign" body. Article IX then declared that "[t]he United States in Congress assembled shall have the sole and exclusive right of determining on peace and war . . . entering into treaties and alliances." This express grant of war and treaty powers alone undermines Justice Sutherland's central premise that

---

be laid "at rest"; he remarked upon the "fallacy" of its "historical argument," and that "the succession of sovereignty from the Crown to the Federal Government has no basis in American history"; Executive Agreement Hearings 17–18. Professor Bickel likewise observed that Sutherland's "grandiose conception never had any warrant in the Constitution, is wrong in theory and unworkable in practice." Ibid. 26.

220. 299 U.S. at 316–317.

221. Chisholm v. Georgia, 2 U.S. (2 Dall.) 419, 470 (1793). For example, the Massachusetts Constitution of 1780, Art. IV, provided, "The people of this commonwealth have the sole and exclusive right of governing themselves as a free, sovereign and independent State, and do, and forever hereafter shall, exercise and enjoy every power, jurisdiction, and right which is not, or may not hereafter be, by them expressly delegated to the United States of America in Congress assembled"; 1 Poore 958.

222. Commager, supra, n. 24 at 111.

these powers were derived from "some other source" than the several states. If the newborn Continental Congress possessed "inherent" war and treaty powers from the outset, the express grant was gratuitous.

Nor did the Founders share Justice Sutherland's views on sovereignty. More pragmatic than he, they spoke, not in terms of sovereignty, but of power; and they were quite clear that the *people*, not even the cherished states, were sovereign. Power flowed from the people, not from the Crown to fill a vacuum. Hear James Iredell in North Carolina: "It is necessary to particularize the power intended *to be given*, in the Constitution, as having *no existence before*."[223] "The people," stated Madison in the Convention, "were in fact, the fountain of all power";[224] a part they conferred upon the individual states; and in the clause, "We, the people of the United States . . . do ordain and establish this Constitution," said Chief Justice Jay, "we see the people acting as sovereigns of the whole country."[225] Sovereignty was taken by the people unto themselves.

When Justice Sutherland cited *Penhallow v. Doane*,[226] he referred solely to the opinion of Justice William Paterson, ignoring the fact that the majority opinions of Justices Iredell and Cushing were to the contrary. The case arose on a state of facts that antedated the adoption of the Articles of Confederation; and Paterson stated that the Continental Congress exercised the "rights and powers of war," and that "States individually did not."[227] This, however, does not tell the whole story. For example, the Continental Congress resolved on November 4, 1775,

> that the town of Charleston ought to be defended against any attempts that may be made to take possession thereof by the enemies of America,

223. 4 Elliot 179.

224. 2 Farrand 476. For similar remarks by George Mason, James Iredell, James Wilson, and others, see Berger, *Congress v. Court* 173 n. 99, 174–175. See also G. S. Wood, *The Creation of the American Republic, 1776–1787*, pp. 329, 362–363, 371–372, 382–383 (Williamsburg, 1969). With justice, therefore, did Professor Philip Kurland dismiss Justice Sutherland's "discovery" that "the presidential powers over foreign affairs derived not at all from the Constitution but rather from the Crown of England"; Kurland, n. 127 at 622. Recall that all roots of presidential power to the Crown prerogative had been cut, supra, Ch. 3, text accompanying nn. 5, 10, 15, and that Madison emphasized the President would have powers that were "given" and "defined"; ibid. at n. 17.

225. Chisholm v. Georgia, 2 U.S. (2 Dall.) 419, 471 (1793).

226. 3 U.S. (3 Dall.) 54 (1795).

227. Ibid. 80–81.

and that the convention or council of safety of the colony of South Carolina, ought to pursue such measures, as to them shall seem most efficacious for that purpose, and that they proceed immediately to erect such fortifications and batteries in or near Charleston, as will best conduce to promote its security, the expence to be paid by said Colony.[228]

Other testimony that each of the Colonies was thought to possess warmaking power is furnished by the July 12, 1776, draft of the Articles of Confederation: "The said Colonies unite themselves . . . and hereby severally enter into a firm League of Friendship . . . binding the said Colonies to assist one another against all Force offered to or attacks made upon them."[229] Indeed, as Justice Chase was to remark in a cognate case, the very fact of delegation of war power by the states to the Congress demonstrates that the states must have "rightfully possessed" it.[230] In the course of time, the states did not "individually" exercise the power of war; but that did not spring from absence of original power but from a voluntary surrender expressed both in the Article IX delegation and in the 1776 draft of Article XIII: "No colony . . . shall engage in any War without the Consent of the United States assembled[231] —a provision that was preserved in Article VI of the Articles as adopted.

Justice James Iredell, whose opinion in *Penhallow* went unnoticed by Sutherland, understood all this full well. Each province, he pointed out, had comprised "a body politic," in no wise connected with the others "than as being subject to the same common sovereign."[232] If Congress, he continued, "previous to the articles of confederation, possessed any authority, it was an authority derived from the people of each province . . . this authority was conveyed by each body politic separately, and not by all the people in the several provinces or States, jointly."[233] And he concluded that the warmaking authority "was not possessed by congress unless given by all the States."[234] In this view he was joined

228. 3 Jour. Contl. Cong. 326 (1775).

229. 5 Jour. Contl. Cong. 546–547 (1776).

230. "Virginia had a right, as a sovereign and independent nation, to confiscate any British property within its territory, unless she had before delegated that power to congress . . . if she had parted with such power it must be conceded that she once rightfully possessed it"; Ware v. Hylton, 3 U.S. (3 Dall.) 199, 231 (1796).

231. 5 Jour. Contl. Cong. 549; Commager, supra, n. 24 at 112.

232. 3 U.S. at 90.

233. Ibid. 92–94.

234. Ibid. 95.

by Justice William Cushing;[235] and both are abundantly confirmed by the specific grants of war and treaty powers to Congress in the Articles of Confederation.

Reliance for "inherent" war and treaty powers that antedate the Articles of Confederation has also been placed[236] upon some remarks of Justice Samuel Chase in *Ware v. Hylton:* "The powers of congress originated from necessity . . . they were revolutionary in their very nature . . . It was absolutely and indispensably necessary that congress should possess the power of *conducting* the war against *Great Britain*, and therefore, if not expressly given by all (as it was by some of the States [who had ratified the Articles in 1778]) . . . Congress did rightfully possess such power."[237] A simpler and more prosaic explanation is at hand. Sitting and working together, the delegates from the Thirteen States—who as early as July 1776 proposed in the draft Articles of Confederation to reduce to writing the necessary delegation by the States to Congress and who agreed to the Articles of Confederation in November 1777—presumably were agreed that the conduct of the war required centralization and considered themselves empowered to authorize the necessary "confederated" acts pending formal adoption of the proposed Articles. Despite his statement respecting "revolutionary" "necessity," Justice Chase himself stated in *Ware v. Hylton* that "all the powers actually exercised by congress, before [the confederation], were rightfully exercised, on the presumption not to be controverted, that they were so authorized by the people they represented, by an express or implied grant."[238]

The invocation of the treaty signed with France by Benjamin Franklin and his fellow commissioners in February 1778, and ratified by Congress in May,[239] little advances the argument for "inherent" national power. Franklin and the other commissioners proceeded to France under express instructions to enter into a treaty with the King of France, carrying with them "letters of credence" (September 1776), running not from the Congress but from "The delegates of the United States of New Hampshire,

235. Justice Cushing stated, "I have no doubt of the sovereignty of the States, saving the powers delegated to Congress . . . to carry on unitedly the common defense in the open war"; ibid. 117.

236. McDougal & Lans 258.

237. 3 U.S. at 232.

238. Ibid.

239. See McDougal & Lans 258; 11 Jour. Contl. Cong. 421, 444, 457 (1778).

Massachusetts Bay" and each of the other enumerated states.[240] Doubtless the delegates from the several states believed themselves authorized to send Franklin in search of an alliance. The resulting treaty, it bears emphasis, was concluded with "the thirteen United States of North America, viz. New Hampshire, Massachusetts Bay," and so forth,[241] scarcely testimony that France thought it was concluding an alliance with a sovereign nation. But give the "revolutionary" central government its widest scope, and it still remains to ask, what relevance do deeds resulting from revolutionary necessity in the absence of an existing national structure have to a subsequent written document, such as the Articles of Confederation, which carefully enumerates the powers granted and reserves all powers not "expressly delegated"?[242] John Jay later wrote of the treatymaking power in Federalist No. 64 that "it should not be *delegated* but . . . with such precautions as will afford the highest security."[243]

Study of the constitutional records convinces that the Founders jealously insisted on a federal government of enumerated, strictly limited powers.[244] In creating first governors, and then the President, they purposely cut all roots to the royal prerogative.[245] Not for them the aureole with which Justice Sutherland endowed the

240. 5 Jour. Contl. Cong. 827, 833; emphasis added. McDougal & Lans 537 therefore say truly that "these early Congresses . . . although controlling foreign policy, essentially functioned as councils of ambassadorial delegates from a group of federated states," a statement that undercuts Sutherland's dictum that the States never had external "sovereignty."

241. 11 Jour. Contl. Cong. 421 (1778). Justice Sutherland also relied on Rufus King's remarks in the Convention (299 U.S. at 317): "The states were not 'sovereigns' in the sense contended for by some. They did not possess the peculiar features of sovereignty—they could not make war, nor peace, nor alliances, nor treaties"; 1 Farrand 323. But this was because they had delegated those functions to the Congress.

Levitan demonstrates that the Continental "Congress was a committee of safety having as its basic aim the defeat of Great Britain. At no time was it viewed, nor did it view itself as a governmental organization having legislative authority." Supra n. 193 at 483. The "record of events leaves no doubts that treaty-making power was exercised by the States"; ibid. 485. The states did not deem the 1778 Franklin treaty "binding on them, until they had individually ratified the treaty"; ibid. 486. The 1776–1787 history, he concludes, "leaves little room for the acceptance of Mr. Justice Sutherland's 'inherent' powers, or in fact 'extra-constitutional' powers theory"; ibid. 496.

That so solid a demonstration of the vulnerability of the Sutherland dicta should not have discouraged further citation is not the least remarkable chapter in the history of *Curtiss-Wright*.

242. Articles of Confederation, Art. II; Commager, supra, n. 24 at 111.

243. *Federalist* at 417; emphasis added.

244. Ch. 3, supra, text accompanying nn. 17, 19–56; and n. 17. For additional citations see Berger, *Congress v. Court* 13–14, 377 n. 52.

245. Ch. 3., supra, text accompanying nn. 5, 10, 15.

President's power over foreign relations. That power was no less circumscribed than the domestic powers, as Madison made clear.[246] A supraconstitutional residuum of powers not granted expressly or by necessary implication was not only furthest from their thoughts,[247] but avowal of such a residuum would have affrighted them and barred adoption of the Constitution.[248] We have the testimony of James Wilson that *all* the "powers naturally connected" with that of declaring war were conferred on Congress.[249] And John Quincy Adams, after serving as Secretary of State and as President, stated: "in the authority given to Congress by the constitution . . . to declare war, all the powers incidental to war are, by necessary implication, conferred upon the Government of the United States." The "war power," he continued, "is strictly constitutional."[250] To conjure up an "inherent" executive power in the teeth of this history is both to shut our eyes to the historical record and to abort the plainly manifested intention of the Founders to create a federal government of limited and enumerated powers.[251]

E. *What Is the Exclusive Presidential Enclave?*

In the entire armory of war powers only one has been exclusively conferred upon the President, the power as "first General" to direct the conduct of war once it has been com-

246. Supra, text accompanying n. 214.

247. In his 1791 Lectures, James Wilson, then a Justice of the Supreme Court, referred to the executive powers granted by the Constitution and to the presidential veto as "a guard to protect his powers against [the Legislature's] encroachment. Such power and such a guard he ought to possess: but a just distribution of the powers of government requires that *he should possess no more*"; 1 Wilson, *Works* 319; emphasis added.

248. See statement of Alexander White, supra, Ch. 3, text accompanying n. 55.

249. Supra, text accompanying n. 8.

250. 12 Cong. Debates 4037–4038 (1836). Compare Justice Harlan's statement: "Chief Justice Marshall, in McCulloch v. Maryland . . . has taught us that the Necessary and Proper Clause is to be read with *all* the powers of Congress, so that 'where the law is not prohibited, and is really calculated to effect any of the objects entrusted to the government'" the Court will not "'inquire into the degree of its necessity . . .'"; Reid v. Covert, 354 U.S. 1, 69 (1957), concurring. So read, the war powers are plenary.

251. An "inherent" presidential war power was dismissed out of hand by Justice Jackson in the Youngstown Case 644–650. See also supra, n. 185. According to Halberstam, Senator Karl Mundt, who attended the conference between President Lyndon Johnson and the Soviet Premier Kosygin at Glassboro, "was appalled to find that the Soviet Union's Kosygin did not have the power to go to war that Johnson seemed to have" Halberstam 590.

menced. Even in this area, the military and naval command were not immune from parliamentary inquiry into the conduct of the war.[252] It is said in a recent Yale memorandum,[253] relying on the schema set forth by Justice Jackson in the *Youngstown* case, that there is an "exclusive" warmaking zone where the President "is authorized to act even against the express will of Congress."[254]

Jackson sketched three categories: First, "when the President acts pursuant to an express or implied authorization of Congress, his authority is at its maximum, for it includes all that he possesses in his own right plus all that Congress can delegate." The steel-seizure, he said, "is eliminated from the first" category "for it is conceded that no congressional authorization exists for this seizure."[255] His second category is "a zone of twilight in which he [the President] may have concurrent authority, or in which its distribution is uncertain." Here again presidential authority is subject to that of Congress. The steel-seizure, said Jackson, "seems clearly eliminated from that class because Congress . . . has covered [the field] by three statutory policies inconsistent with this seizure."[256] Given concurrent powers, as Chief Justice Marshall held in an early war-powers case,[257] a congressional statute must prevail. Remains the third category: "When the President takes measures incompatible with the express or implied will of Congress, his power is at its lowest ebb, for then he can rely only upon his own constitutional power minus any constitutional powers of Congress over the matter." Judicial caution is required in such case lest "by disabling the Congress from acting upon the subject . . . The equilibrium established by our constitutional

252. For parliamentary inquiries into the "conduct" of a war, see supra, Ch. 2, text accompanying nn. 15–23.

253. The memorandum, entitled "Indo-china: The Constitutional Crisis," is reprinted in two parts at 116 Cong. Rec. 15409–15415 (May 13, 1970)—Part I—and ibid. 16478–16481 (May 20, 1970)—Part II—hereafter cited as Yale Memorandum. It was prepared for filing with the Senate by a group of Yale Law School students under the aegis of several eminent professors and former high government officers.

254. Ibid. 16478. The statement in Barenblatt v. United States, 360 U.S. 109, 112 (1959), that Congress "cannot inquire into matters which are within the exclusive province of one of the other branches of the Government" is too broad. Congress can probe into all departments of the Government "to expose corruption, inefficiency or waste"; Watkins v. United States, 354 U.S. 178, 187 (1957). As we have seen, Parliament could inquire into the disbursement of appropriations, the conduct of a war, the manner in which the laws were being executed; and as an auxiliary to the power of impeachment, inquiry knew no limits.

255. 343 U.S. at 635, 638.

256. Ibid. 637, 639.

257. Little v. Barreme, 6 U.S. (2 Cranch) 170, 177–178 (1804).

system" be disturbed.[258] Jackson stressed that where the Court can sustain the President only by holding that his actions were "within his domain and beyond control by Congress," the President's position is "most vulnerable to attack and in the least favorable of possible constitutional postures."[259] And he went on to reject the argument that President Truman's commitment of troops to Korea vested him with power to seize the nation's steel mills.[260] Jackson could find no such power under the "executive power," the "commander in chief" power, or in an "inherent power," which he peremptorily rejected.[261] Consequently, if, following Jackson's analysis, we are to speak of an "exclusive" presidential power "beyond control by Congress," we should keep in mind Jackson's warning that such claims are most difficult to sustain. Where they are raised, the "presidential power [is] most vulnerable to attack and in the least favorable of possible constitutional postures."[262]

Is the role of Commander-in-Chief altogether beyond the control of Congress? This can be confidently affirmed of one set of circumstances only: once war is commenced, Congress can not conduct a campaign;[263] it can not "deprive the President of command of the army and navy." But in the words of Justice Jackson,

258. 343 U.S. at 637. J. N. Moore would diminish Jackson's "lowest ebb" statement on the ground that "Steel Seizure" turned on a domestic issue in which the presidential war power was far from clear (although the President invoked prior "precedents"), and because Myers v. United States, 272 U.S. 52 (1926) struck down a statute which required Senate concurrence in removal of a postmaster; Fulbright Hearings 468. But from the 1789 "removal" debate onward, the power of removal had been thought to belong exclusively to the President. Berger, *Impeachment* 280–283. A statute cannot override a constitutional grant. Be the issue "domestic" or "foreign," the President's "war power" is derived from his role as Commander-in-Chief, and in that capacity he is merely "first General."

259. 343 U.S. at 640.

260. Ibid. 642.

261. Ibid. 641–652.

262. Professor Rostow sets forth the three Jackson classifications in extenso, and considers that the "early history" of our foreign affairs "matches the classification"; Rostow, supra, n. 3 at 862–863. But what of the subsequent history? More and more the President has grasped monopolistic control of military and foreign affairs, from which, by executive agreements, by resort to claims of executive privilege, and the like, Congress is excluded. How does this "match" the exceedingly narrow scope assigned by Jackson to solo presidential power?

263. Former President Taft, who argued for a strong executive power, stated, "When we come to the power of the President as Commander-in-Chief it seems perfectly clear that Congress could not order battles to be fought on a certain plan, and could not direct parts of the army to be moved from one part of the country to another"—a very modest enclave of "exclusivity"; W. H. Taft, "The Boundaries between the Executive, the Legislative and the Judicial Branches of the Government," 25 Yale L.J. 599, 610 (1916).

"only Congress can provide him an army or navy to command."[264] What it gives it can take away, in whole or in part.[265]

Presidential peacetime deployment of the armed forces in troubled areas sharply focuses the problem. Such deployments may invite or provoke attack, dangerously risk American involvement in war,[266] and present Congress with a fait accompli. Testifying in 1951 on behalf of President Truman's plan to station six divisions of American soldiers in Europe, Secretary of State Acheson asserted:

> Not only has the President the authority to use the Armed Forces in carrying out the broad foreign policy of the United States and implementing treaties, but it is equally clear that this authority may not be interfered with by Congress in the exercise of powers which it has under the Constitution.[267]

Acheson spoke ex cathedra, disdaining the citation of authority, but his claim shatters on analysis.

It is Congress that is to "provide for the common defense,"[268] which implies the right to decide what is requisite thereto. Congress also is "to raise and support armies," and by necessary im-

264. 343 U.S. at 644. Another limitation, as Madison observed, is that, although the President can command, the appointment of officers requires Senate consent. 3 Elliot 394. By its power to make rules for the "Government and Regulation of land and naval forces," Congress, said Justice Jackson, "may to some unknown extent impinge even upon command functions"; 343 U.S. at 644. "Presidential power, even in the exercise of the commander-in-chief power, is not autonomous." Moore, supra, n. 196 at 813.

265. Cf. United States v. Hudson & Goodwin, 11 U.S. (7 Cranch) 32, 33 (1812): "the power which congress possesses to create courts of inferior jurisdiction, necessarily implies the power to limit the jurisdiction of those Courts to particular objects." See also Sheldon v. Sill, 49 U.S. (8 How.) 441, 448–449 (1850).

266. For example, on "November 28, 1941, the President and his War Cabinet discussed the question: 'How shall we maneuver them [the Japanese] into the position of firing the first shot . . .' "; Corwin, *Total War* 32. Reveley, supra n. 78 at 1262, states that Wilson and "especially Roosevelt, were forced to resort to deception and flagrant disregard of Congress in military deployment decisions because they were unable to rally congressional backing for action essential to national security." This substitutes a "Great White Father" for constitutional processes. See also Harvard Note, supra, n. 36 at 1785–1787, 1796, 1798.

267. S. Rep. 606, 92d Cong., 2d Sess. 17, 19 (1972). Resort to presidential power over foreign policy cannot supply any *military* power which the Commander-in-Chief lacks. In 1971 Secretary of State Rogers indicated that a congressional attempt "to restrict the President's authority to deploy forces abroad" would be unconstitutional; Fulbright Hearings 499. Notwithstanding, Mr. Rogers would not question "the constitutionality of the right of Congress to bring back the troops from Europe," apparently by virtue of its power over appropriations; ibid. 504. I am baffled by the reasoning which would then deny to Congress a right to stipulate that no part of an appropriation should be used to *send* troops to Europe.

268. U.S. Constitution, Art. I §8(1).

plication it can withhold or withdraw that support.[269] In determining the size of the army it will "support," it is entitled to weigh priorities: shall troops be stationed in Germany or deployed in Cambodia? Indeed, the constitutional mandate that "no appropriation" for support of the armies "shall be for a longer term than two years" implies that it is for Congress to decide at any point whether further appropriations should be made and in what amounts.[270] The duty of Congress, in Hamilton's words, "to deliberate upon the propriety of keeping a military force on foot,"[271] surely comprehends the right to insist that a portion of the military forces should not be kept "on foot" in Vietnam or Europe.[272]

269. Ibid. §8(12); see supra, n. 265. In 1697 the Commons resolved to disband the army, notwithstanding that adherents of the King urged that the nation was still unsettled; and in 1698–1699, they voted to reduce the army; 5 Parl. Hist. Eng. 1167, 1168. See also infra, n. 276.

270. Art. I §8(12). When Gerry expressed fear about the absence of restrictions on the numbers of a peacetime army, Hugh Williamson "reminded him of Mr. Mason's motion for limiting the appropriations of revenue as the best guard in this case"; 2 Farrand 330, 327. In the early days the President was *compelled* to come to Congress for authorization to employ troops abroad because he had to obtain funds to raise and support troops. Only when Congress supplied a standing army was he enabled to escape this necessity; see supra, n. 44.

271. Federalist No. 26 at 163: the Congress "will be *obliged* by this provision, once at least in every two years, to deliberate upon the propriety of keeping a military force on foot; to come to a new resolution on the point . . . They are *not at liberty* to vest in the executive department permanent funds for the support of an army, if they were even incautious enough to be willing to repose in it so improper a confidence." Professor Richard B. Morris concluded that "in limiting military appropriations for 2 years," the Founders "had in mind curbing extensive wars of which they did not approve"; Fulbright Hearings 102.

272. In his testimony before the Senate Foreign Relations Committee, Professor Alexander Bickel stated: "Congress can govern absolutely, absolutely, the deployment of our forces outside our borders and that Congress should undertake to review and revise present dispositions"; Fulbright Hearings 557. For similar views of former Justice Goldberg, Professor Alfred Kelly, and McGeorge Bundy, ibid. 787, 788, 90, 116, 422. The Act of Sept. 16, 1940, 54 Stat. 885, 886, provided that draftees "shall not be employed beyond the limits of the Western Hemisphere." See also Professor R. J. Bartlett, Executive Agreements Hearings 44.

I would dissent from the proposition that to "require congressional approval for every decision to deploy American troops is hardly either desirable or constitutionally required"; Harvard Note, supra, n. 36 at 1798. The Congressional power is plenary, subject to no exceptions. It may be, as a practical matter, that Congress should leave the President free to make some peacetime deployments that cannot possibly lead to involvement in war; but that is a matter of accommodation by Congress, not "inherent" presidential power. In any event, the Harvard writers conclude that "there will be some situations, such as the rushing of troops to Lebanon . . . which, although not involving immediate commitment to combat, so clearly entail the possibility of conflict that prior approval should be sought . . . instead of assuming that the President may deploy American forces as he sees fit and only in the exceptional case need he seek congressional approval, the presumption should be that congressional collaboration is the general rule wherever the use of the military is involved, with presidential initiative being reserved for the exceptional case." What

With the power of appropriation goes the right to specify how appropriated moneys shall be spent. This is not a mere matter of logic but of established parliamentary practice. After 1665, states Hallam, it became "an undisputed principle" that moneys "granted by Parliament, are only to be expended for particular objects specified by itself."[273] The Act of Settlement (1701), for example, provided that appropriations were to be applied "to the several Uses and Purposes by this act directed and intended as aforesaid, and to no other Use, Intent or Purpose whatsoever."[274] The Founders were quite familiar with parliamentary practice;[275] and we may be sure that in reposing in Congress the power of raising revenues and of making and reviewing appropriations for support of the armies they conferred the concomitant right to "specify" the "particular objects" upon which its appropriations are to be expended.[276] So an early Congress read its constitutional

---

the Harvard writers, and Moore, supra, n. 196 at 814, regard merely as the part of wisdom, I consider lies within the constitutional power of Congress to require.

273. 2 Henry Hallam, *Constitutional History of England* 357 (London, 1884). In 1624 "the king consented that the supplies granted should be used solely for purposes designated and spent under the direction of officers accountable to the house of commons"; E. B. Turner, "Parliament and Foreign Affairs, 1603–1760," 38 Eng. Hist. Rev. 172, 174 (1919). For a later example, 1697, see 5 Parl. Hist. Eng. 1168. In 1711 the Commons complained to Queen Anne that the armed "service has been enlarged, and the charge of it increased beyond the bounds prescribed . . . a dangerous invasion of the rights of parliament. The commons must ever assert it as their sole and undoubted privilege, to grant money and to adjust and limit the proportions of it"; 6 Parl. Hist. Eng. 1027. Queen Anne replied that she would "give the necessary directions to redress the Grievances you complain of"; ibid. 1031. In 1697 the Commons resolved to disband the army, notwithstanding opposition by royal adherents. 5 Parl. Hist. Eng. 1167.

The principle remains vital in England; Ivor Jennings, *Parliament* 338, 292 (London, 1957). Sir Edward Seymour was impeached for having applied appropriated funds to public purposes other than those specified; 8 *Howells State Trials* 127–131, Art. 1, 1680 (London, 1810). Compare the proposed investigation by the House of Representatives in 1792 of charges that Secretary of the Treasury Hamilton had violated the terms of an appropriation law; infra, Ch. 6, text accompanying n. 28.

274. 12 & 13 Will. 3, c. 11, §26, 3 Statutes at Large 367 (1758).

275. On a related point, Mason said in the Convention that "he considered the caution observed in Great Britain on this point as the paladium (sic) of public liberty"; 2 Farrand 327. John Dickinson asked in the Convention, respecting the English practice of originating money bills in the Commons, "Shall we oppose to this long experience, the short experience of 11 years which we had ourselves?"; ibid. 278. Madison referred to British appropriation practices in Federalist No. 41 at 265. Compare the assurances of Madison, Marshall, and others in the Virginia Convention that the provision for jury trial carried with it all its attributes under English practice, including specifically, the right to challenge jurors; 3 Elliot 531, 546, 558–559, 573.

276. For English use of appropriations to reduce the armed forces, see Note, "The War-Making Powers: The Intention of the Framers in the Light of Parliamentary History," 50 B.U. L. Rev. 5, 7–8 (1970). See also the Commons' resolution of 1697, supra, n. 273.

powers in enacting a statute that all "sums appropriated by law for each branch of expenditure in the several departments shall be solely applied to the objects for which they are respectively appropriated."[277] The 1971 Act which prohibits use of appropriated funds "to finance the introduction of United States ground combat troops into Cambodia" is in this tradition.[278] If we may safely infer that the long-established parliamentary practice was adopted by the Founders as another "attribute" of the legislature, such statutes do not constitute an invasion of the President's powers as Commander-in-Chief.[279]

There remains the congressional power "to make rules for the government and regulation of the land and naval forces."[280] This was "added from the existing Articles of Confederation"; but the Framers omitted the phrase that followed—"and directing their operations"[281]—having in mind that the President would be Commander-in-Chief and, in the words of the New Jersey Plan, would "direct all military operations."[282] Thus, the Framers separated the presidential direction of "military operations" in time of war from the Congressional power to make rules "for the government and regulations of the armed forces," a plenary power enjoyed by the Continental Congress and conferred in identical terms upon the federal Congress. The word "government" connotes a power "to control," "to administer the government" of the armed forces; the word "regulate" means "to dispose, order, or govern." Such powers manifestly embrace congressional restraint upon deployment of the armed forces. Since the Constitution places no limits on the congressional power to support and to govern the armed forces and to make or withhold

277. Act of Mar. 3, 1809, Ch. 28, 2 Stat. 535. The foregoing history refutes the Executive argument that Congress' attempt "to command the expenditure of moneys that is appropriated for the construction" of the B-70 super-planes "would be a violation of the separation of powers, the invasion of a presidential prerogative under the Constitution!"; Kurland, supra, n. 127 at 630; see also infra, n. 279.

In his sixth Annual Message (Dec. 1, 1836), President Andrew Jackson said that the Constitution "vests the power of declaring for what purposes the public money shall be expended in the legislative department . . . to the exclusion of the executive and judicial"; 3 Richardson 110. "Impoundment" as a means of controlling congressional policy was as yet undreamed of.

278. Special Foreign Assistance Act of 1971, Pub. L. No. 91–652, 84 Stat. 1942, 1943.

279. Compare Justice Jackson's statement: "Congress alone controls the raising of revenues and their appropriation and may determine in what manner and by what means they shall be spent for military procurement"; Youngstown Case, 343 U.S. at 643.

280. U.S. Constitution, Art. I §8(14).

281. 2 Farrand 330; Commager, supra, n. 24 at 114.

282. 1 Farrand 244.

appropriations therefore, arguments addressed to the impracticability of regulating all deployments go to the wisdom of the exercise, not the existence, of the congressional power. In fine, the constitutional distribution of powers refutes Acheson's assumption that the President may deploy the armed forces as he sees fit in disregard of congressional will.

Once war is initiated by Congress or by invasion of American soil, the Commander-in-Chief clause empowers the President to conduct the campaign. But no "first General" may create incidents which embroil the nation in war; he may not provoke, extend, or persist in a war against the will of Congress.[283] After conferring upon Congress the lion's share of the war powers, the Framers hardly contemplated that those powers would be suspended, placed in the deep-freeze once war was commenced. Not only must Congress be consulted before war is begun, it is entitled to be consulted during the war, in Madison's words, whether "a war ought to be commenced, continued or concluded."[284] Shall an expeditionary force be increased from 60,000 to 500,000 men? That involves vast expenditures, the drafting of many men, and if Congress is to plan and legislate intelligently, it must be apprised of the war plans, not merely for the moment but for what must be anticipated. No "first General" was meant to be unaccountable to the legislature. Congress must have access to information if only to perform its own sweeping warmaking functions and protect the nation against costly executive blunders such as the escalation in Vietnam. More "confidently" than Professor Henkin, I would, therefore, maintain that the President's

> powers as Commander-in-Chief are subject to ultimate Congressional authority to "make" the war, and Congress can control the conduct of the war it has authorized . . . he would be bound to follow Congressional

283. See Henkin, supra, text accompanying n. 20. Compare General Douglas MacArthur's crossing of the Yalu River, which drew powerful Chinese forces into the Korean War and contributed to his removal by President Truman. Acheson, supra, n. 77 at 462–466. As "first General," the President must be equally responsible to Congress for expanding a war upon Korea to one on China.

284. *Letters of Helvidius*, 6 Madison, *Writings* 148. Former Under Secretary of State George Ball, testified in 1971 that "it is essential that the Executive and Congress must work closely together not only in the actual conduct of a war but, even more, in shaping the policies that help create the situations that lead to conflict —and, finally, in the hard decision as to whether, when a crisis comes, the United States should react with military means"; Fulbright Hearings 627. And in deciding upon the "use of force," he added, "it is terribly important that the information that is made available to the Congress when it goes to look at these things is the same information and all the same information that is in the hands of the executive"; ibid. 637. To the same effect, J. N. Moore, ibid. 476.

directives not only as to whether to continue the war, but whether to extend it to other countries and other belligerents, whether to fight a limited or unlimited war, today perhaps, even whether to fight a "conventional" or a nuclear war.[285]

Nothing in the foregoing history suggests that in vesting the President with the function of Commander-in-Chief, the Founders intended to reject the Parliamentary practice and to render him unaccountable to Congress in the execution of that function. The fact that they provided for impeachment of the President argues to the contrary, for traditionally impeachment could be preceded by inquiry. Were Congress to enact a law governing deployment of troops abroad, it would be empowered, as Montesquieu stated, to examine "in what manner its laws have been executed." So too, if it appropriated moneys for the conduct of war in Vietnam and sought to investigate rumors that these moneys were being used to wage war in Cambodia and Laos, it would have parliamentary precedent for inquiry whether there had been an impeachable violation of law. Even within the narrow, "exclusive" compass of the Commander-in-Chief function, Congress is historically authorized to inquire into the "conduct" of the war.

No presidential "precedent" mustered by Attorney General Rogers laid claim to a right to withhold information respecting the conduct of a war or the disbursement of appropriations,[286] established categories of parliamentary inquiry. In the words of the Supreme Court,

> the power of inquiry has been employed by Congress throughout our history . . . in determining what to appropriate . . . The scope of the power of inquiry, in short, is as penetrating and far-reaching as the potential power to enact and appropriate under the Constitution.[287]

And if these powers do not reach far enough, there is the all-encompassing power to inquire into executive conduct which is an auxiliary to impeachment.

285. Henkin 108. McGeorge Bundy, a chief adviser of Presidents Kennedy and Johnson, testified, "the constitutional power to declare war clearly includes the power to put limits on any hostilities that are authorized"; Fulbright Hearings 421. He added that Congress "has every right to assert itself on broad questions of place, time, or the size of forces committed . . . and to concern itself with the purposes of any hostilities and the conditions on which they may be continued or ended"; ibid. 422. Professor Bickel deduced from Congress' "power to declare war" that it would "necessarily have the power to declare peace"; ibid. 588. Madison and James Wilson agreed that "executive powers . . . do not include the rights of war and peace"; supra, text accompanying n. 38.

286. Rogers memo 4–29.

287. Barenblatt v. United States, 360 U.S. 109, 111 (1959).

5

PRESIDENTIAL POWERS: FOREIGN RELATIONS

SOMETHING of the wonder that suffuses a child upon learning that a mighty oak sprang from a tiny acorn fills one who peers behind the tapestry of conventional learning and beholds how meager are the sources of presidential claims to monopolistic control of foreign relations.[1] A grandiose formulation of such claims was enunciated by Woodrow Wilson, then president of Princeton University:

> One of the greatest of the President's powers . . . [is] his control, which is very absolute, of the foreign relations of the nation. The initiative in foreign affairs, which the President possesses without any restriction whatever, is virtually the power to control them absolutely. The President . . . may guide every step of diplomacy, and to guide diplomacy is to determine what treaties must be made, if the faith and prestige of the government are to be maintained. He need disclose no step of negotiation until it is complete, and when in any critical matter it is completed the government is virtually committed. Whatever its disinclination, the Senate may feel itself committed also.[2]

Wilson felt no need to advert to the constitutional problems presented by his statement, but apparently regarded it as dogma beyond need of demonstration. In his own person as President of the United States, Wilson was later to suffer a disastrous refutation when the Senate rejected the Versailles Treaty and League of Nations, which he had negotiated according to his dogma. The cost of presidential absolutism came high.[3]

1. The word "monopoly" is borrowed from the caption, "Negotiation a Presidential Monopoly" in Edward S. Corwin's revision of the official *Constitution of the United States of America—Analysis and Interpretation* 412 (Washington, 1953).

2. Woodrow Wilson, *Constitutional Government in the United States* 77–78 (New York, 1908).

3. Wilson was aware that the "spirit of the Constitution" called on the President to keep "himself in confidential communication with the leaders of the Senate while his plans are in course, when their advice will be of service to him and his information of the greatest service to them, in order that there may be veritable counsel and a real accommodation of views instead of a final challenge and contest"; ibid. 139–140.

Today, we are told, war is merely an instrument of foreign policy;[4] four times in this century presidential foreign policy has entangled us in great wars—World Wars I and II, Korea, and Vietnam.[5] As Wilson indicated, the President's foreign policy can present the nation with an all but irreversible fait accompli.[6] At a time when the havoc of war immediately threatens every man, woman, and child, when the sacrifices war requires in property, blood, even life itself, are staggering,[7] it needs to be asked whether the Founders intended to leave such risks for the decision of a single man.[8]

While such risks have been mounting, the executive tendency to shroud the conduct of foreign relations in secrecy has grown

4. "The military machine has simply become an instrument for achieving presidential power objectives." Henry Monaghan, "Presidential War-Making," 50 Bost. U. L. Rev. 19, 31 (1970); W. T. Reveley, "Presidential War-Making: Constitutional Prerogative or Usurpation?" 55 Va. L. Rev. 1243, 1245–1246 (1969). Clausewitz, the pioneer military theorist, regarded war as "a continuation of political commerce"; 1 C. von Clausewitz, *On War* [1832] 23 (London, 1966). Our war in Vietnam is the creature of presidential foreign policy. Secretary of State Rogers agreed that war is "the most disastrous" of "our foreign policies"; Fulbright Hearings 533.

5. Corwin wrote, "Our three wars of outstanding importance prior to World War II were all the direct outcome of Presidential policies in the making of which Congress had but a minor part"; Corwin, *Total War* 13. For Franklin Roosevelt's prewar policy, see Morison 991–1001. The President "has always possessed the power to bring the country to war, if he so chose"; McDougal & Lans 614. "[P]residential hegemony over the shaping of foreign policies . . . lead to the need to use armed forces"; Reveley, supra, n. 4 at 1304.

6. Corwin, *President* 274, refers to the "ability of the President simply by his day-to-day conduct of our foreign relations to create situations from which escape except by the route of war is difficult or impossible." The President may "so conduct the foreign intercourse, the diplomatic negotiations with other governments, as to force a war"; John N. Pomeroy, *An Introduction to the Constitutional Law of the United States* §672 (Cambridge, Mass., 1875). See also Reveley, supra, n. 4 at 1245–1247. Cf. text accompanying n. 2 supra. The President "may conduct a vital phase of foreign policy literally for years without Congressional control, as with our foreign policy toward Japan before the last war, toward Russia during the war, and toward China after the war." Such policymaking "may lead to policies for which there is inadequate support, as with Wilson and, had not Pearl Harbor intervened, conceivably with Roosevelt." Robert A. Dahl, *Congress and Foreign Policy* 173 (New York, 1950).

7. As Hugh Gaitskill, leader of the British Labour Party, said in 1960, "foreign affairs concern the lives and destinies of all of us today"; quoted in P. G. Richards, *Parliament and Foreign Affairs* 72 (London, 1967). In England "it has been abundantly clear to the majority of voters that their well-being and their very existence depends far more upon international developments than on domestic political issues"; ibid. 31.

8. "The conclusion is unavoidable, for example, that in the years preceding Pearl Harbor, President Roosevelt and his advisers believed that many of their foreign policies could not have secured the support of a majority in Congress. Important foreign policies were made without prior or subsequent congressional consent"; Dahl, supra, n. 6 at 178. Dahl adds: "President and State Department believed they had information, experience, and a grasp of issues involved that the Congress and electorate lacked"; ibid. 180.

apace, as is exemplified by numerous "executive agreements" which are not even revealed to the Senate.[9] May information respecting the conduct of foreign affairs—for example, the disbursement of funds appropriated for defense[10] or for foreign aid[11] or the acquisition of foreign bases[12]—be withheld from Congress on the ground that congressional inquiry encroaches on presidential prerogatives?

Because of the widespread ramifications of foreign relations, discussion must perforce be confined to two vital aspects: presidential executive agreements, and whether the Senate may be excluded from knowledge of, and participation in, negotiations as a part of the treatymaking process.[13] Mention only can be made of the legislative shortcomings which have contributed to the all but total takeover of foreign relations by the President, of the need for procedural reform in the Senate if its participation is to be effective.[14] Could we view the matter as an original question, that is, were we drafting or amending a Constitution and free to decide where power is best vested, such factors might persuade that exclusive power over foreign affairs is best lodged in the President. Apart from counter-

9. See n. 123 infra.

10. Judge Learned Hand asked, "is it not possible to argue that Congress, especially now that the appropriations for the Armed Forces are the largest items of the budget, should be allowed to inquire in as much detail as it wishes, not only how past appropriations have in fact been spent, but in general about the conduct of the national defense?" L. Hand, *The Bill of Rights* 17–18 (Cambridge, Mass., 1958). Hand's tentative question, framed in terms of "should be allowed to inquire," can be firmly answered in light of the plenary parliamentary control over the expenditure of appropriations (supra, Ch. 4, text accompanying nn. 272–274), early congressional insistence that appropriations be applied solely to the objects specified (ibid. at n. 277), and the established parliamentary inquiries into the conduct of war (supra, Ch. 2, text accompanying nn. 15–23), and into the disbursement of public moneys; (ibid. at nn. 24–29).

11. See Ervin Hearings 27. Senator J. W. Fulbright, Chairman of the Foreign Relations Committee, testified, "I have made repeated efforts to secure access to the 5-year plan for military assistance for use by the Foreign Relations Committee in its consideration of military assistance under the foreign aid authorization bill." In vain. Ibid.

12. On June 19, 1972, the Senate voted to cut off funds for recently concluded military base agreements with Portugal and Bahrein unless the agreements were submitted to the Senate as treaties. The Executive did not comply with an earlier Senate resolution asking for submission of the executive agreements as treaties, on the ground that they had already been concluded; 118 Cong. Rec. S 9653 (daily ed. June 19, 1972); N.Y. Times, June 20, 1972 at 1, 15. Many millions of dollars were involved.

13. Recall Wilson's 1908 remark that the President "need disclose no step in the negotiation until it is complete . . . [and then] the government is virtually committed"; supra, text accompanying n. 2. True, Congress may reject a treaty, but the shift in policy may have "disastrous consequences for the international structure of power"; Dahl, supra n. 6 at 97.

14. For an excellent discussion of the entire problem, see Dahl, supra n. 6.

vailing considerations, however, if the Constitution provides for Senate participation in treatymaking, the Senate cannot now be barred on the ground that it lacks the wisdom and machinery to participate effectively.[15] "The peculiar circumstances of the moment," said Marshall, "may render a measure more or less wise, but cannot render it more or less constitutional."[16] Accordingly, the focus of discussion will be the constitutionality of presidential monopoly claims. The starting place of course must be the constitutional text itself, in the light of such illumination as is provided by the intention of the Framers and the understanding of the Ratifiers.

The constitutional provisions which confer power upon the President in the premises are three, only one of which is confided to the President alone: authority to receive ambassadors or ministers. This, Hamilton explained in *The Federalist*, is "more a matter of dignity than authority," "without consequence," in order to obviate the "necessity of convening the legislature . . . upon every arrival of a foreign minister"[17]—a slender reed upon which to rest a claim of monopoly of foreign relations. The other two presidential powers—to appoint ambassadors and ministers and to "make" treaties—are conditioned upon the "advice and consent" of the Senate, which is thus intended to participate in these acts. In addition, Congress is given the exclusive power "to regulate commerce with foreign nations . . . to control naturalization,"[18]

15. For improvements in the congressional machinery, see ibid. 146–168. Many consider the presidential policy that involved us in the Vietnam war a monumental folly, among them General Charles de Gaulle. See infra, Conclusion, n. 5. Dahl states that "to the extent that the executive is capable of solving its problems without accepting Congressional collaboration, it must become more and more the democratic shadow" of a "frank dictatorship"; Dahl, supra, n. 6 at 264. See also ibid. 116.

16. Gerald Gunther, *John Marshall's Defense of McCulloch v. Maryland* 190–191 (Stanford, 1969).

17. "The President is also to be authorized to receive ambassadors and other public ministers. This, though it has been a rich theme of declamation, is more a matter of dignity than of authority. It is a circumstance which will be without consequence in the administration of the government; and it was far more convenient . . . than that there should be a necessity of convening the legislature . . . upon every arrival of a foreign minister"; Federalist No. 69 at 451. "Receiving ambassadors," observes Professor Henkin, "seems a function rather than a 'power,' a ceremony which in many countries is performed by a figurehead." And "While making treaties and appointing ambassadors are described as 'powers' of the President (Article II, sect. 2), receiving ambassadors is included in section 3 which does not speak in terms of power but lists things the President 'shall' or 'may' do"; Henkin 41.

18. Arthur Schlesinger, Jr., "Congress and the Making of American Foreign Policy," 51 Foreign Affairs 78, 81–82 (1972). For the several provisions see U.S. Constitution, Art. I §8(1), (3), (4).

plus the power to lay duties and thereby control tariffs. Thus, commercial and tariff treaties were made primarily an object of congressional concern. "From the beginning," Professor Henkin states, "the foreign trade of the United States was near the core of its foreign policy and the power to regulate commerce with foreign nations gave Congress a major voice in it."[19] Looking to the aggregate of powers that affect foreign relations, it is safe to say with Professor Henkin that the "Constitution clearly gave Congress the ultimate foreign relations power, the power to go or not go to war, major legislative powers integral to foreign policy (for example, to regulate foreign commerce), and a spending power that has become a principal tool in foreign as in domestic affairs."[20]

I. NEGOTIATION OF TREATIES

A. *The Text of the Constitution*

Article II, §2 of the Constitution provides that the President

> shall have power by and with the Advice and Consent of the Senate, to make Treaties . . . and he shall nominate, and by and with the Advice and Consent of the Senate, shall appoint Ambassadors, other public Ministers . . .

Section 3 provides that "he shall receive Ambassadors and other public Ministers . . ." From these provisions Justice Sutherland distilled his oft-quoted statement that with respect to

> external affairs . . . participation in the exercise of the power is significantly limited. In this vast external realm . . . the President alone has the power to speak or listen as a representative of the nation. He *makes* treaties with the advice and consent of the Senate; but he alone negotiates. Into the field of negotiation the Senate cannot intrude; and Congress itself is powerless to invade it.[21]

Vainly does one search for "significant limits" in the constitutional text; they are of Sutherland's own contriving.

19. Henkin 69. Henkin also states, "The vast legislative powers of Congress that relate particularly to foreign affairs do not begin to exhaust its authority to make laws affecting foreign relations"; ibid. 76–78. Such comprehensive grants, to put it mildly, are repugnant to the claim that the Senate need not be consulted about foreign relations.

20. Henkin 273. "The solid fact," stated Professor Ruhl J. Bartlett, "is that Congress is the authoritative organ of the government in the determination of foreign policy. The President is the agent of Congress, the spokesman of the United States in diplomatic relations"; Executive Agreements Hearings 19.

21. United States v. Curtiss-Wright Export Corp., 299 U.S. 304, 319 (1936).

As was so often the case, the Framers borrowed the words "advice and consent" from parliamentary practice. They were words of art, reaching deep into history, which were descriptive of *participation in lawmaking*. For example, the statute of 13 Charles II (1661) states: "be it enacted by the King's most excellent Majesty, by and with the Advice and Consent of the Lords and Commons in this present Parliament assembled."[22] When, therefore, those words were employed in the "treaty" phrase, they connoted full participation in the *making* of a treaty,[23] as the history of the treaty clause clearly demonstrates.

Before Justice Sutherland ascended to the bench, he explained: "It will be observed that the advice and consent of the Senate qualifies the power of the Senate to *make*, and not to *negotiate*, treaties."[24] Since no mention whatever of "negotiate" is to be found in the constitutional text, it could hardly be "qualified." What power to "negotiate" a treaty exists derives from the power to "make" a treaty; and since the "make" power is expressly subject to "advice and consent," it follows that the power to "negotiate" a treaty is likewise so qualified. Nor does history disclose an intention to separate the "negotiate" component for independent presidential exercise; to the contrary, as will appear, the Founders intended the Senate to participate in all stages of treatymaking. They knew well enough how to single out a particular function for independent presidential exercise, as when they provided that the President "shall *nominate*, and by and with the Advice and Consent of the Senate, shall *appoint* Ambassadors." The fact that they did not equally provide that "he shall *negotiate*, and by and with the Advice and Consent of the Senate, *make* treaties" speaks volumes against the Sutherland reading. The comparison was tellingly drawn by Senator Henry Cabot Lodge, himself no mean historian:

The carefully phrased section gives the President absolute and unrestricted right to nominate, and the Senate can only advise and consent

22. 2 Stat. at Large 681 (ed. 1758). Professor Arthur Bestor called my attention to this correlation.

23. An early version, 3 Hen. V, 1 Stat. at Large 466 (1415), states: "Our Lord the King, at his Parliament . . . by the Advice and Assent of the Lords Spiritual and Temporal, and at the Request of the Commons . . . hath ordained and established divers Statutes and Ordinances." In the early medieval Parliaments the Commons were merely petitioners, not participants in lawmaking. Berger, *Impeachment* 20–21. When they became participants, they took part in the "advice and consent."

24. George Sutherland, *Constitutional Power and World Affairs* 122 (New York, 1919).

to the appointment of a given person. All right to interfere in the remotest degree with the power of nomination and the consequent power of selection is wholly taken from the Senate. Very different is the wording of the treaty clause. There the words "by and with the advice and consent of" come in after the words "shall have power" and before the power referred to is defined. The "advice and consent of the Senate" are therefore coextensive with the "power" conferred on the President, which is "to make treaties," and apply to the entire process of treaty-making.[25]

As Lodge's analysis indicates, the textual terms are to be scrutinized with greatest care, the more so because the Framers were fastidious draftsmen. What Chief Justice Taney discerned on the face of the Constitution is richly attested by the Convention records: "No word was unnecessarily used, or needlessly added. . . . Every word appears to have been weighed with the utmost deliberation, and its force and effect to have been fully understood."[26]

What does the word "advice" connote? As early as 1806, Senator Anderson pointed out that the "advice should precede the making of the treaty," that the word was employed "for the purpose of obtaining the opinion of the Senate as to the principles upon which the treaty should be made."[27] In 1906 Senator Augustus Bacon developed this analysis: "We do not advise men after they have made up their minds and after they have acted; we advise men while they are considering, while they are deliberating, and before they have determined, and before they have acted."[28] Unless "advice" is so understood, it is superfluous; it would have sufficed to require only Senate "consent" for the "making" of a treaty. So the process was understood by President Washington.[29]

In 1917 Edward S. Corwin countered with the argument that

25. Quoted in Ralston Hayden, *The Senate and Treaties: 1789–1817*, at 17 (New York, 1920). The differentiation emerges even more clearly in an earlier version: "to have with the advice and approbation of the Senate the power of making all treaties . . . to have the nomination . . . subject to the approbation or rejection of the Senate"; 1 Farrand 292. In 1908 Woodrow Wilson considered that such consultation was required by the "spirit of the Constitution"; supra, n. 3.

26. Holmes v. Jennison, 39 U.S. (14 Pet.) 540, 571 (1840).

27. Quoted in Hayden, supra, n. 25 at 202 n. 1.

28. 40 Cong. Rec. 2126. In 1971 Secretary of State Rogers testified that "in the formulation of policy, we feel we should consult and take into consideration and act upon congressional views." "Certainly," he stated, "in the foreign policy field the Congress plays a major role"; Fulbright Hearings 519. Cf. ibid. 530–531. One who has watched the conduct of foreign affairs by the Nixon administration must conclude that there is a wide gap between words and deeds, as we shall find equally in the field of "executive privilege."

29. See infra, text accompanying nn. 66–73; see also infra, text accompanying n. 110, for remarks of Rufus King, who had been a Framer.

"in connection with *appointments* the Senate's function of '*advice and consent*' is discharged by a mere 'yes' and 'no.' " "Advice" does not come too late when it surfaces after a "nomination," for the nomination has in nowise committed the President or the nation.[30] But to be effective, "advice" respecting "making" of a treaty must come before the positions of the negotiating parties have crystallized. In any event, Corwin leaves unanswered why "nomination" was freed of "advice and consent" whereas "treaty-making" was not. He himself later stated that "the Constitutional clause evidently assumes that the President and the Senate will be associated throughout the entire process of making a treaty."[31]

B. *The Understanding of the Founders*

Few are the instances in which deductions from the text are so unmistakably confirmed by the meaning attached to the terms by the Founders themselves. But first a quick recapitulation of the English antecedents earlier set forth so that the reader may view the constitutional provisions against the English background to which the Framers were throughout alive.[32]

As early as December 9, 1621 the House of Commons in a petition to James I stated with respect to matters of peace and war, "we cannot conceive that . . . the state of your kingdom, are matters at any time unfit for our deepest consideration in time of Parliament."[33] It needs constantly to be borne in mind that the Founders were more influenced by the struggle of the Commons in the revolutionary seventeenth century than by subsequent eight-

30. Edward S. Corwin, *The President's Control of Foreign Relations* 183 n. (Princeton, 1917) (hereafter cited as Corwin, *Control*). The distinction was appreciated in the antecedent provision; supra, n. 25.

31. Corwin, supra, n. 1 at 412. Corwin stated that the "significant thing" about the phraseology of the treaty-clause "is that it associates the President with the Senate *throughout the entire process* of treaty-making"; Corwin, *President* 253. McDougal & Lans 553 state: "The Framers assumed . . . that the Senate would participate equally with the President in the active direction of all negotiations and all aspects of foreign policy." See also ibid. 220; see Henkin 131. Compare with the foregoing history Dean Acheson's assertion that "the negotiation of [a treaty] is given to one branch and ratification to another"; Ervin Hearings 264. He considered that the Senate was limited to "exercising its constitutional power to make a treaty by ratifying it"; ibid. 261. Certainly nothing in the text requires the conclusion that the President may *exclude* the Senate from full participation in treatymaking.

32. See supra, Ch. 4, n. 275; Berger, *Impeachment* 87 n. 160, 143 nn. 97, 197, 217–218. Cf. ibid. 4, 30 nn. 107, 89, 98, 99, 101, 122, 171 n. 217. See also infra, n. 47.

33. Joseph R. Tanner, *Constitutional Documents of the Reign of James I, 1603–1625* at 281 (Cambridge, 1960).

eenth-century developments.[34] Parliament, through its power over supplies, constrained James I "to make no treaty without first acquainting parliament and requesting its advice."[35] When "the long parliament was sitting the king informed the members of the alliance he was about to make with the Dutch, and asked for advice."[36] After the Restoration the Commons again "insisted on a share in foreign policy if they were to supply the means of carrying it out"; and the Crown acquiesced. The Lord Chancellor declared in 1763 that "the King . . . hath made your Counsels the Foundation of all His Proceedings" abroad.[38] When negotiations respecting the second partition treaty (1700) were "carried through without the advice of parliament" it impeached those who assisted William in making it.[39] The "participation of parliament in foreign affairs and even its supervision of them was . . . fully recognized" in the Hanoverian period.[40] Christopher Hill concluded that by 1714 "Parliament had established a degree of control over the executive and over all its actions—including foreign policy."[41]

All this was part of the struggle between Parliament and the Crown, which eventuated in parliamentary supremacy.[42] Thereafter came ministerial responsibility to Parliament rather than to

34. See supra, Ch. 2, n. 39; and infra, n. 47.

35. E. B. Turner, "Parliamentary Government and Foreign Affairs, 1603–1760," 38 Eng. Hist. Rev. 172, 174 (1919).

36. Ibid. 175.

37. Ibid. 175.

38. Ibid. 177. "Since Danby's fall [ca. 1678] sprang from the government's foreign policy, the Commons' effective control of this hitherto sacrosanct sphere was again demonstrated." Christopher Hill, *The Century of Revolution, 1603–1714*, p. 230 (New York, 1961). In 1701 the Commons advised the King to act in concert with the States General in treaty negotiations with France to "conduce to their security"; the King responded that he had done so; 5 Parl. Hist. Eng. 1243 (1701). The King communicated the posture of the negotiations, and in closing said that the "safety of England . . . does very much depend upon your Resolutions in this matter"; ibid. 1250. In 1709 both Houses advised Queen Anne as to measures for a secure peace; 6 Parl. Hist. Eng. 788.

39. Turner, supra, n. 35 at 183. In 1715 the Commons "impeached Oxford because . . . he had misrepresented negotiations to the queen and hence to parliament," and so "prevented the just Advice of the Parliament to her Majesty"; ibid. 188. Was it sheer coincidence that James Iredell told the North Carolina Ratification Convention that if the President "has concealed important intelligence" from the Senate and so induced them to consent to a treaty, he could be impeached?; 4 Elliot 127.

40. Turner, supra n. 35 at 188.

41. C. Hill, supra n. 38 at 2. Parliament had emerged "as the leading partner"; Trevelyan 472.

42. Clayton Roberts, *The Growth of Responsible Government in Stuart England* (Cambridge, 1966).

the King, and management of foreign affairs by Ministers who, under orthodox theory, were under the control of Parliament. What such control could mean is illustrated by a resolution passed by the House of Commons in 1782—not without relevance to President Nixon's disregard of the repeal of the Gulf of Tonkin Resolution[43]—condemning the "farther prosecution" of the war with the American colonies on the ground that it was the means of "weakening the efforts of this country against her European enemies" and increasing the "mutual enmity, so fatal to the interests both of Great Britain and America."[44] When the ministry disregarded this resolution, a second resolution declared that "this House will consider as enemies" those who advise the "further prosecution" of the war "for the purpose of reducing the revolted Colonies to obedience by force." Now Lord North yielded and bowed to the opinion of Parliament.[45] The Founders, who cited the ongoing impeachment of Warren Hastings,[46] were hardly unfamiliar with these pages of Hansard.[47]

When the revolting colonies assembled in the Continental Congress and dispensed with an executive, they carried the movement for parliamentary supremacy to its logical conclusion. Experience led them to make an exception for a Secretary of Foreign Affairs, and John Jay was appointed to the post.[48] But he was kept under a tight rein, as the Journals of the Congress disclose. There could be no secrets from Congress: "Any member of Congress shall have access" to the Secretary's books and records, read the resolution.[49] And the Congress more than once appointed a Committee to investigate the Department of Foreign Affairs.[50]

43. Supra, Ch. 4, text accompanying nn. 136–138.

44. 22 Parl. Hist. Eng. 1071, 1085 (1781–1782).

45. Ibid. 1089, 1090, 1107.

46. E.g., George Mason, 2 Farrand 550; John Vining, 1 Annals of Cong. 373 (1789).

47. Hamilton's statement in Federalist No. 69 at 450–451, suggests unfamiliarity with the particulars: "The king of Great Britain is the sole and absolute representative of the nation in all foreign transactions. He can of his own accord make treaties of peace, commerce." But, he emphasized, "In this respect . . . there is no comparison between the intended power of the President and the actual power of the British sovereign. The one can perform alone what the other can do only with the concurrence of a branch of the legislature."

But compare Gouverneur Morris' reminder that in England "the real King [is] the Minister"; 2 Farrand 104. Cf. ibid. 69. Note too the Founders' familiarity with the details of English impeachment practices. Berger, *Impeachment* 54–55, 74–75, 84–85, 88–89. *See also* supra, Ch. 2, n. 162.

48. 19 Jour. Contl. Cong. 43 (1781); 20 Jour. Contl. Cong. 638 (1781).

49. 22 Jour Contl. Cong. 88 (1782).

50. Ibid. 370; 24 ibid. 37 n.

To argue that all this was changed by the constitutional provision for an executive branch and the separation of powers is to lose sight of the development of the treaty clause. The Framers—thirty of the fifty-five had been members of the Continental Congress—[51] began by adopting its practice. As late as August 6, the Convention Committee on Detail draft provided that "the Senate . . . shall have power to make treaties."[52] During the debate Madison "observed that the Senate represented the States alone," and, consequently, "the President should be an agent [not the exclusive agent] in Treaties."[53] As the Convention drew to a close, the Committee of Eleven proposed on September 4 that "the President by and with the advice and Consent of the Senate, shall have power to make Treaties."[54] How this appeared to the Framers may be judged from Rufus King's remark that "as the Executive was here joined in the business, there was a check [on the Senate] which did not exist in [the Continental] Congress."[55] It was the President, therefore, who was finally made a participant in the treaty-making process, which had been initially lodged—after the pattern of the Continental Congress—in the Senate alone. Not the slightest hint is to be found in the Convention records that thereby the President was meant to nose out the Senate from participation in any part of treatymaking. To the contrary, Hamilton explained in Federalist No. 75 that

51. The dual members were Abraham Baldwin, George Clymer, John Dickinson, Thomas Fitzsimons, Benjamin Franklin, Elbridge Gerry, Nicholas Gilman, Nathaniel Gorham, Bedford Gunning, Alexander Hamilton, Jared Ingersoll, Daniel of St. Thomas Jenifer, William S. Johnson, Rufus King, John Langdon, James Madison, James McHenry, Thomas Mifflin, Gouverneur Morris, Robert Morris, William Pierce, Charles Pinckney, Edmund Randolph, George Read, John Rutledge, Roger Sherman, Richard O. Spaight, George Washington, Hugh Williamson, and James Wilson.

The New Jersey Plan proposed to vest in Congress certain powers, "in addition to the powers vested in the United States in Congress, by the present existing articles of Confederation." 1 Farrand 243. In the New York Ratification Convention, Chancellor R. R. Livingston explained that the Continental Congress "have the very same" powers proposed for the new Congress, including the power "of *making* war and *peace* . . . they may involve us in a war at their pleasure"; 2 Elliot 278; emphasis added.

52. 2 Farrand 183.

53. Ibid. 392.

54. Ibid. 498.

55. Ibid. 540. "Not until September 7, ten days before the Convention's final adjournment, was the President made a participant in those powers"; Corwin, supra, n. 1 at 412. Commenting on the concurrence of the two branches to make a treaty, Patrick Henry stated, "the President, as distinguished from the Senate, is nothing"; 3 Elliot 353.

the vast importance of the trust, and the operation of treaties as laws, plead strongly for the *participation* of the whole or a portion of the legislative body in the office *of making* them . . . It must indeed be clear to a demonstration that the *joint possession* of the power in question, by the President and Senate, would afford a greater prospect of security, than the separate possession of it by either of them.[56]

The same point had earlier been made by John Jay in *The Federalist*, and though he appreciated that negotiations with those who preferred to "rely on the secrecy of the President" might arise, he stressed that such secrecy was with respect to "those preparatory and auxiliary measures which are not otherwise important in a national view, than as they tend to facilitate the attainment of the objects of the negotiations." The President, "in forming [treaties must] act by the advice and consent of the Senate."[57] Corwin correctly reads Jay to mean that "occasions" may arise . . . when the *initiation* of a negotiation may require great secrecy and dispatch, and at such times the President must undoubtedly *start the ball rolling;* but otherwise all negotiations of treaties will be the joint concern of President and Senate."[58]

The Ratification Conventions were given to understand that the Senate, without qualification, was to participate in the *making* of treaties. Some cumulative detail may be pardoned because of the importance of this point. In New York, Chancellor R. R. Livingston stated that the Senate "are to form treaties with foreign nations"; and Hamilton explained that "They, together with the President, are to manage all our concerns with foreign nations." Chancellor Livingston repeated that "the Senate was to transact all foreign business."[59] In Pennsylvania, James Wilson said, "nor is there any doubt but the Senate and the President possess the power of making" treaties; and that he was "not an advocate for secrecy in transactions relating to the public; not generally even *in forming* treaties."[60] What should not be withheld from the *public* could

56. Federalist No. 64 at 486, 488; emphasis added.
57. Ibid. 419, 420.
58. Corwin, *President* 253; emphasis added. That is the negative pregnant of Pierce Butler's explanation to the North Carolina Ratification Convention of why the House was not joined in treatymaking: "negotiation always required the greatest secrecy, which could not be expected in a large body"; 4 Elliot 263. A smaller body, i.e., the Senate, was therefore preferred for "negotiation." The need for secrecy was the stock explanation why the House was excluded from treatymaking. See, e.g., 2 Elliot 506, 3 Elliot 509, 4 Elliot 290.
59. 2 Elliot 291, 305, 323.
60. Ibid. 506; emphasis added.

not be withheld from the co-partner in treatymaking. In North Carolina, Samuel Spencer stated that the Senate "are, in effect to form treaties."[61] And speaking to "intercourse with foreign powers," James Iredell said that it is the President's "duty to impart to the Senate every material intelligence he receives." If he "has concealed important intelligence . . . and by that means induced them [the Senate] to enter into measures . . . which they would not have consented to had the true state of things been disclosed to them," impeachment would lie.[62] With good reason, therefore, do even those commentators who construe the President's authority broadly agree that "the Senate was made a participant in his diplomatic powers."[63] Indeed, it would fly in the face of common sense to deduce that the Framers, after taking great precautions, as James Wilson said, to put it beyond the power of a "single man . . . to involve us in such distress [war],"[64] then unraveled all their labors by giving sole control of foreign policy, which can plunge a nation into war, to that very "single man."

61. 4 Elliot 116. See the statement of William Davie, infra, text accompanying n. 152. In the course of a 1790 debate in the First Congress, Michael Stone stated in the House that "the principles of the Constitution" vest "the Senate equally with the President, in the whole business of negotiation"; 1 Annals of Cong. 1085. And, he stated, "If you give an influence to the President superior to the Senate, in anything relating to the intercourse between the United States and foreign nations, you deviate from the principles of the Constitution"; ibid. 1082. Roger Sherman, a Framer, added that "the two bodies ought to act jointly in every transaction which respects the business of negotiation with foreign powers"; ibid. 1085.

62. 4 Elliot 127. William Davie, a Framer, explained to the North Carolina Convention "that jealousy of executive power which has shown itself so strongly in all the American governments, would not admit" of lodging the treaty power in the President alone. And because of "the extreme jealousy of the little states" it became "necessary to give them an absolute equality in making treaties"; ibid. 120. In other words, Senate participation in treatymaking was demanded in order to satisfy small state jealousy. C. C. Pinckney's remark in South Carolina that the Senate was given "the power of agreeing or disagreeing to the terms proposed" by the President, ibid. 265, is opposed to the decided consensus that treaty *making* was a joint function.

63. Corwin, *President* 366, 254. McDougal & Lans, 539 n. 25, state: "The testimony of delegates to the Constitutional Convention clearly indicates the intention of the draftsmen that the Senate participate equally with the President in the step-by-step negotiation of treaties." See also ibid. 207, 220.

Looking at "the constitutional landscape," Corwin concluded that "the legislative power, was evidently intended originally to be the predominant one"; Corwin, *Total War* 158. Recall Madison's "In republican government, the legislative authority necessarily predominates"; Federalist No. 51 at 338.

64. 2 Elliot 528. That acute student of constitutional government, Walter Bagehot, said that the Framers "shrank from placing sovereign power anywhere. They feared it would generate tyranny"; W. Bagehot, *The English Constitution* 218 (London, 1964); see also supra, Ch. 3, n. 8. It is virtually beyond debate that the intention of the Framers was to confer all power connected with warmaking on Congress, leaving to the President only command of the armed forces and authority to repel sudden attack. See Ch. 4, supra, text accompanying nn. 7–45.

C. *Washington's Contemporaneous Construction*

Were the meaning of the constitutional text and the understanding of the Framers and Ratifiers, doubtful, we have the best of contemporaneous constructions[65]—by the presiding officer of the Convention, George Washington, our first President. In August 1789 he advised a Senate Committee that

> [i]n all matters respecting Treaties, oral communications [to the Senate] seem indispensably necessary; because in these a variety of matters are contained, all of which not only require consideration, but some of them may undergo much discussion; to do which by written communications would be tedious without being satisfactory.[66]

Oral communications proved impracticable; but Washington "continued to seek its [the Senate's] advice by message before opening negotiations" and "during their course."[67]

The facts have been beclouded by Corwin, who stated in 1917: "At the outset Washington sought to associate the Senate with himself in the negotiation of treaties, but this method of proceeding went badly and was presently abandoned."[68] So too, McDougal and Lans stated in 1945:

> it is clear the Framers anticipated that the Senate would normally function as an executive council, advising the President or his subordinates during the course of negotiations, as had been the case under the Articles of Confederation. This proposal for continuous consultation or for any significant degree of advance consultation proved to be unworkable and was abandoned during the administration of George Washington.[69]

All that "proved to be unworkable," however, was *oral* consultation with the Senate, and this because such was the awe in which

65. Respect for contemporaneous construction is deeply rooted in the past. In 1454 Chief Justice Prisot stated, "the Judges who gave these decisions in ancient times were nearer to the making of the statute than we now are, and had more acquaintance with it"; Windham v. Felbridge, Y. B. 33 Hen. 4, f. 38, 41 pl. 17, quoted in C. K. Allen, *Law in the Making* 193, 6th ed. (Oxford, 1958). For early American statements to the same effect, see Stuart v. Laird, 5 U.S. (1 Cranch) 299, 309 (1803); Ogden v. Saunders, 25 U.S. (12 Wheat.) 213, 290 (1827).

66. 33 George Washington, *Writings* 373 (Washington, 1939).

67. S. B. Crandall, *Treaties, Their Making and Enforcement* 68, 2d ed. (Washington, 1916); Denna F. Fleming, *The Treaty Veto of the American Senate* 21 (New York, 1930): Washington "adhered to the practice of asking the advice of the Senate before negotiations were opened and during their course."

68. Corwin, *Control*, supra, n. 30 at 85.

69. McDougal & Lans 207.

Washington was held that the Senate felt inhibited from necessary debate by his presence.

In Washington's own view, treaties called for the independent legislative judgment of the Senate. "In treaties," he wrote, the agency of the Senate "is perhaps as much of a legislative nature, and the business may possibly be referred to their deliberations in their legislative chamber.[70] For details of Washington's first and last visits to the Senate, we are indebted to the Journal of Senator William Maclay. Washington told the Senate that "he had called on us for our advice and consent to some propositions respecting the treaty to be held with the southern Indians."[71] Those propositions were stated under seven heads in a paper handed over by Washington. Maclay spoke up: "The business is new to the Senate. It is of importance. It is our duty to inform ourselves, as well as possible, on the subject." Lee wanted to read a particular treaty: "The business labored with the Senate. There appeared an evident reluctance to proceed." Gunn then moved that a treaty with the Creeks be postponed until Monday; his motion was seconded. Maclay noted, "I saw no chance of a fair investigation of subjects while the President of the United States sat there, with his Secretary of War to support his opinions, and overawe the timid and neutral part of the Senate." The motion carried. Washington, Maclay records, was in a "violent fret." Nevertheless, he appeared again on Monday, and again, "shamefacedness, or I know not what, flowing from the presence of the President, kept everybody silent."[72] Oral communication, so uncomfortable to all concerned, was thereupon abandoned. But that Washington continued to seek advice from the Senate "before opening negotiations" is attested by a series of instances collected by Crandall and confirmed by others.[73]

70. 30 Washington, *Writings*, supra, n. 66 at 378.

71. William Maclay, *Sketches of Debates in the First Senate of the United States, 1789–1791* at 122 (Harrisburg, 1880).

72. Ibid., 123–126. See also Hayden, supra, n. 25 at 20–27. Washington himself realized that "it could be no pleasing thing . . . for the President, on the one hand to be present and hear the propriety of his nominations questioned, nor for the Senate, on the other hand, to be under the smallest restraint from his presence from the fullest and freest inquiry into the character of the person nominated"; 30 Washington, *Writings*, supra, n. 66 at 374. That his presence would exercise a similar "restraint" on the Senate's "inquiry" into a *treaty* needs no argument. Henkin 375 fairly sums up that Washington "came seeking immediate yes-or-no answers to several questions about an Indian Treaty; the Senate insisted on a few days to refer it to a Committee and deliberate about it, not in the President's presence."

73. Crandall, supra, n. 67 at 68–69; Hayden, supra, n. 25 at 27–28, 32–34, 40, 47, 51–52, 54–55; Forrest R. Black, "The United States Senate and the Treaty Power,"

To demonstrate "the right of the President to refuse the Senate information with respect to a pending negotiation," Corwin alleges that "this ground was first asserted by Washington against a call by the House of Representatives for information with respect to the negotiation of the Jay Treaty of 1794."[74] This citation is passing strange, for "in fact, all the papers affecting the negotiations . . . were laid before the Senate."[75] The denial to the House was based on Washington's view that the treaty power was vested exclusively in the President and Senate, so that there was no "right in the House of Representatives to demand . . . all the papers respecting a negotiation with a foreign power." Denial of the information to the House because it had no "right" to it, accompanied by delivery to the Senate which had such a "right," constituted recognition of the Senate's right and is poles apart from a precedent for refusal to the Senate. Indeed, Washington emphasized that he had no disposition to "withhold any information . . . which could be required of him . . . as a right," instancing a proposal to impeach by the House,[76] which, parenthetically, recognizes that inquiry is a corollary of impeachment. How scholars can fashion from such unpromising material a right to refuse information to the Senate respecting pending negotiations passes understanding.

A second point later made by Corwin stands no better. For his statement that "the relations of President and Senate in the realm of diplomacy came rapidly to assume a close approach to their present form," he relies on the Jay Treaty as "a prime illustration" of a treaty negotiated "under instructions in the framing of which the Senate had no hand."[77] At this time, the Federalists were in control of the Senate, and four of them—Oliver Ellsworth, George Cabot, Caleb Strong, and Rufus King—"were the backbone of the administration party in the Senate," and "dominated the entire proceeding." They suggested both the mission and the plenipotentiary to Washington, and then pressed Chief Justice John Jay to accept the post.[78] In effect, the Senate acted "through a small number of its members in whom both the executive and a majority of

4 Rocky Mt. L. Rev. 1, 6 (1931). See also supra, n. 67. The practice, however, was not invariable. Hayden, supra, at 37.

74. Corwin, *Control*, supra, n. 30 at 90.

75. 5 Annals of Cong. 760 (1796).

76. Ibid. 760–761. For discussion of the incident, see Berger, Executive Privilege 1085–1086.

77. Corwin, *President* 257.

78. Hayden, supra, n. 25 at 63, 65, 67, 92.

their colleagues had great confidence." In instructing the envoy, "the Senatorial group still exercised a powerful if not a predominant influence."[79] As Hayden observed: "The entire procedure, certainly, is very similar to that by which it later became customary to consult the Senate through the Committee on Foreign Relations before any important negotiation was embarked upon."[80]

D. *Marshall's "Sole Organ" of Foreign Relations*

One of the pillars of the claimed presidential monopoly of foreign relations is John Marshall's famed statement in 1799 that "[t]he President is the sole organ of the nation in its external relations."[81] Upon this statement Justice Sutherland uncritically relied in *United States v. Curtiss-Wright Export Corporation*,[82] and it was later cited by Justice Douglas in *United States v. Pink*.[83] Thus emboldened by "that arch constitutional conservative"[84]—Justice Sutherland—McDougal and Lans concluded that Marshall "indicated the constitutional basis for the consummation of direct Presidential [executive] agreements,"[85] from which the Senate was excluded. So it is that uncritical repetition of a statement torn from its context has raised it to the level of dogma.

Marshall spoke in the House of Representatives to the extradition of one Jonathan Robbins, charged with murder by Great Britain and surrendered to the British authorities without judicial hearing upon the order of President John Adams, who acted under an existing treaty.[86] Adams was under attack on the ground that the matter of surrender was for the courts, not the President. Patently, the participation of the Senate in treaty negotiations or in any other facet of foreign affairs was not remotely involved. The Robbins affair, replied Marshall, involved "a national demand made upon the nation" and was therefore

> not a case for judicial cognizance . . . The President is the sole organ of the nation in its external relations, and its sole representative with

79. Ibid. 71, 72; cf. ibid. 92.
80. Ibid. 73.
81. 10 Annals of Cong. 613 (1800).
82. 299 U.S. 304, 319 (1936).
83. 315 U.S. 203, 229 (1942). More recently, Justice Harlan, after citing Marshall's statement, stated that "there has been no substantial challenge to this description of the scope of executive power"; New York Times v. United States, 403 U.S. 718, 756 (1971), dissenting.
84. McDougal & Lans 255.
85. Ibid. 249–250.
86. Corwin, *Control*, supra, n. 68 at 99.

foreign nations. Of consequence, the *demand* of a foreign nation *can only be made on him*. . . .

He is charged to execute the laws. A treaty is declared to be a law. He must then execute a treaty. . . .

Ought not [the President] to perform the object, although the particular mode of using the means has not been prescribed? Congress, unquestionably, *may prescribe* the *mode,* and Congress *may devolve on others the whole execution* of the contract; but, till this be done, it seems the duty of the Executive department, to execute the contract by any means it possesses.[87]

Corwin justly concluded, "Clearly, what Marshall had foremost in mind was simply the President's role *as instrument of communication* with other governments."[88] Stripped of later interpretive encrustations, Marshall merely affirmed that a demand for extradition under a treaty "can only be made upon" the President; and that he is free to fashion his own means of complying with the treaty and demand until Congress "prescribes the mode." Far from excluding Congress from this "sole organ" area, therefore,

87. 10 Annals of Cong. 613–614; emphasis added. In his influential *President's Control of Foreign Relations,* Corwin stated that the "President is the organ of diplomatic intercourse . . . first, because of his power in connection with the reception and dispatch of diplomatic agents and with treaty making; secondly, because of the tradition of executive power adherent to his office." Corwin, *Control,* supra, n. 30 at 33. It follows, he stated, that "this power is preseumptively his alone," ibid. 35, and from this he glided into the "necessity of preserving to the President his full constitutional discretion in the conduct of our foreign relations"; ibid. 37. But the power to "receive" ambassadors, Hamilton explained, was "without consequence," "more a matter of dignity than authority." See supra, n. 17. By Corwin's own testimony, the treaty-power requires Senate participation in negotiations. Supra, n. 31 and text accompanying n. 58. No "tradition of executive power" can diminish the constitutional provisions nor defeat the intention of the Founders.

Corwin, *Control,* supra, n. 30 at 39, likewise relied on a Marshall dictum in Marbury v. Madison, 5 U.S. (1 Cranch) 137, 165–166 (1803) to bolster the "discretion" of the President "as the organ of communication." Marshall pointed to the Act of Congress for establishing the department of foreign affairs, and said of the Secretary, "This office, as his *duties were prescribed by that act,* is to conform precisely to the will of the President"; emphasis added. It was the President's statutory control of the Secretary in the frame of judicial review that was under discussion, not his total freedom from congressional control. Congress could of course repeal the act; it could not permanently abdicate the powers confided to it, as Corwin himself noted. Corwin, *President* 9. And as we noted, Marshall recognized the overriding power of Congress even with respect to the President's sole power of communication.

88. Corwin, *President* 216, Earlier, Corwin took exception to Marshall's assertion that "Congress may unquestionably prescribe the mode," etc.; Corwin, supra, n. 68 at 102. But if Marshall's statement is to undergird presidential claims, it must be read entire, limited as Marshall confined it. Corwin recognizes that by Act of Congress "complaints for extradition may be lodged with any court of record," but maintains that "the final act of surrender still rests with the discretion of the President"; Corwin, supra, n. 68 at 103. That exclusive enclave is small indeed.

Marshall regarded the exercise of even this power as subject to Congressional control.

E. *Hamilton's Later Views*

Corwin attributes the expansion of the "President's external role . . . in the first instance" to Hamilton, through the medium of his "Pacificus" papers in 1793.[89] Madison entered the lists under the nom de plume "Helvidius"; and John Quincy Adams remarked in 1836 that Madison "scrutinized the doctrines of Pacificus with an acuteness of intellect never perhaps surpassed," and that his "most forcible arguments are pointed with quotations from the papers of *The Federalist* written by Mr. Hamilton."[90] But "history," said Corwin, "has awarded the palm of victory to 'Pacificus,' " meaning that "[b]y his reading of the 'executive power' clause 'Pacificus' gave the President constitutional warrant to go ahead and apply the advantages of his position in a field of power to which they are specially adapted.[91] That "Pacificus' " views were congenial to presidential expansionism is hardly deniable; but whether they afforded a "constitutional warrant" must turn on the validity of his arguments rather than their subsequent adoption by presidents whose purposes they served. For, as Lord Justice Denman stated, "the mere statement and re-statement of a doctrine . . . cannot make it law, unless it can be traced to some competent authority."[92] The magic of Hamilton's name must not obscure the fact that he had executed a *volte-face*, repudiating assurances he had made both in *The Federalist* and in the New York Ratification Convention to procure adoption of the Constitution.

To still objections to the exclusive presidential power to "receive Ambassadors"—the sole foreign affairs power confided to the President alone—Hamilton had earlier assured the people that it "is more a matter of dignity than of authority . . . without consequence."[93] Now, as "Pacificus," he transformed this innocuous

89. Corwin, *President* 217.
90. Ibid. 219, 466 n. 34, quoting J. Q. Adams, Eulogy on James Madison 46 (1836).
91. Corwin, *Total War* 12.
92. O'Connell v. Regina, 8 E.R. 1061, 1143 (1844). Maitland too stated that "some statement about the 13th century does not become true because it has been constantly repeated, that a 'chain of testimony' is never stronger than its first link"; Quoted in C. H. S. Fifoot, *Frederic William Maitland: A Life* 11 (Cambridge, Mass., 1971).
93. See supra, n. 17.

"dignity" into "the right of the executive to decide upon the obligations of the country with regard to foreign nations," so that had there been an "*offensive* and defensive" treaty with France, presidential recognition "of the new government . . . would have laid the Legislature under an obligation . . . of exercising its power of declaring war."[94] The "story as a whole," Corwin observes, "only emphasizes the essential truth of 'Helvidius' ' contention that 'Pacificus' ' reading of the executive power clause contravened, certainly in effect, the express intention of the Constitution that the war-declaring power [plus discretion when to exercise it] should lodge with the legislative authority."[95]

Hamilton also built upon the contrast between Article I, which provides that "all legislative powers herein granted shall be vested in a Congress," and Article II, which declares that "the Executive power shall be vested in a President," brushing aside the enumeration of specific presidential powers that followed as not "derogating from the more comprehensive grant in the general clause."[96] Although the vast bulk of the powers granted by the Constitution are conferred upon Congress, it is the President, according to "Pacificus," who emerges with all but unlimited power. His view, as we have seen, is refuted by the historical record and by his own explanations in *The Federalist*.[97]

These were not the only departures by "Pacificus" from Hamilton's prior representations. Having erected a plenary executive power, "Pacificus" proceeded to whittle down "participation of the Senate in the making of treaties, and the power of the legislature to declare war" because "as exceptions out of the general 'executive power' vested in the President, they are to be construed strictly."[98] Not only does this run counter to the last-minute joinder of the President as a participant in the treaty power, but Hamilton himself had stated in Federalist No. 75 that the treaty power

94. 4 Hamilton, *Works* 442. With good reason, therefore, did Madison say that the reception clause merely provided "for a particular mode of communication . . . for the ceremony of admitting public ministers, of examining their credentials, and of authenticating their title," so that "it would be highly improper to magnify the function into an important prerogative"; 6 Madison, *Writings* 162. "So visionary a prophet," Madison indicated, as would have foretold in 1788 that Hamilton would in 1793 elevate an admittedly inconsequential power to that of imposing on Congress an obligation to declare war, would not have been believed; ibid. 162–163.

95. Corwin, *Total War* 14. See generally, supra, Ch. 4.

96. 4 Hamilton, *Works* 438–439. "The Supreme Court," states Henkin, 43, "has not considered [the executive power clause] as a possible source of constitutional power to conduct foreign relations." See infra, text following n. 187.

97. Supra, Ch. 3, text accompanying nn. 47–55.

98. 4 Hamilton, *Works* 443.

"partake[s] more of the legislative than of the executive character, though it does not seem strictly to fall within the definition of either."[99] Wilson and Madison, far more influential in the Convention than Hamilton, stated that some of the King's prerogatives "were of a Legislative nature. Among others that of war & peace"; and consequently those prerogatives were not "a proper guide in defining the Executive powers." The "only powers," they considered "strictly Executive were those of executing the laws, and appointing officers not appointed . . . by the Legislature."[100] Later Wilson stated that in the distribution of war powers *all* of the powers "naturally connected" with Congress' power to "declare war" were confided to it, leaving to the President only "authority to lead the army."[101] If there was an "exception," it ran the other way, from the plenary warmaking power of Congress for the executive function of "first General." So too, the treaty power, which was lodged in the Senate almost to the end of the Convention, and only then altered to admit presidential participation, hardly reflects a view that it is executive in nature.[102]

After his "Pacificus" papers Hamilton returned to his earlier view, writing in his *Letters of Camillus* that "the organization of

99. Federalist No. 75 at 486.

100. 1 Farrand 65–66, 70.

101. 1 Wilson, *Works* 433, 440. For extended discussion, supra, Ch. 4.

102. In his "Helvidius" letters, Madison reasons: "The natural province of the executive magistrate is to execute the laws, as that of the legislature is to make laws. All his acts, therefore, properly executive, must presuppose the existence of laws to be executed. A treaty is not the execution of laws: it does not presuppose the existence of laws. It is, on the contrary, to have itself the force of a *law*, and to be carried into *execution*, like all *other laws*, by the *executive magistrate*. To say, that the power of making treaties, which are confessedly laws, belongs naturally to the department which is to execute it, is to say that the executive department naturally includes a legislative power. In theory this is an absurdity—in practice a tyranny"; 6 Madison, *Writings* 145. After serving as Secretary of State, Vice President Jefferson wrote in his *Manual of Parliamentary Practice* §52 that "Treaties are legislative acts."

Corwin considered that Madison's view is inconsistent with his position during the "removal" debate in 1789; Corwin, *Control*, supra, n. 30 at 28–29. If Madison's 1789 views were inconsistent with the views he later expressed, the latter were consistent with the 1788 statements that are an index to construction of the Constitution. See Berger, *Congress v. Court* 76–81.

Then too, the issues were entirely different. The Constitution made no provision for removal from office, and there was no explanation by the Framers. Hence, when Madison and others argued that the power ought to be in the Executive, they contradicted neither the express terms of the Constitution nor its history. Hamilton, however, did contradict the evident assumption writ large in the text that "the President and Senate will be associated throughout the making of a treaty"; see text accompanying n. 31 supra. And in his subsequent *Letters of Camillus*, Hamilton stated that because of the "most ample latitude" of the treaty power "it was so carefully guarded; the cooperation of . . . the Sente . . . being required to make any treaty whatever"; 6 Hamilton, *Works* 183.

the power of treaty in the Constitution was attacked and defended with an admission on both sides, of its being of the [legislative] character which I have assigned to it. Its great extent and importance . . . the legislative authority were mutually taken for granted."[103]

Of course Hamilton was free to change *his* mind from time to time; but the meaning of the Constitution, as Jefferson stressed, is "to be found in the explanations of those who advocated it," upon which the people relied in adopting the Constitution.[104] Until the people are given the chance to say whether *they* have changed their minds, Hamilton's shifts can furnish no "constitutional warrant" for an unconfined executive power. It is the unmistakable lesson of history that the President was intentionally given a few enumerated powers, no more.

F. *The 1816 Senate Report*

Another hardy perennial frequently drawn forth in defense of presidential monopoly—by Justice Sutherland[105] and Dean Acheson[106] among others—is an 1816 Report by the Senate Committee on Foreign Relations, which counseled against "interference of the Senate in the direction of foreign negotiations."[107] This warning was based on notions of expediency, as to which men may differ, rather than upon the historical content of the treaty power. Opposed to this Committee Report is a Senate debate in 1806, which

103. 6 Hamilton, *Works,* 185. In this letter Hamilton cited the dissent of George Mason from the Constitution on the ground that "By declaring all treaties supreme laws of the land, the Executive and Senate have, *in many cases,* an *exclusive power of legislation*"; and he comments, "This shows the great extent of the power, in the conception of Mr. Mason: *in many cases* amounting to an *exclusive power of* legislation: nor did he object to the extent"; ibid. 184.

104. Quoted in 4 Elliot 446. So too, Madison clung "to the sense in which the Constitution was accepted and ratified by the Nation . . . And if that be not the guide in expounding it, there can be no security for a consistent and stable government, more than for a faithful exercise of its powers"; 9 Madison, *Writings* 191.

105. United States v. Curtiss-Wright Export Corp., 299 U.S. at 319. See supra, text accompanying n. 21.

106. Ervin Hearings 260. The Report was also cited by Assistant Attorney General Rehnquist, ibid. 431.

107. "[T]he President is the constitutional representative of the United States with regard to foreign nations. He manages our concerns with foreign nations and must necessarily be most competent to determine when, how, and upon what subjects negotiations may be urged with the greatest prospect of success. For his conduct he is responsible to the Constitution. The committee considers this responsibility the surest pledge for the faithful discharge of his duty. They think the interference of the Senate in the direction of foreign negotiations calculated to diminish that responsibility and thereby to impair the best security for the national safety"; quoted in 299 U.S. at 319, and in Ervin Hearings 260.

discloses that the *Senate* then "believed that, constitutionally, it possessed authority to participate in treaty-making at any stage in the process,"[108] a belief later shared by Secretary of State Buchanan and President Polk.[109]

A more important episode is the statement in the Senate by Senator Rufus King in 1818. King had been a member of the Continental Congress, of the Federal Convention where, as a member of the Committee of Detail, he helped draft the final provision for presidential participation in treatymaking, of the Massachusetts Ratification Convention, and of the Senate quadrumvirate, which piloted the Jay Treaty from beginning to end. Said King,

> in respect to foreign affairs, the President has no exclusive binding power, except that of receiving Ambassadors . . . [T]o the validity of all other definitive proceedings in the management of the foreign affairs, the Constitutional advice and consent of the Senate are indispensable . . . [I]n this capacity the Senate may, and ought to, look into and watch over every branch of the foreign affairs . . . they may, therefore, at any time call for full and exact information respecting the foreign affairs . . . To make a treaty includes all the proceedings by which it is made; and the advice and consent of the Senate being necessary in the making of treaties, must necessarily be so, touching the measures employed in making the same.[110]

King rejected the gloss "that the President shall make treaties, and by and with the consent of the Senate ratify the same."[111] Great weight attaches to his explanation, not merely because "he was there," but because it faithfully corresponds to the view that was taken of the treaty power by the Framers, *The Federalist*, the Ratifiers, and by President Washington.

Proponents of expanded presidential power over foreign relations also rely on the *Curtiss-Wright* dicta[112] and "adaptation by usage,"[113] issues earlier discussed in connection with the powers of the Commander-in-Chief and which require no special tie-in to foreign relations.

Here let me note only that for pages on end McDougal and Lans ring the changes on the evils of rule by a one-third Senate minority,[114] and in midstream call on Jefferson's statement in 1816 that

108. Hayden, supra, n. 25 at 203, 199–203.
109. Quoted in Black, supra, n. 73 at 7–8.
110. 31 Annals of Cong. 106–107 (1818).
111. Compare supra, text accompanying note 21.
112. Supra, Ch. 4 nn. 206, 216.
113. Ibid. text accompanying and following n. 155.
114. McDougal & Lans 536–582.

Some men look at constitutions with sanctimonious reverence, and deem them like the ark of the covenant, too sacred to be touched . . . Let us . . . avail ourselves of our reason and experience, to correct the crude essays of our first and unexperienced, although wise, virtuous, and well-meaning councils."[115]

But Jefferson, who had stated that "in questions of power then, let no more be heard of confidence in man, but bind him down from mischief by the chains of the Constitution,"[116] who adhered to the "meaning" of the Constitution as "found in the explanations of those who advocated it" in the Ratification Conventions,[117] was hardly the man to embrace self-appointed revisers of the Constitution. Rather, he must be understood to mean that reverence should not preclude us, in the light of experience, from improving the Constitution in the manner it provides—by amendment.

II. EXECUTIVE AGREEMENTS

A. *Evolution*

Executive agreements are not mentioned in the Constitution, in the Constitutional Convention, in *The Federalist*, or in the Ratification conventions; indeed the term is of comparatively recent vintage.[118] Starting from a trickle,[119] executive agreements made by the President alone—which can involve large financial, and possibly military, commitments[120] and which have invaded the

115. Ibid. 545.

116. Quoted in Charles Warren, *Congress, the Constitution, and the Supreme Court* 153 (Boston, 1925).

117. Supra, Ch. 4, text accompanying n. 194.

118. "Actually there are few documents which bear the title 'executive agreement' . . . But this phrase is used by the Department of State as the title of the series of publications listing important international agreements, negotiated subsequent to 1930, which did not receive Senatorial consent under Article II, Section 2, prior to ratification"; McDougal & Lans 198, n. 16.

119. The power was appraised modestly enough in 1917 by Corwin, *Control*, supra, n. 30 at 125, when he referred to "the President's prerogative in the making of international compacts of a temporary nature and not demanding enforcement by the courts," and prophetically stated that it "is likely to become larger before it begins to shrink."

"Since 1933 there has been a considerable extension in the use of the executive agreement, and it has been employed for purposes never contemplated by statesmen or writers before 1930. This movement was accelerated since the *Curtiss-Wright* decision in 1937, avowing a wide inherent power of the Federal Government to deal with foreign affairs"; Edwin Borchard, "Treaties and Executive Agreements—A Reply," 54 Yale L.J. 616, 649 (1945).

120. Consider, for example, the 435 million dollars in credits and assistance promised to Portugal in return for a 25-month extension of base rights in the Azores; N.Y. Times, April 3, 1972, p. 7. An editorial in the *Times* remarks, "the

area of tariffs and foreign commerce that was made the exclusive province of Congress[121]—have since 1930 mounted to a flood.[122] Many of these agreements the State Department refused to reveal even to the Senate,[123] the constitutional participant in the making of international agreements. Professor Ruhl J. Bartlett reminded us of the Taft-Katsura agreement of 1905, whereby "President Theodore Roosevelt agreed to Japan's control over Korea," and which probably violated "the Korean-American Treaty of 1882."[124] Senate Subcommittee Chairman Stuart Symington had "no knowledge" of "agreements in 1960 with Ethiopia, in 1963 with Laos, in

stationing of American troops abroad and the establishment of military bases . . . can commit the nation to war in some instances as thoroughly as a treaty of alliance"; N.Y. Times, May 1, 1972, p. 32. For secret promises by Admiral Carney to Greece of atomic support, and a secret agreement governing nonwithdrawal of combat troops stationed in Europe, see C. L. Sulzberger, *A Long Row of Candles* 867, 923 (New York, 1969).

121. See supra, text accompanying n. 19. Writing in 1951, Senator Robert Taft stated: "More and more the State Department has assumed to do many things which are beyond its power in the field of trade . . . It has insisted that the Executive have the power to raise and lower tariffs, through reciprocal trade agreements within constantly widening limits . . . Political agreements as important as those made at Yalta have never been submitted to Congress at all"; Fulbright Hearings 262.

122. "The office of the Legal Adviser of the Department of State reports 368 treaties and 5,590 other international agreements concluded by the United States between Jan. 1, 1946 and April 1, 1972"; Henkin 420, n. 1.

123. Indeed, a civil servant, apparently a former officer of the State Department, suggested that "for controversial international acts the Senate method may well be quietly abandoned, and the instruments handled as executive agreements." Wallace McClure, *International Executive Agreements* 378 (New York, 1941).

Professor Philip B. Kurland, Chief Consultant to the Senate Subcommittee on Separation of Powers, stated before that Committee in an exchange with former Secretary of State Dean Acheson that "this committee . . . attempted to secure from the State Department a list, not even the contents, but a list of executive agreements between this country and foreign countries and the State Department has been unwilling to afford that information to this committee. There are some hundred odd such agreements, the contents of which I think are unknown"; Ervin Hearings 268. See also the statement of Senator Sam J. Ervin, Jr., Washington Post, April 25, 1972 at A–7.

"In 1962 Secretary of State Rusk and the Thai Foreign Minister expressed in a joint declaration 'the firm intention of the United States to aid Thailand . . . in resisting Communist aggression and subversion . . .' While this statement may have been no more than a specification of SEATO obligations, the executive branch thereafter secretly built and used bases and consolidated the Thai commitment in ways that would still be unknown to Congress and the electorate had it not been for the indomitable curiosity of Senator Symington and his Subcommittee on Security Arrangements and Commitments Abroad"; Schlesinger, supra, n. 18 at 100–101. See supra, Ch. 1, n. 35.

Former Secretary of Defense Clark Clifford testified before the Senate that executive agreements lead "to excessive secrecy in policy-making, and it can lead to implied national commitments to other nations"; Washington Post, April 25, 1972, at A–7. Compare Madison's statement that "when a treaty is forming, secrecy is proper; but . . . when actually made, the public ought to be made acquainted with every circumstance relating to it"; 3 Elliot 331.

124. Executive Agreements Hearings 21.

1964 with Thailand, in 1966 with Korea, in 1967 with Thailand, and secret annexes to the Spanish bases agreement of 1953."[125] To pile insult on injury, the State Department, Senator Fulbright, Chairman of the Foreign Relations Committee, stated, though "implored" to submit the agreement for bases in Spain as a treaty, declined. Instead, it submits "many agreements dealing with the most trivial matters as treaties"; but, Fulbright ironically told Secretary of State Rogers, "something that is as important as stationing troops and the payment of millions of dollars is proper for an executive agreement."[126] Even apologists for executive agreements agree that secret agreements are undesirable and that they should be subject to debate and the salutary influence of public opinion."[127]

Roused by this state of affairs, the Senate has recently moved to limit presidential circumvention of legislative prerogative by requiring that executive agreements be submitted for information; and it also has considered legislation that would confirm Senate power to veto executive agreements.[128] The vast bulk of executive agreements, 95 percent or more, the Legal Adviser of the State Department said, are tied into Senate or congressional authorization.[129] According to the State Department, they fall into several categories: (1) those made under the authority of a legislative act,

125. Ibid. 69.
126. Fulbright Hearings 529.
127. In the course of vigorous advocacy of executive agreements, McDougal & Lans stated, "No one believes that secret agreements—except to the extent necessitated by war-time exigencies—are desirable . . . debate in the House of Representatives can only be an additional safeguard and provide public education of the highest value"; McDougal & Lans 552–553. "In any situation," they said, "reference of an important international agreement to Congress has the undoubted advantage of stimulating public discussion of the issues involved and permits the Executive's judgment to be questioned and checked by independent critics"; ibid. 555–556. Former Secretary of State Dean Acheson testified that "in most cases a legislative agreement would be better. You bring in the House and you have a much broader basis of support." He related that when he proposed that the UNRRA relief agreement should be an executive agreement, Senator Arthur Vandenberg exploded and "the State Department was scared off"; Ervin Hearings 268. As "a rule, international agreements, as well as treaties, should be entered into only in such a way that the salutary influence of public opinion can be brought to bear on them; the country should not, as a rule, be bound by stipulations of executive agreements without its knowledge and without opportunity to protest"; John Mathews, *American Foreign Relations: Conduct and Policies* 545–546 (New York, 1938).
128. Pub. Law 92–403, 92d Cong. S. 596; 86 Stat. 619 (Aug. 22, 1972). See 118 Cong. Rec. S1904–1910 (daily ed. Feb. 6, 1972); N.Y. Times, May 1, 1972, p. 30. Senator Sam J. Ervin, Jr., introduced a bill that would authorize Congress to veto any executive agreement within sixty days of its transmittal; S. 3475, 92d Cong., 2d Sess. See 118 Cong. Rec. S5787–5788 (daily ed. April 11, 1972). For subsequent developments, see supra, n. 12.
129. Executive Agreements Hearings 59.

(2) those made prior to legislation but expressly made subject to later congressional approval or implementation, (3) those made pursuant to treaty, and (4) those which are derived directly from the President's constitutional powers.[130] The first three groups were sifted and categorized by the State Department,[131] and there exists no good reason why they should not be transmitted to Congress. The problems arise from the fourth category, those said to rest on the President's own constitutional powers.[132] It is therefore necessary to investigate the bases of the "independent" power claims, and to inquire whether resort to those "independent" powers represents an attempt to bypass the treatymaking provisions[133] and whether the proposed bill invades an area exclusively entrusted to the President.

Article II, §2 of the Constitution provides that the President "shall have power, by and with the Advice and Consent of the Senate, to make Treaties." At the adoption of the Constitution, the word "treaties" had a broad connotation; in the words of Nicholas Bailey's (1729) dictionary, a treaty was "an agreement between two or more distinct Nations concerning Peace, Commerce, Navigation, etc." Hamilton construed "treaty" in the broadest terms:

from the *best opportunity of knowing the fact*, I aver, that it was understood by *all* to be the intent of the provision to give that power the most

130. Ibid. 16, 58. Edwin Borchard stated: "Circumstances have forced the Executive, in the conduct of military affairs and certain aspects of foreign relations, to conclude—either with or without congressional authorization—numerous agreements with foreign countries covering the movement of armed forces, the adjustment of claims, protocols, tariff and postal agreements, *modi vivendi* . . . even armistices." These agreements "have dealt either with routine questions, within the President's admitted constitutional powers, or have related to matters which the Senate deemed too unimportant for formal treaty procedure, or which Congress had previously authorized"; E. Borchard, "Shall the Executive Agreement Replace the Treaty?" 53 Yale L.J. 664, 670 (1944).

131. Executive Agreements Hearings 72.

132. Ibid. 16, 58. Cf. United States v. Pink, 315 U.S. 203, 229 (1942). As late as 1940, Green Hackworth, the respected Legal Adviser to the Department of State, stated that "International agreements involving political issues or changes of national policy and those involving international arrangements of a permanent character usually take the form of treaties"; quoted Fulbright Hearings 12. And Attorney General Robert Jackson carefully emphasized that the agreement for exchange of British destroyers for bases "involve[d] no promises or undertakings by the United States that might raise the question of the propriety of incorporation in a treaty"; 39 Ops. Atty. Gen. 484, 488 (1940).

133. A challenge to the constitutionality of an executive agreement which bypasses the Senate's role in treatymaking is made by Professor Henry Steele Commager and Richard B. Morris, Fulbright Hearings 23, 84, 102. "Congress," said former Justice Goldberg, must "act to correct departures from the spirit and letter of the Constitution"; ibid. 788. The important thing, he stated, is to restore "us to our constitutional safeguards"; ibid. 789.

ample latitude—to render it competent to all the stipulations which the exigencies of national affairs might require; competent to the making of treaties of alliance, treaties of commerce, treaties of peace, and every other species of convention usual among nations . . . And it was emphatically for this reason that it was so carefully guarded; the cooperation of two-thirds of the Senate, with the President, being required to make any treaty whatever.[134]

Those indefatigable advocates of executive agreements, McDougal and Lans,[135] state that "there are no significant criteria, under the Constitution . . . or in the diplomatic practice of this government, by which the *genus* 'treaty' can be distinguished from the *genus* 'executive agreement,' other than the single criterion of the procedure or authority by which the United States' consent to ratification [by the Senate] is obtained."[136] It follows that the

134. *Letters of Camillus*, 6 Hamilton, *Works* 183. Compare Story's restatement: "The power 'to make treaties' . . . embraces all sorts of treaties, for peace or war; for commerce or territory; for alliance or succors; for indemnity for injuries or payment of debts; for the recognition and enforcement of principles of public law; and for any other purposes, which the policy or interests of independent sovereigns may dictate in their intercourse with each other"; 2 Joseph Story, *Commentaries on the Constitution of the United States* §1508 (Boston, 1905). The Hamilton-Story view is reflected in Geofroy v. Riggs, 133 U.S. 258, 266–267 (1890): "That the treaty power . . . extends to all proper subjects of negotiation between our government and the government of other nations, is clear . . . It is not perceived that there is any limit to the questions which can be adjusted" subject to constitutional limitations. In Santovincenzo v. Egan, 284 U.S. 30, 40 (1931) it was said that the treaty-making power embraces "all subjects that properly pertain to our foreign relations."

135. The McDougal & Lans article runs to some 250 pages, the bulk of which are devoted to a plea for agreements fashioned by the President with the approval of a majority of both Senate and House as distinguished from consent by two-thirds of the Senate alone. But they break more than one lance for the solo presidential agreements; ibid. 205, 223, 247–251, 311, 317, 338. With respect to the suggestion that the President has a plenary power to "make international agreements on any subject whatever," they state that "It is not necessary . . . to come to a conclusion on this point. What is completely certain is that the powers of the Congress can be superadded to those of the President, and that the two sets of power taken together are plenary"; ibid. 246. Their comment on the argument that executive agreements conduce to the "dangers of 'secret diplomacy' " points up their ambivalence:

> These arguments appear to be rooted in a simple failure to differentiate between the two principal classes of executive agreements: those perfected by the President on his own responsibility, and those made in pursuance of Congressional authorization. The Constitution of the United States is, fortunately, sufficiently flexible that it presents no necessity for choosing between the Scylla of a foreign policy dominated by a Senatorial minority and the Charybdis of simple Presidential agreements. It offers a third and thoroughly democratic alternative: the Congressional-Executive agreement, eliminating both the possibility of arbitrary, injudicious or secret action and the disintegrating effects of minority obstructionism.

Ibid. 552.

136. Ibid. 199. They also say, "Nor does the Constitution state any limitation upon the scope of the subject matter of treaties"; ibid. 220. But McDougal and Lans

express provision for treatymaking by the Senate and President jointly—which embraces "all the stipulations . . . which national affairs might require . . . and every other species of convention" —covers the field.[137] Consequently, as Justice Jackson stated in the *Youngstown* case, where Congress had less clearly preempted the field, the presidential claim of power to make executive agreements is "clearly eliminated."[138] On the historical facts, the question, in the words of Professor Philip Kurland, is: "Should the Constitution really be read to mean that by calling an agreement an executive agreement rather than a treaty, the obligation to secure Senate approval is dissolved?"[139] Inescapably, the answer, to borrow from the Legal Adviser himself, is that, "if certain subject matters have to be dealt with by treaty, there is no option in the Executive to deal with those by executive agreements."[140]

This proves too much, it may be argued, for legislatively sanctioned or approved executive agreements equally fall within the all-inclusive scope of "treaties." Consider, for example, the "detailed arrangements" under the NATO treaty that were "worked out with respect to facilities and that sort of thing, which," said the Legal Adviser, "are really to a certain extent housekeeping matters."[141] Of the same nature are executive agreements to effec-

---

conclude that "all distinctions in the naming of these agreements—'treaties,' 'executive agreements,' or 'Congressional-Executive agreements'—are merely convenient labels"; ibid. 226.

Corwin also considered that "the criteria seem lacking for a nice differentiation of the prerogative under discussion [executive agreements] from the treaty making power, with the result that its curtailment . . . is a problem of practical statesmanship rather than of Constitutional Law"; Corwin, *Control*, supra, n. 30 at 120–121. Given the express provision for Senate participation in treatymaking, the all-embracing coverage of "treaty-making," any exclusion by solo presidential agreements from such participation plainly presents a problem of "constitutional law."

137. Youngstown Case 604. Given that "treaties" cover the field, it is unimportant that the "Constitution does not provide that the treaty-making procedure is to be the exclusive mode"; McDougal & Lans 216. Ordinarily express mention of one mode is thought to exclude another, subject to rebuttal, for example, by a contrary legislative purpose. Here the legislative intention confirms the implication of exclusivity. The treaty power was granted to Senate and President jointly, as Hamilton explained, in order to "afford a greater prospect of security, than the separate possession of it by either of them"; Federalist No. 75 at 488. See supra, text accompanying n. 56.

138. 343 U.S. at 639.

139. Philip Kurland, "The Impotence of Reticence," 1968 Duke L.J., 619, 626. Former Chief Justice Earl Warren stated that "the constitutional role of the Senate in relation to treaties, increasingly is being bypassed through the device of non-treaty agreements between the executive and foreign governments"; N.Y. Times, Feb. 12, 1973, p. 27.

140. Executive Agreements Hearings 79.

141. Ibid. 75.

tuate tariff treaties.[142] Such arrangements, in the words of Henry Steele Commager, represent a "useful method for disposing of routine business that did not rise to the dignity of a treaty."[143] Must the Senate or Congress be burdened by such details? The whole history of congressional delegation teaches that such delegations are within permissible limits.[144]

Let us now examine the fourth category: executive agreements rested on the President's own constitutional powers. Here, allegedly acting "within his own domain and beyond control by Congress," the President's position, in the words of Justice Jackson, is "most vulnerable to attack and in the least favorable of possible constitutional postures."[145] The truth of this statement is strikingly confirmed by the historical-constitutional materials that bear on the treaty power.

In their zeal to forestall obstruction to a World Union after World War II by a "willful," "undemocratic" Senate minority[146] —such as blocked our adherence to the League of Nations—McDougal and Lans consigned to deepest limbo the "assumption that the treatymaking procedure is exclusive." They stamped as vain all "efforts to woo [the] enigmatic meaning" of the treaty clause; the "true intention" of the Framers they considered "a speculative domain of impenetrable obscurity."[147] However impenetrable the intention of the Framers may be in some respects, here they made clear beyond doubt that the specific objective of the treaty clause was to preclude the President from entering into international agreements without the participation of the Senate. This point is so vital, the evidence speaks so plainly, as to bear detailed exposition.

Hamilton, who has been said to reflect the consensus of the Framers,[148] stated in Federalist No. 75 that treaties are

> agreements between sovereign and sovereign . . . the vast importance of the trust, and the operation of treaties as laws, plead strongly for the participation of the whole or a portion of the legislative body in the office of making them . . . it would be utterly unsafe and improper to entrust [the entire power of making treaties] to an elective magistrate

142. Infra, text accompanying notes, 212–213.
143. Fulbright Hearings 23.
144. See supra, Ch. 4, n. 210; Professor R. J. Bartlett, Executive Agreements Hearings 16.
145. See supra, Ch. 4, text accompanying n. 262.
146. McDougal & Lans 187, 535, 563, 565, 567, 569, 575, 602.
147. Ibid. 216–217.
148. Supra, Ch. 4, n. 17.

. . . The history of human conduct does not warrant that exalted opinion of human virtue which would make it wise in a nation to commit interests of so delicate and momentous a kind, as those which concern its intercourse with the rest of the world, to the sole disposal of a magistrate created and circumstanced as would be the President of the United States . . . It must indeed be clear to a demonstration that the joint possession of the power in question, by the President and the Senate, would afford a greater prospect of security, than the separate possession of it by either of them.[149]

A number of Framers spoke to the same effect in the Ratification conventions. James Wilson said in Pennsylvania: "if the powers of either branch are perverted, it must be with the approbation of someone of the other branches of government. Thus checked on each side, they can do no one act of themselves."[150] In South Carolina, C. C. Pinckney said: "Surely there is greater security in vesting this power as the present Constitution has vested it, than in any other body. Would the gentleman vest it in the President alone? If he would, his assertion that the power we have granted was as dangerous as the power vested by Parliament in the proclamations of Henry VIII, might have been, perhaps, warranted . . . [The Senate] joined with the President . . . form together a body in whom can be best and most safely vested the diplomatic power of the Union."[151] In North Carolina, William Davie stated that "jealousy of executive power" would not permit a grant of treaty power to the President alone.[152] Shortly thereafter, Roger Sherman, a delegate to the Constitutional Convention, stated in the First Congress that Senate and President

149. Federalist No. 75 at 486–487, 488. Apparently the point loomed so large in the public mind that it had earlier been made by John Jay in No. 64, and by Hamilton in No. 69. Jay said: "The power of making treaties is an important one, especially as it relates to war, peace and commerce; it should not be delegated but in such a mode, and with such precautions, as will afford the highest security that it will be exercised by men the best qualified for the purpose, and in the manner most conducive to the public good," i.e., as provided by the treaty clause; ibid. 417. In No. 69, Hamilton stated: "The king of Great Britain is the sole and absolute representative of the nation in *all* foreign transactions. He can of his own accord make treaties of peace, commerce, alliance, and of every other description . . . In this respect, therefore, there is no comparison between the intended power of the President and the actual power of the British sovereign. The one can perform alone what the other can do only with the concurrence of a branch of the legislature"; ibid. 450–451; emphasis added.

150. 2 Elliot 466. And he stated: "Neither the President nor the Senate, solely, can complete a treaty; they are checks upon each other, and are so balanced as to produce security to the people"; ibid. 507.

151. 4 Elliot 280–281.

152. Ibid. 120.

ought to act jointly in *every transaction* which respects the business of negotiation with foreign powers . . . There is something more required than responsibility in conducting treaties. The Constitution contemplates the united wisdom of the President and Senate, in order to make treaties . . . The more wisdom there is employed, the greater security there is that the public business will be well done.[153]

Across the vista of forty-five years, Joseph Story restated these views.[154]

Thus, the Founders made unmistakably plain their intention to withhold from the President the power to enter into treaties all by himself, because, as Francis Corbin said in Virginia, "it would be dangerous to give this power to the President alone."[155] Hence, they circumscribed his power over foreign intercourse by requiring Senate participation in "every . . . species of convention usual among nations."[156] To circumvent that careful design by a mere change of labels, by substituting the words "executive agreements" for "treaties"—bearing in mind the absence of "significant criteria" for distinguishing between the two—is to reduce the restrictions so carefully fashioned by the Framers to ropes of sand.[157] McDougal and Lans' answer, that "To ascertain the full extent to which Congressional-Executive and Presidential agreements have become interchangeable with the treaty it is necessary to look . . .

153. 1 Annals of Cong. 1085 (1789), emphasis added; see also supra, text accompanying nn. 46–61.

154. 2 Story supra, n. 134 at §1512:

> Considering the delicacy and extent of the power, it is too much to expect that a free people would confide to a single magistrate, however respectable, the sole authority to act conclusively, as well as exclusively, upon the subject of treaties . . . But however proper it may be in a monarchy, there is no American statesman but must feel that such a prerogative in an American president would be inexpedient and dangerous. It would be inconsistent with that wholesome jealousy which all republics ought to cherish, of all depositaries of power.

See also ibid. §1515.

155. 3 Elliot 509.

156. *Letters of Camillus*, 6 Hamilton, *Works* 183. See supra, text accompanying n. 134.

157. Compare McDougal & Lans, quoted supra, text accompanying n. 136. "As a matter of constitutional construction," Professor Henkin, 179, rejects the suggestion that "the President is constitutionally free to make any agreement on any matter involving our relations with another country" because "it would wholly remove the 'check' of Senate consent which the Framers struggled and compromised to write into the Constitution."

Such analysis was scornfully dismissed by McDougal & Lans, 226, with the statement, "Whether an executive agreement is 'as good as a treaty' or the 'same thing as a treaty' can, furthermore, be of interest only to legal philosophers still in search of Platonic absolutes." To the contrary, it is of interest to pragmatists, who with Washington, Jefferson, and Madison, believe in a constitutional government of limited powers not to be distorted by those in power.

at the actual record of how these instruments have been used in our diplomatic practice,"[158] substitutes for constitutional limitations a presidential power to "adapt" the Constitution to his own purposes, as in the case of solo warmaking.

They maintain, moreover, that

> The Framers themselves explicitly recognized that there are international agreements other than treaties and put this recognition into the document. In Article I, Section 10 the Constitution . . . provides that "No state shall enter into any treaty, alliance or confederation," but continues that "No state shall, without the consent of Congress . . . enter into any agreement or compact with another state, or with a foreign power." Unless one takes the position that the Framers sought to deny to the Federal Government the power to use techniques of agreement made available to the states—an argument completely refuted by the debates at the Convention and by contemporaneous history—the conclusion is inescapable that the Federal Government was intended to have the power to make "agreements" or "compacts."[159]

On the contrary, the fact that the Framers explicitly authorized the states to enter into "agreements" but omitted to do so in the case of the President implies a deliberate decision to withhold that power from him.[160] It is a non sequitur, moreover, to deduce from a grant of power to make "agreements" *with the consent* of Congress, a presidential power to make such agreements without congressional consent, let alone that such a construction would nullify the Founders' unmistakable intention to limit presidential action in the diplomatic area by the requirement of Senate consent. The rule of construction is to carry out, not to defeat, that intention.[161]

So too, the McDougal and Lans appeal to history is misconceived. Of course there was general recognition of the vices of a weak, ineffectual federal government; but to many this did not seem nearly so perilous as a potentially tyrannical central government.[162] It is also true that a woeful deficiency under the Articles of Confederation had been state noncompliance with treaties, and

158. McDougal & Lans 261.

159. McDougal & Lans 221.

160. Compare T.I.M.E. v. United States, 359 U.S. 464, 471 (1959), quoted supra, Ch. 2, n. 138. Then too, the state "agreement" clause was contrived to meet a special situation. See infra, text accompanying nn. 173–174.

161. We "cannot rightly prefer . . . [a meaning] which will defeat rather than effectuate the constitutional purpose"; United States v. Classic, 313 U.S. 299, 316 (1941). In the First Congress, Elbridge Gerry stated, "Why should we construe any part of the Constitution in such a manner as to destroy its essential principles, when a more consonant construction can be obtained?"; 1 Annals of Cong. 473.

162. Berger, *Congress v. Court* 8–10, 31–34, 260–261.

the Constitution therefore made treaties enforceable against the states.[163] But, as Willoughby points out, "in the State ratifying conventions the fact that treaties were to be superior to State constitutions and laws created not a little fear of possible oppression."[164] Well aware of such sentiments, the Framers had taken pains to circumscribe the power.[165] At every turn there was jealous suspicion of a centralized government and insistence upon a grudging, carefully limited grant of enumerated powers.[166] The Framers went so far as expressly to empower the President to ask for written opinions from executive department heads;[167] but under the reasoning of McDougal and Lans, the Framers had no qualms about entrusting to the President "inherent" powers of unlimited scope![168]

Another factor that contributed to insistence on Senate participation in treatymaking was explained by William Davie: because of "the extreme jealousy of the little states" it "became necessary to give them absolute equality [in the Senate] in making treaties,"[169] a statement confirmed by a fellow Framer, Richard Spaight.[170] To conceive that the "little states" would then leave the barn door wide open so that the President could singlehandedly enter into executive agreements without their concurrence is to upend history. McDougal and Lans explain that "The need to propitiate the small states—a rationale whose contemporary invalidity is indicated in a subsequent section [of their article, which dwells on the diminishing importance of State's Rights]—surely might have been adequate reason for failure to state more explicitly the scope of powers conferred" on the House[171] and, by parity of reasoning, on the President. More baldly stated, this is an appeal to repudiate the representations and compromise made to secure the adherence of the small states to the Constitution, a sorry basis for the authors' high-minded plea for a more "democratic" process. In seeking the meaning of constitutional language, it is the understanding of the

163. Ibid. 234–235, 239, 307, 309, 372–373, 380, 381 n. 73.

164. 1 W. W. Willoughby, *The Constitutional Law of the United States* 520 (New York, 1929).

165. See supra, text accompanying nn. 55–64, 134, 149.

166. For example, E. Pierce, speaking generally, stated in Massachusetts: "I believe such a superior power ought to be in Congress. But I would have it distinctly bounded, that every one may know the utmost limits of it"; 2 Elliot 77. See also Samuel Stillman, ibid. 166; supra, Ch. 3, text accompanying nn. 48–55.

167. U.S. Constitution, Art. II, §2(1).

168. The point was made by Justice Jackson in the Youngstown Case, 640–641, concurring; supra, Ch. 3, text accompanying n. 56.

169. 4 Elliot 120. See McDougal & Lans 538.

170. 4 Elliot 27.

171. McDougal & Lans 236.

Framers that is all important. As Justice Iredell, who had fought valiantly but vainly for ratification in North Carolina, said, "We are too apt, in estimating a law passed at a remote period, to combine, in our consideration, all the subsequent events which have had an influence upon it, instead of confining ourselves (which we ought to do) to the existing circumstances at the time of its passing."[172]

Before leaving the state "compact" clause, a word as to the distinction there drawn between a "treaty, alliance or confederation," and an "agreement or compact." How does this square with the comprehensive scope given to the treaty clause by Hamilton? "Agreements" and "compacts" between some states, regulating boundaries, rights of fishery, and the like—of which the Framers were doubtless aware—had been entered into prior to adoption of the Constitution.[173] It is reasonable to infer that the "compact" clause provided for such arrangements, drawing a distinction between them and the more political "treaty, alliance or confederation," which were forbidden to the states absolutely. Given the broad understanding of federal treaties recorded by Hamilton, there is no reason to import into the treaty clause the more restricted reading of "treaty" in the compact clause. It is familiar learning that the same word may have different meanings in the different contexts of the same statute when they are directed to different purposes.[174] In any event, the decisive factor is not so much the content of "agreement" as the fact that sole use of the word in the Constitution was wedded to consent by Congress. It cannot be divorced from such consent to liberate the President from the consent of the Senate required by the treaty clause.

The view here taken is confirmed by the action of President Monroe in 1818. In 1817 his Secretary of State and the British Minister to the United States had exchanged notes providing for a limitation of naval armaments on the Great Lakes and Lake Champlain. Monroe, who had participated in the Virginia Ratification Convention, submitted the agreement to the Senate and inquired whether it

172. Ware v. Hylton, 3 U.S. (3 Dall.) 199, 267 (1796).

173. Abraham Weinfeld, "What Did the Framers of the Federal Constitution Mean by 'Agreements or Compacts'?" 3 U. Chi. L. Rev. 453, 464 (1936). Writing in 1803, Judge St. George Tucker cited the Virginia-Maryland "compact" of 1785 for the regulation of navigation on boundary waters and the like, as an example of the "agreements or compacts" contemplated by the compact clause. 1 W. Blackstone's *Commentaries on the Law of England*, App. at 310, Tucker ed. (Philadelphia, 1803).

174. Atlantic Cleaners & Dyers v. United States, 286 U.S. 427, 433–434 (1932).

is such an arrangement as the Executive is competent to enter into, by the powers vested in it by the Constitution, or is such an one as requires the advice and consent of the Senate. . . .

The Senate, remarks Professor Bartlett, " 'approved and consented to' the arrangement and thus by implication decided it was in the nature of a treaty."[175] Not alone was Monroe doubtful of the extent to which he could step outside the treaty power, but he appropriately concluded that the resolution of a doubtful case in favor of himself was for the Senate, presumably because he did not consider that a shared power could be unilaterally altered.

Let us now turn to executive agreements said to rest on the independent powers of the President, bearing in mind that the Founders' explanation of the treaty power contains not a hint that there was to be *any* exemption from its provision for Senate participation. When asked to enumerate such agreements the Legal Adviser referred to (1) agreements for settlement of American citizens' claims against foreign nations, (2) agreements giving the Soviet government the right to assets of the prior Imperial regime, (3) armistice agreements, and (4) agreements with respect to intelligence operations.[176] These, parenthetically, do not explain the Spanish bases agreement, which involves the promise of many millions of dollars and possible deployment of troops, or the secret Japanese agreement of 1905. Professor Bickel suggests a fifth category, "an executive agreement with the Japanese about cooperation between American troops lawfully stationed in Japan, and Japanese military forces in a series of contingencies. These are tactical arrangements that the commander of troops makes for their safety . . . Congress cannot say nay."[177] Agreed that such tactical arrangement, if made in the midst of war, fall within the "first General's" conduct of a war. But if made in peacetime, they smack of the secret arrangements the British military made with the French prior to World War I;[178] and I would hold that Congress is entitled to know of all such contingent commitments so that it may measure the risks that may be involved. If, as Professor Bickel justly observes, "Congress can say . . . don't station troops in Japan,"[179] if, under its control over deployment and appropriations for the Army, it can direct that troops be with-

175. Executive Agreements Hearings 15.
176. Ibid. 73–75.
177. Ibid. 41–42.
178. Barbara Tuchman, *The Guns of August* 46–55 (New York, 1962).
179. Executive Agreements Hearings 42.

drawn, it is difficult to conceive on what theory the "first General" may conceal from Congress contingent plans for the use of troops so deployed.

For settlement of claims agreements, whereunder claims of Americans against foreign nations may be cut tremendously[180] without compensation, the Legal Adviser invoked the Executive power and the foreign affairs power, that is, resting on his power to recognize foreign countries and receive foreign ambassadors.[181] True it is that in the *Belmont* case,[182] the Litvinov settlement was sustained as an attribute of the power of recognition; but, as Professor Bickel stated, and as will hereafter be developed in detail, one may doubt the claim for exclusive power rested on "a little snippet of a phrase" which authorizes the President to "receive ambassadors."[183] This power, Hamilton was constrained to explain, "is more a matter of dignity than of authority," and "will be without consequence in the administration of government."[184] So flimsy a base offers shaky support for a claim to oust Senate participation in the making of such settlement agreements,[185] considering particularly the confiscatory impact of such settlements on the reimbursement claims of citizens.

The power of the Commander-in-Chief to conclude an armistice may be granted, but as the Legal Adviser noted, "it does not extend to a peace treaty";[186] for, it will be recalled, the Federal Convention flatly rejected a proposal to empower the President to make a peace treaty by himself.[187] As to the "Executive power," that was conceived in terms of a power to execute the laws and slightly enriched by several *enumerated* powers. The fact that the powers to receive ambassadors and to make treaties were expressly enumerated under the "executive power" repels an inference that still other foreign affairs powers were deposited in the words "executive power" themselves.

180. See infra, n. 211.
181. Executive Agreements Hearings 73.
182. Infra, text accompanying n. 211.
183. Executive Agreements Hearings 42.
184. See supra, n. 17.
185. Professor Bickel doubts "that the power to recognize a foreign government, as exercised in the Roosevelt-Litvinov agreement of 1939, is such an independent power" as is beyond the reach of Congress; Executive Agreements Hearings 26–27. President Jackson acknowledged that the power of recognition might at times require congressional consultation; supra, Ch. 4, text accompanying n. 97.
186. Executive Agreements Hearings 74.
187. Supra, Ch. 4. n. 164. Madison and Wilson early laid down that the executive power does not "include the Rights of war and peace"; 1 Farrand 65–66, 70. See Henkin 85, 81.

The "intelligence" agreements were rested by the Legal Adviser on the "Commander-in-Chief power and . . . legislation authorizing," for example, the Central Intelligence Agency.[188] Since Congress is to "support" the Army and "provide for the common defense," it has solid claims to intelligence that may affect such action, the importance of which will hereinafter be discussed. No intimation exists in the constitutional records that Congress was to perform such acts while blindfolded. Such an inference would run counter to the experience of the Framers who sat in the Continental Congress and closely supervised Washington's conduct of the Revolutionary War. That he would have been inhospitable to concealment from Congress by the military may be gathered from his Farewell warning to "avoid the necessity of those overgrown Military establishments which, under any form of government . . . are to be regarded as particularly hostile to Republican Liberty."[189]

The Act which set up the CIA directs it to report to the National Security Council, composed of the President and sundry Secretaries.[190] It neither requires nor prohibits the supply of intelligence to Congress; and it would be a strained construction that would erect a barrier between Congress and an agency of its own creation. Were such a construction adopted, it would be open to Congress to require that information be supplied to it, after the fashion of the Atomic Energy Act.[191] Executive agreements respecting "intelligence" cannot, therefore, be regarded as an "independent" presidential prerogative.

The all-embracing definition of treaties by Hamilton, and the important purposes that underlie the requirement of Senate "consent," justify a *presumption* that a given agreement falls within the treatymaking power. The burden of meeting that presumption, it hardly needs saying, is not satisfied by the invocation of the President's inflated and untenable theories of the Commander-in-Chief and "sole organ" functions. Neither the Senate's nor the President's determination of the issue would be conclusive on conflicting claims of power, but such claims, like all constitutional boundary disputes, should be submitted to the courts.[192]

It remains to consider a remarkable assertion by McDougal and

188. Executive Agreements Hearings 80.
189. 35 Washington, *Writings*, supra, n. 66 at 221–222.
190. 50 U.S.C. §403 et seq.
191. 42 U.S.C. §2252.
192. Infra, Ch. 11.

Lans: where executive "agreements are predicated upon the President's independent constitutional powers, such as in the field of foreign relations, under the separation of powers doctrine, Congressional action might not affect . . . the domestic effect of the agreement."[193] They are aware that "a treaty may be terminated . . . by a Congressional act."[194] but

> if the subject of the [executive] agreement is a matter within the President's special constitutional competence—related, for example, to the recognition of a foreign government or to an exercise of his authority as Commander-in-Chief . . . the separation of powers doctrine might . . . permit the President to disregard the statute as an unconstitutional invasion of his powers.[195]

Thus, an executive agreement, nowhere mentioned in the Constitution, is exalted above a treaty for which explicit provision is made—a treaty may be repealed by Gongress, not so an executive agreement!

The Commander-in-Chief power, as we have seen, is ill-suited to sustain such a claim.[196] Then too, virtually every state constitution had provided that as "Commander-in-Chief" the Governor was to act under the laws of the state, which is to say, subject to legislative governance.[197] Reiterated emphasis in the several Ratifying conventions that the President's major function was to execute the laws,[198] reinforced by the Article II, §3 provision that "he shall take care that the laws be faithfully executed," reflects the same concern and precludes any inference that the Commander-in-Chief clause conferred power which rises above the "lawmaking" powers of Congress. Least of all may such soaring power shelter in the power of "recognition," itself derived from the inconsequential power to receive ambassadors.

The crowning incongruity is McDougal and Lans' appeal to the separation of powers to protect such solo agreements from con-

193. McDougal & Lans 338.

194. Ibid. 334.

195. Ibid. 317.

196. Compare the Supreme Court statement in Tucker v. Alexandroff, 183 U.S. 424, 435 (1902) that the "commander-in-chief" would require statutory authorization for the return under treaty of Russian deserters; see infra, text accompanying n. 202.

197. Article VII of the Massachusetts Constitution of 1780 provides that the Governor shall be "commander-in-chief," and that his powers shall "be exercised agreeably to . . . the laws of the land and not otherwise"; 1 Poore 965–966. For Delaware, Art. 9, ibid. 275; for New Hampshire (identical with Massachusetts), 2 Poore 1288.

198. See supra, Ch. 3, text accompanying nn. 18–23.

gressional invasion. What magic in the dubious, inexplicit presidential solo power calls forth a protection denied to the *express* provision for Senate participation in the all-inclusive treatymaking power? Why does respect for express constitutional provisions exhibit "mechanical filiopietistic" "slavery,"[199] whereas invocation of *implicit* doctrines, such as the separation of powers to shelter a highly dubious interpretation, is free of that taint? The answer lies in a double standard of constitutional interpretation, turning on whose ox is gored.

B. *Supreme Court Decisions*

Constitutional "law" seldom exhibits such frail underpinning as was mustered by McDougal and Lans for judicial recognition of solo presidential executive agreements. Consider their reliance on *Tucker v. Alexandroff*,[200] in which "the Supreme Court intimated by way of dictum that the President was empowered to make agreements permitting passage of foreign troops through the United States and could thereby divest all American officials of jurisdiction over such a military force."[201] The issue presented was whether a member of the Russian navy, who had deserted while awaiting the launching of a Russian warship in Philadelphia, came within a Russian treaty calling for return of deserters from Russian ships. In passing, the Court remarked:

> While no act of Congress authorizes the executive department to permit the introduction of foreign troops, the power to give such permission without legislative assent was probably assumed to exist from the authority of the President as commander-in-chief. . . . It may be doubted, however, whether such power could be extended to the apprehension of deserters in the absence of positive legislation to that effect.[202]

As Corwin said, the question of the validity of "this species of agreement" was "touched upon in rather equivocal terms."[203] If this be judicial recognition of executive agreements, the Court's

199. See supra, Ch. 4, text accompanying n. 162.
200. 183 U.S. 424 (1902).
201. McDougal & Lans 310. The suggestion that the President could "divest all American officials of jurisdiction" is wide of the mark. After a review of the cases the Court stated: "In none of these cases, however, did a question arise with respect to the immunity of foreign troops from the territorial jurisdiction, or the power of their officers over them"; 183 U.S. at 435. The Court, as will appear, gave limited recognition to a presidential assumption that he could "permit the introduction of foreign troops," no more.
202. 183 U.S. at 435.
203. Corwin, *Control*, supra, n. 30 at 118.

emphasis that return of deserters required legislative assent confines it to the narrowest compass.

Next, McDougal and Lans state:

[T]he general powers of the President to make executive agreements seems to have been first touched by the Supreme Court in 1933, in *Monaco v. Mississippi* wherein Chief Justice Hughes stated: "The National Government, by virtue of its control of our foreign relations is entitled to employ the resources of diplomatic negotiations and to effect such an international settlement as may be found to be appropriate, *through treaty, agreement of arbitration, or otherwise.*[204]

The question in *Monaco* was whether a state could be sued by a foreign state without her consent; whether the President could make an executive agreement by himself was not in issue. Hughes's reference to the power of the "National Government" to act does not necessarily imply that the President is authorized to act without the consent of the Senate. A redistribution of constitutional powers should not rest on strained inferences.[205]

McDougal and Lans next summon the *Curtiss-Wright* case.[206] That case, it will be recalled, was later dismissed by Justice Jackson because it "involved, not the question of the President's power to act without congressional authority, but the question of his right to act in accordance with an act of Congress."[207] Justice Sutherland's dictum regarding the President's inherent powers is without historical foundation; his reliance on Marshall for the statement that "participation in the exercise of the power [over external affairs] is significantly limited"[208] all but perverts Marshall's "sole organ" remark.[209]

"The dicta of the *Monaco* and *Curtiss-Wright* cases," McDougal and Lans tell us, "were the capstones of the decisions in the *Belmont* and *Pink* cases, dealing with the validity and interpretation of an assignment of Russian-owned assets in the United States, which was one of several executive agreements

204. McDougal & Lans 310, quoting 292 U.S. 313, 331 (1934).

205. As the Supreme Court stated in Brady v. Roosevelt Steamship Co., 317 U.S. 575, 580–581 (1943), "Such a basic change in one of the fundamentals of the law of agency should hardly be left to conjecture." See also supra, Ch. 3, text accompanying n. 12.

206. McDougal & Lans 255–256, 310.

207. Youngstown Case, 343 U.S. at 635–636 n. 2, concurring. Curtiss-Wright merely held that the congressional delegation to the President was constitutional; 299 U.S. at 327–328.

208. 299 U.S. at 319. For refutation of Sutherland's "inherent" power dictum, see supra, Ch. 4, text accompanying nn. 205–235, 244–251.

209. See supra, text accompanying nn. 81–88.

negotiated when the United States recognized the Soviet government in 1933."[210] In the *Belmcnt* case, Justice Sutherland once more delivered himself of untenable dicta:

in respect of what was done here, the Executive had authority to speak as the sole organ of that government. The assignment and the agreements in connection therewith did not, as in the case of treaties, as that term is used in the treaty making clause of the Constitution . . . require the advice and consent of the Senate.[211]

No account was taken by Sutherland of the history which demonstrates the Founders' intention to withhold from the President the right to enter into international agreements without Senate consent. Instead, he reasoned from *B. Altman & Co. v. United States*[212] that an international compact may be distinguished from a treaty. There a reciprocal agreement had been made with France under authority of the Tariff Act; and the sole question was whether Congress, by permitting a direct appeal to the Supreme Court with respect to treaties, intended to encompass such a compact. In answering this question the Court stated, "True, that under the Constitution . . . the treaty-making power is vested in the President, by and with the advice and consent of the Senate," but it concluded that the reciprocal agreement "was a *compact authorized by the Congress* . . . [and] *such a compact* is a treaty" for the purposes of the appeals statute.[213] In treating the authorized compact as a treaty for the purposes of a special appeals statute, the Court did not purport to sanction executive agreements not authorized by Congress, a jump unhesitatingly made by Justice Sutherland.

Belmont also leaned on the power of "recognition," to which the Litvinov Agreement was incidental.[214] That power was derived

210. McDougal & Lans 311.

211. United States v. Belmont, 301 U.S. 324, 330 (1937). Sutherland disposed of the issue in lordly fashion: that the agreements "were within the competence of the President may not be doubted." Earlier he had stated that "international agreements which are not treaties in the full constitutional sense, are perhaps confined to such as affect administrative matters, as distinguished from policies, and those which are of only individual concern, or of limited scope and duration, as distinguished from those of general consequence and permanent character"; Sutherland, supra, n. 24 at 121.

Borchard, supra, n. 119 at 647, stated that about 5 million dollars were accepted in return for the sacrifice of 300 million dollars in American claims arising out of confiscations in Russia.

212. 224 U.S. 583 (1912).

213. Ibid. 600, 601; emphasis added.

214. United States v. Belmont, 301 U.S. 324, 330–331 (1937).

from the presidential function of "receiving foreign ambassadors,"[215] which Hamilton downgraded as a mere matter of "dignity," of "no consequence." The Framers hardly intended by this inconsequential function to authorize the President to evade Senate consent to treaties for which they so painstakingly provided, particularly treaties of serious import. When recognition might lead to grave consequences, such as war, President Jackson considered that it should be exercised in consultation with Congress.[216] Lincoln went even further. Referring to recognition of "Hayti" and Liberia, he stated "Unwilling . . . to inaugurate a novel policy [recognition] in regard to them without approbation of Congress, I submit for your consideration the expediency of an appropriation for maintaining a chargé d'affaires near each of those new States."[216a] Because recognition has become "a most potent instrument of foreign policy,"[217] it calls for critical reappraisal rather than, as in the misplaced reliance on Marshall's "sole organ" remark, mechanical repetition.

Justice Stone, in an opinion joined by Justices Brandeis and Cardozo, concurred in *Belmont* with a significant reservation:

> We may, for present purposes, assume that the United States, by treaty . . . *could alter the policy* which a *State might otherwise adopt.* It is unnecessary to consider whether the present agreement between the two governments can rightly be given the same effect as a treaty within this rule, for neither the allegations . . . nor the diplomatic exchanges, suggest that the United States has either recognized or declared that any *state policy is to be overridden.*[218]

And so we arrive at *United States v. Pink*,[219] in which the issue reserved by Justice Stone was presented, and where Justice Douglas, citing *Belmont* and *Curtiss-Wright*, stated that the

> Litvinov Assignment was an international compact which did not require the participation of the Senate. . . . Power to remove such obstacles to full recognition as settlement of claims of our nationals . . . certainly is a modest implied power of the President who is the "sole organ of the federal government in the field of international relations."[220]

215. Cf. Henkin 47.
216. Supra, Ch. 4, text accompanying n. 97; cf. supra, text accompanying n. 183.
216a. 6 Richardson 47.
217. Corwin, *President* 230.
218. 301 U.S. at 336; emphasis added.
219. 315 U.S. 203 (1942).
220. Ibid. 229. The government had argued that "The authority of the President to enter into executive agreements with foreign nations without the consent of the

The *Pink* case had no occasion to rule that a presidential agreement could be made against the wishes of Congress; and in fact Justice Douglas said that the executive policy had been "tacitly" recognized by congressional appointment of commissioners to determine American claims against the Soviet fund.[221] The dissent of Chief Justice Stone, in which Justice Roberts joined, is incontrovertible: "we are referred to no authority which would sustain such an exercise of power as is said to have been exerted here by mere assignment unratified by the Senate."[222]

We need only recall Davie's references to the prevalent distrust of executive power,[223] to the jealous insistence by the small states on participation in treatymaking on an equal basis in the Senate,[224] to the fears that surfaced in the Ratification conventions—despite Senate participation—that the power to override state laws might lead to oppression,[225] in order to conclude that without Senate participation the treaty power would not have found acceptance. To allow an executive agreement to override state law or policy on the ground that it represents "a modest implied power" is to ignore the Founders' plain intention to withhold that power from the President.

This is confirmed by Article VI, which makes only "Laws" and "Treaties" the "supreme law of the land" binding upon the states.[226] An executive agreement is not a "treaty" because it lacks the "advice and consent" of the Senate; it is not a "law" because it was not "made" by the Congress.[227] Justice Sutherland all too lightly leapt over these obstacles; while the supremacy of treaties, he said,

---

Senate *is established*," ibid. 208, citing Monaco and Curtiss-Wright; emphasis added. Thus are mere dicta transmuted into "established" law.

221. Ibid. 227–228.

222. Ibid. 249. McDougal & Lans, 310, also rely on Watts v. United States, 1 Wash. Terr. 288, 294 (1870), for the proposition that "an executive agreement between Great Britain and the United States . . . with regard to jurisdiction over San Juan Island, was deemed to modify the Organic Law of the territory as enacted by Congress." Whether one can extract such a holding from the three separate opinions in the case is at least debatable. Whatever the effect of the opinion of a territorial court, it may be doubted that the Supreme Court would allow a presidential agreement to override an Act of Congress. See infra, text accompanying n. 232.

223. See supra, text accompanying n. 152.

224. See supra, text accompanying n. 169.

225. See supra, text accompanying n. 164.

226. For discussion of the "binding" phrase, see Berger, *Congress v. Court* 236–244.

227. Discussing Art. VI, James Iredell stated that "when the Congress passes a law consistent with the Constitution, it is to be binding"; 4 Elliot 179. At this juncture men thought that judges ascertained the law; they did not "make it."

is established by the express language of cl. 2, Art. VI, of the Constitution, the same rule would result in the case of all international compacts and agreements from the very fact that complete power over international affairs is in the national government and is not and cannot be subject to any curtailment or interference on the part of the several states.[228]

Be it assumed that plenary power over "international affairs" resides in the "national government," and it by no means follows that it was vested in the President.[229] Then too, actuated by profound distrust of centralized federal power and deep-seated attachment to local state sovereignty,[230] the people consented to be "bound" *only* by "laws" and "treaties," and, as we have seen, accepted "treaties" only when participation of the Senate was assured.[231] Sutherland would repudiate these assurances in reliance on his impalpable theory of supraconstitutional federal "sovereignty" and "inherent" powers. But the Founders did not fashion a government of limited powers, they did not circumscribe both President and Congress by an enumeration of powers, they did not then go on to reserve all "powers not delegated . . . by the Constitution" only to turn over to the President an unbounded power to set these limitations at naught.

At best, the not so "modest implied power" of the President to enter into such agreements with the tacit consent of Congress amounts to no more than a concurrent power that Congress can curtail by statute, as Justice Jackson reminded us in the *Youngstown* case.[232] Were the issue presented anew by a congressional challenge, embodied in a statute, to presidential entry into executive agreements without its consent, the cases would be far from conclusive.[233] Even *Curtiss-Wright* did not intimate, said Justice

228. United States v. Belmont, 301 U.S. 324, 331 (1937). To the extent that his statement turns on an assumption of supraconstitutional, "inherent" powers, of "sovereignty," it was earlier shown to be untenable; supra, Ch. 4, text accompanying nn. 211–235.

229. Supra, Ch. 4, text accompanying n. 215.

230. For distrust of centralized power, see Berger, *Congress v. Court* 8–9, 31–34; for attachment to state sovereignty, ibid. 260–263, 224.

231. Supra, text accompanying nn. 148–156.

232. 343 U.S. at 637–639, concurring. Given concurrent powers, Chief Justice Marshall held in an early war-powers case, a congressional statute must prevail; Little v. Barreme, 6 U.S. (2 Cranch) 170, 177–178 (1804).

233. Professor Henkin comments that the cases exhibit "the vagaries of judicial incursions [into foreign affairs] that are infrequent and develop no confident mastery"; Henkin 64. At another point he states: "To some extent judicial difference in relation to foreign affairs has been the product of conceptualisms about sacrosanct 'sovereignty,' of unexamined assumptions reflected in incantations about 'war and peace,' of set

Jackson in the *Youngstown* case, that the President "might act contrary to an act of Congress."[234]

When Rufus King, who participated in shaping much of the foregoing history—from the Continental Congress' preclusion of secrecy, through framing presidential participation in treaty-making, to selection of John Jay as plenipotentiary to Britain and programming his mission—stated that the Senate may "at any time call for full and exact information respecting the foreign affairs,"[235] he knew at first hand whereof he spoke. The pattern had been set by the Hanoverian period, in which the "participation of parliament in foreign affairs and even its supervision of them was . . . fully recognized."[236] The constitutional treaty-power clause, Corwin truly said, "evidently assumed that the President and the Senate will be associated throughout the entire process of making a treaty,"[237] the reason, in Hamilton's words, being that "the vast importance of the trust . . . plead[s] strongly for the participation . . . of the legislative body in the office of making them." "Joint possession" of the treaty power, he continued, affords "greater prospect of security, than the separate possession of it by either" Senate or President.[238] There can be no meaningful "participation" in the exercise of a "joint" power by a partner who is kept in total ignorance by the other. Presidential concealment of foreign affairs from the Senate finds no excuse in constitutional history; instead it thwarts the manifest intention of the Founders.

---

habits of thought about international relations, about how they are conducted, about the 'proper' role of courts in regard to them"; ibid. 272.

Neither *Belmont* nor *Pink* presented a conflict between Congress and the President. Were Congress to assert its constitutional powers, by statute or otherwise, the judicial function of policing constitutional limitations should impose the duty of adjudicating the conflicting boundary claims. See infra, Ch. 11.

234. 343 U.S. 635–636 n.

235. Supra, text accompanying n. 110.

236. Supra, text accompanying n. 40.

237. Supra, text accompanying n. 31; and see supra n. 63.

238. Supra, text accompanying n. 56. Henkin, 84, concludes with characteristic understatement that "the theoretical arguments for Congressional primacy [in the field of foreign relations], or at least concurrent authority, are not less persuasive than those for the President." And, he states: "The Executive must learn to conduct foreign relations with less secrecy and greater responsibility. Congress must have a timely, honest, meaningful role, and the flow of information to fulfill it"; ibid. 279.

6

PRESIDENTIAL "PRECEDENTS"

IN Anatole France's delicious satire on the Dreyfus case—wherein the French Army, trapped in false charges on which it condemned Captain Dreyfus to Devil's Island, piled forgery upon forgery to thwart reversal—the Minister of War calls upon the Chief of Staff and is startled to see files of "evidence" stacked to the ceiling. When the Chief proudly informs him that these are proofs of Dreyfus' guilt, the Minister retorts, "Proofs! Of course it is good to have proofs, but perhaps it is better to have none at all." Originally, he continues, the case "was invulnerable because it was invisible. Now it gives an enormous handle for discussion."[1] Deputy Attorney General William P. Rogers would have done well to be guided by this admonition, for the mountain of "precedents" he assembled in his 1957 Memorandum to the Senate (hereafter Rogers memo) crumbles under scrutiny.

The Memorandum was delivered to the Subcommittee on Constitutional Rights in response to its request, addressed to the Attorney General, "as the chief legal officer of our Government," for explanation of the President's authority "to withhold requested information from Congress."[2] As a presumably reasoned presentation of the case for executive privilege,[3] addressed to an "intolerably prolonged" constitutional controversy,[4] such a memorandum, one might anticipate, would evidence more than the ordinary care one expects of the "chief law officer" of the United States.[5] Instead

1. Anatole France, *Penguin Island* 194 (New York, 1933).

2. Memorandums of the Attorney General vii, Senate Committee on the Judiciary (85th Cong., 2d Sess. 1958), herein cited as Rogers memo.

3. Senator Thomas C. Hennings, Chairman of the Subcommittee, stated that it "apparently represent[s] the considered views of the Attorney General on the scope of the power of the President to withold information from the Congress"; ibid. iii.

4. So it was termed by Senator Matthew Neely in 1956; quoted in Robert Kramer and Herman Marcuse, "Executive Privilege—A Study of the Period 1953–1960," 29 Geo. Wash. L. Rev. 623, 827, 867 (1961).

5. The provenance of the Rogers memorandum is curious. In 1949 a subordinate attorney of the Department of Justice, Herman Wolkinson, published "Demands of Congressional Committees for Executive Papers," in three installments, 10 Fed. B.J. 103, 223, 319. Without attribution, the Rogers memorandum reproduces these articles virtually word for word.

it is a farrago of internal contradictions, patently slipshod analysis, and untenable inferences.[6] Notwithstanding, the Memorandum has become a bible for the executive branch; its "precedents" were again cited to Congress in 1971 by Mr. Rogers, then translated to Secretary of State,[7] and by William P. Bundy, former Assistant Secretary of State.[8] So too, when Assistant Attorney General (now Justice) William H. Rehnquist testified on executive privilege before Congress in 1971, he avouched no pre-Convention precedents to show that legislative inquiry into the executive branch could be limited by the Executive, but relied chiefly on the separation of powers and the post-Convention "precedents" unearthed by Rogers for his assertion that the privilege is "firmly rooted in history and precedent."[9] The testimony of such an array of notables may not be ignored; it demands refutation in detail.[10] For, as J. R. Wiggins observed, "Unless historians bestir themselves . . . the lawyers' [that is, Rogers'] summary that has placed 170 years of history squarely behind the assertion of unlimited executive power to withhold information threatens to get incorporated into that collection of fixed beliefs and settled opinions that governs the conduct of affairs. History thereafter may become what the lawyers mistakenly said it was theretofore."[11]

6. For its ill repute with professional opinion, see infra, n. 25. Justice Jackson dismissed his own prior statements as Attorney General as mere advocacy: a "judge cannot accept self-serving press statements of the attorney for one of the interested parties as authority in answering a constitutional question, even if the advocate was himself." Youngstown Case 647. For samples of internal contradictions, see infra, Ch. 7, n. 47.

7. Ervin Hearings 472–473. Testifying in 1971, Secretary of State Rogers said, "When I was Attorney General I gave a long statement on [executive privilege] that is now cited as authority"; Fulbright Hearings 519. "Not surprisingly," Attorneys General have "invariably supported the constitutional right of the executive to withhold information from the Congress"; Joseph Bishop, "The Executive's Right of Privacy: An Unresolved Constitutional Question," 66 Yale L.J. 477, 483 (1957).

8. Ervin Hearings 319. See also Irving Younger, "Congressional Investigations and Executive Secrecy: A Study in Separation of Powers," 20 U. Pitt. L. Rev. 755, 756–763, 771 (1959); Kramer & Marcuse 900.

9. Ervin Hearings 429. The Acting Legal Adviser of the State Department testified in 1971 that "the separation of powers is the foundation of the executive privilege"; ibid 476. See also supra, Ch. 1, n. 54.

"A course of conduct and ex parte pronouncements," justly stated Congressman George Meader in 1958, "do not make law and are not precedents for anything." 104 Cong. Rec. 3850. See supra, Ch. 4, text accompanying n. 73.

10. In addition, "refutation of an argument," as Chief Justice Thomas McKean told the Pennsylvania Ratification Convention, "begets a proof"; 2 Elliot 541. In the First Congress, Fisher Ames said "nearly as good conclusions may be drawn from the refutations of an argument as from any other proof," citing the maxim *destructio unis est generatio alterius;* 1 Annals of Cong. 539.

11. J. R. Wiggins, "Lawyers as Judges of History," 75 Mass. Hist. Soc. Proc. 84, 104 (1963).

Frequent and uncritical repetition of dubious doctrine transforms it into accepted dogma.[12]

It would be tedious and unrewarding to accompany Mr. Rogers on all of his historical peregrinations, so the discussion will be confined to the first fifty years of his historical wanderings, both because they are more nearly contemporaneous with the forging of the Constitution and therefore carry much greater weight than subsequent aberrations,[13] and because if examples culled from this period by Mr. Rogers do not stand up, we are entitled to doubt the efficacy of the rest.[14] Error is not cured by repetition.

Rogers' opening broadside immediately betrays his undependability:

> Nor are instances lacking where the aid of a court was sought to obtain information or papers from a President and the heads of departments. *Courts have uniformly held* that the President and the heads of departments have an uncontrolled discretion to withhold information and papers in the public interest, and they will not interfere with that discretion.[15]

12. One of the earliest and most acute students of the Constitution, St. George Tucker, said of earlier judicial opinions, "where any doubt is entertained of their correctness . . . they ought to receive an early and full discussion; otherwise they will soon acquire the force of *precedents.* These are often more difficult to be shaken than most cogent arguments, when drawn from reason alone"; 1 W. Blackstone, *Commentaries on the Law of England,* Tucker ed. App. 380 (Philadelphia, 1803).

Compare misapplication of Marshall's "sole organ" statement, supra, Ch. 5, text accompanying nn. 81–88, of his "a constitution we are expounding," supra, Ch. 4, text accompanying nn. 183–193; and reliance on Justice Sutherland's "inherent" presidential power over foreign relations, supra, Ch. 4, text accompanying nn. 206–238.

13. Justice William Johnson referred in 1827 to the "presumption, that the contemporaries of the constitution have claims to our deference . . . because they had the best opportunity of informing themselves of the understanding of the framers of the constitution, and of the sense put upon it by the people when it was adopted by them"; Ogden v. Saunders, 25 U.S. (12 Wheat.) 212, 290. See also Stuart v. Laird, 5 U.S. (1 Cranch) 299, 309 (1803) (practice for several years after 1789 "fixed the construction"). What Congressman William Vans Murray said in the House in 1796, "We have all seen the Constitution from its cradle, we know it from its infancy, and have the most perfect knowledge of it and more light than ever a body of men . . . ever had of ascertaining any other Constitution" (5 Annals of Congress 701), was even more true of the First Congress. Respect for a contemporary construction goes back to Coke, and before that to Chief Justice Prisot in the fifteenth century. Berger, *Impeachment* 285. See supra, Ch. 5 n. 65.

14. See statement of Justice Jackson, infra, text accompanying n. 97.

15. Rogers memo 1; emphasis added. Former Assistant Secretary of State William P. Bundy stated in 1971, "if I read the law correctly, the executive privilege could be invoked on anything"; Ervin Hearings 323. The Wolkinson-Rogers reference to "uncontrolled discretion" may have been inspired by Willoughby's statement that, as a result of the controversy over Congress' right to demand information from the President "it is practically established that the President may exercise a full discre-

By Rogers' own testimony this is false; he quotes with apparent approval a commentator's statement that "the legal problems *were never presented* to the courts. Thus *it remains an open question* whether the executive officers must submit all the information which Congress may request." And he himself states that "There has been no Supreme Court decision dealing squarely [or otherwise] with that question."[16]

Before examining Rogers' "precedents" it needs to be emphasized that at no time have Rogers or other executive spokesmen, past or present, taken account of the comprehensive scope of parliamentary inquiry, of the statement by Henry Hallam that, since 1690, "no courtier has . . . ventured to deny this general right of inquiry,"[17] or Montequieu's statement (for all his espousal of the separation of powers) that the lawmaker has the right to examine "how its laws have been executed,"[18] of James Wilson's 1774 eulogy of the Commons' performance as "Grand Inquest," emphasizing that the "proudest ministers . . . have appeared at the bar of the house to give an account of their conduct."[19] Even an advocate may be expected to meet the objections made to his argument by the opposition. Instead Rogers invokes presidential "precedents" which are at best self-serving assertions by one of the claimants in a constitutional boundary dispute, and as such are no more "precedents" than are the claims of one of the parties to a dispute about farm boundaries. Neither branch, as Madison stated, has the "superior right of settling the boundaries between their respective powers."[20] Were it possible for the President to create constitutional power by mere assertion, these "precedents" would yet not bear the construction placed upon them.

---

tion as to what information he will furnish and what he will withhold"; 3 W. W. Willoughby, *The Constitutional Law of the United States* 1488 (New York, 1929). But see infra, n. 25.

16. Rogers memo 62; emphasis added. In Kaiser Aluminum & Chem. Co. v. United States, 157 F. Supp. 939, 944 n. 7 (Ct. Cl. 1958), Justice Reed, sitting by designation, said "The assertion of such a privilege by the Executive, vis-a-vis Congress, is a judicially undecided issue." A former Assistant Attorney General, Dean Robert Kramer, wrote, "no court has yet upheld the power of the Executive branch to withhold information from Congress"; Kramer & Marcuse 903. For additional citations, see Berger, Executive Privilege 1102 n. 309.

17. Supra, Ch. 2, text accompanying n. 21.

18. Supra, Ch. 1, text accompanying n. 14.

19. Supra, Ch. 2, text accompanying n. 111.

20. Federalist No. 49 at 328, quoting Jefferson.

A. *The St. Clair Inquiry*

One of the chief foundations of Rogers' argument for executive privilege is the alleged response of Washington to the House investigation of 1792 into the failure of General St. Clair's expedition against the Indians, the first "precedent" cited for "*Refusals* by our President . . . to Furnish Information. . . ."[21] The House had appointed a Committee to inquire into "the causes of the failure of the late expedition [against the Indians] . . . and to call for such persons, papers . . . as may be necessary to assist their inquiries."[22] The Secretaries of the Treasury and the War Department appeared to make "explanations . . . in person";[23] and all of the St. Clair documents *were turned over*; "not even the ugliest line on the flight of the beaten troops was eliminated."[24] It is another mark of slipshod advocacy that this incident should be cited for a "refusal" of information.[25] Washington's recognition of Congress' right to inquire into the conduct of an executive officer—an established parliamentary practice—is expressed in his letter to General St. Clair:

> As the House of Representatives has been pleased to institute an enquiry into the causes of the failure of the late expedition, I should hope an opportunity would thereby be offered you, of explaining your conduct, in a manner satisfactory to the public and yourself.[26]

So far as the St. Clair incident is a "precedent," it teaches that Washington would not claim privilege to hide a shameful failure within his administration, a lesson that has been lost on several presidential administrations.

21. Rogers memo 4; emphasis added.
22. 3 Annals of Cong. 493 (1792).
23. Ibid. 1106; Rogers memo 4.
24. 6 Douglas Freeman, *Biography of Washington* 339 (New York, 1948–1957). Washington wrote the Secretary of War, April 4, 1792, "You will lay before the House of Representatives such papers from your Department as are requested by the enclosed Resolution"; 32 George Washington, *Writings* 15 (Washington, 1940). Even one critical of the proposed inquiry, W. Smith, stated that "in any case where it shall appear that the Supreme Executive has not done his duty, he should be fully in favor of an inquiry"; 3 Annals of Cong. 491.
25. Rogers memo 4. Rogers' claim of "uncontrolled discretion" has been termed a "remarkable and inexact assertion"; Bishop, supra, n. 7 at 478 n. 5, and "utterly unsupported by any cited case"; Bernard Schwartz, "Executive Privilege and Congressional Investigatory Power," 47 Calif. L. Rev. 3, 13 (1959). Professor Ralph Winter puts no faith in the Rogers memo; Ervin Hearings 301.
26. Dated April 4, 1792; 32 Washington, *Writings*, supra, n. 24 at 15–16.

Washington was even more emphatic in welcoming a rumored investigation into the conduct of the Secretary of the Treasury, Alexander Hamilton.[27] Contemporaneously with the St. Clair investigation, the House, sitting as a Committee of the Whole, debated a number of Resolutions charging the Secretary with grave derelictions, among them, violating the terms of an appropriation law.[28] After vigorous debate Hamilton was acquitted of wrongdoing; but the power to investigate into his official conduct was never questioned. On the contrary, Mr. Lee, who voted against the Resolutions, took as his theme "whether the Secretary of the Treasury had acted legally," and he "dilated on the necessity of the purest and most confidential communication between the Secretary of the Treasury and the Legislature."[29] Madison, an advocate of the Resolutions, declared that "it was the duty of the Secretary, in complying with the orders of the House, to inform the House how the law had been executed . . . to explain his own conduct."[30] An opponent, Elias Boudinot, said that "we're now exercising the important office of the grand inquest of the Nation," and noted that the inquiry was "into the conduct of an officer of the Government in a very important and highly responsible station."[31] Beyond doubt the power of the House to investigate executive conduct in the highest circles was exercised and recognized from the beginning.

The precedential force of the St. Clair incident is not rested on anything Washington said or did but on what Assistant Attorney General Rehnquist described as "an excerpt from Jefferson's notes of the cabinet meeting."[32] The cabinet agreed that the "house was an inquest, & therefore might institute inquiries," but concluded that the President had discretion to refuse papers, "the disclosure of which would injure the public."[33] This discussion was rendered academic by the turnover of all the details

27. "With respect to the fiscal conduct of the S-t-y of the Tr-s-y I will say nothing; because an enquiry, more than probable, will be instituted next Session of Congress into some of the Allegations against him; . . . and because, if I mistake not, he will seek, rather than shrink from, an investigation. . . . No one . . . wishes more devoutly than I do that they may be *probed to the bottom*, be the result what it will"; letter to Pendleton, Sept. 23, 1793, 33 Washington, *Writings*, supra, n. 24 at 95; emphasis added.

28. 3 Annals of Cong. 905, 907 (1792).

29. Ibid. 931, 932.

30. Ibid. 934.

31. Ibid. 947–948.

32. 2 Moorhead Hearings 360.

33. 1 Jefferson, *Writings* 189–190.

of the disastrous expedition. Jefferson's "notes" did not find their way into the government files; there is no evidence that the meditations of the cabinent were ever disclosed to Congress.[34] Indeed it would have been unsettling and unwise to excite the House by a claim of discretion to withhold when all the information was in fact turned over. The "notes" were found among Jefferson's papers after his death and published many years later, under his "Anas," unofficial notes recorded in what he described as "loose scraps of paper."[35] There this "precedent" slumbered until it was exhumed by the Rogers memorandum in 1957. What little precedential value may attach to it vanishes when it is considered that only four year later Washington did not think to invoke the St. Clair "precedent" in the Jay Treaty episode upon which Rogers next relies.[36] Nor did Jefferson himself, as President, invoke it for an incident also cited by Rogers—testimony that St. Clair first emerged as a "precedent" in the mind of Mr. Rogers.

Nevertheless, any statement by so accomplished a lawyer as Jefferson calls for respectful consideration, particularly because, as escaped Mr. Rogers, his "notes" were not the product of arid speculation about the "separation of powers." Bred to the common law, Jefferson turned to English precedent to determine the respective rights of legislature and executive, as his followers have failed to do, preferring to make bricks without straw. In his own words, he "principally consulted the proceedings of the commons in the case of S. Robert Walpole,"[37] furnishing citations to the record on which his conclusions must stand or fall. That he should have come forth with the established view that the House is an "inquest [that] might institute inquiries . . . might call for papers generally" constitutes recognition of the historical practice, which William Pitt summarized in the Walpole debate.[38] But Jefferson's citations for presidential discretion to withhold were less happy.[39] His reliance on the Walpole ministry's reply to the Commons' request for the correspondence with the King of Prussia relating

34. See Lyman's statement in the House in 1796, quoted infra, text accompanying n. 85. During the course of the debate on the Burr-Wilkinson affair in 1810, Mr. Pearson referred to the St. Clair investigation and said, "The power which Congress then exercised had not then been questioned"; 21 Annals of Cong. 1747 (1810).

35. 1 Jefferson, *Writings* 154.

36. Notwithstanding, the Rogers memo, 5, asserts, "the precedent thus set by our first President . . . was followed in 1796" by Washington.

37. 1 Jefferson, *Writings* 190.

38. Ibid. 189. For Pitt, see supra, Ch. 2, text accompanying nn. 91–92.

39. For additional discussion of Jefferson's citations see Berger, Executive Privilege 1082–1084.

to the ongoing war[40] overlooked the fact that the temporizing nature of the reply—the request would be "carefully examined" to determine whether disclosure would be in the public interest —rendered a call for a vote to override the ministry premature. The fact that the Commons at once requested all correspondence with the States General and letters from the Secretary of State to the Minister at The Hague "relating to the State of the War"[41] evidences that Parliament did not concede the last word to its Minister. When Walpole, aware that he had lost the confidence of the Commons, shortly afterward resigned, the Commons by a vote of 202 to 182 asked for all papers "relating to the Convention between Great Britain and Spain" of 1739, a source of dissatisfaction, and met with prompt compliance.[42] This branch of the Walpole proceedings is a precedent against rather than for the Jefferson reading.

Jefferson's citation to John Scrope's refusal to testify about the disbursement of the "Secret Service Money" could not take account of the fact, not revealed in the course of the debate but well-understood by the Commons, that this aged man was an indispensable official on whom Treasury operations hinged, so that he could not be incarcerated.[43] An expendable recalcitrant, Nicholas Paxton, Solicitor of the Treasury, who refused to testify about those moneys was clapped in jail,[44] a fact not noticed by Jefferson. The history Jefferson relied on does not support him; viewed most favorably to his "notes," the Walpole incident constitutes a fleeting departure from the comprehensive parliamentary power of inquiry and established right to participate fully in foreign affairs.

William Pitt, the elder, who spoke in the course of the Walpole proceedings, more faithfully reflected the state of English law than did Jefferson's mistaken reading:

> We are called the Grand Inquest of the Nation, and as such it is our duty to inquire into every step of publick management, either abroad or at home, in order to see that nothing is done amiss.[45]

40. 13 Chandler 104, 107; quoted supra, Ch. 2, text accompanying nn. 64–66.
41. 13 Chandler 107.
42. For detailed discussion see supra, Ch. 2, text accompanying nn. 71–72. Then too, the Commons were accustomed to share fully in foreign affairs; supra, Ch. 5, text accompanying nn. 33–41.
43. Supra, Ch. 2, text accompanying nn. 86–90. In 1691 an account of "Secret Service Money," though "confidential," was produced on demand; ibid. n. 29.
44. Ibid. text accompanying n. 84.
45. 13 Chandler 172, 173.

Member after member spoke for the right and the duty to inquire into the conduct of the administration and its ministers, "from the highest to the lowest."[46] Said one, "shall there be the least Suspicion of Mismanagement and a *British* House of Commons not inquire into it?"[47] Opposition to the inquiry was not based on a denial of the power but on injudicious timing;[48] an opposition spokesman confirmed that no man would deny that "we have a Right to inquire into the Conduct of our publick affairs."[49]

Even the headstrong George III's Minister, Lord North, later had to concede that Parliament had the last word.[50] And so it remained, as Lord Justice Coleridge recognized in 1845, saying it was for the Commons to determine the limits of their own power.[51] At best, finally, Jefferson's mistaken reading of the Walpole proceedings can not be pressed beyond foreign affairs, because Sir William Yonge, an opposition spokesman, conceded that "with regard to *domestic* affairs, we have a much greater latitude; because we may more safely call for *all* Papers relating to any such affair."[52]

B. *The Jay Treaty*

The second major incident cited in the Rogers memorandum for "Refusals by our Presidents" arose out of the Jay Treaty.[53] The House requested Washington to furnish the instructions to the Minister who had negotiated the treaty, apparently because "it was necessary to implement the treaty with an appropriation."[54] Washington refused the papers to the House on the narrow ground that since the treatymaking power was exclusively vested in the President and Senate, "the inspection of the papers asked for can[not] be relative to any purpose under the cognizance of the House . . . except that of impeachment; which the resolution has not expressed." And, he continued, "in fact, all the papers affecting the negotiations . . . were laid before the Senate."[55]

46. Ibid. 93, 94, 96, 101, 139–140, 150, 158, 161, 210.
47. Ibid. 149.
48. Ibid. 161, 192, 195.
49. Ibid. 161. For a similar concession by Horatio Walpole, son of Robert Walpole, see ibid. 195.
50. Supra, Ch. 4, text accompanying n. 101.
51. Supra, Ch. 2, text accompanying n. 102.
52. 13 Chandler 99; emphasis added.
53. Rogers memo 5.
54. Ibid.
55. 5 Annals of Cong. 760–762 (1796).

This, Attorney General Rogers concluded, "established" the principle that "the authority of the President for the conduct of foreign affairs does not oblige him to produce the instructions which had been given to his representatives in negotiating a treaty."[56] Rogers' deduction is without warrant in the facts.

Washington did not lay claim to a power to *withhold from the Congress*, for disclosure had been made to the Senate. Instead he based his withholding, not on *his* constitutional right to do so but on the exclusion of the House from the treaty process. He denied "a *right* in the House of Representatives *to demand* . . . papers respecting a negotiation with a foreign power." Indeed, he emphasized that he had no disposition to "*withhold any information* . . . which could be *required* of him by either House as a *right*."[57] The latter clause constitutes a disclaimer of right to withhold where there is a "right" to demand, as is confirmed by his turnover of the disputed papers to the Senate, which had a "right" to information because its powers embraced the subject matter of treaties.[58] That Washington should thus have attempted to limit the powers of the House rather than to insist on executive privilege to withhold at least suggests a doubt whether he could safely invoke such an executive power. To deduce from this an "established principle" of "authority" to withhold information *from the Senate*, a "historic example of the exercise of Executive privilege,"[59] is totally to misconstrue the Jay incident.

Whether or not the House is authorized to review treaties, a subject that agitated the House far more than the issue of inspection, is for present purposes of no moment. Washington's view that the power of inspection is confined to an expressed intention to impeach put the cart before the horse—it required the House to prejudge the case, to decide to launch impeachment proceedings before obtaining the information upon which such a decision should rest, contrary to familiar grand jury practice.[60] And his

56. Ervin Hearings 555.
57. 5 Annals of Cong. 760–762; emphasis added.
58. In 1971 the Acting Legal Adviser to the State Department agreed that Washington held that "Congress is entitled to have information from the executive branch . . . if that information is reasonably necessary to enable a particular House of Congress to discharge some function confided to it by the Constitution"; Ervin Hearings 475. Manifestly it is not for the President to determine what is "reasonably necessary" for Congress' "discharge" of its own functions.
59. Supra, text accompanying n. 56; Ervin Hearings 473.
60. In the House, Mr. Lyman said that the "power of impeachment . . . certainly implied the right to inspect every paper and transaction in any department, other-

refusal was the more offensive to the House because on prior occasions Washington had forwarded "confidential" information, even respecting pending negotiations, to *both* Senate and House.[61] Insofar as Washington undertook to define the powers of the House, therefore, he was plainly wrong and tactically unwise.[62] Vice President Adams, who had his eyes on the presidency, and upon whom Washington now leaned after the resignations of Hamilton and Jefferson,[63] said after Washington's refusal: "I cannot deny the right of the House to ask for papers . . . My ideas are very high of the rights and powers of the House of Representatives." This, despite his awareness that "these powers may be abused."[64] Adams, it may be added, acted upon this view in 1798 as President when, pursuant to the House's request, he furnished to it "the instructions to the Envoys . . . to the French Republic, request[ing] only that they be considered in confidence until the members of Congress shall have opportunity to deliberate on the consequences of their publication; after which I submit them to your wisdom."[65]

Were no more involved, the incident would be left to moulder

---

wise the power of impeachment could never be exercised with any effect"; 5 Annals of Cong. 601. This reflected English practice, supra, Ch. 2, n. 2 and accompanying text. See supra, Ch. 2, text accompanying nn. 133–135.

61. See infra, text accompanying nn. 72–79. Prior to the Jay Treaty, "Whatever information [Washington] sent to the Senate he submitted also to the Representatives, a course which was in accord with the opinion of Jefferson"; Hayden, supra, Ch. 5, n. 25 at 52.

62. For more detailed discussion, see Berger, Executive Privilege 1086–1087. Madison was astonished by the refusal and wrote James Monroe on April 8, 1796, that Washington "not only ran into the extreme of an absolute refusal, but assigned reasons worse than the refusal itself"; 2 Madison, *Letters and Other Writings* 96–97 (Philadelphia, 1865).

Jefferson had earlier counseled Washington to the contrary. In a diary note dated April 9, 1792, Jefferson refers to Senate readiness to approve the redemption of Algerian captives but mentions that it "was unwilling to have the lower House applied to previously to furnish the money" because this "should let them into a participation of the power of making treaties." Jefferson "observed, that wherever the agency of either, or both Houses would be requisite subsequent to a treaty, to carry it into effect, it would be prudent to consult them previously, if the occasion admitted. That thus it was, we were in the habit of consulting the Senate previously, when the occasion permitted, because their subsequent ratification would be necessary. That there was the same reason for consulting the lower House previously, where they were to be called on afterwards, and especially in the case of money, as they held the purse strings and would be jealous of them"; Saul Padover, *The Complete Jefferson* 1223–1224 (New York, 1943).

63. 2 Page Smith, *John Adams* 878–880 (Garden City, N.Y., 1962).

64. 2 John Adams, *Letters to Abigail Adams* 223 (Boston, 1841), written April 19, 1796.

65. 8 Annals of Cong. 1374–1375 (1798).

in the dusty records. But the Jay Treaty touched off the first full-dress examination of the legislative power to require information from the Executive, in which the House firmly insisted on the right to obtain it. In that debate Madison made a statement that constitutes the most telling bit of historical evidence for presidential withholding, of which no account was taken in the Rogers memorandum:

> [Madison] thought it clear that the House must have a right, in all cases, to ask for information which might assist their deliberations . . . He was as ready to admit that the Executive had a right, under a due responsibility, also, to withhold information, when of a nature that did not permit a disclosure at the time. . . .
>
> If the Executive conceived that, in relation to his own department, papers could not be safely communicated, he might, on that ground, refuse them, because he was the competent though responsible judge within his own department.[66]

This was a surprising remark; it outran Washington's claim, for he challenged only the right of the House to demand information about negotiation of a treaty, while disclaiming a right to withhold information to which either House had a "right." More important, the decided preponderance of sentiment in the House, including the views of most opponents of the House Resolution, ran counter to Madison.

The House had begun with a proposed resolution calling for information,[67] promptly modified by an exception proposed by Edward Livingston for papers that "any existing negotiation may render improper to disclose."[68] This proposal was swiftly engulfed by an elaborate debate whether the House had a constitutional right to review treaties in which the President and Senate had concurred. Mark that this was before Washington had said a word about the matter. The debate ran on for four weeks and is reported in 334 closely printed pages.[69]

The plea of "secrecy" advanced by opponents of the resolution was speedily riddled. Mr. Smith asked, "are these papers

66. 5 Annals of Cong. 773.

67. Ibid. 426. The call was for "a copy of the instructions to the Minister of the United States, who negotiated the Treaty . . . together with the correspondence and other documents relative to the said treaty"; ibid.

68. Ibid.

69. Ibid. 426–760.

secret? No, they are known to thirty Senators, their Secretary and his clerks, to all the officers of Government, and to those of the members of this House who chose to read them."[70] Though Williams opposed the resolution, he said that "he did not think there were any secrets in them. He believed he had seen them all. For the space of ten weeks any member of [the] House might have seen them [in the Senate]."[71] "Secrecy" was clearly a makeweight.

To the fact that the papers had been laid before the Senate may be added the fact, as Livingston pointed out, that "from the first establishment of the Constitution . . . the Executive had been in habits of free communication with the Legislature as to our external relations."[72] Confidential information, he said, had been conveyed to the House respecting a treaty with Algiers and Morocco in 1790,[73] as were instructions that were given to the Commissioners who were to negotiate with Spain, France, and Great Britain in 1793.[74] Mr. Smith referred to the President's transmission of documents of a "confidential nature" respecting the Proclamation of Neutrality in 1793.[75] Mr. Lyman recalled a request for a missing paper in the correspondence between Secretary of State Jefferson and the British Minister which was satisfied,[76] as is corroborated by the debates in the earlier Con-

70. Ibid. 625.

71. Ibid. 642. See also ibid. 588. The House had not been given a share in treaty-making because, in large part, secrecy was thought incompatible with participation of a large popular assembly; see supra, Ch. 5, n. 58. By implication, the fact that the Senate *was* made a participant precluded secrecy as to it.

72. 5 Annals of Cong. 636. Livingston also cited Parliament's request for the instructions to the Duke of Marlborough respecting negotiations of the Barrier Treaty with Holland in 1709, and other relevant correspondence, which the Queen granted; ibid. 634, 754. The opposition acknowledged the incident but sought to discredit it as a reflection of shifting political tides; ibid. 754. But what dispute between administration and opposition is not subject to the same objection? It is the opposition that generally brings scandal to the surface.

73. Ibid. 638. In his closing remarks, Madison said that "A view of these precedents had been pretty fully presented to them by a gentleman from New York [Livingston], with all the observations which the subject seemed to require"; ibid. 781. Livingston had argued for the fullest disclosure.

74. Ibid. 638–639. Washington wrote the Senate *and the House* on Dec. 5, 1793: "On the subjects of mutual interest between this country and Spain, negotiations and conferences are now depending. The public good requiring that the present state of these should be made known to the Legislature in confidence only, they shall be the subject of a separate and subsequent communication." 33 Washington, *Writings* 173 (1940). For additional confidential communications respecting treaties, to both House and Senate, ibid. 330, 374.

75. 5 Annals of Cong. 622.

76. Ibid. 601.

gress,[77] and as was conceded by the opposition.[78] All of which, said Livingston, shows that "on some occasions, it was not deemed imprudent to entrust this House with the secrets of the Cabinet."[79] "Secrecy" was therefore merely a pretext to be given, as Pitt earlier remarked, little weight on the issue of withholding;[80] and it had found small favor with Jefferson.[81]

Although the call for information was so early swallowed up by the debate on the role of the House in review of treaties,[82] there was nonetheless strong and repeated insistence upon the *right* of the House to know, going beyond participation in the treaty process. Mr. Nicholas alluded to the right of the House, as the "grand inquest of the nation," to "superintendence over the officers of Government," and asserted that this right "gave a right to demand a sight of those papers, that should throw a light upon their conduct."[83] Mr. Heath said this right was "founded upon a

77. It was Madison who "thought there was a chasm, which should be filled up"; 4 Annals of Cong. 250 (1794). So the President was requested "to lay before the House the omitted letter, or such parts as he may think proper"; ibid. 251. The entire letter was forwarded by Secretary of State Jefferson; ibid. 256. In 1794 Washington sent to the House a letter from "our Minister at London . . . of a confidential nature," apparently relating to a treaty"; ibid. 462. For other confidential matters forwarded by Washington, from the commissioners at Madrid, see ibid. 595; see also ibid. 674, 713, 437, 393–394.

78. 5 Annals of Cong. 649, 442.

79. Ibid. 638. In defending before the Virginia Ratification Convention the provision in Art. I, §5(3), authorizing each House to keep parts of their Journals secret, John Marshall stated, "In this plan, secrecy is only used when it would be fatally pernicious to publish the schemes of government"; 3 Elliot 223.

80. Supra, Ch. 2, text accompanying n. 92. It needs to be stressed that "secrecy" (from the House) was claimed solely for delicate negotiations. So Smith of South Carolina said, "in the process of negotiation, many things are necessarily suggested, the publication of which may involve serious inconvenience"; 5 Annals of Cong. 441. And Williams observed that "in the negotiations in time of war, confidential communications were necessary"; ibid. 642. It was secrecy from the House, not the Senate, that was contemplated; supra, n. 71.

81. In a diary note of Nov. 28, 1793, Jefferson refers to the "draught of messages on the subject of France and England." Hamilton and Knox objected to disclosure of the whole, Randolph to part. Jefferson records: "I began to tremble now for the whole, lest all should be kept secret. I urged, especially, the duty now incumbent on the President, to lay before the legislature and the public what had passed on the inexecution of the treaty . . . it could *no longer* be considered as *a negotiation pending* . . . The President . . . decided without reserve, that not only what had passed on the inexecution of the treaty should go in as public . . . but also that those respecting the stopping of our corn should go in as public . . . This was the first instance I had seen of his deciding on the opinion of one against that of three others, which proved his own to have been very strong"; Padover, supra, n. 62 at 1270.

82. This was the subject of repeated comment; 5 Annals of Cong. 487, 717, 726.

83. Ibid. 444. So too, Livingston, ibid. 629. This was the English practice; supra Ch. 2, text accompanying nn. 1–54.

principle of publicity essentially necessary in this, our Republic, which has never been opposed."[84] Mr. Lyman added that

The right of calling for papers was sanctioned . . . by the uniform and undeniable practice of the House ever since the organization of the Government . . . the House had the fullest right to the possession of *any* papers in the Executive Department . . . this was the *first time it had ever been controverted.*[85]

Such statements cannot be dismissed as political rodomontade, for Washington, it will be recalled, had turned over the St. Clair papers without reference to the supposed discretion to withhold recorded in Jefferson's undisclosed "notes." Mr. Smith also said that it had been the "custom . . . invariably to ask for *all and every* paper that might lead to information."[86] A number of opponents readily conceded the right. So, Mr. Harper agreed, if information sought by the House "came within its powers," it "in that case would have a *right* to the papers . . . He would demand them and insist on the demand."[87] Another opponent, Mr. Smith of New Hampshire, said that were the papers "necessary" to decide whether to carry the treaty into effect, he

conceived that they not only possessed the right, but it was their duty to call for *all* papers and documents which would enlighten their minds or inform their judgments on all subjects within their sphere of agency. He had always been in favor of such calls.[88]

How little Madison's views reflected those of the House is underscored by its rejection of his motion to substitute for Livingston's exception for "existing negotiations" a broader formula that would except "so much as, in [the President's] judgment, it may not be consistent with the interest of the United States, at this time, to disclose."[89]

84. 5 Annals of Cong. 448.
85. Ibid. 601; emphasis added.
86. Ibid. 622; emphasis added. Brent referred to "calls so often made for information to the Heads of Departments"; ibid. 575.
87. Ibid. 458; emphasis added.
88. Ibid. 593; emphasis added. See also ibid. 501, 613. Only two opponents, N. Smith and Coit, claimed executive discretion to withhold; ibid. 453, 656. When the House finally appropriated funds for the treaty, it "entered upon its journal a resolution to the effect that it enjoyed a constitutional right . . . to request the submission to its inspection of documents pertaining to the negotiation of a treaty"; John C. Miller, *Alexander Hamilton: A Portrait in Paradox* 433 (New York, 1959).
89. 5 Annals of Cong. 438. As Giles said, "a majority of the House, when their sentiments are collected, speak the sense of the House"; ibid. 766. Madison too said that the "meaning of the Constitution would be established, as far as depends on the vote of the House of Representatives"; ibid. 782.

Cognizant of this lengthy debate, Washington, as has been noted, stated that, first, inspection of treaty papers was outside the purview of the House, and, second, the impeachment power which would authorize inspection was not named in the resolution.[90] At once proponents of the resolution were up in arms. Mr. Giles stated that "he would never consent to act upon [the treaty] till the papers deemed material to the investigation were laid upon the table."[91] His allies insisted that the House should consider recording a refutation "for posterity."[92] In the upshot two resolutions were proposed: first, that the House was empowered to consider the expediency of carrying a treaty into effect; and second, that it need not state the purpose for which it required information.[93] The second resolution premised the broad ground stated by Nicholas, the right to inquire into official conduct. Carried by a vote of 57 to 35,[94] the resolutions manifest a decisive rejection of Madison's views. Before, during, and after this incident, the House insisted on plenary access to information from the executive. A highlight later was furnished by John Quincy Adams who, after moving from the Presidency to the House, joined in insistence that "the House had the right to demand and receive *all* the papers" respecting President Polk's instruction to our Minister in Mexico.[95] Both John Adams and his son had great diplomatic careers and knew full well how far the need for secrecy in foreign affairs stretched, and yet both affirmed the House's right to know.

In the face of these historical facts Mr. Rogers, now Secretary of State, unblushingly asserted in 1971 that "It has been commonly *accepted by Congress* . . . since the time of George Washington's presidency that there are certain matters the disclosure of which by the Executive branch would not be in the public interest." And he went on to cite *St. Clair* and *Jay* as "historic examples of the exercise of executive privilege."[96] "Executive

90. Ibid. 761.
91. Ibid. 762.
92. Ibid. 768, 762–763, 765, 767.
93. Ibid. 771–772.
94. Ibid. 782–783.
95. Samuel F. Bemis, *John Quincy Adams and the Union* 532 (New York, 1956); emphasis added. The House Resolution was voted 145 to 15, the purpose being to "air the question whether Polk had conspired with Santa Anna to overthrow the *de facto* Mexican Government on the eve of the [Mexican] War"; Ibid. For an example of similar unanimity in the Tyler administration, see infra, n. 117.
96. Ervin Hearings 473; emphasis added.

privilege" was not asserted in either case; much less was there congressional recognition of such a right to withhold. In *St. Clair* information was furnished without any mention to Congress of such a right; in *Jay* information was withheld from the House only, on the ground that it had no constitutional share in treaty-making. Washington not only gave the information to the Senate but volunteered that he had no disposition to withhold information to which either House had a "right." At best, these were a disputant's claims, immediately rejected by the other, hardly a "precedent" binding on either Congress or the courts.

Here we might halt, after the example of Mr. Rogers' illustrious predecessor, Justice Jackson, who, in the course of his guide to advocacy before the Supreme Court, cautioned the neophyte that "if the first decision cited does not support [the proposition], I conclude that the lawyer has a blunderbuss mind and rely on him no further."[97] Two demonstrably erroneous citations doubly justify dismissal of the Rogers memorandum; but I shall proceed further in order to hammer home that it is utterly unworthy of credence.

C. *The Jefferson Incident*

The Rogers memorandum cites a Jefferson incident as the "first authoritative instance of a President of the United States *refusing* to divulge confidential information."[98] The House had requested information respecting the Burr conspiracy "*except* such as [Jefferson] may deem the public welfare to require not to be disclosed."[99] Despite this dispensation, Jefferson explained that he withheld information given to the government in confidence because "neither safety nor justice will permit the exposing of names."[100] A gratuitous explanation made to justify the withholding of information expressly "excepted" is termed an "authoritative refusal"![101] In labeling this the "first authoritative refusal," Rogers also strips *Jay* and *St. Clair* of authority. As a House Committee said in 1843 respecting a similar Monroe in-

97. Robert H. Jackson, "Advocacy Before the Supreme Court: Suggestions for Effective Case Presentations," 37 A.B.A.J. 801, 804 (1961).

98. Rogers memo 6; emphasis added.

99. Ibid.; emphasis added.

100. Ibid. 6. As will appear, informers enjoy no blanket immunity from disclosure in private litigation. Infra, Ch. 7, text accompanying nn. 76–91.

101. Jefferson "complied with its request, and exceeded it because he was not content to exercise an outright discretion without full explanation of what he withheld and why he withheld it"; Wiggins, supra, n. 11 at 96.

cident in 1825,[102] "the House invested the President . . . with the discretion which he exercised" and it is not to

be presumed that the exercise of discretion by President Monroe, in a case where it *was* conferred upon him, proves that he would have exercised it in a case where it *was not* conferred. This would be a somewhat violent presumption.[103]

Let it be assumed that Jefferson's gratuitous explanation constitutes a claim of power to withhold information from Congress for the purpose of protecting unoffending citizens against injurious exposure. This is morally admirable but it may well be doubted that it is a necessary attribute of executive power. The test of an implied power ordinarily is whether it is "necessary and proper to carry into effect" an express power.[104] The power to withhold information to protect a citizen from defamation is not really "necessary" to carry out any part of the executive power. Nor can it be "proper" on that ground to thwart a recognized legislative power, for the President was not made the chief protector of the public interest[105] against the representative assembly, except to the extent that he exercises the veto power. Protection from either legislative or executive excesses was confided to the courts,

102. The House had merely requested Monroe to furnish, "so far as he may deem compatible with the public interest any correspondence" with respect to the suspension of a naval officer; and Monroe explained that the documents "might tend to excite prejudices"; H. Rep. No. 271, 27th Cong., 3d Sess. 13 (1843); 2 Richardson 278.

103. Ibid. 13–14.

Much stress has been laid on such "exceptions" made by the House, a not unnatural courtesy from one excluded from treatymaking, and occasionally by the Senate, in the words of Assistant Attorney General Rehnquist, under a "practice [which] goes back to the days of Daniel Webster," labeled "a courteous recognition of the authority of the executive branch to withhold information from Congress in the field of foreign relations"; Ervin Hearings 431. But to borrow from Rogers memo 70, "we must not confuse comity and reasonableness . . . with the sometimes asserted right" of the President to withhold.

In fact, the commentary to House Rule 22 explains: "It is usual for the House in calling on the President for information, especially with relation to foreign affairs, to use the qualifying clause 'if not incompatible with the public interest' . . . But in some instances the House has made its inquiries of the President without condition, and has even made the inquiry imperative"; Rules of the House of Representatives 405–406 (80th Cong. [1947]. For rejection by the House of such a qualifying clause in 1798 (after Washington's Jay Treaty refusal) by a vote of 95 to 27, because, according to Edward Livingston, "This was not a time . . . to stand upon trifling punctilios," see 8 Annals of Cong. 1359, 1371. In this resides no "recognition" of presidential "authority" to withhold information.

104. United States v. Curtiss-Wright Export Corp., 299 U.S. 304, 316 (1936). The "genius and spirit of our institutions are hostile to the exercise of implied powers"; Anderson v. Dunn, 19 U.S. (6 Wheat.) 204, 225 (1821).

105. Richard B. Morris, Fulbright Hearings 105.

not to the opposing branch, as Andrew Johnson recognized when he expressed his readiness to execute a statute which he considered unconstitutional.[106] For protection of his "right of privacy" the individual may invoke the process of the courts.[107] Finally, although among the values Jefferson cherished was "a deep respect for the privacy of the individual," it would be a mistake to deduce from his expression of that respect a repudiation of another of his values—"candour and accountability of public officials."[108]

D. *The Jackson Incidents*

Actually, the first unequivocal assertion of power to withhold information from Congress cited in the Rogers memorandum is that of Andrew Jackson in 1835. Coming forty-six years after the Act of 1789, which itself is a reflection of parliamentary practice, and the steadfast congressional insistence on the plenary power to require information, this belated Jacksonian claim on a disputed constitutional issue is a feeble "precedent."

The Andrew Jackson picture is mixed: he alternately furnished and refused information to Congress.[109] The leading incident selected by Rogers concerns Jackson's refusal in 1835 of a Senate request for charges made to the President, which led to the removal of Surveyor-General Gideon Fitz from office, for the purpose of acting on his successor and investigating frauds in sales of public lands.[110] Jackson rejected the request for information respecting such frauds on the ground that it "would be applied in secret session" and thereby deprive a citizen of a "basic right," namely, "that of a public investigation in the presence of his accusers and the witnesses against him.[111] Thus, where Jefferson feared that premature disclosure might do injustice to innocent men, Jackson insisted on public display. Headstrong though he was, Jackson had acknowledged in 1834 that

106. Berger, *Impeachment* 286.

107. Jefferson is a poor witness for executive privilege because he was eager to share information with Congress, even in foreign affairs, supra, nn. 62, 81. As we have seen, he deferred to Congress in the matter of warmaking, supra, Ch. 4, text accompanying nn. 92–93, and was therefore hardly likely to conceal such information from Congress.

108. William Shannon, quoted by Professor R. J. Bartlett, Executive Agreements Hearings 37.

109. Instances are set forth by Wiggins, supra, n. 11 at 80–81.

110. Rogers memo 7.

111. Ibid.

cases may occur in the course of its legislative or executive proceedings in which it may be indispensable to the proper exercise of its powers that it should *inquire* or decide upon the *conduct* of the President or other public officers, and in *every* case its constitutional right to do so is cheerfully conceded.[112]

Fitz was a public officer, and Jackson now arrogated to himself the decision whether the inquiry was "indispensable to the proper exercise" of *Congress'* power, a patently untenable assertion of power. When measured against historical precedents,[113] Jackson was clearly wrong, unless we are to assume that the power to investigate executive conduct is cut off by termination of official service.[114] Given that the "power of Congress to conduct investigations is inherent [and] comprehends . . . probes into departments of the Federal Government to expose corruption, inefficiency or waste,"[115] it would be insufferable were the President able to thwart investigation by removing the official. Jackson's strictures failed to sway his successors, Presidents Polk and Buchanan, for both expressly recognized the plenary power of Congress to investigate suspected executive misconduct.[116]

112. Quoted by Wiggins, supra, n. 11 at 80; emphasis added.

113. For parliamentary and colonial precedents, see supra, Ch. 2. Recall the St. Clair investigation, and that proposed of Secretary of the Treasury Hamilton; supra, text accompanying nn. 21–31.

114. In the impeachment of Senator Blount in 1797, Jared Ingersoll, his counsel, stated, "I certainly shall never contend, that an officer may first commit an offense, and afterwards avoid punishment by resigning his office"; Francis Wharton, *State Trials of the United States* 296 (Philadelphia, 1849). The issue was "squarely raised" in the impeachment of Grant's Secretary of War, W. W. Belknap, and the Senate ruled that "it had not lost jurisdiction by virtue of Belknap's resignation"; 3 W. W. Willoughby, *The Constitutional Law of the United States* 1449 (New York, 1929).

Compare Jackson's erroneous assumption that Congress cannot inquire into the ground for removal of an officer, with Secretary of the Treasury Wolcott's invitation to the House in 1800, after his resignation, to investigate his official conduct (Landis, supra, Ch. 2, n. 1 at 171), a precedent followed by Vice President Calhoun in 1826, when he asked the House to investigate his administration of the War Department; ibid. 177. Then too, Congress has superior facilities to investigate executive derelictions and to compel testimony by subpoena as compared to the limited investigatory power of the President, a fact noted by the House during the Tyler administration; 3 Hinds Precedents 183. And if the derelictions warrant, impeachment can follow and result in disqualification to hold office.

115. Watkins v. United States, 354 U.S. 178, 187 (1957). Compare Sinclair v. United States, 279 U.S. 263, 294 (1929), where the Secretaries of Navy and the Interior had made leases of oil reserves to Sinclair, and the Court declared that the Senate had power to investigate what "was being done by executive departments under the Leasing Act."

116. Referring to a House Resolution which in part related to "alleged abuses in post-offices, navy yards, public buildings," President Buchanan stated to the House on Mar. 28, 1860: "In such cases inquiries are highly proper in themselves and belong equally in the Senate and the House, as incident to their legislative duties

E. *The Tyler Incident*

The Rogers memorandum also invokes "President Tyler's refusal to communicate to the House" reports relative to frauds on the Cherokees.[117] Tyler did not assert an absolute right to withhold;[118] instead he enumerated certain categories of information in reliance on the *evidentiary* privilege recognized in judicial proceedings involving private litigants, saying "these principles are *as applicable* to evidence sought by a legislature as to that required by a court."[119] And he underscored his meaning by claiming, not an absolute, but "a *sound* discretion in complying" with congressional calls.[120] In the field of evidentiary privilege, it needs to be borne in mind, the Supreme Court stated that "judicial control over the evidence in a case cannot be abdicated to the caprice of executive officers," thus leaving no room for a conclusive assertion of a right to withhold.[121]

Notwithstanding the relatively narrow scope of the discretion

---

and being necessary to enable them to discover and to provide the appropriate legislative remedies for any abuse which might be ascertained"; 5 Richardson 614. And he might have added, as a corollary to the power to impeach "all civil officers of the United States"; Constitution, Art. II, §4. For a telling refutation of the Attorney General's reliance on the Polk incident, Rogers memo 11–12, see Wiggins, supra, n. 11 at 101. For Polk's very broad view of the investigative power, see infra, Ch. 8, text accompanying n. 145.

117. Quoted by Wiggins, supra, n. 11 at 80; emphasis added. The House demand was voted 140 to 8, and as the House report emphasizes, "a majority of *both* the great political parties in the House voted for it, after it had been fully discussed"; H. Rep. No. 271, supra, n. 102 at 2; emphasis added.

118. Tyler sent to the House "all the information" except "Colonel Hitchcock's suggestions and projects that dealt with the anticipated propositions of the delegates of the Cherokee Nation; Colonel Hitchcock's views of the personal characters of the delegates were likewise not sent . . . because President Tyler felt their publication would be unfair and unjust to Colonel Hitchcock"; Rogers memo 9. Tyler singled out for "confidential" withholding "incomplete" inquiries so that officials under investigation would not be alerted and defeat them, and that "irremediable injury to innocent parties" flowing from "libels most foul and atrocious" might be avoided prior to establishment of their truth or falsehood; 3 Hinds Precedents 181. And he would withhold the names of those charged so that they might not be exposed to the resentment of those whom they impugned; ibid. 182.

119. 3 Hinds Precedents 182; emphasis added. The sloppiness of the Rogers memo is again illustrated by the reference to "Tyler's refusal to communicate to the House . . . the reports relative to the affairs of the Cherokee Indians and to the frauds which were alleged to have been practiced upon them." Rogers memo 9. To the contrary, Tyler advised the House that he directed that "the report of Lt. Col. Hitchcock concerning the frauds which he was charged to investigate be transmitted to the House . . . and it accordingly accompanies this message." And he assured the House that "all the papers . . . known or supposed to have any relation to [those] alleged frauds . . . are herewith transmitted"; 4 Richardson 225.

120. 3 Hinds Precedents 182; emphasis added.

121. United States v. Reynolds, 345 U.S. 1, 9–10 (1953); see infra, Ch. 7.

claimed by Tyler, the House Committee, reporting back to the House, promptly took issue:

The communication of evidence to a jury is a promulgation of it to the country, and the law so regards it, and it is so in fact. Hence the rule which excludes evidence the disclosure of which would be detrimental to the interests of the State. But this rule is applicable only to judicial, and not to parliamentary tribunals; and the error of the President consists in not having observed the distinction . . . [For] parliamentary tribunals . . . may conduct their investigations in secret, without divulging any evidence which may be prejudicial to the state.[122]

And, addressing itself to Tyler's reliance on English evidentiary privilege precedents establishing that "a minister of the Crown or a head of a Department cannot be compelled to produce any papers or disclose any transaction relating to the Executive functions of the Government, which he declares are confidential, or such as the public interest requires should not be divulged,"[123] the Committee recurred to its earlier distinction, saying that

In the administration of justice between private individuals the courts will not permit that the public safety should be endangered by the production of evidence having such a tendency. But in parliamentary inquiries, where the object is generally to investigate abuses in the administration itself, and where such inquiry would be defeated if the chief of the administration or his subordinates were privileged to withhold the information or papers in their possession, no such rule prevails. The cases are entirely different. In the first, the public safety requires that particular evidence should be suppressed; in the second, the public safety requires that it should be disclosed.[124]

The Committee faithfully reflected English history, to recall only William Pitt's rejection of the suggestion that secrets of State could not safely be disclosed to a parliamentary inquiry.[125]

Thus, Tyler, summing up sixty-five years of experience since the founding of the government, in the most elaborate and

122. 3 Hinds Precedents 185.

123. H. Rep. No. 271, supra, n. 102 at 10; Rogers memo 10. Tyler cited no cases for this proposition; 4 Richardson 223. See infra, Ch. 7 at nn. 32–33.

124. H. Rep. No. 271, supra, n. 102 at 10. "The case for abdicating political [i.e., legislative] checks upon the executive is much weaker than that for saying that the interests of the individual litigant must yield, perhaps only for a time, to the determination by the executive as to what is admissible in evidence . . . Here departmental inefficiency, concealed for [alleged] reasons of public interest, may not merely disappoint individual claims but endanger the whole fabric behind which it shelters—the public interest itself." Clive Parry, "Legislatures and Secrecy," 67 Harv. L. Rev. 737, 740 (1954).

125. Supra, Ch. 2, text accompanying n. 92.

reasoned justification theretofore proffered,[126] claimed no greater discretion vis-à-vis Congress than that rather narrowly accorded to the executive branch in private litigation. Even so, the House immediately and soundly insisted that the policy which may justify the executive in withholding from a private litigant has no application when the issue is whether Congress may demand information for governmental purposes. And, as we shall see, executive withholding from Congress far exceeds the permissible bounds set by the courts in private litigation, where final decision is not left to the bureaucracy but is reserved to the courts. It should also be borne in mind that the Jefferson, Jackson, and Tyler incidents present the "right of privacy" issue which was not given to the President to decide. Not once in the first sixty-five years, if we may rely on Mr. Rogers' exhaustive search for "precedents," did the President assert a right to conceal foreign affairs from the Senate or warmaking moves from Congress.

Thus far we have considered presidential "precedents" for "executive privilege"; it remains to examine a number of non-presidential utterances on which the Rogers memorandum relies.

F. *Marbury v. Madison*

The Rogers memorandum asserts that "Marbury v. Madison defines the limits at which a court must stop when the head of a department invokes the privilege that the information sought from him is confidential and cannot be disclosed," and cites it as an illustration for the "fundamental theory which justifies an uncontrolled discretion in the heads of executive departments."[127] The *Marbury* dictum is far narrower, as Rogers himself proves when he quotes Chief Justice Marshall as saying in the Trial of Aaron Burr that "the principle there [Marbury] decided was that communications *from the President to the Secretary* of State could not be extorted from him."[128] Respect for such a confidential communication hardly gives rise to "uncontrolled discretion" to withhold anything and everything.

The argument for shielding "confidential advice to the President" is itself altogether without historical roots. "Pernicious advice" to the King by his Ministers was a repeated cause of im-

126. Rogers memo 77 states that Tyler's is "one of the best reasoned precedents . . ."

127. Ibid. 32–33.

128. Ibid. 34; emphasis added.

peachment;[129] and Francis Corbin in the Virginia Ratification Convention, Henry Pendleton in South Carolina, and James Iredell in North Carolina alluded to such "advice" as within the scope of impeachment.[130] Given impeachable "advice," inquiry whether it was communicated cannot be barred on constitutional grounds, whatever may be the merits of the practical arguments for confidentiality. Practical desiderata cannot be converted into constitutional dogma.[131]

Chief Justice Marshall made no breach in the "advice" doctrine but rather obliquely confirmed it. But first it is important to isolate the actual issue. Counsel for Marbury sought to obtain information whether his commission was recorded in the office of the Secretary of State, and Attorney General Levi Lincoln, the Secretary at the time of the transaction, declined to answer "as to any facts which came officially to his knowledge while acting as Secretary of State." This was rejected by Marshall on the ground that "There was nothing confidential required to be disclosed. If . . . he thought anything was communicated to him in confidence he was not bound to disclose it . . . but that the fact whether such commissions had been in the office or not could not be a confidential fact; it is a fact which all the world have a right to know."[132] Lincoln answered. Thus, the "confidentiality" remark was pure dictum; and, as Rogers noted, Marshall, in the *Burr* trial, confined it to "communications *from* the President to the Secretary."[133] So far as Marbury may be a precedent, it does not shelter a communication *to the President;* in fact Marshall held in *Burr* that a private letter *to* President Jefferson from General James Wilkinson, who was implicated in the Burr conspiracy,[134] was subject to subpoena, and that production could be required.[135]

Corwin deduced from the Lincoln interchange that "a high executive official is not bound to divulge matters regarding which he is a confidant of the President," and that "the question at

129. Berger, *Impeachment* 71.
130. Ibid. 89 n. 169; 71 n. 91.
131. Speaking of "communications by an adviser to a Government official," Philip Kurland found it "difficult to find a place in the Constitution for a statute or a judicial ruling which would sustain that as a privilege"; Ervin Hearings 377.
132. 5 U.S. at 142–144.
133. Rogers memo 34; emphasis added.
134. Morison 369.
135. See discussion of Burr trial, infra, text accompanying nn. 140–169.

issue was whether the Supreme Court could require an official to answer, but the doctrine is equally applicable to the case of an investigation by a congressional committee."[136] Even within *judicial* compass, as we have seen, this reads *Marbury* much too broadly. In truth, *Marbury* is utterly irrelevant to *congressional* inquiry. That was a suit by a private individual, and Marshall stated that the "province *of the court* . . . is not to inquire how the executive or executive officers perform duties in which they have a discretion."[137] Precisely that function, however, does lie within the *province of the legislature*, as parliamentary history makes clear, and as Montesquieu and James Wilson perceived. President Washington, it will be recalled, welcomed an investigation of the Secretary of the Treasury, and he turned over all documents in the investigation of General St. Clair. The congressional power to investigate into the executive branch was confirmed by the Supreme Court in *McGrain v. Daugherty*.[138] No comparable judicial power exists, as Marshall justly remarked. The claim that communications and advice to the President by his advisers are shielded from congressional inquiry is without constitutional warrant. Whether Congress should respect such advice as a matter of comity, as it has done from time to time, is something else again.

G. *The Trial of Aaron Burr*

1. *Production of Documents*

Secretary of State Rogers, testifying before a Senate Committee in 1971, alluded to "President Jefferson's refusal to comply with Chief Justice Marshall's subpoena in the trial of Aaron Burr."[139] Apparently this was patterned after Corwin's statement that Jefferson "refus[ed] to respond to Chief Justice Marshall's subpoena in Aaron Burr's Trial for Treason."[140] This is demonstrably wrong.

Preliminarily it needs once more to be emphasized that in any event judicial power over the President is not the measure of con-

136. Corwin, *President* 138.
137. 5 U.S. at 168–170; emphasis added.
138. 273 U.S. 135 (1927).
139. Ervin Hearings 473.
140. Corwin, *President* 139. At another point Corwin alludes to "Jefferson's defiance of the *subpoena duces tecum*, which Chief Justice Marshall issued during the trial of Aaron Burr for treason ordering the President to produce certain documents in court"; ibid. 383. For additional discussion of Burr, see infra, Epilogue at nn. 49–73.

gressional power. The judicial power in question was the general power to compel testimony, and Marshall held that the President was not exempted from that authority.[141] The source of congressional power is the inquisitorial function and the fact that the President was made subject to impeachment. Iredell exulted in the provision that made the President triable.[142] Congress, said Corwin, "has power to investigate his every official act."[143] President Andrew Jackson "cheerfully conceded" the constitutional right of Congress to "inquire or decide upon the conduct of the President."[144] No British minister was exempt from inquiry, and inquiry without a power to compel testimony would be enfeebled.[145]

Notwithstanding that *Burr* is thus irrelevant to congressional investigation, consideration of the case will point up Rogers' inveterate tendency to distort the cases. According to his memorandum, Marshall ruled that the President "was free to keep from view such portions of the letter which the President deemed confidential in the public interest."[146] At the outset it is necessary to separate what Jefferson wrote to his counsel[147] from what he did. In fact Jefferson went a long way toward full compliance.[148]

The argument had revolved almost entirely about a letter to Jefferson from General Wilkinson; and it had been argued for Jefferson that it was

141. See infra, text accompanying nn. 154–156.

142. 4 Elliot 109.

143. Corwin, *President* 365; cf. supra, Ch. 2.

144. Quoted supra, text accompanying n. 112.

145. "Without the power to investigate—including of course the authority to compel testimony . . . Congress could be seriously handicapped in its efforts to exercise its constitutional functions"; Quinn v. United States, 349 U.S. 155, 160–161 (1955).

146. Rogers memo 35.

147. See 9 Jefferson, *Writings* 55–62 n. 1, for his correspondence concerning the subpoena.

148. Jefferson, on June 12, 1807, wrote George Hay, the United States District Attorney, that he had delivered the papers to the Attorney General, and instructed the War and Navy Departments to review their files with a view to compliance. 1 David Robertson, *The Trial of Aaron Burr* 210–211 (Philadelphia, 1808). On June 17, 1807, Jefferson wrote Hay that "the receipt of these papers [by Hay] has, I presume, so far anticipated, and others this day forwarded will have substantially fulfilled the object of a subpoena from the District Court of Richmond"; ibid. 254.
When Jefferson learned that the Attorney General did not have the Wilkinson letter that Burr had subpoenaed, he wrote Hay on June 23, 1807, "No researches shall be spared to recover this letter, & if recovered, it shall immediately be sent on to you"; 9 Jefferson, *Writings* 61. Hay advised the court that "When we receive General Wilkinson's letter, the return will be complete"; 1 Robertson 256. Jefferson also stated that if Burr should "suppose there are any facts within the knowledge of the heads of the departments or of myself . . . we shall be ready to give him the benefit of it, by way of deposition"; 1 Jefferson, *Writings* 57. Notwithstanding Jefferson's attempts to comply with the subpoena, Rogers states that Jefferson "paid no attention to the subpoena"; Rogers memo 35.

improper to call upon the president to produce the letter of Gen. Wilkinson, because it was a private letter, and contained confidential communications, which the president ought not and could not be compelled to disclose. It might contain *state secrets,* which could not be divulged without endangering national safety.[149]

Mark that this was not so much a claim for "confidentiality" per se as against disclosure of "state secrets" which might endanger the "national safety," a much narrower ground. Jefferson left it to his counsel, George Hay, "to withhold communication of any parts of the letter which are *not directly material* for the purposes of justice."[150] Hay emphasized that he was willing to disclose the entire letter to the court, and to leave it to the court to suppress so much of the letter as was not material to the case.[151] This was reemphasized on his return to the subpoena duces tecum wherein he supplied a copy of the letter

excepting such parts thereof as are, in my opinion, not material for the purposes of justice, for the defense of the accused, or pertinent to the issue now about to be joined. . . . The accuracy of this opinion I am willing to refer to the judgment of the court, by *submitting the original letter* to its inspection.[152]

149. United States v. Burr, 25 Fed. Cas. 30, 31 (No. 14692d) (C.C. Va. 1807); emphasis added.

150. 1 Robertson, supra, n. 148 at 210; emphasis added.

Because Jefferson had thus devolved on Hay the exercise of "discretion" to withhold nonmaterial parts of the letter, United States v. Burr, 25 Fed. Cas. 55, 65 (No. 14693) (C.C. Va. 1807), Chief Justice Marshall said: "the *president* has assigned no reason whatever for withholding the paper called for. The propriety of withholding must be decided by *himself,* not by another for him. Of the weight of the reasons for and against producing it, he is himself the judge. It is their operation on *his* mind, not on the mind of others, which must be respected by the court"; United States v. Burr, 25 Fed. Cas. 187, 192 (No. 14694) (C.C. Va. 1807); emphasis added. In other words, the *initial* judgment of need to withhold must be made by the President, not left to a subordinate.

151. Thus, Hay said: "The application made by the defendant is that testimony which concerns himself should be adduced; that what tends to his own just defense and exculpation may be brought forward. Is it right that he should have more? Is it proper, fair or right that he should have the liberty of going through the whole letter, as well those parts which do not relate to him as those which do, for the purpose of making unfavorable impressions on the public mind . . . making public confidential communications respecting private characters, and thereby producing controversies and violent quarrels? *I wish the court to look at the letter* and see whether it does not contain what ought not to be submitted to public inspection"; 2 Robertson, supra, n. 148 at 509; emphasis added.

152. 25 Fed. Cas. 187, 190 (No. 14694) (C.C. Va. 1807); emphasis added. Marshall said, "I do not think that the accused ought to be prohibited from seeing the letter"; ibid. 192. Rogers himself states that "Judge [sic] Marshall made it clear that if a letter in the possession of the President material to the trial contains matter —'which it would be imprudent to disclose, which it is not the wish of the executive to disclose; such matter, *if it be not immediately* and essentially applicable to the

Far from asserting a claim of absolute privilege, therefore, counsel for Jefferson was perfectly willing to leave it to the court to determine whether portions of the letter were in fact not material. He insisted only that the portions so adjudged should be withheld from the defendant. To this the defendant objected that the court could not judge whether the confidential portions were relevant to the defense until that defense was fully disclosed, and that defendants were not required to make such disclosure until they had put in their case.[153]

It was on this state of facts that Chief Justice Marshall ruled

> that the president of the United States *may be subpoenaed* and *examined as a witness*, and *required to produce* any paper in his possession, is not controverted . . . The president, although subject to the general rules which apply to others, may have sufficient motives for declining to produce a particular paper, and those motives *may be such* as to restrain the court from enforcing its production . . . I can readily conceive that the president might receive a letter which would be improper to exhibit in public, because of the manifest inconvenience of its exposure. The occasion for demanding it ought, in such a case, be very strong, and to be fully shown to the court before its production *could be insisted on*.[154]

And, referring to private letters sent to the President respecting matters of public concern, Marshall stated that they "ought not *on light ground* to be forced into public view."

> Yet it is a very serious thing, if such letter should contain any information material to the defense, to withhold from the accused the power of making use of it . . . I cannot precisely lay down any general rule for such a case. *Perhaps* the court ought to consider the reasons, which would induce the president to refuse to exhibit such letter as conclusive on it, *unless* such letter could be shown to be *absolutely necessary* in the defense. The president may himself state the particular reasons which may have induced him to withhold a paper, and the court would unquestionably allow their full force to those reasons. At the same time, the *court could not refuse* to pay proper attention to the affidavit of the accused. But on objections being made by the president to the pro-

point, will, of course, be suppressed' "; Rogers memo 36; emphasis added. In short, Marshall would exclude only irrelevant or immaterial matter, not the entire letter. Whether the adversary should inspect the entire letter is hereinafter discussed.

153. 2 Robertson, supra, n. 148 at 516. Note also Luther Martin's statement on behalf of Burr that "the *personal* attendance of the president was dispensed with only on the condition that the [Wilkinson] letter should be produced"; ibid. at 514.

154. United States v. Burr, 25 Fed. Cas. 187, 191–192 (No. 14694) (C.C. Va. 1807); emphasis added.

duction of a paper, the court would not proceed further in the case without such an affidavit as would *clearly shew the paper to be essential* to the justice of the case . . . [T]o induce the court to take any definite and decisive step with respect to the prosecution, founded on the *refusal of the president* to exhibit a paper, for reasons stated by himself, the *materiality* of that paper *ought to be shown*."[155]

Materiality to the defense, in short, would overcome presidential refusal to disclose. And Marshall concluded that "I do not think that the accused ought to be prohibited from seeing the letter."[156]

Plainly this contradicts Rogers' statement that Marshall "ruled that the President was free to keep from view such portions of the letter which the President deemed confidential in the public interest. The President alone was judge of what was confidential."[157] For Marshall asserted judicial power to decide whether a presidential claim of privilege had merit, and that a claim of secrecy in the "public interest" would have to yield to the necessities of the accused. Rogers' statement that "the President may in his own discretion withhold documents from a court"[158] is further discredited by the all but universal rule in private litigation that whether disclosure must be made by the executive branch cannot be left to the caprice of executive officers.[159]

2. *Personal Attendance by the President*

As the Rogers memorandum states, Marshall claimed for the courts "the right to issue a subpoena against the President"; and

155. Ibid. 192; emphasis added.

156. Ibid. Lest it be thought that the rule in civil cases may be narrower, note Marshall's statement that "if this might be likened to a civil case, the law is express on the subject. It is that either party may require the other to produce books or writings in their possession or power which contain evidence pertinent to the issue"; ibid. 191. We need look no further than United States v. Reynolds, 345 U.S. 1, 9–10 (1953), for confirmation that "judicial control over evidence in a case cannot be abdicated to the caprice of executive officers."

157. Rogers memo 35. After Marshall delivered the foregoing opinion, Jefferson sent a copy of the Wilkinson letter, "excepting such parts as he deemed he ought not permit to be made public," United States v. Burr, 25 Fed. Cas. 187, 193 (No. 14694) (C.C. Va. 1807), thereby complying with Marshall's preliminary requirement that the President himself must decide the propriety of withholding. But Burr no longer pressed the matter. Beveridge says, "Perhaps the favorable progress of the case relieved Burr's anxiety. It is possible that the 'truce' [with Marshall] so earnestly desired by Jefferson was arranged." 3 Albert J. Beveridge, *Life of John Marshall* 522 (Boston, 1919). The Marshall opinion, however, stands and speaks for itself; it announced the paramount power of the court to decide the claim of privilege for itself.

158. William P. Rogers, "Constitutional Law: The Papers of the Executive Branch," 44 A.B.A.J. 941, 1012 (1958).

159. See infra, Ch. 7.

the subpoena that issued required the President "to personally attend."[160] Jefferson objected that personal attendance would disrupt performance of his executive functions, for he could be haled to far-off St. Louis, to one court after another.[161] But he offered to testify by deposition, stating that if Burr should "suppose there are any facts within the knowledge of the heads of the departments or of myself . . . we shall be ready to give him the benefit of it, by way of deposition."[162] This was a plea of serious administrative inconvenience, not a claim of absolute immunity from judicial process. No such claim was made by his counsel; to the contrary, as Marshall stated, the "attorney for the United States avowed his opinion that a general subpoena might issue to the president."[163] Not satisfied to rest on concession, Marshall left no doubts on this score: "In the provisions of the constitution, and of the statutes, which give the accused the right to compulsory process of the courts, there is no exception whatever."[164] He rejected the reservation in the law of evidence for the King—which was based on the ground that it was "incompatible with his dignity to appear under the process of the court"—because the "principle of the English constitution that the king can do no wrong" was inapplicable to our government whereunder "the president . . . may be impeached and removed from office." And, Marshall added, "it is not known ever to have been doubted, but that the chief may be served with a subpoena ad testificandum."[165] Fully alive to the

160. Rogers memo 36, 35.

161. United States v. Burr, 25 Fed. Cas. 55, 69 (No. 14693) (C.C. Va. 1807).

162. Ibid.

163. 1 Robertson, supra, n. 148 at 180. Jefferson's counsel, Alexander McRae, conceded that "a subpoena may issue against him [the President] as well as against any other man"; ibid. 181.

164. Ibid. This reflected James Wilson's statement in the Pennsylvania Ratification Convention: "not a *single privilege* is annexed to his character; far from being above the laws, he is amenable to them in his private character as a citizen, and in his public character by impeachment"; 2 Elliot 480. Another Framer, Charles Pinckney, speaking in the Senate on March 5, 1800, of the express congressional privilege from arrest, stated:

> it was never intended to give Congress, or either branch, any but specified, and those very limited, privileges. They [the Framers] well knew how oppressively the power of undefined privileges had been exercised in Great Britain, and were determined no such authority should ever be exercised here . . . Let us inquire why the Constitution should have been so attentive to each branch of Congress . . . and have shewn so little to the President . . . in this respect . . . No privilege of this kind was intended for your Executive, nor any except that which I have mentioned for your Legislature. 3 Farrand 385.

165. United States v. Burr, 25 Fed. Cas. 30, 34 (No. 14,692d) (C.C. Va. 1807). The Supreme Court stated in 1972 that in Burr, "Chief Justice Marshall, sitting on Circuit,

gravity of the issue, Marshall was at pains to put beyond doubt that a subpoena could reach the President. His subpoena, far from offending the mores of the time, responded to contemporary egalitarianism and met with approval, even from the Republicans.[166] As the foremost apostle of a democratic society, Jefferson could not very well publicly put the President above the law.

In weighing Marshall's judgment it needs to be kept in mind that he knew the problems of government at first hand: he had been a member of the Virginia Assembly and had taken vigorous part in obtaining ratification of the Constitution in Virginia; he had been a member of Congress, defended the Jay Treaty, been a member of the "XYZ mission to France," and had served as Secretary of State under John Adams.[167] As Charles Beard stated, Marshall "had better opportunities than any student of history or law today to discover the intention of the framers of the federal Constitution."[168] Greater light was not given to a present-day President.

What of the defiance threatened by Jefferson in his letters to the district attorney: the court had no "controul over the executive"; force was given by the Constitution to him, not the courts; the executive had the superior means to "protect itself from enterprises of force" attempted by the other departments. This was part and parcel of his total rejection of *Marbury v. Madison* and the doctrine of judicial review, which he denounced as "not law."[169]

opined that in proper circumstances a subpoena could be issued to the President"; Branzburg v. Hayes, 408 U.S. 665, 689 n. 26.

Rejection of royal immunity had been underlined in the North Carolina Ratification Convention by James Iredell. 4 Elliot 109, quoted supra, Ch. 2, n. 126.

166. "For the first time, most Republicans approved of the opinion of John Marshall. In the fanatical politics of the time there was enough of honest adherence to the American ideal that all men are equal in the eyes of the law, to justify the calling of a President, even Thomas Jefferson, before a court of justice"; 3 Beveridge, supra, n. 157 at 450.

Writing in 1803, before the Burr trial, St. George Tucker, the prominent Republican editor of Blackstone, and later judge of the Virginia Court of Appeals, stated: "In the trial of Mr. Thomas Cooper [before Justice Chase] . . . for a libel against the President . . . under the sedition law, it is said that Mr. Cooper applied to the court for a subpoena to summon the president as a witness on his behalf, and that the court refused to grant one. Upon what principle the application was refused (notwithstanding this article [for compulsory process]) I have never been able to obtain satisfactory information"; Tucker's Blackstone, supra, n. 12 at App. 358. For Chase's high-handed conduct of such trials, see Berger, *Impeachment* 224–251.

167. 12 *Dictionary of American Biography* 315.

168. Charles Beard, *The Supreme Court and the Constitution* 108 (Englewood Cliffs, N.J., 1962).

169. 9 Jefferson, *Writings* 55–62; 3 Henry S. Randall, *Life of Jefferson* 211–212 (New York, 1858). Randall states that "Jefferson in no way publicly challenged [the court's] authority"; ibid. 218.

But, as with Stalin's cynical query, "How many battalions has the Pope?," the respect due to Marshall's opinion cannot be measured by his lack of battalions to enforce a judicial decree. Command of the armed forces was not given the President in order that he might resist judicial decrees but rather to enforce them. The effect of Marshall's opinion as law is not a whit diminished by Jefferson's private threats of resistance. Jefferson's view was not that of the Founders; history confirms Marshall: the final word as to the "law" was given to the courts, the "ultimate interpreter" of the Constitution.

H. *Executive Shielding of Subordinates*

Not the least of Rogers' misreadings of law and history is his assertion that "heads of departments may not be compelled to attend a trial," and that they "are subject . . . to the direction of the Presidents of the United States. They are not subject to any other directions." Given a subpoena, he maintains, "The President may intervene and direct the Cabinet officer or department not to appear; the person subpoenaed would then advise the court of the President's order and abstain from appearing altogether."[170] As long ago as 1838 *Kendall v. United States* rejected an analogous claim. The Postmaster General, acting on presidential instructions, refused to pay moneys owed by the United States for carriage of mails. Congress then passed a law directing payment, and when this was refused by the Postmaster General, mandamus was brought against him to compel payment. Although the executive power is vested in the President, the Supreme Court declared:

> it by no means follows that every officer in every branch of that department is under the exclusive direction of the President . . . it would be an alarming doctrine, that Congress cannot impose upon any executive officer any duty they may think proper, which is not repugnant to any rights secured and protected by the constitution.

The contrary principle, said the Court, would clothe "the President with a power entirely to control the legislation of congress, and paralyze the administration of justice."[171] Whether the rights asserted by a department head are "protected by the Constitution" was not of course left for final decision by the President, but committed to the "ultimate interpreter" of the Constitution, the judiciary.

170. Rogers memo 38, 2.
171. 37 U.S. (12 Pet.) 524, 610, 613 (1838).

From the first the courts exercised the power to bring department heads into court, as the mandamus action against the Secretary of State in *Marbury v. Madison* testifies. Marshall left no doubts about the power of the courts to compel an officer to obey the law:

If one of the heads of departments commits any illegal act . . . it cannot be pretended that his office alone exempts him from being sued in the ordinary mode of proceeding, and being compelled to obey the judgment of the law.[172]

That doctrine was dramatically reaffirmed in our own time in *Youngstown Sheet & Tube Co. v. Sawyer*, wherein the Secretary of Commerce was restrained from executing President Truman's decision to seize strike-threatened steel mills in order to assure continued production during the war.[173] And when the same Mr. Sawyer, now joined by the Solicitor General, in another case, was recalcitrant, arguing that "courts cannot 'coerce' executive officials," both speedily learned better. Judge Prettyman, writing on behalf of the Court of Appeals, which held them in contempt, affirmed that "government officials are bound to obey the judgment of a court just as are private citizens."[174]

These cases had no occasion to consider the inquisitorial power of Congress. Parliamentary history, as we have seen, discloses that executive officers—Ministers or their subordinates—were brought before Committees of Inquiry without a by-your-leave.[175] And the Founders left no doubt that the Congress required no leave from the President in order to reach his subordinates. An officer, said Madison in the First Congress, "may be removed even against the will of the President" by means of an impeachment, notwithstanding, added Elias Boudinot, "he should be supported by all the power of the Executive."[176] In 1792 the Secretaries of the Treasury

172. 5 U.S. (1 Cranch) 137, 170 (1803). Marshall asked, "Is it to be contended that the heads of departments are not amenable to the laws of their country?" Further, "to what purpose are powers limited, and to what purpose is that limitation committed to writing, if these limits may, at any time, be passed by those intended to be restrained?"; ibid. 176.

173. 343 U.S. 579 (1952).

174. Sawyer v. Dollar, 190 F. 2d 623, 633–634 (D.C. Cir. 1951); motion for stay denied, 341 U.S. 912 (1951). See also Bowman Dairy Co. v. United States, 341 U.S. 214, 221 (1951).

175. See generally supra, Ch. 2. For instances of inquiries of subordinates, see Nicholas Paxton, ibid. text accompanying n. 84; Matthew Prior and Thomas Harley, ibid. at nn. 48–52; Peter Pett and William Penn, ibid. at n. 15.

176. 1 Annals of Cong. 372, 468 (1789); for additional citations, see Berger, *Impeachment* 101 n. 228 and 140.

and War Departments appeared before Congress to make "explanations" in person of the defeat of General St. Clair.[177] In 1944, the Senate Truman Committee served subpoenas upon Secretary of the Navy James Forrestal and Attorney General Francis Biddle, who complied therewith.[178] The congressional power of inquiry, it cannot be unduly emphasized, is coextensive with its power to impeach "all civil officers." Like the other executive claims of immunity from disclosure and inquiry, the latter-day claims that no subordinate may appear before Congress against the will of the President[179] is a product of wishful thinking which flies in the face of history.

Another facet of such ill-considered views is the Rogers critique of Marshall's decision in *Burr* as "unsound, for the reason" that the President "is in a position to completely disregard the court's subpoena or order. Since such disregard brings contempt upon a court, it would appear wise for the court not to issue such a futile order or command."[180] What an extraordinary statement to come from the chief law enforcement officer under "a government of laws and not of men"! Long since the Supreme Court said that "no officer of the law may set that law at defiance with impunity. All the officers of the government, from the highest to the lowest are creatures of the law, and are bound to obey it."[181] Despite the crucial situation presented by judicial intervention in President Truman's seizure of the steel plants, he complied with the Court's mandate.[182] The fact that *such suits can be brought* against a subordinate demonstrates that court orders are far from "futile."[183] When Chief Justice Marshall was told in an early case that "there was no means of compelling" the United States to pay costs, he

177. 3 Annals of Cong. 1106 (1792).

178. Congressman George Meader, 104 Cong. Rec. 3849 (1958).

179. Former Secretary of State Dean Acheson stated that a call for the appearance of a subordinate "isn't legal"; Ervin Hearings 267. Secretary of Defense Melvin Laird declined to permit a subordinate to appear before a Senate Committee and insisted that the "desired testimony . . . should be furnished by my designated representative"; ibid. 6, 449.

180. Rogers memo 36.

181. United States v. Lee, 106 U.S. 196, 220 (1882).

182. Truman "publicly promised to comply with any decision the Supreme Court might make . . . Mr. Truman kept his promise"; Glendon A. Schubert, *The Presidency and the Courts* 313 n. 31 (Minneapolis, 1957).

183. In Marbury v. Madison, 5 U.S. (1 Cranch) 137, 171–172 (1803), Chief Justice Marshall pointed out that in 1794 the Secretary of War appeared in response to a motion for mandamus made by Attorney General Randolph, and that both the Secretary and "the highest law officer of the United States" thought the mode of relief appropriate. The matter is recounted in 11 Annals of Cong. 923–925 (1802). Compare the remarks of Congressman Bayard; ibid. 615.

replied, "That would make no difference, because we are to presume they would pay them, if bound by law so to do."[184] That view has governed the Court into our own times.[185] Presidential disrespect for a decree is more likely to bring the President rather than the Court into "contempt."

I. *Inferences from the Creation of Foreign Affairs Department*

First, the Rogers memorandum states:

> One of the most powerful arguments to be found anywhere for the right of the President and *the heads of departments* to withhold confidential papers . . . in their discretion . . . is contained in the history dealing with the creation of the Department of Foreign Affairs by the Continental Congress in 1782.[186]

Under that Congress, the memorandum correctly states, "every Member thereof was entitled to see anything he wanted to see in the records of that Department." And because some members of the Continental Congress were later members of the First Congress, Rogers concludes that:

> The Members who sat in the New Congress in 1789 could not have been unfamiliar with the fact that during the existence of the Continental Congress its Members had been entitled to see all kinds of secret data. The conclusion is therefore inescapable that the founders of our Government, and those who sat in the First Congress, meant to give no power to the Congress to see secret data *in the executive departments* against the wishes of the President. That was a power which the Continental Congress had and which the framers of the Constitution meant for the new Congress, created by the Constitution, not to have.[187]

This "powerful argument" and its "inescapable conclusion" simply will not stand up. The claim of withholding power for *all* the "heads of departments" runs afoul of the Act of 1789, which expressly requires the Secretary of the Treasury to supply information required by Congress. So far as it has any validity, the Rogers argument must be confined to the Department of Foreign Affairs, now the Department of State.

The relations of the Continental Congress with the Secretary of

184. United States v. Hooe, 7 U.S. (3 Cranch) 73, 90 (1805).

185. In Glidden Co. v. Zdanok, 370 U.S. 530, 571 (1962), the Court adverted to the cases in which it had "asserted jurisdiction . . . despite persistent and never-surmounted challenges to its power to enforce a decree . . . this Court may rely on the good faith of state governments or other bodies to respond to its judgments."

186. Rogers memo 140; emphasis added.

187. Ibid. 140, 141; emphasis added.

Foreign Affairs, according to Rogers, closely resembled the intimate relation of Parliament with its own Ministers,[188] and yet it jealously insisted on access to all "secrets" in that Department. Why should the former members of the Continental Congress have become more trusting with a new Department, set up in a separate executive branch, than with the old, over which they had plenary control? The fact is that the Framers began by following the older model, that is, the treaty powers were reposed in the Senate alone, and only at the last minute was the President admitted to participation as a "check" on the Senate, not to displace it.[189] This hardly indicates a purpose to authorize presidential withholding of foreign affairs information from Congress. By the time of the Hanoverian Kings, Parliament had achieved full participation in foreign affairs, and with it the right to be kept informed,[190] the corollary being that the King no longer enjoyed a plenary power to withhold information. Now the Rogers memorandum would endow the President with a power no longer enjoyed by the King, in the teeth of Hamilton's declaration that the powers of the President in this area were "much inferior" to those of the King,[191] and of the purpose of the Founders to cut all roots of the executive in the royal prerogative.[192] "The vast importance of the trust," said Hamilton, required "joint possession" of the treaty power,[193] and this alone repels an inference that the President was empowered to conceal information from his "leading partner."[194] A Convention which carefully reduced the war powers of the Executive to those of a "first General" did not undo its labors by authorizing him to withhold from Congress—the warmaker—information as to moves which could embroil the nation in war. In short, the inferences drawn by Rogers from the history of the Continental Congress run contrary to all intendments.

Second, Attorney General Rogers argued that "the Executive privilege . . . could be traced back to section 2 of the Act of July 27, 1789, 1 Stat. 28, establishing the Department of Foreign Affairs."[195] Presumably he reasoned like McDougal and Lans that

188. Ibid. 140–141.
189. Supra, Ch. 5, text accompanying nn. 48–56.
190. Ibid. at nn. 32–41.
191. Federalist No. 69 at 448, 451.
192. Supra, Ch. 3 n. 5; ibid., text accompanying nn. 13, 42.
193. Fully quoted supra, Ch. 5, text accompanying n. 56.
194. So Trevelyan 472 described Parliament. Madison explained in Federalist No. 51 at 338 that "the legislature necessarily predominates."
195. Paraphrased by Kramer & Marcuse 895 n. 772.

while the duties of the Secretary of the Treasury were prescribed in the statute establishing his office and in supplementary statutes, which further directed him to submit reports to Congress upon request, his counterparts in the War and State Departments were placed under the administrative direction of the President and freed of the obligation to report to Congress.[196]

No word expressly "freeing" the Secretary of an obligation to furnish information to Congress is to be found in the Act which established the Department of Foreign Affairs. Apparently both Rogers and McDougal and Lans infer such a dispensation from the omission in the Act of an express duty to furnish information to Congress such as was imposed upon the Secretary of the Treasury. But this overlooks the peculiar provenance of the Treasury provision. It was Hamilton, the prospective Secretary of the Treasury, who drafted the provision making it the duty of the Secretary to *report* and furnish information to Congress, hoping, it has been said, by this "sweeping mandate . . . wholly without limitation" to "fasten onto every conceivable activity of the Administration."[197] The original provision did not contemplate that the Secretary would wait for a *request* for information, and it was heatedly resented as an *intrusion* into the business of legislation.[198] Since there was no dispute about existence of the power to call for information, but rather recognition of its essentiality,[199] Hamilton's proposal was watered down to the familiar duty to furnish information upon legislative request. No parallel attempt at "interference of an Executive officer in business of legislation"[200] was encountered in the framing of the Foreign Affairs statute, so there was no occasion similarly to curtail the "intrusion."[201] To extract from this understandable omission an abandonment of a cherished legislative power is to attribute to the First Congress an intention to surrender the right to be informed about foreign affairs which had been exercised both by Parliament and the Continental Congress, and to shield the President from accountability which no Minister had dared disclaim.[202] Such an attribution is refuted by the records.

The principle which animated the First Congress was stated by

196. McDougal & Lans 305.
197. Louis Koenig, *The Invisible Presidency* 58 (New York, 1960).
198. Supra, Ch. 2, text accompanying nn. 143–146.
199. Ibid. at nn. 147–150.
200. Mr. Page, 1 Annals of Cong. 594.
201. For other factors, see Berger, Executive Privilege 1062.
202. See supra, Ch. 3, text accompanying n. 12.

Roger Sherman: "as we need information to act upon, we must procure it where it is to be had."[203] Fisher Ames said that the House was to "act upon the best knowledge of circumstances," and in the case of finance, the "Secretary is presumed to have the best knowledge of the subject."[204] There is no hint that this reasoning was limited to financial matters; instead, the principle lies at the root of all inquiry. Indeed, the "first volume of the *Annals of Congress* records that 'Secretary for Foreign Affairs Jefferson attended agreeably *to order*, and made the necessary explanations . . .' "[205] In 1854 Attorney General Caleb Cushing, notwithstanding his "zeal for executive power,"[206] advised the President that

> By express provision of law, it is made the duty of the Secretary of the Treasury to communicate information to either House of Congress when desired; and it is practically and by legal implication the same with other secretaries, and with the Postmaster and Attorney General.[207]

Finally, since the Treasury Act of 1789 arose out of the need for information in order to deal with the fledgling nation's chaotic financial affairs;[208] the First Congress had no occasion to consider Congress' power to inquire into the conduct of executive officers as a concomitant of its power to impeach. We may not attribute to Congress an intention to abandon that power with respect to all of the Departments but that of Treasury; and if we would, Congress yet could not abdicate its power.

Third, another restrictive argument was based by Corwin on terminological differences between the Acts creating the Treasury Department and those creating the Departments of War and of Foreign Affairs. Congress, he stated, specifically recognized

> the responsibility of [the latter] departments to the President, but not so with the act of organizing the Department of Treasury, the head of which is required to "perform all services relative to finances as he shall be directed to perform—" directed, that is, by Congress. Nor is the reason underlying this difference far to seek. The State and War Departments are principally, although not exclusively, organs of the President in the exercise of functions which are assigned to him by the

203. 1 Annals of Cong. 607.

204. Ibid. 595. Page took for granted that information would be forthcoming from "any other officer"; quoted supra, Ch. 2 n. 147.

205. Quoted Corwin, *President* 360; emphasis added.

206. Ibid. 250.

207. 6 Ops. Atty. Gen. 326, 333 (1856). "Congress," summed up Cushing, "may at all times call on them [the Departments] for information or explanation in matters of official duty"; ibid. 344.

208. See Berger, Executive Privilege 1062.

Constitution itself, while the Treasury Department is primarily an instrument for carrying into effect Congress' constitutional powers in the field of finance.[209]

The fact that the 1789 Acts made the Secretaries of War and of Foreign Affairs expressly responsible to the President does not signify that the other branches were not. Speaking of "the actual conduct of foreign negotiations, the *preparatory plans of finance* . . . the direction of the operations of war," and so forth, Hamilton said that "The persons . . . to whose immediate management these different matters are committed, ought to be considered as assistants or deputies of the chief magistrate . . . and ought to be subject to his superintendence."[210] That "superintendence" and the correlative responsibility of cabinet heads to the President were reasons advanced in the First Congress for presidential "removal" power across the board.[211] So the "superintendence" argument proves too much. Moreover, the power of Congress over foreign commerce was no less plenary than "in the field of finance"; and, as Professor Henkin observes, at this time "the foreign trade of the United States was near the core of its foreign policy and the power to regulate commerce with foreign nations gave Congress a major voice in it."[212] Why should Congress retain its grip on financial affairs and abdicate with respect to "foreign policy"? Nevertheless, Professor Henkin, following in Corwin's footsteps, states that "from the beginning Congress itself gave the President control of foreign affairs";[213] and he apparently regards the Foreign Affairs Act as an authorization to "withhold" information respecting foreign affairs "even from Congress."[214]

There are solid reasons for rejection of a construction of the several Acts of 1789 that would restrict congressional participation in, and access to information about, foreign affairs. Parliament, it bears repeating, had come to enjoy comprehensive participation in the making of foreign policy; and the colonists made the Continental Congress the sole repository of foreign affairs, conduct of which it delegated to its Secretary of Foreign Affairs under strict control. The First Congress was not intent on

209. Corwin, *President* 97.
210. Federalist No. 72 at 468–469; emphasis added.
211. 1 Annals of Cong. 379, 462, 465, 474, 490, 499, 512. "Each head of a department is and must be the President's *alter ego* in the matters of that department"; Myers v. United States, 272 U.S. 52, 133 (1926). See also Rogers memo 3, 55.
212. Henkin 69.
213. Ibid. 365 n. 89.
214. Ibid. 46, 300 n. 20.

surrendering cherished prerogatives to the newly created executive branch, which influential Framers had considered merely an instrument for execution of the laws made by Congress.[215] Instead, the 1789 debate on the new departments is rife with distrust of the President and the department heads.[216] Moreover, the members of the 1789 Congress who had been members of the Continental Congress had earlier had access to all the information involved in the delicate treatymaking with France, Holland, and England. Such access militates strongly against the argument that they would *sub silentio* endorse a doctrine that executive insulation of information from Congress was indispensable to the conduct of foreign affairs.

Certainly Jefferson, as Secretary of Foreign Affairs, made no claim that the Act of 1789 had released his office from accountability to Congress, for, as we have seen, he attended the First Congress "*agreeably to order*, and made the necessary explanation."[217] Washington also took for granted that the Senate was entitled to be consulted and to participate in treatymaking,[218] notwithstanding that he had approved the several Acts of 1789. During his administration, also, the House investigated the conduct of General St. Clair, and despite the parallel "dispensation" in the 1789 War Department Act, the Secretary of War appeared before the House to make explanations. Later Rufus King, whose experience ran from the Continental Congress through the federal and Massachusetts Conventions and participation in Senate instructions to John Jay respecting the British Treaty, and who was hardly ignorant of the several Acts of 1789, affirmed that the Senate was empowered to "call for full and exact information respecting the foreign affairs."[219] No one countered with the renunciation allegedly embodied in the Act of 1789; nor was the argument made in the oft-cited Senate Report of 1816, recommending on policy grounds that foreign affairs be left to the President.[220] Finally, Attorney General Cushing, confirming Jefferson's earlier assumption, advised the President that by "implication of law" all Secre-

215. Supra, Ch. 3, text accompanying nn. 18–24.

216. For the First Congress' suspicion of executive "intrusion," see supra, Ch. 2, text accompanying nn. 144–149. Note too, Gerry's remark, "If the doctrine of having prime and great ministers of state was once well established, he did not doubt but we should soon see them distinguished by a green or red ribbon, or other insignia of Court favor and patronage"; 1 Annals of Cong. 601. See also Mr. Page; ibid. 594.

217. Corwin, *President* 360; emphasis added.

218. Supra, Ch. 5, text accompanying nn. 66–73.

219. Ibid., text accompanying n. 110.

220. Ibid. n. 107.

taries were under the duty expressly placed upon the Secretary of the Treasury by the Act of 1789,[221] presumably not unaware that the several Acts of 1789 were very differently phrased. These facts, to my mind, preclude a differentiation between the Acts of 1789 which would shut off the traditional legislative right to participate in the *making* of foreign policy, necessarily based upon full information, and to inquire into executive conduct across the board.

J. *House Rule* 22

Assistant Attorney General Rehnquist stated to Congress that "Hinds *Precedents* discloses a most significant limitation on resolutions of inquiry in the House of Representatives . . . A resolution of inquiry had to be limited to facts, i.e. whether or not certain action had been taken by the executive and could not call for opinions, or the reason why the executive had taken a certain course of action."[222] That does not tell the whole story. To come within the "immediate consideration" contemplated by Rule 22(5)—"All resolutions of inquiry, addressed to the heads of executive departments shall be reported to the House within one week after presentation"—a resolution was required to call for facts only.[223] Notwithstanding, however, the House can "by resolution . . . ask for an opinion of the head of the Department" outside the Rule.[224]

K. *The American Tradition against Secrecy*

No discussion of the Rogers "precedents" would be complete without notice of the fact that they run counter to the deep-seated American tradition against secrecy in public affairs. James Wilson, explaining to the Pennsylvania Ratification Convention the exclusion of the House from treatymaking, said that it would be improper to entrust the secret and delicate negotiations, "especially in time of war . . . to any great number of persons." For my part," he continued,

> I am not an advocate for secrecy in transactions relating to the public; not generally even in forming treaties, because I think that the history of the diplomatic corps will evince, even in that great department of

221. Supra, n. 207 and accompanying text.
222. Ervin Hearings 436.
223. 3 Hinds Precedents 174, 168.
224. Ibid. 175.

politics, the truth of an old adage, that "honesty is the best policy," and this is the conduct of the most able negotiators.[225]

In 1846 President Polk wrote the House, "I am fully aware of the strong and correct public feeling which exists throughout the country against secrecy of any kind in the administration of the Government."[226] That the feeling endures was attested by Assistant Attorney General Rehnquist in 1971: "the claim of executive privilege is an unpopular one, both within and without Congress."[227]

Once, and once only, did the Framers authorize secrecy: Article I, §5(3) requires Congress to keep and publish Journals, except "such parts as may in their [each House] judgment require secrecy." This provision did not have smooth sailing in the Convention; initially six states were for it, four states against, and one was divided.[228] Wilson, whose state, Pennsylvania, voted against it, stated that "The people have a right to know what their Agents are doing or have done, and it should not lie in the option of the Legislature to conceal their proceedings." George Mason thought "it would give a just alarm to the people."[229] Toward the end of the Convention, Mason and Elbridge Gerry pressed for publication of "all the proceedings of the House," and the "other side" countered that "cases might arise where secrecy might be necessary in both Houses—Measures preparatory to a declaration of war."[230]

Such attempts to quiet fears of secrecy by restrictive readings were echoed in the Ratification Conventions. In Virginia Patrick Henry demanded an explanation "why Congress should keep their proceedings secret," and opined that "the liberties of a people never were . . . secure when the transactions of their rulers may be concealed from them." He recognized the need for temporary withholding of "such transactions as relate to military operations or affairs of great consequence, the immediate promulgation of which might defeat the interest of the community." But he con-

225. 2 Elliot 506. As Justice Wilson, lecturing in 1791, stated, "That the conduct and proceedings of representatives should be as open as possible to the inspection of those whom they represent, seems to me, in republican government, a maxim of whose truth or importance the smallest doubt cannot be entertained"; 1 Wilson, *Works* 421.

226. 4 Richardson 434.

227. Ervin Hearings 428.

228. 2 Farrand 257.

229. Ibid. 260.

230. Ibid. 613.

cluded that to "cover with the veil of secrecy the common routine of business, is an abomination."[231] Mason also argued that the provision "enables them to keep the negotiations about treaties secret. Under this veil they may conceal anything and everything."[232] To set such fears at rest, John Marshall referred to the British practice invoked by Patrick Henry and asked:

> When debating on the propriety of declaring war, or on military arrangements, do they deliberate in the open fields? No sir . . . In this plan, secrecy is only used when it would be fatal and pernicious to publish the schemes of government.[233]

Not satisfied, Mason urged, "why not insert words that would exclude ambiguity and danger?"[234]

In the North Carolina Ratification Convention, William Davie, a member of the Federal Convention, explained that under the provision "they would conceal nothing, but what it would be unsafe to publish."[235] And James Iredell added that

> in time of war it was absolutely necessary to conceal the operations of government; otherwise no attack on an enemy could be premeditated with success . . . that it was no less imprudent to divulge [to the public] our negotiations with foreign powers.[236]

These remarks testify to the apprehension that was generated by an *express* congressional authorization to conceal information from the public, and they explain resort to a restrictive reading to allay such fears. In light of the denial to the representative body —then more trusted than the executive[237]—of limitless power to conceal, how can intention be derived of an *implied* grant to the executive to keep "anything and everything" secret? Rather, the

231. 3 Elliot 170.
232. Ibid. 404.
233. Ibid. 233, 170, 222. In the Massachusetts Convention, Samuel Perley asked, "Would it . . . have been prudent for . . . General Washington, previous to the American army's taking possession of Dorchester Heights, to have published to the world his intention of doing so? No . . ."; 2 Elliot 52. Mason stated, "In matters relative to military operations and foreign negotiations secrecy [from the public] was necessary sometimes"; he called attention to the Articles of Confederation exception from publication of parts "relating to treaties, alliances, or military operations, as, in their judgment, require secrecy"; 3 Elliot 459, 404. In the upshot, the Virginia Convention proposed an amendment cast in the Confederation terms; ibid. 659–660. Madison had stated that "when a treaty is forming, secrecy is proper; but when actually made, the public ought to be acquainted with every circumstance relating to it"; ibid. 331.
234. Ibid. 404.
235. 4 Elliot 72.
236. Ibid. 73.
237. Supra, Ch. 3, text accompanying nn. 1, 9.

express authorization for discretionary secrecy by Congress and the omission to make similar provision for the President indicates an intention to withhold such authority from him.[238]

Concealment by the President *from Congress* raises quite different operative consideration than secrecy of the Journals. Article I permitted concealment *from the public*, and, as Madison explained to the Virginia Convention, "There never was any legislative assembly without a discretionary power of concealing important transactions the publication of which might be detrimental to the community."[239] So the colonists held when by Article IX of the Articles of Confederation they provided that the Congress "shall publish the Journal of their proceedings monthly, except such parts thereof relating to treaties, alliances or military operations as in their judgment require secresy."[240] No similar precedent exists for presidential withholding of information *from the legislature*. To the contrary, parliamentary history discloses that ministerial communication to Parliament on request was the established practice, as the Framers well knew. What might momentarily be concealed from the public *had* to be divulged to Congress if that partner in government was to participate in making the momentous decisions which alone were to be kept secret temporarily.

From time to time apologists for executive privilege point to the fact that the Federal Convention conducted its proceedings under a rule of secrecy.[241] The fact that the Convention deliberated in secret is quite irrelevant, for in the Constitution it provided for *limited secrecy by the Congress* alone, thereby excluding executive secrecy. It is illuminating, however, to consider the secrecy of the Convention in its own frame. In seeking to draft a new Constitution, the delegates to the Convention stepped outside their mandate to alter and amend, not discard, the Articles of Confederation.[242] If we may judge from widespread criticism of that departure in the Ratification Conventions, the Convention probably would have blown up had the arrogation come to light. Forty years later Madison said that "no Constitution would ever

238. Supra, Ch. 5, n. 160. As Charles Pinckney remarked in 1800, the Framers conciously withheld from the President privileges granted to Congress; supra, n. 164.

239. 3 Elliot 409.

240. Commager 115.

241. See, e.g., testimony of Assistant Attorney General Rehnquist; Ervin Hearings 425.

242. Carl van Doren, *The Great Rehearsal* viii (New York, 1948); Morison 305–306.

have been adopted by the Convention if the debate had been made public."[243] It is not easy to conclude that commitment of the nation to a cataclysmic war must be governed by the same considerations. Even so, Jefferson wrote to Adams, "I am sorry they began their deliberations by so abominable a precedent as that of tying up the tongues of their members. Nothing can justify this example but the innocence of their intentions, & ignorance of the value of public discussions."[244] With Henry Steele Commager, one may safely conclude that

> The generation that made the nation thought secrecy in government one of the instruments of Old World tyranny and committed itself to the principle that a democracy cannot function unless the people are permitted to know what their government is up to.[245]

In sum, the case for congressional inquiry may be restated in the words of the Supreme Court in *McGrain v. Daugherty:*

> In that period ["Before and when the Constitution was framed and adopted"] the power of inquiry—with enforcing process—was regarded and employed as a necessary and appropriate attribute of the power to legislate—indeed, was treated as inhering in it. Thus there is ample warrant for thinking as we do, that the constitutional provisions which commit the legislative functions to the two houses are intended to include this attribute to the end that the function may be effectively exercised.[246]

That "attribute," as our survey of parliamentary practice has shown, embraced comprehensive inquiry into executive conduct and affairs without a trace of executive denial of the right. Against this the Rogers memorandum erects a phantom barrier of self-serving "precedents" behind which, as in the case of the facade of villages built by Potemkin for his mistress, Catherine the Great,

243. 3 Farrand 479. Madison considered that secret discussion enabled men to yield to the force of argument.

244. Ibid. 76. In the Virginia Ratification Convention Patrick Henry stated, "it would have given more general satisfaction, if the proceedings of the Convention had not been concealed from the public eye"; 3 Elliot 170. Cf. Grayson, ibid. 340.

245. New York Review of Books, Oct. 5, 1972, p. 7.

246. 273 U.S. 135, 175 (1927); see also ibid. 161, and Quinn v. United States, 349 U.S. 155, 160–161 (1955). In McGrain the Court determined that Congress was empowered to investigate "the administration of the Department of Justice . . . and particularly whether the Attorney General and his assistants were performing or neglecting their duties"; 273 U.S. at 177. True, it was the brother of the Attorney General, an Ohio banker, who had been summoned; but it can hardly be deduced therefrom that the Attorney General himself, the object of the investigation, was exempt from inquiry. Historically inquiries were directed at members of the executive, not at private persons, although they too were from time to time summoned.

there is nothing. "Historical fact," J. R. Wiggins justly stated, "is overwhelmingly at war with the law as the Attorney General prefers to view it."[247]

A good part of the criticisms here set forth was published in 1965; prior to the publication, an editor who had read the manuscript and knew Mr. Rogers, then in private life, requested permission to submit it to him so that he might point out particulars in which the criticisms were unfair or erroneous. This was done; after about two weeks the manuscript was returned without a word. In the intervening eight years no member or former member of the executive branch and, to the best of my knowledge, no proponent of executive privilege, has published a refutation of those criticisms of the Rogers "precedents." Continued adherence by high-ranking members of the executive branch to these "precedents" exhibits, in this light, cynical reliance on the modern propaganda tenet: repeat it often enough and it will be believed.[248]

247. Supra, n. 11 at 83.

248. Patrick Buchanan, "Mr. Nixon's most conservative speech writer," was asked "whether it is really that easy to change public opinion," and "replied, 'Yes. Drip by drip by drip. It wears them down.' " *Newsweek*, Jan. 15, 1973, p. 43.

7

EXECUTIVE PRIVILEGE COMPARED WITH EVIDENTIARY PRIVILEGE

A. *Introductory*

It is paradoxical that the claim of "uncontrolled" discretion to withhold information from Congress should first have been asserted after a claim of absolute discretion to withhold military secrets from a private litigant had been rejected by the Supreme Court: "judicial control over the evidence in a case cannot be abdicated to the caprice of executive officers."[1] Why should an executive determination be more conclusive against Congress when it requires information as a preliminary to legislation or appropriation or seeks to ferret out corruption or inefficiency? If the law were as privilege adherents would have it, a private litigant would enjoy greater rights to information than does Congress, and this though President Tyler, summarizing the first sixty-five years of experience, pushed the claim of executive privilege no further than the recognized categories of evidentiary privilege. True, thus far the only sanction for nondisclosure in private litigation has been a choice between producing the information or losing the action; the government has not actually been *compelled* to produce information,[2] because a party who obtains judgment has little need to press on for disclosure. But, when an administrator is faced with a choice between disclosure or defeat, particularly when the stakes are high, there will be few instances in which he will deem nondisclosure more important than victory. It is hardly conceivable, for example, that, if the government sued Lockheed Corporation for repayment of its $250,000,000 loan, it would stubbornly refuse to disclose some "candid interchange" among its subordinates at the cost of losing the suit.

Tyler's invocation of evidentiary privilege was rebutted by the

1. United States v. Reynolds, 345 U.S. 1, 9–10 (1953).
2. Joseph Bishop, "The Executive's Right of Privacy: An Unresolved Constitutional Question," 66 Yale L.J. 477, 483 (1957).

House Committee because, although the public interest in withholding information may rise above that of a particular litigant, the need for investigating "abuses in the administration itself" rises higher than the privilege lest the investigatory function be defeated.[3] It would be anomalous to conclude that Congress may compel executive disclosure in private litigation by consenting to suit against the United States,[4] that it can waive the privilege of withholding "state secrets" from such litigants,[5] and yet that it is powerless to protect the nation by requiring disclosure to itself.

For purposes of comparison it will be useful first to pull together the threads of the several claims of privilege against Congress. After an extended survey, Mr. Irving Younger, a proponent of executive privilege, categorized the various claims of privilege as follows:

(1) A house of Congress or Congress as a whole has no power to legislate on the particular matter;
(2) foreign affairs require the withholding of certain information;
(3) the innocent must be protected;

3. Supra, Ch. 6, text accompanying n. 124. "The case for abdicating political [i.e., legislative] checks upon the executive is much weaker than that for saying that the interests of the individual litigant must yield, perhaps only for a time, to the determination by the executive as to what is admissible in evidence . . . Here departmental inefficiency, concealed for reasons of public interest [?], may not merely disappoint individual claims but endanger the whole fabric behind which it shelters—the public interest itself"; Clive Parry, "Legislatures and Secrecy," 67 Harv. L. Rev. 737, 740 (1954).

4. "No suit can be maintained against the United States . . . without express authority of Congress." Stanley v. Schwalby, 162 U.S. 255, 270 (1896); United States v. Clarke, 33 U.S. (8 Pet.) 436, 444 (1834).

5. Halpern v. United States, 258 F. 2d 36, 43 (2d Cir. 1958).

A remarkable argument to the contrary was advanced in a concurring opinion by Circuit Judge Wilkey, Soucie v. David, 448 F. 2d 1067, 1082–1083 (D.C. Cir. 1971). Speaking with reference to information sought by a member of the *public* under the Freedom of Information Act, he declared that if the exemption for intra-agency communications afforded by the Act did not embrace the case at bar, "the executive may still assert a constitutional privilege on the ground that Congress may not compel by statute disclosure of information which it would not be entitled to receive directly upon request." He reasoned that "Obviously Congress could not surmount constitutional barriers . . . by conferring upon any member of the general public a right which Congress, neither individually nor collectively, possesses. Water does not naturally rise higher than its source." His authority for the statement that Congress would not be entitled to the information is a self-serving article by Attorney General Rogers, and another by a lately resigned Assistant Attorney General and an employee of the Department of Justice; ibid. 1081. No one knew better than Marshall the scope of the separation of powers, having participated in defense of the Constitution against onslaughts by Patrick Henry in the Virginia Ratification Convention, yet he was untroubled by it in the Burr case.

If a judicial compulsion to furnish executive information to a private litigant is not in violation of the separation of powers, a congressional demand for similar information also does not invade the executive prerogative.

(4) the identity of sources of confidential information should not be disclosed;
(5) administrative efficiency requires secrecy. The warp and woof are perfect; there is no gap.
Any exigency will justify withholding from Congress.[6]

Younger's first category purports to reflect the Jay Treaty episode; in Younger's own words, "Washington had withheld the requested papers, not because prudence dictated secrecy, but because Washington thought the House had no right to them."[7] Consequently, there was no occasion to decide whether the President had a "right" to withhold in the face of a "right" to demand. Indeed, Washington stated that, given a legislative "right" to require information, he was "disposed" to furnish rather than withhold it. Younger's second category is drawn from the St. Clair investigation, wherein Washington turned over all the documents, without disclosing reservations entertained by his cabinet about hypothetical future situations.[8] The third category, protection of the innocent, was first assigned by Jefferson as a gratuitous explanation to the House respecting the Burr conspiracy.[9] One who studies Senator McCarthy's perversion of congressional investigations must appreciate Jefferson's prophetic assertion of the need to screen "rumors, conjectures, and suspicions," and his conclusion that justice will not "permit exposing of names."[10] But here we are examining the historical basis of a claimed executive power —what power was granted, not what ought to be. The President was not constituted the Protector of the People against the Congress; that function was confided to the courts.[11]

Younger's fourth category, "the identity of sources of confidential information," is traceable to President Tyler's statement; it surfaced in our time when Attorney General Robert Jackson refused FBI reports and names of confidential informants to a House Committee in 1941.[12] Tyler, drawing on the presidential duty to "take care that the laws be faithfully executed," deduced an "obligation . . . to inquire" how executive subordinates perform

6. Irving Younger, "Congressional Investigations and Executive Secrecy: A Study in Separation of Powers," 20 U. Pitt. L. Rev. 757, 773 (1959).
7. Ibid. 758.
8. Supra, Ch. 6, text accompanying nn. 21–37.
9. Ibid. at nn. 98–108.
10. Younger, supra, n. 6 at 758; Rogers memo 6; 1 Richardson 412 (Jan. 22, 1807).
11. Cf. Marshall v. Gordon, 243 U.S. 521 (1917); Jurney v. McCracken, 294 U.S. 125 (1935).
12. Rogers memo 22, 10.

their duties, and concluded that "to require from the Executive the transfer of this discretion to [Congress] is equivalent to the denial of its possession by him and would render him dependent upon that branch in the performance of a duty purely executive."[13] On his reasoning, however, the power of inquiry into executive conduct would be denied to the legislature in the performance of a recognized legislative function. Historically it was given to the legislature to police executive conduct, and executive supervision of subordinates must yield to that power. Experience, moreover, has shown that the executive is not the best supervisor of executive misconduct, all too frequently seeking to block discovery.[14]

Attorney General Jackson reasoned that disclosure would (1) prejudice law enforcement; (2) be a breach of faith with confidential informants and thereby impair future efficiency; and (3) interfere with the president's duty to "take care that the laws be faithfully executed."[15] Implicit in Jackson's "prejudice law enforcement" is the untenable assumption that law enforcement is the exclusive concern of the Executive. As *maker* of the laws which it is given the President to enforce, Congress is entitled to conclude that the public interest in a particular disclosure outweighs the conduct of a particular prosecution. Even if that judgment be unwise, it is not rendered unconstitutional. In part, the argument that disclosure to Congress may prejudice law enforcement may be met by submission of investigative reports for confidential treatment by Congress. For years FBI reports were delivered to Senator McCarran and so treated.[16] Jackson's "breach of faith" argument was spectacularly undercut by the Nixon administration. When three employees of the Committee to Reelect the President requested that FBI interviews with respect to the Watergate conspiracy be conducted in private, presumably to

13. Ibid. 10; 3 Hinds Precedents 181.

14. See the Walpole cover-up of corruption, supra, Ch. 2, text accompanying nn. 76–81. Writing of the Teapot Dome scandal, Professor Felix Frankfurter stated, "For nearly two years the efforts to uncover wrongdoing in the disposal of our public domain were hampered by every conceivable obstruction on the part of those in office"; Frankfurter, "Hands off the Investigations," 38 New Republic 329, 330 (1924). The same may be said of efforts to stall investigation of tax frauds in the Bureau of Internal Revenue during the Truman administration, and of the improper influence that led to the Dixon-Yates contract during the Eisenhower administration. See Clark Mollenhoff, *Washington Cover-Up* 36–38, 60–78 (New York, 1962).

15. 40 Ops. Atty. Gen. 45 (1941); Rogers memo 22. Jackson also instanced "gross injustice to innocent individuals," discussed supra, text accompanying nn. 10–11.

16. Senator McCarran stated that "For years as chairman of the Judiciary Committee, I had the FBI files handed to me"; 99 Cong. Rec. 2156 (Mar. 20, 1953).

escape the chilling eye of White House counsel John Dean, the FBI files were later forwarded to Dean, who then delivered them to the Committee, which thereupon called upon the hapless employees for an accounting.[17] Thus did the White House make a mockery of the "sanctity" of the files upon which President Nixon had laid such great stress.[18] The conclusion is irresistible that this "sanctity" is a political shibboleth, ignored when disregard will advance administration purposes and invoked only to block much needed investigation.

It is no mean feat to erect on Jackson's third category—the duty to execute the laws—a barrier which precludes the lawmaker from inquiry how its laws have been executed, a traditional attribute of legislative power."[19] When Attorney General Jackson donned judicial robes, he expressed abhorrence of secret evidence employed to exclude the alien wife of a citizen, and said, "the menace to the security of this country, be it as great as it may, from this girl's admission is as nothing compared to the menace to free institutions inherent in procedures of this pattern."[20] This change of attitude, which accompanied his translation from partisan advocate to impartial arbiter, underscores the need heavily to discount self-serving statements by the Attorney General or other high officials as "precedents" for curtailment of congressional powers.[21]

Younger's fifth category, "administrative efficiency requires secrecy," derives from President Eisenhower's letter of May 17, 1954, to the Secretary of Defense, then under fire by Senator McCarthy, advising that executive employees must "be in a position to be completely candid in advising with each other on official matters," and that this "candid interchange" would be impaired by disclosure to Congress.[22] Since 1954 this newly coined doctrine has mushroomed like the black cloud of an atomic explosion; it has become the favorite bureaucratic gambit to block disclosure.[23] For the moment let it suffice that the doctrine can

17. Los Angeles Times, Mar. 13, 1973, p. 1; Washington Post, Mar. 15, 1973, p. A-8.

18. "[T]he sanctity of these files must be maintained"; N.Y. Times, Mar. 16, 1973, p. 22.

19. Supra, Ch. 3, text accompanying nn. 15–16, 18–24, 28–30, 58–59.

20. United States ex rel Knauff v. Shaughnessy, 338 U.S. 537, 551 (1950), dissenting.

21. This was Jackson's own view; supra, Ch. 6, n. 6.

22. Mollenhoff, 45–46. For the circumstances from which this directive arose, see ibid. 41–54.

23. These developments are discussed infra, Ch. 8.

summon no historical precedent. President Jackson's refusal to reveal a statement he made *to his Cabinet*[24]—what Marshall termed "secrets of the cabinet"[25]—is poles apart from an unlimited discretion to withhold any and every communication between several million subordinate employees in the interest of "administrative efficiency."[26] An assumption that such communications may be concealed from Congress would have shielded Fall, Denby, and Daugherty from congressional investigation and have enabled them to despoil Teapot Dome, all in the guise of taking "care that the Laws be faithfully executed"![27] If Congress is to inquire whether a given operation is "efficient," as the Supreme Court, walking in the path of historical tradition, held it is authorized to do,[28] it cannot be left to the executive branch to determine that "efficiency" forecloses legislative scrutiny. Withholdings that border on the grotesque were produced during the Eisenhower regime when the executive branch proceeded on the contrary premise.[29]

In examining the evidentiary and executive privilege materials that follow, we should be alert to what Professor Wade, an acute observer of the English administrative scene, called the "civil servant's occupational love of secrecy," the "official instinct of hiding as much as possible from the public gaze."[30] He reported that

24. Younger, supra, n. 6 at 772–773.

25. Marbury v. Madison, 5 U.S. (1 Cranch) 137, 170 (1803).

26. In Conway v. Rimmer, 1 All E. R. [1968] 874, 910, Lord Pearce differentiated cabinet correspondence "from trivial correspondence with or within a ministry." It needs to be borne in mind that "secrets of the cabinet" can not be shielded from inquiry into "pernicious advice" and subsequent impeachment.

27. This was the view of Congressman Richard M. Nixon in 1948 when he rejected President Truman's refusal of information to a congressional committee "for this very good reason, that would mean that the President could have arbitrarily issued an Executive Order in . . . the *Teapot Dome* case, or in any other case denying the Congress information it needed to conduct an investigation of the executive department"; 94 Cong. Rec. 4783 (April 22, 1948).

Speaking with reference to illegal tampering during the Truman administration with tax cases in the Bureau of Internal Revenue and the Tax Division of the Department of Justice, Mollenhoff stated, "It had been vital to learn the nature of advice and recommendations of both high-level and low-level officials on settlements of huge tax cases . . . Caudle [Assistant Attorney General] and White House aide Matthew Connolly could have claimed that their communications were 'confidential executive business.' As it was, the Caudle-Connolly communications were actually used as the basis of criminal charges on which Caudle and Connolly were convicted"; Mollenhoff 36–38, 50.

28. The "power of Congress to conduct investigations is inherent in the legislative process . . . It comprehends probes into departments of the Federal Government to expose corruption, inefficiency or waste"; Watkins v. United States, 354 U.S. 178, 187 (1957).

29. See infra, Ch. 8.

30. H. W. R. Wade, *Administrative Law* 18 (2d ed., Oxford, 1967).

Mr. Justice Devlin said that Crown privilege was becoming a serious obstruction to justice, and both he and the Court of Appeal were clearly convinced that privilege was being claimed for documents which could be made available without the least damage to the public interest. As we shall see, this has now been officially admitted.[31]

Equally farfetched claims have been made by American officialdom against the Congress. But in private litigation the bureaucracy has met with upsets.

B. *Evidentiary Privilege*

Chief Justice Marshall, it will be recalled, held on the *Trial of Aaron Burr* that, though the Executive might have serious reason for declining to produce a document, such reason would have to yield if the defendant could "clearly show the paper to be essential to the justice of the case."[32] Marshall was not blazing new trails. In 1775, an English court, sitting in Calcutta on a state trial, had overruled the objections of Governor and Council of the East India Company, that production of Council proceedings might expose "secrets of the utmost importance to the interest and even to the safety of the state," saying that "the papers and records of all the public companies in England . . . the East India House, are liable to be called for, where justice requires . . . and [are] continually given in evidence."[33] And in 1789, shortly after the adoption of the Constitution, that holding was re-echoed in an English admiralty case involving a seizure by British authorities of lumber of American origin, the importation of which was forbidden by statute. The shipowner claimed that he had vainly sought to obtain a copy of an order in council (and of relevant documents) which had suspended the statute. The court found it unnecessary to decide the issue, but said in passing that,

In any cause where the crown is a party, it is to be observed, that the crown can no more withhold evidence of documents in its possession,

31. Ibid. 243 (1st ed., Oxford, 1961). "It has several times happened that evidence for which the Crown at first claimed privilege has since been produced in court and shown to be quite innocuous"; ibid. 245. In Conway v. Rimmer, supra, n. 26 at 915, Lord Upjohn stated that "some really trivial correspondence between some ministry and a subject or local authority has been withheld." And Lord Pearce, alluding to past privilege claims, referred to "the complete lack of common sense a general blanket protection of wide class may lead"; ibid. 910.

32. Supra, Ch. 6, text accompanying nn. 155–156.

33. Trial of Maharajah Nundocomar, 20 Howell's State Trials 923, 1057 (Supreme Court of Judicature, Bengal, 1776) (London, 1809–1826).

than a private person. If the court thinks proper to order the production of any public instrument, that order must be obeyed.[34]

Such an "order in council," issued in the prosecution of a hard-fought war, comes close to being a "state secret"; yet the court experienced no qualms and took mandatory disclosure for granted, thereby indicating that an absolute privilege for government documents was then judicially undreamed of, that there was as yet no common law of executive privilege in litigation.

It is important to bear in mind, as the House of Lords reminded us in *Conway v. Rimmer* (1968), that the "public interest" is not solely identified with governmental objections to disclosure. There is the competing "public interest that the administration of justice shall not be frustrated by the withholding of documents which must be produced if justice is to be done." It is not for the Minister, "who has no duty to balance those interests," said Lord Reid, to make a conclusive claim against disclosure, but the balancing, rather, is for the courts.[35] Any exception which deprives the court of this balancing function makes the judgment of an interested party conclusive.

For present purposes a rather cursory survey of the several categories of evidentiary privilege must suffice.[36]

1. *Secrets of State: Military and Foreign Affairs*

There are statements from which it might be inferred that in the area of military and foreign affairs an absolute privilege of nondisclosure exists.[37] These statements, however, require reevaluation in light of later developments.

Military Secrets. The government's claim for protection of military secrets once led to summary rejection of a plea for disclosure.[38] But the Supreme Court held in *United States v. Reynolds* that such claims are not conclusive on the court, saying that "the court itself must determine whether the circumstances are appropriate for the claim of privilege."[39] In that case the widows of

34. The Ship Columbus, 1 Collectanea Juridica 88, 92 (1789).

35. 1 All E. R. [1968] 874, 880, 887; see also ibid. 890, 891, 893, 901, 914.

36. For more extended discussion see 8 J. H. Wigmore, *Evidence*, §§2367–2379 (Boston, 1940). James Moore, *Federal Practice*, §§26.61 (New York, 1972).

37. Dayton v. Dulles, 254 F. 2d. 71, 77 (D.C. Cir. 1957).

38. See, e.g., Firth Sterling Steel Co. v. Bethlehem Steel Co., 199 Fed. 353 (E.D. Pa. 1912).

39. 345 U.S. 1, 8 (1953). Such scrutiny is the more essential because as a former General Counsel of the Army remarked, "there is not much information in the files of the State and Defense Departments—of a sort likely to attract congressional

civilian passengers on a crashed military plane which carried secret electronic equipment sought discovery of the Air Force's investigation report. Discovery was denied because plaintiffs had made "dubious showing of necessity" in light of an "available alternative."[40] But the Court emphasized that "judicial control over the evidence in a case cannot be abdicated to the caprice of executive officers"; that "a complete abandonment of judicial control would lead to intolerable abuses." Notwithstanding, the Court carved out a narrow enclave: on occasion it may be possible to satisfy the court that "there is a reasonable danger that the compulsion of the evidence will expose military matters which, in the interest of national security, should not be divulged," in which case the court should not insist upon examination even *in camera*.[41] This judicial wariness of executive representations is essential.

Possibly to temper the blunting of judicial scrutiny in critical areas, *Reynolds* stated that privilege "is not to be lightly invoked . . . [the claim must be] lodged by the head of the department . . . after actual personal consideration by that officer."[42] Reliance on "actual personal consideration" by the Secretary of Defense, for example, of the numerous calls for information by private litigants is illusory. How the department head arrives at his decision was graphically portrayed by Wigmore (who did a stint with the Army in Washington):

> The subordinate at that lowest point, obsessed by the general dogma against disclosure, prepares a reply denying the application; he will usually not have the initiative or courage to propose an exceptional use of discretion in favor of granting the application. This draft reply is sent up, "through channels" (as the phrase goes), past two or more intervening superiors (each one treating it in routine fashion), till it reaches the Departmental head or other chief officers whose signature is necessary. Arriving in a ponderous pile of daily draft correspondence [plus quasi-judicial opinions, legal, economic, or technical memoranda, drafts of proposed legislation or regulations, or of proposed testimony before congressional committees], it receives the necessary signature without further consideration.[43]

---

interest—which could not with some plausibility be given a security classification, if the executive wished to withhold it on that ground [or on any ground]"; Bishop, supra, n. 2 at 487.

40. 345 U.S. at 11.
41. Ibid. 10. For further discussion, see infra, Epilogue at nn. 107–125.
42. Ibid. 7–8.
43. 8 Wigmore, *Evidence* 793.

One who has seen government service, whether in upper or lower echelons, can confirm that the picture is lifelike.

The *Reynolds* requirement that the head of the department must give the litigant's request for disclosure "actual personal consideration" runs counter to the pioneer conclusion of the Attorney General's Committee on Administrative Procedure that agency heads "cannot, and they should not . . . determine in every instance whether or not action is required.[44] If the department head does shunt more important matters aside in order to consider disclosure requests that present "technical or complex" matters, he will, as a veteran administrator observed in another connection, usually take the staff proposals "on compulsory faith"; "staff recommendations will inevitably be taken as prima facie correct."[45] Certification by the department head that he has "personally" considered the matter must in most cases, therefore, be an empty formality if only because of the relentless pressure of far more important affairs.[46]

An arresting illustration is afforded by the earlier discussed Rogers memorandum. When one considers its numerous internal contradictions,[47] its concatenation of authorities which crumble

44. Report of the Attorney General's Committee on Administrative Procedure, S. Doc. No. 8, 77th Cong., 1st Sess., 18–22 (1941), quoted in Walter Gellhorn and Clark Byse, *Administrative Law: Cases and Comments* 19 (4th ed., Brooklyn, 1960).

45. Warner Gardner, quoted in Gellhorn and Byse, supra, n. 44 at 25, 27.

46. After calling attention to a particularly harsh refusal to exercise the Attorney General's discretion to release a deportable alien on bond because a "very subordinate official . . . (not the Attorney General himself) said that Zydok's [the alien] dossier showed involvement with the Communists" though "there was no disclosed evidence of subversive activities," Gellhorn & Byse, ibid. 819–820, point out that "the Attorney General's judgment is rarely brought to bear on these matters, or, indeed, on any other individual cases in the deportation process." This was confirmed by Justice Black in Jay v. Boyd, 351 U.S. 345, 366 (1956) (dissenting): "The Court concedes . . . that the Attorney General does not personally exercise discretion in these cases. Therefore, the 'unfettered discretion' . . . is the unfettered discretion of inquiry officers."

47. Compare his quotation of the Act of 1789 requiring the Secretary of the Treasury to furnish information to Congress as "may be required" (Rogers memo 47) with his statement that, "Up to now, Congress has not passed such a law"; ibid. 4; his statement that "courts have uniformly held that the President and the heads of departments have an uncontrolled discretion to withhold the information" (ibid.) with his quotation that "the legal problems which are involved were never presented to the courts"; ibid. 62.

Corwin is cited by him as confirming "the soundness of the actions of our Presidents and the decisions of the courts which lodges in the executive branch the power to determine what information to divulge and what to keep secret" (ibid. 43), despite a quotation from Corwin on the same page: "Nevertheless, should a congressional investigating committee issue a subpoena duces tecum to a Cabinet officer ordering him to appear with certain adequately specified documents, and should he fail to do so, I see no reason why he might not be proceeded against for contempt of the house which sponsored the inquiry."

under scrutiny, it is scarcely conceivable that either the Attorney General or even his chief assistants could have studied it.[48] The fact that it was submitted to Congress in its woefully inadequate state over the signature of the Deputy Attorney General, in response to a formal request for a legal opinion on a long-standing controversy between Congress and the President, should make us skeptical of certification by department heads on such lesser issues as the need to withhold information from a litigant in the public interest. Certainly the record of unflagging departmental opposition to disclosure on any and all grounds does not conduce to confidence in executive determinations that information must be withheld.[49] Whether it be "military secrets" or "candid interchange" of opinions, whenever the bureaucracy is "given a blank cheque," it yields, as Professor Wade remarked, "to the temptation to overdraw."[50]

Then too, as Judge Albert Maris stated in the court below, there is no "danger to the public interest in submitting the question of

48. Justice Jackson, concurring in McGrath v. Kristensen, 340 U.S. 162, 176 (1950), rejected a "foggy" opinion, probably rendered by himself as Attorney General, to Secretary of War Stimson, saying that "it would be charitable to assume" that "the *nominal* author of the Opinion [did not] read it"; ibid. 177; emphasis added.

49. For instances, see supra, n. 14.

We may perceive in another context how far administrative obstinacy, even persistence in wrongheadedness can go. In the sequel to United States ex rel Knauff v. Shaughnessy, 338 U.S. 537 (1950) (sustaining bar to admission of foreign wife of American serviceman), the House, "after considering the objections of the Department of Justice," unanimously passed a private bill for Mrs. Knauff's relief. While like action was pending in the Senate, the Immigration officials hastily brought her to Idlewild Airport for passage to Germany, and were halted only twenty minutes before departure by a stay issued by Justice Jackson. He stated that this departmental action was calculated to "defeat any effort" to obtain Supreme Court review of her petition for habeas corpus, and to "circumvent any action by Congress—which the Department has vigorously opposed—to cancel her exclusion"; Gellhorn & Byse, supra, n. 44 at 812–813.

Another illustration of administrative persistence in defiance of Congress is afforded by Heyer Products Co. v. United States, 140 F. Supp. 409, 411, 412 (Ct. Cl. 1956). Heyer had testified before a Senate Committee that an Ordnance Center had made an award to the high bidder though Heyer's bid was $116,730 lower. The Senate Report said that Ordnance had failed to "give convincing explanations" of the rejection of the low bid. Thereafter Heyer bid again, was again the low bidder, and again the same higher bidder was preferred. After investigation, the Senate Committee reported that this "is a shameful story." Judicial review was unavailable because of the "standing to sue" doctrine.

50. H. W. R. Wade, *Administrative Law* 285 (2d ed., Oxford, 1967). For documentation of administrative heel-dragging in the wake of Reynolds, see Paul Hardin, "Executive Privilege in the Federal Courts," 71 Yale L.J. 879, 881–887 (1962). The "executive continues to withhold from court inspection much that could not be classed as military secrets" (ibid. 896); and Professor Hardin states that "Without being unduly cynical, one can surmise that in many of the cases the information is really being withheld in order to gain advantage in the suit or to avoid official embarrassment or simply to avoid troublesome interruption of bureaucratic routine"; ibid. 884.

privilege to the decision of the courts. The judges . . . are public officers whose responsibility under the Constitution is just as great as that of the heads of the executive departments."[51] No branch has enjoyed greater confidence of the American people than the judiciary,[52] and it is singular that there should be any qualms about permitting the courts to weigh any administrative claims for secrecy. In a notable decision, *Conway v. Rimmer* (1968),[53] the House of Lords, sharply restricting overbroad remarks in an earlier case,[54] stressed that the "final responsibility lies" with the court, not the objecting minister.[55] The Lords emphasized that the courts have the power of private inspection (in chambers) "and should clearly use it when necessary";[56] and though aware of *Reynolds'* disclaimer of *in camera* inspection in exceptional circumstances,[57] they went on to cite Justice Scrutton's inspection of documents in *Asiatic Petroleum Co. v. Anglo-Persian Oil Co.*, notwithstanding that the Admiralty had objected that disclosure would be "detrimental to the interests of the State and of possible assistance to the enemy."[58] There is no more reason to look for disinterested administrative judgment in military affairs than in other categories, as to which the House of Lords, with British understatement, said, "the fact that the privilege was sought shows that it is not easy for the department concerned to make an objective appraisal of the matter."[59]

Wigmore justifiably asked, "is it to be said that even this much of disclosure [*in camera*] cannot be trusted? Shall every subordinate in the department have access to the secret, and not the presiding officer of justice?" To leave the final determination in bureaucratic hands, he continues, is to furnish governmental officials "too ample opportunities for abusing the privilege. The lawful limits are extensible beyond any control, if its applicability is

51. Reynolds v. United States, 192 F. 2d 987, 997 (3d Cir. 1951). Judge Maris' views were adopted by the dissenters, Black, Frankfurter and Jackson, JJ., in United States v. Reynolds, 345 U.S. 1, 12 (1953).

52. Madison stated in the Virginia Ratification Convention, "were I to select a power which might be given with confidence, it would be the judicial power"; 3 Elliot 535. For similar statements, see Berger, *Impeachment* 102 n. 232.

53. 1 All E. R. 874. See supra, n. 35 and accompanying text.

54. Duncan v. Cammell Laird & Co. [1942] A.C. 624.

55. 1 All E. R. 906, 898.

56. Ibid. 896, 900, 916.

57. Ibid. 887.

58. Ibid. 899, 907.

59. Ibid. 910; see supra, text accompanying n. 35.

left to the determination of the very official whose interest it may be to shield a wrongdoing under the privilege."[60] That ever-present possibility, so often realized in practice, dictates that courts should not too readily sacrifice the interests of justice in reliance on administrative representations,[61] that they should feel free to inspect the documents *in camera*.

A post-*Reynolds* case that underscores the need for judicial scrutiny of privilege claims for military secrets is *Halpern v. United States*.[62] The statute authorized withholding of a patent if the government believed secrecy was required in the national interest but afforded a right to compensation. In 1941, Halpern revealed to the government a discovery with important military implications whereby "an object may escape observation or detection by radar." His patent was withheld, though deemed otherwise allowable, because as late as 1956 the Commissioner of Patents found secrecy essential. Compensation was denied by the administration, whereupon Halpern filed suit and was met among other things by a plea of privilege for "state secrets." Recovery for the secret he himself had discovered was opposed because the secret had to be preserved! The Second Circuit rejected this claim saying, first, that there could be a trial *in camera*, and, second, that

> the scope of the privilege of the United States with respect to state secrets, like its similar privilege to withhold the identity of confidential informants, "is limited by its underlying purpose . . ." [T]he privilege relating to state secrets is inapplicable when disclosure to court per-

60. 8 Wigmore 799 (Boston, 1940). Not "every subordinate" has access to military secrets, but subordinates undeniably do handle them and consult tiers of superiors. This has received judicial recognition. Matters of "rarest secrecy" must often be duplicated by subordinates and thus become "known to one or more stenographers or file clerks or photographers or other craftsmen, and likely as not to others"; United States v. Certain Parcels of Land, 15 F.R.D. 224, 232 (S.D. Cal. 1954). Obviously the Secretary himself cannot keep all "state secrets" under lock and key. From time to time we learn that subordinates leak such secrets to hostile nations. Moreover, today, "hundreds of thousands of civilians are engaged in secret activities of the greatest military importance, whether at military laboratories such as Fort Monmouth or civilian agencies like the Atomic Energy commission . . . [not to mention the numerous subcontractors] . . ."; Telford Taylor, *Grand Inquest* 107 (New York, 1955). Compare the claim of secrecy made against the House for papers that could be seen in the Senate; supra, Ch. 6, text accompanying nn. 70–71.

61. By objections to inspection *in camera* the ministries were "enabled to suppress the evidence altogether. This is a highly dangerous power, since it enables the executive to deprive a litigant of his legal rights"; Wade, supra, n. 30 at 283.

In Carr v. Monroe Mfg. Co., 431 F. 2d 384, 389 (5th Cir. 1970), the court alluded to the "special danger in the government official having the power to define the scope of his own privilege, free of supervision by the courts."

62. 258 F. 2d 36, 44 (2d Cir. 1958).

sonnel in an *in camera* proceeding will not make the information public or endanger the national security.[63]

Judicial common sense rather than "state secret" fetishism carried the day, and prevented what would have been a gross injustice. No case since *Halpern* has criticized or proceeded in disregard of its holding.[64]

Foreign Affairs Secrets. "Foreign affairs" no more require an absolute privilege than do "military secrets." Wigmore cites *United States v. Burr* for "recognition of privilege" for correspondence which "might have involved international relations with Spain and France,"[65] but in this he is plainly mistaken. At an early stage of the proceeding Chief Justice Marshall, referring to an *answer* to General Wilkinson's letter, said,

> the propriety of requiring the answer to this letter is more questionable. It is alleged that it most probably communicates orders showing the situation of this country with Spain . . . *If* it contain matter *not essential to the defense,* and the disclosure be unpleasant to the executive, it certainly ought not to be disclosed. This is a point which will appear on the return.[66]

No further mention of this letter is made, and from the government attorney's later statement to the court that, "when we receive General Wilkinson's letter, the return will be complete," it may be inferred that this answer was not withheld.[67]

A 1958 case, *Dayton v. Dulles*, did, however, declare that withholding was permissible where "disclosure would adversely affect our internal security or the conduct of our foreign affairs. The cases and common sense hold that the courts cannot compel the Secretary to disclose information garnered by him in confidence

63. Ibid. 44. The court stated that a trial *in camera* should be had if it "can be held without running any serious risk of divulgence of military secrets"; ibid. 45, but it would appear that the court regarded the risk as negligible. "It should not be difficult to obtain a court reporter and other essential court personnel with the necessary security clearance. If necessary, the stenographers who are now writing letters concerning the invention [and often handling and filing the "secrets"] for the Department of the Navy can be utilized to record the testimony"; ibid. 43.

64. Halpern was cited approvingly in Henrik Mannerfried v. Teegarden, 23 F.R.D. 173, 176 (S.D. N.Y. 1959).

65. 8 Wigmore, supra, n. 65 at §2738, p. 785 n. 6, citing United States v. Burr, 25 Fed. Cas. 30 (No. 14692d) (C.C. Va. 1807). But note that Wigmore assumes the necessity for secrecy only "for acts of pending international negotiations or military precautions against foreign enemies," and even here he insists that courts should determine whether secrecy is necessary; 8 Wigmore 789, 799.

66. 25 Fed. Cas. at 37; emphasis added.

67. See supra, Ch. 6, n. 148. Marshall's subsequent opinion was confined to General Wilkinson's letter. 25 Fed. Cas. at 190–193.

in this area."[68] Plaintiff sought a passport to India in order to accept a position as research physicist at the University of Bombay. The Secretary of State denied the passport on the basis of confidential information that plaintiff had been a member of the Rosenberg ring and was going abroad to advance the Communist cause. He stated in the course of the trial that it would be detrimental to internal security and to our foreign relations to disclose the source of his information,[69] thus denying to Dayton a constitutional right on the basis of secret evidence. In affirming the denial, Judge Prettyman relied on *Chicago & Southern Air Lines v. Waterman S.S. Corp.*,[70] which held that an order of the President approving an order of the Civil Aeronautics Board which denied an overseas route was unreviewable. He quoted Justice Jackson's statement that

> The President, both as Commander-in-Chief and as the Nation's organ for foreign affairs, has available intelligence services whose reports are not and ought not to be published to the world. It would be intolerable that the courts, without the relevant information, should review and perhaps nullify actions of the Executive taken on information properly held secret.[71]

Dayton was overruled on the ground that the *statute* did not authorize withholding of a passport on those grounds,[72] from which it follows that the Secretary could not draw on presidential powers over "foreign affairs." Moreover, Prettyman's reliance on Jackson's *Waterman* opinion overlooked Jackson's later expression of abhorrence for the use of "secret evidence" to exclude the alien wife of a citizen.[73] It is difficult to conceive why "foreign relations"

68. 254. F. 2d 71, 77 (D.C. Cir)
69. Ibid. 72–74.
70. 333 U.S. 103, 111 (1948).
71. Quoted 254 F. 2d at 75.
72. Dayton v. Dulles, 357 U.S. 144 (1958), relying on Kent v. Dulles, 357 U.S. 116, 128 (1958): the statute did not give the Secretary "unbridled discretion to grant or withhold a passport from a citizen for any substantive reason he may choose." Later the Court denied that Congress "can grant the Executive totally unrestricted freedom of choice" even in the field of foreign relations; Zemel v. Rusk, 381 U.S. 1, 17 (1965).
73. Supra text accompanying n. 20. It was said in Pan-American World Airways v. CAB, 392 F. 2d 483, 492 (D.C. Cir. 1968), that "though *Waterman* has not been overruled by the Supreme Court, its apparently sweeping contours have been eroded by recent Circuit Court opinions."

Whatever the impact of *Waterman* on evidentiary privilege, a statute requiring disclosure to Congress would stand on a different footing. Justice Jackson himself regarded *Waterman* as an example of "wide definition of presidential powers *under* statutory authorization"; the earlier *Curtiss-Wright*, he said, did not intimate that should enjoy an absolute shield from disclosure to the detriment of a litigant when "military secrets" under the *Reynolds* case do not.[74] This is not to suggest blanket disclosure but rather the exercise of an informed judgment by the court, *in camera* if need be, bearing in mind Jackson's statement with respect to bureaucratic claims that disclosure threatens "national security": "security is like liberty in that many are the crimes committed in its name."[75]

2. *Informers*

The "informer's privilege" is in reality the government's privilege to withhold the identity of informers in order to encourage them to communicate information of law violations to enforcement officers.[76] Attorney General Jackson, it will be recalled, asserted that informers would not reveal if their confidence was not preserved.[77] If their secret charges, however, are to be made the basis of a proceeding to blast the rights of others, fairness demands that their confidence be disclosed.[78] It is a perversion of values to be more solicitous of the faceless informer than of the victims who are crushed by his charges.[79] When Jackson ascended to the bench, he observed:

> The plea that evidence of guilt [for exclusion of immigrants] must be secret is abhorrent to free men, because it provides a cloak for the malevolent, the misinformed, the meddlesome, and the corrupt to play the role of informer undetected or uncorrected.[80]

---

the President "might act contrary to an Act of Congress"; Youngstown Case 343 U.S. 579, 635–636 n. 2 (1952), concurring.

74. In Republic of China v. National Union Fire Ins. Co., 142 F. Supp. 551, 553 (D. Md. 1956), the government refused to "supply any memoranda of certain conversations between the American and British representatives" because it "would be prejudicial to our foreign relations." The court said, "Here, as in the Reynolds case, the necessity for the disclosure of the information requested is dubious and the reason for sustaining the claim of privilege is clear"; ibid. 557.

75. United States ex rel Knauff v. Shaughnessy, 338 U.S. 537, 551 (1951), dissenting opinion, in which Black and Frankfurter, JJ. concurred. See also supra, n. 61.

76. Roviaro v. United States 353 U.S. 53, 60–61 (1957). It had earlier been held that the informer's privilege must give way: "If what is asked is useful evidence to vindicate the innocence of the accused or lessen the risk of false testimony or is essential to the proper disposition of the case, disclosure will be compelled"; Wilson v. United States, 59 F. 2d 390, 392 (3d Cir. 1932).

77. Supra, text accompanying n. 15.

78. Robert B. McKay, "The Right of Confrontation," 1959 Wash. U. L.Q. 122, 146–160. "If the aim is to protect the underground of informers, the FBI report need not be used. If it is used, then fairness requires that the names of the accusers be disclosed"; United States v. Nugent, 346 U.S. 1, 14 (1953); Douglas and Black, JJ. dissenting.

79. McKay, supra, n. 78 at 150.

80. United States ex rel Knauff v. Shaughnessy, 338 U.S. 537, 551 (1950), dissent-

Such procedures are reminiscent of the days when Venice lived in terror of anonymous accusations dropped into the Lion's Mouth.[81] Suspicion of secret information is heightened when one learns from time to time that FBI informants are proven unreliable.[82]

Possibly such considerations led the Supreme Court to declare in *Roviaro v. United States* that "Where the disclosure of an informer's identity, or of the contents of his communication, is relevant and helpful to the defence of an accused, or is essential to a fair determination of a cause, the privilege must give way."[83] It was a *civil* case, *Greene v. McElroy*,[84] which indicated that a hurtful determination based upon secret evidence was unconstitutional. Greene was vice-president of an engineering firm which had a government contract that was the source of almost all of its business. The government revoked his security clearance on the basis of undisclosed confidential information,[85] and the firm was compelled to discharge him or lose the contract. Greene, who had received a salary of $18,000 a year, was reduced to taking a job at

ing opinion, in which Black and Frankfurter, JJ. concurred. See also supra, text accompanying n. 20.

81. Our soil was not thought favorable for transplantation of that practice. In 1802 Congressman Nicholson referred to "Venice, where the vilest wretch was encouraged as a secret informer, and the lion's mouth was ever gaping for accusation"; 11 Annals of Cong. 824 (1802).

82. Justice Frankfurter alluded in his memorandum in Mesarosh v. United States, 352 U.S. 808, 811 (1956), to a "statement by the Government that it 'now has serious reason to doubt' testimony given in other proceedings by Mazzei, one of its specialists on Communist activities." And he stated in Jay v. Boyd, 351 U.S. 345, 373 (1956), that "we can take judicial notice of the fact that in conspicuous instances, not negligible in number, such 'confidential information' has turned out to be either baseless or false. There is no reason to believe that only these conspicuous instances illustrate the hazards inherent in taking action affecting the lives of fellow men on the basis of such information. The probabilities are to the contrary"; dissenting opinion. Dean McKay has furnished citations for still other "indications of unreliability on the part of an appreciable number of regularly employed informants who were apparently regarded by the FBI as 'sources known to be reliable.' " McKay, supra, n. 78 at 152. Alan Barth, *Government by Investigation* 84–90 (New York, 1955).

83. 353 U.S. 53, 60–61. Roviaro adds that, "The problem is one that calls for balancing the public interest in protecting the flow of information against the individual's right to prepare his defense. Whether a proper balance renders nondisclosure erroneous must depend on the particular circumstances of each case, taking into consideration the crime charged, the possible defenses, the possible significance of the informer's testimony, and other relevant factors"; ibid. 62.

Professor Edmund Morgan stated that "If a privilege to suppress the truth is to be recognized at all, its limits should be sharply determined so as to coincide with the limits of the benefits it creates"; foreword to *ALI Model Code of Evidence* 7 (Philadelphia, 1942).

84. 360 U.S. 474 (1959).

85. Greene had been given three security clearances since World War II (ibid. 476); he testified under oath and produced a number of witnesses who testified as to his good character; no evidence to the contrary was introduced; ibid. 478–479.

$4,000, the only one he could find, for the denial of security clearance barred him from numerous plants all over the country. Chief Justice Warren stated:

Certain principles have remained relatively immutable in our jurisprudence. One of these is that where governmental action seriously injures an individual, and the reasonableness of the action depends on fact findings, the evidence used to prove the Government's case must be disclosed to the individual so that he has an opportunity to show that it is untrue . . . We have formalized these protections in the requirements of confrontation and cross examination. They have ancient roots . . . This Court has been zealous to protect these rights from erosion. It has spoken out not only in criminal cases . . . but also in all types of cases where administrative and regulatory actions were under scrutiny.[86]

The informer cases are now legion; and there has been a tendency to restrict disclosure to cases of real need for the informer's evidence, to exclude disclosure of information used for search and seizure warrants and the like.[87] But, if there is no "absolute" right to disclosure of an informer,[88]

The law is clearly established that the [informer's] privilege . . . is a qualified one, not absolute, limited by the underlying purpose of the privilege as balanced against the fundamental requirement of fairness and disclosure in the litigation process.[89]

And, continued the Court of Appeals for the Fifth Circuit, "the balancing of interest test that [Roviaro] established has been applied to civil cases as well."[90] That balancing of course is for the court, not the executive branch.[91]

86. Ibid. 496–497. Goldberg v. Kelly, 397 U.S. 254, 270 (1969) invoked a vital portion of the Greene statement. The "right of confrontation is an essential and fundamental requirement" of a "fair trial"; Pointer v. Texas, 380 U.S. 400, 404–405 (1965).

87. For citations to the cases see *Modern Federal Practice*. "Witnesses" Sec. 216. In United States v. Hurse, 453 F. 2d 128, 131 (8th Cir. 1972), the court sanctioned an *in camera* hearing where the informer led to a search and arrest.

88. McCray v. Illinois, 386 U.S. 300, 310–311 (1967).

89. Hodgson v. Charles Martin Inspectors of Petroleum, 459 F. 2d 303, 305 (5th Cir. 1972); see also Riley v. United States, 411 F. 2d 1146, 1151 (9th Cir. 1969): the informer's "privilege is not absolute."

90. 459 F. 2d at 305.

91. The privilege "must be granted or denied by the trial judge in the exercise of sound judicial discretion"; Riley v. United States, 411 F. 2d 1146, 1151 (9th Cir. 1969).

"Where no significant security interests would be jeopardized by disclosure of sources of adverse information, it is difficult to justify withholding sources of whatever information is relied upon for the administrative decision"; Gonzalez v. Freeman, 334 F. 2d 570, 580 n. 21 (D.C. Cir. 1964).

3. *Confidential Information*

Confidential information may be categorized roughly as that procured by governmental investigation and that turned over on a statutory guarantee of confidential treatment.

Investigation Reports. Investigative reports enjoy "no absolute executive privilege";[92] they "have not ordinarily, without more, supported claims of privilege."[93] No investigation reports have been more respectfully treated than those of the FBI. Yet even FBI reports have been denied judicial shelter;[94] and *Ex parte Sackett* illustrates why the claim of privilege for such reports must be viewed with reserve. *Sackett* was a private suit for damages under the Sherman Act in which it was discovered that the defendant had destroyed certain papers that had been copied by the FBI. The FBI declined to bring forth the papers on the ground that "it was against public policy to produce such documents because they were part of the confidential and official files."[95] The mere transfer of ordinary papers to the FBI, in other words, sanctifies them and puts them beyond the reach of profane hands.[96] Disclosure has been ordered of an investigation report by the Alien Property branch of the Department of Justice,[97] of a naval investigation of a collision,[98] of an Air Force Inspector General's report of a collision,[99] and of confidential appraisal reports.[100] And if FBI operatives testify at a criminal trial, their written reports must be produced.[101]

92. Timken Roller Bearing Co. v. United States, 38 F.R.D. 57, 64 (N.D. Ohio E.D. 1964).

93. Boeing Airplane Co. v. Coggeshall, 280 F. 2d 654, 660–661 (D.C. Cir. 1960). See also FTC v. Bramman, 54 F.R.D. 364, 367 (W.D. Mo. W.D. 1972).

94. Zimmerman v. Poindexter, 74 F. Supp. 933 (D. Hawaii 1947). Here the Army was ready to turn over the files bearing on the plaintiff's imprisonment but the Department of Justice objected to inclusion of FBI reports. See also United States v. Cotton Valley Operators Comm., 9 F.R.D. 719 (W.D. La. 1949), affirmed by an equally divided Court, 339 U.S. 940 (1950).

95. 74 F. 2d 922 (9th Cir. 1935). The refusal to turn over was sustained by virtue of a regulation promulgated under the "housekeeping" statute, a refusal that Congress has since barred. See infra, text accompanying nn. 115–117.

96. See supra, text accompanying nn. 17, 18. With good reason does Professor Hardin say that "it is appalling for persons in public service to permit bureaucratic routine and a petty proprietary attitude toward 'confidential' files to outweigh elementary considerations of justice"; Hardin, supra, n. 50 at 901.

97. Royal Exchange Assur. v. McGrath, 13 F.R.D. 150 (S.D. N.Y. 1952).

98. Bank Line, Ltd. v. United States, 76 F. Supp. 801 (S.D. N.Y. 1948).

99. Eastern Airlines v. United States, 110 F. Supp. 491 (D. Del. 1952).

100. United States v. Certain Parcels of Land, 15 F.R.D. 224 (S.D. Cal. 1954).

101. Jencks v. United States, 353 U.S. 657 (1957). The subsequent Jencks Act restricts disclosure to "statements" as there defined, but as Justice Brennan, Chief

It would take us far afield to explore the variant problems that have been thrown up in this field; for present purposes it suffices that investigative reports do not enjoy an absolute privilege, that it is for the courts to say whether disclosure must be made.

Statutory Assurances of Confidential Treatment. To encourage disclosure of private data for administrative purposes[102] certain statutes provide for confidential treatment, for example, for income tax returns, trade secrets, and patent applications.[103] Often these are not airtight assurances: the income tax statute provides for inspection upon the order of the President under regulations of the Secretary of the Treasury; the Patent Act makes patent applications available in "such special circumstances as may be determined by the Commissioner" of Patents. There might be no occasion to examine such statutes in the frame of disclosure to Congress, for it can expressly provide for inspection by its committees, as it has in the case of income tax returns,[104] but for an incident involving a comparable statute upon which President Theodore Roosevelt relied in withholding information from Congress in 1909.

The Senate had by resolution directed the Attorney General to inform the Senate whether he had brought suit against the United States Steel Corporation on account of its absorption of Tennessee Valley Coal and Iron Company, if not, to state why not, and to furnish any legal opinion he had rendered. Roosevelt informed the Senate that the Attorney General orally advised him there were insufficient grounds for suit, accompanying it with details of an interview between the President and Judge Gary and Henry Frick, the heads of United States Steel Corporation (in itself a titillating tidbit), and that he had instructed the Attorney General to make no explanation to the Senate of his reasons for non-action.[105] Such an acquisition by the giant of the steel industry patently raised a question whether it was in violation of the Anti-trust law, a question in which the lawmaker had a legitimate

---

Justice Warren, Justices Black and Douglas concurring, stated: "Congress took particular pains to make it clear that the legislation 'reaffirms' that [Jencks] decision's holding"; Palermo v. United States, 360 U.S. 343, 361 (1959).

102. 8 Wigmore 761.

103. Income tax: 68A Stat. 753, 26 U.S.C. §6103 (1954); trade secrets: 38 Stat. 717 (1914), 15 U.S.C. §46(f) (1958); patent applications: 35 U.S.C. §122 (1958).

104. Int. Rev. Code of 1954 §6103(d).

105. Rogers memo 16–17.

interest. Legislative inquiry into execution of the laws, we have seen, was an established parliamentary practice; it had been recognized by Montesquieu; it was implicit in the duty imposed upon the President by the Constitution to "take care that the Laws be faithfully executed," a duty which ran directly to the lawmaker. This is now beyond dispute since the Supreme Court, in the wake of the Teapot Dome investigations, held that "the administration of the Department of Justice . . . and particularly whether the Attorney General and his assistants were performing or neglecting their duties" was within the jurisdiction of Congress.[106] Roosevelt was therefore arrogating to himself a power to deny to Congress the right to exercise an established legislative attribute.

But it was the next step which brings the incident into the frame of confidential treatment. Balked in the attempt to obtain the information from the Attorney General, the Senate Judiciary Committee summoned the head of the Bureau of Corporations to appear with the documents in the case. Again Roosevelt intervened, and in a private explanation stated: "Some of these facts . . . were given to the Government under the seal of secrecy and cannot be divulged, and I will see to it that the word of this Government to the individual is kept sacred."[107] Thus, Roosevelt cast himself in the role of protector of the individual against Congress, a role that was not given to him but to the courts. On his theory, promises of confidential treatment to "informers" should be equally "sacred," yet that is not the case.

Apparently Roosevelt relied on the Act of 1903 which made the President "responsible for making public so much of the [corporations] information collected for him as he (the President) sees fit."[108] To the mind of Attorney General Rogers, the Senate therefore sought records, "which by express provision of law the President had the right not to make public."[109] Congress, however, scarcely intended to curtail its own established right of inquiry by its authorization to withhold information from the public.[110]

106. McGrain v. Daugherty, 273 U.S. 135, 177 (1927).
107. Rogers memo 17.
108. Ibid. 49, 18.
109. Ibid. 49.
110. Compare the English rule that "statutes do not bind the Crown in the absence of express provision or necessary implication"; Wade, supra, n. 30 at 269—still less the Parliament.

A number of courts have held that statutes restricting the use of confidential information do not deprive the courts of access for purposes of administering justice.[111] As one said on the issue of "secrecy": "we are confident that it will as wholeheartedly be respected and as sedulously preserved by the juvenile court as it will be by the officers of the welfare department."[112] Here, as in the case of "informers," who likewise rely on nondisclosure of their identity, there is need for "balancing the public interest in protecting the flow of information against the individual's right to prepare his defense."[113] Statutory assurances which cannot bar the courts lest they impede the administration of justice, and which are designed by the legislature merely to safeguard against prying by members of the public, need not be contrued to deny access to the legislature. And there is no more necessity to read into statutes which expressly bar production in the courts[114] a congressional intention to bar its own access.

4. *The "Housekeeping" Privilege*

Insofar as the "housekeeping privilege rested on the statute which authorized department heads to make regulations for the custody and use of departmental papers and records,[115] it has been decently interred by a 1958 amendment which provides that that statute "does not authorize withholding from the public."[116] The statute "cannot be construed to establish authority in the executive departments to determine whether certain papers and records are privileged . . . It cannot bar a judicial determination of the question of privilege or a demand for the production of evidence found not to be privileged."[117]

111. Boeing Airplane Co. v. Coggeshall, 280 F. 2d 654, 662 (D.C. Cir. 1960) ("The secrecy imposed by statute on these documents does not provide immunity from subpoena duces tecum). Bell v. Banker's Life & Cas. Co., 327 Ill. App. 321, 64 N.E. 2d 204 (1945). Cf. Blair v. Oesterlein Mach. Co., 275 U.S. 220, 227 (1927); Maryland Cas. Co. v. Clintwood Bank, Inc. 155 Va. 181, 193, 154 S.E. 492, 496 (1930); State v. Church, 35 Wash. 2d 170, 175, 211 P. 2d 701, 703–704 (1949) (even though use in a criminal prosecution would make the information public); State ex rel Haugland v. Smythe, 25 Wash. 2d 161, 168–169, 169 P. 2d 706, 710 (1946).

112. Haugland v. Smythe, supra, n. 111 at 169; see supra, text accompanying nn. 51–52, 60.

113. See supra, n. 83.

114. For illustrations see 8 Wigmore 770–773 (Boston, 1940).

115. 5 U.S.C. §22 (1965).

116. 72 Stat. 547 (1958), 5 U.S.C. §22 (1965).

117. NLRB v. Capitol Fish Co., 294 F. 2d 868, 875 (5th Cir. 1961); United States v. Certain Parcels of Land, 15 F.R.D. 224, 230 (S.D. Cal. 1954); Bank Line v. United States, 76 F. Supp. 801 (S.D. N.Y. 1948).

5. *Intradepartmental "Candid Interchange"*

The claim that communications between members of the executive branch must be sheltered from discovery in private litigation so that they may be completely candid in advising with each other on official matters is not deeply rooted in the law. In England "candid interchange" at a high official level obtained recognition in 1841 in *Smith v. East India Co.*;[118] and in 1942 it was given sweeping extension in *Duncan v. Cammel, Laird & Co.*, which made the ministerial judgment not to disclose conclusive.[119] Thereby "free reign was given to the tendency to secrecy which is inherent in the public service,"[120] with the not surprising result that the privilege was abused. Privilege for "candid interchange" would be claimed, in the words of Lord Radcliffe, for "everything however commonplace that has passed between one civil servant and another."[121] A rising tide of dissatisfaction finally led the House of Lords to repudiate the privilege in *Conway v. Rimmer* (1968),[122] where the Lords "shattered" the "candid interchange" argument "without mercy."[123] Lord Hodson stated that it is "impossible to justify the maintenance of the doctrine laid down" in *East India* "in its widest form."[124] One Lord after another rejected the contention that the possibility of future disclosure would affect candor.[125] It cannot be too readily assumed, therefore, as Circuit Judge Wilkey did, that the candor doctrine is rooted in "common sense."[126]

118. 1 Phill. 50, 55, 41 E.R. 550, 552 (1842).

119. 1 All E.R. 587 (1942). For searching criticism of the undesirable consequences of this rule, see H. W. R. Wade, *Administrative Law* 240–248 (1st ed., Oxford, 1961). "English experience," states Wade, "has shown the truth of the United States Supreme Court's statement that 'a complete abandonment of judicial control would lead to intolerable abuses.'" Wade, supra, n. 30 at 283–284, citing United States v. Reynolds, 345 U.S. 1 (1953).

120. Wade, supra, n. 30 at 285.

121. Glasgow Corp. v. Central Land Board [1956] Scots Law Times 41.

122. 1 All E.R. [1968] 874.

123. H. W. R. Wade, "Crown Privilege Controlled At Last," 84 L. Q.R. 171, 172 (1968). Wade remarks that this achievement "can fairly be said to be the culmination of a widespread movement of legal opinion"; ibid. 173.

124. 1 All E.R. at 904.

125. Lord Morris, ibid. 891. Said Lord Hodson, "It is strange if civil servants alone are supposed to be unable to be candid in their statements made in the course of duty without the protection of an absolute privilege denied other fellow subjects"; ibid. 904. "There are countless teachers at schools and universities," said Lord Pearce, "countless employers of labour, who write candid reports, unworried by the outside chance of disclosure"; ibid. 912. See also Lord Upjohn, ibid. 915.

126. Soucie v. David, 448 F. 2d 1067, 1080 (D.C. Cir. 1971), concurring.

American cases were few;[127] and when Wigmore came to sum up, he stated that the scope of the privilege beyond secrets "in the military or international sense is by no means clearly defined; and furthermore, that it has not become a matter of precedent or even of debate in more than a few jurisdictions"; and that "ordinarily there are [not] any matters of fact, in the possession of officials, concerning *solely the internal affairs of public business*, civil or military, which ought to be privileged from disclosure."[128] The doctrine first achieved prominence in private litigation through an opinion by Justice Reed, sitting by designation, in *Kaiser Aluminum & Chemical Corp. v. United States*.[129] The documents sought were opinions rendered by staff members concerning a proposed sale of aluminum plants. Although the court relied on the "policy of open, frank discussion between subordinate and chief concerning administrative action," it assimilated the request for discovery to an attempt "to probe the mental processes of the administrator in reaching his conclusion," —a debatable analogy—and set to one side the disclosure of "primary facts upon which conclusions are based." Reed reaffirmed that "The power must lie in the courts to determine executive privilege in litigation, and went on to say that the privilege for intradepartmental advice would very rarely have the importance of diplomacy or security. It does not have in this case." The court, however, declined to examine the document because the record did not show the need.[130] The holding, therefore, was confined to opinions which were thought a part of the decisional process, excluding "primary facts upon which conclusions are based." Since then it has been held that there is "no absolute executive privilege from disclosure of administrative reports and internal communications."[131] Instead, the prevailing opinion in this area is that "It is for the Court, and not the governmental agency or executive branch, to determine whether documents

127. E.g. United States v. Six Lots of Ground, 27 Fed. Cas. 1097 (No. 16, 299) (C.C. La. 1872), 234, 236 (correspondence between the attorney general and district attorney as to dismissing a writ of error, held confidential).

128. 8 Wigmore on Evidence, 788–789 (Boston, 1940); emphasis added.

129. 157 F. Supp. 939, 946 (Ct.Cl. 1958).

130. Ibid. 946, 947. For further discussion, infra, Epilogue at nn. 30–48.

131. Timken Roller Bearing Co. v. United States, 38 F.R.D. 57, 64 (N.D. Ohio E.D. 1964); see also Rosee v. Board of Trade, 36 F.R.D. 684, 689 (N.D. Ill. E.D. 1965).

sought to be withheld under a claim of privilege are entitled to protection of that privilege."[132]

Across the entire spectrum of privilege, in fine, "the policy of American courts . . . [is] to weigh, independently of the evaluation of an executive officer, the need for any asserted governmental privilege."[133] "No official or agency," said the Court of Appeals for the District of Columbia, "can be given absolute authority to determine what documents in his possession may be considered by the court in its task."[134]

132. Sperandeo v. Milk Drivers & Dairy Employees Local, 334 F. 2d 381, 384 (10th Cir. 1964).

133. Carr v. Monroe Mfg. Co., 431 F. 2d 384, 388 (5th Cir. 1970).

134. Committee for Nuclear Responsibility v. Seaborg, 463 F. 2d 788, 794 (D.C. Cir. 1971).

8

WITHHOLDING INTRADEPARTMENTAL COMMUNICATIONS FROM CONGRESS

A. *The "Candid Interchange" Doctrine*

While the courts were shrinking the scope of executive privilege in private litigation, the executive branch began staking out its boldest claim to withhold information from Congress, for the first time articulating the "principle" that communications and conversations between employees of the executive branch must be withheld from Congress so that they may "be completely candid in advising with each other." This sweeping claim had its origin in a 1954 directive by President Eisenhower[1] in the midst of the Senate probe of Senator Joseph McCarthy's charges against the Army, and is therefore of quite recent vintage. It need hardly be said that it is altogether without historical foundation. Though the worm was long in turning, though Eisenhower's belated recoil from McCarthy's mounting effrontery is understandable,[2] our distaste for McCarthyism should not lead us too quickly to conclude that what was bad for McCarthy necessarily is good for the country.

Under the chairmanship of Senator John L. McClellan, the Senate Committee was conducting hearings into the McCarthy-Army imbroglio; the Army alleged that McCarthy and his chief counsel, Roy Cohn, had improperly used the power of his subcommittee to obtain preferential treatment for Cohn's pal, Private G. David Schine, and that McCarthy and Cohn "had launched a vindictive probe of the Army security programs in reprisal against those who had not cooperated to grant special treatment to Private Schine." Senator McCarthy countercharged that the

1. The directive is reprinted in 100 Cong. Rec. 6621, and in Mollenhoff 45–46, a thoroughgoing account of the growth of the "candid interchange" doctrine during the Eisenhower years.

2. For details see Alan Barth, *Government by Investigation* 48–66 (New York, 1955); Telford Taylor, *Grand Inquest* 87, 112–135, 266–269 (New York, 1955).

Army attempted to "blackmail his investigating committee into dropping its investigation of the Army loyalty-security set-up by threatening to circulate an embarrassing report about Cohn and Schine."[3] Nationally televised, the hearings brought into sharp focus the bullying, brutal tactics of McCarthy and "completely destroyed his public image."[4]

The Eisenhower directive was engendered by McCarthy's attempt to elicit from Defense Department Deputy General Counsel John Adams details as to a meeting which had taken place at the Department of Justice with Attorney General Herbert Brownell, Deputy Attorney General William P. Rogers, Presidential Assistant Sherman Adams, and other high officials to discuss means of halting the McCarthy investigation. Adams testified that he was present at the meeting, but later refused under "instructions" to recount the conversation.[5] If the subject of the meeting is accurately stated, the discussion was of more serious import than McCarthy suspected. Executive scheming to interfere with the course of a parliamentary investigation would in all likelihood have been viewed as an impeachable encroachment on the prerogatives of Parliament; and such offenders were dealt with harshly.[6] It was to meet this situation that Eisenhower issued his directive, garbed in the separation of powers,[7] and accompanied by an Attorney General's memorandum[8] which was a resumé of the "precedents" and arguments later embodied in the Rogers memorandum.

Assume that the strategy meeting was properly shielded, the high-level conversations resemble the "secrets of the cabinet"[9] which might deserve shelter on practical grounds, hardly to be extended to communications between millions of subordinates. The evil spawned by the directive was precisely this extension of concealment to the lower tiers of the bureaucracy, often invoked for sheer trivialities or to block exposure of administrative neglect or corruption, thus fulfilling Telford Taylor's early prophecy that congressional committees would "frequently be shut off from access to documents to which they are clearly entitled by tradi-

3. Mollenhoff 42–43.
4. Ibid. 48.
5. Ibid. 41–42.
6. Berger, *Impeachment* 70.
7. Mollenhoff 45–46.
8. Ibid. 211–221.
9. Supra, Ch. 7, text accompanying n. 25.

tion, common sense and good governmental practice,"[10] let alone by the plenary scope of parliamentary investigation in which the congressional inquiry power is rooted.

It was not long in dawning on harried administrators that here was a beautiful, fresh invitation to withholding, as was unwittingly disclosed by Acting Director Saccio of the International Cooperation Administration: "*if ICA wanted to apply the 'executive privilege' GAO* [General Accounting Office, the watch-dog of Congress] *would not see one thing* because practically every document in our agency has an opinion or a piece of advice."[11] The Department of Agriculture sought to withhold "initialed file copies of an amendment" because "they related solely to its internal operations,"[12] thus expanding Saccio's evaluation to the affixing of an initial. So too, Agriculture refused to submit a Farm Population Estimate which had been withdrawn from distribution and destroyed.[13] Even privilege proponents labeled this a "trivial matter," an "awkward recourse to the Executive privilege."[14] What had once been exceptional soon hardened, in the words of a friend of the privilege, Senator Wayne Morse, into a "uniform practice," a "blanket policy."[15] So, the Department of the Interior advised a House Committee that, while the sought-for documents "did not contain any information which the Department would be unwilling to make available to Congress, it, nevertheless, considered itself bound to 'honor the principle which had been followed from the beginning of our Government.' "[16] Thus, a claim born of desperation in 1954 had ripened by 1956 into a time-honored "principle," which like the Juggernaut rode over a request for information that confessedly there was no reason to withhold.[16a]

10. Taylor, supra, n. 2 at 133.
11. Kramer & Marcuse 852. See supra, Ch. 7, n. 39.
12. Kramer & Marcuse 658–659.
13. Ibid. 877.
14. Ibid. 911.
15. Ibid. 851–852. A number of withholdings of intradepartmental communications will be found in ibid. 647–648, 654–656, 658, 660, 664, 667, 842.
16. Ibid. 660.
16a. "The Eisenhower directive ushered in the greatest orgy of executive denial in American history. From June 1955 to June 1960 there were at least 44 instances when officials in the executive branch refused information to Congress on the basis of the Eisenhower directive—more cases in those five years than in the first century of American history . . . What had been for a century and a half sporadic executive practice employed in very unusual circumstances was now in a brief decade hypostatized into sacred constitutional principle"; Arthur M. Schlesinger, Jr., *The Imperial Presidency* 158–159 (Boston, 1973).

Recurring charges of mismanagement, which more than once have proven too true, underscore the need for full inquiry, "interdepartmental candor" notwithstanding. There was the incident of the rejection of a low bid on a projected grain elevator in Pakistan and negotiation of a contract with a company which had submitted a bid nearly $1,000,000 higher under dubious circumstances. At the end of the hearings, which resembled nothing so much as an administrative obstacle course, the Director of Foreign Operations Administration told the committee that all proposals had been canceled, that a new contract could be awarded upon open bidding, and that certain parties would be ineligible to bid to avoid conflicts of interest.[17] Of this, a former Assistant Attorney General said that "The FOA Grain Storage Elevator in Pakistan incident shows how embarrassing and damaging it may become to the concept of the Executive privilege, if a congressional investigation, originally strongly resisted by an agency, proves to have been justified."[18] More important, the incident shows that if the executive may censor what Congress may see, it can arrest a badly needed investigation. There is yet another cost: inevitably the suspicion arises, as Senator J. W. Fulbright remarked on another occasion, that the invocation of executive privilege may constitute "a cover up for a mistake rather than a means of protecting crucial intelligence."[19] Proponents of privilege observed that, while "the interests to be protected by the withholding of information may be important; still they may be outbalanced by the suspicions and adverse inferences which follow the claim of privilege."[20]

How richly such suspicions can be justified is illustrated by the Dixon-Yates case, where the claim of privilege for interdepartmental communications sought to conceal maladministration

17. Kramer & Marcuse 828–829, 838.

18. Ibid. 911. In an investigation of the Laos foreign aid program it developed that several officials had conflicts of interest, that a government employee had accepted bribes, that others had "questionable dealings"; the Subcommittee concluded that "ICA failed to investigate diligently charges of impropriety and failed to take significant remedial action even after reliable evidence was obtained"; ibid. 850. For additional details see Mollenhoff 154–159.

19. Kramer & Marcuse 910–911. On another occasion a similar inference was drawn by Representative Fountain, ibid. 878; and after considerable pressure the Department of Agriculture turned over the information rather than suggest the possibility that it was "damaging to the Department"; ibid. 880. "When the charge was made that certain withheld documents were damaging to him, [President] Jackson immediately ordered them revealed"; Younger, supra, Ch. 7, n. 6 at 775. See infra, n. 34.

20. Kramer & Marcuse 910.

that cried out for airing. The case arose out of the contract between the Atomic Energy Commission and the Mississippi Valley Generating Company for the construction of a power plant and the sale of electric power to the United States.[21] It was entered into at the request of President Eisenhower,[22] who avowedly desired to revise the government's approach to the public power program and to encourage private power development.[23] Adolphe H. Wenzell, an officer of First Boston, which was interested in financing the project, had prepared certain financial studies in connection with the contract while he was employed in the Bureau of the Budget.[24] The Supreme Court later stated that he was "the real architect of the final contract," and that in numerous instances he "seemed to be more preoccupied with advancing the position of First Boston or the sponsors than with representing the best interests of the Government."[25] The Kefauver Senate Committee undertook an investigation of this transaction, whereupon President Eisenhower declared that it was "open to the public."[26] Although the President had "waived" his directive in this case so that "every pertinent paper or document could be made available to the Committee," Mr. R. J. Hughes, Director of the Budget, who had denied that Wenzell had played a dual role in the contract, declined to furnish a report made by Wenzell as adviser to the Bureau of the Budget, on the ground that it was a "confidential document."[27] Only when Eisenhower, prodded at a press conference, declared that if Wenzell had "brought in a definite recommendation," he would be "very delighted to make that public," did the Budget Director yield.[28]

Some ugly facets of executive handling of the matter emerged. On instructions from the Bureau of the Budget, the Atomic Energy Commission had deleted the name of Wenzell from a release that purported to be a full chronology of events in the development of the contract.[29] Sherman Adams, the Assistant to the President, asked the chairman of the Securities and Exchange Commission, sub rosa, to postpone hearings on the financing of the contract

21. Ibid. 689–690.
22. Ibid. 713.
23. United States v. Mississippi Valley Generating Co., 364 U.S. 520, 526 (1961).
24. Ibid. 523–524; Kramer & Marcuse 690.
25. 364 U.S. at 552, 558.
26. Kramer & Marcuse 690–691.
27. Ibid. 691; Mollenhoff 64, 66.
28. Kramer & Marcuse 692.
29. Mollenhoff 64, 73.

until the House completed action on a tie-in appropriation of $6,500,000, presumably because Wenzell was to be a witness before the SEC and disclosure of his role "could have had a devastating impact on the appropriation."[30] Throughout, as Clark Mollenhoff has tellingly shown, Eisenhower exhibited a lamentable unawareness of the scandal his subordinates sought to sweep under the rug.[31] Can it be maintained that protection for such "candid interchange" is of greater public benefit than plenary congressional investigation which exposed the maladministration over persistent executive heel-dragging and deception?[32] Rather, the knowledge that every such recommendation or communication will be open to scrutiny serves as an excellent deterrent to chicanery.

Another example, drawn from the last days of the Eisenhower administration and the inception of that of Kennedy, is the withholding by the International Cooperation Administration of records respecting the administration of foreign aid in Peru. After Chairman Porter Hardy's House subcommittee had obtained information from outside sources that there was mismanagement and corruption in that program, he asked ICA for all documents. Eisenhower ordered that they be withheld, and subsequently directed the Secretary of the Treasury to ignore a statutory cut-off of funds which was invoked by Hardy, on the ground that the statute was an unconstitutional encroachment on his prerogative.[33]

This was the posture of affairs when President Kennedy took office. Although he was publicly committed to full disclosure to Congress and the people,[34] such is the bureaucratic infatuation with secrecy that the State Department obstinately persisted in

30. Ibid. 65, 70–72. President Eisenhower is not, of course, to be charged with knowing concealment of scandals in his administration; rather his trust was abused by his subordinates; though it can hardly be gainsaid that he was bumbling throughout, making no attempt to come to grip with the facts and charges that were constantly being aired in the newspapers and brought directly to his attention by a lively press corps. Mollenhoff 67–68, 158–164. Responsibility in this, the highest quarter, cannot therefore be counted on to cleanse the Augean stable.

31. Ibid. 68–70, 73–74. For similar obliviousness in the face of searching criticism of the Laos scandal, see ibid. 158–159, 162–164.

32. See supra, Ch. 7, n. 14.

33. Mollenhoff 172–173, 234–235.

34. Ibid. 178, 186. A behind-the-scenes glimpse was furnished by Lee White, then special counsel to President Kennedy. Kennedy saw that this was not a matter of intrinsic importance and that it raised a "presumption that the administration was trying to conceal wrong-doing [that] was very nearly irresistible," and therefore ordered a turn-over of the required information; 1 Moorhead Hearings 46–47. See supra, n. 19.

the Eisenhower course and instructed subordinates not to answer.[35] Hardy then revealed malodorous details of incompetence, conflicts of interest, laxity, and illegal diversion of funds;[36] whereupon Kennedy intervened and directed that the information be furnished to Congress.[37] These were the documents, the release of which Attorney General Rogers had said "would gravely impair the proper functioning and administration of the executive branch of the Government."[38] Kennedy sharply limited resort to executive privilege,[39] an example followed by President Johnson.[40] The fact that during those eight years executive towers did not topple, that prophecies of doom were not realized,[41] goes far to riddle the claim that blanket protection of "candid interchange" is an indispensable condition of good government. That administration is not really threatened by disclosure to Congress is further shown by the testimony of Robert E. Keller, Deputy Comptroller General, that though some agencies resist the turnover of "candid interchange" to GAO, "there are certain agencies where anything in the department is open to us, whether it is an evaluation report, a source selection, a board report, an internal staff-memo, or some other document."[42]

In fact, Eisenhower's claim that "candid interchange" among subordinates is indispensable to good government is an untested assumption. It is disproved by the fact that our nation flourished and prospered from 1789 to 1954 without benefit of an iron curtain for "candid interchanges," that the Peru foreign-aid documents withheld by Eisenhower because disclosure allegedly "would gravely impair" administration were released by Kennedy without untoward result.[43] And it is again disproved by the practice of some agencies to turn over internal reports and memoranda

35. Mollenhoff 178, 183.
36. Ibid. 184, 187–189.
37. Ibid. 185–186.
38. Ibid. 186.
39. See Study by Library of Congress, infra, App. A, summarized in relevant part, infra, n. 107.
40. Ervin Hearings 34, 35, infra, App. A. During Kennedy's first year, the claim of privilege was not used at all; ibid. 34.
41. Kramer & Marcuse 906, had opined that free congressional inspection of executive documents would cause the executive branch to "disappear from our polity leaving in its place another unfortunate example of government by legislators." See also Younger, supra, Ch. 7, n. 6 at 771.
42. Ervin Hearings 309, 310–314; see also 8 Moorhead Hearings 3081. If matters of national security present different problems, that still does not warrant the claim for blanket concealment of *all* internal communications.
43. Supra, text accompanying nn. 33–38.

to GAO. Indeed, the former Legal Counsel to the Department of Justice points to the "vast outpouring of data, reports, letters . . . which flow from the executive to Congress,"[44] practically all of which, Acting Director Saccio of ICA stated with respect to ICA, have "an opinion or piece of advice."[45]

In England, Professor Wade pointed out that

> In private life candid reports have to be made by many professional men . . . yet they do not shrink from giving honest opinions because there is a distant chance that their report may one day have to be disclosed. Lord Radcliffe said in the House of Lords: "I should myself have supposed Crown servants to be made of sterner stuff."[46]

That view was repeatedly reiterated in the House of Lords in *Conway v. Rimmer* (1968).[47] A former special counsel to Presidents Kennedy and Johnson, Lee White, and later Chairman of the Federal Power Commission, stated: "just about anyone who reduces any thoughts to writing today recognizes the inherent danger that it will be reproduced. I take it that this is a fact of life that we are prepared to adapt to and accept."[48]

It has been urged that employees "must be free to disagree with their superiors without being subject to later hearings as to whether they were right or whether they were wrong."[49] The subordinate who was "right" will not complain of disclosure, for that only vindicates his judgment. Frequently it is healthy to disclose that the chief ignored the sound advice of a subordinate who, for example, better resisted "influence" than a politically oriented chief. Often too, subordinates who differ with their superiors are eager to voice their differences.[50] A striking illustra-

44. N.Y. Times, Mar. 23, 1973, p. 35.

45. Supra, text accompanying n. 11.

46. H. W. R. Wade, *Administrative Law* 246 (1st ed., Oxford, 1961), citing Glasgow Corp. v. Central Land Board [1956] Scots Law Times 41.

47. 1 All E.R. [1968] 874. Lord Morris regarded the suggestion that "future candour" would be affected as "of doubtful validity. Would the knowledge that there was a remote chance of possible enforced production really affect candour?"; ibid. 891. Lord Upjohn could not justify the "candour" privilege "when those in other walks of life which give rise to equally important matters of confidence in relation to security and personnel matters as in the public service can claim no such privilege"; ibid. 915. See also supra, Ch. 7, n. 125. Consider the embarrassing communications that are disclosed in antitrust cases, or in the "cloaking" cases under the Trading with the Enemy Act.

48. 1 Moorhead Hearings 49.

49. Kramer & Marcuse 887, quoting Assistant Attorney General Hansen.

50. When the Department of Justice waived the "candid interchange" rule, a former attorney of the Antitrust Division testified that "he was critical of the proposed settlement of the *A.T.&T.* case, and that he refused to sign the proposal consent decree"; Kramer & Marcuse 889 n. 746. The interest of Congress in the execution of

tion is furnished by testimony of sundry generals and admirals before a Senate investigation of why a $6,500,000,000 contract for the "TFX experimental plane" was awarded to General Dynamics Corporation rather than to Boeing Company. As recounted by Clark Mollenhoff, the decision was strongly influenced by political considerations; it ran against the almost unanimous disapproval of the Services. A Report by the Senate Committee on Government Operations—dominated by Democrats and criticizing a Democratic administration—stated that the methods whereby Secretary of Defense Robert McNamara arrived at his decision were "capricious, lacking in depth, and without factual substantiation."[51] A number of "subordinates" appeared before the Committee in opposition to the Secretary, and before long one head, that of Admiral George W. Anderson, Chief of Naval Operations, rolled.[52] The aftermath fulfilled the most gloomy predictions; and it underscores how unreasonable it is to ask Congress to appropriate such astronomical sums without being apprised of conflicting views of departmental experts.

In 1972, Ernest Fitzgerald revealed a two-billion-dollar cost overrun on the Lockheed Aircraft Corporation's C-5a transport plane contract, and was cashiered for his pains.[53] Not long after, Gordon Rule, the civilian director of procurement control of the Navy Materiel Command, testified that "Grumman won the F-4 contract by cutting its bid by $500-million, pretty much the amount it now wants if it is to continue building the airplane." Rule also stated that "the Navy was 'sold a bill of goods' when it contracted with Litton to build helicopter assault ships of $133-

---

the antitrust laws surely justifies inquiry into what ingredients entered into a consent decree with one of the most important of the antitrust defendants.

51. Clark Mollenhoff, *The Pentagon* 402, 385–402 (New York, 1972). For the confirmatory appraisal by the GAO, see ibid. 399–400.

52. N.Y. Times, May 7, 1963, p. 1 (Western ed.). The N.Y. Times, Oct. 19, 1973, p. 13, reports that "In another round of running debate about whether the natural gas industry understates its revenues, two Federal Power Commission economists challenged before Congress today the reliability of statistics compiled by their own agency." John Wilson, Chief of Economic Studies, told a Senate hearing that FPC figures on gas reserves not under sales contract were 'grossly inadequate.' " In view of repeated charges that "fixing" in the highest quarters has been prevalent during the Nixon administration, it may be healthy and desirable that the facts be permitted to emerge from the mouths of nonpolitical subordinates.

Hanson Baldwin, noted military analyst, wrote that "Objections or dissent, even to Congress are discouraged, muted or, when possible, stifled"; quoted in Mollenhoff, supra, n. 51 at 390. Compare the cases of Ernest Fitzgerald and Gordon Rule in 1973, infra, text accompanying nn. 53, 54.

53. N.Y. Times, March 1, 1973, p. 73.

million per copy, with Litton now demanding $294-million each." He was banished to a bureaucratic Siberia.[54] Of course it is most comforting to a department head to present to the world a picture of unruffled unanimity, even at the cost of stifling dissent. And loyalty to the chief is a bureaucratic axiom. But loyalty to the nation must rise higher, as Sir Charles Trevelyan demonstrated when, at the outset of his career in India, he exposed the corruption of his chief.[55] Only unreasoning devotion to the "old school tie" tradition can condemn the official who tells Congress of very serious deficiencies in his department. True, the official may be mistaken; but the important thing is to keep the channels of communication open against the chance that his may be the voice of wisdom. As to the subordinate who was "wrong," a commentator who was then in government service said, "it is self-evident that the hapless Department head who is criticized for a bad decision will use his authority to rid himself of the advisor who gave incompetent advice."[56] If this be so, the basis of "candid interchange"—the protection of the subordinate's freedom to speak candidly—goes down the drain.

Against the debatable assumption that fear of disclosure to Congress may inhibit "candid interchange" and seriously impair administration, there is the proven fact that such exchanges have time and again served as the vehicle of corruption and maladministration so that, to borrow from Lord Morris, "a greater measure of prejudice to the public interest would result from their non-production."[57] If we elevate the "candid interchange" claims to the status of respectable policy, there are weighty countervailing policy considerations which heavily tip the scales, and which an era given to "balancing" competing considerations may not ignore.

"Once it has been ascertained that a responsible official . . . has made a mistake," it has been asked, why should Congress seek to determine "whether the mistake . . . was caused by faulty

54. Wall Street Journal, Jan. 10, 1973, p. 14; N.Y. Times, Jan. 21, 1973, sec. 4, p. 16. "Four Army sergeants who organized a ring that systematically defrauded non-commissioned officers clubs in Vietnam told Senate investigators today that the Army was incapable of uncovering such wrong-doing by itself." Sergeant W. O. Wooldridge told the Senate Committee that " 'command influence' was so pervasive that it was 'quite often exerted to hush up investigation' "; N.Y. Times, May 9, 1973, p. 18.

55. John Clive, *Macaulay* 318 (New York, 1973).

56. Conrad O. Philos, "The Public's Right to Know and the Public Interest—A Dilemma Revisited," 19 Fed. B.J. 41, 54 (1959).

57. 1 All E.R. at 901. See Mollenhoff 50.

internal advice?"[58] Often the "mistake" emerges only when we learn of the "internal advice"; for example, in *Dixon-Yates* the mistake came to the surface only when Congress uncovered the conflicting interests of Wenzell, the key "internal adviser." If Congress is to expose corruption and negligent administration, it cannot stop with pinning mistakes on the head, who more often than not is totally unaware of their presence. The efficiency of a vast department turns on the operations of its sprawling components, operating tier on tier; and its deficiencies are not always apparent to the overburdened head, as one Congressional investigation after another has revealed.[59] The objectionable handling of grain elevator benefits to Billie Sol Estes by the Department of Agriculture in 1962—he was subsequently convicted—was unknown to an upright Secretary, Orville Freeman.[60] It was more important to trace the conflicts of interest and negligent administration that operated behind the scenes in the Pakistan Elevator case than to pin responsibility for rejecting the low bid on the head. As Senator Sam J. Ervin said, "sometimes you have to go below the top man to find out what foolish decisions the top man is making."[61] Let the statement of Rodney Leonard, who served as Administrator of Consumer Marketing Service, flash a warning:

> I discovered during my service in the Department of Agriculture that many officials and employees of the Department seek to minimize information made available to the public in order to shield their decisions and actions from questioning, and frequently to cover up mistakes and misjudgments in the administration of public programs.[62]

Not for a moment should it be forgotten that the "power of Congress to conduct investigations," in the words of the Supreme Court, "comprehends probes into departments . . . to expose corruption, inefficiency or waste."[63]

58. Kramer & Marcuse 915.
59. See supra, Ch. 7, n. 14.
60. Time Magazine, May 25, 1962, p. 24. Harrison Wellford tells of an interview in 1969 with the Secretary of Agriculture, Clifford Hardin, respecting a proposed study of concealment in the Pesticide Division: "The Secretary appeared diffident and a little confused . . . a covey of aides . . . rushed to intercept all questions thrown his way"; Ervin Hearings 599–600.
61. Ibid. 330. Chairman Emanuel Celler asked in another situation, "how can we find there has been dereliction unless we know some of those facts?"; Kramer & Marcuse 887. "The question," said former Justice Goldberg, "is, What happened? Did the President get adequate advice? Did he follow the advice?"; 1 Moorhead Hearings 18.
62. Ervin Hearings 484.
63. Watkins v. United States, 354 U.S. 178, 187 (1957).

Apart from unearthing "corruption, inefficiency or waste," Congress is historically authorized to inquire into how its laws are being executed, to police disbursements of appropriations, to seek information in order to legislate and appropriate intelligently. The high-handed fashion in which these functions have been balked by the executive branch, even in defiance of statute, is well-illustrated by a 1958 case which has become a festering "precedent." The Act of 1921 directs every department and establishment of the government to furnish to the Comptroller General (head of the General Accounting Office) "such information regarding the powers, duties, activities, organization, financial transactions, and methods of business of their respective offices as he may from time to time require of them."[64] The papers to which the Comptroller is thereby entitled, the Attorney General said in 1925, "would seem to be a matter solely for his determination,"[65] that is, no administrator can decide for him what he may see. Acting under this statute, the Comptroller General requested a report upon the Air Force Ballistics program, made in 1958 by the Inspector General to the Secretary of the Air Force.[66] The purpose of that report was to "evaluate the management concept" of that program.[67] Access to the report was refused,[68] not because of the absence of statutory coverage,[69] not because of threats to military security,[70] but because of a desire to improve "self-criticism,"[71] a claim which had been rejected by the courts in the field of private litigation.[72] Early in our history, in 1828,

64. 42 Stat. 26 (1921), 31 U.S.C. §54 (1958). In §204a of the Legislative Reorganization Act of 1970, this was spelled out: "The Comptroller General shall review and analyze the results of Government programs and activities carried out under existing law, including the making of cost benefit studies"; 84 Stat. 1168.

65. 34 Ops. Atty. Gen. 446, 447 (1925).

66. Hearings on Availability of Information from Federal Departments and Agencies before a Subcommittee of the House Committee on Government Operations, Part 16, p. 3578 (85th Cong., 2d Sess., 1958); hereinafter cited as Moss Hearings.

67. Ibid. 3677, 3635.

68. Ibid. 3573, 3578. For citations to a row of similar withholdings see Berger, Executive Privilege 1312.

69. The Air Force Secretary conceded that the statutory powers of the Comptroller General are "so broad that executive privilege is the only possible major exception to them"; ibid. 3684.

70. Ibid. 3641.

71. Ibid. 3676, 3572.

72. The "Government claims a new kind of privilege. Its position is that the proceedings of boards of investigation of the Armed Forces should be privileged in order to allow the free and unhampered *self-criticism* within the service necessary to obtain maximum efficiency . . . I can find no recognition in the law of the existence of such a privilege"; Brauner v. United States, 10 F.R.D. 468, 472 (E.D. Pa. 1950); emphasis added. Brauner was reversed in United States v. Reynolds, 345

the Secretary of War, upon request, furnished confidential reports of the Inspector General of the Army.[73]

The Air Force Secretary took the position that in order to encourage the confidence of those who divulged information to the Inspector it was necessary to conceal their identity.[74] This was not a miniscule operation; the Inspector General's office employed the services of 3,139 employees and in fiscal 1959 twenty-four million dollars was expended on its operations—more than was then being spent on some of the independent agencies.[75] Beyond doubt Congress had a legitimate interest before appropriating more moneys for the operation to know whether it was efficiently operated, and whether the giant ballistics program was being adequately monitored. The Inspector General agreed that it was "important to the Congress" to be assured by "an independent evaluation" that his office "is doing a thoroughly adequate job in its surveys of management concepts."[76] And he stated that "the report itself is in the nature of a summary of a great deal of information which was deevloped in the course of the survey. Literally we developed a 5-foot shelf of information and data."[77] The Air Force Secretary refused to make available "the back-up material that is collected in the investigation," and at first transmitted a two-and-a-half-page "summary" of the Inspector General's Report, and then provided a thirty-five-page typewritten "statement of facts contained in the report."[78] Every lawyer knows that lawyers and judges frequently draw quite different "statements of fact" from a record, and that so much of the record as is relied on must be certified to an appeals court so that it can check assertions of fact against the record itself. Indeed, the Inspector General conceded that "for a thorough understanding of a survey that the Inspector General has made, it is *necessary to be thoroughly conversant with all of this* material."[79] To insist, therefore, that GAO had to proceed on the basis of the

U.S. 1, 11 (1953), but on the ground that no adequate predicate had been laid for disclosure of "military secrets." See also Circuit Judge Clark, concurring in Bank Line v. United States, 163 F. 2d 133, 139 (2d Cir. 1947).

73. Philip R. Collins, "The Power of Congressional Committees of Investigation to Obtain Information From the Executive Branch: The Argument for the Legislative Branch," 33 Geo. L.J. 563, 572 (1951).

74. Moss Hearings 3660.

75. For citations see Berger, Executive Privilege 1113.

76. Moss Hearings 3654.

77. Ibid. 3643.

78. Ibid. 3582, 2711.

79. Ibid. 3643; emphasis added.

truncated Air Force "statement of facts" manifestly frustrated the statutory purpose to provide for an independent evaluation of the Inspector General's monitoring.

The investigator, Senator John McClellan stated in another context, must determine "what information was available and upon what basis that final decision was made."[80] More recently Senator Charles Mathias observed that if the "advice and consent" of the Senate is to be meaningful, Congress "must have access to the same information the President has—access to the documents, the recommendations, the advisers."[81] This is confirmed from the executive side by George Ball, former Under Secretary of State. Speaking of the sensitive use-of-force decisions, he stated, "it is terribly important that the information that is made available to the Congress . . . is the same information and all of the same information that is in the hands of the executive."[82] "I can see no conceivable reason," said former Justice Goldberg, "why the chairman of the appropriate committees of Congress cannot be furnished copies of executive reports and memorandums essential to the performance of congressional responsibilities."[83]

The Air Force Secretary's justification for withholding the Inspector General's report verges on the absurd: effective performance of the delegated duty required him to withhold details of performance from his principal, Congress.[84] "[P]olicing of its own performance," said Assistant Attorney General Rehnquist in 1971, requires the uninhibited "collection of information."[85] Let that be assumed and it yet must yield to the paramount power of Congress to probe "corruption, inefficiency or waste in the Federal departments."[86] The military forces, moreover, are notori-

80. Kramer & Marcuse 836.

81. Ervin Hearings 17.

82. Fulbright Hearings 637. Former Assistant Secretary of State W. P. Bundy acknowledged that if he had to pass "on important legislative problems affecting international relations without the benefit of the views . . . of the President's advisors on foreign affairs," he "wouldn't feel wholly happy about it," but sought refuge in the "separation of powers"; Ervin Hearings 330.

83. 1 Moorhead Hearings 13.

84. This is not a thing of the past. In 1971 former Assistant Secretary of State Bundy testified: "internal audits are an example of the executive branch conducting a self-inquiry . . . we felt that we could not keep the efficiency of the process of self-audit if the auditors thought that everything they said would be revealed." Bundy withheld audits from GAO "in order to protect the toughness and efficiency of the audits"; Ervin Hearings 326. Such arguments would carry little weight with the Securities & Exchange Commission in an investigation of corporate audits by private accounting firms.

85. Ibid. 440.

86. See supra, Ch. 2, n. 159; Ch. 7, text accompanying nn. 13–14.

ously incapable of policing the vast sums they administer. So Chairman F. Edward Hebert of a House Armed Services Subcommittee found after nearly ten years of investigation into military spending.[87] The testimony of Ernest Fitzgerald respecting a two-billion-dollar aircraft cost overrun and of similar practices in the Navy by Gordon Rule was earlier noted.[88] To add a bizarre note, there is Cambodia's bland acknowledgment that $100,000,000 of American aid was expended on 100,000 men who never served in an alleged army of 300,000,[89] recalling Nikolai Gogol's "Dead Souls," the tale of a sharper whose stock in trade was a roster of dead serfs. If these be the fruits of the "tough," "efficient" internal audits, which former Assistant Secretary of State William P. Bundy considers need to be protected from congressional supervision,[90] God help these United States! In fact it is Congress, as we have seen, that was made the ultimate judge of efficient performance;[91] and Congress may conclude, even at the cost of "candid interchange," that it must have complete access to all documents that bear on that function. Balancing necessities of government, as is essential in weighing conflicting claims of power—without for a moment conceding that the executive claim has any constitutional validity—the question is whether the alleged executive desire to improve its performance shall be permitted to outweigh the congressional duty to ferret out inefficiency and corruption,

87. Mollenhoff 145. President Kennedy told Hebert that the administration "felt it needed the help and prodding of a committee of Congress to cut billions in wasteful defense spending"; ibid. 190.

On July 16, 1959, Hebert charged that the Defense Department, with the approval of President Eisenhower, had barred GAO from seeing certain requested reports. GAO had found gross overcharges and excessive profits ranging as high as 140 percent; it referred one case to the Department of Justice for prosecution. Herbert concluded that "they don't want us to find out where the bodies are buried"; Washington Daily News, July 16, 1959, p. 3.

In 1963 Secretary of Defense Robert McNamara cited to a Joint Congressional subcommittee "several instances of expensive programs that were retained beyond their usefulness, and of overlapping of weapons and equipment." N.Y. Times, Mar. 29, 1963, p. 3. Such instances recur with monotonous regularity and a thick volume would not suffice to catalogue them. See Clark Mollenhoff, *The Pentagon* (New York, 1972).

88. See supra, text accompanying nn. 53–54.

89. "The Minister of Information acknowledged . . . that because of payroll padding by military commanders, the Government had 'at times' paid salaries to as many as 100,000 non-existent soldiers . . . a total of $2-million a month . . . [This] is only part of the web of military corruption . . . Since the United States foots the bill for virtually the entire Cambodian budget . . . it is the United States, in effect, that is paying for the graft"; N.Y. Times, Jan. 7, 1973, Sec. 4, p. 3.

90. Supra, n. 84.

91. Compare supra, text accompanying n. 63; and Ch. 7, text accompanying nn. 13–14.

to legislate and appropriate intelligently. It is a perversion of values to require that Congress stumble in the dark so that executive subordinates can indulge in "candid interchange."

In truth, "candid interchange" is but another of a string of shallow rationalizations to justify withholding of information in the particular instance, "instant history." Several examples will further serve to make this clear. In 1958, Chairman Lyndon Johnson of the Senate Preparedness Subcommittee requested copies of the "Killian and Gaither panel reports," which had been prepared at President Eisenhower's request to assess the nation's military status. Who better than Congress, empowered by the Constitution "to provide for the common defense" and to make appropriations for that purpose, was entitled to know about the nation's military status? Yet Eisenhower refused on the ground that a turnover would "violate the confidence of the advisory relationship."[92] Killian and Gaither were not members of the federal establishment, but outsiders who were unlikely to be called on to prepare another report, and whose subsequent "candor" would no more be inhibited than that of a geologist who makes a highly confidential report to an oil company. A similar example was cited by Senator Fulbright: Sir Robert Thompson was employed by the President to make a report on Vietnam for a fee running into tens of thousands of dollars. The Committee on Foreign Relations requested the report on December 1969, and was refused by the State Department on the ground that it "was prepared for the President personally."[93]

Behind the complacent assumption that the executive branch alone may have access to the Thompson Report, to FBI files,[94] and indeed to all information gathered by the executive branch that it chooses to withhold, lurks something resembling the assertion of a proprietary interest in the information,[95] an assumption that

92. Quoted in Milton Carrow, "Governmental Nondisclosure in Judicial Proceedings," 107 U. Pa. L. Rev. 166, 167 (1958).

A Department of Justice refusal to furnish documents resting on the confidential relation of the turnover by American Tel. & Tel. was promptly made ridiculous by A.T. &T's voluntary turnover, supplemented by turnovers made by the Department of Defense and the Federal Communications Commission; Kramer & Marcuse 887, 891, 913.

93. Ervin Hearings 477.

94. See supra, Ch. 7, text accompanying nn. 17–18.

95. As Senator Charles Mathias stated, "When any branch of government comes to possess such vast power over such a vast and vital body of information it comes, inevitably, to regard that information as its own exclusive property, and employs it, inevitably for its own ends"; Ervin Hearings 16.

Congress and the people may see only so much as the President considers is good for them. But the vast information-gathering apparatus was created by Congress and is paid for by the people, to whom it belongs. Thompson, as Senator Fulbright emphasized, was "hired by public funds to make a report on a matter of great public interest."[96] It is precisely because the Executive is thus equipped to gather information, said Justice Story, that it was wisely placed under a duty to supply it to Congress.[97]

From time to time it is suggested that the problem can be obviated by Congress' creation of its own information-gathering machinery. In desperation, the Senate Foreign Relations Committee once hired and sent its own staff to Southeast Asia to obtain information that was being withheld by the Executive. This, Senator Fulbright testified, is "time-consuming and costly," it "is like creating a new State Department."[98] To duplicate the vast executive apparatus would be intolerably costly and impose a needless burden on the backs of the taxpayers, altogether out of proportion to the benefits that allegedly flow from secrecy.

"Executive privilege won't kill you," Roger C. Cramton, recently Assistant Attorney General, reassuringly states. Those who insist that Congress needs more information, he says, labor under a "staggering misconception. The practical fact is that Congress gets most of the information it wants from the executive branch." "Except," says Mr. Cramton, "possibly in the foreign and military area, Congress is not hindered in making legislative judgments by the failure of the executive to provide relevant information."[99] That is a tremendous "except." The supply of information about importation of nuts and bolts does not compensate for suppression of the Pentagon Papers, of five-year projections for astronomical foreign aid.[100] It does not make up for ten years of agonized escalation in Vietnam while Congress and the people were kept in the

96. Ibid. 478.

97. 2 Joseph Story, *Commentaries on the Constitution of the United States* §1561 (Boston, 1905).

98. Ervin Hearings 206.

99. N.Y. Times, Mar. 23, 1973, p. 35.

100. "Congress is being asked to appropriate $4 billion the next ten years to finance military aid . . . Unless the Foreign Relations Committee is to operate in the dark in authorizing this large expenditure, it has a right to know what obligations this country would incur in giving this help and whether military officials plan to increase this assistance or taper it off. For these purposes, the five-year plans worked out in the Pentagon for each recipient country are relevant, even indispensable documents"; N.Y. Times, Sept. 6, 1971, p. 16. See also 8 Moorhead Hearings 3103.

dark as to dismal expert evaluations; for secret agreements with foreign powers for bases, troop commitments and military aid running into hundreds of millions. It does not balance the deception of Congress and the nation, the falsification of records respecting 3,500 air raids on Cambodia in which more than 100,000 tons of bombs were dropped in 1969–1970, raids authorized by President Nixon at a time when the administration repeatedly insisted that it respected Cambodian neutrality.[101] Nor does the supply of innocuous information in bulk balance President Nixon's refusal to release White House documents to the Senate and the Special Prosecutor which may confirm or refute oral testimony that he himself was implicated in the Watergate cover-up.[102]

Who would be satisfied to receive mountains of statistics about growing deposits while the banker's alleged embezzlement was concealed? Common sense would be revolted by the suggestion that a banker under investigation should be permitted to decide what books and documents the examiner may inspect so that "future candor" of bank subordinates may not be inhibited.[103] An investigation of executive conduct which can obtain only such documents as the executive chooses to furnish, be the doctrinal pretext what it may, is crippled from the start. Such withholding aborts the whole purpose of legislative oversight; it flies in the face of the parliamentary history from which the congressional power of inquiry is derived; it is an arrant denial of the judicially recognized power to investigate "corruption, inefficiency or waste." And, in the words of Senator Fulbright, it makes the executive "judge and jury in cases of its own malfeasance and failures of judgment."[104]

101. N.Y. Times, July 17, 1973, p. 1; ibid. July 18, 1973, p. 1; ibid. July 21, 1973, p. 1; ibid. July 23, 1973, p. 30; ibid. July 24, 1973, pp. 4, 33.

When it came to light, Assistant Secretary of Defense Jerry W. Friedheim stated, "Obviously it was a blunder of some magnitude . . . we weren't smart enough" to foresee that Major Hal M. Knight would reveal all to the Senate; ibid. July 21, 1973, p. 1. No lesson learned, no reason to conclude that such "blunders," if that word can describe willful concealment and falsification, will not be repeated with more fastidious measures of deception.

102. Infra, text accompanying nn. 135–138; Newsweek, July 30, 1973, pp. 12–16.

103. The English have rejected a different standard for the government's employees; supra, text accompanying nn. 46–47.

104. This is astoundingly exemplified by President Nixon's withholding of taped recordings of conversations with White House aides charged with complicity in the Watergate cover-up:

> I personally listened to a number of them. The tapes are entirely consistent with what I know to be the truth . . . However, as in any verbatim recordings of

B. *"Candid Interchange" in the Nixon Administration*

Claims of executive privilege lay relatively dormant during the Kennedy-Johnson administrations, possibly because both presidents had learned at first hand of the resentment refusals of information stirred in Congress.[105] Kennedy was not disposed to lock horns in behalf of a "future candor" principle when intrinsically unimportant matters were involved.[106] Possibly, too, both Kennedy and Johnson so effectively concealed crucial matters, for example, the increasing involvement in Vietnam, that Congress had no clue as to what to ask for. But as Congressman John E. Moss remarked in 1963, "The powerful genie of executive privilege momentarily is confined but can be uncorked by future Presidents."[107]

> informal conversations, they contain comments that persons with different perspectives and motivations would inevitably interpret in different ways.

N.Y. Times, July 24, 1973, p. 19.
What defendant would not vastly prefer to have judge and jury rely on *his* construction of "informal conversations" rather than to leave interpretation to "the different perspectives and motivations" of judge or jury?

105. Attorney General Robert Kennedy, who "had been associated with a congressional committee for five or six years and had battles with the executive branch of the government regarding obtaining information," said, "it is terribly important to insure that the executive branch of the government is not corrupt and that they are efficient, that the legislative branch of the government has the ability to check on what we are doing in the executive branch of the government . . . In the last analysis the group that can best check and insure that [the executive branch] is handling its affairs properly is the Congress"; Mollenhoff 198–199. Why the congressional experience of Mr. Nixon and his vigorous condemnation of President Truman's withholding in 1948 did not conduce to a similar attitude is matter for conjecture. Does the difference derive from a more absolutist conception of the presidential role?

A former Assistant Attorney General and proponent of executive privilege, Robert Kramer, stated, "undue secrecy may seriously cripple the legislature and promote official arrogance and inefficiency as well as fiscal laxity . . . government without investigation might easily turn out to be democratic government no longer"; Kramer & Marcuse 915–916.

106. See testimony of Lee White, special counsel to President Kennedy; 1 Moorhead Hearings 46–47; see supra, n. 34.

107. Memorandum, Foreign Operations and Government Operations Subcommittee (H.R.) Part V, Executive Privilege, p. 49 (August 1963; unpublished). Congressman John E. Moss stated that "in a review of instances of withholding from the Congress between 1955 and 1960, 44 cases developed where [Eisenhower's] May 17, 1954 letter was relied upon as an absolute authority . . . by any one within the executive department who desired to refuse information to the Congress"; Ervin Hearings 333.

A study by the Government and General Research Division of the Library of Congress (reprinted, Cong. Rec. H.2243–2246, March 28, 1973, set out infra, in Appendix A) states that President Kennedy invoked executive privilege once, and his administration refused information to congressional committees "three times, apparently without Presidential authority." President Johnson did not invoke execu-

Uncorking by President Nixon was hardly to be anticipated in light of his earlier vigorous attack on executive privilege when a Congressman:

> The point has been made that the President . . . has issued an order that none of this information can be released and that, therefore, the Congress has no right to question the judgment of the President. I say that the proposition cannot stand from a constitutional standpoint.[108]

As President, he advised Congressman Moss in 1969 of his belief that

> the scope of executive privilege must be very narrowly construed . . . this administration is dedicated to insuring a free flow of information to the Congress and the news media—and thus, to the citizens . . . I want open government to be a reality in every way possible.[109]

And in a memorandum to department heads, he stated:

> The policy of this administration is to comply to the fullest extent possible with Congressional requests for information . . . this administration will invoke [executive privilege] only in the most compelling circumstances and after a rigorous inquiry into the actual need for its exercise.[110]

As this is being written (July 1973), President Nixon has formally invoked executive privilege some eight or more times, including his much-criticized refusal of the taped White House conversations with his aides; and his subordinates have refused information to Congress on fifteen other occasions in apparent violation of his own orders.[111] Under the Nixon directive laying

---

tive privilege, but there were two refusals by members of his administration; ibid. It is said that two-thirds of the refusals to furnish information to Congress have come in the last twenty years, about one-third in the four and one-half years of the Nixon presidency; N.Y. Times, Aug. 20, 1973, p. 31. This testifies to a rapidly accelerating tendency to executive secrecy.

108. 94 Cong. Rec. 4783 (1948). In a newspaper conference on Jan. 31, 1973, President Nixon replied to a question by Clark Mollenhoff, "you were quite critical of executive privilege in 1948 when you were in Congress?" "I certainly was." N.Y. Times, Feb. 1, 1973, p. 20.

109. Ervin Hearings 36.

110. Ibid.

111. See supra, n. 107; Ervin Hearings 5–6, 310–314. Four times are recounted in the Library of Congress study, infra, Appendix A. For March 12, 1973, directive, infra, text accompanying n. 112; for June 7, 1973, bar to access to presidential papers, and July 7, 1973, ditto, see N.Y. Times, July 15, 1973, p. 36; for bar to tapes of recorded presidential conversations with White House aides, see Newsweek, July 30, 1973, pp. 12–16; and for bar to disclosure to court of White House files of conversations with the dairy industry which allegedly led to a price adjustment of $500-million in exchange for $422,000 in contributions to the Nixon re-election

down that "Executive privilege will not be used without specific Presidential approval," and reserving to himself "Presidential decision to invoke Executive privilege,"[112] such refusals, Assistant Attorney General Rehnquist indicated, were unauthorized and therefore of doubtful legality.[113] Some of these refusals came after interminable stalling;[114] and when first an exasperated Senate Committee and then a House Committee invoked a statutory cut-off of funds to end two such protracted withholdings of information, President Nixon at last invoked executive privilege to shield the withholdings.[115]

Instead of being "very narrowly construed," executive privilege has been expanded in truly extraordinary fashion by President Nixon, and all in the name of "well-established precedent." Thus, on March 12, 1973, he directed that no "member or former member" of his White House staff shall appear before Congress.[116] On April 10, Attorney General Kleindienst, by another ipse dixit, extended this immunity from the White House staff to the two and one-half million federal employees. The President, he asserted, is empowered to forbid federal employees to testify before Con-

campaign, see N.Y. Times, July 28, 1973, p. 9. The White House claim of absolute privilege was rejected in a private litigation by District Judge William B. Jones, who directed the government to show the files to the court; ibid.

112. Ervin Hearings 36–37.

113. Among the fifteen refusals was a denial of the Pentagon Papers to the Senate Committee on Foreign Relations by Secretary of Defense Melvin Laird, on the ground that "it would be clearly contrary to the national interest," without asserting executive privilege. Asked to comment on this, Assistant Attorney General Rehnquist implied that the withholding was unauthorized because an administrator can "withhold information . . . only on the basis of executive privilege," that is, with the approval of the President; 3 Moorhead Hearings 781–782. He agreed that under the Nixon directive "there is no authority for an executive agency or department to refuse outright to give Congress information"; Ervin Hearings 441. See Macomber, supra, Ch. 1, n. 32.

114. It is impossible in small compass to brush in details of such interminable foot-dragging. See, for example, the fruitless attempts from May 21, 1969, to July 28, 1971, to obtain the Five-Year Plan for the Military Assistance program, which at long last led the Senate Foreign Relations Committee to invoke a statutory cut-off of funds only to be met by President Nixon's invocation of executive privilege"; Ervin Hearings 40–46. For a comment by Senator Sam J. Ervin on such other incidents; ibid. 6. See also the experience of the Symington Subcommittee; ibid. 216. For similar stalling tactics encountered by GAO, see 8 Moorhead Hearings 3044–3074. Comptroller General Elmer B. Staats testified that President Nixon's withholding policy has had a "crippling effect" on the work of the General Accounting Office, and has caused "tremendous delays in making information available to us"; Washington Star, April 11, 1973, p. A-2. Senator Ervin justly commented that these practices reflect "contempt for congressional requests for information." Ervin Hearings 6.

115. Ervin Hearings 45–46; N.Y. Times, Mar. 17, 1972, p. 7.

116. N.Y. Times, Mar. 13, 1973, p. 16.

gress under any circumstances and to block congressional demands for *any* document within the executive branch. He could, Kleindienst claimed, order his aides not to testify "even when called upon to impeach the President."[117]

The Nixonian rationale for his freshly minted claims of privilege again illustrates that the appetite for power grows by what it feeds on. Consider the claim of privilege for the White House staff, alleged by Mr. Nixon to be "rooted in the Constitution" and "designed to protect communications within the executive branch."[118] Before White House counsel, John Dean, was "fired" from the White House under the cloud of Watergate, he had advised a Senate Committee which sought the attendance of a White House aide, Peter Flanagan, that "Under the doctrine of separation of powers, and long established historical precedents, the principle that members of the President's immediate staff not appear and testify before congressional committees with respect to performance of their duties is firmly established."[119] The fragility of such "precedents" is illustrated by the fact that not many weeks later, after Flanagan had appeared before the Committee in order to save the confirmation of Mr. Kleindienst as Attorney General, Mr. Dean proclaimed exactly the opposite: there never has been such a "blanket immunity."[120] Mr. Nixon's March 12th pronouncement constituted still another *volte face*, eloquent testimony of how history is tailored to the occasion.[121]

As this is being revised for press, President Nixon argues in the courts that the principle of "confidentiality" is vital to maintenance of the presidency and separation of powers, that to make even one departure by disclosure to the grand jury in the pending Watergate investigation is to damage the principle "irreparably." His advisers, he maintained, must be "uninhibited . . . candid . . . free-wheeling," otherwise they "will always be speaking in

117. Washington Star, April 11, 1973, p. A-2; Washington Post, April 11, 1973, p. 1. According to White House Press Secretary Ronald Ziegler, Mr. Kleindienst "was expressing administration policy"; Washington Post, April 12, 1973, p. 8.

118. N.Y. Times, Mar. 23, 1973, p. 16.

119. Wall Street Journal, April 13, 1972, p. 5.

120. On April 20, 1972, Mr. Dean, commenting on concerns expressed in a Federation of American Scientists Newsletter about the extension of executive privilege beyond confidential communications between the President and his immediate counsellors, wrote to the Director of the Federation of American Scientists, Dr. Jeremy J. Stone: "The precedents indicate that no recent president has ever claimed a 'blanket immunity' that would prevent his assistants from testifying before the Congress on any subject"; Washington Post, Mar. 26, 1973, p. A-23.

121. For the repeated changes in course, see N.Y. Times, July 15, 1973, p. 36.

a eunuch-like way, rather than laying it on the line."[121a] "Laying it on the line" scarcely reflects the "aye, aye, sir" tradition by which Acting Director of the FBI Patrick Gray felt himself bound,[121b] the "mine not to reason why" rule of conduct to which one member after another of the Executive branch testified in the Senate Watergate hearings.[121c] The air of sanctity with which the principle is being invested justifies a further historical comment.[121d]

That no such "principle" obtained in the practice of Parliament is made immediately apparent by its inquiry in 1714 as a prelude to the impeachment of the Earl of Oxford and other high Ministers. Among the witnesses examined were Thomas Harley, brother of Oxford, and Matthew Prior, envoys to France, who were interrogated as to their instructions by the Ministers to negotiate a secret treaty behind the back of their Dutch allies.[121e] Here was an occasion when disclosure was disgraceful, for the resultant treaty of Utrecht, said William Pitt, left an indelible stain on English honor.[121f] Yet a claim of privilege to withhold was not breathed.

A reflection of this history is found in the Jay Treaty incident, instanced by Secretary of State William Rogers for the proposition that the President need "not produce the instructions which had been given to his representatives in negotiating a treaty. It seems clear that they constituted *advice within the Executive Branch* on official matters."[121g] Refused by Washington to the House on the ground that it was not empowered to participate in the treaty-making process, this internal "advice" *was furnished to the Senate*,[121h] testimony that Washington did not conceive even *his own communications* sancrosanct.

In truth, there are no "long established precedents" for the prin-

121a. N.Y. Times, Aug. 23, 1973, p. 28. But see infra, Epilogue at nn. 5–7.

121b. N.Y. Times, Aug. 12, 1973, sec. 4, p. 2.

121c. "The 10 weeks of hearings brought witness after witness who by his own account was afraid to speak his mind to Mr. Nixon, or who beat around the bush when he got up the nerve"; Wall Street Journal, Aug. 10, 1973, p. 6.

121d. See supra, Ch. 6, text accompanying nn. 129–138.

121e. Supra, Ch. 2, text accompanying nn. 48–53, and n. 53.

121f. Quoted in Winston Churchill, *Marlborough: His Life and Times* 890 (New York, 1968).

121g. Ervin Hearings 555; emphasis added. For the insistence of former President John Quincy Adams that the House was entitled to receive the complete instructions of President Polk to our Minister in Mexico, see supra, Ch. 6, text accompanying n. 95.

121h. Supra, Ch. 6, text accompanying nn. 53–59. For President Monroe's repeated supply of "confidential" communications, see App. D. See also John Adams, supra, Ch. 6, text accompanying n. 65.

ciple of "confidentiality." President Nixon himself could do no better than to invoke the refusal of ex-President Truman in 1953 to turn over some papers to a House Committee,[121i] which an indulgent Committee did not pursue. The instances mustered by Assistant Attorney General Rehnquist in 1971 went back no farther than the Truman administration, that is, about 1950. In the words of now Justice Rehnquist, "these precedents are all of recent origin,"[122] grounded on the "principle" that such intimate advisers "ought not to be interrogated as to conversations or discussion had with the President or advice given and recommendations made to the President."[123] The dubiety of constitutional sanction for a claim of "confidentiality" has been earlier noticed;[124] assume arguendo that it has constitutional warrant and it is yet a pretty leap from "confidentiality" to immunity for mere physical proximity to the President—membership in the White House staff.

To turn from abstract principle to concrete cases, consider the blanket immunity claimed for Henry Kissinger, the Nixon foreign policy adviser, whose take-over of high-level State Department functions is open and notorious, to mention only his negotiations for a rapprochement with China and Russia, and the peace negotiations with Vietnam.[125] It results that the nominal head of foreign affairs, the Secretary of State, who, in Marshall's words, is the "confidential agent" of the President,[126] enjoys no "blanket immunity" but is accountable to and appears before Congress, whereas the White House *eminence grise* claims to be completely shielded by executive privilege.[127] The conclusion is irresistible that the "confidentiality" test has been supplanted by geographical location: a "confidential agent" located at Foggy Bottom is

121i. New York Times, July 8, 1973, p. 23.

122. Ervin Hearings 426.

123. 2 Moorhead Hearings 363.

124. Supra, Ch. 6, text accompanying nn. 129–138.

125. It was Kissinger, George Reedy rightly emphasized, "not [Secretary of State] Rogers who went over to meet the Foreign Minister of the Chinese Government . . . quite obviously he was acting in the capacity . . . of . . . the Secretary of State"; Ervin Hearings 458. W. Averell Harriman, former Under Secretary of State, testified that Kissinger "certainly is assuming some of the responsibilities of the Secretary of State. The Secretary of State normally is supposed to be the President's most intimate advisor on foreign policy and if he is called I see no reason why Dr. Kissinger should not respond"; ibid. 363.

126. Marbury v. Madison, 5 U.S. (1 Cranch) 137, 166 (1803).

127. Ervin Hearings 22. Counsel to the President John Dean advised the Chairman of a House Subcommittee, in response to his request for the appearance of Kissinger, Herbert Klein, and Dean, that "as members of the immediate staff of the President" they must decline; 3 Moorhead Hearings 896.

accountable; one located in the White House is not. However valid the invocation of privilege for "confidential communications" to the President, it cannot shelter mere location in the White House.

The influence of the White House advisers, said Senator Charles Mathias, a member of the President's own party, "upon foreign policy is far greater than that of any members of the Senate or even of the executive department."[128] Moreover, Mr. Kissinger is in fact "a great deal more than a personal adviser to the President," as Senator Fulbright pointed out. He "presides over a staff of 54 'substantive officers' and a total staff of 140 employees. In addition, Mr. Kissinger serves as chairman of six interagency committees dealing with the entire range of foreign policy and national security issues," including the National Security Council.[129] Consequently, his claimed immunity from accountability extended far beyond confidential communications to and from the President; it shielded activities which on no theory should be insulated from inquiry; and, in the words of Senator Fulbright, it "undercuts Congressional oversight and the advisory role of the Senate in making foreign policy."[130] Thus, the "confidential" communications "precedent" has become the cloak for a vastly expanded "privilege" having no relation to "confidential communications."[131]

128. Ervin Hearings 17.

129. Ibid. 21–22. The "officers of the National Security Council staff report directly to Dr. Kissinger. The budget justification prepared by the National Security Council states that 'An Assistant to the President is the principal supervisory officer of the Council. Dr. Kissinger is listed in the United States Government Organization Manual, along with the NCC 'staff secretary,' as one of the two 'officials' of the National Security Council"; 25 Fed. Amer. Scientists Newsletter, no. 3, p. 2 (March 1972).

130. Ervin Hearings 22. Arthur J. Goldberg, former Justice and then Ambassador to the United Nations, stated, "we have an intolerable situation now where basic issues of foreign policy are formulated . . . and Congress is denied the opportunity to explore the facets of the foreign policy"; Fulbright Hearings 792. He agreed that the expansion of the privilege for "personal communications between the President and a Secretary . . . to a great bureaucracy of 500 . . . or 5000 men" is "an absurdity"; ibid. 793. Lyndon Johnson's Press Secretary, George Reedy, stated about the Kissinger situation that this is "a new type of agency which just happens to be housed within the confines of the President's residence"; ibid. 454. Compare McGeorge Bundy, ibid. 432. Former Under Secretary of State Harriman said that Kissinger "is very much involved in policy-making" and should be on call by Congress; Ervin Hearings 359.

131. In justice to the Nixon administration, it must be noted that the claim had been made by an Associate Special Counsel to President Lyndon Johnson, who refused to appear before a congressional committee on the ground that "It has been

Even less defensible was the expansion of executive privilege to shield another White House adviser, Peter Flanagan. Mr. Flanagan was caught up in the International Telephone and Telegraph scandal, which turned on the charge that the Justice Department settled three antitrust suits against ITT in exchange for a $400,000 guarantee by the corporation of the expenses of the 1972 Republican National Convention. Surely it was within the scope of legitimate inquiry to question any White House aide who allegedly had some contact with ITT's efforts to obtain the settlement,[132] to probe into the possibility of corrupt influence. Nevertheless, the "White House rejected an invitation for Mr. Flanagan to appear before the Committee . . . claiming executive privilege" on the basis of "the principle that members of the President's immediate staff not appear and testify before congressional committees with respect to the performance of their duties."[133] Again, "confidentiality" was not in question, for "conversations" between President Nixon and Mr. Flanagan about the ITT settlement for an election fund quid pro quo are too scandalous to be entertained.

But it is President Nixon's claim of immunity for the now fallen John Dean himself, by his statement of March 11, 1973, forbidding members of his staff to appear before Congress,[134] that brings the extravagance of his claims into high relief. Prior to the November 1972 election, five men laden with eavesdropping equipment were caught inside the Democratic National Headquarters at Watergate in Washington. A former White House aide, E. Howard Hunt, and G. Gordon Liddy, counsel to Nixon's Reelection Committee, were implicated; all seven were convicted for wiretapping conspiracy. The Reelection Committee, testimony showed,

---

firmly established, as a matter of principle and precedents, that members of the President's immediate staff shall not appear . . . This limitation . . . is fundamental to our system of government"; Ervin Hearings 474. How trippingly "firmly established" and "fundamental" fall from executive lips, and this for "precedents" that the executive branch traced no further back than the Truman administration!

132. N.Y. Times, April 15, 1972, p. 1. Part of the same pattern is exhibited by the indictment of former Attorney General John Mitchell and former Secretary of Commerce Maurice Stans, for accepting $200,000 in cash as a Nixon campaign contribution in return for which they were to intercede with the Securities and Exchange Commission, then conducting an investigation of the donor, Robert L. Vesco. Time, May 21, 1973, pp. 21–22. Compare McGrain v. Daugherty, 273 U.S. 135, 177 (1927), which sustained a Senate investigation, arising out of the Teapot Dome frauds, whether the "Attorney General and his assistants were performing or neglecting their duties."

133. Wall Street Journal, April 13, 1972, p. 5.

134. N.Y. Times, Mar. 13, 1973, p. 16.

had allotted $89,000 to finance the wiretapping, part of a scheme to subvert the electoral process.[134a] This is not the place to set out the mind-boggling details that were unfolded during the summer of 1973. Suffice it to say that a massive cover-up of the break-in, designed to obstruct justice, was masterminded by White House aides. By his own testimony John Dean participated, and he implicated the President himself.[135] White House denials ensued, and when the Senate Committee sought access to White House documents and secretly recorded tapes of conversations with the President, Mr. Nixon again invoked executive privilege.

Executive resistance to exposure of maladministration that Congress has encountered again and again does not inspire confidence in executive discretion to determine that no investigation is needed, or that it must be limited. Consider the statement by President Nixon on August 29, 1972, with respect to the Watergate scandal:

> Within our own staff, under my direction, Counsel to the President, Mr. Dean, has conducted a complete investigation of all leads which might involve any present members of the White House staff or anybody in the Government. I can say categorically that his investigation indicates that no one in the White House staff, no one in this administration, presently employed, was involved in this very bizarre incident.[136]

Subsequently a number of members of his administration confessed that they *were* involved in this incident. Not the least "bizarre" aspect of Watergate is the fact that the "administration was forced to admit that former Presidential counsel John Dean had told essentially the truth when he insisted that he had never made a formal report to the President on his supposed Watergate investigation, as Mr. Nixon himself had maintained."[137] Since then Mr. Dean has admitted his own complicity in the cover-up

134a. Former Attorney General Richard G. Kleindienst characterized it as a "fantastic event . . . in addition to being a felony, if you can think of anything worse, it also went to the very heart of our political system"; N.Y. Times, Aug. 8, 1973, p. 16. In the words of Max Lerner, it involved "the resolve of a small group to keep the President and themselves in power by clandestine means, even if it involved wiretapping, secret survaillance, political espionage. These . . . are the core corruption of power"; Lerner, "A Corruption of Power," Boston Herald American, April 24, 1973, p. 30.

135. For condensed version of Dean's testimony, see N.Y. Times, July 1, 1973, Sec. 4, p. 1.

136. Reprinted in N.Y. Times, April 18, 1973, p. 16.

137. Newsweek, May 28, 1973, p. 26; see also ibid. May 14, 1973, p. 34.

and, in testimony before the Senate, implicated the highest officers of the White House.[138]

Be it assumed that some constitutional footing for executive privilege exists, it should extend at most to *official* acts, not to unofficial acts[138a] of a candidate campaigning for re-election with the aid of a Reelection Committee that, according to testimony, sought to corrupt the election.[139] Still less should a misguided conception of the separation of powers be interposed to bar investigation of criminal conduct,[140] for the express provisions for indictment and impeachment of the President constitute an *exception* to the separation of powers. Mr. Nixon's appeal to the example of Washington overlooks the fact that Washington, upon learning that an inquiry into the conduct of his "intimate adviser," Alexander Hamilton, Secretary of the Treasury, was rumored, stated: "No one . . . wishes more devoutly than I do that [the allegations] may be probed to the bottom, be the result what it will."[141] He would have welcomed, not impeded, the interrogation of Mr. Dean.

President Nixon's rationalization of the claimed immunity for Dean has at least the merit of novelty. He asserted that "the man-

138. For summary of Dean's testimony see N.Y. Times, July 1, 1973, sec. 4, p. 1. For earlier cover-ups, see supra, n. 23.

138a. So it has been held in cases involving "evidentiary" privilege: Rosee v. Chicago Board of Trade, 36 F.R.D. 684, 690 (N.D.Ill. 1965); United States v. Procter & Gamble Co., 25 F.R.D. 485, 490 (D. N.J. 1960).

139. For details see J. Anthony Lukas, "The Story So Far," N.Y. Times, July 22, 1973, mag. sec., p. 1.

140. On April 10, 1973, Attorney General Richard Kleindienst told a Senate Committee that "even if a Member of the President's staff is accused of a crime he should not appear and testify if the President invokes executive privilege and directs him not to"; Washington Star, April 11, 1973. President Nixon apparently thought better of it, because on May 22, 1973, he directed that "executive privilege will not be invoked as to any testimony concerning possible criminal conduct in the matters presently under investigation, including the Watergate affair and the alleged cover-up"; N.Y. Times, May 23, 1973, p. 28.

On Aug. 17, 1973, Mr. Nixon's counsel advised the United States District Court, in a suit brought by Special Prosecutor Archibald Cox, to obtain taped recordings of conversations between the President and members of the White House staff implicated or charged with participating in the Watergate conspiracy, that the President's interest in preserving confidentiality rises above the need for criminal prosecution; N.Y. Times, Aug. 18, 1973, p. 3. This with respect to a conspiracy to subvert the electoral process that has shaken the nation, in which he himself was implicated by the sworn testimony of John Dean, his White House counsel, which testimony might be confirmed or denied by the tapes; N.Y. Times, July 15, 1973, p. 36. The repeated changes of presidential course suggest large doubts as to the scope of the claimed privilege.

141. Letter to Pendleton, Sept. 23, 1793; 33 George Washington, *Writings* 95 (Washington, 1940).

ner in which the President exercises his assigned executive powers is not subject to questioning by another branch of the Government," and deduced that "If the President is not subject to such questioning it is equally inappropriate that members of his staff not [sic] be so questioned for their roles are in effect an extension of the President.[142] Mr. Nixon overlooked that inquiries by Parliament, in which, the Supreme Court held, the congressional power of inquiry is rooted, had their inception in inquiries preliminary to impeachment. The Constitution makes the "President, Vice President and all civil officers impeachable." James Iredell adverted in the North Carolina Ratification Convention to the maxim that the King can do no wrong, and exulted in the "happier provision" which made the President himself "triable."[143] The executive, it should never be forgotten, was not looked at with awe but with apprehension.

Even the headstrong Andrew Jackson acknowledged in 1834 that

> cases may occur in the course of [Congress'] proceedings in which it may be indispensable to the proper exercise of its power that it should inquire or decide upon the conduct of the President or other public officers, and in every case its constitutional right to do so is cheerfully conceded.[144]

The sweeping scope of congressional inquiry was more powerfully stated by President Polk in 1846:

> If the House of Representatives, as the grand inquest of the nation, should at any time have reason to believe that there has been malversation in office by an improper use or application of public money by a public officer, and should think proper to institute an inquiry into the matter, *all the archives and papers* of the Executive Department, public or private, would be subject to inspection and control of a committee of their body and *every facility* in the power of the Executive *be afforded* to enable them to prosecute the investigation.

Polk "cheerfully admitted" the right of the House, as an auxiliary to its power of impeachment,

> to investigate the conduct of *all* public officers under the Government . . . the power of the House in the pursuit of this object *would penetrate*

142. N.Y. Times, Mar. 13, 1973, p. 16.

143. 4 Elliot 109. See also George Nicholas and Francis Corbin in the Virginia Convention; 3 Elliot 17, 516.

144. Quoted in J. R. Wiggins, "Government Operations and the Public's Right to Know," 19 Fed. B.J. 62, 80 (1959).

into the most secret recesses of the Executive Departments. It could command the attendance of any and every agent of the government, and compel them to produce all papers, public or private, official or unofficial, and to testify on oath to tell all facts within their knowledge.[145]

Much closer in time to the Founders, these statements of Jackson and Polk, rather than the self-serving declaration of Truman in 1953, are the true "precedents" by which the President should be guided.

In light of the fact that impeachment embraces "all civil officers" the immunity that President Nixon sought to wrap around Dean falls to the ground. Assume that a presidential immunity exists, it is yet not shared by the President's subordinates, as a line of suits against cabinet members, stretching from *Marbury v. Madison* through the "Steel Seizure case" testifies.[146] Impeachment, said Elias Boudinot in the First Congress—"almost an adjourned session" of the Constitutional Convention—[147] enables the House "to pull down an improper officer, although he should be supported by all the power of the Executive." The point was made over and over again, among others, by Abraham Baldwin, one of the Framers.[148] It would be wondrous strange if the House could "pull down" an officer without the President's permission but could not question him before doing so. Untroubled by such considerations, Attorney General Kleindienst asserted on April 10, 1973, that the President could order his aides not to testify, "even when called upon to furnish evidence to impeach the President."[149] Assistant Attorney General Robert Dixon went on to affirm on May 8th that President Nixon could assert executive privilege even in a proceeding involving his own impeachment.[150] Even on the vulnerable premise that the privilege is founded on the separation

145. 4 Richardson 435, 434; emphasis added. Edward Corwin concluded that "Congress has the power to investigate his [President's] every official act"; Corwin, *President* 365.

146. 5 U.S. (1 Cranch) 137 (1803); 343 U.S. 579 (1952). See Land v. Dollar, 190 F 2d 623 (D.C. Cir. 1951); Corwin, *President*, 513, n. 78.

147. Charles Warren, *Congress, the Constitution, and the Supreme Court* 99 (Boston, 1925).

148. 1 Annals of Cong. 468; similiter, Samuel Livermore, ibid. 478. "Favoritism," said Abraham Baldwin, could not protect a man from the power of the House "in despite of the President" to "drag him from his place"; ibid. 558; see John Lawrence, ibid. 482.

149. Washington Star, April 11, 1973, p. A-2; cf. Washington Post, April 11, 1973, p. 1.

150. N.Y. Times, May 9, 1973, p. 28.

of powers, impeachment is plainly an *exception* thereto, as the Founders well understood.[151] By impeachment Congress could call the executive to account. Mr. Kleindienst's rationalization that the Senate needs neither "facts nor evidence" to impeach the President, "all it needs . . . is votes,"[152] will not satisfy those who would accord due process to the lowliest felon. It would be a supreme irony of fate were Kleindienst's assertion to haunt the President.

"Candid interchange" is yet another pretext for doubtful secrecy. It will not explain Mr. Nixon's claim of blanket immunity for members of his White House staff on the basis of mere membership without more; it will not justify Kleindienst's assertion of immunity from congressional inquiry for two and one-half million federal employees. It is merely another testimonial to the greedy expansiveness of power, the costs of which patently outweigh its benefits. As the latest branch in a line of illegitimate succession, it illustrates the excesses bred by the claim of executive privilege. And in practice it has realized Lord Pearce's pregnant observation: "what a complete lack of common sense a general blanket protection of wide class may yield."[153] The problem will not be met by pruning a branch here and there; the axe must be put to the root of a claim that is altogether without constitutional warrant, leaving it to the good sense of Congress and the people—and, if need be, the courts—to work out an accommodation for such matters as confidential communications between the President and his immediate advisers, excluding any communications with respect to illegal acts. To leave it with the executive branch to decide is to court more of the "horrors" revealed by recent history.[154]

151. Elias Boudinot said in the First Congress that impeachment was one of the "exceptions to a principle," i.e., to the separation of powers; 1 Annals of Cong. 527.

152. Washington Star, April 11, 1973, p. A-2.

153. Conway v. Rimmer, 1 All E.R. [1968] 874, 910.

154. Professor Arthur Schlesinger, Jr., stated, "The secrecy system has become much less a means by which Government protects national security than a means by which the Government safeguards its reputation, dissembles its purposes, buries its mistakes, manipulates its citizens, maximizes its power and corrupts itself"; quoted by Curt Matthews, St. Louis Post-Dispatch, Feb. 26, 1973, sec. 1–12B, p. 1.

9

THE COST OF SECRECY

> If we advert to the nature of Republican Government, we shall find that the censorial power is in the people over the Government, and not in the Government over the people.
> — James Madison*

WHILE we were upbraiding the Russians for dropping an Iron Curtain in Eastern Europe, a succession of presidents were interposing a web of deception between the people and the facts, concealing from them the ill-starred decisions which plunged the nation ever deeper into the quagmire that was Vietnam. Whether the American people would have made wiser decisions had the facts been disclosed to them may be problematical; but incontrovertibly Congress and the people were denied the opportunity for full debate that might have turned the scales. When one weighs the costs—55,000 dead, 300,000 wounded or maimed, one hundred or more billion dollars, and a spiraling inflation which has touched off an international crisis—it can hardly be gainsaid that the people were entitled to be told what our real aims were and to weigh whether they were worth the ever-mounting sacrifices that were foreseen in the inner circle. For this we need not call on the wisdom of hindsight, because contemporary records amply set forth the ingredients of decision and the doubts that gnawed at the decisionmakers.[1] Instead of candid disclosure we had, to borrow from James Reston, escalation by stealth.[2]

* 4 Annals of Cong. 934 (1794).

1. This chapter is based largely upon the documents published by the New York Times, edited by Neil Sheehan and others, *The Pentagon Papers* (New York, 1971). With Justice Black, I consider that in "revealing the workings of the government that led to the Vietnam War," the Times nobly fulfilled the purposes of the Founders; United States v. New York Times, 403 U.S. 713, 717 (1971), concurring. The story was filled out by reference to David Halberstam, *The Best and the Brightest* (New York, 1972).

2. Quoted in Halberstam 570. The Chairman of the Senate Foreign Relations Committee, Senator Fulbright, stated: "President Johnson went out of his way to

A. *Saigon: A Tottering Ally*

George Ball, who almost alone in that inner circle exhibited the wisdom of hindsight at the moment of decision, has said that our military efforts "flounder[ed] so long and inconclusively" because "there was no adequate indigenous political base on which our power could be emplaced."[3] Very early, in 1954, the Joint Chiefs of Staff (hereinafter JCS) laid down as a precondition for military aid to the Diem regime: "It is absolutely essential that there be a reasonably strong, stable military government in control."[4] Diem's regime, reported American intelligence sources in 1959, "is in fact essentially authoritarian"; according to intelligence sources, "the war began largely as a rebellion in the South against the increasingly oppressive and corrupt regime" of Diem.[5]

In 1961, Secretary of Defense Robert McNamara perceived that "Success will depend on factors many of which are not within our control—notably the conduct of Diem himself."[6] Periodically secret intelligence reports described "the gulf between the mandarin ruler and the apathetic peasantry."[7] McNamara noted in 1963 that the "repressive" Diem government "is becoming increasingly unpopular," and before long Diem was overthrown with American connivance.[8] The successor government, in the words of McNamara, was "the greatest source of concern. It is indecisive and drifting."[9] Reporting in March 1964, McNamara stated that "the situation has unquestionably been growing worse"; large groups "are now showing signs of apathy and indifference"; the viability of the Khanh government is "uncertain"; it constituted "an extremely weak base which might at any moment collapse," all of which undercut "the present policy—the South Vietnamese must

---

conceal from Congress and the public what he really had in mind in 1964"; Fulbright Hearings 450. He further said: "One of the most striking revelations to emerge from the Pentagon Papers was the extraordinary secrecy with which the inner circle of the Johnson administration made their fateful decisions in 1964 and 1965 . . . the almost total exclusion of Congress from the policy-making process"; Ervin Hearings 23.

3. G. W. Ball, "Have We Learned or Only Failed?" N.Y. Times, April 1, 1973, Mag. Sec., pp. 12, 13.
4. Pent. Pap. 14.
5. Ibid. 71, 67.
6. Ibid. 149.
7. Ibid. 164.
8. Ibid. 211, 194–232.
9. Ibid. 271.

win their own fight."[10] Like the rerun of a badly worn film, General Maxwell Taylor reported in August 1964 that "the government is ineffective, beset by inexperienced ministers who are jealous and suspicious of each other," and not trusted by Khanh; the "population is confused and apathetic"; Khanh had no "popular support."[11] President Johnson was led to ask in September, "can we really strengthen the GVN," the government of Vietnam.[12] On the occasion of the coup which brought General Ky and General Thieu into power, General Taylor lectured them like schoolboys, saying, "we Americans are tired of coups," and that the military plans "are dependent on government stability."[13] John McNaughton, Assistant Secretary of Defense, reported in September 1964 that the situation "is deteriorating," and "promises to lead to . . . more rapid deterioration. . . . War weariness was apparent."[14]

General Taylor stated in November 1964: "After a year of changing and ineffective government, the counter-insurgency program country-wide is bogged down and will require heroic treatment to assure revival"; and added, "it is impossible to foresee a stable and effective government under any name in anything like the near future"; we "sense the mounting feeling of war weariness and hoplessness which pervade South Vietnam." Further,

> This chronic weakness is a critical liability to future plans. Without an effective central government with which to mesh the U.S. effort the latter is a spinning wheel unable to transmit impulsion to the machinery of the GVN.[15]

In June 1965 General Taylor reported the "very tenuous hold the new government" of Thieu and Ky "had on the country."[16] In June also, General Westmoreland reported that the South Vietnamese "desertion rates are inordinately high," as were the battle losses; in the words of the Pentagon study, the South Vietnamese forces were "devoured by the enemy."[17] McNamara noted in July 1965 Westmoreland's report that South Vietnamese battalions

10. Ibid. 279–281.
11. Ibid. 293.
12. Ibid. 315.
13. Ibid. 379–381; Halberstam 509.
14. Pent. Pap. 355.
15. Ibid. 370–371.
16. Ibid. 413.
17. Ibid. 410, 409.

were "being chewed up and . . . showing some signs of reluctance to engage in offensive operations."[18] No improvement was noted by McNamara in November 1965: "the Ky 'government of generals' is . . . not acquiring wide support or generating actions; pacification is thoroughly stalled"; there is "increased infiltration . . . and willingness of the Communist forces to stand and fight."[19] In opposition to further increases in the war effort, McNamara wrote in October 1966 that, despite the bombing program, "we find ourselves . . . if anything worse off. This important war must be fought and won by the Vietnamese themselves . . . But the discouraging truth is that . . . we have not found the formula, the catalyst, for training and inspiring them into effective action." The rural population believe that "the GVN is really indifferent to the people's welfare"; there is "corruption high and low."[20] At length McNamara concluded, in May 1967, that we are under no "obligation to pour in effort out of proportion to the effort contributed by the people of South Vietnam or in the face of coups, corruption, apathy or other indications of Saigon failure to cooperate effectively with us."[21] Of all this nary a word seeped out to the public. The people were entitled to know that the Saigon regime the administration was ostensibly bent on saving had, in the words of George Ball, "constantly to be propped up like a drunk by a lamppost."[22]

B. *Bombing*

"Fear that South Vietnam was politically disintegrating," Ball correctly states, "was the decisive argument for initiating our ill-conceived air offensive in early 1965."[23] After World War II, a Strategic Survey team had concluded that allied bombing of Germany had been "surprisingly ineffective, rallied German morale and spurred industrial production."[24]

The bombing of North Vietnam, as the inner circle soon learned, was to achieve similar results. In part the decision to bomb sprang from a desire to avoid the commitment of ground combat troops,

18. Ibid. 456.
19. Ibid. 488.
20. Ibid. 543, 546.
21. Ibid. 583.
22. Ball, supra, n. 3 at 43.
23. Ibid. 40. General Taylor despaired of improving Saigon effectiveness and turned to bombing as a will-breaking device; Pent. Pap. 390; see also ibid. 314, 352.
24. Halberstam 495.

and in part it derived from the illusion, to quote Stewart Alsop, "that wars can be won cheaply by dropping bombs from airplanes."[25] General Taylor, however, had foreseen in August 1964 that bombing the North to prevent the collapse of the Khanh regime in the South, "increases the likelihood of U.S. involvement in ground action."[26] On the eve of the bombing program McNaughton advised McNamara that the situation probably could not be "bottomed out (a) without extreme measures against [North Vietnam] and/or (b) without deployment of large numbers of U.S. (and other) combat troops inside SVN."[27]

Conceived "to break the will" of North Vietnam,[28] after the fashion of Nazi terror-bombing of Rotterdam and London, the objective soon shifted to interdiction of troops and supplies. In neither case was the objective realized. In April 1965 John McCone, Director of the Central Intelligence Agency, stated that the "strikes to date have not caused a change in the North Vietnamese policy of directing Viet Cong insurgency, infiltrating cadres and supplying material. If anything the strikes . . . have hardened their attitude."[29] This was the burden of a November 1965 report by the Defense Intelligence Agency, with elaborate explanations based on the rural nature of the area and subsistence economy, so that assumptions based upon interdiction bombing of highly developed industrial nations were misleading.[30] The failure to interdict infiltration of men and materiel into South Vietnam was acknowledged by McNaughton in January 1966,[31] and documented by a team of forty-seven scientists, who in the summer of 1966 made a secret study of the bombing program at McNamara's suggestion under the aegis of the Institute for Defense Analysis. The team went on to discount rosy estimates that increase and expansion of the bombing would be more productive.[32] McNamara confirmed in October 1966 that the bombing program had not "significantly affected infiltration or cracked the morale of Hanoi.

25. Stewart Alsop, book review, N.Y. Times, Jan. 28, 1973, Book Rev. sec.
26. Pent. Pap. 314.
27. Ibid. 433.
28. Ibid. 390, 394, 476.
29. Ibid. 440. Sir Robert Thompson reported that the bombing "is unifying North Vietnam"; ibid. 579. Over the years there was a stream of gloomy intelligence appraisals which prophetically read the portents. Some will appear in this narrative. For others see ibid. 180, 330–331, 459, 474, 475, 476–478, 494, 535, 550. See also Halberstam 278–279, 307, 356, 485.
30. Pent. Pap. 469.
31. Ibid. 472.
32. Ibid. 483–484; 502–506.

There is agreement in the intelligence community on these facts," for which he supplied an Appendix.[33] And, in November 1966, he concluded: "in spite of an interdiction campaign costing at least $250 million per month at current levels, no significant impact on the war in South Vietnam is evident."[34] Against the disappointing results of the bombing had to be weighed the costs summarized by McNamara on May 19, 1967: "it costs American lives; it creates a backfire of revulsion and opposition by killing civilians; it creates serious risks; it may harden the enemy."[35]

This, it hardly needs to be said, was not the view of the military. McNamara noted in October 1966 that "General Westmoreland, as do the JCS, strongly believes in the military value of the bombing program."[36] More and larger doses of the same was recommended by the military. Then there was the school impatient of all restrictions, led by General Curtis LeMay, who would "bomb them into the Stone Age,"[37] to preserve our "reputation" as a guarantor against Communist "aggression." Strategic bombing, McGeorge Bundy wrote to President Johnson in May 1967, "does tend to divide the U.S.," and the apparent majority support for the bombing "rests upon an erroneous belief in its effectiveness as a means to end the war."[38] By May 1967 McNamara had come to see that "The picture of the world's greatest super-power killing or seriously injuring 1,000 noncombatants a week, while trying to pound a tiny backward nation into submission on an issue whose merits are hotly disputed, is not a pretty one."[39] All such doubts and intelligence were concealed from Congress and the public at at a time when the war effort was being rapidly escalated.

C. *Commitment of Combat Troops*

On April 1, 1965, President Johnson decided on the use of ground troops for offensive action because, though the bombing had just begun, the administration perceived that "it was not going to stave off collapse in the South."[40] Up to this time the

33. Ibid. 543, 550; see also ibid. 577.
34. Ibid. 555. Bombing costs rose in 1966 to $1.2 billions, with little more accomplishment than about 20,000 civilian casualties; ibid. 523.
35. Ibid. 579.
36. Ibid. 548.
37. Halberstam 462.
38. Pent. Pap. 570.
39. Ibid. 580.
40. Ibid. 382.

mission of the small body of American troops had been employed for defense of small enclaves;[41] now "the President approved a change of mission . . . to permit their more active use," and the deployment of 18,000 to 20,000 more troops.[42] And, with duplicity that was to find repeated illustration as the pressure to conceal mounted, he stated (in paraphrase by the National Security Action Memorandum) his desire that

> premature publicity be avoided by all possible precautions. The actions themselves should be taken as rapidly as practicable, but in ways that should minimize any appearances of sudden change in policy . . . The President's desire is that these movements and changes should be understood as being gradual and wholly consistent with existing policy.[43]

But the change from defense of a few enclaves to the offensive, shortly to emerge as Westmoreland's "search and destroy,"[44] was "wholly [*in*]consistent with existing policy"; and both Congress and the people were entitled to be informed of the drastic shift.

In 1954 General Matthew Ridgway, the hero of Korea, sensible of the pressure for an American take-over of the war in Vietnam, dispatched a picked team to investigate the needs such a take-over would engender. He found that from 500,000 to 1,000,000 men would be needed, "plus enormous construction costs" for bases, port facilities, and the like. The idea of intervention was abandoned.[45] General Taylor had advised President Kennedy in November 1961 that, "if the first contingent is not enough to accomplish the necessary results, it will be difficult to resist the pressure to reinforce . . . there is no limit to our possible commitment (unless we attack the source in Hanoi)," an attack that was thought to present the risks of bringing China and Russia into the conflict.[46] In February 1964 General Taylor objected that the placing of "any considerable number of Marines in areas beyond those presently assigned . . . would be [a] step in reversing long-standing policy of avoiding commitment of ground combat forces in South Vietnam. Once this policy is breached, it will be very difficult to hold the line."[47] McCone, Director of CIA, a proponent

41. Ibid. 401, 411.
42. Ibid. 382; Halberstam 574.
43. Pent. Pap. 383.
44. Ibid. 411.
45. Halberstam 143–144.
46. Pent. Pap. 141. McNaughton wrote in March 1965, "Once U.S. troops are in, it will be difficult to withdraw them . . . without admitting defeat"; ibid. 437.
47. Halberstam 546.

of intensive bombing, advised in April 1965 that we "can expect requirements for an ever-increasing commitment of U.S. personnel without materially improving the chances of victory . . . we will find ourselves mired down in combat in the jungle in a military effort that we cannot win, and which we will have extreme difficulty in extracting ourselves.[48]

Such prophecies were speedily realized. There was first the precipitous rise in demands for combat troops. In April 1965 it was considered that 82,000 men would "accomplish the 'victory strategy.' "[49] Westmoreland's requests for troops jumped to 175,000 in June, to 275,000 in July, to 443,000 in December, and to 542,000 in June 1966, all of which were not disclosed to the public.[50] And Assistant Secretary of Defense Alain Enthoven reported in May 1967, on the basis of analytical studies, that "the size of the force we deploy has little effect on the rate of attrition of enemy forces," and that the military "has ignored this type of information in discussing force levels."[51] It took Westmoreland's request for an additional 206,000 troops after the shattering enemy Tet offensive in early 1968 to shock Johnson into a realization that this was a bottomless pit. Now Clark Clifford, McNamara's successor as Secretary of Defense, asked, if "we follow the present course in SVN, could it ever prove successful even if vastly more than 200,000 troops were sent?"[52] All this was the result, to borrow from McNaughton, of an "enormous miscalculation,"[53] a failure to take counter-escalation into account.

Emmett John Hughes tells us that in March 1965, McGeorge Bundy rejected the possibility that North Vietnam would retaliate "by matching the American air escalation with their own ground escalation."[54] Yet in contrast to the dismal prognosis for South

48. Pent. Pap. 441. Ball, too, predicted "almost certainly a protracted war involving an open-ended commitment of U.S. forces, mounting U.S. casualties, no assurance of a satisfactory solution, and a serious danger of escalation at the end of the road . . . Once we suffer large casualties, we will have started a well-nigh irreversible process. Our involvement will be so great that we cannot—without national humiliation—stop short of achieving our national objectives"; ibid. 450.

49. Ibid. 407.

50. Ibid. 459. According to Halberstam, Westmoreland told Eugene Black in 1965 that "we must not take away this war from the Vietnamese. If we did, we would be in the same position as the French, and it would be hopeless." Beyond 175,000 American troops, "they would give up the war, and it would get worse and worse"; Halberstam 597.

51. Pent. Pap. 573.

52. Ibid. 597–598.

53. Ibid. 491.

54. Halberstam 528.

Vietnamese efforts, there was constant recognition of the "great" progress of the Viet Cong, of their high motivation and morale.[55] Said General Taylor in November 1964:

> The ability of the Viet Cong continuously to rebuild their units and to make good their losses is one of the mysteries of the guerilla war . . . Not only do the Viet Cong units have the recuperative powers of the phoenix, but they have an amazing ability to maintain morale.[56]

It did not amaze the intelligence community. Intelligence analyses of the time stated that the primary sources of Communist strength in South Vietnam arose out of the revolutionary social aims of the Communists and their identification with the nationalist cause during the independence struggle with France in the 1950's.[57] Opposed to this fervor was a string, as George Ball puts it, of "practical-minded juntas that succeeded one another in Saigon [and] blithely pursued the corrupt politics that came naturally to them,"[58] indifferent to the peasantry which was the backbone of the nation. The administration resolutely shut its eyes to the political maxim that "you can't beat somethin' with nuthin'."

Slowly Westmoreland learned (August 1966) that "we must not underestimate the enemy, nor his determination. The war can continue to escalate."[59] Again, in April 1967, Westmoreland, asking for an additional 100,000 troops, stated that "counter-action" must be anticipated; whereupon President Johnson asked, "When we add divisions can't the enemy add divisions? If so, where does it all end?" To which Westmoreland could make no good answer.[60]

The answer was *stalemate*. McCone, we have seen, had warned that we would be "mired down" in inextricable jungle warfare.[61] "No one can assure you," wrote Ball to Johnson on July 1, 1965, "that we can beat the Viet Cong or even force them to the conference table on our own terms, no matter how many hundred thousand *white, foreign* (U.S.) troops we deploy." The alternative to limiting our liabilities, he counseled, "is almost certainly a protracted war involving an open-ended commitment of U.S. forces, mounting U.S. casualties, no assurance of a satisfactory solution,

55. Pent. Pap. 190, 272, 282.
56. Ibid. 372.
57. Ibid. 242.
58. Ball, supra, n. 3 at 40.
59. Pent. Pap. 501.
60. Ibid. 567.
61. Supra, text accompanying n. 48.

and a serious danger of escalation at the end of the road."[62] Recommending increased deployments in November 1965, McNamara cautioned that they "will not guarantee success. U.S. killed in action can be expected to reach 1,000 a month, and the odds are even that we will be faced in early 1967 with a 'no-decision' at an even higher level."[62a] In April 1966 William Bundy, Assistant Secretary of State, said: "As we look a year or two ahead, with a military program that would require major further budget costs—with all their implications for taxes and domestic programs —and with steady or probably rising casualties, the war could well become an albatross around the Administration's neck at least equal to what Korea was for President Truman in 1952."[63] McNamara concluded in October 1966 that "The prognosis is bad that the war can be brought to a satisfactory conclusion within the next two years . . . The solution lies in girding openly, for a longer war."[64] CIA advised in March 1968 that the addition of 200,000 troops would merely spell more stalemate.[65] The situation was summed up by Assistant Secretary of Defense, Alain Enthoven, who headed the Pentagon Office of Systems Analysis:

> While we have raised the price to NVN of aggression and support of the VC, it shows no lack of capability or will to match each new escalation. Our strategy of "attrition" has not worked. Adding 206,000 men to a force of 525,000 . . . at an added cost to the U.S. of $10-billion per year raises the question of who is making it costly for whom . . . We have achieved stalemate at a high commitment.[66]

Only the military could not learn. Reporting that the surprise enemy Tet offensive early in 1968 "was a very near thing," that the American troops would now "be hard pressed to meet adequately all threats," that "we must be prepared to accept some reverses," General Wheeler, Chairman of the JCS, had but one solution—yet another 200,000 troops.[67] "It is amazing," recently stated Stewart Alsop, "how consistently the advice of the military

62. Pent. Pap. 449–450. He continued, "No one has demonstrated that a white ground force of whatever size can win a guerrilla war—which is at the same time a civil war between Asians—in jungle terrain in the midst of a population that refuses cooperation to the white forces (and the South Vietnamese) and thus provides a great intelligence advantage to the other side"; ibid.

62a. Ibid. 489, 490.

63. Ibid. 474–475.

64. Ibid. 549. For his dismal evaluation of the state of affairs, see ibid. 543.

65. Ibid. 599.

66. Ibid. 600–601.

67. Ibid. 617, 620.

to the President has been bad advice."[68] A telling illustration is Admiral U. S. Grant Sharp's prediction that the bombing of North Vietnam's oil installations would "bring the enemy to the conference table or cause the insurgency to wither from lack of support." The intelligence agencies questioned whether the oil depot bombing would have the predicted effect; and in the event McNamara pointed out to the military the glaring discrepancy between their optimistic estimates and their disappointing results.[69]

More disturbing was the readiness of the military to suppress intelligence that might militate against their advice. Under General Paul Harkins, Halberstam states, "the facts would be fitted to Washington's hopes," the intelligence reports "were edited down by the operations people, and the Vietcong capability was always downgraded and reduced."[70] A massive 1965 CIA intelligence estimate predicted that "the Viet Cong, and in particular the North Vietnamese, had an enormous capacity to escalate if the United States bombed." By the time it left the office of General Taylor, now ambassador at Saigon, "the paragraphs which told of the North Vietnamese response were missing."[71] A flabbergasting example, if we may credit Halberstam's account, concerns General Westmoreland. At his request, Colonel William Crossen, a top intelligence officer, did an estimate of the enemy capacity for reinforcement and, greatly surprised by his figures, rechecked, only to conclude that the enemy had "an amazing capacity and

68. Alsop, supra, n. 25. Alsop instances "The Navy and Army officers on the spot pooh-poohed any danger of a successful Japanese strike against Pearl Harbor. The Joint Chiefs unanimously favored MacArthur's 'go north' policy in Korea; they supported the Bay of Pigs plan; they favored a 'surgical strike' against Cuba; and they unanimously supported the disastrous 1965 escalation in Vietnam." The generals "simply suffer from a professional deformation, and this deformation discourages the timidities and dubieties which should be very much a part of the decision-making process"; ibid.

69. Pent. Pap. 476–478, 480–481. Compare Sharp's admission in January 1968 that, despite the bombing, "the enemy has been able to replace or rehabilitate many of the items damaged or destroyed, and transport inventories are roughly at the same level they were at the beginning of the year." The enemy efforts had merely been made more "costly"; ibid. 614. Compare Air Force Secretary Brown's recommendation for "bombing of military targets without the present scrupulous concern for collateral civilian damage and casualties," notwithstanding he acknowledged that it would not "be likely to reduce NVN capability in SVN substantially below the 1967 level," and that North Vietnam would probably "be willing to undergo these hardships"; ibid. 606.

70. Halberstam 186.

71. Ibid. 508. During the trial of Daniel Ellsberg, a Central Intelligence analyst, Samuel Adams, testified that he had attended conferences in Saigon and Hawaii and at the agency, in which the military purposely diminished estimates of enemy strength in Vietnam; N.Y. Times, Mar. 7, 1973, p. 1.

capability of reinforcing." "Impossible," said Westmoreland; upon being assured that the figures had been checked and double-checked, he said, "Jesus, if we tell this to the people in Washington we'll be out of the war tomorrow! We'll have to revise it downward."[72] Confirmation of such incidents has just come from within the Army itself. Major General Daniel O. Graham, who moved to the Defense Intelligence Agency, stated that the "relatively recent realization of military leaders that they should not try to bend intelligence to support their pet projects has improved the quality of strategic military estimates."[73]

Another hurtful concealment was of the estimates that this would be a long and costly war, as Michael V. Forrestal, a White House aide, advised President Kennedy in February 1963.[74] General Taylor informed McNamara in January 1964 that "it would be unrealistic to believe that a complete suppression of the insurgency can take place in one or even two years. The British effort in Malaya is a recent example of a counter-insurgency effort which required approximately ten years."[75] According to Halberstam, Westmoreland stated in June 1965 to Eugene Black, for reiteration in Washington: "if I get the troops I ask for and all the breaks . . . it will take six or seven years to turn it around."[76] At the same time, the Chairman of the JCS, General Earle Wheeler, told President Johnson, Halberstam recounts, that "to drive the last Vietcong out of Vietnam it will take seven hundred, eight hundred thousand, a million men and about seven years," and even then "we would have to keep a major force there for perhaps as long as twenty or thirty years,"[77] as Korea was to prove. That these 1965 estimates were not far off is disclosed by Westmoreland's advice to Johnson in April 1967 that, with 565,000 men, "the war could well go on for three years," and with "650,-000 men, it could go on for two years."[78] In the result the war went on for almost seven years, until 1973. But congressional critics, such as Senator Ernest Gruening, were told by President Johnson that six months of bombing would get the enemy to the table, an estimate also leaked to the press.[79]

72. Halberstam 545.
73. N.Y. Times, April 11, 1973, p. 9.
74. Pent. Pap. 113.
75. Ibid. 275.
76. Halberstam 597.
77. Ibid. 596–597.
78. Pent. Pap. 568.
79. Halberstam 577–578.

D. *American Objectives*

What were the objectives for which the nation was being asked to sacrifice untold lives and money? They were confused and shifting. One was ostensibly the right of "self-determination," the right of the people of South Vietnam "to determine their own future."[80] Before the 1964 election, when Lyndon Johnson was opposing Senator Barry Goldwater—the advocate of full-scale bombing of North Vietnam—as the candidate of reason and restraint, Johnson was speaking out against "committing a good many American boys to fighting a war that I think ought to be fought by the boys of Asia to help protect their own land."[81] The genuineness of such expressions was impeached by Johnson's instruction to Ambassador Henry Cabot Lodge to knock "down the idea of neutralization wherever it rears its ugly head,"[82] that is, a neutralist coalition with the Communist forces which might invite the United States to leave, never mind that it might bring peace to the war-weary Vietnamese. Self-determination is also hardly reconcilable with the statement in a position paper submitted by William Bundy on November 24, 1964: "The United States would seek to control any negotiations and would oppose any independent South Vietnamese efforts to negotiate."[83]

A more candid appraisal emerged in January 1965, with the expression by McNamara and McNaughton that our objective was "not to 'help friend' but to contain China."[84] The military, and with only little less zeal, the inner circle, were wedded to the "falling domino" theory that if South Vietnam went, all the rest of Southeast Asia would fall to the Communists.[85] The "domino" theory had been rejected in November 1964 by George Ball, and it was strongly challenged in January 1965 by the CIA.[86] By May 1967 that theory no longer seemed tenable to McNamara.[87]

Another motive was to protect our reputation as a guarantor. McNamara stated in March 1964 that, in the eyes of the world,

80. Pent. Pap. 583.
81. Ibid. 310–311.
82. Ibid. 285, 244. See infra, n. 109.
83. Ibid. 375. Compare the imposition of conditions for a halt of bombing known to be tougher than Hanoi could accept; ibid. 470. See also infra, n. 105.
84. Pent. Pap. 342.
85. Ibid. 254–255; see also ibid. 572.
86. Ibid. 325, 254.
87. Ibid. 583.

"the South Vietnam conflict is regarded as a test case of U.S. capacity to help a nation meet the Communist war of liberation."[88] Better attuned to realities, George Ball heavily discounted "the effect of [a settlement] on the credibility of our commitments around the world," noting in particular that "the principal anxiety of our NATO Allies is that we have become too preoccupied with an area that seems to them an irrelevance and may be tempted in neglect to our NATO responsibilities"; that they would "be inclined to regard a compromise solution in South Vietnam more as new evidence of American maturity than of American loss of face." Our role in the war, he continued, was "perceptively [sic] eroding the respect and confidence with which other nations regard us."[89]

In March 1965 McNaughton quantified our aims:

70%—To avoid a humiliating defeat (to our reputation as a guarantor).
20%—To keep SVN (and the adjacent territory) from Chinese hands.
10%—To permit the people of SVN to enjoy a better, freer way of life. . . .
NOT—to "help a friend" . . .[90]

Changing course in May 1967, McNamara downgraded fears of the "falling dominoes," and emphasized that "(1) Our commitment is only to see that the people of South Vietnam are permitted to determine their own future. (2) This commitment ceases if the country ceases to help itself." No longer should our goal be "to guarantee that the self-chosen government is non-Communist." Grasping the nettle at last, he said that we have no obligation "to pour out an effort out of proportion to the effort contributed by the people of South Vietnam or in the face of corruption, apathy or other indications of Saigon failure to cooperate effectively with us."[91]

To this the JCS strongly objected, intruding into the area of political judgment for which they had no special competence and which, under our theory of government, was reserved to the civilians. They asserted that McNamara "fails to appreciate the full

88. Ibid. 284, 438.
89. Ibid. 452–454.
90. Ibid. 432. By January 1965 McNaughton had come to believe that "the US end is solely to preserve our reputation as a guarantor," and that it was time to scale down our victory aims; ibid. 492.
91. Ibid. 583. President Eisenhower had written to Diem in 1954 that the United States would help the Vietnamese only if they would and could help themselves; Ball, supra, n. 3 at 50.

implications for the free world of failure" in Vietnam. Nothing less than "a significant escalation of the war with a call-up of reserves" was needed.[92] But it was the generals who grossly misconceived world opinion,[93] as was to be revealed when President Nixon ordered full-scale bombing of Hanoi, to the horror of the world.[94] In "the eyes of mankind," justly concluded George Ball, "our poor, wretched opponents . . . came eventually to be seen as the valiant underdogs, and we the blundering bully,"[95] once again underscoring Clemenceau's aphorism that war, let alone the underlying political judgments, is too important to be left to the generals.

We can only conjecture whether the course of events would have been changed had the foregoing facts been spread before Congress

92. Pent. Pap. 538. The potent behind-the-scenes influence of the military may be gathered from the Pentagon analysts' remark that the President did not adopt the McNamara approach in view of the need to keep "the military 'on board' in any new direction for the U.S. effort in Southeast Asia." This, remarks Hedrick Smith, "is evidently an allusion to reports at the time that some high-ranking officers were in the mood to threaten resignation if the McNamara policy was adopted"; ibid. 515.

In October-November 1964, a number of bombing options were under consideration, among them a "limited-duration selective bombing campaign as a last effort to save the South . . . accompanied [by] a propaganda campaign about the unwinnability of the war given the [Saigon] ineptness, and then [to seek] negotiations through compromise and neutralization when the bombing failed." Because of "forceful objections" by Admiral Mustin, the representative of the Joint Chiefs, this was "downgraded in the final paper presented to the National Security Council," in the words of the Pentagon analyst, "rejected before [it was] fully explored"; ibid. 323–324.

93. Prime Minister Harold Wilson wrote Johnson on Nov. 3, 1965, respecting proposed bombing of oil targets near Hanoi and Haiphong: "as seen from here, the possible military benefits that may result from this bombing do not appear to outweigh the political disadvantages that would seem the inevitable consequence. . . . I remain convinced that the bombing of these targets without producing decisive military advantage . . . may only increase the difficulty of reaching an eventual settlement . . . if this action is taken we shall have to dissociate ourselves from it . . . the effect on public opinion in this country—and I believe throughout Western Europe—is likely to be such as to reinforce the existing disquiet and criticism that we have had to deal with"; ibid. 449. This dealt a body blow to the rationale that we were acting to protect our reputation as a guarantor. As McNaughton observed, "since it is our *reputation* that is at stake, it is important that we do not construe our obligation to be more than do the countries whose opinions of us *are* our reputation"; ibid. 492. Under the guise of preserving our reputation with the world, we were undertaking measures from which it shrank.

Alistair Buchan, for many years director of the Institute of Strategic Studies, then Commandant of the Imperial Defense College, and now professor of international relations at Oxford, expressed in The Times of London "the anger and contempt which President Nixon's resumption of bombing in North Vietnam arouses in this country." He labeled it a "cruel act of technological bad temper"; N.Y. Times, Jan. 6, 1973, p. 29.

94. See infra, Appendix C (Palme)

95. Ball, supra, n. 3 at 13; and see supra, text accompanying n. 39.

and the people.[96] But undeniably they were deprived of the choice which was theirs to make. They had a right to know that the success of our intervention was dependent upon a succession of shaky, corrupt satrapies, that our aims were open to grave doubt, that one measure after another had proved ineffective, that the cost of attaining our objectives would be steeply mounting casualties and billions of dollars, that the military estimated that the war would be protracted beyond the imagining of the man in the street, and that the inner circle itself bleakly saw stalemate at ever higher levels. Given the frightful stakes, it suffices, in the words of Neil Sheehan, that "knowledge of these policy debates and the dissents from the intelligence agencies might have given Congress and the public a different attitude toward the publicly announced decisions of the successive administrations."[97]

Instead of disclosure there was a web of deception, because there was awareness in the inner circle of public uneasiness.[98] So, for example, McNaughton outlined a plan in September 1964, which would "create as little risk as possible of the kind of military action which would be difficult to justify to the American public."[99] In March 1965 McNaughton wrote: "Large U.S. troop deployments are blocked by 'French defeat' and 'Korea' syndromes."[100] It was rather disclosure of the deployments that was blocked, witness the rise from 82,000 to 443,000 troops in a matter of months. Johnson himself cautioned after the meeting of "100 people" at the Honolulu conference of February 9, 1966: "I don't want to have come out of this meeting that we have come up and added on X divisions and Y battalions or Z regiments or D dollars because one good story about how many billions are going to be spent can bring us more inflation."[101] In the event, inflation was born of concealment of precisely such facts and the inescapable need to finance massive expenditures as we went along. It was because Johnson refused to look economic realities in the face and to take Congress and the

96. Perhaps the prevailing fear of Communist aggression would have carried all before it. Pent. Pap. 651.

97. Ibid. xiii.

98. See, e.g., supra, text accompanying n. 43. Shortly after Johnson's election in November 1964 the N.Y. Times stated, "if the Asian war is to be converted into an American war, the country has a right to insist that it be told what has changed so profoundly in the last two months to justify it"; Pent. Pap. 646.

99. Ibid. 356.

100. Ibid. 433.

101. Ibid. 496. Cf. Halberstam 456.

people into his confidence that we are now haunted by inflation.[102] At length McNaughton was driven to write to McNamara, in May 1967, that "a feeling is widely and strongly held that 'the Establishment' is out of its mind."[103]

Three years earlier, McNaughton, knowing that military action against North Vietnam "would be difficult to justify to the American public," yet recommending action "likely at some point to provoke a military DRV response," cautioned in what is surely a jewel of American double-speak that "During the next two months, because of the lack of 'rebuttal time' before elections to justify particular actions which may be distorted to the U.S. public, we must exercise special care."[104] In the vernacular, keep these provocative actions under wraps until after the election. Examples of Johnsonian duplicity are too numerous to catalogue. One example must suffice. When the shift from enclave defense to offensive ground operations was under active discussion and in immediate contemplation, President Johnson could tell the press, "I know of no far-reaching strategy that is being suggested or promulgated."[105] Indeed, when the State Department Press Officer, Robert McCloskey, let the cat out of the bag in June 1965 by a statement that the American forces "would be available for combat support," he was repudiated by a White House statement: "There has been no change in the mission of the United States ground combat units . . . The primary mission of these troops is to secure and safeguard important military installations."[106] This though the Commandant of the Marine Corps had blurted out in April that "the marines were not in Vietnam to 'sit on their

102. Halberstam 603–610; Edwin L. Dale, Jr., "What Vietnam Did to the American Economy," N.Y. Times, Jan. 28, 1973, sec. 3, p. 1.

103. Pent. Pap. 534.

104. Ibid. 356, 357.

105. Ibid. 400. Compare supra, text accompanying n. 43. Consider Johnson's attempt to obtain public support for the air war by striking a position of compromise, stating that he offered to negotiate "without posing any preconditions," about which the Pentagon study states, the moves masked publicly unstated conditions that "were not 'compromise' terms, but more akin to a 'cease and desist' order that, from [the enemy] point of view was tantamount to their surrender"; Pent. Pap. 388. In November 1964, it "was stressed that the US should define its negotiating position 'in a way which makes Communist acceptance unlikely' "; ibid. 324–325. In a memorandum of Dec. 3, 1965, McNaughton outlined the conditions upon which the United States should insist and commented that they amounted to "capitulation by a Communist force that is far from beaten"; ibid. 471. See also Johnson's dissimulation with respect to the enemy Tet offensive, ibid. 592; cf. ibid. 596, 616, 561; Halberstam 599.

106. Pent. Pap. 411.

dittyboxes . . . they were there to kill Vietcong,' " as was soon attested by a "search and destroy operation" on June 27.[107] Notwithstanding, Johnson could reply on July 28 to a question whether the deployment of additional troops in Vietnam implied "any change in the existing policy of relying mainly on South Vietnamese to carry out offensive operations and using American forces to guard installations and act as emergency back-up," "it does not imply any change in policy whatever."[108] Such unblushing assertions go beyond the President's failure to confide in Congress and the people; they spell, to use the ugly word, deception.[109] For me the lesson of Vietnam is that Executive secrecy nourishes the very arrogance of power which the Founders sought to avoid; it shields gigantic miscalculations, and in the end it conduces to one-man decisionmaking that cost the nation dear.

E. *Suppression of the Pentagon Papers*

"The story of the Pentagon Papers," said Justice Douglas, "is a chronicle of suppression of vital decisions to protect the reputations and political hides of men who worked an amazingly successful scheme of deception on the American people."[110] When Senator J. W. Fulbright, Chairman of the Senate Foreign Relations Committee asked, on November 11, 1969, for a copy of the Pentagon Papers in aid of the Committee's "review of Vietnam policy issues," Secretary of Defense Melvin Laird replied that "it would clearly be contrary to the national interest" to supply them.[111] Since then an impressive array of former members of the Kennedy and Johnson administrations—the period covered by the Pentagon Papers—and a roster of members of the intelligence community,

107. Ibid. 410, 401, 404–405.

108. Ibid. 416; cf. ibid. 463, 467, 457.

109. Halberstam 655, 661, 599. Johnson's Press Secretary, George Reedy, later stated, "President Johnson went out of his way to conceal from the Congress and the public what he really had in mind in 1964. How he could ever run the campaign he did in 1964, and have in mind what he evidently did have in mind, is beyond belief"; Fulbright Hearings 450–451. See supra, n. 2, and text accompanying nn. 81–82.

110. Gravel v. United States, 408 U.S. 606, 647 (1972), dissenting.

111. Ervin Hearings 37–39. Assistant Attorney General Rehnquist testified that this was "not a claim of executive privilege," 3 Moorhead Hearings 782, which, under the President's instructions could "not be used without specific Presidential approval"; Ervin Hearings 37. Laird's letter made no reference to such approval, and, said Rehnquist, might well be regarded as unauthorized; Ervin Hearings 442. See also supra, Ch. 1, n. 32; Ch. 8, n. 113.

past and present, have testified, in the trial of Daniel Ellsberg, that publication of the Papers by the *New York Times* in June 1971 was not injurious to the national interest.[112]

The military argument to the contrary proved vulnerable. For example, General William G. Dupuy, a prosecution witness, testified that a 1968 JCS "memorandum on the effects of the Communist Tet offensive in the spring of that year could have helped Hanoi plan last year's [1972] Tet offensive." On cross-examination, he conceded that, by March 1969, Hanoi could have purchased the same information in a report written by General William Westmoreland from the Government Printing Office, a report that Dupuy himself had helped to edit.[113] Under pressure from the trial judge, the prosecution produced exculpatory evidence from its own files. One Department of Defense analysis of a volume of Pentagon Papers concluded that "review of this volume does not show that its compromise would effect in any way national defense interests in 1969 or today." With respect to another volume, a Defense Department evaluation stated: "Since virtually all the information presented in this volume has been in the public domain prior to 1969, it would be difficult, if not impossible, to assess the contents of the volume as having any effect whatsoever on national defense as of 1969."[114] Similar conclusions, the *New York Times* states, were drawn in the analyses of eight other vol-

112. Lieut. Col. Edward A. Miller, Office of Security Review, Department of Defense, N.Y. Times, Feb. 4, 1973 (News of the Week Section) p. 10; McGeorge Bundy, one of the architects of the Vietnam policy, N.Y. Times, Mar. 10, 1973, p. 1; Arthur Schlesinger, Jr., Kennedy adviser, Boston Eve. Globe, Mar. 13, 1973, p. 10; John Kenneth Galbraith, N.Y. Times, Mar. 13, 1973, p. 13; Allen S. Whiting, formerly director of the office of research and analysis of the Far East Section of the State Department, Washington Star, Mar. 15, 1973, p. D-10; Adrian S. Fisher, former deputy-director of the United States Arms Control and Disarmament Agency, N.Y. Times, Mar. 29, 1973, p. 12; William Gerhard of the National Security Agency, who was assigned by the Defense Department to prepare analyses of the Pentagon Papers for the Ellsberg case, N.Y. Times, April 3, 1973, p. 16.

113. N.Y. Times, Jan. 20, 1973, p. 15. Dupuy was also controverted by Samuel Adams, a CIA analyst. N.Y. Times, Feb. 21, 1973, p. 1. Major General Paul F. Gorman testified that disclosure of a certain "execute message" from the JCS, dated Nov. 10, 1966, could damage the national defense, but was refuted by a report by Admiral U. S. G. Sharp, published in 1969, which "had more detail about the same 'execute message' than the Pentagon papers had"; N.Y. Times, Feb. 10, 1973, p. 9. An illuminating illustration of the need heavily to discount built-in military secretiveness was afforded by Gorman's statement that "as far as he was concerned, a geography book, public opinion polls and transcripts of Congressional hearings—all public information—could be helpful to foreign intelligence analysts"; N.Y. Times, Feb. 10, 1973, p. 9.

114. N.Y. Times, Feb. 1, 1973, p. 5.

umes by the Department of Defense and the State Department;[115] and it reported that Judge Matthew Byrne, the trial judge, stated that "much of the Government's own analyses showed that the disclosure of some of the documents had not in fact injured the national defense."[116]

However the impact on the national interest of disclosure to the *public* may be viewed, withholdings of the Pentagon Papers from the Senate Foreign Relations Committee and from Congress is something else again. Congress, as we have seen, was intended to be the senior partner in the new federal government, the chief agent in waging, continuing, and terminating war. It was therefore entitled to be advised of all the relevant facts that bear on those functions, in particular of the elaborate study that revealed the bankruptcy of the long-drawn, secret war policy. It is a measure of executive arrogance that refusal of this study to Congress was made in the name of the "national interest." Nowhere in the Constitution or in the several Conventions does it appear that the Founders looked to the President to protect the "national interest" against the Congress. The provision for impeachment of the President by the Congress alone suggests that it was Congress that was to protect the nation against the President.

"It is terribly important," said former Under Secretary of State George Ball, "that the information that is made available to Congress when it goes to look at these things is the same information and all of the same information that is in the hands of the executive."[117] Former Justice Goldberg, Ambassador to the United Nations during the Johnson regime, stated, "we would be in a better position as a nation if a study of this character had been submitted to responsible committees of Congress."[118] One who has studied the documents published in the Pentagon Papers must find it difficult to come to a contrary conclusion. Thus, the *constitutional right* of Congress to be fully informed and consulted with respect to all matters pertaining to warmaking is fortified by practical con-

115. Ibid.
116. N.Y. Times, Feb. 4, 1963, p. 25.
117. Fulbright Hearings 637.
118. 1 Moorhead Hearings 25. Speaking of one volume of the Pentagon Papers, a section dealing with Kennedy's hopes to withdraw American troops, Arthur Schlesinger, Jr., a Kennedy adviser, stated, "had this volume been disclosed earlier we would have been spared much blood and agony in southeast Asia"; Boston Eve. Globe, Mar. 13, 1973, p. 10.

siderations that speak against secrecy. Secrecy deprived Congress and the people of their options, with calamitous consequences.[119]

The appeal to the "national interest" by the Nixon administration for withholding the Pentagon study was, I suggest, a cover-up for a felt need to suppress a study that might disenchant the American public with President Nixon's continuance of the war. It attempted to stifle criticism of the wisdom of carrying on a war that had toppled the Johnson administration, that was to cost another 20,000 lives and to result in a peace that is already falling apart as these lines are written. Whether this was too high a price to pay for Nixon's Carthaginian "peace with honor" may be left to historians.[120]

119. Vietnam richly confirms Congressman John E. Moss's statement that "the branch of government which successfully asserts control over information is going to dominate the government"; Ervin Hearings 332.

120. George Ball stated that we have "made a desert of much of the area; and in view of all the napalm and defoliants, more than one million refugees, and 1.3 million casualties—and particularly with memories still fresh of the Christmas bombing when we used civilian deaths as an instrument of diplomacy—we should be neither surprised nor outraged if the phrase 'peace with honor' evokes derisive echoes in some precincts of the world"; Ball supra, n. 3 at 52. Mr. Nixon bought his "honor" dear.

10

PRACTICAL ARGUMENTS FOR EXECUTIVE PRIVILEGE EXAMINED

BEFORE we assay the practical arguments for executive privilege it is well to recall that the wisdom of an allocation of power is not a test of its constitutionality.[1] Only when the constitutional provisions are ambiguous or equivocal may considerations of policy tip the scales. So clear is the grant of comprehensive inquisitorial power to Congress, the absence of any intention of the Founders to curtail that power and to confer any executive immunity from such inquiry, as to obviate the need to balance policy considerations. Even so, examination of competing policy pulls will confirm the wisdom of the parliamentary practice embodied in the constitutional grant of "legislative power."

By far the best argument that has been made for executive discretion to withhold information from Congress is that of Professor Joseph W. Bishop, a former Deputy General Counsel of the Army.[2] If his views understandably are colored by his experience, they are far removed from the swollen claims of Rogers, Nixon, and Kleindienst.[3] Bishop concluded that "whereas the present situation is quite tolerable ['not inimical to good government'] unlimited congressional access to executive information (whether 'secrets of state' or merely 'official information') would almost certainly be intolerable."[4]

Over the years the vast bulk of congressional requests for infor-

1. Gerald Gunther, *John Marshall's Defense of McCulloch v. Maryland* 190–191 (Stanford, 1969).

2. Joseph Bishop, "The Executive's Right of Privacy: An Unresolved Constitutional Question," 66 Yale L.J. 477 (1957). Professor Bishop did not explore the constitutional problems.

3. Although Bishop stated in 1971 that "Information can justifiably be withheld from Congress . . . only in very exceptional ["rare"] cases," Ervin Hearings 499, one wonders whether he would regard President Johnson's concealment of the Vietnam escalation, and the suppression of the Pentagon study, ibid. 30, 37–38, as "very exceptional."

4. Bishop 486.

mation have met with compliance,[5] from which we may conclude that "merely 'official information'" was freely turned over without "intolerable" consequences. The fact that the Peruvian foreign aid information, withheld by President Eisenhower because disclosure would be harmful in the extreme, was immediately delivered by President Kennedy with salutary rather than "intolerable" consequences suggests that considerable skepticism is in order.[6] Since Professor Bishop wrote, we have had years of "escalation by stealth" in Vietnam, and the suppression of the Pentagon study of the escalation, which cast grave doubt on the policy as well as its concealment; we have had secret agreements for Spanish bases and aid,[7] the 1969–1970 secret bombing in Cambodia, of which Congress was kept in the dark. Congress no less than the President, as Justice Douglas observed, is "trustee of the national welfare,"[8] and as cotrustee it is richly entitled to know and participate in matters that so profoundly affect the "national welfare." A study of the instances in which executive privilege was invoked[9] should persuade that the consequences that might flow from disclosure were not nearly of the same order of magnitude as the "intolerable" consequences of concealment and suppression of the escalation in Vietnam and secret bombing in Cambodia. Then there was the attempt to shield members of the White House staff from inquiry as to their involvement in the Watergate conspiracy,[10] the greatest executive scandal in American history. But let us look more closely at the "practical considerations" advanced by Professor Bishop.

First, he argues, "congressional control over appropriations and legislation is an excellent guarantee that the executive will not lightly reject a congressional request for information."[11] Repeatedly the very administration under which he served lightly rejected such requests,[12] notwithstanding congressional power to curtail appropriations. Attorney General Richard Kleindienst had the hardihood to taunt Congress in April 1973, to abolish or cut appropriations for certain executive functions or to impeach the

5. Assistant Attorney General Rehnquist, Ervin Hearings 421.
6. Supra, Ch. 8, text accompanying nn. 33–38.
7. Supra, Ch. 5, text accompanying n. 126.
8. Youngstown Case, 343 U.S. at 629, concurring.
9. Library of Congress Study, Cong. Rec. Mar. 28, 1973, H.2244–2245; infra, Appendix A.
10. Supra, Ch. 8, text accompanying nn. 116, 134.
11. Bishop 486.
12. Supra, Ch. 8, text accompanying nn. 11–33, 64–79.

President if it disapproved of presidential conduct.[13] Indeed, soon after the Bishop article appeared, a congressional committee, frustrated by the refusal of the Eisenhower administration to furnish information respecting allegedly corrupt administration of Peruvian foreign aid, invoked a statutory cutoff of foreign aid funds. Thereupon Attorney General Rogers furnished an opinion to the President that the cutoff was unconstitutional because it was beyond the power of Congress, directly or indirectly, to compel the disclosure of information that the President "considers contrary to the national interest."[14] Eisenhower then directed the Secretary of the Treasury to disburse funds for the functions affected by the cutoff provision, in disregard of the statute. This was truly an extraordinary performance: Eisenhower and Rogers declared a statute unconstitutional—a power to be exercised rarely if at all[15]—on the dubious theory that the statute encroached on an alleged constitutional power to withhold information. It is a reproach to Congress that it did not turn to the courts to set the Eisenhower directive aside, for the presidential appetite for power has been fed by precisely such reluctance to challenge the encroachment.[16]

Second, argues Professor Bishop, "Congress may not be a safe repository for sensitive information." "Most Congressmen," he continues, "are, of course, quite as trustworthy as most executive officials, but there can be no 'security program' for legislators . . . no assurance that the seniority system will not place such a security risk in the chairmanship of an important committee."[17] Against speculation that a "security risk" may rise to "the chairmanship of an important committee," there is hard evidence that Congress is to be trusted. Allen Dulles, the respected Director of the Central Intelligence Agency, wrote:

> It is also often said that Congress can't keep a secret. Past history belies this. The Manhattan Project, through which the atomic bomb was developed . . . was a well-kept secret in a vital area of our national defense . . . From almost ten years of experience in dealing with the

13. N.Y. Times, April 11, 1973, p. 1.
14. Mollenhoff, 172–174, 235.
15. See Berger, Executive Privilege 1114–1117; Berger, *Impeachment* 285–291.
16. On June 29, 1972, Senator Stuart Symington quoted to the Senate my 1965 prediction: "Until Congress faces up to the fact that the swelling tide of Executive Privilege claims can be stemmed only by decisive Congressional action, executive claims will continue to clog Congressional performance of vital functions"; Cong. Rec. S10587 (June 29, 1972).
17. Bishop 486.

Congress, I have found . . . that secrets can be kept and the needs of our legislative bodies met. In fact, I do not know of a single case of indiscretion that has resulted from telling these [congressional] committees the most intimate details of CIA activities, and that included the secret of the U-2 plane.[18]

Because the legend of congressional untrustworthiness dies hard, the reader will indulge some cumulative evidence. Former Justice Goldberg, who served as Secretary of Labor and as Ambassador to the United Nations, stated with reference to "sensitive materials" received by the "Armed Services Committee and Foreign Affairs Committee": "I have seen very little disclosure that would be harmful to the national security interests of our country, emanating from such congressional sources."[19] Deputy Under Secretary of State William B. Macomber testified with respect to regular briefings of members of Congress by the State Department: "We have never had a leak out of that group of any consequence, with one possible inadvertent exception."[20] And Senator Stuart Symington, who served for nineteen years on the Armed Services Committee and eleven years on the Foreign Relations Committee, stated that "there has never been a leak out of either Committee."[21]

If there has been an infrequent congressional "leak," the executive branch, despite its "security program," has known dreadful leaks, for example, the delivery by Rosenberg of atomic secrets to Soviet Russia.[22] And, although I consider that in disclosing the Pentagon Papers, Daniel Ellsberg acted in response to a loyalty to the nation that rose above loyalty to the Defense Department,[23] the fact remains that this was a "leak" which the "security program" did not prevent. Abram Chayes, formerly Legal Adviser to the State Department, stated that during his tenure leaks of

18. Allen Dulles, *The Craft of Intelligence* 241 (New York, 1963).
19. 5 Moorhead Hearings 1456.
20. 3 Ibid. 922.
21. Ervin Hearings 224.
22. See Rosenberg v. United States, 346 U.S. 273 (1953). On Oct. 11, 1963, the New York Times (West. ed.), p. 1, reported that an Army sergeant who had been assigned to the National Security Agency had committed suicide when under investigation for security violations, having allegedly "delivered the nation's most sensitive codes and communications secrets to the Russians."

During John Adams' presidency, Secretary Wolcott, a member of his cabinet, was supplying Alexander Hamilton, Adams' inveterate enemy, "with confidential governmental communications"; 2 Page Smith, *John Adams* 1043 (Garden City, N.Y., 1962).

23. Cf. General Matthew R. Ridgway, "A Code of Loyalty," N.Y. Times, May 2, 1973, p. 43.

classified information repeatedly occurred.[24] In a 1971 colloquy with John R. Stevenson, Legal Adviser to the State Department, Senator John Sparkman asked, "don't you have to take the risk of leakage . . . with everybody you deal with, even the people in your department . . . apparently there are leaks all through the Government."[25] There is an aura of self-righteousness, little aided by the Watergate disclosures, about the executive determination that it alone can be trusted with "secrets." "Bureaucrats," no less than Congressmen, Professor Bishop recognizes, act both "from the best and worst of motives."[26]

In "the heat of partisan passion" the national interest, Bishop stated, may run "a very poor second to considerations of faction." As an example, he cites Senator Burton K. Wheeler's revelation of "the Navy's occupation of Iceland [during World War II] while the operation was still in progress and the ships vulnerable to attack by submarines," apparently because Wheeler was an "extreme isolationist."[27] Wheeler's viewpoint is not adequately described as factional partisanship. There was room for legitimate difference of opinion whether President Roosevelt was exceeding his constitutional authority that is being paralleled in current criticism of President Nixon's continued bombing of Cambodia notwithstanding the "peace" with Vietnam. I would not suggest that one who acts from deep conviction may jeopardize the lives of troops in transit; but is the alternative to one such incident to conceal from Congress hostile entry into a foreign country until after the event? President Nixon's entry into Cambodia without prior consultation with Congress raised a great outcry. "Factionalism" is not of course peculiar to Congress. President Johnson's concealment of the Vietnam escalation because he believed that Congress would jettison his "Great Society" program in favor of prosecution of the war, whereas he wanted both "guns and butter,"[28] may equally be viewed as "factional." By their very nature great issues are factional; they divide the nation and require the disclosure so that the issues may be fully debated, the indispensable prerequisite to a democratic consensus. If it be assumed that some "sensitive" information must be withheld,

24. Affidavit filed in the Trial of Daniel Ellsberg (1972–1973).
25. Executive Agreements Hearings 77.
26. Bishop 477.
27. Ibid. 486.
28. Halberstam 594, 604.

that scarcely justifies the wholesale withholding of minor, even trivial, matters reported in the Kramer and Marcuse collection.

Assume that some secrets are of such gravity as to require that disclosure be restricted to few. For this we have the suggestion made by William Pitt in the course of the Walpole debate:

There are Methods, Sir, for preventing Papers of a very secret Nature from coming into the Hands of the Servants attending, or even of all the Members of our Secret Committee. If his Majesty should by Message acquaint us that some of the Papers sealed up and laid before us required the utmost Secrecy, we might refer them to our Committee, with an Instruction for them to order only two or three of the Number to inspect such Papers, and to report from them nothing but what they thought might be safely communicated to their whole Number. By this Method, I hope, the Danger of a Discovery would be effectually removed; therefore this Danger cannot be a good Argument against a Parliamentary Inquiry.[29]

One hundred years later a congressional committee picked up the suggestion that the "secrets" be transmitted to a select few designated by the legislature:

Information . . . may be referred to a committee under the charge of secrecy until an examination of it can be made, when, if the committee concur in opinion with the Executive, its publication may be dispensed with. This is the true parliamentary course. It furnishes, at once, a security against secret abuses and the irresponsibility of the public officers and agents, which would follow the denial of the right of the House to demand information, and at the same time protects the State against the discovery of facts important for the time to be concealed.[30]

Pitt's suggestion was acted upon by Secretary of State Dulles when he showed Senators Taft and Sparkman confidential material respecting a nominee for high office.[31] So too, Secretary of State Acheson was accustomed to consult with Senators Arthur Vandenberg and Tom Connally on important matters.[32] This is not the ideal solution for it is open to the charge that it merely

29. 13 Chandler 173–174.

30. H.R. Rep. No. 271, 27th Cong., 3d Sess., p. 7 (1843).

31. Alan Barth, *Government by Investigation* 37–38 (New York, 1955). Hamilton, said Madison, complained "of the House because the members did not go to his office and ask information, instead of requiring it to be publicly reported"; 3 Annals of Cong. 947 (1793).

32. Ervin Hearings 262–263.

makes two more privy to the secrecy of the inner circle—the Congress remains in the dark. But these are two who have been elevated to positions of high trust by their legislative colleagues and who enjoy their confidence. Perhaps some secrets—the building of the atom bomb by the Manhattan Project—require nothing short of such rigorously limited access.

But wider access to grave secrets might be patterned on the practice of the British Parliament during World War II. The Executive took the Parliament into "confidence very fully," subject to security checks applicable to the Executive; and an English writer remarks that during World War II the "high quality" of security was "astonishing" in light of the extent to which "Parliament was privy to the details" and "continuous publication to between six and fourteen hundred persons."[33] It must be emphasized, however, that Parliament vigorously policed alleged breaches of its security by Members and "constituted itself the jealous guardian of its own orders of secrecy."[34] Congress has tended to be lax in this respect, and if it is to insist on sharing secrets of great import it must accept the responsibility of preserving their secrecy.[34a] For the infrequent maverick who does not heed a congressional injunction of secrecy, the Congress has at hand censure, even expulsion. A member of the House was "censured for divulging secret correspondence" in the early days of the Republic;[35] and censure of a member has often been employed over the years.[36] Indeed, the Rules of the Senate provide for a more severe penalty: expulsion. Rule XXXVI, §3 provides that "all confidential communications made by the President . . . to the Senate shall be . . . kept secret"; and §4 provides that "any Senator . . . who shall disclose the secret . . . shall be liable . . . to suffer expulsion from the body." It would need few censures, expulsions, or possibly contempts[37] to bring home to members of

33. Clive Parry, "Legislation and Secrecy," 67 Harv. L. Rev. 737, 741 (1954).

34. Ibid. 762, 768.

34a. Although the leaks from the Senate Select Committee investigating Watergate in the summer of 1973 were not of this order, they exhibited lax enforcement. But leaks from the prosecution of the Watergate conspiracy and from the grand jury were little less frequent. As this is being written, Vice President Agnew complains bitterly about leaks from the Justice Department respecting an investigation into his alleged criminal conduct while Governor of Maryland. N.Y. Times, Aug. 22, 1973, pp. 24, 32.

35. 5 Annals of Cong. 443 (1796).

36. See 6 Hinds Precedents, Index "Censure" 249–250.

37. The power of Parliament to commit its own members for contempt reaches back to the sixteenth century and was judicially recognized in Burdett v. Abbott, 14 East. 1, 104 E. R. 501, 555, 557 (K.B. 1811). I found no case in which Congress

Congress that breaches of secrecy will not be tolerated; and wholehearted enforcement would go a long way to alleviate executive distrust.

A last point remains to be noticed: may the Executive impose a requirement of concealment from the public as a condition of disclosure to Congress, as was attempted by President Hoover, and later by the younger Hoover as Acting Secretary of State?[38] Congress, not the President, was given a limited power to conceal from the public;[39] to it was left the determination of what had to be concealed. This was the view of President John Adams. Transmitting to both Houses the instructions to and dispatches from the Envoys to France, pursuant to the House's request, Adams asked that they

> be considered in confidence until the members of Congress . . . shall have had opportunity to deliberate on the consequences of their publication; after which time I submit them to your wisdom.[40]

---

attempted to hold a member in contempt, although there is a statement by Congressman Findley in 1793, asserting the most sweeping contempt power:

> It is solely in the power of the House to punish all contemptuous or indecent treatment of its authority . . . We might have ordered him [Secretary of the Treasury, Alexander Hamilton] to the bar of this House and obliged him to make proper acknowledgments.

3 Annals of Cong. 963 (1793).

Article I, §5(2) of the Constitution provides that "Each House . . . may punish its members for disorderly behaviour, and . . . expel a member." A dictum stressing punishment for "disorderly behavior" or for "refusal to obey some rule on that subject made by the House for preservation of order" appears in Kilbourn v. Thompson, 103 U.S. 168, 189–190 (1880). Earlier, Justice Johnson, implying a general congressional power to punish *non*-members for contempt in the face of the express grant limited to members, explained that "the exercise of the powers given over their own members, was of such a delicate nature, that a constitutional provision became necessary to assert or communicate it . . . [S]ome such provision was necessary to guard against [the states'] mutual jealousy since every proceedings would indirectly affect the honor or interests of the state which had sent him"; Anderson v. Dunn, 19 U.S. (6 Wheat.) 204, 233 (1821).

In the Convention records, Edmund Randolph's scheme for a Constitution contains a "quaere how far the right of expulsion may be proper"; 2 Farrand 140. That "quaere" dropped from sight. Two Wilson drafts contain the statement "may expel a member, but not a second time for the same offense." From this last we may conclude that expulsion for an "offense," minimally against the respective houses, was contemplated. What is the effect of the "punishment for disorderly behavior" phrase? I suggest that expulsion for "disorderly conduct" was deemed too drastic, and the sanction was limited to punishment short of expulsion. It does not follow that Congress is powerless to "punish" for an "offense" of a different order. The power to expel comprehends a power to impose a less severe sanction, e.g., confinement for contempt in defying an injunction to preserve secrecy in a matter touching national security. This was the power historically exercised by Parliament, and there is no evidence that the Framers intended to deny it to the Congress.

38. Rogers memo 21; Kramer & Marcuse 842.

39. Supra, Ch. 6, text accompanying nn. 228–245.

40. April 3, 1798, quoted in Fulbright Hearings 192.

Executive imposition of a condition upon disclosure that Congress must conceal the information from the public usurps a power that was confided to Congress alone.

Third, Professor Bishop argues for preservation of privacy for derogatory information in executive files.[41] This is truly a compelling consideration.[42] But, distressing as needless publicity of such matters has often been, it is an issue of decency, of protection of the individual against what Taylor has termed "indecent exposure."[43] The citizen's protection against Congress has not been given to the executive departments,[44] root and branch the creation of Congress.[45] Historically the claim of an inherent executive power to withhold "derogatory" materials stands on none-too-solid ground. Even a claim of privilege against self-incrimination was rejected by the Walpole Select Committee.[46] And Jefferson's gratuitous explanation of a withholding which the House had left in his discretion—that it was for the protection of the innocent—scarcely adds up to a presidential assertion of a *right* to withhold, let alone congressional recognition of that right.[47]

This tenderness for "derogatory" information ill becomes an executive branch that time after time has placed the individual in cruelly humiliating circumstances without disclosure for the protection of his interest;[48] and has not hesitated to reveal the most "derogatory" information when it served its own political purposes. Thus, Attorney General Herbert Brownell summarized in "considerable detail" on television a "Top Secret" FBI report after the death of Harry Dexter White, Assistant Secretary of the

41. Bishop 487.
42. Barth, supra, n. 31 at 32, 37.
43. Telford Taylor, *Grand Inquest* 85 (New York, 1955).
44. Supra, Ch. 6, text accompanying nn. 104–108. Professor Richard Morris stated in 1971 that he would "hesitate to accept the role of the President as the chief protector of our liberties"; Fulbright Hearings 105. That hesitation is multiplied when one considers the illegal infringements on individual rights that President Nixon contemplated in the name of "national security"; N.Y. Times, July 29, 1973, Sec. 4, p. 1; ibid. July 31, p. 23.
45. The "chief executive departments are all the work of the first and succeeding Congresses. No constitutional duty demanded their institution; no constitutional duty demands their continuance." J. M. Landis, "Constitutional Limitations on the Congressional Power of Investigation," 40 Harv. L. Rev. 153, 196 (1926). This is even more plain in the case of the "independent" agencies which were meant to be an "arm of Congress."
46. 13 Chandler 224–225.
47. Supra, Ch. 6, text accompanying nn. 98–108.
48. United States *ex rel* Knauff v. Shaughnessy, 338 U.S. 537 (1950), discussed supra, Ch. 7, n. 49; Greene v. McElroy, 360 U.S. 474 (1959), discussed supra, Ch. 7, text accompanying nn. 84–86; Bailey v. Richardson, 182 F. 2d 46 (D.C. Cir. 1950).

Treasury, to show that White, who had denied these charges under oath before a House Committee, "was known to be a Communist Spy," an incident which Alan Barth described as "flogging the dead body" of White.[49] In 1954 the Department of Agriculture called Wolf Ladejinsky, an agricultural attache in Tokyo, a "security risk," and "departed from precedent in previous security cases in making information on Ladejinsky available . . . information derogatory to Ladejinsky."[50] Clark Mollenhoff, who investigated the case, reported that Ladejinsky had been cleared on the same evidence by the State Department, and that Harold Stassen, head of Foreign Operations Administration, stated that "there was no evidence that Ladejinsky had ever been sympathetic to any communist causes in the nineteen years he had been employed as an economist by the government."[51] In 1973 White House counsel, John Dean, turned over to the Committee to Reelect the President FBI files of interviews with Committee employees in connection with the Watergate investigation, who were then called to account by the Committee.[52] It is not necessary to maintain that "Congress is the paladin of civil liberties and the executive their foe,"[53] for it suffices that the pot cannot call the kettle black. This is not to suggest that reputations of innocent men are to be flung to the dogs but rather to question whether the Executive can lay claim on either moral or legal grounds to being the sole and final judge of what Congress may safely see. Here as elsewhere the individual must look to the courts for protection against both the President and Congress.

I would not intimate that judicial protection renders congressional self-improvement unnecessary. Congressional lynching-bees have lessened respect for Congress and have shaken the deep-seated conviction of the American people that they "must look to representative assemblies for protection of their liberties."[54] The sadistic spectacle of Senator McCarthy publicly lashing the

49. Barth, supra, n. 31 at 91–92, 131.
50. Mollenhoff 81, 85.
51. Ibid. 81.
52. Los Angeles Times, Mar. 13, 1973, p. 1. The Justice Department agreed to make raw FBI reports and material from FBI wiretaps available to the Liddy-Hunt "plumbers," the investigative unit set up by President Nixon in the White House; Newsweek, May 14, 1973, p. 33. Liddy and Hunt were convicted for participation in the Watergate conspiracy.
53. Bishop 489.
54. Myers v. United States, 272 U.S. 52, 294–295 (1926), Brandeis, J., dissenting, joined by Holmes, J.

helpless General Zwicker, for example, was revolting to a sense of fair play.[55] All this to make political hay at the cost of hapless public servants. A step in the right direction was taken by the House in the Fair Play rules of 1955;[56] but it was only a beginning. Not just better rules, but a heightened sense of responsibility for their enforcement and a halt to the unjustified smearing of public officials are required. The quest for inefficiency and corruption or for information need not be converted into a witchhunt with ill-considered resort to the pillory. Respect for the individual, it can not too often be emphasized, is the cornerstone of democracy; and when Congress permits its own members unjustly to tear the individual down it erodes confidence in its capacity to govern. We are entitled to look to Congress itself for protection from its irresponsible members, and resort to the courts for protection against them should be a last ditch and, hopefully, unnecessary step. Happily high-minded members of the Congress have become aware of the problem and favor corrective measures. Senator Sam J. Ervin, Jr., Chairman of the Senate Subcommittee on Separation of Powers, suggested that the Executive ought to withhold "raw and unevaluated evidence. Such evidence has a distinct bearing upon the privacy of individual citizens and its disclosure rarely accomplishes anything other than the destruction of the privacy of those citizens in very sensitive areas of their lives."[57] I would join in this suggestion, not on the basis of a constitutional right to withhold or because executive moral superiority better qualifies it to judge, but in order to make a start toward protection of privacy by *both* branches. And, since Senator Ervin's suggestion comes as a matter of grace, it should not be converted into an iron curtain but should leave room for accommodation in the exceptional case.

Finally, our solicitude to guard against the misuse of derogatory information in executive files must not blind us to the fact that

absence of a legislative check—or of any publicity—may promote gross irresponsibility or carelessness in an executive agency—which is especially dangerous in a police agency such as the FBI. So long as its

55. McCarthy told General Zwicker that "he was unfit to wear the uniform on which were sewn the General's decorations for heroism in the service of his country"; Taylor, supra, n. 43 at 87.

56. See Frank Newman, "Some Facts on Fact-Finding by an Investigatory Commission," 13 Ad. L. Bull. 120, 123 (1960–1961).

57. Ervin Hearings 440.

reports are kept confidential, appraisal of its methods, its sources, its reliability, and its judgment is extremely difficult.[58]

This was confirmed in the wake of Watergate by the then Acting Director of the FBI, William D. Ruckelshaus:

There must be effective oversight of all F.B.I. activities. This essential review and check should come from both the executive and legislative branches of our Government. In my opinion, legislative oversight is not sufficient today and needs to be strengthened.[59]

Fourth, Professor Bishop argued that the interchange of opinions which precedes a policy decision requires shelter, that subordinates who advise superiors "should be able to present unpalatable facts and make unpopular arguments without fear of being dragooned by the first Congressman who needs a headline."[60] Earlier the policy considerations which weigh heavily against this argument were set forth in detail. They have just received spectacular demonstration in the testimony of the former Director and present Deputy Director of CIA, Richard Helms, and Lieutenant General Vernon Walters, respecting efforts by the White House staff to use them for the purpose of limiting the FBI investigation of the Watergate conspiracy.[61] Who would argue that such interdepartmental communications should find shelter under the "candid interchange" doctrine?

The "most compelling illustration," said Professor Bishop, is found in the "operations of the employee security system," citing the Army's repulse of Senator McCarthy's attempt to subpoena individual members of the Appeals Board employed in the screening of employee security cases.[62] On the hunt for "any members of the old Administration who hid communists," Senator McCarthy was rebuffed because the "loyalty boards were quasi-judicial in character."[63] A Special Senate Committee which later looked into the Army-McCarthy imbroglio rejected immunity from subpoena but indicated that there "may be subjects on which they should not be forced to testify," spelled out by the

58. Barth, supra, n. 31 at 39.
59. N.Y. Times, June 16, 1973, p. 12.
60. Bishop 487.
61. N.Y. Times, June 4, 1973, p. 24.
62. Bishop 487–488; Kramer & Marcuse 671–674.
63. Kramer & Marcuse 672, citing S. Rep. No. 2507, 83d Cong., 2d Sess. 60 (1954).

minority as freedom from testifying as to "the reasons for their judicial determinations."[64] If we accept the premise that these appeals boards were exercising judicial functions, as now appears requisite,[65] then their immunity from probing into the processes whereby they arrived at their decisions seems clear. Manifestly, however, this example does not stretch to exclude every internal communication by every governmental subordinate. And if we look closely at the theoretical underpinning of the "mental processes" doctrine, other considerations emerge which should suggest that it should be closely confined.

The doctrine originated in *United States v. Morgan*, wherein the Secretary of Agriculture had been "questioned at length regarding the process by which he reached the conclusions of his order, including the manner and extent of his study of the record and his consultation with subordinates." The proceeding, said the Supreme Court, "has a quality resembling that of a judicial proceeding . . . it was not the function of the court to probe the mental processes of the Secretary."[66] When we translate this into the field of *congressional* inquiry, two factors need to be taken into account. Undoubtedly the *courts* were meant to be "independent," not accountable to Congress for the *judgments* which they rendered;[67] and the separation of powers protects them in this respect. But a Department to which Congress has confided a complex of quasi-judicial, quasi-legislative, and executive functions is not a branch of the judiciary; at best it enjoys the privileges of the executive branch, and as we have seen, "executive privilege" is not one of them. Where such powers are conferred on an independent agency, the agency, the Supreme Court held, is not an "arm or eye of the executive"; indeed it "must be free from executive control."[68] Congressional inquiry is not, therefore, barred by the separation of powers. The *Morgan* case, it needs to be borne in mind, decided that a *court* could not probe the "mental processes" of an administrator in a private litigation. But the scope of congressional inquiry into executive conduct, and even

64. Kramer & Marcuse 674–675.

65. Greene v. McElroy, 360 U.S. 474, 496–497 (1959).

66. 313 U.S. 409, 422 (1941). The rule is not absolute; there are occasions when an administrator may be required to explain his decision. Citizens to Preserve Overton Park v. Volpe, 401 U.S. 402, 420 (1971).

67. Berger, *Congress v. Court* 117–118.

68. Humphrey's Executor v. United States, 295 U.S. 602 (1935), discussed supra, Ch. 2, text accompanying n. 186.

more into conduct of agencies outside the executive branch, vastly transcends that of the courts.[69]

It is also worth recalling that in 1667 the House of Lords examined Lord Chief Justice Holt and Justice Eyres as to the basis of a certain opinion they had rendered; and that in 1689 the House of Commons similarly examined Lord Chief Justice Pemberton and Justice Thomas Jones.[70] Although such examinations of the *judiciary* were barred by our Constitution, they suggest that there is no historical or constitutional basis for the view that similar insulation is *inherent* in administrative judges. At best it is a product of convenience, and is not to be extended in derogation of the historical legislative power of inquiry beyond the function of sitting in judgment.

When a Department head sits in judgment, does a report filed by a subordinate, for example, an Examiner's report, come within the immunity for the head's "mental processes"? That report was arrived at quite independently of the head's "mental processes"; today administrative practice contemplates that the Examiner's report will be made available for purposes of review.[71] The *Morgan* case tells us that "much was made of [the Secretary's] disregard of a memorandum from one of his officials who, on reading the proposed order, urged considerations favorable to the market agencies."[72] This indicates that the "mental processes" of the Secretary did not include the work product of a subordinate; and that there was no bar to access to a subordinate's dissenting view.

Professor Bishop's summary of preliminary mechanics employed by the executive branch in handling legislative inquiries further illuminates the problem. First, "no fishing expeditions are allowed," but congressional investigators "must define with reasonable precision . . . the character of the documents they wish to see."[73] This is a remarkable requirement, coming after the executive branch prevailed upon the courts to discard the "colorful and nostalgic slogan 'no fishing expeditions' " and to clothe an administrative agency with a "power of inquisition" so that it can "investigate merely on suspicion that the law is being

69. Supra, Ch. 6, text accompanying n. 137.
70. S. A. Ferrall, *The Law of Parliament* 332, 316 (London, 1837).
71. Administrative Procedure Act §8; 5 U.S.C. §557 (1967).
72. United States v. Morgan, 313 U.S. 409, 422 (1941).
73. Bishop 489.

violated."[74] Thus, the traditional power of the "Grand Inquest" would now be saddled with a limitation that the newcomer in government found galling. Assistant Attorney General Hansen "admitted that it might be difficult for a subcommittee to make demands for specific documents without having examined the files,"[75] as Professor Schwartz learned when he was cast in the role of investigator.[76]

For his second point, Professor Bishop lays down that:

> *No "raw" files are to be released.* The files requested will be screened by the legislative liaison officer or one of his assistants, who will remove any documents which, in his judgment . . . should not go outside the executive branch. There can be no blinking the fact that this affords an opportunity for serious abuse . . . [I]t is most certainly unjustifiable to remove part of a file simply because it betrays administrative stupidity or inertia [or worse]. The temptation to indulge in such an abuse is, of course, considerable.[77]

In the less polite parlance that callous government attorneys employ when the shoe is on the other foot, the executive is accustomed to "stripping the files." Consider the raucous outcries that would fill the air were government attorneys to uncover such a practice in a subpoena enforcement proceeding![78]

Finally, what of the possible "abuses" so cheerfully conceded? Professor Bishop first concludes that the risks of such abuse are "less than the risk inherent in giving Congress free access to executive files."[79] Free access may carry with it the exceptional risk that some irresponsible member of Congress may trumpet a "military secret" to the world, but such risks surely are outweighed by the perils of concealing executive derelictions in a multi-million executive establishment which administers and dis-

74. United States v. Morton Salt Co., 338 U.S. 632, 642 (1950).

75. Kramer & Marcuse 890.

76. Bernard Schwartz, "Executive Privilege and Congressional Investigatory Power," 47 Calif. L. Rev. 3, 4 (1959).

77. Bishop 489–490.

78. Norman G. Cornish, Deputy Staff Director of the House Foreign Operations and Government Information Subcommittee, recounted a written certification by the Secretary of State that he had transmitted a complete file to a House Subcommittee. A subordinate, called upon to testify, stated: "Oh yes, sir, we spent half the night going through this thing and cleaning it out and clearing it and taking out all of the things, which we were instructed to take out. So, sure, there are papers missing from this file"; Hearings on Availability of Information to Congress before a Subcommittee of the Committee on Government Operations 148 (H.R. 93d Cong., 1st Sess. [1973]).

79. Bishop 490.

burses vast sums, or of hiding some ill-advised foreign adventure.[80] As Senator Stuart Symington, former Secretary of the Air Force, stated: "the risk of failure of executive branch policies and programs occasioned by their revelation to Congress is much to be preferred as against the risk of vital damage inflicted on a democratic system because of failure to disclose the truth."[81] Second, suggests Professor Bishop, competent department heads learn about "honesty as a policy in their dealings with Congress."[82] Some very competent department heads, even the President himself, have failed to learn that "homely maxim" as the stealthy escalation in Vietnam, the secret bombing of Cambodia reveal.

A last practical consideration: after noting the secrecy that surrounds the deliberations of "judges in their chambers, and of grand juries," Taylor concludes that "the executive branch, too, may claim that it is not required to plan and conduct all of its operations in a goldfish bowl."[83] Certainly the alternative is not to conduct all its operations in a darkroom, as has tended to become the rule. For such operations as really demand a darkroom, disclosure to Congress need not mean disclosure to the public, for Congress can take steps to keep such matters confidential. Disclosure of war and foreign affairs to Congress is not a matter of grace but of right, because the bulk of the war powers and at least an equal share in foreign relations were given to Congress. Grand jury proceedings are an exception to "this nation's historic distrust of secret proceedings," deeply rooted in our history and long antedating the adoption of the Constitution.[84] If only there were a like tradition of "executive" secrecy! Then too, the grand jury is an investigating tribunal of constantly changing members,

80. In 1971 Senator Symington referred to the fact that until the Senate sent investigators into Laos, the public was told that "what we were spending in Laos was $52 million. Now recently, the Secretary of State has come out with a figure of $350 million." He estimated that the bombing of the Ho Chi Minh Trail "runs over a billion dollars by itself. Inasmuch as the Secretary of Defense has testified . . . that he was not conducting military operations in Laos, it is clear that the operation in Laos is being conducted by the Central Intelligence Agency . . . you not only have a war going on in Laos, which the American taxpayer is financing with no knowledge whatever on his part of what's going on, you also have a secret war being operated under executive privilege, because the Director of the Central Intelligence Agency . . . reports through the National Security Council directly to the President"; Ervin Hearings 226. The recently disclosed sustained secret bombing in Cambodia is cut from the same cloth.

81. Ervin Hearings 219.

82. Bishop 490.

83. Taylor, supra, n. 4 at 86.

84. In re Oliver, 333 U.S. 257, 273 (1948); 1 Sir William S. Holdsworth, *History of English Law* 322 (3d ed., London, 1922).

having no built-in yearning to conceal its own mistakes or misdeeds.[85] Nor does the comparison of judicial deliberations with those of executive employees stand any better. All told, there are some 500 to 600 federal judges as against upward of 2,500,000 federal employees. The problems of safeguarding these two against corruption, inefficiency, and waste are simply incommensurable.[86]

It is farfetched to compare the conference of two lowly subordinates, or of a subordinate with a lower echelon chief, with consultation between the President and a member of his cabinet, or of a Justice with his immediate aide. And it needs emphasis that not even a judge is beyond the scope of legislative investigation, else the impeachment power would be shackled. The oft-cited example of Judge Louis Goodman's refusal on behalf of himself and his fellow district judges in California to testify before a congressional committee, apparently as to their conduct of judicial proceedings,[87] reflects the view that "such an examination of a judge would be destructive of judicial responsibility."[88] But this spells no immunity from investigation into judicial misconduct, for example, acceptance of a bribe for a favorable de-

85. Justice Douglas reminded us that commissions "tend to acquire a vested interest in that role." Hannah v. Larche, 363 U.S. 420, 499 (1960), dissenting. A sympathetic observer of the administrative process, Senator Paul Douglas, remarked that administrators "do not like to admit mistakes, and they naturally protect their own class"; quoted in Walter Gellhorn and Clark Byse, *Administrative Law: Cases and Comments* 182 (Brooklyn, 1960).

86. The fact that the executive branch cannot peer into congressional files, as is noted by Taylor, supra, n. 43 at 105, and Bishop 478, derives from the fact that there is no historical executive analogue of the legislative power of the Grand Inquest to inquire into executive conduct, no precedent for reversal of the roles. See supra, Ch. 7, text accompanying nn. 13–14.

87. Barth, supra, n. 31 at 80; Taylor, supra, n. 43 at 96–97.

88. United States v. Morgan, 313 U.S. 409, 422 (1941). Even here, as Karl Llewellyn said,

> It is well to remember that neither secrecy of the court's deliberation or later secrecy about what went on during that deliberation rests in the nature of things or in any ordinance of God. The roots of each are either practical or accidental, and it is only either ignorance or tradition which makes us feel that we have here something untouchable, a semiholy arcanum. We tend to forget that in common law history the centuries of the Year Books rest on a practice of conference, consultation, and decision going on in open court before ears and eyes of counsel, the bar at large, and the apprentices . . . Thus the storied sanctity of the conference room represents to me as pragmatic and nonmystic a phase of appellate judicial work as the handling of the docket. Our modern fetish of secrecy reminds me of the shock German lawyers displayed at the notion of such dangerous things as published dissenting opinions.

K. Llewellyn, *The Common Law Tradition* 324 n. 308 (Boston, 1960).

cision, maladministration of bankruptcy proceedings, and the like, as a number of judicial impeachments testify.[89]

The plain fact is that the executive branch was *meant* to operate in a goldfish bowl, to be accountable to the legislature. That is one of the presuppositions of democratic government, perceived from the outset. The alternative to a "goldfish bowl" cannot be uncontrolled executive discretion to withhold from Congress for, as the past twenty years teach, that conduces to a mushrooming cloud of concealment. Dress it as decorously as you will, in the last analysis executive discretion to determine what Congress shall see empowers the executive branch to determine how far it needs to be investigated. "If men were angels" then we could safely lodge that power in the subject of investigation.

89. Berger, *Impeachment* 56–57; Joseph Borkin, *The Corrupt Judge* (New York, 1962).

11

JUDICIAL REVIEW

A. *Introductory*

Essentially the controversy about executive privilege is a boundary dispute, bottomed on irreconcilable claims to constitutional power. Pitted against claimed "uncontrolled" executive discretion to withhold information is a claimed plenary congressional power to demand it. It is remarkable that the issue has never been submitted to the courts, for ours is a land, as de Toqueville early observed, where "scarcely any political question arises . . . that is not resolved, sooner or later, into a judicial question."[1] The necessity of submitting this "intolerably prolonged controversy" to the courts was perceived by Senator Matthew Neely in the 1950's.[2] Since then others have taken up the thought, among them Senator J. W. Fulbright,[3] former Justice Arthur J. Goldberg,[4] Assistant Attorney General (now Justice) William H. Rehnquist,[5] a number of academicians,[6] and now President Nixon himself.[7]

1. 1 Alexander de Tocqueville, *Democracy in America* 280 (New York, 1945). "By the very nature of our Constitution," said Justice Frankfurter, "practically every political question eventually, with us, turns into a judicial question"; Felix Frankfurter, "Chief Justices I Have Known," 39 Va. L. Rev. 883, 895 (1953).

2. Kramer & Marcuse 867. Republican Senator Carlson agreed with Senator Neely; ibid. In 1956 a Senate Committee recommended that "steps be taken by the several committees to provide a test in the courts to determine the respective powers of Congress and the executive agencies"; ibid. 877.

3. Ervin Hearings 208, 211. For other utterances to the same effect see Memorandum, Foreign Operations and Government Information Subcommittee (H.R.) (August 1963), p. 48 (unpublished).

4. Fulbright Hearings 775. Mr. Goldberg spoke to the presidential making of unconstitutional wars, but the issue remains one of constitutional boundaries. See also 5 Moorhead Hearings 1445.

5. 2 Moorhead Hearings 379, 381.

6. Professor Norman Dorsen: "If the President refuses to give certain information, obviously the ultimate remedy has to be in the courts, and . . . the Congress . . . has to go to court and fight it out and not accede to the generalized claims of confidentiality"; 3 Moorhead Hearings 860. Professor J. N. Moore: where "the President acts in opposition to the limits of Congressional authorization you maximize the likelihood that the Court will say the issue is justiciable"; Fulbright Hearings 480. In 1965, I sought to furnish an underpinning for such views; Berger, Executive Privilege 1333–1362.

7. Infra, text accompanying n. 28.

What are the alternatives to impartial arbitrament of this increasingly exacerbated controversy? Before Attorney General Richard Kleindienst went into retirement, he told the Senate: "You've got all kinds of remedies . . . cut off funds, abolish most of what we can do or impeach the President,"[8] tongue-in-cheek advice by one who felt quite confident that the opposition could not muster the two-thirds vote needed to override presidential vetoes or to impeach. Let it be assumed that the Watergate developments which have since engulfed the White House make Mr. Kleindienst's "remedies" not quite so unlikely as they seemed before the bubble burst, are they wise? Of impeachment—a last resort—more will be said later. To abolish the Department of Defense because it refuses to furnish Congress with information respecting Laos, projected military aid plans, and the like is a cure worse than the disease. Even resort to curtailment of funds, the cutoff of appropriations, represents regress to primitive self-help; it would substitute the battle-axe for temperate adjudication of conflicting claims to constitutional power.

What it can mean was starkly illuminated by the recent congressional attempt, by a rider to an appropriation bill, to cut off funds for the continued bombing of Cambodia. To veto the bill, said George H. Mahon, Chairman of the House Appropriations Committee, would bring "the U.S. Government to a screeching, grinding unacceptable halt at midnight on June 30." Senate majority leader Mike Mansfield said, "If the President doesn't want to stop the bombing but does want to stop the government, that is his business." An "appalled GOP topsider told Newsweek's chief Congressional correspondent Samuel Sheffer . . . 'It's like two gunmen in a narrow alley, approaching from either end and wondering who's going to step aside.' "[8a] Luckily the confrontation was defused by the President's promise to halt the bombing on August 15, 1973, in return for deletion of the cutoff rider. Government by cliff-hanger is a wretched alternative to judicial arbitrament of a constitutional boundary dispute.

Notwithstanding that the constitutional argument for executive privilege, in my judgment, has little or no historical or constitutional footing, that the Executive has repeatedly decided the issue in its own favor, I would yet not have the Congress impose its construction on the President by *force majeure*, unless the courts

8. N.Y. Times, April 11, 1973, p. 17.
8a Newsweek, July 9, 1973, p. 27.

avert their countenance from the dispute and leave Congress no alternative. It is to avoid such self-help that we turn to the courts.[9]

Consideration of appropriation cutoffs to enforce the will of Congress must also take into account the determined resistance of President Eisenhower. In 1960, when Congress invoked a statutory cutoff of foreign-aid funds because the executive had withheld information, Attorney General Rogers advised Eisenhower that this was an "unconstitutional condition," an invasion of his presidential prerogative to withhold information. Thereupon, Eisenhower instructed the Secretary of the Treasury to disregard the cutoff and to draw on federal funds to meet the required payments,[10] itself an invasion of Congress' exclusive right to specify the purpose for which appropriations are to be applied,[11] as the recent "impoundment" cases have been confirming.[12]

It is a startling notion that the President, who by the terms of Article II, §3, "shall take care that the Laws be faithfully executed," may refuse to execute a law on the ground that it is unconstitutional. To wring from a duty faithfully to execute the laws a power to defy them[13] would appear to be a feat of splendid illogic. There are early cases[14] and presidential utterances which speak against it. Even the stubborn Jackson, according to Roger Taney, a member of his Cabinet, "never expressed a doubt as to the duty and obligation upon him in his Executive character to carry into execution any Act of Congress regularly passed, whatever his own opinion might be of the constitutional question."[15]

9. The importance of "settling grievances peacefully in the courts" was stressed in United States v. Mississippi, 380 U.S. 128, 144 (1965).

10. Mollenhoff 173–174.

11. Supra, Ch. 4, text accompanying nn. 268–279.

12. See infra, n. 135.

13. Rogers memo 3–4, 48–49.

14. "To contend that the obligation imposed upon the President to see the laws faithfully executed implies a power to forbid their execution, is a novel construction of the Constitution, and entirely inadmissible"; Kendall v. United States, 37 U.S. (12 Pet.) 524, 613 (1838). Earlier it had been said: "The president . . . cannot control the statute, nor dispense with its execution, and still less can he authorize a person to do what the law forbids. If he could, it would render the execution of the law dependent on his will and pleasure"; United States v. Smith, 27 Fed. Cas. 1192, 1230 (No. 16,342) (C.C. N.Y. 1806). Still earlier, in 1794, Sedgwick said on the floor of the House: "There was, in fact, in no instance an authority given to the Executive to repeal a Constitutional act of the Legislature"; 4 Annals of Cong. 570. Even in the field of foreign relations, where the President moves somewhat more freely, "it was intimated that the President might act in external affairs without congressional authority, but not that he might act contrary to an act of Congress." Youngstown Case 549, 635–636 n. 2 (Jackson, J. concurring).

15. Quoted in 1 Charles Warren, *The Supreme Court in United States History* 224 (Boston, 1922). President Polk said of a statute that "it is binding upon all de-

In the midst of his struggle with the Reconstruction Congress, Andrew Johnson, who had earlier condemned the Civil Rights Act as unconstitutional, said it was "now the law of the land" and "will be faithfully executed" until declared unconstitutional by courts.[16] That this must be so with respect to laws affecting the rights of third persons seems clear. The courts were made the "ultimate interpreter" of the Constitution;[17] to them was left the protection of individual rights against governmental impairment.[18]

Does it necessarily follow that the President is equally bound to execute a law which encroaches on *his* constitutional power? The issue was presented on the impeachment of Andrew Johnson, when Congress sought to limit his power to remove the Secretary of War, Edwin M. Stanton, in the face of a long-standing interpretation by the First Congress that this was the exclusive prerogative of the President,[19] as the Supreme Court later held in *Myers v. United States*.[20] Even so, concluded Edward Corwin:

> No one doubts that the President possesses prerogatives which Congress may not constitutionally invade; but neither does any one doubt that he is under obligation "to take care that the laws be faithfully executed." And, he was endowed by the Constitution with a qualified veto upon acts of Congress with the idea among others that he might then protect his prerogatives from legislative curtailment. But this power being exercised, this power of self-defense is at an end; and once a statute has been duly enacted, whether over his protest or with his approval, he must promote its enforcement.[21]

---

partments of the Government, and especially upon the Executive, whose duty it is 'to take care that the laws be faithfully executed' "; 4 Richardson 432.

16. David M. Dewitt, *The Impeachment and Trial of Andrew Johnson* 96–97 (New York, 1967). So too, in Mississippi v. Johnson, 71 U.S. (8 Wall.) 475, 492 (1866), where it was sought to prevent President Johnson from carrying out the military occupation for which the Reconstruction Act provided, Attorney General Henry Stanbery told the Court that, though the President had vetoed the Act as unconstitutional, he felt after repassage that he was under a duty "faithfully to carry out and execute these laws."

17. See Berger, *Congress v. Court* 27–28 n. 97, 55–56, 96, 182–183; Powell v. McCormack, quoted infra, text accompanying n. 109.

18. Berger, *Congress v. Court* 16–21.

19. Berger, *Impeachment* 280–283.

20. 272 U.S. 52 (1926).

21. Corwin, *President* 79. For an earlier expression to the same effect see 3 W. W. Willoughby, *The Constitutional Law of the United States* 1503–1504 (New York, 1929).

That view won my concurrence in an earlier examination of the conflict between Congress and the Executive in the domain of executive privilege;[21a] but further study and reflection have persuaded me that Corwin's view is mistaken.

To begin with, Corwin washes out his postulate that "the President possesses powers which Congress may not constitutionally invade" by denying him the right effectually to resist such invasion. Repassage over a veto was not designed to free Congress from constitutional limitations; it cannot render constitutional that which is unconstitutional. Moreover, although the President must "take care that the laws be faithfully executed," the question arises whether a law contrary to the Constitution is such a "law." By the terms of Article VI, only laws made "in pursuance" of the Constitution, that is, laws consistent therewith, are the "supreme law of the land" and therefore "binding."[22] This logic, it may be urged, extends equally to laws affecting the rights of third persons.[23] But since protection of individual rights was confided to the courts for an attack against such impairments, the challenge to unconstitutional enactments in such case may be left to individual suits. The distinction was drawn by Johnson's great counsel, former Justice Benjamin B. Curtis: "if a law is passed over his veto which he believes to be unconstitutional, and that law affects the interests of third persons, those whose interests are affected must take care of them." But, when "a question arises whether a particular law has cut off a power confided to him by . . . the Constitution, and he alone can raise that question, and he alone can cause a judicial decision to come between the two branches of the Government to say which of them is right," then he may raise the question.[24]

To this, Curtis' co-counsel, William M. Evarts, added an argument which proceeded from the oath that the Constitution requires from the President alone: "I . . . will, to the best of my ability,

21a. Berger, Executive Privilege 1115–1117.

22. Berger, *Congress v. Court* 228–244.

23. In truth, a law beyond the powers conferred was for the Founders no law at all, undeserving of obedience; Berger, *Impeachment* 287–288.

24. *The Trial of Andrew Johnson*, Congressional Globe, 40th Cong., 2d Sess., Supp. 126–127. See also William J. Groesbeck, ibid. 314.

There is an area of overlap, where an invasion of the prerogatives of a branch, e.g., impoundment of appropriated funds by the President, may be injurious to the rights of a third person as well as in derogation of exclusive congressional power. But Congress should not be left to the accident of litigation by a third person for the protection of its own rights.

preserve, protect, and defend the Constitution . . ." Central to the constitutional scheme is the separation of powers, the principle that each of the three branches is confined within its own boundaries and will exercise no powers not confided to it.[25] Hamilton stated in Federalist No. 51 that to maintain the separation of powers each department is given the "necessary constitutional means and personal motives to resist encroachments of the others."[26] Only the veto power, it may be countered, was "given" to the President. Agreed that a veto exhausts presidential power when the issue is the *wisdom* of the legislation. But the object of the Framers was to prevent *"encroachment"*; and they were too practical to limit the President's power to "defend" the Constitution against a breach of its very essence: the separation of powers. Preservation of that separation goes to the very existence and functioning of the constitutional scheme. With Evarts, I would therefore hold that the presidential oath to "protect and defend the Constitution" posits both a right and a duty to protect his own constitutional functions from congressional impairment. And the test of that right of course cannot be that Congress and the academicians consider that his claim is without color of law, for that judgment is finally reserved to the courts. Nor does the presidential determination that a law is unconstitutional constitute the last word, as Assistant Attorney General Rehnquist recognized. The right of the President stretches no further, to borrow the words of now-Justice Rehnquist, than "to take appropriate steps to have the law tested."[27] Indeed, President Nixon himself stated on March 15, 1973, with reference to the executive privilege issue, that if the Senate "want a court test, we would welcome it. Perhaps this is the time to have the highest court of this land make a definitive decision with regard to this matter."[28] And so we come to judicial review.

B. *The Contempt Power*

The time-honored legislative means of procuring documents or testimony is issuance of a subpoena, enforceable by exercise of the contempt power on noncompliance. In the words of Pro-

25. Ibid. 339. His view was accepted by Senators Grimes and Reverdy Johnson; ibid. 423, 431.
26. *Federalist* at 337.
27. 2 Moorhead Hearings 381.
28. N.Y. Times, Mar. 16, 1973, p. 22.

fessor Joseph Bishop, "Congress undoubtedly has power to punish contempts . . . by the simple forthright process of causing the Sergeant at Arms to seize the offender and clap him into the common jail of the District of Columbia or the guardroom of the capitol police."[29] This need not be regarded as unseemly or punitive but merely as the mechanism that opens the door to judicial review. Once the recalcitrant official is in Congress' custody he can obtain his freedom by filing a petition with a court for a writ of habeas corpus, which poses the issue of Congress' constitutional power to insist that the information be supplied.

The legislative contempt power has its roots deep in parliamentary history and was employed by Congress from the beginning.[30] The House of Commons imprisoned Nicholas Paxton, Solicitor of the Treasury, during the course of the Walpole inquiry for refusal to answer.[31] In 1793 Congressman Findley stated: "It is solely in the power of this House to punish all contemptuous or indecent treatment of its authority . . . We might have ordered him [Secretary of the Treasury Alexander Hamilton] to the bar of this House and obliged him to make proper acknowledgments."[32] Recognition of the power by the Supreme Court is found in 1821 in *Anderson v. Dunn*,[33] and was thus summarized by it in *McGrain v. Daugherty:* "The power of inquiry—with the power to enforce it—is an essential and appropriate auxiliary to the legislative function," resting on the history of the legislative power prior to the adoption of the Constitution.[34]

But Attorney General Rogers would restrict the force of these cases to citations against *private* individuals: "the reason the court found a legislative power to summon private persons for inquiry, in connection with the exercise of the legislative function, was because of a practice, long continued, of summoning private persons before the House of Congress."[35] *McGrain* did in fact hold

29. Bishop 484. Corwin, *President* 436, was of the same opinion.
30. Raoul Berger, "Constructive Contempt: A Post-Mortem," 9 U. Chi. L. Rev. 602, 611, 620 (1942).
31. 13 Chandler 224–225.
32. 3 Annals of Cong. 963. An 1859 Massachusetts case sustained the power of the legislature to "imprison" an official "for contempt" for refusing to produce papers, saying that as "the grand inquest for the Commonwealth, [it] . . . has power to inquire into official conduct of all officers of the Commonwealth"; Burnham v. Morrissey, 80 Mass. (14 Gray) 226, 230, 239 (1859).
33. 19 U.S. (6 Wheat.) 204, 233–234.
34. 273 U.S. 135, 174 (1927); see also ibid. 175; Jurney v. MacCracken, 294 U.S. 125 (1935).
35. Rogers memo 64.

that a private person, Mal Daugherty, an Ohio banker and brother of Attorney General Harry Daugherty, could be summoned by the Senate in an investigation into the Attorney General's conduct of the Department of Justice. But the Court sustained the jurisdiction of Congress to inquire into "the administration of the Department of Justice . . . and particularly whether the Attorney General and his assistants were performing or neglecting their duties."[36] To insist that investigation whether the Attorney General was "neglecting" his duties must proceed without the Attorney General is to stage Hamlet without the Dane.[37] Parliament exhibited no tenderness toward the highest Minister. The first one in line for interrogation, subject to protection against self-incrimination, is the officer himself. We go for information, said the Supreme Court, to "those who best can give it and who are most interested in not doing so."[38] If we want information, said Roger Sherman in 1789, "we must get it out of this officer," the Secretary of the Treasury,[39] reflecting a long course of parliamentary inquiry into executive conduct to which not the highest Minister made demur.

The parallel and little older power of the courts to hold the highest officer in contempt is hardly controvertible. Marshall entertained no doubts about the judicial power to *compel* an officer to obey the law:

> If one of the heads of departments commits any illegal act, under color of his office . . . it cannot be pretended that his office alone exempts him from . . . being compelled to obey the judgment of the law.[40]

When Secretary of Commerce Charles Sawyer and Solicitor General Philip Perlman were recalcitrant and argued that "courts

36. 273 U.S. 135, 177. For a detailed critique of Rogers' analysis of McGrain v. Daugherty, see infra, App. B.

37. Indeed the District Court had held the inquiry improper because it saw "no reason why the information . . . cannot be obtained *without calling outsiders*"; Ex parte Daugherty, 299 Fed. 620, 640 (S.D. Ohio 1924); emphasis added.

38. United States v. Morton Salt Co., 338 U.S. 632, 642 (1950); McGrain v. Daugherty, 273 U.S. 135, 163.

39. 1 Annals of Cong. 607. See similar expression by Fisher Ames, supra, Ch. 2, n. 148.

40. Marbury v. Madison, 5 U.S. (1 Cranch) 137, 170 (1803). Marbury was decided as political lightning crackled about the Court. But Marshall justly pointed out in 1794 that the Secretary of War appeared in response to a motion for a mandamus made by Attorney General Randolph, and that both the Secretary and "the highest law officer of the United States" thought the mode of relief appropriate; ibid. 171–172. The matter is recounted in 11 Annals of Cong. 923–925 (1802). See remarks of Congressman James Bayard; ibid. 615.

cannot 'coerce' executive officials," a Court of Appeals held them in contempt, stating that "government officials are bound to obey the judgment of a court just as are private citizens."[41] This merely reaffirmed the doctrine long since declared in *United States v. Lee:* "No officer of the law may set that law at defiance with impunity. All the officers of the government, from the highest to the lowest, are creatures of the law and are bound to obey it."[42] The power of the Grand Inquest to inquire is no less important than the judicial power to enforce the laws,[43] and, given its jurisdiction to inquire into executive conduct and call officers before it, it may equally resort to the contempt power to enforce its demands.

Then there is the provision of Section 134a of the Legislative Reorganization Act of 1946, which authorizes every standing committee and subcommittee "To require by subpoena or otherwise the attendance of such witnesses . . . as it deems desirable."[44] Here is no exemption from the plenary power of the committee to determine which witnesses it deems "desirable." An exemption from broad statutory language must be proven, not assumed. Finally, Assistant Attorney General Rehnquist agreed in 1971 with Congressman John Moss that Congress has "power to punish what it might deem to be contempt of the Congress by an officer of the Government who refused to appear and supply information."[45]

The contempt route to a test of congressional power of inquiry offers a not inconsiderable advantage. When one who is in the custody of Congress seeks his freedom via a petition for a writ of habeas corpus on the ground that Congress lacks power to arrest and confine him, the courts can hardly leave him to rot in jail on the theory that it presents a "political question."[46]

41. Land v. Dollar, 190 F. 2d 623, 633, 638 (D.C. Cir. 1951).
42. 106 U.S. 196, 220 (1882).
43. Cf. Lord Chief Justice Denman, supra, Ch. 2, n. 4.
44. 60 Stat. 831; 2 U.S.C. §190b.
45. 2 Moorhead Hearings 379. And though he considered that Congress "is without a remedy as against the President himself," he stated: "That is not to say that the member of the executive branch who himself has custody of the documents for which the President is seeking to assert executive privilege might not be at least a compellable witness in the sense that he would have to respond to a subpoena"; ibid. 385. Mr. Rehnquist properly reserved judicial review; ibid. 379.
46. Professor Alexander Bickel stated: "it is very difficult to find your way to holding that the habeas corpus is a political question because there is a man under

Among the alternatives open to Congress, the use of a subpoena enforceable by the contempt power represents a tried remedy, deeply rooted in history. But there are those for whom the contempt power seems too drastic;[47] and for them resort to the courts for enforcement of the subpoena may seem more desirable. Let us then consider that approach.

C. *Judicial Enforcement of a Subpoena*

A suit by Congress against a member of the executive branch to enforce a subpoena would proceed after the fashion made familiar by the statutes that created the various administrative agencies. Such a suit raises a number of questions: (1) does it present a "case or controversy"? (2) does Congress have "standing to sue"? (3) does it present a nonjusticiable "political question"?[48]

1. *"Case or Controversy"*

More than one hundred years ago, when the Treasury Department appeared in opposition to the Attorney General, the Court stated shortly that "where the United States is a party, and is represented by the Attorney General . . . no counsel can be heard in opposition on behalf of any other of the departments of the government."[49] Today suits wherein a "part of the government

---

confinement and I think it would be decided, yes"; Executive Agreements Hearings 41. Those vigorous proponents of executive privilege, Kramer & Marcuse, state that

> A case or controversy could arise if Congress cited for contempt pursuant to 2 U.S.C. §194, a Government official who had refused to comply with a demand for information and criminal proceedings were thereupon instituted, or if Congress exercised its own contempt powers and directly ordered the arrest of the official without invoking the assistance of the courts, and the prisoner sought relief by way of habeas corpus.

Kramer & Marcuse 903.

47. Senator J. W. Fulbright stated in 1971, "Not for a moment would I wish to impose so drastic a procedure on Mr. Kissinger or any other official of our Government"; Ervin Hearings 29. Writing in 1965, I too shrank from a possible repulse of the Sergeant-at-Arms by a cordon of federal soldiers; Berger, Executive Privilege 1333. But President Nixon's welcome of a court test, supra, text accompanying n. 28, banishes such concerns.

48. For more detailed discussion of some aspects of these questions, see Berger, Executive Privilege 1333–1362.

49. The Gray Jacket, 72 U.S. (5 Wall.) 342, 371 (1866). In Globe & Rutgers Fire Ins. Co. v. Hines, 273 Fed. 774, 780 (2d Cir. 1921) the court, proceeding from the premise that "the same person cannot be both plaintiff and defendant in the same action," denied recovery to an insurer who had paid for an injury by a Central Railroad float to a New York Central Railroad tug because both roads had been taken over by the United States Railroad Administration, which had organized the roads "into a unified national system of transportation under a single head."

appears before" the courts "fighting another part" are a commonplace;[50] yet such conflicts have received little analysis in terms of "case or controversy."

In private litigation, it has been said that the same party cannot be both plaintiff and defendant, for "in that event, there is no real case or controversy";[51] and the Supreme Court has stated that where one person owns the stock of the opposing corporations there is no controversy because he is "the *dominis litis* on both sides."[52] But when one branch, for example, Congress, which enjoys complete autonomy, stubbornly opposes the position taken by another branch, the Executive, maintaining that the latter is unconstitutionally invading its prerogatives, the facts are at war with a technical assumption that the two branches are the "same person" or that there is a "*dominis litis*" who controls the litigation. Apart from the "people," to whom an appeal on this issue is unfeasible and remote, there exists no organ but the courts which can arbitrate their differences.

In the area of public law the courts have moved away from earlier doctrinaire analysis. Thus, in *ICC v. Jersey City* a railroad sought a rate increase which the ICC authorized over the protests of Jersey City and the federal Price Administrator, who had intervened, alleging that the increase was "in violation of the Stabilization Act." The Court emphasized that the controversy was "between two governmental agencies as to *whether* the powers

50. FTC v. Ruberoid Co., 343 U.S. 470, 482–483 (1952) (Jackson, J., dissenting). See Federal Maritime Bd. v. Isbrandtsen Co., 356 U.S. 481 (1958); Secretary of Agriculture v. United States, 347 U.S. 645 (1954); United States ex rel Chapman v. FPC, 345 U.S. 153 (1953); ICC v. Inland Waterways Corp., 319 U.S. 671, 683 (1943); Miguel v. McCarl, 291 U.S. 442, 450 (1934); Summerfield v. CAB, 207 F. 2d 200 (D.C. Cir. 1953).

Such actions have been termed "routine" in the state courts. Note, "Judicial Resolution of Administrative Disputes Between Federal Agencies," 62 Harv. L. Rev. 1050 (1949). See State Bd. of Educ. v. Levit, 52 Cal. 2d 441, 343 P. 2d 8 (1959) (proceeding by Board of Education to compel the Director of Finance to comply with its order to print books); Morss v. Forbes, 24 N.J. 341, 132 A. 2d 1 (1957) (suit by county prosecutor to enjoin Legislative Committee from demanding confidential information).

51. Defense Supplies Corp. v. United States Lines Co., 148 F. 2d 311, 312–313 (2d Cir. 1945). This was a "dispute about the proper allocation of government funds between different parts of the government," i.e., between a government corporation and the United States; ibid. 313 n. 5. The statute had directed that suits should proceed under principles "obtaining in like cases between private parties" and the court reserved the "question whether such an action, even if authorized by statute, would be justiciable"; ibid. 312, 313 n. 5. The Defense Supplies rule was applied in United States v. Easement & Right of Way, 204 F. Supp. 837, 839–840 (E.D. Tenn. 1962).

52. South Spring Hill Gold Mining Co. v. Amador Medean Gold Mining Co. 145 U.S. 300, 301 (1892).

of the one or the other are *preponderant in the circumstances*."[53] That is precisely the issue presented by the conflicting constitutional claims of Congress and the President. The resolution of such intragovernmental disputes among departments and agencies that involve the fortunes of major statutory schemes intersecting at points of great national importance should not hinge on the accident that the suit is initiated by a private party rather than by a governmental agency which claims that its functions are being impaired by another agency or department.

So the Court apparently concluded when it passed on a suit initiated by a department that complained of just such impairment. In *United States ex rel. Chapman v. Federal Power Commission*, the Secretary of the Interior petitioned to set aside a license granted by the FPC to a private power company on the ground that his "duties relating to the conservation and utilization of the Nation's water resources" were "adversely affected by the Commission's order." Without mention of "case or controversy," the Court held that the Secretary had standing to sue.[54] Implicit in this holding is the assumption that there existed a "controversy," for without it there could be no federal jurisdiction.[55] Recognition "of the legitimate interest of public officials and administrative commissions . . . *to resist* the endeavor to prevent the enforcement of statutes in relation to which they have official duties"[56]—that is, to prevent impairment of their functions—more clearly implies that such resistance contains the kernel of a "controversy."

There is no historical compulsion to read the "case or con-

53. 322 U.S. 503, 523–524 (1944); emphasis added. Cf. ibid. 519. In ICC v. Inland Waterways Corp., 319 U.S. 671, 683 (1943), the Attorney General did not participate because "of a conflict in litigation between coordinate agencies . . . the Agricultural Adjustment Administration and the Interstate Commerce Commission." Compare the attack by the Price Administration on the ICC in Alabama v. United States, 56 F. Supp. 478, 483 (W.D. Ky. 1944), because of "failure properly to interpret and apply its constitutional and statutory authority to protect interstate commerce from undue and unreasonable burdens from intrastate commerce and also by its failure to accommodate the exercise of its powers to the congressional policies embodied in the Emergency Price Control Act."

54. 345 U.S. 153, 156 (1953). Justice Frankfurter stated that the case involved "a conflict of view between two agencies of the Government having duties in relation to the development of national water resources"; ibid. 155. Cf. United States ex rel. Chapman v. FPC, 191 F. 2d 796, 800 (4th Cir. 1951).

55. The presence of "parties having adverse legal interests" continues to be the criterion of "case or controversy." Aetna Life Ins. Co. v. Haworth, 300 U.S. 227, 240–241 (1937). Cf. Public Util. Comm'n v. United States, 355 U.S. 534, 536 (1958); Stephenson v. Stephenson, 249 F. 2d 203, 208 (7th Cir. 1957).

56. Coleman v. Miller, 307 U.S. 433, 442 (1939); emphasis added.

troversy" phrase restrictively. If, with Justice Frankfurter, we look to "matters that were the traditional concern of the courts at Westminster,"[57] we find that those courts took a very broad view of such matters. For centuries they had encouraged *attacks by strangers* on actions of officials in *excess of jurisdiction* through the medium of writs of prohibition, of "relator" actions, that is, proceedings brought by the Attorney General "at the relation of some other person" against "any public authority which is abusing its power."[58] Suits by the Attorney General to keep an official within bounds have long been accepted as a staple of judicial business,[59] and, in the words of Judge Jerome Frank, they present

57. Ibid. 460, dissenting. Elsewhere I have shown that Justice Frankfurter's restrictive reading is without historical foundation. Berger, "Standing to Sue in Public Actions: Is It a Constitutional Requirement?" 78 Yale L.J. 816 (1969). Restrictive as was the Frankfurter reading, he yet recognized the standing of "those who have some specialized interest of their own to vindicate, apart from a political concern which belongs to all"; Coleman v. Miller, 307 U.S. 433, 464 (1939), dissenting. He later stated that " 'standing' to challenge official action is more apt to exist when that action is not within the scope of official authority than when the objection to the administrative decision goes only to its correctness . . . The objection to judicial restraint of an unauthorized exercise of powers is not weighty"; Joint Anti-Fascist Refugee Committee v. McGrath, 341 U.S. 123, 156–157 (1951), concurring. The "courts of Westminster" gave it no weight at all.

58. For citations, see Berger, "Standing to Sue" 819–820, 826.

59. Goddard v. Smithett, 69 Mass. (3 Gray) 116, 125 (1854); Attorney General v. Trustees of Boston Elevated Ry., 319 Mass. 642, 652, 67 N.E. 2d 676, 685 (1946): "The Attorney General represents the public interest, and as an incident to his office he has the power to proceed against public officers to require them to perform the duties that they owe to the public in general, to have set aside such action as shall be determined to be in excess of their authority, and to have them compelled to execute their authority in accordance with law." See also McMullen v. Person, 102 Mich. 608 (1894); State ex rel. Young v. Robinson, 112 N.W. 269, 272 (Minn. 1907); State v. Cunningham, 81 Wis. 440, 51 N.W. 724 (1892). In the federal domain the Attorney General may bring suit "by virtue of his office." United States v. San Jacinto Tin Co., 125 U.S. 273, 280, 284 (1888); Sanitary District v. United States, 266 U.S. 405, 426 (1925).

Although the Attorney General in England could bring suits to "restrain breaches of statutory duty and excess of powers conferred by statute," such suits were generally confined to local authorities; he can not obtain an injunction "against the Crown or a Crown servant acting in that behalf"; S. A. de Smith, *Judicial Review of Official Action* 344 (London, 1959). The latter bar flowed from sovereign immunity, cf. H. W. R. Wade, *Administrative Law* 14 (Oxford, 1961), rather than the absence of a "controversy." A "local authority" in the English unitary, as opposed to our dual federal-state, system is a part of the one government, cf. ibid. 22; and thus English law early provided for adjudicating disputes between one part of the government and another. The place of an injunction against the Crown and its servants is taken by a "declaration," i.e., declaratory judgment, and a litigant can "be sure that it will be respected by the government"; ibid. 226. See ibid. 87, 92–93. Crown immunity, as we have noted, has little relevance in this respect to the development of our institutions; Marshall maintained from the outset that "heads of departments" were "amenable to the laws"; Marbury v. Madison, 5 U.S. (1 Cranch) 137, 164 (1803). Then too, defiance of Parliament can be speedily met by a vote of no confidence. See infra, text accompanying nn. 67–68.

an "actual controversy."[60] There were, in addition, the centuries-old "informers" actions which went beyond *making available* process to challenge extrajurisdictional official conduct, and offered financial *inducements to strangers* to prosecute such actions. By means of a "very large" number of statutes, "the public at large was encouraged to enforce obedience to statutes by the promise of a share of the penalty imposed for disobedience."[61] Such informers had "no interest whatever in the controversy other than that given by statutes";[62] they were artificial "adversaries," created for the purpose of curbing official action in excess of jurisdiction.

All of the foregoing—suits by strangers, informers, relators, and the Attorney General—fit handily into orthodox notions of "case or controversy." A "case," Marshall stated, is a "suit instituted according to the regular course of judicial procedure."[63] The enumerated suits were entertained in "regular course" by the courts of Westminster, and were, therefore, "cases."[64] A "controversy" is presented, in the words of Chief Justice Taney, when there is a "real dispute between the plaintiff and defendant," the antithesis of an "interest in the question" which is "one and the same."[65] Given that Congress maintains the President is un-

60. Associated Industries v. Ickes, 134 F. 2d 694, 704 (2d Cir. 1943). See Reade v. Ewing, 205 F. 2d 630, 632 (2d Cir. 1953).

61. 4 Sir William Holdsworth, *A History of English Law* 356 (2d ed., London, 1937).

62. Marvin v. Trout, 199 U.S. 212, 225 (1905): "Statutes providing for actions by a common informer, who himself had no interest whatever in the controversy other than that given by statute, have been in existence hundreds of years in England, and in this country ever since the foundation of our Government." The use of such actions to police official misconduct is noted by Blackstone, who refers to suits for forfeitures against persons who "being in particular offices . . . neglect to take the oaths to the government; which penalty is given to him that will sue for the same"; 2 Sir William Blackstone, *Commentaries on the Law of England* (Oxford, 1765–1769) 437. A New York informer's statute of 1692 to restrain privateers and pirates provided for one-half the recovery of fines against an "Officer that shall Omitt or neglect his duty herein"; P. Martin and C. Baker, 1 *Supreme Court of the Judicature of the Province of New York, 1691–1704*, p. 30 n. 77, 71 n. 74 (New York, 1959).

63. So states Muskrat v. United States, 219 U.S. 346, 356 (1911).

64. "[O]ne touchstone of justiciability to which this Court has frequently had reference is whether the action sought to be maintained is of a sort 'recognized at the time of the Constitution to be traditionally within the power of the courts in the English and American judicial system' "; Glidden Co. v. Zdanok, 370 U.S. 530, 563 (1962).

65. Lord v. Veazie, 49 U.S. (8 How.) 251, 254 (1850). More recently the Supreme Court said that there is a "controversy" where there is "a dispute between parties who face each other in an adversary proceeding . . . [who] had taken adverse positions with respect to their existing obligations"; Aetna Life. Ins. Co. v. Haworth, 300 U.S. 227, 242 (1937). There "is an actual controversy . . .

lawfully depriving it of rights conferred upon it by the Constitution, and the charge is controverted, there is such a "real dispute,"[66] far more so than that presented by an "informer's" suit; and there is no "common interest" in obtaining the same decision. If we do not find precedents for a suit by Parliament against a Minister it is because of the peculiar development of English institutions. At a time when Ministers were servants of the Crown, accountable only to the King, Parliament finally bent them to its will by a series of impeachments.[67] After they became accountable to Parliament, they could in orthodox theory be toppled by a vote of no confidence. The Framers discarded the "omnipotent parliament" of Blackstone[68] and the royal prerogative,[69] replacing them by a Congress and President of *limited* powers, intended to be kept in bounds by the judiciary. In so doing they scarcely contemplated that enforcement of these limits in a suit by a stranger, informer, or relator would present a "controversy," whereas no "controversy" would exist when either branch complained that its own functions were being impaired by action of the other branch in excess of the power conferred by the Constitution. Rather, the presumption is that all channels that would conduce to checking jurisdictional excesses would be kept open.[70]

It remains to consider the explanation by the Supreme Court in *Flast v. Cohen* of "cases and controversies" primarily as defining "the role assigned to the judiciary in a tripartite allocation of

---

where one side makes a claim of a present, specific right and the other side makes an equally definite claim to the contrary"; Stephenson v. Stephenson, 249 F. 2d 203, 208 (7th Cir. 1957).

66. In a concurring opinion in State v. Cunningham, 81 Wis. 440, 486, 51 N.W. 724, 730 (1892), in which the rest of the court apparently concurred, Judge Pinney said of a suit by the state on the relation of the Attorney General against the Secretary of State, invoking the original jurisdiction of the Supreme Court: "We have, then, all the essential elements of a judicial controversy proper for the determination of a court of justice. There is a controversy between the state, as a political organization suing by its attorney general, and the respondent, in relation to the discharge of a purely ministerial duty, concerning matters respecting the sovereignty . . . of the state . . . which is matter cognizable in this court"; ibid. 81 Wis. at 507, 51 N.W. at 737. See also the remarks of Judge George Wythe of Virginia in 1782, infra, text accompanying n. 128.

67. The story is recounted in Zechariah Chafee, *Three Human Rights in the Constitution* 98–140 (Lawrence, 1956); 1 Sir William Holdsworth, *A History of English Law* 380–384 (3d ed, London, 1922); Clayton Roberts, *The Growth of Responsible Government in Stuart England* (Cambridge, 1966).

68. Berger, *Congress v. Court* 28–30.

69. Supra, Ch. 3, n. 5.

70. Cf. Berger, *Impeachment* 287–288.

power to assure that the courts will not intrude into areas committed to the other branches of government."[71] Authority to decide the scope of intersecting powers about which the executive and legislative branches are in dispute was not "committed" to either. Still less can there be "intrusion" when both Congress and President unite in submitting the long-standing dispute to the courts. Moreover, litigation that challenges unconstitutional action by Congress or the President does not constitute an "improper judicial interference" with, or "intrusion" into, the domain of the other branches. No authority to act in excess of powers conferred was granted to those branches; instead the courts were authorized to check such excesses.[72] An executive usurpation does not change character when it is challenged by Congress; a judicial check thereof remains a judicial function, not an intrusion, though undertaken at the call of either Congress or the President. No hint that judicial restraints of legislative or executive usurpations was to hinge on the nature of the suitor is to be found in the records of the Constitutional Convention.

Finally, whatever the immunity of the President himself, it is not shared, as Assistant Attorney General Rehnquist recognized, by a subordinate who, for example, "has custody of the documents for which the President is seeking to assert executive privilege."[73] On the view that the official is wrongfully withholding information to which Congress is constitutionally entitled, the official may be regarded as a wrongdoer who is "stripped of his official or

71. 392 U.S. 83, 95 (1968). The Court was careful to separate the issue of "capacity to sue" from the question whether it had Article III jurisdiction of the subject matter: "when standing is placed in issue in a case, the question is whether the person whose standing is challenged is a proper party to request an adjudication of a particular issue and not whether the issue itself is justiciable"; ibid. 99–100. The distinction was drawn in the Tileston and Willing cases; infra at nn. 77–78. Flast goes on to state that, whether "a particular person is a proper party to maintain the action does not, by its own force, raise separation of powers problems related to improper judicial interference in areas committed to other branches"; 392 U.S. at 100. Then, after stating that "in deciding the question of standing, it is not relevant that the substantive issues in the litigation might be non-justiciable," Flast declares that it is "necessary to look to the substantive issues . . . to determine whether there is a logical nexus between the status asserted and the claim sought to be adjudicated"; ibid. 101–102. How the irrelevant thus becomes relevant passes my understanding.

72. Berger, *Congress v. Court* 8–16; see statement by Marshall, C.J., infra, text accompanying n. 116. Justice Frankfurter stated, "No institution in a democracy . . . can have absolute power. Nor can the limits of power be finally determined by the limited power itself"; Pennekamp v. Florida, 328 U.S. 331, 355–356 (1946).

73. 2 Moorhead Hearings 385.

representative character and is subjected in his person to the consequences of his individual conduct.[74] A suit between Congress and such an individual wrongdoer should plainly present a "case or controversy."

2. *Standing to Sue*

When we turn from "case or controversy" to "standing to sue" the scene shifts from a constitutional imperative to a judge-made rule unmentioned in the Constitution and which, in its American form, is of relatively recent origin. At the adoption of the Constitution "standing" was neither a term of art nor a familiar doctrine.[75] The Supreme Court, however, has stated that "the requirement of standing is often used to describe the constitutional limitation on the jurisdiction of this Court to 'cases' and 'controversies.' "[76] This confuses two quite different concepts: "cases or controversies" refer to the limited *jurisdiction* or authority of the federal courts to entertain an action; whereas "standing" refers to the right of a litigant to invoke judicial succor, that is, his *capacity to sue*, given a suit that falls within the jurisdiction of the court. That differentiation was drawn by the Supreme Court itself in *Tileston v. Ullman:*

> Since the appeal must be dismissed on the ground that appellant has no standing to litigate the constitutional question . . . it is unnecessary to consider whether the record shows the existence of a genuine case or controversy essential to the exercise of the jurisdiction of this court.[77]

So too, in *Willing v. Chicago Auditorium Ass'n* there was "no lack of a substantial interest in the plaintiff in question," that is,

74. Ex parte Young, 209 U.S. 123, 160 (1908). Marbury v. Madison, 5 U.S. (1 Cranch) 137, 190 (1803): "If one of the heads of departments commits any illegal act, under color of his office, by which an individual sustains an injury, it cannot be pretended that his office alone exempts him from being sued in the ordinary mode of proceeding."

75. Louis Jaffe, "Standing to Secure Judicial Review: Public Actions," 74 Harv. L. Rev. 1265, 1270 (1961), states that he encountered "no case before 1807 in which the standing of the plaintiff is mooted." And the standing of a private individual to enforce a "public right" was first squarely presented in 1897"; ibid. 1271–1272. As late as 1955, an English writer examining the availability of the writ of certiorari could say that the subject of *locus standi* had not been "treated in a satisfactory way by any one, judge or jurist." D. C. M. Yardley, "Certiorari and the Problem of Locus Standi," 71 L.Q. Rev. 388, 393 (1955).

76. Barrows v. Jackson, 346 U.S. 249, 255 (1953). It has been said that "standing to sue is an element of the federal constitutional concept of 'case or controversy' . . ."; Charles A. Wright, *Federal Courts* 36 (St. Paul, 1963). And see infra, n. 84.

77. 318 U.S. 44, 46 (1943).

standing, but Justice Brandeis concluded that "still the proceeding is not a case or controversy."[78]

That "case or controversy" and "standing to sue" are not interchangeable terms will further emerge from examination of standing in two of its important aspects: whether a litigant has suffered an injury that amounts to a "legal wrong," and whether he is invoking a wrong done to another rather than his own. Of that aspect of standing which pertains to attempts to assert the right of another, the Supreme Court said in a constitutional context that judicial abstention rests not on "principles ordained by the Constitution" but rather on "rule[s] of practice," exceptions to which have been made "where there are weighty countervailing policies."[79] The more vexing aspect of standing, which is identified with the absence of legal injury (*damnum absque injuria*),[80] corresponds to failure to state a cause of action. At common law a plaintiff might allege a real enough injury, presenting an actual dispute between adverse litigants—the core of "case or controversy"—and yet fail because his cause fell outside the existing writs. So, contracts under seal were enforceable in actions of covenant from earliest times whereas a parol contract had to wait for enforcement for several centuries.[81] Until 1603 there could be a real enough "controversy," an actual dispute between truly adverse parties arising out of an oral contract, and yet no remedy. It was this situation that was summed up in *damnum absque injuria*, an injury for which at the moment the law provided no remedy. Failure to state a cause of action is not therefore jurisdictional; it "calls for a judgment on the merits and not for a dis-

78. 277 U.S. 274, 289 (1928). For a similar differentiation in the field of conflicts, between the jurisdiction of a court over the subject matter—the power confided by a state to decide in the premises—and the capacity of a party to sue, see Albert Ehrenzweig, *Conflict of Laws* 35, 71, 72, 120 (St. Paul, 1962). Compare Chief Justice Marshall's question in Osborn v. Bank of the United States, 22 U.S. (9 Wheat.) 737, 823 (1824): "Has this legal entity a right to sue? Has it a right to come . . . into any court?"

79. United States v. Raines 362 U.S. 17, 22 (1960); Poe v. Ullman, 367 U.S. 497, 503–504 (1961).

80. In the classic federal example, Tennessee Elec. Power Co. v. TVA, 306 U.S. 118, 140 (1939), eighteen power companies sought to enjoin operation of the TVA, asserting a lack of constitutional power. The Court held that the plaintiffs lacked standing because the "damage consequent on competition, *otherwise lawful*, is in such circumstances *damnum absque injuria*"; emphasis added. Whether the competition was "lawful" was the very heart of the case, and that question "cannot be assumed away"; Alexander Bickel, "Foreword: The Passive Virtues," 75 Harv. L. Rev. 40, 44 (1961). Cf. Wright, supra, n. 76 at 38.

81. J. H. Baker, "New Light on *Slade's Case*," 1971, Camb. L.J. 213, 236.

missal for want of jurisdiction."[82] In other words, "a court may have jurisdiction over the subject matter of an action though the complaint therein does not state a claim upon which relief can be granted."[83] It muddies analysis, in fine, to confuse the *jurisdictional* phrase "case or controversy" with "standing to sue," which merely refers to a litigant's capacity to sue, or to confuse "standing" with failure to state a cause of action.

So far as concerns attacks on official action in excess of jurisdiction, "standing," I have shown elsewhere, is without roots in the practice of the "courts of Westminster," to which Justice Frankfurter turned as a guide.[84] Here it suffices to say that such attacks in suits by strangers, relators, the Attorney General, and informers, discussed above, demonstrate that these courts did not impose the restrictions which Frankfurter mistakenly attributed

82. Bell v. Hood, 327 U.S. 678, 682 (1946); see also Romero v. International Terminal Operating Co., 358 U.S. 354, 359 (1959). Dissenting in Smith v. Sperling, 354 U.S. 91, 98 (1957), Justice Frankfurter objected that the Court was "confounding the requirements for establishing a substantive cause of action with the requirements of diversity jurisdiction."

As regards public actions, I would dissent from Professor Herbert Wechsler's view that the judicial power extends to all cases arising under the Constitution "only when the standing law, decisional or statutory, provides a remedy to vindicate the interest that demands protection"; H. Wechsler, "Toward Neutral Principles of Constitutional Law," 73 Harv. L. Rev. 1, 6 (1959), assuming that by such "interest" he meant a "personal stake." My reading in the records of the several Conventions turned up no limitation beyond Madison's proposal to confine Article III to cases of a "judiciary nature," by which he presumably meant cases which had theretofore been entertained by the courts. Suits by strangers were of that nature. To make existence of a "remedy" a component of the Article III power raises still other problems. Suppose there is a deprivation of constitutional rights for which no "remedy," statutory or decisional, exists, can it be that such a case "arising under the Constitution" lies outside the "judicial power"? Can it be that an invasion of constitutional rights would be without remedy? If the Constitution provides its own "remedy" in such cases we are engaged in circular reasoning. Suppose that the Court proceeds to fashion a new remedy—Marshall laid claim in Marbury v. Madison, 5 U.S. (1 Cranch) 137, 163 (1803), to the common law power to fashion a remedy for the protection of every right—and suppose that the *existence* of a remedy is an indispensable element of "judicial power," is not this the creation of bootstrap jurisdiction? Analytically the Article III "judicial power" is jurisdictional, and to make it depend upon the availability of remedies is to leave the jurisdiction at the mercy of Court or Congress, who can then contract it at will. The judicial power is best viewed as a grant of jurisdiction of the subject matter described in Article III, which exists independently of whether a litigant can state a cause of action.

83. Weiss v. Los Angeles Broadcasting Co., 163 F. 2d 313, 314 (9th Cir. 1947).

84. Berger, "Standing to Sue," supra, n. 57. Justice Frankfurter told us to look to the business of the "courts of Westminster when the Constitution was framed" in order to determine the scope both of "justiciable controversy" and "standing to sue." He regarded "standing" as a "limitation 'on the judicial power' . . ."; Joint Anti-Fascist Refugee Committee v. McGrath, 341 U.S. 123, 150 (1951) (concurring). Pennsylvania R.R. v. Dillon, 335 F. 2d 292, 294 (D.C. Cir. 1964): "Allegation of a legally protected right is a constitutional predicate of standing to attack government action."

to them. To the contrary, they welcomed such suits because, as Justice Brett much later explained,

the real ground of the interference by prohibition is not that the defendant below is individually damaged, but that the cause is drawn in *aliud examen* that the public order in administration of law is broken. And inasmuch as the duty of enforcing such order is imposed on the superior courts, and the issue of a writ of prohibition is the means given to them by law of enforcing such order, it seems to us that upon principle . . . it must be their duty to issue such a writ whenever they are clearly convinced by legal evidence, by *whomsoever brought* before them, that an inferior court is acting without jurisdiction or exceeding its jurisdiction.[85]

The case for the "standing" of Congress to complain of an impairment of its functions by executive action in excess of jurisdiction stands stronger than that of a stranger who has no interest whatsoever of his own. Without taking account of the learning here summarized, the Supreme Court, in *United States ex rel. Chapman v. Federal Power Commission*, struck out in this direction. The Secretary of the Interior was allowed to attack an order of the FPC, granting a license to a private power company to construct a dam, on the ground that it encroached on a responsibility that a statute had confided to him, namely, the duty of marketing surplus power developed at federal hydroelectric plants.[86]

Recognition of the "interest" of a public officer in protection of

85. Worthington v. Jeffries, L.R. 10 C.P. 379, 382, 383 (1875); emphasis added.
English courts continue to be hospitable to suits by strangers; recently they have entertained two mandamus actions, one to compel the Commissioner of Police to enforce the anti-gaming laws, R. v. Metropolitan Police Commissioner (C.A.) 1 All E.R. [1968] 763, and a second to compel him to enforce anti-pornography laws, Reg. v. Police Commissioner, ex p. Blackburn (C.A.) 1 Q.B. [1973] 241. In the former, Lord Denning, M.R., stated it was "an open question whether [Blackburn] has a sufficient interest to be protected"; but the court, after examining the merits and determining that no order was necessary, found no need to decide the issue of standing (pp. 769, 775, 777). A similar result followed in the second case, but Lord Denning took the occasion to say: "Mr. Blackburn has served a useful purpose in drawing the matter to our attention," and Lord Justice Phillimore concurred that "Mr. Blackburn has done a public service in bringing the whole situation into the open." A third case, Blackburn v. Attorney General (C.A.) 2 All E.R. [1971] 1380, involved a suit for a declaration that entry into the Common Market would be in breach of law. Again the court ruled against Blackburn on the merits, and Lord Denning, one of the most respected of present-day English jurists, reserved the question of standing, but stated that "I would not myself rule him out on the ground that he has no standing (p. 1383) and commended him: "Blackburn—as he has done before—has shown eternal vigilance in support of law."

86. 345 U.S. 153 (1953). The facts are set out in more detail in United States ex rel. Chapman v. Federal Power Commission, 191 F. 2d 796 (4th Cir. 1951).

his functions from impairment represented no innovation. The agency which protests that another administrator is unlawfully encroaching on *its* jurisdiction has an immediate interest that transcends an interest in general law enforcement such as a stranger was permitted to assert: it seeks protection from interference with its functions. The Supreme Court has recognized "the legitimate interest of public officials and administrative commissions, federal and state, to resist the endeavor to prevent enforcement of statutes in relation to which they have official duties."[87] An agency which has a "duty" to perform has a "correlative right . . . to protection in performance of its function."[88] The right of Congress to protect one of its most vital functions from impairment rises at least as high as the standing of state senators to maintain the "effectiveness of their votes."[89] The functions confided to Congress are more vital and essential, more deserving of protection from impairment than those of any agency or officer; and no instrumentality of government is more justified in challenging official misconduct than is the representative body elected by the people.

Were "standing" more limited at common law than history indicates, it is yet not a limitation embodied in the Constitution as is "case or controversy"; and, since Congress is not confined to traditional forms or remedies, it is free to go beyond the common law. Over the years Congress has afforded an array of remedies unknown to the common law; and it would hardly be argued that those who were given newly created rights have no standing because the courts of Westminster had not enforced such rights in 1789.[90] To the contrary, the Supreme Court gave

87. Coleman v. Miller, 307 U.S. 433, 442 (1939). "Innumerable cases recognize the standing of an administrative or executive official to defend the constitutionality of the legislation which he is charged with administering or enforcing." Henry Hart and Herbert Wechsler, *The Federal Courts and the Federal System* 162 (Brooklyn, 1953).

88. Brewer v. Hoxie School Dist. No. 46, 238 F. 2d 91, 104 (8th Cir. 1956). In Summerfield v. CAB, 207 F. 2d 200, 203 (D.C. Cir. 1953), wherein the board fixed an airmail transportation rate for a carrier, it was held that "The Postmaster General is a party in interest by reason of the duties in respect to mail pay imposed upon him by the statute."

89. Coleman v. Miller, 307 U.S. 433, 438 (1939), quoted in Baker v. Carr, 369 U.S. 186, 208 (1962).

90. Congress is not confined to traditional forms or remedies. Aetna Life Ins. Co. v. Haworth, 300 U.S. 227, 240 (1937). Compare such new remedies as the Federal Declaratory Judgment Act, and the Fair Labor Standards Act, which authorizes the Secretary of Labor to sue for recovery of minimum wages on behalf of an employee and to make a turnover of the recovery; Sec. 1b, 52 Stat. 1069 (1938),

express sanction to the right of Congress to confer standing as a representative of the public interest upon one who could assert no "legal right" himself.[91] Taking note of "informers'" statutes, and doubtless aware of "relators" actions, Judge Jerome Frank drew from *FCC v. Sanders Brothers Radio Station*, and *Scripps-Howard Radio v. FCC*[92] the proposition that "Congress can constitutionally enact a statute conferring on any non-official person [and a fortiori upon itself] . . . authority to bring a suit to prevent action by an officer in violation of his statutory powers . . . Such persons, so authorized are, so to speak, private Attorney Generals."[93] When this statement appeared in 1943, those who were under the spell of the Court's earlier statements regarded it as a daring break with tradition, whereas in fact it is solidly rooted in the common law. Some continue to doubt the broad power of Congress in the premises;[94] but it is difficult to see how the power of Congress to confer standing by statute can be open to question when its power to create informers actions is beyond doubt. Both Justices Douglas and Harlan have referred to the right of Congress to confer standing;[95] and I would conclude with Professor Charles A. Wright that, "Where suit by the United States [or one of its branches] is expressly authorized by Act of Congress, there is no problem of standing; Congress has power to authorize the United States to be guardian of the public interest by bringing

29 U.S.C. §216 (1959). One need only mention such "rights" as were created by the Federal Employees Liability Act. "When Congress transmutes a moral obligation into a legal one by specially consenting to suit, it authorizes the tribunal . . . to perform a judicial function" within the meaning of Art. III; Glidden Co. v. Zdanok, 370 U.S. 530, 567 (1962). See also supra, n. 82.

91. Scripps-Howard Radio v. FCC, 316 U.S. 4, 14 (1942); FCC v. Sanders Brothers Radio Station, 309 U.S. 470, 477 (1940).

92. Supra, n. 91.

93. Associated Industries v. Ickes, 134 F. 2d 694, 704 (2d Cir. 1943); *vacated as moot*, 320 U.S. 707 (1943).

94. In the Hearings on S. 2097 Before the Subcommittee on Constitutional Rights of the Senate Committee on the Judiciary, 89th Cong., 2d Sess. 498 (March 1966), Professor P. G. Kauper stated that "absent a showing of injury" to the suitor in some "specific or concrete way," he would not suppose that Congress has the power to direct the federal courts to take jurisdiction of such citizen's suits; ibid. 502. And see the remarks of Professor A. S. Miller; ibid. 509.

95. Congress "has broad authority to determine who has standing to protest the action of administrative agencies"; W. O. Douglas, "The Bill of Rights Is Not Enough," 38 N.Y.U. L. Rev. 207, 225 (1963). Justice Harlan, who questions the wisdom of broadening the standing of strangers, stated that "any hazards to the proper allocation of authority among the three branches of the Government would be substantially diminished if public actions had been pertinently authorized by Congress and the President"; Flast v. Cohen, 392 U.S. 116, 131–132 (1968), dissenting.

suits."[96] Any doubts as to congressional "standing" to complain of executive impairment of its functions can therefore be set at rest by statute.

3. *Political Questions*

Introductory. It has been generally assumed that courts will not adjudicate conflicting claims to power by the legislative and executive branches because they present a "political" and therefore nonjusticiable question.[97] That assumption requires re-examination in light of the quakelike shakeup of the entire doctrine by *Baker v. Carr*, the "reapportionment" case,[98] and *Powell v. McCormack*, which reversed the exclusion of Adam Clayton Powell from the House.[99] In the wake of each of these cases there followed a flood of commentary, criticism, and theorizing.[100] No single theory, it is said, explains all the cases;[101] and it would go far beyond the bounds of this section to attempt a synthesis which thus far has eluded others. For me, the two cases themselves constitute the springboard from which analysis must take off.

All that the political question doctrine "can defensibly imply," wrote Professor Herbert Wechsler, "is that the courts are called upon to judge whether the Constitution has committed to another agency of government the autonomous determination of

96. C. Wright, supra, n. 76 at 60.

97. After referring to Eisenhower's directive limiting Senator McCarthy's efforts to obtain information from the Army, Judge Learned Hand queried, "is it not possible to argue that Congress, especially now that the appropriations for the armed forces are the largest items of the budget, should be allowed to inquire in as much detail as it wishes, not only how past appropriations have in fact been spent, but in general about the conduct of the national defense? Nevertheless, would you not, like me, guess the Court would refuse to pass on the controversy?" L. Hand, *The Bill of Rights* 17–18 (Cambridge, Mass., 1958). See also Alan Barth, *Government by Investigation* 17 (New York, 1955); Telford Taylor, *Grand Inquest* 87 (New York, 1955), citing still other writers. Had Hand been familiar with the solid historical background for parliamentary inquiry into the disbursement of appropriations and the conduct of a war, his speculations might have turned the other way. See infra, n. 127.

98. 369 U.S. 186 (1962).

99. 395 U.S. 486 (1969).

100. E.g. Symposium, 72 Yale L.J. 7 et seq. (1962); Phil C. Neal, "Baker v. Carr: Politics in Search of Law," 1962, Sup. Ct. Rev. 252; "Comments on Powell v. McCormack," 17 UCLA L. Rev. 1, 58–191 (1969), hereinafter cited as UCLA Comments.

101. Fritz Scharpf, "Judicial Review and the Political Question: A Functional Analysis," 75 Yale L.J. 517, 566 (1966); Note, "The Supreme Court as Arbitrator in the Conflict Between Presidential and Congressional War-Making Powers," 50 Bost. U. L. Rev. 78, 84 (1970).

the issue raised."[102] Attempting to rationalize the welter of cases, *Baker v. Carr* set forth "six" categories of political questions,[103] but in fact it gave preponderant weight to the "commitment" factor when it stated that the "nonjusticiability of a political question is primarily a function of the separation of powers," that is, the determination of the issue was confided to another branch.[104] There is considerable agreement that *Powell v. McCormack* turned pretty largely on the "commitment" issue.[105] In *Powell* the House argued that, by the terms of Article I, §5(1), "each House shall be the judge of the . . . qualifications of its own members."[106] That grant, replied the Court, "is limited to the standing qualifications prescribed in the Constitution," namely age, citizenship, and residence. When the House excluded Powell for misconduct, the Court held, it acted beyond the power conferred upon it;[107] in other words, the power to "judge" does not permit the Congress to add to the constitutional "qualifications."[108]

The Court proceeded from the premise that it is the "ultimate interpreter of the Constitution," vested with the "responsibility" to decide "whether the action of another branch . . . exceeds whatever authority has been committed."[109] The exercise of this

102. Wechsler, supra, n. 82 at 7–8. In Baker v. Carr, 369 U.S. at 246, Justice Douglas, concurring, said, "Where the Constitution assigns a particular function wholly and indivisibly to another department, the federal judiciary does not intervene."

103. "Prominent on the surface of any case held to involve a political question is found a textually demonstrable constitutional commitment of the issue to a coordinate political department; or lack of judicially discoverable and manageable standards for resolving it; or the impossibility of deciding without an initial policy decision of a kind clearly for nonjudicial discretion; or the impossibility of the court's undertaking independent resolution without expressing lack of the respect due coordinate branches of government; or an unusual need for unquestioning adherence to a political decision already made; or the potentiality of embarrassment from multifarious pronouncements by various departments on one question"; 369 U.S. at 217. See infra, text accompanying nn. 151–152.

104. Ibid. 210.

105. S. K. Laughlin, UCLA Comments, supra, n. 100 at 102; Terrance Sandalow, ibid. 173; R. B. McKay, ibid. 124.

106. 395 U.S. at 513–514.

107. Ibid. 550.

108. Berger, *Impeachment* 105.

109. 395 U.S. at 521, citing Baker v. Carr, 369 U.S. 186, 211 (1962):

> An essential ingredient of our rule of law is the authority of the courts to determine whether an executive official or agency has complied with the Constitution or with the mandate of Congress which define and limit the authority of the executive. Any claim to executive absolutism [e.g., absolute right to determine the scope of executive privilege] cannot override the duty of the

power, for example, when Congress has exceeded its "legislative" bounds is familiar; on what ground is Congress to be exempted when it dons its "judicial hat"? The internal management of Congress is surely not more important than its power to legislate for the whole nation. Nor is the "legislative power" less exclusive than its power to judge of membership qualifications merely because Congress is not expressly authorized to "judge" which subject of legislation is to be preferred.[110] The "judicial power" itself is "limited" to categories beyond which the federal courts may not stray. It cannot be that the congressional power to "judge" alone is unlimited.

Deference to Congress does not lead the Court to stay its hand when legislation transgresses constitutional bounds. So too, deference to its right to manage its internal affairs must yield to the right of the states and electorate to choose their own representatives except as limited by the Constitution,[111] to the right of the individual member of Congress to be protected against deprivation of office except in accordance with law,[112] the essence of due process, and to the basic principle that ours is a government of enumerated and limited powers. "It is far more important," Justice Douglas said, "to be respectful to the Constitution than to a coordinate branch of government."[113]

In all this *Powell* is solidly anchored in *Marbury v. Madison:* "It is emphatically the province and duty of the judicial department to say what the law is."[114] Marshall had spoken strongly to this effect in 1788, as a leader in the drive to blunt Patrick Henry's opposition to the adoption of the Constitution in the Virginia Ratification Convention:

> court to assure that an official has not exceeded his charter or flouted the legislative will.

Committee for Nuclear Responsibility v. Seaborg, 463 F. 2d 788, 793 (D.C. Cir. 1971).

110. "It should make no difference whether Congress exceeds its authority in the course of its constitutionally committed power to legislate, or in the course of its constitutionally committed power to judge the qualifications of its members. In either case, it is the right and duty of the Supreme Court to declare the unconstitutionality of the act"; D. T. Weckstein, UCLA Comments, supra, n. 100 at 85–86.

111. "A fundamental principle of our representative democracy is, in Hamilton's words, 'that the people should choose whom they please to govern them' "; Powell v. McCormack, 395 U.S. at 547.

112. Cf. R. B. McKay, UCLA Comments, supra, n. 100 at 122; D. T. Weckstein, ibid. 85: Powell "established the inapplicability of the political question doctrine in cases and controversies involving infringements of constitutional rights."

113. Massachusetts v. Laird, 400 U.S. 886, 894 (1970), dissenting.

114. 5 U.S. (1 Cranch) 137, 177 (1803).

To what quarter will you look for protection from an infringement on the Constitution, if you will not give the power to the judiciary? There is no other body that can afford such a protection.[115]

And, as he stated in *Marbury*, "To what purpose are powers limited, and to what purpose is that limitation committed to writing, if these limits may, at any time, be passed by those intended to be restrained?"[116] A challenge to this analysis rejects judicial review itself.

But the issue thus posed by *Powell* was not really a "political question"—a question of "justiciability"—but rather, as Professor Robert G. Dixon observed, a question of "jurisdiction."[117] Whether the House's power to "judge the qualifications" of its members went beyond the enumerated qualifications or was limited thereto goes to the *extent of power* conferred by the Constitution, a question of "jurisdiction" pure and simple. Just as the "commitment" of "legislative power" to Congress does not foreclose judicial inquiry as to the scope of the power committed, so the grant of power to "judge" of membership qualifications does not bar judicial review of the extent of that power. Analysis in terms of "political question" only confuses the classic issue: judicial interpretation of the scope of a constitutional grant of power. And if power to decide in the premises, including the scope of the power, is "committed" to another branch, it follows that the power is withheld from the courts; and that issue does not pose a question of "political" deference to that branch but a lack of *judicial* jurisdiction. In this area at least the "political question" label is a misnomer, more apt to mislead than to enlighten.

It needs to be borne in mind that a "Constitution is a political instrument. It deals with government and governmental powers . . . It is not a question whether the considerations are political, for nearly every consideration arising from the Constitution can be so described."[118] "From the beginning," said Professors Felix

115. 3 Elliot 554.

116. 5 U.S. at 176. For documentation of the Founders' intention to make the Court the "final" interpreter of the Constitution, see Berger, *Congress v. Court* 188–197.

117. UCLA Comments, supra, n. 100 at 110.

118. Melbourne v. Commonwealth of Australia, 74 Commw. L.R. 31, 82 (1947) (Dixon, J.). This had been anticipated by de Toqueville: "The American judge is brought into the political arena independently of his own will . . . The political question which he is called upon to resolve is connected with the interest of the suitors and he cannot refuse to decide it without abdicating the duties of his post. Alexander de Toqueville, *Democracy in America* 101 (New York, 1945).

Frankfurter and J. M. Landis, "the Court had to resolve what were essentially political issues—the proper accommodation between the states and the central government,"[119] an accommodation that had vastly greater importance for the Founders than that between the several branches of the federal government.[120]

If the assertion of a right to obtain or withhold information be deemed "political," that "does not mean it presents a 'political question.' "[121] Judicial resolution of the executive privilege controversy will not "risk embarrassment of our government abroad or grave disturbance at home."[122] It will not embroil the Court in the "overwhelmingly party or intraparty contests" such as Justice Frankfurter feared might flow from the reapportionment decision,[123] for, as the clinical examples earlier set out show, information withholdings seldom are "strongly entangled in popular feeling."[124] When one compares the "violently partisan nature" of the reapportionment controversy,[125] the "political" overtones of executive resistance to a congressional request for an Inspector General's report seem like flutterings over teacups.

Boundary Dispute between Two Branches. The "commitment" doctrine has little relevance to a dispute between two branches as to their respective constitutional boundaries, for the power finally to decide whether Congress has a plenary right to demand information or whether the President has "uncontrolled discretion" to refuse it plainly was "committed" to neither. Essentially this is a dispute about the scope of intersecting powers; if one branch has the claimed power the other branch necessarily has not. One branch cannot finally decide the reach of its own power when the result is to curtail that claimed by another. Neither of the two departments, said Madison in Federalist No. 49, "can pretend to an exclusive or superior right of settling the boundaries between their respective powers."[126] "Some arbiter," said Justice

119. Felix Frankfurter and J. M. Landis, *The Business of the Supreme Court* 318 (New York, 1927).

120. For the Founders' fervent attachment to the states, see Berger, *Congress v. Court,* Index "State Sovereignty."

121. Baker v. Carr, 369 U.S. 186, 209 (1962); Louis Jaffe, "Standing to Secure Judicial Review: Public Actions," 74 Harv. L. Rev. 1265, 1304 (1961).

122. Baker v. Carr, 369 U.S. at 226.

123. Ibid. 324 (dissenting).

124. Ibid. 267.

125. Thomas Emerson, "Malapportionment and Judicial Power," 72 Yale L.J. 64, 65 (1962).

126. Federalist No. 49 at 328. True, Madison also said that no provision was made "for a particular authority to determine the limits of the constitutional division of

Jackson, "is almost indispensable when power is . . . balanced between different branches, as the legislative and executive . . . Each unit cannot be left to judge the limits of its own power."[127] In at least one pre-1787 case, *Commonwealth v. Caton*, Judge George Wythe, mentor of Jefferson, took for granted the justiciability of a dispute between the Virginia Senate and House of Delegates. The dispute lay at the bottom of an appeal from a conviction for treason; and Wythe unhesitatingly assimilated the duty "to protect one branch of the legislature, and, consequently, the whole community, against the usurpations of the other," to the judicial duty to protect "a solitary individual against the rapacity of the sovereign."[128] It speaks volumes on whether a dispute between different branches of government was deemed "justiciable" in 1782 that so eminent a jurist and scholar should not have experienced the slightest qualms on that score. No men-

---

power between the branches of the government. In all systems there are points which must be adjusted by the departments themselves, to which no one of them is competent. If it cannot be determined in this way, there is no resource left but the will of the community"; 1 Annals of Cong. 500–501 (1789). But Madison by no means expressed the general viewpoint. In the same debate on the "removal" power, Elbridge Gerry, also a Framer, said that if the President and Senate differ, "let it go before the proper tribunal; the judges are the Constitutional umpires on such questions"; 1 Annals of Cong. 473. For other similar statements in that debate, see Berger, *Congress v. Court* 147–148.

After a lifetime in government, Madison himself concluded that that function must fall to the courts. Although he affirmed the right of each department to interpret its own powers and to act upon that interpretation "without involving the functions of any other" department, he then said, "it may always be expected that the judicial branch . . . will . . . most engage the respect and reliance of the public as the surest expositor of the Constitution, as well in questions . . . concerning the boundaries between the several departments of the Government as in those between the Union and its members"; 4 James Madison, *Letters and Other Writings of James Madison* 349–350 (Philadelphia, 1867).

127. Robert H. Jackson, *The Struggle for Judicial Supremacy* 9 (New York, 1949). Compare Hand, supra, n. 97 at 3: "No provision was expressly made, however, as to how a 'Department' was to proceed when in the exercise of one of its own powers it became necessary to consider the validity of some earlier act of another 'Department.' Should the second accept the decision of the first that the act was within the first's authority, or should it decide the question *de novo* according to its own judgment? A third view prevailed . . . it was a function of the courts to decide which Department was right, and that all were bound to accept the decision of the Supreme Court."

In Youngstown Case 597 Justice Frankfurter, concurring, stated: "The judiciary may, as this case proves, have to intervene in determining where the authority lies between the democratic forces in our scheme of government," i.e., between Congress and the President. Citing Youngstown, the court in Berk v. Laird, 429 F. 2d 302, 304 (2d Cir. 1970), answered in the affirmative the question whether the courts "have the power to make a particular kind of constitutional decision involving the division of powers between the legislative and executive branches." See also Judge Learned Hand, supra, Ch. 1, n. 45.

128. 4 Call 5, 8 (Va. 1782).

tion of "political questions" was made in the several Conventions; that is a judicial construct of a later time.

Thus far no case has decided that a legislative-executive conflict is nonjusticiable. In the course of an elaborate and acute analysis of the "political question" cases, Professor Fritz Scharpf concluded that "the political question also has had no place when the Court was presented with conflicting claims of competence among the departments of the federal government."[129] That statement is confirmed by the cases. In the aftermath of the Civil War, the Supreme Court held in *United States v. Klein* that a congressional attempt to deprive it of jurisdiction to review a provision curtailing the effect of a presidential pardon "impairs the executive authority," thus jumping into a "political" thicket with both feet.[130] The Supreme Court has also acted "as umpire between Congress and the president"[131] in *Myers v. United States*,[132] where it permitted the Attorney General to attack a congressionally enacted statute limiting the President's removal power. As Justice Frankfurter later remarked, "on the Court's special invitation Senator George Wharton Pepper, of Pennsylvania, presented the position of Congress [in opposition to the Attorney General] at the bar of this Court."[133] In *Youngstown Sheet & Tube Co. v. Sawyer*[134] the President had directed the Secretary of Commerce to seize and operate most of the nation's steel mills, on the ground that a strike called by the steel unions jeopardized the continued production of steel indispensable to the national defense. The seizure was held invalid because, in the words of Justice Burton, the President "invaded the jurisdiction of Congress."[135]

129. Scharpf, supra, n. 101 at 585.

130. 80 U.S. (13 Wall.) 128, 145, 148 (1871).

131. Nathaniel Nathanson, "The Supreme Court as a Unit of the National Government: Herein of Separation of Powers and Political Questions," 6 J. Pub. L. 331, 332 (1957).

132. 272 U.S. 52 (1926). Citing Myers, a "privilege" proponent, Irving Younger, "Congressional Investigations and Executive Secrecy: A Study in Separation of Powers," 20 U. Pitt. L. Rev. 755, 777 n. 100 (1959), stated that "we should not forget that the Supreme Court has decided disputes between Congress and the President under its general power to hold the other two departments within the ambit of the Constitution."

Another example is furnished by The Pocket Veto Case, 279 U.S. 655, 676 (1929), wherein the Court passed on "the reciprocal rights and duties of the President and of Congress." Hatton W. Sumners was amicus for the House Judiciary Committee.

133. Wiener v. United States, 357 U.S. 349, 353 (1958).

134. 343 U.S. 579 (1952).

135. Ibid. 660. A row of decisions by lower courts, setting aside presidential impoundments of funds appropriated for purposes specified by Congress (in suits by

It would be anomalous in the extreme to hold that the rights of Congress can be asserted against the Executive by a third person but that Congress itself cannot be heard in defense of its own rights. The "public interest in responsible and realistic constitutional decisions," as Professor Sharpf observed, "is much too serious to be left unprotected against the accidents of ordinary litigation."[136] If the central "power" issue is "political," the taint is not removed because it is presented in a private litigation. That "which is essentially a judicial question . . . in suits between private parties [or between them and the executive] . . . is not different in a suit between the States."[137] Consideration of the right to test confinement of an official under a congressional contempt by a habeas corpus proceeding[138] confirms this analysis. If conflicting claims to power between Congress and President present a "political question," a shift in *procedure*—from a habeas corpus for illegal confinement to a suit by Congress to enforce its demand —cannot transform the *subject matter:* that remains "political."[139] Justiciability cannot be made to turn on the accident of remedy. Nor can we accept the view that habeas corpus is available to test the confinement of a private individual by Congress but not of an executive officer. To conclude alternatively that such controversies are unjusticiable in any type of proceeding would be to permit Congress to imprison executive officers without hin-

---

persons affected) has just been well summarized by District Judge Gerhard A. Gesell (U.S. Dist. Ct. for Dist. Col.):

> When Congress directs that money be spent, and the President, as chief executive, declines to permit the spending, the resulting conflict is not political. We are a government of law, not of men, and the law must be determined and upheld.

N.Y. Times, Aug. 4, 1973, p. 21; see also ibid. Aug. 1, 1973, p. 14.

In Gravel v. United States, 408 U.S. 606, 661 (1972), Senator Mike Gravel resisted a grand jury subpoena to his aide respecting Gravel's disclosure of the Pentagon Papers. The Senate filed an amicus brief, and Justice Brennan, dissenting, stated that the Executive "seeks the aid of the judiciary . . . to extend its power of inquiry and interrogation into the privileged domain of the legislature." Another conflict between Congress and the Executive.

136. Scharpf, supra, n. 101 at 528–529.

137. Pennsylvania v. West Virginia, 262 U.S. 553, 591 (1923).

138. See remarks of Assistant Attorney General Rehnquist, supra, text accompanying n. 45.

139. Compare ICC v. Brimson, 154 U.S. 447, 486 (1894): "We cannot assent to any view of the Constitution that concedes the power of Congress to accomplish a named result, indirectly, by particular forms of judicial procedure, but denies its power to accomplish the same result, directly, and by a different proceeding judicial in form."

drance, short of a file of marines.[140] The suggestion that the Executive may resist the Sergeant-at-Arms would invite the "trial of physical strength" that the Court condemned.[141] In short, the courts, said *Baker v. Carr*, "cannot reject as 'no law suit' a bona fide controversy as to whether some action denominated 'political' exceeds constitutional authority."[142] For, said Chief Justice White in another "political question" case, it is the "ever present duty" of the courts "to enforce and uphold the applicable provisions of the Constitution as to each and every exercise of governmental power."[143] That duty is not eliminated by the fact that action in excess of jurisdiction injures a coordinate branch rather than the individual. To the contrary, the centrality of the separation of powers to our democratic system and to the protection of individual rights dictates that such injuries to a coordinate branch *must* be halted by the judiciary.[144] It is precisely at this point that enforcement of constitutional "limits" is most urgently required for the preservation of our democratic society.

Following in the path of the Court in *Powell*, which summoned "basic principles of our democratic system"—the right of the people to "choose whom they please to govern them"—in order to buttress its jurisdictional analysis,[145] let us glance at the no less important right of the people to be informed. Executive secrecy shrouded "escalation by stealth" in Vietnam, the ugly cover-up of Watergate, and accompanying attempts to corrupt the election process. "Nothing so diminishes democracy as secrecy," Justice Douglas reminded us; "information to the people," he quoted Jefferson, "is the most certain and legitimate engine of government."[146] Indeed, information is the bloodstream

140. The courts "will not stand impotent before an obvious instance of a manifestly unauthorized exercise of power"; Baker v. Carr, 369 U.S. at 217.

141. United States v. Texas, 143 U.S. 621, 641 (1892).

142. 369 U.S. at 217; see also ibid. 230.

143. Pacific States Tel. & Tel. Co. v. Oregon, 223 U.S. 118, 150 (1912).

144. In protecting one branch of the legislature "against the usurpation of the others," Judge George Wythe emphasized that he was thus protecting "the whole community"; supra, text accompanying n. 128.

145. 395 U.S. at 547–548.

146. Gravel v. United States, 408 U.S. 606, 641 (1972), dissenting. And in his concurring opinion in United States v. New York Times, 403 U.S. 713, 724 (1971), Justice Douglas stated: "Secrecy in government is fundamentally antidemocratic, perpetuating bureaucratic errors. Open discussion [based on full information] and debate of public issues are vital to our national health." It is therefore puzzling that he should say in Gravel, with respect to the issue of "executive privilege," a chief "tool of suppression," 408 U.S. at 642, that "the federal courts do not sit as an *ombudsman,* refereeing the disputes between the other two branches." This sets the seal on suppression by the Executive unless Congress picks up a battle-axe. Cf.

of democracy; he who can shut it off controls our lives, as the progressive escalation in Vietnam alone should teach. Justice Potter Stewart aptly summarized the issue in a comment on the Executive refusal to release conflicting agency and departmental reports about the wisdom of a contemplated underground atomic explosion in Amchitka:

a nuclear test that engendered fierce controversy within the Executive Branch . . . would be precisely the kind of event that should be opened to the fullest possible disclosure consistent with the legitimate interests of national defense. Without such disclosure, factual information available to the concerned Executive agencies connot be considered by the people or evaluated by the Congress. And with the people and then their representatives reduced to a state of ignorance, the democratic process is paralyzed.[147]

Here, as in *Baker v. Carr*, to borrow from Professor Archibald Cox, "refusal to act would have the effect of legitimizing the evil";[148] it would leave with the Executive the power of paralyzing the democratic process. That is too high a price for comporting with the demands of "delicacy."

"Manageable Standards" and "Enforceable Remedy." For Professor Dixon the issue was not whether there was no "commitment" to Congress, but "should the judiciary proceed to *exercise* the jurisdiction it concededly posseses"; this is not a "simple matter of right or wrong" but of "delicacy," the "core of the nonjusticiability idea," "what courts can and cannot do effectively," which hinges on a "manageable standard for decision" and "enforceable remedy."[149] This represents a turn from what *is* to what *ought* to be; for in *Powell* the Court stated that the "other arguments that this case presents a political question depend in great measure on the textual commitment question."[150] Understandably, commentators have concluded that the "six" criteria of justiciability have been reduced to one;[151] and Professor Dixon

infra, text accompanying n. 148. He himself condemned a carte blanche to the executive branch "to insulate information from public scrutiny"; Environmental Protection Agency v. Mink, 410 U.S. 73, 110 (1973), dissenting.

147. Environmental Protection Agency v. Mink, 410 U.S. 73, 94–95 (1973).

148. Archibald Cox. "The Role of the Supreme Court in American Society," 50 Marq. L. Rev. 575, 591 (1967). See also Weckstein, UCLA Comments, supra, n. 100 at 83; C. E. Rice, ibid. 103; L. D. Asper and S. J. Rosen, ibid. 72; McKay, ibid. 122; Scharpf, supra, n. 101 at 585.

149. Dixon, UCLA Comments, supra, n. 100 at 111, 112, 116.

150. 395 U.S. at 521 n. 43.

151. Laughlin, UCLA Comments, supra, n. 100 at 102; Sandalow, ibid. 173; cf. McKay, ibid. 124.

himself despondently stated that the *Powell* approach "virtually kills the political question concept without saying so."[152] A requiem, however, may be premature, so let us examine the executive privilege dispute in the frame of "manageable standards" and "enforceable remedy."

The presidential claim of constitutional authority to withhold information from Congress presents nothing like the thorny "standards" problem posed by "reapportionment." Reapportionment," said Justice Douglas, "as our experience shows, presented a tangle of partisan politics in which geography, rural constituencies, and numerous other non-legal factors play varying roles . . . Yet we held the issues were justiciable."[153] In contrast, the claim of executive power to withhold information from Congress can be measured by the long inquisitorial practice of Parliament, which ranged across the entire gamut of government, with the aid of the fact that there is not the slightest intimation in the records of the several Conventions of an intention to curtail the recognized power of the Grand Inquest in any respect. To the extent that the Court feels impelled to make inroads on the sanction given that practice by the Founders, it can look to the judicial experience of dealing with claims of "executive privilege" in private litigation. In almost every category of such claims there exist judicial precedents; so that unlike the uncharted "reapportionment" tangle the task will not require the formulation of new standards but rather the adaptation and application of the old. Viewed in terms of fitness for judicial determination, the basic issues of fact and law are not appreciably altered by the fact that it is the Attorney Harry Daugherty rather than his brother Mally who is asked about the Attorney General's conduct in office.

If the issue be phrased in Justice Frankfurter's terms, the difficulty of "finding appropriate modes of relief,"[154] courts have entered decrees in private litigation directing the executive branch to make requested information available; the framing of such a decree in a dispute between Congress and the President presents no greater difficulty. A Court which did not boggle at

152. Dixon, ibid. 110. R. F. Bischoff refers to "the cavalier manner in which the opinion in [Baker v. Carr] treated past decisions and interpretations in the interest of a necessary solution of a fundamental problem of the mid-twentieth century"; Bischoff, ibid. 158.

153. Oregon v. Mitchell, 400 U.S. 112, 138 (1970), dissenting and concurring.

154. Baker v. Carr, 369 U.S. at 278; Jaffe, supra, n. 121 at 1304.

the formidable remedial difficulties[155] posed by reapportionment[156] should not shy from requiring an executive officer to deliver information or from declaring that he is under a duty to do so. Compared with the complexities involved in reapportionment this is a marvelously simple judicial order, differing little from countless orders which direct public officers to do or refrain from doing something. On my view of the historical records, there is no constitutional authorization to withhold *any* information from Congress. Assume that the constitutional boundaries are more blurred than I consider them to be, the task of pricking out the withholding boundaries is no more complicated—if indeed as complicated—than the determination of the scope of the "commerce" clause or the content of "due process."

The question of "remedy" in *Powell* was treated by Professor Dixon in terms of the House's potential *defiance* of the Court's declaratory judgment: how could the House be compelled to pay Powell's back salary and restore his seniority?[157] The Court, as Dean McKay stated, ordinarily has "not shrunk from unpopular decision or even from clash with another branch of the federal government."[158] Of the latter, the not infrequent decisions holding congressional enactments unconstitutional afford a familiar example, including the federal income tax, the child labor legislation, the New Deal decisions.[159] The school desegregation decision was entered in the teeth of massive opposition in the South and, as experience has since demonstrated, of barely submerged hostility in the North, so that nineteen years after

155. Professor Alexander Bickel points out that "the decisive factor in Colegrove could not well have been the difficulty or uncertainty that might attend enforcement of a judicial decree. A judicial system that swallowed *Brown v. Board of Education* [desegregation] and *Cooper v. Aaron* would hardly strain at *Colegrove v. Green* or *Baker v. Carr*"; Alexander Bickel, "The Durability of Colegrove v. Green," 72 Yale L.J. 39, 40 (1962). The Court itself acknowledged in Brown v. Board of Education, 347 U.S. 483, 495 (1954), that "the formulation of decrees in these cases presents problems of considerable complexity." Justice Douglas remarked that "Adjudication is often perplexing and complicated. An example of the extreme complexity of the task can be seen in a decree apportioning water among the several states"; Baker v. Carr, 369 U.S. at 245, concurring.

156. Emerson, supra, n. 125 at 75–80; cf. Allen P. Sindler, "Baker v. Carr: How to 'Sear the Conscience' of Legislators," 72 Yale L.J. 23, 32–38 (1962).

157. Dixon, UCLA Comments, supra, n. 100 at 131. Justice Frankfurter stated in Baker v. Carr, 369 U.S. at 270, dissenting, there is "nothing judicially more unseemly nor more self-defeating than for this Court to make *in terrorem* pronouncements, to indulge in empty rhetoric."

158. McKay, UCLA Comments, supra, n. 100 at 124.

159. Scharpf, supra, n. 101 at 552.

the decision desegregation still proceeds with "all deliberate speed." In truth the likelihood of "disobedience" has not been a compelling factor in "political question" cases.[160] When Marshall was told in 1805 that "there was no means of compelling" the United States to pay costs, he replied, "that would make no difference, because we are to presume that they would pay them, if bound by law so to do."[161] Later he decided against Georgia in spite of the high probability that the order would be disregarded, undeterred by President Jackson's reported assurances that he would not lend his aid to enforcement.[162] Today, as in 1892, the Court "cannot decline the exercise of [its] jurisdiction upon the inadmissible suggestion that action might be taken by political agencies in disregard" of its judgment.[163]

The historical records make clear that the Court was made the "ultimate interpreter" of the Constitution; and as a corollary it was contemplated that its "final" interpretations would be obeyed.[164] Disobedience by either Congress or the President would set at naught the carefully wrought constitutional "limits." To make effectiveness of those limits turn on the likelihood of disobedience to a decree is to feed defiance of law and to reopen the argument that each branch is free to construe the Constitution for itself, particularly with respect to its own powers.[165] That argument is at odds with the intention of the Founders, given recognition by Congress from the beginning.[166] Lincoln's defiance of Chief Justice Taney's decree in *Ex parte Merryman*, so often invoked, presented an extraordinary situation, an attempt im-

160. Ibid. 551.

161. United States v. Hooe, 7 U.S. (3 Cranch) 73, 90.

162. Scharpf, supra, n. 101 at 550; Worcester v. Georgia, 31 U.S. (6 Pet.) 515 (1832). 1 Charles Warren, *The Supreme Court in United States History* 205, 217, 219 (Boston, 1922).

163. McPherson v. Blacker, 146 U.S. 1, 24 (1892).

164. Berger, *Congress v. Court* 188–196.

165. Hand, supra, n. 97 at 29–30, regarded such "finality" as a necessity of government, as indeed the Founders foresaw; Berger, *Congress v. Court* 219.

166. See remarks in the "removal" debate in the First Congress, collected in Berger, ibid. 147–148.

In 1876 the House cited one Kilbourn for contempt and committed him to the district jail. He then sued out a writ of habeas corpus; the district court ordered that he should be brought into court. "Some of the Representatives urged that the writ should be disregarded, but cooler counsels prevailed, and the House honored the writ by directing the Sergeant-at-Arms to produce 'the body of said Kilbourn before said court' "! Taylor 46–47. The Senate responded to a similar order in Jurney v. McCracken, 294 U.S. 125, 143 (1935).

Congress cannot at one and the same time invoke the aid of the President to limit presidential incursions on its powers and refuse to honor judicial mandates directed to it.

mediately after the outbreak of the Civil War to prevent armed secessionists from operating in Maryland.[167] When Congress assembled it accepted Lincoln's measures "willy-nilly,"[168] and it may be assumed that he represented popular opinion. Per contra, on the anti-secrecy issue, the generally acknowledged need for full and free flow of information[169] unites Congress, the people, and the press against the President. Here defiance of a decree by the President would do more to discredit the President than the Court; it would mark him as one who claims to be above the law; and, on the premise that the judgment of the Court represents the law, as Marshall stated, it would render him impeachable for action in contradiction of law.[170] For present purposes, however, talk of possible disobedience is academic, because President Nixon has stated that he "welcomes" the submission of the controversy to the courts.

There remains the recurring suggestion that the controversy should be resolved at the polls.[171] It is unrealistic to assume, however, that refusals to furnish reports respecting the Inspector General's investigation of the Air Force, or of foreign aid to Laos or Pakistan can be blown up to campaign proportions. Often the issues are stale by the time a national campaign comes round. "Withholding" issues, barring the extraordinary case such as Watergate, are unlikely to arouse sufficient popular interest to affect the course of the campaign,[172] and generally must be lost in the swirling clash of larger issues. There is, moreover, a "strong

167. Ex parte Merryman, 17 Fed. Cas. 144, 153 (No. 9487) (C.C. Md. 1861); H. C. Hockett, *The Constitutional History of the United States, 1826–1872*, 280 (New York, 1939). Lincoln's view in a normal situation may be gathered from his Springfield address on the Dred Scott decision, June 26, 1857: "We think its [the Court's] decision on constitutional questions, when fully settled, should control . . . we shall do what we can to have it overrule itself. We offer no resistance to it"; Arthur Goodhart, "Lincoln and the Law," 50 A.B.A.J. 433, 439 (1964). He echoed this sentiment in his First Inaugural Address; 6 Richardson 9.

168. Supra, Ch. 4, text accompanying n. 104.

169. President Nixon himself stated that "when information which properly belongs to the people is systematically withheld by those in power, the people soon become ignorant of their own affairs, distrustful of those who manage them and eventually incapable of determining their own destinies"; N.Y. Times, Mar. 21, 1972, p. 13.

170. Impeachment, stated Blackstone, is provided so "that no man shall dare assist the crown in contradiction to the laws of the land"; 1 Blackstone, supra, n. 62 at 244.

171. Kramer & Marcuse 626; Younger, supra, n. 132 at 784; cf. Taylor, supra, n. 97 at 87.

172. Henry Steele Commager observed that "the people can not be expected to understand somewhat technical questions like the division of authority between Congress and the Executive"; Fulbright Hearings 68.

American bias in favor of judicial determination of constitutional and legal issues."[173] The Founders contemplated, in Madison's words, that the courts would be "an impenetrable bulwark against every assumption of power in the Legislative or Executive."[174] It would be passing strange to conclude that a citizen may invoke that protection against a twenty-dollar fine,[175] but that it is unavailable to protect a branch of the government from impairment of a function that is vital for preservation of our democratic system. The President no less than Congress must be protected against such impairment, as when the Reconstruction Congress sought to deprive Andrew Johnson of his power to remove a refractory member of his cabinet.

In sum, the political question doctrine, in my opinion, interposes no obstacle to judicial determination of the rival legislative-executive claims to receive or withhold information. The power to decide these claims plainly has not been lodged in either the legislative or executive branch; equally plainly, the jurisdiction to demark constitutional boundaries between the rival claimants has been given to the courts. The criteria for judgment whether a claim of "executive privilege" is maintainable can be found in parliamentary practice and, if need be, in the private litigation cases. And the framing of a remedy is attended by no special difficulties but rather falls into familiar patterns. Each of the parties seeks power allegedly conferred by the Constitution and each maintains that interference by the other with the claimed function will seriously impair it, the classic situation for judicial arbitrament. Arbitrament by the courts is the rational substitute for eyeball to eyeball confrontation, such as was narrowly averted with respect to the continued bombing of Cambodia. It is functioning admirably in the controversy over presidential "impounding" of funds appropriated for specified purposes, and there is no reason to believe that it would be less effective were Congress to assert its rights directly. To avoid adjudication by resort to the leaky doctrine of "political questions" is to throw Congress back on its own resources, among them impeachment of the President for encroachment on its prerogatives, for subversion of the Constitution.

173. Jaffe, supra, n. 121 at 1302.

174. 1 Annals of Cong. 439. Earlier Hamilton had stated in Federalist No. 78 at 508 that the courts were "the bulwarks of a limited constitution against legislative encroachments." Jefferson, too, welcomed the "check" which a Bill of Rights "puts in the hands of the Judiciary"; 5 Jefferson, *Writings* 81.

175. Frank v. Maryland, 359 U.S. 360 (1959).

When Congress proceeded along that path with President Andrew Johnson, Chief Justice Salmon Chase was of the opinion that the conflicting claims of constitutional power had better have been submitted to the courts.[176] Impartial adjudication promises a better solution than trial of its own cause by a Congress whose temper has been frayed by protracted controversy.

176. Berger, *Impeachment* 300.

CONCLUSION

EACH GENERATION tends to read history in the focus of its own preoccupations; each thinks that it enjoys a special vantage point. So it is that a contemporary re-evaluation of the protracted information-withholding controversy inevitably is colored by the extraordinary events of our time. Secret executive agreements that make commitments of unknown magnitude; presidential warmaking and bombing hooded in secrecy; escalation by stealth in Vietnam in the teeth of bleak intelligence estimates not disclosed to the nation; "White House Horrors"—the words are those of John Mitchell, former partner and Attorney General of President Nixon—spreading a miasma of encroachments on individual rights. These events have confirmed Patrick Henry's warning that secrecy in government is an "abomination"; it is a main instrument in the corruption and arrogation of power.[1] If the nation has not relearned that lesson from the secret escalation in Vietnam, from the bold attempt to corrupt the electoral process that surfaced in Watergate,[2] it is unteachable.

Another lesson to be learned from the past forty years of implicit trust in the wisdom of the President is that he, no less than Congress, may prove sadly deficient in vision.[3] Arthur Schlesinger, who sat close to the throne while some of the fateful commitments

1. Supra, Ch. 6, text accompanying nn. 231–232.

2. Of Watergate, Nixon's former Attorney General, Richard Kleindienst, stated that "it went to the very heart of our political system . . . an act of such heinous nature"; N.Y. Times, Aug. 8, 1973, p. 12.

3. Former Ambassador John Kenneth Galbraith stated: "Over the last half-decade Fulbright, Morse, Gruening, Kennedy, Cooper, Church, Hatfield and McGovern have surely been more sensible than the senior officials of the Department of State. On the average, I think we are safer if we keep foreign policy under the influence of men who must be re-elected"; Galbraith, "Book Review," N.Y. Times, Oct. 8, 1972, sec. 7, pp. 1, 12. The matter was well summed up in S. Rep. No. 797, 90th Cong., 1st Sess., p. 14 (1972): "Congress, it seems clear, was deficient in wisdom during the 1920's and 1930's, but so were Presidents Harding, Coolidge, Hoover and —prior to 1938—Roosevelt. Just as no one has a monopoly on vision, no one has a monopoly on myopia either."

were being made, stated that "in retrospect, Vietnam is a triumph of the politics of inadvertence";[4] and, if we may credit General de Gaulle, a triumph of wrongheadedness.[5] Perhaps the decisions would not have been better had they been debated in Congress; but, as George Reedy, Press Secretary to President Lyndon Johnson observed, they could not have "been much worse."[6] Executive decisionmaking suffers from a deep-seated malady; as Reedy pointed out, it lacks the benefit of "adversary discussion of the issues"; the "so-called debates are really monologues in which one man is getting reflections of what he sends out."[7] It is not easy to say nay to an overpowering President. What was true of the Johnson inner circle is no less true of the Nixon subordinates as the Watergate Hearings have disclosed.[8] Unquestioning acceptance of decisions rather than criticism and dissent were the rule.

4. Quoted in Alistair Buchan, "Questions About Vietnam," in R. Falk, ed., 2 *The Vietnam War and International Law* 35, 38 (Princeton, 1969).

5. Consider President Kennedy's disregard of the informed advice of President Charles de Gaulle. On the occasion of his visit to France, in May 1961, Kennedy "made no secret of the fact that the United States was planning to intervene [in Indochina]." De Gaulle recorded that he told Kennedy "he was taking the wrong road" that would lead to "an endless entanglement . . . We French have had experience of it. You Americans . . . want to . . . revive a war which we have brought to an end. I predict that you will sink step by step into a bottomless military and political quagmire"; C. de Gaulle, *Memoirs of Hope, Renewal and Endeavor*, quoted in N.Y. Times, Mar. 15, 1972, p. 43.

Buchan observed of our Vietnam involvement, "one cannot fail to be impressed by the slapdash manner in which decisions of profound importance were taken"; Buchan, supra, n. 4 at 38.

6. Ervin Hearings 460, 464; see also Robert Dahl, *Congress and Foreign Policy* 245 (New York, 1950) (assessment of Roosevelt's war policy).

7. Ervin Hearings 465–466. Reedy states of some of the meetings of the Johnson cabinet and of the National Security Council that "every one [was] trying desperately to determine just what it is that the President wants to do"; ibid. 466. Former Attorney General Ramsey Clark stated that "he had been wrong not to speak out against the Vietnam war . . . in President Johnson's cabinet while the war was expanding"; and he is quoted as saying, "there is too much tendency in the executive branch not to argue with policy"; N.Y. Times, Aug. 16, 1972, p. 7. Of course, there is the occasional maverick like George Ball, Under Secretary of State, who persisted in opposition to the Vietnam escalation in the face of an inner circle consensus.

8. The Wall Street Journal, Aug. 10, 1973, p. 6, stated that "The 10 weeks of [Watergate] hearings brought forth witness after witness who by his own account was afraid to speak his mind to Mr. Nixon." As the Acting Director of the FBI, L. Patrick Gray, explained, he had been in the Navy where the tradition was "Aye, Aye, Sir." N.Y. Times, Aug. 12, 1973, sec. 4, p. 2. Moreover, as Derek Bok points out, "The central staff may not be responsive enough to the will of the people and not open enough to debate and discussion with those holding contrary points of view. Without adequate checks and balances, executive officials can easily succumb to the temptation of using the levers of power in unorthodox [or illegal] ways to accomplish what they know [or think] is right"; Boston Sunday Globe, July 22, 1973, p. 44.

A democratic system rests on full access to information and accountability to the people. Speaking of an executive refusal to disclose conflicting agency reports, Justice Potter Stewart said that, when "the people and their representatives are reduced to ignorance the democratic process is paralyzed.[9] Our Constitution provides for congressional participation "in the great decisions that spell life and death to the Nation."[10] Meaningful participation is possible only on the basis of full information; without knowledge of the alternatives that have been spread before the President, and withheld from Congress, legislative decisionmaking stumbles in the dark. When based on full information, the participation of Congress insures that the issues will be aired instead of being decided in a hall of mirrors where courtiers echo the desires of the monarch.[11]

With all its shortcomings, its fumbling, disorganization, susceptibility to manipulation, shrinking from responsibility, Congress yet has one great redeeming feature: it is the national forum of debate.[12] Here ideas can be tested in the crucible of open discussion; here debate can bring into the open risks that executive advisers have overlooked or underestimated; it may show that the supposed advantages of a recommended course of action are outweighed by the concomitant risks. At all times there will be dissident voices, unçowed by a strong presidential personality or by the current of popular opinion. A George Norris, Borah, La Follette, or Wayne Morse, like Winston Churchill in the 1930's, will cry alarm. Debate also substitutes the experience of the many for that of the one. The wise old Franklin, at the close of the Constitutional Convention, adjured the strong-willed delegates to

9. Environmental Protection Agency v. Mink, 410 U.S. 73, 95 (1973), more fully quoted supra, Ch. 11, text accompanying n. 147.

10. Cf. Henry Steele Commager, Fulbright Hearings 46; see supra, Ch. 9.

11. George Reedy said of presidential advisers, "you can be . . . certain that none of the people close to him . . . are going to apply sceptical judgment ["to the information upon which the President is acting"]. At least they aren't going to apply sceptical judgments and remain close to him very long"; Fulbright Hearings 443. In the White House, Halberstam observed, "no one tells the President he is wrong"; Halberstam 456–457; see supra, n. 8; Epilogue at nn. 5–8.

12. "Congressional inquiry, discussion and debate ought to serve a second function: facilitating a rational decision by the electorate *outside* the Congress"; Dahl, supra, n. 6 at 125. Woodrow Wilson stated, "even more important than legislation is the instruction and guidance in political affairs which the people might receive from a body which kept all national concerns suffused in a broad daylight of discussion." W. Wilson, *Congressional Government* 297 (Boston, 1913). See also supra, Ch. 1, n. 18.

swallow their remaining differences on the assumption that the collective judgment is more reliable than that of any one member.[13] Whether the people will be swayed is not so important as that they should have the opportunity to hear opposition views, to have an informed choice of options, to be alerted to possible consequences of massive commitments rather than to have commitments saddled on them by secret one-man decisions. Above all, debate may serve to secure the consent of the people. A Vietnam war hawk, Senator John Stennis, speaking in favor of a bill that would require congressional authorization for the waging of war, said: "Vietnam has shown us that by trying to fight a war without the clear-cut prior support of the American people we may not only risk military ineffectiveness but we also strain, and can shatter, the very structure of the Republic."[14]

Whatever the merits of debate, this is a requirement of a democratic society. Those who are to bleed and die have a right to be consulted, to have the issues debated by their elected representatives; for a nation of two hundred million cannot be convened in a town meeting. Unlike the totalitarian nations we have not placed our faith in a Fuehrer, a Big Brother; a benign dictatorship is not for us.[15] "With all its defects, delays or inconveniences," said Justice Jackson, "men have discovered no technique for long preserving free government except that the Execu-

13. 2 Farrand 641–643. As Senator Bacon said in 1906:

> There are Senators here who have been here for a generation and whose advice and counsel would be valuable to any president . . . An election to the Presidency does not ipso facto endow one with all knowledge and all wisdom, and it is not an unreasonable suggestion that in the aggregate of ninety Senators, many of them men of large experience, there is more knowledge of public affairs, more of correct judgment of the requirements of the public interests than is possessed by any one man in the United States, whoever he may be.

40 Cong. Rec. 2137.

14. Fulbright Hearings 706. In 1971 Secretary of State Rogers told the Senate, "If there is one lesson we have learned from this involvement in Vietnam, it is that we need congressional support and we need public support"; ibid. 511. That lesson was imperfectly learned, as the continued bombing of Cambodia against the will of Congress and a large segment of the public testifies. And it betrays the extraordinary assumption that the executive *could* wage a large war *without* public or congressional support.

15. Those indefatigable proponents of executive agreements, McDougal & Lans, 577–578, stated: "Government by a self-designated elite—like that of benevolent despotism or of Plato's philosopher kings—may be a good form of gevernment for some peoples, but it is not the American way." The reference was to a minority of the elected Senate, who were constitutionally authorized to differ. See also Philip Kurland, "The Impotence of Reticence," 1968 Duke L.J. 619, 625–628.

tive be under the law, and that the law be made by parliamentary deliberations."[16] Experience with strong royal authority, said Sir Denis Brogan, taught the English that the worst elected chamber was better than the best royal antechamber.[17] That lesson should not be lost on the viewers who heard the testimony of the White House camarilla in the Watergate Hearings.

Against free congressional inquiry it is customary to pit the spectre of McCarthyism. But the spectacle of Senator McCarthy whip-lashing innocent victims, revolting as it was, was not nearly so costly to the nation as the "escalation by stealth" in Vietnam or the conspiracy to corrupt the electoral process that burst upon our vision at Watergate. A generation so given to "balancing" competing policies should ask whether the occasional excesses of congressional investigations were as damaging to the nation as the evils which have flowed from unrestricted secrecy.[18]

He who controls the flow of information rules our destinies. So much Vietnam alone should prove. It was not the design of the Founders that the people and the Congress should obtain only so much information as the President concluded was fitting for them to have.[19] As a partner—the senior partner—in the conduct of our government, Congress is entitled to share *all* the information that pertains to its affairs. The basic presupposition of our society was the widest access to information except, in the words of John Marshall, when disclosure would be attended by "fatally pernicious" consequences. Given, as James Iredell said, that the officers of the government—the President included—are the "servants and agents of the people," it is a contradiction in terms to con-

16. Youngstown Case 655, concurring. Justice Brandeis stated, and history confirms, that "In America, as in England, the conviction prevailed then that people must look to their representative assemblies for the protection of their liberties"; Myers v. United States, 272 U.S. 52, 294 (1926), dissenting, joined by Holmes, J.

17. Paraphrased by Willard Hurst in interview with Israel Shenker, N.Y. Times, Feb. 27, 1972, p. 18.

18. Here I would say, as Professor Alexander Bickel said in the context of the war powers, "I do believe in constitutional arrangements and in their wisdom, and since the departure from them over the past 10 years has worked as badly as it has, I think the risk I would like to take is the constitutional risk, is the risk of the original arrangement"; Fulbright Hearings 579.

Former Justice Goldberg stated, "There will be abuses and there will be problems but we have to pay a price for the larger question which is adequate information to Congress so that Congress can perform its constitutional duties"; ibid. 794.

19. To leave to the President the determination in any particular case whether the public interest permits disclosure is to "leave open the possibility that the President may abuse his prerogative, especially in instances where the information would reflect unfavorably on him or his administration of the nation's affairs"; Telford Taylor, *Grand Inquest* 101 (New York, 1955).

clude that the agent may dole out information to his principal. The perils of that course were underscored by a great early American statesman, Edward Livingston:

> No nation ever yet found any inconvenience from too close an inspection into the conduct of its officers, but many have been brought to ruin, and . . . slavery . . . only because the means of publicity had not been secured.[20]

20. Reynolds v. United States, 192 F. 2d 987, 995 (3d Cir. 1951). Lord Acton stated, "nothing is safe that does not show it can bear discussion and publicity." Quoted in A. S. Miller and D. S. Sastri, Secrecy and the Supreme Court: On the Need for Piercing the Red Velour Curtain, 22 Buffalo L. Rev. 799 (1973).

EPILOGUE

THE LANDMARK decision in the Grand Jury "tapes" case by the Court of Appeals for the District of Columbia brought the problems herein studied into high relief.[1] And it reaffirmed some principles which badly needed to be brought home to the executive branch. At issue was the effect of a subpoena to the President for tape recordings of conversations Mr. Nixon had with some of those implicated in the Watergate conspiracy and cover-up. Among other things, the tapes would either confirm or refute the testimony of former White House counsel John Dean that the chief aides of President Nixon as well as the President himself were involved in the cover-up.[2] When judicial enforcement of the subpoena was sought, White House counsel strenuously argued that, in the absence of absolute confidentiality for the conversations of the President, "it would be simply impossible for any President of the United States to function. The creative interplay of open and spontaneous discussion is essential in making wise choices on grave and important issues . . . The issue in this case is nothing less than the continued existence of the Presidency as a functioning institution."[3] After the rejection of that claim by the courts, and the great outcry over Nixon's discharge of Special Prosecutor Archibald Cox, the President bowed to the decree; the tapes have since been surrendered to Chief Judge John J. Sirica and, as might be expected, the presidency continues "as a functioning institution"

1. The case in the District Court before Chief Judge John J. Sirica is entitled Grand Jury Subpoena v. Richard M. Nixon, 360 F. Supp. 1 (D.D.C. 1973). The opinions of the Court of Appeals have not yet been officially reported, and references herein are to the slip opinions in the three cases disposed of by one opinion, Nixon v. Sirica and Cox, No. 73–1962, United States v. Sirica and Nixon, No. 73–1967, and In re Grand Jury Proceedings, No. 73–1789 (D.C. Cir. Oct. 12, 1973).

There are three opinions in the Court of Appeals, that of the five-judge majority per curiam opinion, hereinafter cited as Ct. App., those of dissenting Judge MacKinnon, and of dissenting Judge Wilkey, hereinafter cited as MacKinnon and Wilkey, respectively. All are separately paginated.

2. The information sought is described in Appendix II to Ct. App. at 48–53.

3. Nixon Brief in Opposition, District Court 33–34.

—as it did for the many years before the theory of "absolute confidentiality" was dreamed of.[4]

Since that argument was pressed upon the courts, we have had two pretty examples in practice of "the creative interplay of open and spontaneous discussion . . . on grave and important issues." The first was an order by Chief White House aide General Alexander Haig to Deputy Attorney General William Ruckelshaus to dismiss Special Prosecutor Cox—after Attorney General Elliot Richardson refused to do so and resigned—a dismissal held illegal by Judge Gerhard Gesell.[5] When Ruckelshaus demurred, Haig reportedly replied, "Your Commander-in-chief is giving you an order."[6] The second incident involved the refusal of Attorney General Richard Kleindienst to carry out an order "abruptly" given to him by presidential aide John Ehrlichman to drop the appeal of an antitrust case against International Telephone and Telegraph Corporation. Within minutes came a call from President Nixon himself to Kleindienst, in which he reportedly stated: "Listen, you son of a bitch, don't you understand the English language? Don't appeal that goddam case, and that's all there is to it."[7] Such are the realities of "spontaneous interplay," examples of discussions that, in the words of Judge MacKinnon, "must be informal, candid and blunt."[8]

4. This is par for the course. After the Symington Senate Committee had discovered that the executive branch had been waging a secret war against the Pathet Lao in northern Laos, and the administration "was finally forced to confirm the story in closed session," it then opposed making it public, "predicting all manner of dire consequence if the facts were known." Publication ensued; and as a Committee counsel later observed, "None of the parade of horrors which the State Department imagined did in fact occur." Arthur Schlesinger, Jr., *The Imperial Presidency* 203 (Boston, 1973).

So too, the government represented that unless publication of the Pentagon Papers was halted, "the nation's security will suffer immediate and irreparable harm." Among the evils that that Top Secret stamp was designed to avert were "a definite break in diplomatic relations affecting the defense of the United States, an armed attack against the United States or its allies, a war, or the compromise of military or defense plans or intelligence operations, or scientific or technological developments vital to the national defense." Schlesinger states that "In the third year after the publication of the Pentagon Papers not a single one of these calamities had taken place"; ibid. 345–346.

The Schlesinger book reached me after my text and notes had gone to the printer, so I could only avail myself of the wealth of fresh materials and insights in this Epilogue.

5. N.Y. Times, Nov. 15, 1973, p. 1. See also Raoul Berger, "Was Cox Fired Illegally," Washington Star-News, Nov. 4, 1973.

6. N.Y. Times, Oct. 28, 1973, sec. 4, p. 2.

7. Newsweek, Nov. 12, 1973, p. 29; N.Y. Times, Oct. 30, 1973, p. 33; N.Y. Times, Nov. 1, 1973, p. 33.

8. MacKinnon 27. Compare these drill-sergeants' "orders" with Judge Wilkey's solicitude that "To breach his privacy would unquestionably have a 'chilling effect' on

White House counsel did "not question the power of the court to issue a subpoena to the President," but maintained that this power "does not impose on the Executive any concurrent obligation to disclose that information."[9] This violates the jural postulate that a power and hence a right to demand information carries with it a correlative duty to comply.[10] And it reduces the power to mere words, for the judiciary was not meant to go through empty rituals but, among other things, to police the excesses of the Executive.[11] Finally, presidential counsel revived the argument of Attorney General Stanbery in *Mississippi v. Johnson* that "the President of the United States is above the process of any court or the jurisdiction of any court to bring him to account as President."[12] And they maintained that "the courts are without power to compel compliance with a decision overruling a claim of privilege by the President."[13]

It is to the credit of the American people that they perceived in the subsequent discharge of Special Prosecutor Cox an "intolerable assault upon the courts,"[14] covert disobedience of the court's decree. The consequent "firestorm"—the term is that of General Haig—[15] that swept over the White House led to speedy capitulation. The President lost no time in having his counsel, Professor Charles Alan Wright, advise Chief Judge John J. Sirica that "This President does

those who would otherwise counsel and confide in the President with complete candor and honesty"; Wilkey 11.

The fact is that Mr. Nixon flinches from "face-to-face argument"; he withdraws "from the provocations of criticism and argument"; Schlesinger, supra, n. 4 at 216, 218. In the words of Tom Charles Huston, who served a year as domestic security planner in the White House, President Nixon "abhors confrontations, most particularly those based on philosophical convictions"; ibid. 218. "Instead of exposing himself to the chastening influence of debate," says Schlesinger, Nixon "organized the executive branch and the White House in order to shield himself as far as humanly possible from direct question or challenge"; ibid. 222. Schlesinger asks, "who in [Nixon's] cabinet talked back to him . . . The fate of those who tried was instructive. Messrs. Hickel, Romney, Laird, Connally, Peterson, Finch had vanished from the cabinet by inaugural day 1973"; ibid. 220. That encouragement of free and candid interchange should be attributed to this man is farcical.

9. Nixon Brief in Opposition in the District Court, p. 6.

10. Speaking of "all citizens," the Supreme Court stated, "It is their unremitting obligation to respond to subpoenas"; Watkins v. United States, 354 U.S. 178, 187 (1957).

11. Cf. Berger, *Congress v. Court* 14–18. For fear of presidential excesses, see Berger, *Impeachment* 99–100.

12. Supra, n. 9 at 7–8.

13. Ibid. 29.

14. The phrase is that of Chesterfield H. Smith, president of the American Bar Association. N.Y. Times, Oct. 23, 1973, p. 45.

15. Time, Nov. 5, 1973, p. 13.

not defy the law . . . he will comply in full with the orders of the court."[16] It cannot be otherwise. The Founders adopted judicial review in order to effectuate the "limits" laid down in the Constitution and to restrain executive as well as legislative excesses.[17] Presidential defiance of the courts subverts the rule of law; it undermines the basic supremacy of law and constitutes a long step toward the very tyranny and dictatorship the Founders meant to prevent.

In ruling against Mr. Nixon's imperial claims, the Court of Appeals followed the example of Chief Justice Marshall, correctly reading him to hold that "The court was to show respect for the President in weighing [his] reasons [for nondisclosure], but the ultimate decision remained with the court."[18] In fact, Marshall had gone beyond the "tapes" decree, which directed the district court to review the tapes *in camera*, whereas Marshall held that he would not prohibit a defendant from seeing a private letter written by General Wilkinson to President Jefferson if it was really needed in his defense. Of this more will be said hereafter.

Not overawed by the President, the courts in the "tapes" case reaffirmed two great principles. First, the courts are the "ultimate interpreter" of the Constitution, and that means of the scope of the powers conferred on each branch.[19] Second, the President is not above the law so construed, and like every other citizen is under a duty to comply. In the words of James Wilson, "the most powerful magistrate should be amenable to the law . . . No one should be secure while he violates the Constitution and laws," as Mr. Nixon at last was constrained to acknowledge.[20] Thus, the prolonged ordeal of Watergate has brought forth at least one great benefit: the firm articulation of these principles in the teeth of thinly veiled threats of presidential disobedience.

At the risk of being captious it needs, however, to be noticed that the Court of Appeals treated the issue of "confidentiality" too gin-

16. Ibid. p. 18.

17. Berger, *Congress v. Court* 13–18; supra, Ch. 3, text accompanying nn. 27–28, 48–55.

18. Ct. App. 16, 27.

19. "Any claim to executive absolutism cannot override the duty of the court to assure that an official has not exceeded his charter"; ibid. 24. See also Powell v. McCormack, quoted supra, Ch. 11, text accompanying n. 109.

20. 1 Wilson, *Works* 425; supra, text accompanying n. 16. On Mar. 11, 1972 Nixon, addressing the National Conference on the Judiciary, said: "The only way that justice can truly be done in any society, is for each member of that society to subject himself to the rule of law—neither to set himself above the law in the name of justice nor to set himself outside the law in the name of justice"; Schlesinger, supra, n. 4 at 263.

gerly; it referred to the broad sweep of "judicial recognition" that "the candor of Executive aides and functionaries would be impaired" were they inhibited by fear of later disclosure.[21] Such "recognition" is best viewed in the frame of the two lengthy dissenting opinions of Judges MacKinnon (65 pages) and Wilkey (79 pages), Nixon appointees, a point that would have gone unmentioned but for the fact that both sedulously tread in the footsteps of Attorney General Rogers, citing his memorandum, relying on his "precedents,"[22] quoting from an article written by him when Attorney General,[23] and, in short, treating as gospel mere advocacy for one of the parties to a dispute, which should carry no weight with a court, as was pointed out by Justice Jackson.[24] The MacKinnon-Wiley dissents call for close attention because they represent an attempt to clothe with judicial respectability arguments which thus far have been no more than the advocacy of executive lawyers.

On such an issue accuracy is a sine qua non. Judge Wilkey, however, delivered himself of demonstrably erroneous statements. Thus, he stated that "in Reynolds [United States v. Reynolds, 345 U.S. 1 (1953)] the Supreme Court dealt only with this long established (custom or statute according to Mr. Justice Reed) privilege of confidentiality."[25] In fact, the Supreme Court made no mention whatsoever of that issue, notwithstanding that the claim of privilege for confidential communications had been rejected in the courts below,[26] but stated instead that the Secretary of the Air Force "invoke[d] the privilege against revealing military secrets,"[27] and addressed this issue only, not "confidentiality." An-

21. Ct. App. 22.

22. Among them St. Clair, Jay Treaty, etc., so dear to the heart of Rogers, but now drawn from the so-called Truman memorandum, MacKinnon 5 et seq. Apparently this is the memorandum later published as a series of articles by the unsung Herman Wolkinson, and then adopted by Rogers in haec verba to become the Rogers memorandum. Supra, Ch. 6, n. 5.

"According to [Clark] Mollenhoff, the Department of Justice examined the [Truman] memorandum, found it unsupported by law or by court cases and discarded it as of no value"; Schlesinger, supra, n. 4 at 156.

23. Judge Wilkey draws from these "precedents" in the Rogers memorandum, Wilkey 35, 40, and from Rogers' article, Wilkey 33.

24. Supra, Ch. 6, n. 6. This was perceived before the Revolution by Arthur Lee, who brushed aside Blackstone's view on "representation" on the ground that "The British constitution is not to be new modelled by every *court* lawyer. [footnote] *Mr. Blackstone is solicitor to the Queen*"; B. Bailyn, *The Ideological Origins of the Revolution* 171 (Cambridge, Mass., 1967).

25. Wilkey 7.

26. Infra, text accompanying nn. 39–41.

27. United States v. Reynolds, 345 U.S. 1, 6 (1953).

other negligent citation is his statement that Reynolds "held that military secrets *were* at stake, and even *in camera* inspection would not be permitted."[28] In fact, that issue was not decided:

> where necessity is dubious, *a formal claim of privilege . . . will have to prevail.* Here necessity was greatly minimized by an available alternative, which might have given respondents the evidence to make out their case . . . By their failure to pursue that alternative, respondents have posed the privilege question with the formal claim of privilege set against a dubious showing of necessity.
>
> There is nothing to suggest that the electronic equipment, in this case, had a causal connection with the accident. Therefore, it should be possible for respondents to adduce the essential facts as to causation *without resort to material touching upon military secrets.*[29]

Thus, the Court never reached the question whether "military secrets *were* at stake" because respondent's failure to show "necessity" for the secrets had to yield to the "formal claim of privilege." Neither time nor space permit the multiplication of such examples, so I shall limit myself to several more grandiose Wilkean flights.

A. *Wilkey's "Common Sense–Common Law" Privilege*

At the outset Judge Wilkey builds on "the common sense–common law privilege of Governmental confidentiality." His allusion under the heading "Dual Origin of the Privilege Asserted" indicates that he views the "common law" as one pillar of his defense of "absolute privilege."[30] This becomes the "age-old" "ancient governmental privilege of confidentiality," "long established custom."[31] For "custom" Judge Wilkey relies on an incautious statement by Justice Reed,[32] sitting by designation on the Court of Claims in *Kaiser Aluminum and Chemical Corp. v. United States.*[33] Of "custom" in its strict legal sense, that is, immemorial usage, there is of course no trace.[34] The earliest English cases on

28. Wilkey 8.
29. United States v. Reynolds, 345 U.S. at 11; emphasis added.
30. Wilkey 3, 14. At p. 24 he states that the asserted privilege "derives both from the . . . separation of powers and from the common sense–common law . . . privilege of confidentiality." He asserts that this "privilege of confidentiality" existed long before the Constitution of 1789, and might be deemed an inherent power of any government"; ibid. 4. So far as an executive privilege to withhold information from the legislature is concerned, Judge Wilkey is rebutted by parliamentary history; supra, Ch. 2.
31. Wilkey 7, 9.
32. Ibid. 7.
33. 157 F. Supp. 939, 944 (Ct. Cl. 1958).
34. C. K. Allen, *Law in the Making* 130 (Oxford, 1958).

governmental privilege in the courts that I could find, in 1775 and 1789—the latter involving an Order in Council in the midst of the Revolutionary War—rejected the claim of privilege.[35] A privilege for confidential communications on a high level first occurs in *Smith v. East India Co.* (1841);[36] and that doctrine was repudiated by the House of Lords in 1968.[37] Coming fifty-three years after adoption of the Constitution, *East India* was no part of the common law to which the Framers looked, so that the claim of "common law" footing is therefore without historical foundation.

In the United States the courts had directed the turnover by the government of a variety of internal reports prior to *Kaiser Aluminum*,[38] to which Justice Reed did not refer. Nor did he notice that, when the government contended in the *Reynolds* case in the District Court for a privilege based on the need for "free and unhampered self-criticism within the [armed] service necessary to obtain maximum efficiency," Judge Kirkpatrick stated that "the Government claims a new kind of privilege . . . I can find no recognition in the law of the existence of such a privilege."[39] On appeal, the Court of Appeals for the Third Circuit refused to recognize the claim that a disclosure "would have a deterrent effect upon the much desired objective of encouraging uninhibited statements," saying that "such a sweeping privilege . . . is contrary to sound public policy."[40] The case was reversed on other grounds: military secrets, the necessity for which respondent failed to prove.

35. Supra, Ch. 7, text accompanying nn. 33–34. Note that the East India Co. had governmental functions. See Smith v. East India Co., 1 Phil. 50, 54, 41 E.R. 550, 551–552 (1841).

36. Smith v. East India Co. ibid. To be sure *Smith* was anticipated by Charles Dickens, *Sketches by Boz* (1836). A candidate for election to the office of parish beadle, Captain Purday "brought forward certain distinct and specific charges relative to the management of the workhouse," whose overseer also aspired to be beadle. The captain

> boldly expressed his total want of confidence in the existing authorities, and moved for "a copy of the recipe by which the paupers' soup was prepared, together with any documents relating thereto." This the overseer steadily resisted; he fortified himself by precedent, appealed to the established usage, and declined to produce the papers, on the ground of the injury that would be done to the public service, if documents of a strictly private nature, passing between the master of the workhouse and the cook, were thus to be dragged to light on the motion of any individual member of the vestry.

Quoted 59 A.B.A.J. 1435 (1973).

37. Conway v. Rimmer, 1 All E.R. 874; for discussion see supra, Ch. 7, text accompanying nn. 122–126.

38. Supra, Ch. 7, text accompanying nn. 97–101.

39. Sub nom. Brauner v. United States, 10 F.R.D. 468, 472 (E.D. Pa. 1950); see also Cresmer v. United States, 9 F.R.D. 203, 204 (E.D. N.Y. 1949), quoted infra, n. 120a.

40. Reynolds v. United States, 192 F. 2d 987, 994, 995 (3d Cir. 1951).

Not a word was said by the Court about confidentiality. On the other hand, the three dissenting Justices, Black, Frankfurter, and Jackson, endorsed the opinion of the Court of Appeals.[41] So we have approval of that court's rejection of the "confidentiality" claim, and complete silence on the issue by the majority of the Supreme Court. Such was the state of the law when *Kaiser Aluminum* came down in 1958, hardly a basis for a claim of "long established," "age-old" custom or doctrine.

Justice Reed did not point to cases that had established the "custom." On the contrary, in his immediately following citation to the congressional history—both Judges MacKinnon and Wilkey rely heavily on the congressional parallel—[42] Reed stated that "The assertion of such a privilege by the Executive vis-a-vis Congress is a judicially undecided issue."[43] So there was no "custom" on the congressional side. On the evidentiary privilege side, Reed stated that "When the United States is a party, whether or not, or to what extent, there is a 'privilege' . . . is an unsettled question."[44] Again no "custom." On the critical issue whether there is an absolute privilege in the courts, Reed held that "confidential intra-agency advisory opinions" are "privileged . . . but not absolutely."[45] By Judge Wilkey's own testimony, the "common law" answer to the "basic issue . . . *who decides* the scope of the Executive Privilege, the Judicial Branch or Executive Branch?"[46] gives no comfort to presidential claims of exclusive power to decide. For he concludes that "In summary of the common sense–common law privilege of Governmental confidentiality . . . the *courts do decide* whether the privilege exists and the *courts do decide* as to its scope."[47]

Throughout, Judge Wilkey weds "common sense" to his appeal to the "common law." "Common sense" is cruelly tried by his insistence, against the background of the "tapes" case, upon absolute confidentiality for evidence that either may prove or disprove charges that Mr. Nixon was implicated in the Watergate conspiracy. Rather, common sense suggests that nondisclosure

41. 345 U.S. at 12.
42. MacKinnon 17; Wilkey 34–41.
43. 157 F. Supp, at 944 n. 7.
44. Ibid. 945. See also Wigmore, supra, Ch. 7, text accompanying n. 128.
45. 157 F. Supp, at 946.
46. Wilkey 2, 3, 78.
47. Ibid. 14. Judge MacKinnon also states that "the courts have recognized only a qualified, not an absolute, privilege where the government has resisted disclosure solely on the ground of protesting the confidentiality of the deliberative process"; MacKinnon, 32.

feeds the suspicion that has sapped the confidence of the nation.[47a] Moreover, one cannot lightly conclude that Judge Wilkey has a monopoly of common sense and that all the judges, the Justices, and the Lords who held the other way had none.[48]

This historical background undercuts the overconfident claims that protection for "confidential interchange" is deeply rooted. In practice such protection has nourished unbounded claims for secrecy for anything and everything, and when invoked against Congress has actually hampered the informed performance of its functions. The unproven judicial *assumption* that protection of "confidential communications" is a necessity of government requires reexamination. Just as a Presidency *can* function without the unlimited privilege for confidential communications claimed by President Nixon, so, I venture to predict, the tiers upon tiers of the bureaucracy will get on very well without the shelter for "candid interchange" first fashioned by Eisenhower and uncritically accepted by the courts. At every step the courts need to ask, rather, what is the *subject matter* for which secrecy is sought? Will disclosure really injure the public interest, or instead, will nondisclosure envelope in secrecy that to which free access is needed? Courts must begin with a *presumption against* rather than for secrecy, and put the burden on the government to rebut it. Secrecy in government runs counter to our tradition; time and again it has proved to be an "abomination"; and it is to be admitted only after the government has been put to proof that it is essential for the good of the nation, not merely for that of a President and his "Plumbers."

B. *The Burr Case*

Both Judges MacKinnon and Wilkey are wide of the mark in their version of the *Burr* case. So Judge MacKinnon states that "the President, through his attorney, *refused* to disclose certain passages,"[49] when in fact the attorney offered to show the whole letter both to court and opposing counsel. On such matters it is

47a. A conservative Republican Senator, Barry Goldwater said that Nixon chose to "argue on very nebulous grounds like executive privilege and confidentiality when all the American people wanted to know was the truth"; N.Y. Times, Dec. 18, 1973, p. 31.

48. In the Reynolds case there were District Judge Kirkpatrick; veteran Circuit Judges Maris, Goodrich, and Kalodner; dissenting Justices Black, Frankfurter, and Jackson—the majority of the Court confined itself to "military secrets." The House of Lords was unanimous in Conway v. Rimmer, supra, Ch. 7, text accompanying nn. 121–126.

49. MacKinnon 37; emphasis added.

fruitless to cite opinions of others; the facts of record must speak for themselves. The matter in issue was a letter or letters from General Wilkinson to President Jefferson. Jefferson gave the government attorney, George Hay, "discretion" to withhold parts of the Wilkinson letter "which are not directly material for the purposes of justice."[50] Hay then offered to show the letters to counsel for Burr; "he was willing that Mr. Botts, Mr. Wickham and Mr. Randolph should examine them. He would depend on their candor and integrity to make no improper disclosure; and if there should be any difference of opinion, as to what were confidential passages, the *court should decide*."[51] But Luther Martin, of counsel for Burr, "objected to this as a secret tribunal" and claimed the right to hear the Wilkinson letter "publicly."[52] Then Hay said, "I wish the court to look at the letter and say whether it do not contain what ought not to be submitted to *public* inspection."[53] Thus, Hay claimed no right to withhold the letter either from defense counsel or the court, but only from *the public*. The facts belie a "refusal" by the Jefferson attorney to "disclose certain passages" to court and counsel.

Allegations of "refusal" generally turn on a letter written by Jefferson to Hay on September 7, transmitting the Wilkinson letter with some deletions for which he claimed privilege. To understand the significance of this letter it is necessary to recall some background more fully stated in an earlier chapter.[54] In a nutshell, on September 4 Marshall, sitting as a trial judge, had ruled that a showing of defendant's pressing need for a document would overcome presidential claims that disclosure would be contrary to the public interest. Quite correctly Judge MacKinnon's five brethren who joined in the majority opinion read Marshall to hold that

> The court was to show respect for the President in weighing [his] reasons but the ultimate decision remained with the court.[55]

The proof was earlier set forth in Marshall's own words,[56] and may here be drastically compressed. Given a presidential claim that disclosure should be withheld, Marshall stated in the course of an extended opinion that

50. 1 Robertson 210.
51. 2 Robertson 501–502; emphasis added.
52. Ibid. 502.
53. Ibid. 509; emphasis added.
54. Supra, Ch. 6, text accompanying nn. 148–156.
55. Ct. App. 16, 27.
56. Supra, Ch. 6, text accompanying nn. 154–155.

The occasion for demanding it ought in such case to be very strong . . . before *its production could be insisted on* . . . Such a letter . . . ought not *on light ground to be forced into public view.*

Given strong grounds, therefore, "production could be insisted on." Perhaps, Marshall continued, the court ought to consider the presidential reasons "as conclusive . . . *unless* such letter could be shown to be absolutely *necessary in the defence*,"[57] in which case, it follows, the President's representation would *not* be "conclusive."

For the purpose of weighing presidential representations against defendant's needs Marshall had stated that "the president has assigned no reason for withholding the paper called for. The propriety of withholding it must be decided by himself, not by another for him,"[58] that is, only the President himself could make the claim of privilege. To meet this requirement, as a preliminary to the judicial balancing of the facts, Hay, on September 9, "*presented* a certificate from the president [dated September 7], annexed to a copy of General Wilkinson's letter, excepting such parts as he deemed he ought not to permit to be made public."[59] That is all that the reports of the trial contain on the subject.

From this Judge MacKinnon concludes that Marshall "accepted" the excisions, that they "were not contested."[60] And Judge Wilkey adds that Marshall did "not discuss *President Jefferson's final assertion* of 7 September."[61] Here Judge MacKinnon can call on Jefferson's biographer, Dumas Malone, who states: "The document was accepted without comment. Thus there was an assertion and recognition of a degree of executive privilege."[62] Such conclusions are dubious in the extreme. Hay's "presentation" of the letter needs first to be considered in terms of litigation mechanics. The letter had been supoenaed by Burr; and it would be his counsel who would introduce it in evidence. There is no mention of an offer of the letter in evidence by Burr's counsel, and I shall essay an explanation later. Earlier, Luther Martin, of counsel for Burr, answering an objection—"if this evidence [the letter] came, what would be done with it?"—replied: "The answer is obvious; that it

57. 2 Robertson 535–536; emphasis added.
58. Ibid. 536. Marshall added, "of course it is to be understood that he has no objection to the production of the whole if the attorney has not"; ibid. 537.
59. United States v. Burr, 25 Fed. Cas. 187, 192–193 (No. 14,694) (C.Ct. Va. 1807); emphasis added.
60. MacKinnon 38.
61. Wilkey 53.
62. Letter to N.Y. Times, Nov. 26, 1973, p. 30.

must be retained by the court *till* it is wanted,"[63] at which point it could be called for by counsel for the purpose of introduction in evidence. That, it is reasonable to infer, is what happened when Hay "presented" the letter—it was held "till wanted."

Here we must pause to compare Judge Wilkey's statement that "the full 12 November [Wilkinson] letter was never produced"[64] with what actually happened. Hay stated that "he had that letter and would produce it; but he added, that in general Wilkinson's letters, there was much matter which ought not to be *made public* . . . He was willing to put the letter in the hands of the court instead of filing it with the clerk . . . It would be extremely improper to submit the whole of the letters to *public* inspection. He was content to put them in the hands of the clerk confidentially, and he [the clerk] could copy all those parts *which had relation to the cause*."[65] This, be it noted, was not a claim for "confidential" treatment, but for relevance and materiality. In fine, Hay offered to submit the "whole" letter to Marshall.

Jefferson's submission of September 7 was merely in compliance with Marshall's requirement that Jefferson himself must claim privilege as *a preliminary to Marshall's application* of the September 4 ruling to the facts. Until Burr renewed his insistence on the entire original letter,[66] there was no occasion for Marshall to rule whether Burr's need for it overcame Jefferson's claim that the deleted portions should not be disclosed. It is for this reason, to borrow from Judge Wilkey, that Marshall "said nothing and he did nothing."[67]

Why did Burr's counsel make no further ado about the Wilkinson letters? About this we can only conjecture. Burr's counsel had rejected an offer to look at the whole letter and insisted upon *public* disclosure, from which we may infer that they did not consider the letter as very vital to the defense. At almost any time they could have had those portions "which had relation to the cause"; and Marshall had refused to prohibit them from seeing the whole letter. Then there were the developments which may have sug-

63. 1 Robertson 169; emphasis added.

64. Wilkey 54.

65. 2 Robertson 501; emphasis added.

66. On September 4, before Marshall handed down his ruling of that day, "Mr. Burr said that he would not be satisfied with a copy of part of the letter"; 2 Robertson 514.

67. Wilkey 54. In Judge MacKinnon's words, "these excisions were not contested"; MacKinnon 38. When Judge Wilkey states, however, that Marshall "shied away from making a final order to the Chief Executive to produce the full text of correspondence" (ibid. 2), he distorts the facts of record, that is, that Hay simply "presented" the deleted letter to the court in compliance with its order.

gested that they could dispense with it altogether. On September 1 Burr had been acquitted of the treason charge without the benefit of the Wilkinson letter;[68] his counsel may have anticipated a similar favorable outcome on the misdemeanor charge, as shortly transpired when a verdict of "not guilty" was entered on September 15.[69] So viewed, the letter may have lost whatever importance it had for Burr.

Much more important is the question: what was the effect of "presenting" Jefferson's deletions upon the earlier Marshall opinion? Such presentation in compliance with Marshall's requirement for Jefferson's personal claim of privilege as a preliminary to Marshall's balancing of the claim against Burr's needs can hardly be transformed into Marshall's silent withdrawal of the careful opinion he had delivered but a few days earlier. There Marshall laid down as a rule for the guidance of both sides that a showing of pressing need for a document would outweigh presidential claims that it should not be divulged. Jefferson's compliance with Marshall's requirement as a preliminary to application of that rule to the facts did not alter the rule. It is a violent presumption that Marshall *sub silentio*, without apparent reason, suddenly overruled his opinion, particularly when the opinion gathered up the views he had earlier expressed throughout the trial.

On June 12 Marshall had stated:

> The court would not lend its aid to motions obviously designed to manifest disrespect to the government; but the *court has no right to refuse its aid* to motions for papers to which the accused may be entitled, and which *may be material to his defence* . . . [I]f they may be important in his defence; if they *may safely be read* at the trial; would it not be a *blot* in the page, which records the judicial proceedings of this country, if, in a case of such serious import as this, the accused should be *denied the use* of them?[70]

Later that day he returned to the subject:

> That there may be matter, the production of which the court would not require, is certain; *but* that, in a capital case, the accused ought, in some form, to have the benefit of it, if *it were really essential* to his defence, is a position which the court *would very reluctantly deny* . . . There is certainly nothing before the court which shows, that the letter in ques-

68. 2 Robertson 446–447.
69. Ibid. 539.
70. 1 Robertson 183–184; emphasis added.

tion contains any matter the disclosure of which would endanger the public safety.[71]

Observe that it was not "confidentiality" but danger to the public safety that the court would weigh. And Marshall summed up that, were the government to obtain a guilty verdict,

all those, who were concerned in it, should certainly regret, that a paper, which the accused believed to be *essential to his defense*, which may, for aught that now appears, be essential, *had been withheld from him*. I will not say that this circumstance would, in any degree tarnish the reputation of the government; but I will say, that it would justly *tarnish the reputation of the court*, which had given its sanction to its being withheld. Might I be permitted to utter one sentiment, with respect to myself, it would be to deplore, most earnestly, the occasion which should compel me to look back on any part of my official conduct with so much *self-reproach* as I should feel, *could I declare*, on the information now possessed, that the *accused is not entitled* to the letter in question, if it should really be important to him.[72]

Views so deeply felt, so often repeated, so firmly restated on September 4 rebut a facile presumption that Marshall jettisoned them on mere receipt of the September 7 letter. It was not for this that he thrust from him conduct that would "tarnish the reputation of the court" and fill him with "self-reproach." Stronger evidence than Jefferson's mere compliance with Marshall's requirement that the President himself claim privilege is needed to prove that Marshall silently abandoned views so strongly held. There is none.

Against this background Judge Wilkey errs in stating that "the court never directly decided the question of the scope of the President's asserted privilege . . . nor did it determine who should decide the scope of the privilege."[73] For Marshall very plainly ruled that, whatever the scope of the privilege, however important the factors on which the privilege claim would be based, it would have to yield to the essential needs of the accused. And equally clearly he indicated that it was for the court to decide the effect to be given the privilege claim. True, there was no occasion to apply the rule thus announced to the facts because Burr counsel apparently concluded that they no longer needed the letter. But that in nowise diminishes the effect of Marshall's declaration of the applicable rule.

71. Ibid. 186–187; emphasis added.
72. Ibid. 188; emphasis added.
73. Wilkey 42.

C. *The Separation of Powers*

The "common law–common sense" argument is but one branch of Judge Wilkey's plea for absolute confidentiality. The second is the separation of powers: no authority, including Marshall, has dealt "with the separation of powers issue at all."[74] Judge Wilkey appeals for confirmation on this score to conflicts between the President and Congress.[75] As has earlier appeared, this is an appeal to a mirage, which vanishes as we approach the historical facts.[76] Consider Judge Wilkey's inference from the St. Clair investigation and the Jay Treaty: "The historical evidence shows that Washington *rejected* the demands of *Congress* squarely on the ground of separation of powers."[77] St. Clair rebuts a *rejection* of congressional demands because in fact *all* the documents required by Congress were turned over.[78] So too, the Jay treaty documents were turned over to the Senate,[79] which scarcely comports with a rejection of a demand by *Congress*. True, they were refused by Washington to the House, but this was because he considered that the House was excluded from treatymaking and therefore had no "right" to the papers. His emphasis that he was not disposed to "withhold any information . . . which could be *required* of him by either House as a *right*,"[80] coupled with his turnover to the Senate, explodes Judge Wilkey's reading that *Jay* rested on the separation of powers. Washington, be it remembered, had signed the Act of 1789 which made it the duty of the Secretary of the Treasury to supply information to Congress on demand. It therefore needs some evidence that he had belatedly awakened to the alleged bar the separation of powers interposed. Here, as elsewhere, Judge Wilkey has been entrapped by too slavish devotion to the Rogers memorandum,[81] by neglect to take account of criticism to which it has been subjected.

Another key bit of evidence invoked for this separation point by

74. Ibid. 3.
75. Ibid. 17–24. Parenthetically, Judge Wilkey states that "submitting a dispute between two co-equal Branches to the third Branch would recognize that the Judiciary is 'more equal' than the other two"; ibid. 17. The unhappy alternative is to leave the President in the saddle, to leave with him the last word, whereby he becomes "more equal"; see supra, Ch. 11, text accompanying n. 148.
76. Supra, Ch. 6.
77. Wilkey 17; emphasis added.
78. Supra, Ch. 6, text accompanying n. 24.
79. Ibid. at n. 55; cf. ibid. at nn. 70–71.
80. Ibid. at n. 57; emphasis added.
81. Rogers memo 4 et seq.

Judge Wilkey is the creation in 1789 of the Foreign Affairs Department without express provision for congressional access to its papers.[82] It would be tedious to recapitulate the details of this incident, set forth earlier in Chapter 6. Faithfully following the untenable Rogers analysis,[83] Judge Wilkey concludes that this incident "vividly demonstrates [the Framers'] understanding of the separation of powers as established by the Constitution."[84] How then are we to explain that the self-same First Congress imposed an unmistakable duty on the Secretary of the Treasury to furnish information pertaining to his office?[85] Is the Treasury exempt from the play of that principle? Judge Wilkey pointed to the "revulsion and opposition in the House" to the original Treasury Bill as "based on the separation of powers."[86] To be sure, resentment of Hamilton's "intrusive" proposal that the Secretary should on his own initiative "report" to the House derived from the House's jealousy for its exclusive power of appropriation.[87] The House rebuffed intrusion into its exclusive domain; but it had no fear that legislative inquiry into executive conduct was in violation of the separation of powers. That is evidenced by the enacted Treasury Bill, signed by Washington, which expressly makes it

> the duty of the Secretary . . . to make report, and give information to either branch of the legislature . . . (*as he may be required*) respecting *all matters* . . . which shall *appertain to his office*.[88]

The First Congress acted on the premise that information was to be procured from those officials who had it;[89] and the Treasury Act flatly contradicts Judge Wilkey's notion that Congress could not demand information from the executive branch. Who knew better than Washington and the First Congress whether such a requirement violated the separation of powers? Surely not Judge Wilkey.

Judge MacKinnon quotes from the 1791 Lectures of James Wilson that "The independence of each power consists in this, that *its proceedings . . . should be free from the remotest influence,*

82. Wilkey 27–30.
83. For Rogers' analysis see supra, Ch. 6, text accompanying nn. 186–188.
84. Wilkey 33.
85. Supra, Ch. 2, text accompanying n. 141a. In 1854 Attorney General Caleb Cushing advised the President that "By express provision of law, it is made the duty of the Secretary of the Treasury to communicate information to either House of Congress when desired; and it is practically and by legal implication the same with the other secretaries"; 6 Ops. Atty. Gen. 326, 333 (1856).
86. Wilkey 32.
87. Supra, Ch. 6, text accompanying nn. 197–201.
88. Act of July 31, 1789, 1 Stat. 65–66; emphasis added.
89. Supra, Ch. 6, text accompanying nn. 203–205.

direct or indirect, of either of the other two powers."[90] Wilson, however, was no arid doctrinaire; he was cognizant that "the house of representatives . . . form the grand inquest of the state."[91] Well did he know what was permitted to the Grand Inquest, for he had written that the House of Commons "have checked the progress of arbitrary power . . . [in their] character of grand inquisitors of the realm. The proudest ministers of the proudest monarchs . . . have appeared at the bar of the house, to give an account of their conduct."[92] And he later wrote that as Grand Inquest the House of Representatives "will know the evils which exist, and the means of removing them";[93] it will know because it can inquire. And Judge MacKinnon may be reminded that the Grand Cham of the separation of powers, Montesquieu, had stated that the legislature must be enabled to inquire how its laws were being executed,[94] a reflection of the established English practice. "Independence," in short, was not designed to insulate the executive from legislative inquiry.

Apparently Judge Wilkey considers that Marshall was oblivious to the separation of powers point: Marshall "did not refer to a possible constitutional basis."[95] Yet Wilkey notices that, although Marshall voiced "great respect for the President," he stated that "the reputation of the court would be tarnished if it refused aid to an accused in procuring papers which he deemed essential for his defense,"[96] a statement instinct with awareness that "independence" of the President does not place him beyond reach of the courts. Moreover, in a letter to Hay, which Hay read to the court on June 16, Jefferson asserted his right "to decide, independently of all other authority, what papers . . . the public interests permits to be communicated."[97] Notwithstanding, Marshall held on September 4 that the real needs of the accused must prevail; and as Judge Wilkey notices, though apparently unaware of its significance, Marshall said, "I do not think that the accused ought to be

90. MacKinnon 43.

91. 1 Wilson, *Works* 415. Madison stated in Federalist No. 48 at 321 that, "unless these departments be so far connected and blended as to give each a constitutional control over the others, the degree of separation which the maxim requires . . . can never in practice be duly maintained." For additional citations, see Berger, *Impeachment* 192 n. 53.

92. Supra, Ch. 2, text accompanying n. 111.

93. 1 Wilson, *Works* 415.

94. Supra, Ch. 1, text accompanying n. 14.

95. Wilkey 44.

96. Ibid. 45.

97. 1 Robertson 210.

prohibited from seeing the letter."[98] In other words, the duty of the court could not give way to the claims of presidential independence.

At the conclusion of Marshall's September 4 ruling, Hay stated that "*he would produce the letter* under the restrictions ordered by the court," that is, "no copy of it to be taken for public exhibition."[99] Defiance of the court cannot be distilled from this, the last statement on this subject to the court by Jefferson's attorney. Care must be taken to distinguish Jefferson's fulminations in private from his *acts of compliance*, and to bear in mind that, as his biographer Randall tells us, Jefferson "in no way publicly challenged [the court's] authority."[100] As the foremost apostle of a democratic society, Jefferson could not very well put the President above the law and thus fulfill the fears of the Founders. Albert Beveridge states that "For the first time, most Republicans approved of the opinion of John Marshall. In the fanatical politics of the time there was enough of honest adherence to the American ideal that all men are equal in the eyes of the law, to justify the calling of a President, even Thomas Jefferson, before a court of justice."[101] In any event, constitutional law is not drawn from presidential letters but out of the decisions of the courts.

It would be strange indeed were Marshall—who had argued for judicial review in the Virginia Ratification Convention: "To what quarter will you look for protection from an infringement on the Constitution, if you will not give the power to the judiciary"[102] —utterly oblivious to the threshold question posed by the separation of powers. Few arguments made for executive privilege but could with equal plausibility be made for the proposition that Congress too is the best judge of what it may enact. One who had declared an Act of Congress unconstitutional in *Marbury v. Madison* would hardly conclude that presidential insistence on privacy rose higher.[103] The reasonable inference is that to the mind of Mar-

98. Wilkey 53.

99. 2 Robertson 537; emphasis added.

100. 3 Henry S. Randall, *Life of Jefferson* 268 (New York, 1858).

101. 3 Albert J. Beveridge, *Life of John Marshall* 450 (Boston, 1919). See statement of James Wilson, supra, text accompanying n. 20.

102. 3 Elliot 553–554.

103. In the Grand Jury "tapes" case the Court of Appeals referred to Gravel v. United States, 408 U.S. 606 (1972)—wherein the Court examined the protection expressly accorded to members of Congress by the "speech and debate clause"—and justly stated: "If separation of powers doctrine countenances such a close review of assertions of an express constitutional privilege, the doctrine must also comprehend judicial scrutiny of assertions of Executive privilege which is *at most* implicit in the Constitution"; Ct. App. 25.

shall the separation of powers did not constitute a bar to his rulings. It is very difficult to believe, in short, that the separation of powers, like Brunhilde, hidden by a curtain of magic fire, had to wait for discovery and rescue by a twentieth-century Siegfried.

D. *Courts Can't Coerce President*

Following the Rogers memorandum once again, Judge Wilkey emphasized that "the court has no physical power to enforce its subpoena should the President refuse to comply," hence "what purpose is served by determining whether the President is 'immune' from process? It can hardly be questioned that in any direct confrontation between the Judiciary and the Executive, the latter must prevail."[104] Judge Wilkey reckoned without the American people, who gave judgment in the "firestorm" that engulfed the White House after the Cox discharge. Despite the massive labors of dissenting Judges MacKinnon and Wilkey, President Nixon was constrained to appear in court by Charles Alan Wright and assure Chief Judge Sirica that the President "does not defy the law," that he "will comply in full with the orders of the court."[105]

E. *Military and State Secrets*

One of the fuzzy areas of evidentiary privilege, "military and state secrets," has received all too little attention. For Judge MacKinnon it is crystal clear: "Once the court is satisfied that military or state secrets are at stake, its inquiry is at an end,"[106] citing the *Reynolds* case. This is overstated, for the Supreme Court also said that "It may be possible to satisfy the court, from all the circumstances of the case, that there is a reasonable danger that compulsion of the evidence will expose military secrets which, in the interest of national security should not be divulged."[107] Not "military secrets" simpliciter, but only those which the court is satisfied "in the interest of national security should not be divulged," are to be sheltered. Even this was phrased too freely. Before we regard the law as frozen by the *Reynolds* dictum—the Court was not

104. Wilkey 64. This was the view of Mr. Nixon himself: it is "inadmissible for the courts to seek to compel some particular action from the President"; Schlesinger, supra, n. 4 at 271. It may be ventured that the Founders would have been horrified by the suggestion that because command of the armed forces was given to the President he could defy the courts.

105. Time, Nov. 5, 1973, p. 18.

106. MacKinnon 26.

107. 345 U.S. at 10.

called on to decide the issue, in what was almost a case of first impression,[108] because plaintiff, it held, had an alternative—we should take into account that when a blank check is given to the executive branch in any area of information-withholding, it is invariably greatly overdrawn.[109]

To leave the final determination in bureaucratic hands, Wigmore concluded, is to furnish governmental officials "too ample opportunities for abusing the privilege. The lawful limits of the privilege are extensible beyond any control, if its applicability is left to the determination of the very official whose interest it may be to shield a wrongdoing under the privilege."[110] English experience, our own recent experience under the Freedom of Information Act, the absurd appeals to privilege during the Eisenhower administration[111]—all exhibit the irresistible impulse of bureaucrats to resist every and any demand for information. It is an occupational disease, a professional infatuation with secrecy. Presumably such considerations led the Court to state that "judicial control over evidence in a case cannot be abdicated to the caprice of executive officers."[112] "Caprice" plays no less a role in executive denials of "military and state" information; it needs equally to be subject to careful check. As a former General Counsel of the Army, Professor Joseph Bishop, remarked, "there is not

108. At ibid. p. 1, n. 26; the Court cited to Totten v. United States, 92 U.S. 105 (1875). There suit was brought for espionage services under a secret contract between the spy and President Lincoln. The Court said that both parties "must have understood that the lips of the other were to be forever sealed . . . This condition . . . was implied from the nature of the employment"; the "*existence* of a contract of that kind is itself not to be disclosed"; ibid. 106–107; emphasis added. In short, an implicit term of the contract was nondisclosure of its existence. The "opinion turned," the Second Circuit noted, "primarily on the breach of contract which the Court found occurred by the very bringing of the action"; Halpern v. United States, 258 F. 2d 36, 44 (2d Cir. 1958).

109. An English scholar refers to the "civil servants' occupational love of secrecy," the "official instinct of hiding as much as possible from the public gaze"; H. W. R. Wade, *Administrative Law* 16 (1st ed., Oxford, 1961). "The instinct of bureaucracy, as Max Weber pointed out, was 'to increase the superiority of the professionally informed by keeping their knowledge and their intentions secret.' The concept of the 'official secret' was 'the specific invention of bureaucracy,' and officials defended nothing so 'fanatically' as their secrets"; Schlesinger, supra, n. 4 at 337.

110. 8 Wigmore, §2389 at 799 (3d ed., Boston, 1940).

111. For illustrations under the Freedom of Information Act see the 21st Report by the House Committee on Government Operations on "Administration of the Freedom of Information Act" (H. Rept. No. 92–1419, 1972, pp. 20–42). For the English experience, see supra, Ch. 7, text accompanying nn. 120–125; for examples from the Eisenhower period, see supra, Ch. 8, text accompanying n. 11 et seq.

112. 345 U.S. at 9–10. For, as Schlesinger asks, "if the Presidency had exclusive control over the secrecy system, was not the system foredoomed to end up in secrecy for secrecy's sake?" Schlesinger, supra, n. 4 at 360.

much information in the files of the State and Defense Departments—of a sort likely to attract congressional interest—which could not with some plausibility be given a security classification, if the executive wished to withhold it on that ground."[113] The silly and mountainous expansion of "top secret" classifications and the like[114] needs no rehearsing here; and it confirms that administrators cannot be trusted to determine what may be divulged.

To gain a firmer grip on the scope of permissible "military" secrecy, let us recur to the *express* constitutional provision for discretionary secrecy for the Journals of Congress, and recall Marshall's explanation in the Virginia Ratification Convention to allay fear of secrecy: "In this plan, secrecy is only used when it would be *fatal and pernicious* to publish the schemes of government."[115] Since the executive claim of privilege is without express sanction and at most is implicit in the Constitution, it can hardly be urged that it was to have greater scope than the express congressional privilege.[116]

Marshall later reechoed this view in the *Burr* case. The Burr conspiracy involved delicate relations with foreign states; Jefferson had informed Congress that Wilkinson's letter disclosed a plan to attack Mexico.[117] Even so, Marshall indicated that disclosure might be withheld only if it "would endanger the public safety," a factor that the court would weigh for itself. It needs to be remembered that to the mind of the Nixon administration "national defense" and "national security" were virtually synonymous;[118] that Justice Jackson stated that "security is like liberty in that many crimes are committed in its name."[119] Contemporary point was given to this statement by the White House "Plumbers'" break-in into the offices of Daniel Ellsberg's psychiatrist in the name of "national security"; and John Ehrlichman's unreadiness to draw the line under "national security" short of murder.[120]

113. Bishop 487.

114. "A former Pentagon security officer, William G. Florence, testified that there were 20 million classified documents (including copies) in the defense security system, of which 'less than one-half of 1 per cent . . . actually contain information qualifying even for the lowest defense classification. . . . In other words, the disclosure of information in at least 99½ per cent of these classified documents could not be prejudicial to the defense interest of the nation"; Schlesinger, supra, n. 4 at 344.

115. Supra, Ch. 6, text accompanying n. 233; emphasis added.

116. See supra, n. 103.

117. 1 Richardson 414.

118. Schlesinger, supra, n. 4 at 349.

119. United States ex rel Knauff v. Shaughnessy, 338 U.S. 537, 551 (1950) (dissenting; Black and Frankfurter, JJ., concurred).

120. Schlesinger, supra, n. 4 at 265.

Few would cavil at the plea that submarine plans, plans for an atomic bomb, the time and place of a Normandy invasion, and the like should not be revealed to a litigant.[120a] But a judge must be satisfied that this is actually the type of secret for which nondisclosure is sought. With Wigmore, I consider that the issue of examination *in camera* should always be left to the court.[121] Who would prefer to trust a "secret" to Ehrlichman, Haldemann, Dean, and the sorry procession of White House intimates that trooped before the Senate Watergate Committee, rather than to Chief Judge John Sirica.

The shelter fashioned for "military and foreign affairs" secrets is largely a product of untested assumptions, an uncritical adoption of executive representations. Against such self-serving claims we may balance the sober, dispassionate advice of a long-time high officer of the State Department, latterly Ambassador to the United Nations, Charles W. Yost. "National security," he states,[122]

> is a godsend. It enables a government official to justify keeping his actions and intentions secret even when they might lead the nation into war.
>
> Genuine considerations of national security may require secrecy in regard to the character and deployment of certain weapons. In my thirty-five years in foreign affairs, however, I almost never found that the public disclosure of political measures or plans could be truthfully said to jeopardize national security or be more than temporarily inconvenient.

Once "national security" has come to be accepted as a cloak for the conduct of foreign affairs, it is all too likely that public officials will find it irresistibly convenient for cloaking also some of their more far-out domestic activities [e.g., the White House "Plumbers"]. In fact, once they slip into the national security psychosis, they easily begin to equate, as we have so often seen, the nation's security with their own political power or their partisan aims.[123]

120a. In 1949 a veteran of the bench, District Judge Galston, stated, "In the absence of a showing of a war secret, or secret in respect to munitions of war, or any secret appliance used by the armed forces, or any threat to the national security, it would appear to be unseemly for the Government to thwart the efforts of a plaintiff"; Cresmer v. United States, 9 F.R.D. 203, 204 (E.D.N.Y.)

121. 8 Wigmore supra, n. 110 at 799.

122. "Security Cloak Has Way of Deceiving the Deceiver," Baltimore Sun, Nov. 3, 1973, p. 17. See also Schlesinger, supra, n. 4 at 335–336.

123. "By the 1960s and 1970s," says Schlesinger, "the religion of secrecy had become an all-purpose means by which the American Presidency sought to dissemble its purpose, bury its mistakes, manipulate its citizens, and maximize its power"; supra, n. 4 at 345.

This is the voice of disinterested experience, not of bureaucrats with a built-in urge to hide which they disguise with incantatory phrases such as "national security," "national defense," "military secrets," and the like. It behooves the courts to look behind such incantations and examine closely the alleged need for nondisclosure.

Apparently the Court of Appeals in the Grand Jury "tapes" case was alive to such considerations and declared that

> Insofar as the President makes a claim that certain material may not be disclosed because the subject matter relates to national defense or foreign relations, he may decline to transmit that portion of the material and ask the District Court to reconsider whether *in camera* inspection of the material is necessary. The Special Prosecutor is entitled to inspect the claim and showing and may be heard thereon, in chambers. If the judge sustains the privilege, the text of the government's statement will be preserved in the Court's records under seal.[124]

The corollary is that the judge may find that "inspection is necessary" and rule *against* the claim and decide for himself whether the claimed privilege should be allowed. The criterion should be that of Marshall: whether disclosure would "endanger the public safety." In this the Court of Appeals had been anticipated in 1958 by the Second Circuit Court of Appeals in *Halpern v. United States*. Halpern's radar "secret" had been appropriated by the government in World War II without compensation. His postwar suit for compensation was met among other things by a claim of privilege for "state secrets," the secret that had been his own. But the Court of Appeals sensibly held that "the privilege relating to state secrets is inapplicable when disclosure to court personnel in an *in camera* proceeding will not make the information public or endanger the national security."[125]

From the earliest days of the Republic judges have enjoyed great confidence.[126] They do not have the inveterate bureaucratic urge to reach for the "top-secret" stamp, the congenital instinct to shield their mistakes or misdeeds under the guise of "national security"; above all, they can impartially determine whether disclosure will in fact endanger the national safety; and they are subject to review, not shielded by an iron curtain.

124. Ct. App. 38.
125. The case is discussed supra, Ch. 7, text accompanying nn. 62–64.
126. For the Founders' confidence in the judiciary, see citations in Berger, *Congress v. Court*, Index, "Judiciary, confidence in." For complementary distrust of a President, see Berger, *Impeachment* 99–100.

Finally, the claim of absolute privilege for the confidential conversations of the President needs to be viewed in much wider perspective, for it is merely an offshoot of the much broader Eisenhower claim of privilege for *all* communications between members of the executive branch.[127] The follies to which that 1954 directive gave rise have been described aptly by Arthur Schlesinger as "the greatest orgy of executive denial in American history."[128] Presumably alive to such excesses and those that disfigure the administration of the Freedom of Information Act, the Court of Appeals in the Grand Jury "tapes" case wisely concluded:

> If the claim of absolute privilege was recognized, its mere invocation by the President or its surrogates could deny access to all documents in all the Executive departments to all citizens and their representatives, including Congress, the courts as well as grand juries . . . The Freedom of Information Act could become nothing more than a legislative statement of unenforceable rights. Support for this kind of mischief simply cannot be spun from incantation of the doctrine of the separation of powers.[129]

Executive privilege needs to be lifted from the field of legal esoterica and viewed in terms of underlying reality: as a shield for executive unaccountability. The Founders were well aware that it was by means of legislative inquiry that Parliament brought Ministers of the Crown to book and curbed executive excesses. They approved of the Grand Inquest of the Nation, which encompassed the original power of inquiry as a prelude to impeachment, inquiry into the most secret recesses of the executive branch. Our own system of "checks and balances" is dependent upon information; a Congress kept in ignorance is impotent to "check." Without accountability the President threatens to behave as an elected emperor, enthroned for four years, whose "mandate" may not be questioned.[130] The steady expansion of executive privilege claims

127. See supra, Ch. 8, text accompanying n. 1. Among the items to be withheld under the Eisenhower directive, the Attorney General explained, were "inter-departmental memoranda, advisory opinions, recommendation of subordinates, informal working papers, material in personnel files" etc.; Schlesinger, supra, n. 4 at 156. In practice *intra*-departmental matters also fell under the ban.

128. Schlesinger, supra, n. 4 at 158.

129. Ct. App. 27.

130. In the Revolutionary period "faith ran high that a better world . . . could be built where authority was distrusted and held in constant scrutiny"; Bailyn, supra, n. 24 at 319. This explains, I suggest, why the Grand Inquest of the Nation found such casual acceptance by the Founders.

in the twenty years since the Eisenhower administration first invoked "uncontrolled discretion" to withhold information from the courts as well as Congress should serve to warn that such uncurbed power imperils our democratic system. It is therefore the concern of everyman.

APPENDIX A

STUDY PREPARED BY THE GOVERNMENT AND GENERAL RESEARCH DIVISION OF THE LIBRARY OF CONGRESS

Reprinted from the Congressional Record H. 2243–2246
(March 28, 1973)

THE PRESENT LIMITS OF "EXECUTIVE PRIVILEGE"

(A study prepared under the guidance of the House Foreign Operations and Government Information Subcommittee)

May 17, 1954, was an important day on Capitol Hill. On that day, two separate political battles shifted emphasis, and the new emphasis of each controversy still is causing political problems.

In the Supreme Court Building Chief Justice Earl Warren issued the court's unanimous decision in *Brown v. Board of Education* holding that separate education is not equal education. In the Senate Office Building John Adams, the Army's general counsel, delivered a copy of a letter from President Dwight D. Eisenhower to Secretary of Defense Charles Wilson directing the Secretary to tell all his subordinates not to testify about advisory communications during the hearings of a special subcommittee of the Senate Government Operations Committee.[1]

Both important developments of May 17, 1954, had roots deep in the history of the United States. In the future both would effect the political development of the nation. The results of the Supreme Court's school desegregation decision are widely discussed in popular literature and scholarly studies and have become a part of current history. But there is comparatively little current knowledge about the developments that flowed from President Eisenhower's May 17, 1954, letter. Possibly, that letter and the political conflict of which it is a part are more important to the study of the American form of democratic government with three branches than is the widely studied school desegregation issue.

President Eisenhower's May 17, 1954, letter brought a new dimension to the interactions between the Legislative and Executive Branches of the Federal government which are part of our separate-but-coordinate system. His letter, and its accompanying memorandum purporting to list historic examples of Presidential assertion of the right of "executive privilege," became the basis for an extension of the claim of "executive privilege" far down the administrative line from the President.[2] Eight years later there was an attempt to bring "executive privilege" back into proper perspective, but

Footnotes at end of article.

the effort has not been a complete success even though it involved three Presidents.

There are many privileges exercised by the executive head of the United States Government, ranging from the free use of the mountain retreat at Camp David (or Shang-ri-la as President Franklin D. Roosevelt christened it) to a funeral with full military honors. But *the* "executive privilege" has come to mean a claim of authority to control government information.[3] This "executive privilege" to control the dissemination of information has been asserted against the public[4] and against the courts,[5] but the claim of an "executive privilege" which was the basis of the President's May 17, 1954, letter is the claim of authority to withhold information from the Legislative Branch of the Federal government. And the authority claimed in President Eisenhower's May 17, 1954, letter was extended throughout the Executive Branch to include agencies administered by persons appointed by the President with the advice and consent of the U.S. Senate. This claim of control over government information is in addition to the power exercised by Presidents to protect their immediate White House staff—their personal advisers, in effect, over whose appointment the Congress has no confirming power.

The Separation of Powers and the Control of Information.

The conflict between the Legislative and Executive Branches of the Federal government over access to information begins with the first clause of the first section of the first article of the Constitution of the United States. Article I, Section I states that "all legislative Powers herein granted shall be vested in a Congress of the United States. . . ." The power to legislate carries with it the power to investigate[6] and the clash between the executive and the legislature over access to information almost always has occurred in connection with a Congressional investigation.

In fact, the earliest attempt by the Congress to investigate brought on a conflict over the authority of the executive to withhold information. The House of Representatives in 1792 appointed a committee to investigate General St. Clair's military disaster in the Northwest and empowered the committee to "call for such persons, papers, and records, as may be necessary to assist their inquiries."[7] This demand for information by the first Congress and the reaction to it by the first President was brought up 162 years later in connection with President Eisenhower's letter of May 17, 1954. A memorandum from the Attorney General which accompanied the letter listed the call for information in the St. Clair caper as the first example of Presidential assertion of "executive privilege."[8] The memorandum states that President Washington called a Cabinet meeting and the group decided that "neither the committee nor House had a right to call upon the head of a Department who and whose papers were under the President alone."[9]

Not only did this first Congressional investigation result in a confrontation over legislative access to Executive Branch information but it also provided a vehicle for the first major factual error in the memorandum accompanying the May 17, 1954, letter, discussing what has come to be called "executive privilege." Far from being an example of Presidential assertion of "executive privilege," the St. Clair episode was an example of Congress effectively asserting its right of access to information. A Cabinet meeting was held and the question of Presidential power over records was discussed, as reported in the memorandum, but the full text of Thomas Jefferson's notes of that meeting shows that it was decided "there was not a paper which might not be properly produced."[10] In fact, an historian-newsman who analyzed the precedents listed in the memorandum for withholding information from the Congress concluded that, in most of the examples, "the Congress prevailed, and got precisely what it sought to get."[11]

The assertion of an "executive privilege" to withhold information from the legislature is rooted in the opening words of Article II of the Constitution: "The executive power shall be vested in a President of the United States of America" and in the last clause in Section 3 of Article II: "He shall take care that the laws be faithfully executed."[12]

This Constitutional grant of power is both vague and complicated, the language raising more questions of how the power shall be exercised than it answers.[13] In the past 18 years, however, there have been some major changes in Congressional-Executive relationships which clarify the practice—if not the principle—of "executive privilege."

The Recent Growth of "Executive Privilege"

After May 17, 1954, the Executive Branch answer to nearly every question about the authority to withhold information from the Congress was "yes," they had the authority. And the authority most often cited was the May 17, 1954, letter from President Eisenhower to Secretary of Defense Wilson.[14] Not only was the letter cited, but usually the claim of authority included the accompanying memorandum from Attorney General Herbert Brownell, supposedly prepared in the Department of Justice.

The letter and the memorandum were involved in a controversy between Senator Joseph McCarthy (R., Wis.) and the United States Army over the propriety of the Senator's pressure tactics as chairman of the Permanent Subcommittee on Investigations of the Senate Committee on Government Operations. During two days of testimony at special hearings called to give McCarthy and the Army a forum for their fight, Army Counsel John Adams mentioned a meeting in the Attorney General's office attended by top White House staff members.[15]

When Subcommittee members tried to get more information from Adams about what went on at the high-level meeting, Joseph N. Welch of Boston, the Army's special counsel for the Army-McCarthy hearings, said Adams had been instructed not to testify any further about the meeting.[16] That was on Friday, May 14, 1954. When Subcommittee members insisted that Adams testify, Welch asked for and was granted a recess until the following Monday.

On Monday, Adams gave the Subcommittee the letter of instructions from the President to the Secretary of Defense, accompanied by a memorandum supposedly prepared officially in the Department of Justice over the weekend. In fact, the memorandum consisted only of excerpts and paraphrases from a 1949 article printed in the *Federal Bar Journal* and written by Herman Wolkinson, a Justice Department research lawyer.[17] Two years later the Justice Department presented to another Congressional subcommittee what appeared to be an expanded memorandum supporting their position on "executive privilege,"[18] but it was merely the text of the Wolkinson article.[19]

There was a favorable public response to President Eisenhower's firm stand against disclosing conversations in his official family. Newspapers which were later to inveigh against the excesses of "executive privilege" praised the President's letter of May 17, 1954. The *New York Times*, for instance, editorialized against Senator McCarthy's use of legislative powers to encroach upon the Executive Branch "in complete disregard of the historic and Constitutional division of powers that is basic to the American system of Government."[20] And the *Washington Post* called the memorandum which was made public in connection with the President's letter "an extremely useful document," concluding that the President's authority under the Constitution to withhold information from Congress "is altogether beyond question."[21]

But the May 17, 1954, letter from the President, with its accompanying memorandum, soon became the major vehicle for spreading a claim of Presidential authority throughout the Executive Branch. The letter referred only to a specific series of conversations between Presidential appointees, restricting access to information about those conversations only to one specific Subcommittee of the Congress. Four months later, however, the May 17, 1954, letter was extended to cover more than the President's personal appointees and more than the specific Subcommittee's hearings.

In August, 1954, the U.S. Senate established a select committee to determine whether Senator McCarthy was guilty of conduct "unbecoming a member of the United States Senate" and asked two Army generals to testify about their conversations in connection with McCarthy's activities. Major General Kirke B. Lawton refused to testify on the advice of counsel that the May 17, 1954, "directive" applies to "this or any other" committee.[22] Senator Arthur V. Watkins (R., Utah), the chairman of the select committee, asked Secretary of Defense Charles Wilson for clarification and received a letter stating:

"As a matter of legal application, the Attorney General advises me that the principles of the Presidential order of May 17, 1954 are as completely applicable to any committee as they were to the Committee on Government Operations.[23]

Telford Taylor, in his study of Congressional investigatory powers at the time of the Army-McCarthy controversy, commented:

"If President Eisenhower's [May 17, 1954] directive were applied generally in line with its literal and sweeping language, congressional committees would frequently be shut off from access to documents to which they are clearly entitled. . . . It is unlikely, therefore, that this ruling will endure beyond the particular controversy that precipitated it."[24]

He proved a poor prophet, in this case. President Eisenhower's May 17, 1954, letter became the major authority cited for the exercise of "executive privilege" to refuse information to the Congress for the next seven years of his administration[25] and it established a pattern which the three Presidents after Eisenhower have followed.

"Executive Privilege" Limited

President John F. Kennedy bent, although he did not break, the pattern of "executive privilege" claims by officials far down the administrative line from the President. He had been in office for one year when a special Senate subcommittee held hearings on the Defense Department's system for editing speeches of military leaders. When the Subcommittee asked the identity of the military editors who had handled specific speeches, President Kennedy wrote a letter to Secretary of Defense Robert S. McNamara directing him and all personnel under his jurisdiction "not to give any testimony or produce any documents which would disclose such information."[26] The similarity of President Kennedy's letter of February 8, 1962, and President Eisenhower's letter of May 17, 1954, stopped there, for Kennedy added:

"The principle which is at stake here cannot be automatically applied to every request for information. Each case must be judged on its own merits."[27]

There was no legal memorandum attached to President Kennedy's letter, although one was available. A 169-page study of "executive privilege" cases through 1960 had been prepared by two lawyers in the Department of Justice and printed in two issues of the *George Washington Law Review*.[28] The study, reminiscent of Herman Wolkinson's article in the *Federal Bar Journal* which was used as the back-up memorandum for President Eisenhower's May 17, 1954, letter, discussed executive responses to legislative inquiries from 1953 through 1960 and described some of the cases in which "executive privilege" was claimed. The new study called the exercise of "executive privilege" awkward and embarrassing—but not improper—and concluded:

"This power, like most other Presidential powers, therefore, must be delegated to other officials. The question is how far down the administrative line can this delegation proceed.[29]

President Kennedy's answer was: it cannot. His position was clarified in an exchange of correspondence with Congressman John E. Moss (D., Calif.) who, as chairman of the Foreign Operations and Government Information Subcommittee and its predecessor special subcommittee, had been leading the fight against government secrecy for nearly six years. Moss wrote that President Kennedy's letter of February 8, 1962, "clearly stated that the principle involved could not be applied automatically to restrict information," but he urged clarification "to prevent the rash of restrictions on government information which followed the May 17, 1954, letter from President Eisenhower."[30] President Kennedy, whose staff had gone over a draft of the Moss letter before it was sent formally, replied on March 7, 1962:

"Executive privilege can be invoked only by the President and will not be used without specific Presidential approval."[31]

Soon after Lyndon B. Johnson was elected President, Congressman Moss asked him to limit the use of "executive privilege" as had President Kennedy. In a letter of March 31, 1965, Moss discussed the spread of the use of "executive privilege" following President Eisenhower's letter and contended that, as a result of President Kennedy's limitation of the use of the authority, "there was no longer a rash of 'executive privilege' claims to withhold information from the Congress and the public." Moss expressed to President

Johnson the hope that "you will reaffirm the principle that 'executive privilege' can be invoked by you alone and will not be used without your specific approval."[32] President Johnson, in a letter of April 2, 1965, to Congressman Moss, reaffirmed the principle, stating flatly that "the claim of 'executive privilege' will continue to be made only by the President."[33]

Congressman Moss repeated the procedure soon after President Richard M. Nixon took office, asking him to "favorably consider a reaffirmation of the policy which provides, in essence, that the claim of 'executive privilege' will be invoked only by the President."[34] Two months after receiving the letter from Congressman Moss, President Nixon issued a memorandum to the heads of all executive departments and agencies stating that "executive privilege will not be used without specific Presidential approval." He buttressed his memorandum with a letter to Congressman Moss stating:

"I believe, as I have stated earlier, that the scope of executive privilege must be very narrowly construed. Under this Administration, executive privilege will not be asserted without specific Presidential approval."[35]

President Nixon's memorandum of March 24, 1969, spelled out procedural steps to govern the invocation of "executive privilege." First, he stated, anyone who wanted to invoke "executive privilege" in answer to a request for information from a "Congressional agency" had to consult the Attorney General. If the Attorney General and the department head agreed that "executive privilege" should not be invoked, the information requested should be released to the Congress. If, however, either or both of them wanted the issue submitted to the President, "the matter shall be transmitted to the Counsel to the President, who will advise the department head of the President's decision." If the President decided to invoke "executive privilege," the memorandum concluded, "the department head should advise the Congressional agency that the claim of Executive privilege is being made with the specific approval of the President."[36]

This was the first time that a step-by-step procedure was set up for invoking "executive privilege" against Congressional inquiries. It was not, of course, the first time that a President had promised to make the final decisions on the use of "executive privilege," but neither was President Kennedy's decision that only he should refuse information to the Congress, a Presidential first. On April 14, 1909, President William H. Taft issued Executive Order 1062 stating:

"In all cases where, by resolution of the Senate or House of Representatives, a head of a Department is called upon to furnish information, he is hereby directed to comply with such resolution, except when, in his judgment, it would be incompatible with the public interest, in which case he should refer the matter to the President for his direction."

No information is available on the results of President Taft's Executive Order 1062, but there is information from public sources on the results of the Kennedy-Johnson-Nixon limitation of the use of "executive privilege."

The Limits of Limitation

Has the Executive Branch claim of power to refuse information to Congress been severely limited since President Kennedy exercised "executive privilege" but said it would be used only by the President, judging each case on its merits? To answer the question, public sources were researched from 1962 through 1972 to determine the instances in which the Executive Branch refused documents or testimony to Congressional committees. The instances of invocation of "executive privilege" covered might or might not involve the issuance of a subpoena or a formal resolution requesting information. What has been focused upon is a publicly-recorded request for information by a Congressional committee and a publicly-reported refusal by an Executive Branch official to grant that request. That which was sought might be a document, a witness, or both. The refusal may or may not have been accompanied by a reason for the denial. The invocation of "executive privilege" has been interpreted for the purposes of this study to refer to a refusal of information to a Congressional committee or subcommittee by an Executive Branch agency or official. It does *not* include instances in which Presidential aides, serving in the White House Office, have refused to appear before Congressional committees.

Sources used in this study were the *New York Times*, the *Washington Post*, the *Washington Evening Star*, the *Congressional Record*, the *Congressional Quarterly* reports and almanacs, and printed hearings of Congressional committees. Following is the result:

Kennedy administration. Exercise of "executive privilege" by the President:

1. State and Defense Department witnesses directed not to give testimony or produce documents at hearings of the Senate Special Preparedness Subcommittee on Military Cold War Education which would identify individuals who reviewed specific speeches. (Committee on Armed Services, United States Senate, *Military Cold War Education and Speech Review Policies*, 87th Congress, Second Session, pp. 338, 369–370, 508–509, 725, 730–731 and 826).

Refusal by Executive Departments and Agencies To Provide Documents or Testimony

1. The Food and Drug Administration refuses to comply with a request from the House Interstate and Foreign Commerce Committee for files on MER-29 drug (*New York Times*, 6/21/62).

2. The State Department refuses to provide a copy of a working paper on the "mellowing" of the Soviet Union to the Senate Foreign Relations Committee (*New York Times*, 6/27/62).

3. General Maxwell D. Taylor appears before the House Subcommittee on Defense Appropriations and refuses to discuss the Bay of Pigs invasion as "it would result in another highly controversial, divisive public discussion among branches of our Government which would be damaging to all parties concerned." (*Congressional Record*, 4/4/63, p. 5817).

Johnson administration. Refusals by Executive Departments and Agencies to provide documents or testimony:

1. The Department of Defense refuses (April 4, 1968) to supply a copy of the Command Control Study of the Gulf of Tonkin incident to the Senate

Foreign relations Committee (Committee on the Judiciary, United States Senate, *Executive Privilege: The Withholding of Information by the Executive*, 92nd Congress, First Session, p. 39). This source hereafter cited as Senate Judiciary Committee hearings, *Executive Privilege.*

2. Treasury Under Secretary Joseph W. Barr refuses to testify before Senate Judiciary Committee on the nomination of Abe Fortas to be Chief Justice (*Congressional Record*, 9/18/68, p. 27518 and *Washington Post*, 9/17/68).

Nixon administration. Exercise of "executive privilege" by the President:

1. The Attorney General refuses (November 21, 1970) to give Congressman L. H. Fountain, chairman of the Intergovernmental Relations Subcommittee of the House Government Operations Committee, reports furnished by the Federal Bureau of Investigation to evaluate scientists nominated to serve on advisory boards of the Department of Health, Education and Welfare (Committee on Government Operations, U.S. House of Representatives, *U.S. Government Information Policies and Practices—The Pentagon Papers*, Part 2, 92nd Congress, First Session, pp. 362–363).

2. The Department of Defense refuses (August 30, 1971) to supply foreign military assistance plans to the Senate Foreign Relations Committee (Senate Judiciary Committee hearings, *Executive Privilege*, pp. 45–46).

3. The State Department refuses (March 15, 1972) to give the House Foreign Operations and Government Information Subcommittee the Agency for International Development country field submissions for Cambodian foreign assistance for the fiscal year 1973 (*New York Times*, 3/17/72; *Congressional Record*, 3/16/72, pp. H2148–H2149).

4. The United States Information Agency refuses (March 15, 1972) to give the Senate Foreign Relations Committee all USIA Country Program Memoranda (*Congressional Record*, 3/16/72, pp. H2148–H2149).

Refusals by Executive Departments and Agencies To Provide Documents or Testimony

1. The Department of Defense refuses (June 26, 1969) to supply the five-year plan for military assistance programs to the Senate Foreign Relations Committee (Senate Judiciary Committee hearings, *Executive Privilege*, p. 40).

2. The Defense Department refuses to provide a copy of "Commitment Plan 1964" between U.S. and Thailand to the Senate Foreign Relations Committee (*New York Times*, 8/9/69).

3. The Department of Defense refuses (December 20, 1969) to supply the "Pentagon Papers" to the Senate Foreign Relations Committee (Senate Judiciary Committee hearings, *Executive Privilege*, pp. 37–38).

4. Secretary of Defense Melvin Laird declines invitation to appear before Senate (Foreign Relations) Disarmament Subcommittee (*New York Times*, 3/19/70).

5. Department of Defense General Counsel J. Fred Buzhardt refuses in hearings (March 2, 1971) to release an Army investigation report on the 113th Intelligence Group requested by Senate Constitutional Rights Subcommittee (Senate Judiciary Committee hearings, Executive Privilege, pp. 402–405).

6. The Department of Defense refuses (April 10, 1971) to supply continuous monthly reports on military operations in Southeast Asia to the Senate Foreign Relations Committee (Senate Judiciary Committee hearings, Executive Privilege, p. 47).

7. The Department of Defense refuses (April 19, 1971) to allow three designated generals to appear before the Senate Constitutional Rights Subcommittee (Senate Judiciary Committee hearings, *Executive Privilege,* p. 402).

8. The Department of Defense refuses (June 9, 1971) to release computerized surveillance records and refuses to agree to a Senate Constitutional Rights Subcommittee report on such records (Senate Judiciary Committee hearings, *Executive Privilege,* pp. 398–399).

9. The State Department refuses (March 20, 1972) to supply Senate Foreign Relations Committee with a copy of "Negotiations, 1964–1968: The Half-Hearted Search for Peace in Vietnam" (*Washington Post,* 3/20/72).

10. Treasury Secretary John Connally refuses to testify before Joint Economic Committee on matter of the Emergency Loan Guarantee Board refusing to supply requested records on the Lockheed loan to the Government Accounting Office (*Washington Evening Star,* 4/27/72).

11. Benjamin Forman, Department of Defense Assistant General Counsel, appears before the Senate Foreign Relations Committee but refuses to discuss weather modification efforts in Southeast Asia (*Washington Post,* 7/27/72).

12. Henry Ramirez, chairman of Cabinet Committee on Opportunities for the Spanish Speaking, refuses to testify before House Judiciary Subcommittee on Civil Rights (*Congressional Quarterly,* 8/12/72, p. 2017).

13. SEC Chairman William J. Casey refuses to turn over Commission investigative files on ITT to the House Interstate and Foreign Commerce investigative subcommittee (*Washington Evening Star/Daily News,* 11/1/72).

14. HUD Secretary George Romney declines invitation to appear before the Joint Economic Committee to testify on Federal housing subsidies (*Washington Post,* 12/6/72).

15. Department of Defense refuses to turn over documents requested by the House Armed Services Committee on unauthorized bombing raids of interest to the committee as part of hearings on the firing of Gen. John D. Lavelle (*Washington Post,* 12/19/72).

Conclusions

President Kennedy exercised the Presidential claim of "executive privilege" one time when he directed witnesses not to identify speech reviewers in testimony before the Senate subcommittee investigating military cold war education policies. Six separate refusals to provide information to the subcommittee were involved in the President's single action.

After the Kennedy directive, however, Executive Branch officials in his administration refused to provide information to Congressional committees three times, apparently without Presidential authority.

In the Johnson Administration "executive privilege" was not claimed by President Johnson, but there were two refusals by appointees in his administration to provide information to Congressional committees after President

Johnson's letter of April 2, 1965, stating that "the claim of 'executive privilege' will continue to be made only by the President."

President Nixon personally and formally invoked the claim of "executive privilege" against Congressional committees four times after his memorandum of March 24, 1969, stating that "executive privilege" will not be used without specific Presidential approval. After the memorandum was issued there were, however, 15 other instances in the Nixon Administration in which documents or testimony were refused to Congressional committees without Presidential approval.

This public record of the controversies over Congressional access to Executive information after three Presidents limited the use of "executive privilege," raises a number of questions. Were the Executive Branch officials who apparently refused information to Congressional committees 20 times in violation of the orders of three Presidents, actually acting under orders? Is it possible that three Presidents ordered information withheld 20 times from Congressional committees and left no evidence of their orders?

Contrariwise, is it possible that, in 20 instances, Executive Branch officials were ignoring the clear orders of three Presidents? Or possibly, is there some of both: Executive Branch officials refusing information to Congressional committees with the tacit understanding—at least by the White House staff if not the President, himself—of what was going on?

There are many other problems which can be raised in addition to these three alternatives, such as the question of what formal action the Congress or one of its constituent units must take to assert the Legislative Branch's right of access to information by the Constitution, and the question of whether the Legislative vs. Executive conflict over access to government information may be regarded as a partisan political fight having little to do with the evolution of a system of government based on three coordinate branches.

The fact that there is much more conflict over Congressional access to Executive Branch information when the two branches are controlled by different political parties gives substance to the view that "executive privilege" is a partisan problem. There were, for example, 19 cases of refusal of information to Congressional committees under the first four years of the Republican Nixon Administration working with a Democratic Congress, but there were only six refusals of information in seven years of the Kennedy and Johnson Administrations when both branches were controlled by the same political party. An additional indication of the partisan nature of the conflict is that there were some 34 instances of information refused in response to Congressional requests during the last five years of the Eisenhower Administration, after he issued his letter of May 17, 1954.[37] In that period, the Executive and Legislative Branches were under control of different political parties.

Partisan the problem is, but not purely partisan. It can come up when both branches are under control of the same political party—witness the six cases in the Kennedy and Johnson Administrations—and the partisan makeup of the two branches may merely sharpen the conflict and not make it less of a problem to be solved as the governmental system evolves.

President Nixon, in fact, did more to regularize the flow of information to

Congress on controversial subjects than did his predecessors. He issued the first orders setting up a step-by-step procedure to be followed in his administration before "executive privilege" could be invoked. And his memorandum of March 24, 1969, moved toward an answer to the question of what type of formal action the Congress must take to demand information before "executive privilege" would be asserted.

His memorandum referred throughout to a "Congressional agency"[38] requesting Executive Branch information. By this language, apparently he was recognizing that a Congressional committee or subcommittee—or, possibly, the chairman of either—could make a formal request for information that might result in the claim of "executive privilege." He did not require a resolution of the House or Senate, as did President Taft, nor did he leave the problem completely in limbo, as did Presidents Kennedy and Johnson.

There is some additional information to indicate which of three alternatives—violation of a Presidential order, secret Presidential approval or both—explain the fact that the limitation on the use of "executive privilege" apparently has been ignored. It is possible that the five cases in the Kennedy and Johnson Administrations in which information was refused, apparently without Presidential approval, in fact had Presidential approval but this fact has been kept from public knowledge.

This is not the case in the Nixon Administration. President Nixon's memorandum requires a potential "executive privilege" case to go through the Office of Legal Counsel in the Department of Justice. The "executive privilege" expert in that office is Herman Marcuse, one of the authors of the *George Washington Law Review* study of "executive privileges" from 1953 to 1960 (see footnote 28). Marcuse has stated that only the cases of "executive privilege" listed above were handled in the office and approved by President Nixon since his memorandum.[39]

There is a possibility that, in all three administrations, the cases of refusal of information to Congress, apparently in violation of Presidential orders, did not result from formal confrontations between the two branches of government. Assistant Attorney General William H. Rehnquist, who was in charge of the Office of Legal Counsel, testified after two years' experience under President Nixon's "executive privilege" memorandum that "agencies which seek to withhold information are complying with the procedures set forth in the memorandum."[40] By the time of his testimony, there already had been one formal Presidential use of the claim of "executive privilege" and eight other cases in which, public records show, testimony or documents had been refused to Congressional committees.

Rehnquist downgraded refusals of information to Congress which had not had the stamp of Presidential approval, arguing that no real confrontation over access to information occurs in many cases because they are mere discussions at the staff level between Executive agencies and Congressional committees. And in other cases, he testified, a witness would mention the possibility that a request for particular information might raise the spectre of "executive privilege." Rehnquist added:

"But such a statement, of course, is by no means tantamount to the President's authorizing the claim of privilege. It is simply a statement by a department head or his representative that he is prepared to recommend a claim of privilege to the President should the demand for information not be settled in a mutually satisfactory manner to both the agency and the chairman of the committee or subcommittee involved."[41]

None of the 15 Nixon Administration cases or refusal of information to a Congressional committee without the formal, Presidential citation of "executive privilege" seems to fit the Rehnquist criteria. While the committees or subcommittees involved may not have taken a formal vote to demand the testimony or documents in each case the request for information did come up in hearings or as part of a formal request from the chairman.

If the 15 Nixon Administration cases involved formal, direct requests for information and if there are no secret Presidential orders directing the invocation of "executive privilege," it seems that Executive Branch officials violated the Presidential directive 15 times. When interpreting orders in government administration, however, one bureaucrat's violation may be another bureaucrat's compliance. Those who want to withhold information from the Congress will do everything possible to make it difficult for Congress to get what it needs. That is apparent from the 34 instances occurring in five years when the Executive Branch wrapped itself in President Eisenhower's letter of May 17, 1954, as a cloak of "executive privilege." That cloak no longer exists, but the bureaucracy that used it is little changed. And the top-level policy makers apparently are happy to use the bureaucracy's tactics of delay and obfuscation to prevent Congress from getting at information which might embarrass their agency or their administration.

While the Kennedy-Johnson-Nixon statements limiting the invocation of "executive privilege" may state clearly to Congressional readers that information will not be refused without specific Presidential approval, they may also state to Executive Branch readers that they should be careful when claiming "executive privilege" but they can use other techniques to block Congressional access to information.

Thus, the use of the claim of "executive privilege" has been severely limited but the limitation has not opened new file drawers to Congress. In fact, the Presidential statements have been limitations in name only.

Footnotes

1. U.S. Congress. Senate, Committee on Government Operations. Special Subcommittee on Investigations. *Special Senate Investigation on Charges and Countercharges Involving: Secretary of the Army Robert T. Stevens, John G. Adams, H. Struve Hensel and Senator Joe McCarthy, Roy M. Cohn, and Francis P. Carr.* Hearings, 83rd Congress, 2d session. Washington: U.S. Govt. Print. Off., 1954, pp. 1169–1172.

2. H. Rept. 84–2947, p. 90.

3. H. Rept. 86–2084, p. 37.

4. *Ibid.*, p. 36.

5. *Marbury v. Madison* (1 Cranch 137) and the conspiracy trial of Aaron Burr are the classic historical cases. *Kilbourn v. Thompson* (103 U.S. 168), *McGrain v. Daugherty* (273 U.S. 135), *ex rel. Touhy v. Ragan* (340 U.S. 462) and *U.S. v. Reynolds* (345 U.S. 1) are modern cases which have considered court access to Executive Branch information. When President John F. Kennedy limited the use of "executive privilege" to the President alone (see below), he was asked by the Attorney General whether the limitation applied only to congressional requests for information. Theodore C. Sorenson, Special Counsel to the President, replied in a letter of March 30,

1962, to the Attorney General that the policy "relates solely to inquiries directed by the Congress or its committees to the Executive Branch" and does not have any application to "demands, made in the course of a judicial or other adjudicatory proceeding, for the production of papers or other information in the possession of the Government."

6. Library of Congress. Legislative Reference Service. *The Constitution of the United States of America—Analysis and Interpretation.* Washington: U.S. Govt. Print. Off., 1964, p. 105.

7. *Ibid.*

8. U.S. Congress. House. Committee on Government Operations. Special Subcommittee on Government Information. *Availability of Information from Federal Departments and Agencies.* Hearings, 85th Congress, 2d session. Washington: U.S. Govt. Print. Off., 1958, p. 3911.

9. *Ibid.*

10. J. Russell Wiggins, "Government Operations and the Public's Right to Know," *Federal Bar Journal,* XIX (January, 1959), p. 76.

11. *Ibid.*, p. 82.

12. Senator Sam Ervin (D.-N.C.), the United States Senate's acknowledged constitutional expert, explains:

"Although the Constitution is silent with regard to the existence of executive privilege, its exercise is asserted to be an inherent power of the President. Its constitutional basis allegedly derives from the duty imposed upon the President under article II section 3 to see that the laws are faithfully executed. The President claims the power on the grounds that it is necessary in order to provide the executive branch with the autonomy needed to discharge its duties properly. Inasmuch as the "President alone and unaided could not execute the laws * * *" but requires "the assistance of subordinates" (*Myers* v. *U.S.*, 272 U.S. 117 (1926)), the alleged authority to exercise executive privilege has thereby been extended in practice to the entire executive branch."*

* U.S. Congress. Senate. Committee on the Judiciary. Subcommittee on Separation of Powers. *Executive Privilege: The Withholding of Information by the Executive.* Hearings, 92d Congress, 1st session. Washington: U.S. Govt. Print. Off., 1971, p. 2.

13. Edward S. Corwin. *The President: Office and Powers.* New York: New York University Press, 1968, pp. 4 and 5.

14. H. Rept. 86–2084, p. 117.

15. U.S. Congress. Senate. Committee on Government Operations. Special Subcommittee on Investigations, *op. cit.*, p. 1059.

16. *Ibid.*, pp. 1169–1172.

17. H. Rept. 86–234, p. 64, note 1.

18. U.S. Congress. House. Committee on Government Operations. Special Subcommittee on Government Information. *op. cit.*, p. 2894; another, modified version and the original also found in U.S. Congress. Senate. Committee on the Judiciary. Subcommittee on Constitutional Rights. *Freedom of Information and Secrecy in Government.* Hearings, 85th Congress, 2d session. Washington: U.S. Govt. Print. Off., pp. 63–270.

19. Herman Wolkinson, "Demand of Congressional Committees for Executive Papers," *Federal Bar Journal,* X (April, July, October, 1949), pp. 103–150.

20. New York *Times,* May 18, 1954, p. 28.

21. Washington *Post,* May 18, 1954, p. 14.

22. U.S. Congress. Senate. Select Committee to Study Censure Charges Against Senator Joe McCarthy. *Hearings, Select Committee to Study Censure Charges Against Senator Joe McCarthy, August 31 through September 17, 1954.* 83rd Congress, 2d session. Washington: U.S. Govt. Print. Off., 1954, p. 167.

23. *Ibid.*, p. 434.

24. Telford Taylor. *Grand Inquest.* New York: Simon & Schuster, 1955, p. 133.

25. H. Rept. 86–2084, p. 177.

26. U.S. Congress. Senate. Committee on Armed Services. Special Preparedness Subcommittee. *Military Cold War Education and Speech Review Policies.* Hearings, 87th Congress, 2d session. Washington: U.S. Govt. Print. Off., 1962, pp. 508 and 509.

27. *Ibid.*

28. Robert Kramer and Herman Marcuse, "Executive Privilege—A Study of the

Period 1953–1960," *George Washington Law Review*, XXIX (April, June, 1961), pp. 623–718, 827–916.

29. *Ibid.*, p. 911.

30. U.S. Congress. Senate. Committee on the Judiciary. Subcommittee on Separation of Powers. *op. cit.*, p. 34.

31. *Ibid.*

32. *Ibid.*, p. 35.

33. *Ibid.*

34. *Ibid.*, p. 36.

35. *Ibid.*

36. *Ibid.*, p. 37.

37. H. Rept. 86–2084, pp. 5–35.

38. U.S. Congress. Senate. Committee on the Judiciary. Subcommittee on Separation of Powers. *op. cit.*, p. 36.

39. Telephone interview, August 22, 1972.

40. U.S. Congress. House. Committee on Government Operations. Foreign Operations and Government Information Subcommittee. *U.S. Government Information Policies and Practices—The Pentagon Papers.* Hearings, 92d Congress, 1st session. Washington: U.S. Govt. Printing Office, 1971, p. 365.

41. *Ibid.*, p. 366.

APPENDIX B

ROGERS' MISINTERPRETATION OF McGRAIN V. DAUGHERTY ET AL.

The Attorney General misconceives the effect of *McGrain v. Daugherty*; Rogers memo 71. In the interest of clarity each of his propositions will be treated separately. The Attorney General states: "How is the United States Supreme Court likely to decide the issue concerning the *withholding of confidential papers* by the executive branch from Congress and its committees? The case of *McGrain v. Daugherty* points to the following conclusions:

(a) The Houses of Congress have, in the past exceeded their powers, both with respect to their attempted punishment for contempt of private persons and of a United States official, and the Supreme Court did not hesitate to reject the improper assertions of congressional power"; ibid., citing *Kilbourn v. Thompson*, 103 U.S. 168 (1880), and *Marshall v. Gordon*, 243 U.S. 521 (1917), emphasis added.

In fact, *McGrain* rejected *Kilbourn's* historically unsound intimations that "neither house of Congress has power to make inquiries and exact evidence in aid of contemplated legislation"; 273 U.S. at 171; compare ibid. at 174. *McGrain* explained further that in *Kilbourn* "the resolution contained no suggestion of contemplated legislation; that the matter was one in respect to which no valid legislation could be had; that the bankrupt's estate and the trustee's settlement were still pending in bankruptcy court," and, consequently, that the House had exceeded its powers and assumed to exercise clearly judicial power; ibid at 171. Mr. Justice Frankfurter remarked in *United States v. Rumely*, 345 U.S. 41, 46 (1953), upon the "inroads" made by *McGrain* upon *Kilbourn*.

Marshall v. Gordon, 243 U.S. 521 (1917), is even further afield. *McGrain* explains that there the issue was whether the House could punish for contempt a district attorney who sent an "irritating" letter to a Committee Chairman, and the Court emphasized that the "power to make inquiries and obtain information by compulsory process was not involved"; 273 U.S. at 173. All that was decided in *Marshall,* said *McGrain,* was that the House could not punish for contempt because the letter "was not calculated or likely to affect the House in any of its proceedings or in the exercise of any of its functions"; ibid. Both *Kilbourn* and *Gordon* are therefore totally irrelevant to the "withholding of confidential papers by the executive branch from Congress" when it seeks information in aid of legislation, appropriation or investigation of executive conduct.

The Attorney General states: "(b) Ever since 1796, the executive branch has asserted the right to say 'no' to the Houses of Congress, when they have requested confidential papers which the President or the heads of departments felt obliged to withhold, in the public interest. Since 1800, court decisions have uniformly held that the president or heads of departments need not give testimony or produce papers which, in their judgment, require secrecy"; Rogers memo 71. This paragraph suggests that the courts have "uniformly" sustained executive refusals to furnish infomation to Congress. Certainly the case of *McGrain v. Daugherty* contains not the slightest intimation to this effect. No case has so held—see supra, Ch. 6, n. 16 and accompanying text—and no case cited by the Attorney General supports such a proposition. There is no absolute executive privilege to withhold even from private litigants; see infra, Ch. 7.

The Attorney General states that: "(c) Never in our entire history has either House of Congress taken any steps to enforce requests for the production of testimony or documents which have been refused by the executive branch.

"The foregoing, in the words of the Supreme Court in the *Daugherty* case, point 'to a practical construction, long continued, of the constitutional provisions respecting their powers,' *by the executive* and legislative branches. The long-continued practice of the executive branch, and the passage of no law by Congress to change that practice argue, persuasively for the possession of such a power, under the Constitution by the executive. The United States Supreme Court is not likely to ignore more than 150 years of legislative acquiescence in the assertion of that power"; Rogers memo 71, emphasis added. The suggestion that *McGrain* approves a practical construction "by the executive branch," perverts its meaning. The Supreme Court, after alluding to the fact that *both houses* of Congress early took the Colonial view that the power of inquiry was an "essential auxiliary" to the "legislative function," concluded that the *congressional,* not the executive, "practice . . . falls nothing short of a practical construction, long continued, of the constitutional provisions respecting *their powers,* and therefore should be taken as fixing the meaning of those provisions, if otherwise doubtful"; 273 U.S. at 174, emphasis added. Having approved this "essential auxiliary" for the purposes of sustaining the summoning of witnesses in an investigation of the Department of Justice, *McGrain* scarcely intended to approve a claim of executive privilege to withhold information that would abort it.

Again, the Attorney General's statement that Congress has passed "no law to change that practice" is belied by the facts. See supra, Ch. 2, text accompanying nn. 140–152; infra, Ch. 8, text accompanying n. 64.

For comment on the "150 years of legislative acquiescence," see supra, Ch. 2, text accompanying nn. 172–177.

APPENDIX C

EDITORIAL

New York Times, January 8, 1973, p. 38.

. . . As Others See Us

O Wad some Pow'r the giftie gie us
To see oursels as others see us!
It wad frae monie a blunder free us
An' foolish notion.

—*Robert Burns*

The image of the United States in the eyes of the world today—in the wake of President Nixon's intensive twelve-day bombing attack against the heavily populated Hanoi-Haiphong area of North Vietnam—is one that no American can regard with equanimity. From Stockholm to Sydney, from Turtle Bay to Tokyo, reports of the bombing have been received with horror and nearly universal condemnation. Just across the border, the Canadian House of Commons has voted unanimously to deplore the United States action.

The respected French newspaper *Le Monde* called the raids an "abomination" and likened them to the Nazi bombing of Guernica. Japan's largest circulation daily, normally friendly to the United States, described this country as a "blinded giant," adding that "nothing is more grotesque" than Washington's claim that the attacks were aimed at establishing peace. In Buenos Aires, the attacks were labeled "genocide."

Secretary General Kurt Waldheim of the United Nations called in United States Ambassador Bush to voice his concern while at the Vatican Pope Paul VI expressed "profound bitterness over the all too many victims that this long conflict has reaped in either camp, and particularly those who were sacrificed in the recent frightful exacerbation of hostilities."

Premier Olof Palme of Sweden, who compared the blitz against North Vietnam with Nazi massacres of World War II, and the new Labor Prime Minister of Australia, Gough Whitlam, were the most verbally unrestrained official critics of the American action. The diplomatic rebuffs they received from Washington could not stifle the widespread belief that their comments reflected the unexpressed feelings of many of this country's closest friends and allies abroad.

Chancellor Willy Brandt of West Germany maintained a diplomatic silence but he was quoted by friends as saying he found the bombing policy "disgusting and unfathomable." In Britain, the usually restrained Labor Party leader Roy Jenkins, another strong friend of this country, described the aerial assault as "one of the most cold-blooded actions in recent history." French officialdom discretely muted its obvious disapproval in hope of preserving a useful mediating role in the revived negotiations but President Pompidou criticized the bombing before a diplomatic gathering.

The cessation of bombing north of the 20th Parallel and the resumption of peace talks today offer the United States a chance to begin to redeem itself in the eyes of the profoundly disillusioned and embittered world. It is an opportunity that must not be lost. The implications of this worldwide censure extend far beyond Indochina, vitally affecting this country's ability to lead its allies and others toward the generation of peace that President Nixon has repeatedly promised.

APPENDIX D

MESSAGES OF PRESIDENT JAMES MONROE

WASHINGTON, *January 28, 1822.*

To the House of Representatives:

In compliance with the resolution of the 2d instant, I transmit a report of the Secretary of State, with all the documents relating to the misunderstanding between Andrew Jackson, while acting as governer of the Floridas, and Eligius Fromentin, judge of a court therein; and also of the correspondence between the Secretary of State and the minister plenipotentiary of His Catholic Majesty on certain proceedings in that Territory in execution of the powers vested in the governor by the Executive under the law of the last session for carrying into effect the late treaty between the United States and Spain. Being always desirous to communicate to Congress, or to either House, all the information in the possession of the Executive respecting any important interest of our Union which may be communicated without real injury to our constituents, and *which can rarely happen except in negotiations pending* with foreign powers, and deeming it *more consistent* with the principles of our Government in cases submitted to my discretion, as in the present instance, to hazard error by the *freedom of the communication rather than by withholding* any portion of information belonging to the subject, I have thought proper to communicate every document comprised within this call.

JAMES MONROE.

2 Richardson 113; emphasis added.

WASHINGTON, *May 4, 1822.*

To the House of Representatives of the United States:

In compliance with a resolution of the House of Representatives of the 19th of April, requesting the President "to cause to be communicated to the

House, if not injurious to the public interest, any letter which may have been received from Jonathan Russell, one of the ministers who concluded the treaty of Ghent, in conformity with the indications contained in his letter of the 25th of December, 1814," I have to state that having referred the resolution to the Secretary of State, and it appearing, by a report from him, that no such document had been deposited among the archives of the Department, I examined and *found among my private papers a letter of that description marked "private" by himself.* I transmit a copy of the report of the Secretary of State, by which it appears that Mr. Russell, on being apprised that the document referred to by the resolution had not been deposited in the Department of State, delivered there "a paper purporting to be the duplicate of a letter written by him from Paris on the 11th of February, 1815, to the then Secretary of State, to be communicated to the House as the letter called for by the resolution."

On the perusal of the document called for I find that it communicates a *difference of opinion between Mr. Russell and a majority of his colleagues* in certain transactions which occurred in the negotiations at Ghent, touching interests which have been since satisfactorily adjusted by treaty between the United States and Great Britain. The view which Mr. Russell presents of his own conduct and that of his colleagues in those transactions will, it is presumed, call from the two surviving members of that mission who differed from him a reply containing their view of those transactions and of the conduct of the parties in them, and who, should his letter be communicated to the House of Representatives, will also claim that their reply should be communicated in like manner by the Executive—a claim which, on the principle of equal justice, could not be resisted. The Secretary of State, one of the ministers referred to, has already expressed a desire that Mr. Russell's letter should be communicated, and that I would transmit at the same time a communication from him respecting it.

On full consideration of the subject I have thought it would be improper for the Executive to communicate the letter called for *unless the House, on a knowledge of these circumstances, should desire* it, in which case the *document called for shall be communicated,* accompanied by a report from the Secretary of State, as above suggested. I have directed a copy to be delivered to Mr. Russell, to be disposed of as he may think proper, and have caused the original to be deposited in the Department of State, with instruction to deliver a copy to any person who may be interested.

JAMES MONROE.

2 Richardson 138–139; emphasis added. For other instances where Monroe furnished "confidential" interchanges between subordinates, see message of Dec. 31, 1818, ibid. 49; Feb. 6, 1819, ibid. 52.

BIBLIOGRAPHY

BOOKS

Acheson, Dean. *Present at the Creation* (New York, Norton, 1969).
Adams, John. *Letters to Abigail Adams*, 2 vols. (Boston, Little, Brown, 1841).
Allen, Sir C. K. *Law in the Making*, 6th ed. (Oxford, Clarendon Press, 1958).
ALI Model Code of Evidence (Philadelphia, American Law Institute, 1942).
Bagehot, Walter, *The English Constitution* (London, Watts, 1964).
Bailey, T. A. *The Man in the Street* (New York, Macmillan, 1948).
Bailyn, Bernard. *The Ideological Origins of the American Revolution* (Cambridge, Mass., Harvard University Press, 1967).
Barth, Alan. *Government by Investigation* (New York, Viking, 1955).
Beard, Charles. *The Supreme Court and the Constitution* (Englewood Cliffs, Prentice-Hall, 1962).
Bemis, Samuel F. *John Quincy Adams and the Union* (New York, Knopf, 1956).
Berger, Raoul. *Congress v. the Supreme Court* (Cambridge, Mass., Harvard University Press, 1969).
———. *Impeachment: The Constitutional Problems* (Cambridge, Mass., Harvard University Press, 1973).
Beveridge, Albert J. *Life of John Marshall*, 4 vols. (Boston, Houghton Mifflin, 1916–1919).
Blackstone, Sir William. *Commentaries on the Law of England* (Oxford, 1765–1769).
Borkin, Joseph. *The Corrupt Judge* (New York, Potter, 1962).
Bowen, Catherine Drinker. *The Lion and the Throne* (Boston, Little, Brown, 1957).
Boyer, A. *History of the Impeachment of the Last Ministry* (London, 1716).
Butterfield, Sir Herbert. *George III and the Historians* (London, Macmillan, 1969).
Campbell, Lord John. *Lives of the Chief Justices of England*, 4 vols. (New York, Cockcroft, 1874).
Chafee, Zechariah. *Three Human Rights in the Constitution* (Lawrence, University of Kansas Press, 1956).
Chandler, Richard. *History and Proceedings of Parliament from 1621 to the Present*, 14 vols. (London, 1743).
Churchill, Winston. *Marlborough: His Life and Times*, abridged ed. (New York, Scribner's, 1968).
Clarke, Mary R. *Parliamentary Privilege in the American Colonies* (New Haven, Yale University Press, 1943).
Clausewitz, Carl von. *On War* [1832] (London, Routledge & Kegan Paul, 1966).
Clive, John M. *Macaulay* (New York, Knopf, 1973).
Coke, Sir Edward. *Commentaries on Littleton* (London, 1628).
Commager, Henry Steele. *Documents of American History*, 7th ed. (New York, Appleton, 1963).

BIBLIOGRAPHY

Corwin, Edward S. *The Doctrine of Judicial Review* (Princeton, Princeton University Press, 1914).

———. *The President's Control of Foreign Relations* (Princeton, Princeton University Press, 1917).

———. *The President : Office and Powers*, 3d ed. (New York, New York University Press, 1948).

———. *Total War and the Constitution* (New York, Knopf, 1947).

———. *Twilight of the Supreme Court: A History of a Constitutional Theory* (New Haven, Yale University Press, 1934).

———, editor. *The Official Constitution of the United States of America—Analysis and Interpretation*, rev. ed. (Washington, Government Printing Office, 1953).

Crandall, S. B. *Treaties: Their Making and Enforcement*, 2d ed. (Washington, Byrne, 1916).

Dahl, Robert A. *Congress and Foreign Policy* (New York, Harcourt Brace, 1950).

Davis, K. C. *Administrative Law Text*, 3d ed. (St. Paul, West, 1972).

Dewitt, David M. *The Impeachment and Trial of Andrew Johnson* (New York, Russell, 1967).

Dimock, Marshall. *Congressional Investigating Committees* (Baltimore, Johns Hopkins Press, 1929).

Doren, Carl van. *The Great Rehearsal* (New York, Viking, 1948).

Dulles, Allen. *The Craft of Intelligence* (New York, Harper & Row, 1963).

Eberling, E. J. *Congressional Investigation* (New York, Columbia University Press, 1928).

Ehrenzweig, Albert. *Conflict of Laws* (St. Paul, West, 1962).

Elliot, Jonathan. *Debates in the Several State Conventions on the Adoption of the Federal Constitution*, 2d ed., 4 vols. (Washington, J. Elliot, 1836).

Farrand, Max. *The Framing of the Constitution of the United States* (New Haven, Yale University Press, 1913).

———. *The Records of the Federal Convention of 1787*, 4 vols. (New Haven, Yale University Press, 1911).

The Federalist. *The Federalist* (New York, Modern Library, 1937).

Ferrall, S. A. *The Law of Parliament* (London, 1837).

Fifoot, C. H. S. *Frederic William Maitland: A Life* (Cambridge, Mass., Harvard University Press, 1971).

Fleming, Denna F. *The Treaty Veto of the American Senate* (New York, Putnam, 1930).

France, Anatole. *Penguin Island* (New York, Modern Library, 1933).

Frankfurter, Felix, and James M. Landis. *The Business of the Supreme Court* (New York, Macmillan, 1927).

Freedman, Max, ed. *Roosevelt and Frankfurter: Their Correspondence, 1928–1945* (Boston, Little, Brown, 1967).

Freeman, Douglas. *Biography of Washington*, 7 vols. (New York, Scribner's, 1948–1957).

Gellhorn, Walter, and Clark Byse. *Administrative Law: Cases and Comments*, 4th ed. (Brooklyn, Foundation Press, 1960).

Gibbon, Edward. *The History of the Decline and Fall of the Roman Empire*, 6 vols. (New York, Nottingham, n.d.).

Goebel, Julius, Jr. *History of the Supreme Court of the United States*, vol. 1 (New York, Macmillan, 1971).

Goodman, Walter. *The Committee* (New York, Farrar, Strauss, 1968).

Gunther, Gerald, ed. *John Marshall's Defense of McCulloch v. Maryland* (Stanford, Stanford University Press, 1969).

Halberstam, David. *The Best and the Brightest* (New York, Random House, 1972).

Hallam, Henry. *Constitutional History of England,* 3 vols. (London, John Murray, 1884).

Hamilton, Alexander. *Works,* ed. H. C. Lodge, 12 vols. (New York, Putnam, 1904).

Hand, Learned. *The Bill of Rights* (Cambridge, Mass., Harvard University Press, 1958).

Hart, Henry, and Herbert Wechsler. *The Federal Courts and the Federal System* (Brooklyn, Foundation Press, 1953).

Hayden, Ralston. *The Senate and Treaties: 1789–1817* (New York, Macmillan, 1920).

Henkin, Louis. *Foreign Affairs and the Constitution* (Mineola, N.Y., Foundation Press, 1972).

Hill, Christopher. *The Century of Revolution, 1603–1714* (New York, Norton, 1961).

Hinds, Asher C. *Precedents of the House of Representatives,* 8 vols. (Washington, Government Printing Office, 1907).

Hockett, H. C. *The Constitutional History of the United States, 1826–1872* (New York, Macmillan, 1939).

Holdsworth, Sir William. *A History of English Law,* 12 vols. (London, Methuen, 1903–1938).

Howell's State Trials. Cobbett's Collection, 35 vols. (London, Bagshaw, 1809–1826).

Hurst, J. Willard. *Justice Holmes on Legal History* (New York, Macmillan, 1964).

Jackson, Robert H. *The Struggle for Judicial Supremacy* (New York, Knopf, 1949).

Jefferson, Thomas. *Manual of Parliamentary Practice.*

———. *Writings,* ed. P. L. Ford, 10 vols. (New York, Putnam, 1892–1899).

Jennings, Sir Ivor. *Parliament,* 2d ed. (Cambridge, Cambridge University Press, 1957).

Koenig, Louis. *The Invisible Presidency* (New York, Rinehart, 1960).

Ladd, Bruce. *Crises in Credibility* (New York, New American Library, 1968).

Llewellyn, Karl. *The Common Law Tradition* (Boston, Little, Brown, 1960).

McCloskey, Robert G. *The Modern Supreme Court* (Cambridge, Mass., Harvard University Press, 1972).

McClure, Wallace. *International Executive Agreements* (New York, Columbia University Press, 1941).

McConachie, L. G. *Congressional Committees* (New York, Crowell, 1898).

McGaffin, W., and E. Knoll. *Anything But the Truth: The Credibility Gap* (New York, Putnam, 1968).

McRee, G. J. *Life and Correspondence of James Iredell,* 2 vols. (New York, Appleton, 1857–1858).

Maclay, William. *Sketches of Debates in the First Senate of the United States, 1789–1791* (Harrisburg, 1880).

Madison, James. *Letters and Other Writings,* 4 vols. (Philadelphia, Lippincott, 1865–1867).

———. *Writings,* ed. G. Hunt, 9 vols. (New York, Putnam, 1900–1910).

Malone, Dumas. *Jefferson and His Times,* 4 vols. (Boston, Little, Brown, 1948–1970).

Martin, P., and C. Baker. *Supreme Court of the Judicature of the Province of New York, 1691–1704* (New York, New York Historical Society, 1959).

Mathews, John. *American Foreign Relations: Conduct and Policies* (New York, Appleton, 1938).
Miller, John C. *Alexander Hamilton: Portrait in Paradox* (New York, Harper, 1959).
Mollenhoff, Clark. *The Pentagon* (New York, Pinnacle Books, 1972).
———. *Washington Cover-Up* (Garden City, N.Y., Doubleday, 1962).
Montesquieu, C. de S. *The Spirit of the Laws*, 2 vols. (American translation, Philadelphia, 1802).
Moore, James. *Federal Practice* (New York, Bender, 1972).
Morison, Samuel Eliot. *Oxford History of the American People* (New York, Oxford University Press, 1965).
Notestein, W., F. H. Relf, and H. Simpson. *Commons Debates: 1621*, 7 vols. (New Haven, Yale University Press, 1935).
Owen, J. B. *The Rise of the Pelhams* (London, Methuen, 1957).
Padover, Saul. *The Complete Jefferson* (New York, Duell, Sloan, 1943).
Paterson, Caleb P. *Constitutional Principles of Thomas Jefferson* (Austin, University of Texas Press, 1953).
Pepys, Samuel. *Diary*, 7 vols. (New York, Dodd, Mead, 1904).
Petyt, W. *Miscellania Parliamentaria* (London, 1680).
Pomeroy, John N. *An Introduction to the Constitutional Law of the United States*, 3d ed. (Cambridge, Mass., Hurd and Houghton, 1875).
Poore, Ben P. *Federal and State Constitutions, Colonial Charters*, 2 vols. (Washington, Government Printing Office, 1877).
Randall, Henry S. *Life of Jefferson*, 3 vols. (New York, Derby & Jackson, 1858).
Richards, P. G. *Parliament and Foreign Affairs* (London, Allen & Unwin, 1967).
Richardson, James D. *Compilation of the Messages and Papers of the Presidents, 1787–1897*, 10 vols. (Washington, Government Printing Office, 1897).
Roberts, Clayton. *The Growth of Responsible Government in Stuart England* (Cambridge, Cambridge University Press, 1966).
Robertson, David. *The Trial of Aaron Burr*, 2 vols. (Philadelphia, 1808).
Robinson, J. A. *Congress and Foreign Policy Making* (Homewood, Ill., Dorsey Press, 1962).
Rossiter, Clinton. *The Supreme Court and the Commander in Chief* (Ithaca, Cornell University Press, 1951).
Schouler, James. *History of the United States*, 6 vols. (New York, Dodd, Mead, 1891).
Schubert, Glendon A. *The Presidency in the Courts* (Minneapolis, University of Minnesota Press, 1957).
Schlesinger, Arthur M., Jr. *The Imperial Presidency* (Boston, Houghton Mifflin, 1973).
Schwartz, Bernard. *A Commentary on the Constitution of the United States*, 2 vols. (New York, Macmillan, 1963).
Sheehan, Neil, et al. *The Pentagon Papers* (New York, Bantam Books, 1971).
Smith, Page. *John Adams*, 2 vols. (Garden City, N.Y., Doubleday, 1962).
Smith, S. A. de. *Judicial Review of Official Action*, 2d ed. (London, Stevens, 1959).
Story, Joseph. *Commentaries on the Constitution of the United States*, 5th ed., 2 vols. (Boston, Little, Brown, 1905).
Sullivan, J. W. N. *The Limitations of Science* (New York, New American Library, 1952).

Sulzberger, C. L. *A Long Row of Candles* (New York, Macmillan, 1969).
Sutherland, George. *Constitutional Power and World Affairs* (New York, Columbia University Press, 1919).
Taft, William H. *The Chief Magistrate: His Powers* (New York, Columbia University Press, 1916).
Tanner, Joseph R. *Constitutional Documents of the Reign of James I—1603–1625* (Cambridge, Cambridge University Press, 1960).
Taylor, Telford. *Grand Inquest* (New York, Simon & Schuster, 1955).
Tocqueville, Alexander de. *Democracy in America, 2 vols.* (New York, Knopf, 1945).
Trevelyan, Sir G. M. *Illustrated History of England* (London, Longmans, 1956).
Trial of Andrew Johnson. Congressional Globe (40th Cong., 2d Sess., supp., 1868).
Tuchman, Barbara. *The Guns of August* (New York, Macmillan, 1962).
Tucker, St. George, ed. *Blackstone's Commentaries*, 5 vols. (Philadelphia, 1803).
Wade, H. W. R. *Administrative Law*, 1st ed. (Oxford, Oxford University Press, 1961).
———. *Administrative Law*, 2d ed. (Oxford, Oxford University Press, 1967).
Warren, Charles. *Congress, the Constitution, and the Supreme Court* (Boston, Little, Brown, 1925).
———. *The Making of the Constitution* (Cambridge, Mass., Harvard University Press, 1947).
———. *The Supreme Court in United States History*, 3 vols. (Boston, Little, Brown, 1922).
Washington, George. *Writings*, ed. J. Fitzpatrick, 39 vols. (Washington, Government Printing Office, 1940).
Wharton, Francis. *State Trials of the United States* (Philadelphia, Carey & Hart, 1849).
Wigmore, John H. *Evidence*, 3d ed., 10 vols. (Boston, Little, Brown, 1940).
Willoughby, W. W. *The Constitutional Law of the United States*, 2d ed., 3 vols. (New York, Baker Voorhis, 1929).
Wilson, James. *Works*, ed. R. G. McCloskey, 2 vols. (Cambridge, Mass., Harvard University Press, 1967).
Wilson, Woodrow. *Congressional Government* (Boston, Houghton Mifflin, 1913).
———. *Constitutional Government in the United States* (New York, Columbia University Press, 1908).
Wiseman, H. V. *Parliament and the Executive* (London, Routledge & Kegan Paul, 1966).
Wright, Charles A. *Federal Courts* (St. Paul, West, 1963).

ARTICLES

Alsop, Stewart. Book review, *New York Times*, January 28, 1973, Book review sec.
Ball, George W. "Have We Learned or Only Failed," *New York Times*, April 1, 1973, Mag. sec., p. 12.
Baker, J. H. "New Light on *Slade's Case*," 1971, Camb. L.J. 213.
Berger, Raoul. "Constructive Contempt: A Post-Mortem," 9 U. Chi. L. Rev. 602 (1942).
———. "Executive Privilege v. Congressional Inquiry," 12 UCLA Law Rev. 1044, 1287 (1965).

———. "Standing to Sue in Public Actions: Is It a Constitutional Requirement?" 78 Yale L.J. 816 (1969).
———. "War-Making by the President," 121 U. Pa. L. Rev. 29 (1972).
———. "Was Cox Fired Illegally," *Washington Star-News*, November 4, 1973, p. B-3.
Bickel, Alexander. "Foreword: The Passive Virtues," 75 Harv. L. Rev. 40 (1961).
———. "The Durability of Colegrove v. Green," 72 Yale L.J. 39 (1962).
Bishop, Joseph. "The Executive's Right of Privacy: An Unresolved Constitutional Question," 66 Yale L.J. 477 (1957).
Black, F. R. "The United States Senate and the Treaty Power," 4 Rocky Mt. L. Rev. 1 (1931).
Borchard, Edwin. "Shall the Executive Agreement Replace the Treaty?" 53 Yale L.J. 664 (1944).
———. "Treaties and Executive Agreements—A Reply," 54 Yale L.J. 616 (1945).
Buchan, Alistair. "Questions About Vietnam," in 2 R. Falk, ed., *The Vietnam War and International Law* 35 (Princeton, 1969).
Carrow, Milton. "Governmental Nondisclosure in Judicial Proceedings," 107 U. Pa. L. Rev. 166 (1958).
Collins, Philip. "The Power of Congressional Committees of Investigation to Obtain Information From the Executive Branch: The Argument for the Legislative Branch," 39 Geo. L.J. 563 (1951).
"Comments on Powell v. McCormack," 17 UCLA Law Rev. 58 (1969) by L. D. Asper and S. J. Rosen, R. F. Bischoff, R. G. Dixon, S. K. Laughlin, R. B. McKay, C. E. Rice, Terence Sandalow, and D. T. Weckstein.
Corwin, Edward S. "Judicial Review in Action," 74 U. Pa. L. Rev. 639 (1926).
———. "The President's Power," in D. Haight and L. Johnston, eds., *The President: Role and Powers* 361 (Chicago, Rand, McNally, 1965).
———. "The Steel Seizure Case: A Judicial Brick Without Straw," 53 Colum. L. Rev. 53 (1953).
Cox, Archibald. "The Role of the Supreme Court in American Society," 50 Marq. L. Rev. 575 (1967).
Curtis, Charles P. "Review and Majority Rule," in E. Cahn, ed., *Supreme Court and Supreme Law* 170 (Bloomington, University of Indiana Press, 1954).
Dale, E. L. "What Vietnam Did to the American Economy," *New York Times*, January 28, 1973, sec. 3.
Douglas, W. O. "The Bill of Rights Is Not Enough," 38 N.Y.U. L. Rev. 207 (1963).
Emerson, Thomas. "Malapportionment and Judicial Power," 72 Yale L.J. 64 (1962).
Frankfurter, Felix. "Chief Justices I Have Known," 39 Va. L. Rev. 883 (1953).
———. "Hands Off the Investigations," 38 *New Republic* 329 (1924).
Galbraith, J. K. Book review, *New York Times*, October 8, 1972, sec. 6.
Galloway, George. "The Investigative Function of Congress," 21 Am. Pol. Sci. Rev. 47 (1927).
Goebel, Julius, Jr. "Constitutional History and Constitutional Law," 38 Colum. L. Rev. 355 (1938).
———. "Ex Parte Clio," 54 Colum. L. Rev. 450 (1954).

Hamilton, Walton. "The Path of Due Process of Law," in C. Read, ed., *The Constitution Reconsidered* (New York, Columbia University Press, 1938).

Hardin, Paul. "Executive Privilege in the Federal Courts," 71 Yale L.J. 879 (1962).

Hurst, J. W. Discussion in E. Cahn, ed., *Supreme Court and Supreme Law* 74 (Bloomington, University of Indiana Press, 1954).

Jackson, Robert H. "Advocacy Before the Supreme Court: Suggestions for Effective Case Presentation," 37 A.B.A.J. 801 (1961).

Jaffe, Louis. "Standing to Secure Judicial Review: Public Actions," 74 Harv. L. Rev. 1265 (1961).

Kramer, Robert, and Herman Marcuse. "Executive Privilege—A Study of the Period 1953–1960," 29 Geo. Wash. L. Rev. 623, 827 (1961).

Kurland, Philip. "The Impotence of Reticence," 1968 Duke L.J. 619.

Landis, James M. "Constitutional Limitations on the Congressional Power of Investigation," 40 Harv. L. Rev. 153 (1926).

Legal Adviser, Department of State. "The Legality of the United States Participation in the Defense of Vietnam," 75 Yale L.J. 1085 (1966).

Levitan, David. "The Foreign Relations Power: An Analysis of Mr. Justice Sutherland's Theory," 55 Yale L.J. 467 (1946).

Lofgren, Charles. "War-Making Under the Constitution: The Original Understanding," 81 Yale L.J. 672 (1972).

Lucas, J. Anthony. "The Story So Far," *New York Times*, July 22, 1973, Mag. sec.

McDougal, Myres, and Asher Lans. "Treaties and Congressional-Executive or Presidential Agreements: Interchangeable Instruments of National Policy," 54 Yale L.J. 181, 534 (1945).

McKay, Robert B. "The Right of Confrontation," 1959 Wash. U. L.Q. 122.

Mathews, Craig. "The Constitutional Power of the President to Conclude International Agreements," 64 Yale L.J. 345 (1955).

Monaghan, Henry. "Presidential War Making," 50 Bost. U. L. Rev. 19 (1970).

Moore, J. N. "The National Executive and the Use of the Armed Forces Abroad," in 2 R. Falk, ed., *The Vietnam War and International Law* 808 (Princeton, 1969).

Nathanson, Nathaniel. "The Supreme Court as a Unit of the National Government: Herein of Separation of Powers and Political Questions," 6 J. Pub. Law. 331 (1957).

Neal, P. C. "Baker v. Carr: Politics in Search of Law," 1962, Sup. Ct. Rev. 252.

Newman, Frank. "Some Facts on Fact-Finding by an Investigatory Commission," 13 Ad. L. Bull. 120 (1960–1961).

Parry, Clive. "Legislatures and Secrecy," 67 Harv. L. Rev. 737 (1954).

Philos, Conrad D. "The Public's Right to Know and the Public Interest—A Dilemma Revisited," 19 Fed. B.J. 41 (1959).

Plumb, J. H. "Notes From London," *New York Times*, June 6, 1973, sec. 6.

Potts, C. S. "Power of Legislative Bodies to Punish For Contempt," 74 U. Pa. L. Rev. 691 (1926).

Putney, Albert. "Executive Assumptions of the War-Making Power," 7 National U. L. Rev. 1 (1927).

Ratner, Leonard. "The Co-ordinated Warmaking Power—Legislative, Executive and Judicial Roles," 44 S. Cal. L. Rev. 461 (1971).

Reveley, W. T. "Presidential War-Making: Constitutional Prerogative or Usurpation?" 55 Va. L. Rev. 1243 (1969).

Ridgway, General Matthew R. "A Code of Loyalty," *New York Times*, May 2, 1973.
Rogers, William P. "Constitutional Law: The Papers of the Executive Branch," 44 A.B.A.J. 941 (1958).
Rostow, Eugene V. "Great Cases Make Bad Law: The War Powers Act," 50 Tex. L. Rev. 833 (1972).
Scharpf, Fritz. "Judicial Review and the Political Question: A Functional Analysis," 75 Yale L.J. 517 (1966).
Schlesinger, Arthur, Jr. "Congress and the Making of American Foreign Policy," 51 Foreign Affairs 78 (1972).
———. *Wall Street Journal*, March 30, 1973.
Schwartz, Bernard. "Executive Privilege and Congressional Investigatory Power," 47 Calif. L. Rev. 3 (1959).
Sindler, Allen P. "Baker v. Carr: How to 'Sear the Conscience' of Legislators," 72 Yale L.J. 23 (1962).
Symposium. On Baker v. Carr, 72 Yale L.J. 1 (1962).
Taft, William H. "The Boundaries between the Executive, the Legislative and the Judicial Branches of the Government," 25 Yale L.J. 599 (1916).
Turner, E. B. "Parliament and Foreign Affairs, 1603–1760," 38 Eng. Hist. Rev. 172 (1919).
Wade, H. W. R. "Crown Privilege Controlled at Last," 84 L.Q.R. 171 (1968).
Warren, Charles. "Presidential Declarations of Independence," 10 Bost. U. L. Rev. 1 (1930).
Warren, Earl. "Building the Peace," *New York Times*, February 12, 1973.
Wechsler, Herbert. "Toward Neutral Principles of Constitutional Law," 73 Harv. L. Rev. 1 (1959).
Weinfeld, Abraham. "What Did the Framers of the Federal Constitution Mean by 'Agreements or Compacts'?" 3 U. Chi. L. Rev. 453 (1936).
Wiggins, J. R. "Lawyers as Judges of History," 75 Mass. Hist. Soc. Proc. 84 (1963).
———. "Government Operations and the Public's Right to Know," 19 Fed. B.J. 62 (1959).
Wolkinson, Herman. "Demands of Congressional Committees for Executive Papers," 10 Fed. B.J. 103, 223, 319 (1949).
Wormuth, Francis. "The Nixon Theory of the War Power: A Critique," 60 Calif. L. Rev. 623 (1972).
———. "The Vietnam War: The President versus the Constitution," in R. Falk ed., 2 *The Vietnam War and International Law* (Princeton, 1969) 711.
Yost, Charles W. "Security Cloak Has Way of Deceiving the Deceiver," *Baltimore Sun*, November 3, 1973, p. 17.
Younger, Irving. "Congressional Investigations and Executive Secrecy: A Study in Separation of Powers," 20 U. Pitt. L. Rev. 755 (1959).
Yardley, D. C. M. "Certiorari and the Problems of Locus Standi," 71 L.Q. Rev. 388 (1955).

NOTES

Note. "Congress, the President and the Power to Commit Forces to Combat," 81 Harv. L. Rev. 1771 (1968).
Note. "Judicial Resolution of Administrative Disputes Between Federal Agencies," 62 Harv. L. Rev. 1050 (1949).
Note. "The Supreme Court as Arbitrator in the Conflict Between Presidential and Congressional War-Making Powers," 50 Bost. U. L. Rev. 78 (1970).

BIBLIOGRAPHY

Note. "The War-Making Powers: The Intention of the Framers in the Light of Parliamentary History," 50 Bost. U. L. Rev. 5 (1970).

CONGRESSIONAL HEARINGS AND REPORTS

Hearings. On Availability of Information from Federal Departments and Agencies before a Subcommittee of the House Committee on Government Operations (85th Cong., 2d Sess., 1958).

Hearings. On Availability of Information to Congress before Subcommittee of the House Committee on Government Operations (93d Cong., 1st Sess., 1973).

Hearings. On Commitments to Foreign Powers before Senate Committee on Foreign Relations (92d Cong., 1st Sess., 1971).

Hearings. On Executive Privilege: The Withholding of Information by the Executive before Senate Subcommittee on Separation of Powers (92d Cong., 1st Sess., 1971).

Hearings. On Transmittal of Executive Agreements to Congress before Senate Foreign Relations Committee (92d Cong., 1st Sess., 1971).

Hearings. On U.S. Government Information Policies and Practices before a Subcommittee of the House Committee on Government Operations (92d Cong., 1st Sess., 1971–1972).

Hearings. On S.2097 before the Senate Subcommittee on Constitutional Rights (89th Cong., 2d Sess., 1966).

Hearings. On War Powers Legislation before Senate Committee on Foreign Relations (92d Cong., 1st Sess., 1971).

Report. House Report No. 271 (27th Cong., 3d Sess., 1843).

Report. Senate Report No. 797 (90th Cong., 1st Sess., 1967).

Report. Senate Report No. 606 (92d Cong., 2d Sess., 1972).

Report. 21st Report by House Committee on Government Operations on "Administration of the Freedom of Information Act," H. Rept. No. 92-1419 (1972).

OPINIONS OF THE ATTORNEY GENERAL

6 Ops. Atty. Gen. 326 (1856).

34 Ops. Atty. Gen. 446 (1925).

39 Ops. Atty. Gen. 484 (1940).

40 Ops. Atty. Gen. 45 (1941).

MISCELLANEOUS

American State Papers, Foreign Relations (1789–1815), vol. 1 (Washington, Gales and Sendon, 1832).

Memorandums of the Attorney General, "The Power of the President to Withhold Information from the Congress," Senate Subcommittee on Constitutional Rights (85th Cong., 2d Sess., 1958).

Study. "The Present Limits of 'Executive Privilege,'" prepared by the Government and General Research Division, Library of Congress, reprinted Congressional Record, H. 2243–2246 (March 28, 1973).

Memorandum on Executive Privilege. Foreign Operations and Government Operations Subcommittee of the House, part V (August 1963, unpublished).

GENERAL INDEX

GENERAL INDEX

GENERAL INDEX

INDEX OF CASES

INDEX OF CASES

Bei Fragen zur Produktsicherheit wenden Sie sich bitte an:
If you have any questions regarding product safety,
please contact:

Walter de Gruyter GmbH
Genthiner Straße 13
10785 Berlin
productsafety@degruyterbrill.com